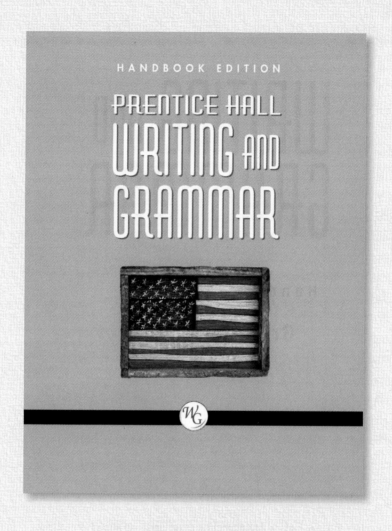

HANDBOOK EDITION

PRENTICE HALL

WRITING AND GRAMMAR

Grade Eleven
Handbook Edition

PEARSON

Prentice
Hall

Upper Saddle River, New Jersey
Boston, Massachusetts

WRITING AND GRAMMAR

Handbook Edition

Grade Eleven

ISBN 0-13-201002-X

2 3 4 5 6 7 8 9 10   10 09 08 07

Go Online

PHSchool.com

Use *Writing and Grammar,* your textbook online!

 Includes every grammar exercise in this book!

- instant feedback on interactive grammar exercises
- interactive writing tools and writing tutorials
- access to the *Prentice Hall Online Essay Scorer*

Interactive Textbook is also available on CD-ROM.

Go on-line to get instant help on the Writing and Grammar Web site!

- additional grammar practice opportunities
- scoring rubrics with scored student models for different modes of writing

Here's how to use the Writing and Grammar Web site:

Look for these Web Codes in your book:

efg-1101
efg-1102

Here's how to use Web Codes:

1. Go on-line. Enter URL: PHSchool.com

2. If you want instant feedback on interactive grammar exercises, enter Web Code: efg-1102

   Choose the appropriate chapter from the menu that appears.

3. If you want to review writing rubrics and scored student models, enter Web Code: efg-1101

   Choose the appropriate chapter from the menu that appears.

Program Authors

The program authors guided the direction and philosophy of *Prentice Hall Writing and Grammar: Communication in Action*. Working with the development team, they contributed to the pedagogical integrity of the program and to its relevance to today's teachers and students.

Joyce Armstrong Carroll

In her forty-year career, Joyce Armstrong Carroll, Ed.D., has taught on every grade level from primary to graduate school. In the past twenty years, she has trained teachers in the teaching of writing. A nationally known consultant, she has served as president of TCTE and on NCTE's Commission on Composition. More than fifty of her articles have appeared in journals such as *Curriculum Review, English Journal, Media & Methods, Southwest Philosophical Studies, Ohio English Journal, English in Texas,* and the *Florida English Journal*. With Edward E. Wilson, Dr. Carroll co-authored *Acts of Teaching: How to Teach Writing* and co-edited *Poetry After Lunch: Poems to Read Aloud*. Beyond her direct involvement with the writing pedagogy presented in this series, Dr. Carroll guided the development of the Hands-on Grammar feature. She co-directs the New Jersey Writing Project in Texas.

Edward E. Wilson

A former editor of *English in Texas*, Edward E. Wilson has served as a high-school English teacher and a writing consultant in school districts nationwide. Wilson has served on the Texas Teacher Professional Practices Commission and on NCTE's Commission on Composition. With Dr. Carroll, he co-wrote *Acts of Teaching: How to Teach Writing* and co-edited the award-winning *Poetry After Lunch: Poems to Read Aloud*. In addition to his direct involvement with the writing pedagogy presented in this series, Wilson provided inspiration for the Spotlight on Humanities feature. Wilson's poetry appears in Paul Janeczko's anthology *The Music of What Happens*. Wilson co-directs the New Jersey Writing Project in Texas.

Gary Forlini

Gary Forlini, a nationally known education consultant, developed the grammar, usage, and mechanics instruction and exercises in this series. After teaching in the Pelham, New York, schools for many years, he established Research in Media, an educational research agency that provides information for product developers, school staff developers, media companies, and arts organizations, as well as private-sector corporations and foundations. Mr. Forlini was co-author of the *S.A.T. Home Study* program and has written numerous industry reports on elementary, secondary, and post-secondary education markets.

National Advisory Panel

The teachers and administrators serving on the National Advisory Panel provided ongoing input into the development of *Prentice Hall Writing and Grammar: Communication in Action.* Their valuable insights ensure that the perspectives of teachers and students throughout the country are represented within the instruction in this series.

Dr. Pauline Bigby-Jenkins
Coordinator for Secondary English
  Language Arts
Ann Arbor Public Schools
Ann Arbor, Michigan

Lee Bromberger
English Department Chairperson
Mukwonago High School
Mukwonago, Wisconsin

Mary Chapman
Teacher of English
Free State High School
Lawrence, Kansas

Jim Deatherage
Language Arts Department
  Chairperson
Richland High School
Richland, Washington

Luis Dovalina
Teacher of English
La Joya High School
La Joya, Texas

JoAnn Giardino
Teacher of English
Centennial High School
Columbus, Ohio

Susan Goldberg
Teacher of English
Westlake Middle School
Thornwood, New York

Jean Hicks
Director, Louisville Writing Project
University of Louisville
Louisville, Kentucky

Karen Hurley
Teacher of Language Arts
Perry Meridian Middle School
Indianapolis, Indiana

Karen Lopez
Teacher of English
Hart High School
Newhall, California

Marianne Minshall
Teacher of Reading and Language Arts
Westmore Middle School
Columbus, Ohio

Nancy Monroe
English Department Chairperson
Bolton High School
Alexandria, Louisiana

Ken Spurlock
Assistant Principal
Boone County High School
Florence, Kentucky

Cynthia Katz Tyroff
Staff Development Specialist
  and Teacher of English
Northside Independent School District
San Antonio, Texas

Holly Ward
Teacher of Language Arts
Campbell Middle School
Daytona Beach, Florida

Grammar Review Team

The following teachers reviewed the grammar instruction in this series to ensure accuracy, clarity, and pedagogy.

Kathy Hamilton
Paul Hertzog
Daren Hoisington
Beverly Ladd

Karen Lopez
Dianna Louise Lund
Sean O'Brien

CONTENTS IN BRIEF

CONTENTS
PART 1: WRITING

Chapter 4 Narration

Autobiographical Writing 32

Student Work
IN PROGRESS

Featured Work:
"Train Tracks"
by Lauren Mizock
Whitney Young Magnet School
Chicago, Illinois

INTEGRATED
SKILLS

Chapter 5 Narration

Short Story 48

Student Work
IN PROGRESS

Featured Work:
"Too Much Information"
by Ben Spoer
Santa Monica High School
Santa Monica, California

INTEGRATED SKILLS

INTEGRATED SKILLS

Chapter 8 Persuasion

Advertisement 92

Student Work IN PROGRESS

Featured Work:
"The International Language
Training Center"
by Catherine Johns
Bel Air High School
El Paso, Texas

INTEGRATED SKILLS

Student Work
IN PROGRESS

Featured Work:
"The Real Deal With Mexican
Food" by Vanessa Serna
Bel Air High School
El Paso, Texas

INTEGRATED
SKILLS

Student Work
IN PROGRESS

Featured Work:
"Notes From the Footlights"
by Hilary Odom
Athens High School
Athens, Texas

INTEGRATED SKILLS

Chapter 11 Exposition

Problem-and-Solution Essay.. 138

Student Work IN PROGRESS

Featured Work:
"Zap the Zombie Syndrome"
by Jennifer Tufts
Broken Arrow High School
Broken Arrow, Oklahoma

INTEGRATED SKILLS

Student Work

IN PROGRESS

Featured Work:
"The Armed Forces: The Right
Choice for Some Seniors"
by Shira Pinsker
Miami Palmetto High School
Pinecrest, Florida

INTEGRATED SKILLS

Chapter 13 Research

Research Paper 170

Student Work IN PROGRESS

Featured Work:
"Augusta Savage: Artist of the Harlem Renaissance"
by Rebecca Potter
Central High School
Omaha, Nebraska

INTEGRATED SKILLS

Chapter

14 Response to Literature 298

Student Work IN PROGRESS

Featured Work:
"Sandra Cisneros: Modern-Day Heroine" by J. B. Nelson
Hart High School
Newhall, California

INTEGRATED SKILLS

Chapter 15 Writing for Assessment 208

Student Work
IN PROGRESS

Featured Work:
  "Relative Causes
of the American Revolution"
  by Margaret Boehme
  Buena High School
  Ventura, California

INTEGRATED SKILLS

Chapter 16

Workplace Writing 218

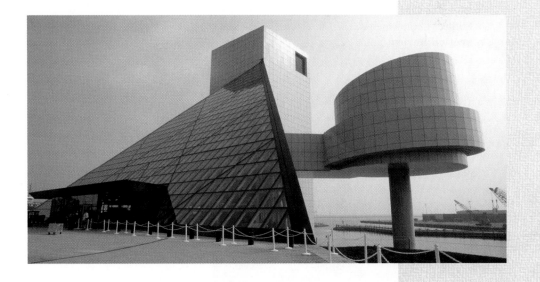

PART 2: GRAMMAR, USAGE, AND MECHANICS

PART 3: ACADEMIC AND WORKPLACE SKILLS

Writing

Harry Cohen: Builder, Jack Beal, © Christie's Images, Ltd., 1999

Writing in Everyday Life

You may not be aware of how heavily you rely on writing every day. At home, you might jot down a "To Do" list, take a phone message, send a letter or an e-mail, or fill out an application or order form. At school, you might write to answer a test question, produce a research report, take notes during a lecture, or generate ideas for a new project. Every time you pick up a pen or pencil or use a keyboard, you are writing.

▲ **Critical Viewing** What kind of writing do you think the students in this photograph might be doing? **[Speculate]**

What Are the Qualities of Good Writing?

Ideas Your ideas are the heart of your writing. Ordinary ideas turn into ordinary writing. Intriguing ideas turn into intriguing writing. Whatever you write, give it a fresh perspective. Use details to help readers see your topic in a new way.

Organization For writing to be effective, it must be presented in a way that readers can follow and understand. Every kind of writing should have a basic structure—a pattern or an organization. Choose a structure, and use it consistently throughout a piece of writing. Make sure readers have the information they need to understand each new piece of information or each new idea you introduce. Conclude your writing by wrapping up any loose ends and leaving the reader with something to think about.

Voice When you call a friend on the telephone, your friend can probably recognize your voice, even though he or she can't see your face. Make your writing voice as distinctive as your speaking voice. Observe the conventions of written English, but give your writing a personal touch that makes it your own.

Word Choice The words you choose influence the effectiveness of your writing. Choose vivid, precise words to communicate your experiences. Use words with powerful connotations to communicate feelings and reactions. Word choice involves more than learning a lot of new words. It involves learning to use the words you already know.

Sentence Fluency Effective writing has a rhythm—a flow. Write sentences that can be read aloud without difficulty or awkwardness.

Conventions Conventions refer to the grammatical correctness of a piece of writing. Don't let errors in grammar, usage, mechanics, and spelling interfere with your message. Carefully proofread all your writing.

Reflecting on Your Writing

Writing involves asking yourself questions and then making the answers real. Here are some questions that can lead you to discover more about the writer in you:

- What kind of writing do you like best? Least?
- What kind of writing would you like to try?
- Where is your favorite place to write?
- At what time of day do you get your best writing ideas?
- What book would you most like to have written?

A Walk Through the Writing Process

Writing can take many forms: It can be a note to a friend, a movie review, an employment application, or a formal college essay. Whatever your final product, the writing process—a systematic approach to writing that includes prewriting, drafting, revising, and editing—can help you write anything better.

▲ Critical Viewing
How can a thoughtful approach to the process of writing help improve your final product?
[Analyze]

Types of Writing

One way to analyze types of writing is by **modes**—the forms that writing takes. The list on this page shows the modes of writing that you'll encounter in this book.

Another way to think about the writing that you do is to analyze its audience and purpose. Some writing is **reflexive;** it is from yourself and for yourself. Poems and journals are often reflexive. Because it is self-sponsored, reflexive writing is more thoughtful and exploratory and allows you to learn as you write. In contrast, some writing is **extensive;** it is for others based on assignments from others. Extensive writing is frequently school-sponsored and includes short stories, research papers, and other class-based writing. When you write extensively, you adopt a more authoritative tone.

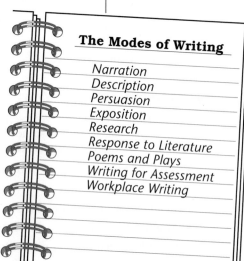

The Modes of Writing

Narration
Description
Persuasion
Exposition
Research
Response to Literature
Poems and Plays
Writing for Assessment
Workplace Writing

The Process of Writing

These are the stages of the writing process:

- **Prewriting** is freely exploring topics, choosing a topic, and beginning to gather and organize details before you write.
- **Drafting** is getting your ideas down on paper in roughly the format you intend.
- **Revising** is correcting any major errors and improving the writing's form and content.
- **Editing and proofreading** is polishing the writing and fixing errors in grammar, spelling, and mechanics.
- **Publishing and presenting** is sharing your writing.

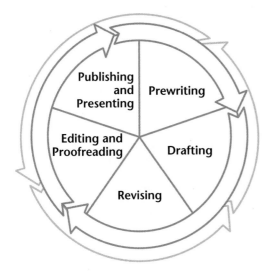

These steps may seem sequential, but writers often jump back to earlier stages as they work. For example, during the drafting stage, you may discover that a topic needs further research, or during revision, you may want to include more of your prewriting work. You may even put down a piece of writing in the prewriting stage, save it in your portfolio, and come back to it several weeks later.

A Guided Tour

Use the information in this chapter to take a guided tour of the writing process. As you read, you'll get to know some of the parts of the process and consider the strategies that effective writers use. Think about how you can apply these techniques when you take a piece of writing from start to finish.

What Is Prewriting?

When you face a blank page, you may be intimidated by its emptiness. Just as athletes "warm up" before running a marathon, writers use certain techniques to loosen their creative muscles. Many of these mental stretches are performed in the prewriting stage. Each writing chapter will offer you several strategies for getting started.

Choosing Your Topic

You'll find that your writing is usually more successful when you write about a subject that is meaningful to you. Prewriting strategies allow you to consider several ideas before choosing a topic to develop into a full piece of writing. The sample strategies here offer you suggestions for generating writing topics.

SAMPLE STRATEGY

Jotting a Quicklist Fold a piece of paper into three columns. Down the length of the first column, list people, places, and things that come to mind. List for several minutes. When you are finished, unfold the second column. In this column, list descriptive words for each of the people, places, and things in your first column. Finally, open the last third of the paper. Use this column to jot down examples or incidents related to your first two columns. When you are finished, choose one set of the items, descriptions, and examples as a topic.

MAKING A QUICKLIST

Noun	Adjective	Example
Terry	funny	His impressions of famous people
Janet	loyal	She kept in touch after I moved
the track	grueling	Last week's championship meet

Learn More

For additional prewriting strategies suited to specific writing tasks, see Chapters 4–16.

Narrowing Your Topic

Artists and photographers do more than just reflect what is seen. They focus on a particular aspect to give a unique viewpoint. Similarly, you as a writer will narrow your topic so that you can bring your own unique viewpoint into focus. You will find a topic-narrowing activity in each lesson. Use it to bring your broad topic into focus.

SAMPLE STRATEGY

Applying the Questions of Classical Invention Classical invention is a strategy used by the ancient Greeks to explore a topic. They created categories of questions and found that the answers to those questions helped them understand a subject more fully.

To apply their technique to your writing, take a closer look at your topic and all the specific ideas it may include. Jot down your broad topic at the top of a list. Then, use the questions associated with classical invention to examine the different facets of your topic.

Review your response to each of these questions, looking for links among the details. Draw arrows between connected ideas, and jot down notes that explain the connection you see. Use one of these connections as your narrowed topic.

CLASSICAL INVENTION

TESTIMONY
What do credible sources
say about the topic?

CIRCUMSTANCE
What makes it possible?
What makes it impossible?

RELATIONSHIP
What are the causes and effects?
What is its opposite?

COMPARISON
How is the topic similar to
or different from connected topics?

DEFINITION
Define and divide it into parts.

Considering Your Audience and Purpose

To be sure your writing is effective, consider two key elements: your **audience,** or the people you expect to reach; and your **purpose**, the reason you are writing.

Considering Your Audience Before you write, imagine the people you expect will read your work. Think about what your readers know and feel about your topic. Then, try to connect on your audience's level. Include language and details that will appeal to your readers.

Use an audience profile like the one below to analyze your audience. Keep your responses in mind as you draft.

AUDIENCE PROFILE	
What does my audience already know?	
What do they need to know?	
What details will interest or influence my audience?	

Considering Your Purpose Just as a knowledge of your audience will direct the language and details you include, your purpose should factor into the planning of your writing. Following are some common purposes for writing, along with suggestions for achieving these specific goals:

- **Writing to inform:** Include facts and examples that teach your readers. Write objectively; avoid including your opinion.

- **Writing to persuade:** Include reasons and arguments to convince readers to adopt your position.

- **Writing to entertain:** Include humorous situations, anecdotes, or exaggerations that your audience will enjoy.

Gathering Details

Before an artist paints a picture, he or she might sketch the scene to identify the details to be included. As a writer, spend time gathering details that you will use in your work. Once you begin drafting, you can draw upon as many or as few of the details as you need when you write, but the time you spend gathering them gives you the opportunity to make that decision. Each writing chapter offers a strategy for gathering details for specific modes of writing.

SAMPLE STRATEGY

Using the Reporter's Formula

Whether you are writing fiction or non-fiction, include enough details to make your subject clear. For example, if you are writing a short story, gather information about characters, setting, and plot events. If you are writing a factual report, gather clear, detailed information about your subject. Take a tip from professional journalists: Use the Reporter's Formula to gather details about different aspects of your topic. To do this, address the 5 *W*'s: *who, what, when, where,* and *why.*

Reporter's Formula

Who	are the people involved or affected?
What	were the specific reasons it happened? What evidence is there to support this conclusion?
When	did the events take place or the situation develop? When did it start, and when did it end?
Where	did the events take place? Where was the impact greatest?
Why	did it happen?

SAMPLE STRATEGY

Completing a Hexagonal Chart When writing about literature, use a hexagon like the one shown here to gather details about different aspects of the literature. Using this organizer will help you write a thoughtful, thorough analysis rather than a superficial summary.

For each segment of the hexagon, follow the directions in the chart. When possible, include references to the work to support your ideas.

▶ **APPLYING THE PREWRITING STRATEGIES**

PLOT — Summarize or paraphrase the work.
PERSONAL ALLUSION — Note ideas or experiences the selection suggests to you.
EVALUATION — Decide whether you liked the work.
THEME — State the message the work conveys.
LITERARY ALLUSION — Name other literature with a similar theme.
ANALYSIS — Cite evidence to support the theme.

1. Make a quicklist. Identify the topic you would choose based on this exercise.
2. Choose a topic such as loyalty or courage. Use classical invention to narrow your topic to one with a specific focus.
3. Create two different audience profiles for an essay you might write about learning to drive.
4. Use the Reporter's Formula to gather details about an event.
5. Complete a hexagon for a short story you have read.
6. Make an outline to identify details you would include in a pamphlet about weekend vacations.

What Is Drafting?

Shaping Your Writing

Focus on the Form Each form of writing has a specific set of goals or purposes—persuasion convinces, exposition explains, and narrative tells a story. Whatever your final product, keep the focus of your specific form in mind as you draft.

Grab Your Readers' Interest With a Powerful Lead Choose a powerful or intriguing opening statement or question to grab your readers' interest from the very start. This "lead" will introduce your writing style to your readers and set the tone for the rest of your writing.

Providing Elaboration

As you add details to your draft, your writing will become vivid and textured for your readers. Try the SEE method to add dimension and depth to your writing.

SAMPLE STRATEGY

Use the SEE Method The SEE method of Statement, Extension, and Elaboration allows you to shed light on a subject by providing a more complete analysis or description. First, start with a statement, or main idea. Then, write an extension by restating or explaining the first sentence. Elaborate further by providing even more detail about the main idea. Look at this example:

STATEMENT: Rosalie and Joe are truly world travelers.

EXTENSION: They have visited cities on six continents.

ELABORATION: From hiking in the Andes and then visiting the museums of Paris to traveling through the jungles of Africa and then enjoying the lights of Broadway, this couple has taken more trips than you can imagine.

▶ **APPLYING THE DRAFTING STRATEGIES**

Complete each of the sentences below. Then, use the SEE method to elaborate on each one.
a. If I had an extra hour every day, I would ___?___.
b. Something I'm really happy about is ___?___.

2.3 *What Is Revising?*

Color-Coding Clues for Revision

When you see writing as a process, you give the revision stage the attention it deserves. Review your writing by asking focused questions. The word **ratiocination** (rash´ ē äs ə nā´ shən) means "to think logically." Color-coding your draft with a system of color-coded clues will help you logically identify specific issues in your writing. Look at these sample revision strategies suited to color-coding:

- circling "to be" verbs
- bracketing sentence beginnings
- underlining vague words

Once you have isolated these elements, you can make decisions about revising your writing. As you work through the revision sections of Chapters 4–16, you will find strategies for revising structure, paragraphs, sentences, and word choice.

Writers in
ACTION

F. Scott Fitzgerald once said about writing and revising, "To have something to say is a question of sleepless nights and worry and endless ratiocination of a subject—of endlessly trying to dig out the endless truth, the essential justice. . . ."

Revising Your Overall Structure

Like the beams and supports that provide the structure for a house, the organization of your writing provides its framework. If the structure is sound or logical, the rest will stand strong. As you revise, you may decide to strengthen the structure of your writing by reordering or adding paragraphs.

SAMPLE STRATEGY

▶ **REVISION STRATEGY**
Cut and Paste

Whether or not you are working on a word processor, you can use the cut-and-paste technique to evaluate the organization of your draft. By experimenting with different paragraph organizations, you may discover a better order for your ideas. You may realize you have missed a key point, or you may choose to eliminate an entire paragraph. Follow these steps:

For electronic editing: Make a copy of your file by using the Save As feature of your word-processing program. Insert double returns between paragraphs, and then cut, copy, and paste until you find the best presentation for your ideas.

For manual editing: Make a photocopy of your essay. Cut paragraphs out of the photocopied draft and rearrange them to discover which sequence is most effective.

Revising Your Paragraphs

After reviewing the structure of your writing, take a closer look at the paragraphs that elaborate your ideas. Each paragraph in your writing should present a specific idea.

Learn More

To see more strategies for revision, see the writing chapters in this textbook.

SAMPLE STRATEGY

▶ **REVISION STRATEGY**
Color-Coding Clues to Evaluate Coherence

For each topical paragraph in a draft, highlight the topic sentence in yellow. Underline in blue the sentences that restate the idea. Underline in red the sentences that support or illustrate the statement. Then, review your work. Decide whether sentences that are not underlined can be revised to create a stronger connection to the topic sentence or whether they should be eliminated. In the example shown here, the writer deleted a sentence that strayed from the paragraph's main idea.

Revising Your Sentences

Sometimes, perception is everything. When writing is presented in short sentences, ideas seem choppy. In contrast, readers may judge writing that includes long, complex sentences to be equally convoluted. Strive to mix short sentences with longer ones.

EVALUATING COHERENCE

The Thanksgiving Day parade was exciting. We arrived at 6 A.M. to get good spots along the parade route. We found a terrific location near the bleachers. Standing in the cold, we passed the time by meeting other spectators who had come to see the parade. Finally, the parade began to march past us. Bands blared, cymbals crashed, and dancers twirled batons high in the air. We cheered for almost two hours. When it was all over, the street was covered with confetti, and we were thrilled to have been part of the experience.

SAMPLE STRATEGY

▶ **REVISION STRATEGY**
Tracking Sentence Lengths

To evaluate the variety of sentence lengths in your writing, note the number of words in a representative paragraph. Count the words in each sentence and note the number in the side margin. Use these tips for revision:

Evaluate
- Do you notice a pattern of short or long sentences?

Revise
- Break a sequence of short sentences by combining a few. To make a series of long sentences less weighty, introduce a short sentence.

Revising Your Word Choice

Choosing the most precise and powerful words will make your writing clean and direct. As you revise each piece of writing you do, check to see whether each word is the best one for your purpose. In the writing chapters, you will learn specific strategies for revising word choice.

SAMPLE STRATEGY

▶ REVISION STRATEGY
Color-Coding to Strengthen the Use of Nouns

When you use a noun, use the most precise noun, rather than trying to describe a vague noun with a string of adjectives. To evaluate your use of nouns, go through a draft, circling adjectives in blue and underlining the nouns they modify in red. Then, determine whether replacing the noun is in order.

Vague Noun Supported by Adjectives	Precise Noun
mixed breed dog lazy person	mutt loafer

Peer Revision

Even professional writers ask for the opinions of others as they revise a work. Each writing lesson offers specific suggestions for having a peer or several peers review your work.

Provide a Specific Task Focus your peer reviewers' comments to get the most specific feedback possible. Look at these suggested discussion starters:

Focusing the Peer Review	
Purpose	**Ask**
Evaluate an introduction	What is memorable about the opening paragraph?
Analyze word choice	Which words are most descriptive?

▶ APPLYING THE REVISION STRATEGIES

Apply each of the revision strategies to the first draft of an essay you've recently written. After you've revised, point out to a partner the techniques that worked well for you.

🔲 Research Tip

Get in the habit of consulting a thesaurus to find the precise words to strengthen your writing.

2.4 *What Are Editing and Proofreading?*

Whether you are writing a note to a friend or a research paper, you want to convey your ideas clearly to your readers. Mistakes in spelling, grammar, usage, or mechanics can distract from this goal. Once you are satisfied with the content of your writing, proofread to make your final draft error-free.

Focusing on Proofreading

To help you develop good proofreading skills, each writing chapter offers a specific focus. Look at your draft with this suggested topic in mind. However, always review your work to correct all errors you see. These are the broad categories for proofreading:

Take a Close Look at Your Spelling Use a dictionary to check the spelling of any word about which you are in doubt. If a dictionary is not available, consider replacing the word in question with a word you know is spelled correctly.

Follow the Conventions of Grammar Look for common grammar errors in your writing. For example, check subject-verb agreement, look to see that each sentence expresses a complete thought, and confirm that you have used pronouns correctly.

Check the Facts If your writing includes details you have incorporated from outside sources, be sure you have included the information correctly. Use the checklist at the right to focus your fact-checking work.

Confirm Legibility If you have written your final draft by hand, make sure that each word is legible. When making corrections or insertions, do so neatly.

Learn More

For extensive coverage of grammar, usage, and mechanics conventions, see Part 2.

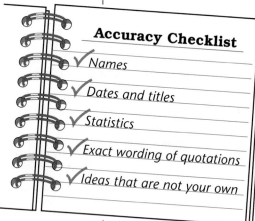

Accuracy Checklist

✓ Names

✓ Dates and titles

✓ Statistics

✓ Exact wording of quotations

✓ Ideas that are not your own

▶ **APPLYING THE EDITING AND PROOFREADING STRATEGIES**

1. Using a draft of a paper you've recently written, use the proofreading suggestions on this page.
2. Jot down two errors you frequently make in your writing. With a partner, discuss strategies you could use to recognize these errors during the proofreading stage.

2.5 *What Are Publishing and Presenting?*

Moving Forward

This walk through the writing process gives you an overview of the strategies and techniques that are available to you as part of the writing process. Each of the chapters in the writing section will teach you strategies suited to specific forms of writing.

Building Your Portfolio To track your own progress, keep your finished writing products in a folder, box, or other organized container. In addition to providing a record of your writing growth, your portfolio can also serve as a place where you keep unfinished writing, thought-provoking ideas, clippings, or photographs that may inspire future writing projects.

PORTFOLIO

Reflecting on Your Writing Each piece of writing you complete will teach you something about yourself, your topic, and your own unique writing process. Questions at the end of each chapter will prompt you to reflect on your writing by considering what you have learned and how you have learned it.

Assessing Your Writing At the end of each chapter, you will find a rubric, or set of criteria, on which you can evaluate your own work. Refer to the rubric throughout the writing process to make sure you are addressing the main points of the specific mode. Then, use the rubric to assess your final draft.

▶ APPLYING THE PUBLISHING AND PRESENTING STRATEGIES

1. Choose one of the prewriting activities you developed during this introductory walk-through. Put it in your portfolio to build into a fully developed piece of writing at a later time. Discuss with a partner why you chose the activity you did.
2. To begin reflecting on your writing process, jot down your response to one of these questions. Add your reflection to your portfolio:

   • Which of the strategies or activities did you find most useful or usable? Explain.

   • What are your strengths as a writer?

Sentences, Paragraphs, and Compositions
Structure and Style

▲ **Critical Viewing**
In what way can
this picture repre-
sent the way sen-
tences and para-
graphs are used in
writing? **[Connect]**

What Are Sentences, Paragraphs, and Compositions?

The **sentence** is the basic unit of writing. It expresses a complete thought. To develop and explain an idea, however, you need to join related sentences in a paragraph.

A **paragraph** is a group of sentences that share a common topic or purpose. Each paragraph is a logical unit of expression focused on a single main idea or thought.

In the same way that sentences in a paragraph share a common topic or purpose, so, too, do paragraphs in a composition. A **composition** is a group of related paragraphs that develop a main idea. The paragraphs fit together like the pieces of a puzzle to present a complete picture.

There are many types of compositions, including essays, reports, and autobiographical narratives. Even short stories (not usually referred to as compositions) are organized in paragraphs with a shared focus.

3.1 ## *Sentence Combining*

Controlling Your Sentences

The sentence is the basic building block of your paragraphs. By controlling the length and structure of your sentences, you can improve the variety and appeal of your writing. A series of short sentences can produce a choppy, repetitive effect. By combining two or more short sentences, you can show connections between events, stress important information, and create a smooth flow of ideas.

Inserting Words and Phrases

One method of combining sentences is to take key information from one sentence and insert it into another. Sometimes, you may have to change the form of certain words and use additional punctuation.

EXAMPLE: **Jacob Coxey was a political reformer.** He showed his concern for monetary policy by naming his son Legal Tender Coxey.

COMBINED: Jacob Coxey, **a political reformer,** showed his concern for monetary policy by naming his son Legal Tender Coxey.

EXAMPLE: Coxey led one of the first protest marches on Washington. **The march occurred in 1894.**

COMBINED: **In 1894,** Coxey led one of the first protest marches on Washington.

▷ **Exercise 1** Combining With Words and Phrases Combine each pair of sentences by inserting key information from one sentence into the other. Add commas as necessary.

1. The march began in Massillon. Massillon is a town in Ohio.
2. Jacob Coxey advocated the use of paper money. He was a member of the Greenback party.
3. In 1878, Jacob Coxey started his own business as a scrap-iron dealer. Jacob Coxey was twenty-four when he started his own business.
4. Coxey urged a huge road-improvement project to create jobs. He was a champion of the unemployed.
5. Coxey was the wealthiest man in Massillon, Ohio. He had a fortune of $200,000.

Using Compound Elements

Two or more short sentences may have common elements that can be combined. For example, sentences that have the same or similar verbs may be combined into one sentence having a **compound subject.**

EXAMPLE: **Betsy Ross** is famous as a heroine of the American Revolution. **Molly Pitcher** is also a heroine of the Revolution.

COMBINED: **Betsy Ross and Molly Pitcher** are famous as heroines of the American Revolution.

In a similar way, sentences that have the same subject may be combined into one sentence that has a **compound verb.**

EXAMPLE: During the American Revolution, Deborah Sampson **disguised** herself as a man. She **fought** in several skirmishes. She was **wounded** twice.

COMBINED: During the American Revolution, Deborah Sampson **disguised** herself as a man, **fought** in several skirmishes, and was **wounded** twice.

This process of compounding works equally well with other parts of the sentence. Examine the combined sentences below:

COMPOUND PREPOSITIONAL PHRASE: Parts of the bicycle were lying **on the floor, on the bench, in the driveway,** and **on the kitchen table.**

COMPOUND DIRECT OBJECT: Corey had purchased **tires, rims, brake pads,** and a **new padded seat.**

> **Exercise 2** Using Compound Sentence Elements Combine each pair of sentences using compound elements.
> 1. Benjamin Franklin was well known for his inventions. He was also well known for his scientific experiments.
> 2. Franklin invented bifocals and the lightning rod. He did not invent the bicycle.
> 3. Noah Webster listened to the way Americans spoke throughout the East and the South. He recorded examples of usage in his notebook.
> 4. I may want to read more about Noah Webster. I could also read more about Benjamin Franklin.
> 5. *Poor Richard's Almanack* was written by Benjamin Franklin. *The Autobiography* was written by Benjamin Franklin.

�“ Learn More

For additional information about prepositional phrases, see Section 19.1; for additional information about direct objects, see Section 18.3.

▼ **Critical Viewing** In this painting, Benjamin Franklin, John Adams, and Thomas Jefferson combine ideas in writing the Declaration of Independence. For what reasons would you combine sentences in a paragraph? **[Connect]**

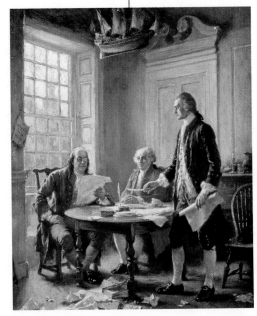

Forming Compound Sentences

A **compound sentence** consists of two or more main clauses. To combine two related sentences, rewrite them as a compound sentence, expressing each idea in its own main clause. The clauses in such a sentence may be linked by a comma and a coordinating conjunction such as *and, but, for, nor, or, so,* and *yet.*

EXAMPLE: The plots of early musicals were silly. The characters were based on stereotypes.

COMBINED: The plots of early musicals were silly, **and** the characters were based on stereotypes.

You may also use a semicolon or a semicolon and a conjunctive adverb such as *however, furthermore,* and *consequently.* Notice that you are not simply linking two ideas, you are expressing a relationship between them.

EXAMPLE: Musicals have always aimed to delight audiences. Some musicals have attained the level of art.

COMBINED: Musicals have always aimed to delight audiences; **furthermore,** some have attained the level of art.

ⓠ Learn More

For additional information about compound sentences, see Section 19.4.

Coordinating Conjunctions			Conjunctive Adverbs	
and	nor	yet	accordingly	however
but	or		consequently	instead
for	so		finally	therefore
			furthermore	thus

▶ **Exercise 3** Forming Compound Sentences Combine each pair of sentences using the strategy in parentheses.

1. Parliament imposed a tax on tea to help ease the financial trouble of the British East India Company. The colonists did not react favorably to the tax. (comma and coordinating conjunction)
2. The Tea Act of 1773 was the last straw for many colonists. Colonists in disguise dumped tea into Boston Harbor. (comma and coordinating conjunction)
3. Most of the colonists took sides in the American Revolution. Some remained neutral. (semicolon and conjunctive adverb)
4. The king was outraged by the behavior of the colonists. He encouraged Parliament to pass harsher laws. (semicolon and conjunctive adverb)
5. Parliament shut down the port of Boston. No ship could enter or leave the harbor. (comma and coordinating conjunction)

Using Subordination

When combining sentences, you can use a subordinate clause to express an idea that provides additional information about your main idea. A **subordinate clause** is a group of words that includes a subject and a verb but that does not express a complete thought. To add more information about a noun or pronoun in the main clause, use a subordinate clause beginning with a relative pronoun such as *who, whom, whose, which,* or *that.*

EXAMPLE: George Washington appointed the first Cabinet. **It included Thomas Jefferson.**

COMBINED: George Washington appointed the first Cabinet**, which included Thomas Jefferson.**

To add more information about a verb, an adjective, or an adverb in the main clause, use a subordinate clause beginning with a subordinating conjunction such as *after, although, as, because, before, if, in order that, unless, until, where,* or *wherever.*

EXAMPLE: Jefferson had served his country in many roles. **He was appointed secretary of state in 1790.**

COMBINED: Jefferson had served his country in many roles **before he was appointed secretary of state in 1790.**

SOME SUBORDINATING CONJUNCTIONS		
after	because	that
although	before	when
as if	even if	whenever
as soon as	in order that	while

Learn More

For additional information about clauses, see Section 19.3; for additional information about pronouns, see Section 17.1.

▶ **Exercise 4** Using Subordination Combine each pair of sentences using subordinate clauses.

1. In 1776, Thomas Paine published a pamphlet called *Common Sense.* The pamphlet fanned the fires of revolution.
2. Patrick Henry urged armed resistance to England. Most of the other speakers argued for compromise.
3. Congress sent Benjamin Franklin to France in 1776. His task was to enlist aid for the American Revolution.
4. John Adams was serving as a delegate to the Second Continental Congress. His wife, Abigail, wrote him letters urging him to promote women's rights.
5. Thomas Jefferson was a brilliant writer. He was chosen to write the Declaration of Independence.

3.2 *Writing Effective Paragraphs*

Main Idea and Topic Sentence

The main idea of many paragraphs is stated in a **topic sentence.** This topic sentence is supported or explained by the other sentences in the paragraph. Facts, details, restatements, and explanations are used to develop the paragraph's main idea.

When the main idea is suggested but not directly stated, then the paragraph has an **implied main idea.** In a paragraph with an implied main idea, the facts and details provide the information that allows a reader to infer the point of the paragraph.

▲ **Critical Viewing** What statement can you make that pulls together the details in this picture? **[Synthesize]**

WRITING

from **Gardening**
Bailey White

The first winter, I could relax only a little. Bermuda grass can establish itself during a winter and get away from you the following spring. So every evening at dusk, I would stalk up and down my garden like a demented wraith, peering at the ground for each loathed blue-green blade, my cloak billowing in the wind and my scarf snagging on the bare gray branches of last summer's sunflowers.

> In this paragraph, the stated topic sentence is shown in blue italics.

from **My Bondage and My Freedom**
Frederick Douglass

When I was about thirteen years old, and had succeeded in learning to read, every increase of knowledge, especially respecting the free states, added something to the almost intolerable burden of the thought—"I am a slave for life." To my bondage I saw no end. It was a terrible reality, and I shall never be able to tell how sadly that thought chafed my young spirit.

> In this paragraph, all the sentences work together to develop the unstated main idea of the paragraph: The more the author learned, the more he realized the injustice of his situation.

> **Exercise 5** Identifying a Stated Topic Sentence Identify the stated topic sentence of the paragraph.

The devastation of World War I left many people with a feeling of uncertainty and disillusionment. They no longer trusted the ideas and values of the world out of which the war had developed. Artistic traditions were abandoned in favor of experimentation. Social values were questioned and challenged. In a variety of ways, people sought to find new ideas that better suited twentieth-century life.

> **Exercise 6** Identifying an Implied Topic Sentence Identify the implied topic sentence of the following paragraph.

Although William Faulkner never finished high school, he read a great deal and developed an interest in writing from an early age. In 1918, he enlisted in the British Royal Flying Corps and was sent to Canada for training. However, World War I ended before he had a chance to see combat, and he returned to Mississippi. A few years later, longing for a change of scene, Faulkner moved to New Orleans. There, he became a friend of Sherwood Anderson. In 1926, Faulkner returned to Oxford, Mississippi, to devote himself to his writing.

Writing a Topic Sentence

Many of the paragraphs you write will be organized around a topic sentence. In a **topic sentence,** you state the main idea that will be developed in a paragraph. Although the details and explanations that you provide in the rest of the sentences of the paragraph are what give your composition depth and form, the topic sentences are the framework on which the composition is built.

To write a topic sentence, review the details you will use. Group related details. For each group, make a single statement that expresses what they mean all together. Polish this statement into a topic sentence.

◀ **Critical Viewing** What do you think this construction worker would say about the importance of a solid framework? **[Connect]**

Writing Supporting Sentences

Use **supporting sentences** to develop, support, or explain the key idea expressed in a topic sentence. You can support or develop the idea using one or more of the following strategies:

Use Facts Facts are statements that can be proved. They support your key idea by providing proof.

FACT: Our school building is open from 7:00 A.M. to 5:00 P.M.

Use Statistics A statistic is a fact, usually stated in numbers.

STATISTIC: At least 60 percent of the students use the building after regular classroom hours.

Use Examples, Illustrations, or Instances An example, illustration, or instance is a specific thing, person, or event that demonstrates a point.

ILLUSTRATION: Last week, three clubs had meetings in the cafeteria at four o'clock.

Use Details Details are the specifics—the parts of the whole. They make your point or main idea clear by showing how all the pieces fit together.

DETAIL: Each club has a specific amount of time to meet but would like more.

▶ **Exercise 7** Writing a Topic Sentence Write a topic sentence for the following paragraph.

   People used to describe the United States as a "melting pot" to suggest that individuals of different ethnic backgrounds came to the United States and blended into a single American culture. Today, many Americans argue that the "melting pot" metaphor is no longer accurate. They say that the United States is a society in which many cultures exist side by side, retaining their individual identities. New images that are used to represent the country's diversity include a *tapestry,* a *mosaic,* and a *quilt.*

▶ **Exercise 8** Writing Supporting Sentences

1. Write two more supporting sentences to add to the above paragraph.
2. Write four sentences that support the following statement after you complete it:
   ___?___ is the most interesting sport to watch.

Placing Your Topic Sentence

Evaluate each paragraph to determine whether to place your topic sentence at the beginning, in the middle, at the end, or to leave it unstated. Placing your topic sentence at the beginning of the paragraph focuses your readers' attention before you present your details. You may choose to place it in the middle when you need to lead into it with background information. Placing your topic sentence at the end of the paragraph summarizes the details you have supplied. Leaving it unstated allows readers to synthesize the information you have presented; this is often a more sophisticated approach.

Paragraph Patterns Sentences in a paragraph can be arranged in a variety of patterns. One of these patterns is the TRI pattern.

TOPIC SENTENCE: You state your key idea.

RESTATEMENT: You interpret your key idea—put it into other words.

ILLUSTRATION: You support your key idea with an illustration or an example.

T	Our town doesn't need a new parking lot.
R	We have enough parking to meet everyone's needs.
I	On any weekday, the municipal lot is only half full. On Saturdays, the busiest day, the longest wait for a parking spot is ten minutes.

Once you have identified the basic elements of your paragraph, experiment with variations of the TRI pattern, such as TIR, TII, or ITR, until you are satisfied with the effect.

Exercise 9 Placing a Topic Sentence Use the TRI pattern, or a variation, to arrange the sentences below in a paragraph. Then, revise the paragraph, using another variation of TRI. You may add transitions and additional sentences as needed.

Many of the merchants in town are willing to hire teens for part-time work after school.

The local day-care center is always looking for volunteers.

After-school clubs provide a forum for students to meet others with similar interests.

No teen in our town can honestly say he or she has nothing worthwhile to do after school.

3.3 *Paragraphs in Essays and Other Compositions*

Unity and Coherence

In a paragraph or composition that has **unity,** all the parts are clearly connected to a single main idea. In a unified composition, the topic sentence of each paragraph connects to the main idea, or **thesis statement,** of the composition. Within a unified paragraph, each sentence connects to the topic sentence or implied main idea of the paragraph.

In a **coherent** composition, ideas follow a logical order and the connections between ideas are clear. Paragraphs are arranged so that one leads logically to the next. Sentences within paragraphs are ordered so that readers can easily follow the flow of ideas.

Unity

When you plan a composition, identify your main points—the topic sentences you will use for your paragraphs. Read each one, and make sure it is relevant to the main idea of your composition. As you draft, be cautious that you do not begin to insert ideas that occur to you but that are unrelated to the main idea. As you revise your composition, evaluate the topic of each paragraph and how relevant it is to the main idea of the composition. As you revise each paragraph, delete any sentences that do not clearly connect to the topic sentence of the paragraph.

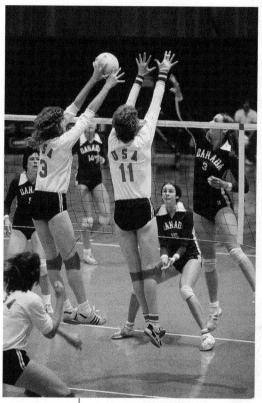

▲ Critical Viewing
Why do the members of a team need to focus on a common purpose?
[Draw Conclusions]

> **Exercise 10** Planning a Unified Composition Read the planned main idea or thesis, shown in bold. Then, evaluate each of the planned paragraphs. Identify the sentence that should be eliminated to improve the unity of the composition.

Equal funding should be provided for girls' and boys' sports.

- Many girls participate in sports.
- Individual sports have more long-term benefits than team sports.
- Participation in sports benefits girls as well as boys.
- Federal law prohibits gender discrimination in educational programs, including athletics.

> **Exercise 11** Revising a Paragraph for Unity Identify
which sentence should be eliminated to improve the unity of
the following paragraph.

   Wearing a bike helmet is just good sense. Studies show that
bike helmets reduce the risk of head injury by 85 percent!
Other common injuries from bike accidents include broken
wrists and lacerations. States with helmet laws have reported
a reduction in head injuries from bike accidents, ranging
between 20 and 40 percent. Although inconvenient, or perhaps
even uncomfortable, bike helmets are worth the trouble.

Coherence

Organize and Show Connections The key to coherence
is organization. Order your ideas logically, and use transitional
words and phrases to keep connections clear as you move from
one idea or detail to the next. The type of organization you
choose when you write depends on your topic and purpose.

Types of Organization	Possible Reasons to Use	Words That Show Connections
Chronological	to narrate; to explain a process	before, after, during, meanwhile, first, next, finally
Spatial	to describe	above, below, behind, next to, near, within, outside
Comparison and Contrast	to show similarities and differences; to evaluate	however, in contrast, similarly, conversely
Cause and Effect	to analyze; to explain reasons and results	accordingly, as a result, consequently, therefore
Order of Importance	to persuade; to describe; to evaluate	furthermore, significant-ly, moreover, most of all

> **Exercise 12** Revising for Coherence Revise this para-
graph to create coherence. Reorganize sentences, add transitions, and make other minor changes as needed.

   Americans called the purchase of the land that is now
Alaska "Seward's Folly." Today, Alaska enjoys a vital tourist
industry and is an important source of oil. The land was not
expensive. William Seward purchased the land from Russia in
1867 for two cents an acre. Many Americans believed the area
to be nothing but a barren wasteland.

The Parts of a Composition

A composition is a group of paragraphs that all work together to develop a single focus. In most compositions, this single focus is expressed in a thesis statement. The rest of the paragraphs in the composition are organized to develop that thesis statement. Whatever organizational strategy you choose, it will have a beginning, a middle, and an end. In writing, these parts are called the *introduction*, the *body*, and the *conclusion*.

Introduction

The **introduction** serves two purposes: It captures readers' attention with a strong lead, and it introduces the focus of the composition in a thesis statement. The **lead** is the first sentence. It can be a startling observation, an intriguing statement, or a quotation. The **thesis statement** declares what you intend to show or prove in your composition. Frequently, the thesis statement is followed by another sentence or two that extend the thesis statement by indicating how it will be shown or proved.

Body

The **body** of a composition is the part that develops, explains, and supports the key idea expressed in the thesis statement. Organize the body paragraphs in a logical order, and make sure that each paragraph is related to your thesis.

Conclusion

The **conclusion** is the final paragraph of the essay. Like the introduction, it serves two purposes. First, it should restate the thesis and sum up the support. Second, it should leave readers with a memorable statement, a call to action, or a thought.

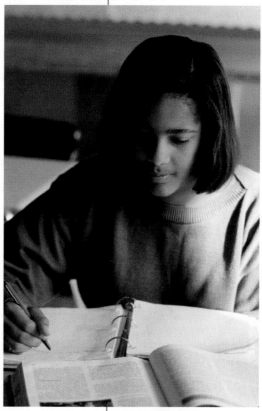

▲ Critical Viewing
How can a knowledge of the parts of a composition make you a more effective writer? [Connect]

Exercise 13 Planning a Composition On a separate sheet of paper, outline the parts of a composition on a topic related to a subject you are studying in science or social studies. Write a thesis statement and a possible lead for the introduction. Write a topic sentence for each of several paragraphs.

Types of Paragraphs

Functional Paragraphs

Functional paragraphs, as their name suggests, perform specific functions. They may not have a topic sentence, but they are unified and coherent because the sentences (if there is more than one sentence) are clearly connected and follow a logical order. Functional paragraphs can be used for the following purposes:

To arouse or sustain interest A few vivid sentences can work together to capture a reader's attention.

To indicate dialogue One of the conventions of dialogue is that a new paragraph begins each time the speaker changes.

To make a transition A short paragraph can help readers move between the main ideas in two topical paragraphs.

WRITING MODEL

from **The Pig**
Barbara Kimenye

. . . He was still worried about the state his filing system must be in today, for having once called in at the Headquarters, merely to see if the youngster who had replaced him needed any advice or help, he had been appalled at the lack of order. Papers were scattered everywhere, confidential folders were open for all the world to read, and his successor was flirting madly with some pinbrained girl at the other end of the newly installed telephone.

The visit had not been anything near a success, for not even his former colleagues showed anything but superficial interest in what Kubka had to say.

So there he was, destined to waste the remainder of his life in the little cottage beside the Kalasanda stream, with plenty indeed to look back on, but not very much to look forward to, and his greatest friend, Yosdfu Mudkasa, was away in Buddu County on business.

> This paragraph makes a transition from the paragraph that looks back on the character's former place of employment to the paragraph that tells about his present situation.

Paragraph Blocks

Sometimes, you may develop a single idea over several paragraphs. The paragraphs in this "block" all support the same key idea or topic sentence but contain too much information to include in one paragraph because that paragraph would become long and unmanageable. By breaking the development of the idea into separate paragraphs, you make your ideas clearer.

USING PARAGRAPH BLOCKS

Topic of Composition
Many students have difficulty fitting required classes into their schedules.

Supporting Topic Sentence: Required classes should be offered more frequently.

> **Paragraph 1** – Statistics of how frequently offered and how many students
> **Paragraph 2** – Suggestion of how frequently should be offered and how many students could be accommodated
> **Paragraph 3** – Summary of impact on school budget

PARAGRAPH BLOCK

Supporting Sentence 2: Students should be allowed more scheduling flexibility.

Exercise 14 **Analyzing Functional Paragraphs** Look through essays and speeches in your literature book and in other sources to find examples of each type of functional paragraph. Make a photocopy of each example. Mark the functional paragraph with a brace, and label it by the function it performs.

Writing Style

Developing Style

Your personal style is the way you present yourself to the world. Writing style is the way you express yourself in writing. Just as you might choose different styles of clothing for different occasions, you can use different writing styles for different purposes. The qualities that contribute to writing style are diction, tone, and sentence variety.

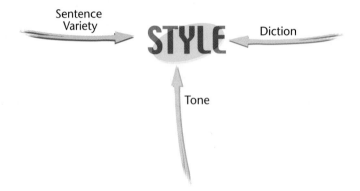

Sentence Variety The lengths and structures of the sentences you use contribute to the effect of your writing. Longer, more complex sentences create a sophisticated, mature style. Shorter, more direct sentences create emphasis and vary the rhythm of your writing. In most types of writing, use a variety of lengths and structures to keep the writing from becoming monotonous.

Diction Diction refers to word choice. The words you choose contribute to the overall effect, or style of a paragraph. You can use words with positive connotations or associations for an upbeat style, or you can use words with negative connotations if you are trying to make a point about a problem or situation. The sounds of words can also contribute to the style of a paragraph.

Tone Tone is the attitude you take when you write about your subject. You may write about your topic with objectivity, with dismay, or with humor. If you are writing an explanation of a process, your paragraphs will have a serious, formal tone. If you are writing a letter to a friend, your paragraphs will have a casual, friendly tone.

Exercise 15 Analyzing Styles Read the excerpt from "The Pig" on page 28. Describe the style of the writing, using specific examples of sentence variety, diction, and tone.

Formal and Informal English

Different types of writing require different levels of formality. When writing a letter or note to a friend, you might use language in a casual way—similar to the way you use everyday speech. When writing a report or a business letter, you would use formal English—following all the conventions of correct grammar and usage.

Using the Conventions of Formal English

You should use formal English for most of your school assignments, such as reports, persuasive essays, and test responses. When writing in formal English, observe the following conventions:

- Do not use contractions.
- Do not use slang.
- Use standard English usage and grammar.

Using Informal English

Informal English is the everyday speech that people use in conversation. Often, informal English is used in dialogue to express certain patterns of speech. You might also use informal English when writing friendly letters, humorous anecdotes, or journal entries. When writing in informal English, you can

- use contractions.
- use popular expressions and slang.

FORMAL ENGLISH:	I am writing to request information about the current status.
INFORMAL ENGLISH:	What's new? Drop me a line and let me know.

▶ **Exercise 16** Using Formal and Informal English On a separate sheet of paper, rewrite the following sentences. Use formal English for those written in informal English. Use informal English for those written in formal English.
1. So, what's your reaction to the flick?
2. I can't stand the food that place dishes up.
3. I am writing to suggest an alternative to your plan.
4. Those who shared the experience agreed that it was exhilarating.
5. I'm boggled by how tricky this problem is!

Narration
Autobiographical Writing

Autobiography in Everyday Life

You flick on the television to see your favorite rock musician being interviewed about the evolution of his band. You are riveted to the set as the story of his success unfolds. Learning the truth about an event from an eyewitness or reading a book whose events actually happened grabs our interest because we are invited to share part of someone's life.

Every day, you share bits and pieces of your life. Whether you spin the story of your game-winning soccer goal or explain what occurred during a school trip to the nation's capital, you are telling bits and pieces of the story of your life. When you retell a part of your life story, you are sharing an autobiographical narrative.

▲ Critical Viewing
What details of this water adventure might you expect to read in an autobiographical narrative? [Analyze]

What Is Autobiographical Writing?

Autobiographical writing tells a true story about an important period, experience, or relationship in the writer's life. Effective autobiographical writing includes

- a series of events that involve the writer as the main character.
- details, thoughts, feelings, and insights from the writer's perspective.
- a conflict or an event that affects the writer.
- a logical organization that tells the story clearly.

To preview the criteria upon which your autobiographical writing may be evaluated, see the Rubric for Self-Assessment on page 46.

Types of Autobiographical Writing

You can choose from one of the following forms of autobiographical writing to share your personal experience:

- **Autobiographical sketches** often include information about a writer's early life and personal qualities or achievements.
- **Memoirs** are accounts of a writer's relationship with a person, place, or animal.
- **Reflective essays, personal narratives**, or **autobiographical incidents** share a writer's personal experience and provide the writer's reactions to the experience.
- **Anecdotes** are brief and usually humorous accounts of single events that provide some insight into life in general.

Writers in
ACTION

While much of her writing is fiction inspired by the events of her life, Julia Alvarez's book Something to Declare *tells the actual stories and conflicts that have framed her life. In this quotation, she explains how the events of her own autobiography influence her approach to writing:*
"I came into English as a ten-year-old from the Dominican Republic. . . . My own island background was steeped in a tradition of storytelling that I wanted to explore in prose."

PREVIEW
Student Work
IN PROGRESS

Lauren Mizock, a high-school student at Whitney Young Magnet School in Chicago, Illinois, wrote an autobiographical narrative about the experience of riding a commuter train. In this chapter, you will see how Lauren used prewriting, drafting, and revising strategies to write her narrative "Train Tracks."

Prewriting

Choosing Your Topic

Autobiographical writing draws on specific events or incidents that have significance to you. To help you choose a memorable experience for your writing, use these strategies:

Strategies for Generating a Topic

1. **Personal Experience Timeline** On a timeline, plot dates and descriptions of memorable experiences or events. After you complete the timeline, review your experiences and choose one of special significance as your topic.

2. **Photographs and Memories** Look through a family album or a personal photo collection you have kept. Jot down notes about the experiences in your life that the photographs depict. Choose one, and expand upon it.

3. **Observation Notebook** For the next few days, keep a journal of what you see and observe wherever your life takes you—at school, at home, at work, at the mall. Choose one incident or event to describe in a piece of autobiographical writing. The sample below shows how Lauren Mizock used an observation notebook.

Try it out! Use the interactive Personal Experience Timeline in **Section 4.2**, online or on CD-ROM.

Student Work
IN PROGRESS

Name: Lauren Mizock
Whitney Young Magnet School
Chicago, IL

Using an Observation Notebook

Lauren Mizock, a high-school student from Chicago, Illinois, used an observation notebook to find a topic for her autobiographical sketch "Train Tracks." She decided to write about her job.

...I've just learned to stir-fry vegetables. This new skill makes me feel independent. . . .

...The argument in social studies class made me wonder: What do I really think about students being denied the right to work after school?

...At night, I really like time to devote to winding down from the events of the day.

TOPIC BANK

f you are having trouble finding a topic, consider these possibilities:

1. **Narrative About an Achievement** Focus on a specific goal that you have worked hard to achieve. In a narrative, tell how you set your sights and met a difficult challenge.

2. **True-Friends Narrative** Tell the true story of how you met a friend who has had an influence on your life. Include your experiences, thoughts, and feelings to show how your friend has affected you.

Responding to Fine Art

3. Sports often provide a good framework for autobiographical writing. Let *Out at Third* spark your own writing ideas. Consider professional sports events you have attended, or choose an incident from your own athletic experience to describe in an autobiographical essay.

Out at Third, Nelson Rosenberg, The Phillips Collection, Washington, DC.

Responding to Literature

4. Read the opening lines of Walt Whitman's "Song of Myself." Use Whitman's inspirational poetry to reflect on your life. Write a narrative about a life experience that illustrates the line "I celebrate myself, and sing myself." You can find more of the poem in *Prentice Hall Literature, Penguin Edition,* The American Experience.

Timed Writing Prompt

5. Sometimes we plan adventures. Other times, adventures take us by surprise. Write about an adventure you have had. Include how the adventure began and what made it exciting and unusual. **(30 minutes)**

Narrowing Your Topic

The more focused your topic is, the sharper the image you can create for your readers. Before you begin drafting, focus your topic by making a list to isolate an episode.

Isolate an Episode

Take the time to list all of the events related to your topic. Review the list, and choose a significant event that you could develop into an effective piece of autobiographical writing. For example, if you are writing a reflective essay, choose an episode that shows how your experience provided you with an insight. Note how Lauren Mizock narrowed her topic by isolating an episode.

Student Work
IN PROGRESS

Name: Lauren Mizock
Whitney Young Magnet School
Chicago, IL

Isolating an Episode

Lauren generated a list of all the events surrounding her after-school job. She narrowed her topic by choosing to develop one idea—waiting for the train.

Getting ready to go to work.
↓
Walk across town.
↓
Wait for train.
↓
Ride train.
↓
Get to work.
↓
Begin to paint.

Considering Your Audience and Purpose

Your audience is your readers—the people with whom you intend to share your narrative. Keep their experiences in mind as you write. You may need to include characterizations of the people you describe or explanations of the places you include. For example, if you describe a speech that you gave at a local library, you may need to tell your readers how and why you were invited to speak.

Your purpose—your reasons for writing a narrative—will also guide the types of details you choose to include. If you want to entertain, include humorous elements. In contrast, if you want to share a serious insight, replace humor with an analysis of your experiences.

Gathering Details

You are the best source of information for your autobiographical writing. Begin by gathering details from your own recollections. Use freewriting as a way to get started.

Freewrite to Gather Details

Freewriting is one way to gather details from memory. Give yourself a time limit of ten or fifteen minutes. As you write, let the memory of one detail lead to the next. At this stage, do not worry about organization or sentence structure. Concentrate on remembering everything you can. Later, you'll be able to shape your writing correctly.

When you finish freewriting, review what you've written to identify other information you'll want to collect. Use these ideas:

Using the Power of Observation Review your freewriting to identify people and places that you can observe. Study the real-life characters and settings further by looking at photographs, visiting settings, or interviewing people who played a part in your experience. Jot down additional details that can be used in your narrative.

Adding Factual Information Some autobiographical incidents may require research beyond your memory or power of observation. For example, if you are describing your trip to a city in another state, you may need to incorporate facts like climate or tourist spots so your readers will understand the incident you describe. Do not assume that your experience has provided you with this knowledge; a reference book can give you the details you need to make your writing accurate.

Interactive Textbook

Get instant help! For assistance gathering details, use the interactive Adding Factual Information activity in **Section 4.2,** online or on CD-ROM.

4.3 **Drafting**

Shaping Your Writing

Like all narratives, an autobiographical narrative tells a story that has a beginning, a middle, and an end. To maintain your readers' interest, establish the proper pacing for each of these parts.

Begin With a Compelling Lead

Sometimes, a simple but poignant sentence can provide just the right amount of information to build the reader's curiosity. Look at these opening sentences:

EXAMPLES: My grandfather handed me a silver box, and suddenly the room became silent.

I think my dog would write me a good recommendation.

Devise a simple sentence to hook your readers. Then, let the rest of your essay develop the point you've introduced.

Organize to Develop Pacing

To keep up the pace of your writing, balance descriptions with events that move the plot along. In the diagram shown here, notice how plot events leading up to the climax add to the conflict and raise interest in the character's success. Be sure your narrative includes a conflict, and keep these tips for each stage of the plot in mind as you draft:

- In the *exposition*, provide background to help your readers understand the narrative to follow.

- Develop the *rising action* by identifying the problem and building toward the *climax* of the narrative.

- In the *falling action*, tie up any loose ends that remain by describing events that follow the climax.

- Use the *resolution* to show the insight you gained from your experience.

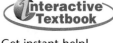

Get instant help! To draft your narrative, use the Essay Builder, accessible from the menu bar, on-line or on CD-ROM.

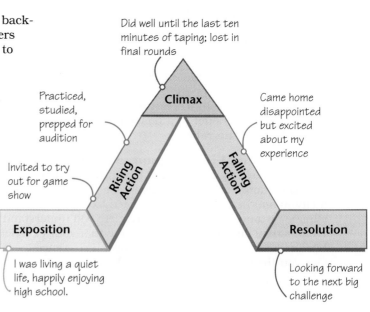

Did well until the last ten minutes of taping; lost in final rounds

Practiced, studied, prepped for audition

Climax

Came home disappointed but excited about my experience

Invited to try out for game show

Rising Action

Falling Action

Exposition

Resolution

I was living a quiet life, happily enjoying high school.

Looking forward to the next big challenge

Providing Elaboration

As you write your draft, look for places to develop your narrative by adding details that bring your experience to life for your readers. Include details that reveal your thoughts and feelings, as well as details about people and places. One way to add such elaboration is to "explode a moment."

Add Details by Exploding a Moment

When you "explode a moment," you expand a description by telling more about what happened, what it looked like, or how the people involved reacted. Cut several "explosion" shapes from construction paper. Your shapes, like those shown in the student model, should be large enough to write on. After you draft a paragraph or two, pause and look for places where you can "explode a moment" by using elaboration. Write the details you want to add on the colored-paper explosions, and paste them lightly on your draft. You can incorporate these details when you revise.

Student Work

IN PROGRESS

Name: *Lauren Mizock*
Whitney Young Magnet School
Chicago, IL

Exploding a Moment

Lauren pasted explosions into the second paragraph of her draft where she wanted to add details about her thoughts and reactions.

I sit down between a homeless man and a young professional man. The homeless man is in layers of gray, tattered clothes. *Once, his clothes were new.* The urban commuter is wearing a bright white shirt and a silk tie. It is a cleanliness that is as important an element of his daily uniform as his silk tie. *it gleams in the sunlight* As a teenage painter, decked in red, *and splattered with paint* my presence completes a Chicago social rainbow on that bench.

4.4 *Revising*

Revision is your chance to polish your writing. Add details that make people and settings more vivid, make dialogue more realistic, and improve the flow of your writing. Begin your revision by evaluating the overall structure of your narrative.

Revising Your Overall Structure
Write a Strong Conclusion

The conclusion of your narrative is your opportunity to sum up main points and leave your readers with a strong final impression. An especially appropriate way to end a piece of autobiographical writing is to step back from the experiences you've described and take a moment to explain the significance of the ideas, event, or situation that is central to your essay.

▶ REVISION STRATEGY
Evaluating Your Conclusion

Review your conclusion to identify what it accomplishes. It may end with a thought-provoking question, it may provide an insight you've gained from the experience, or it may do little more than indicate the end of the essay. Take this opportunity to improve your conclusion. Consider these solutions:

- **Make a Bridge to the Present** If you wrote about a memory, conclude your narrative with an observation from your current point of view. By showing a contrast or a connection between the past and the present, you can emphasize the influence that the experience has had.

- **Provide an Insight** Review your prewriting notes to recall your purpose for writing and your reasons for choosing a writing topic. Consider how the event was significant, how it affected or changed your life, or how it let you see others differently. Finish your paper by addressing these issues in the closing paragraphs.

▼ Critical Viewing Why do you think the words *bridge, road, path,* and *journey* frequently appear in titles of autobiographies? **[Hypothesize]**

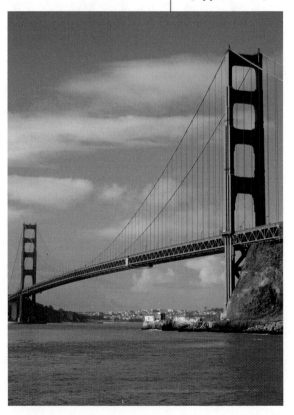

4.5 Editing and Proofreading

Before you finalize your autobiographical writing, proofread it to correct errors. Mistakes in grammar, spelling, or mechanics in your writing may distract your readers from the ideas you want to convey. Proofread your draft to make your final copy error-free.

Focusing on Your Spelling

As you proofread your essay, double-check to make sure that you have spelled words correctly. Use the following methods to catch misspellings:

- Reread your paper, and circle any words that you are unsure how to spell. Don't leave accuracy to chance; find the correct spelling in a dictionary.

- If you worked on a computer, run your paper through the spell-check function. Don't rely solely on the software, however. Reread your paper to find words that are not identified by a spell checker.

- Review the spelling of proper nouns, including the names of people and places.

Timed Writing Hint

If you make the same spelling errors over and over, practice writing those words correctly. You'll be more likely to avoid those errors on exams.

Grammar in Your Writing
Avoiding Usage Errors With *It's* and *Its*

It's and *its* look similar and sound the same, but the two different spellings indicate different meanings. Review the following examples to become familiar with the rules of usage for them.

It's is a contraction that stands for the words "it is."

EXAMPLE: It's time to hand in your papers. (It is time to hand in your papers.)

Its is a possessive pronoun. Like *his* or *hers*, *its* shows ownership.

EXAMPLE: The dog wagged its tail. (The dog wagged his tail.)

Find It in Your Writing As you proofread your autobiographical narrative, check to make sure that you have used *it's* and *its* correctly.

For more on miscellaneous problems in usage, see Chapter 25.

4.6 Publishing and Presenting

Building Your Portfolio

Sharing your essay is an effective way to provide insights into your personal history, your beliefs, and your unique point of view. Consider these ideas for sharing your work:

1. **Create an Illustrated Edition** Present your final draft in an illustrated version. Use photographs or illustrations to enhance the ideas in your writing.

2. **Post Your Essay** Create a bulletin board display of your essay and those of your classmates. Have each writer supply a short commentary about the event or idea that inspired the writing.

Reflecting on Your Writing

Take a few minutes to write about the process of writing an autobiographical essay. Use these suggestions to spark your reflection. Then, add your comments to your portfolio.

- Identify an insight that you gained as a result of writing this essay.

- Explain the strategies you used to make changes between your first and final draft.

Internet Tip

To see model essays scored with this rubric, go on-line: PHSchool.com Enter Web Code: efk-1101

Rubric for Self-Assessment

Use these criteria to evaluate your autobiographical writing:

	Score 4	Score 3	Score 2	Score 1
Audience and Purpose	Contains details that engage the audience; provides a clear insight about an experience	Contains details appropriate for an audience; addresses a clear reason for writing	Contains few details that appeal to an audience; gives a reason for writing	Is not written for a specific audience or purpose
Organization	Organizes events to create an interesting narrative	Presents a clear sequence of events	Presents a confusing sequence of events	Presents no logical order of events
Elaboration	Contains rich details that create vivid characters; uses dialogue that develops characters and plot	Contains details that develop character and describe setting; uses dialogue	Contains characters and setting; uses some dialogue	Contains few or no details to develop characters or setting; uses no dialogue
Use of Language	Uses an excellent variety of sentence beginnings; contains no errors in grammar, punctuation, or spelling	Uses a good variety of sentence beginnings; contains few errors in grammar, punctuation, and spelling	Introduces some variety in sentence beginnings; contains some errors in grammar, punctuation, and spelling	Uses monotonous pattern of sentence beginnings; has many errors in grammar, punctuation, and spelling

Connected Assignment *Firsthand Biography*

Somewhere between telling your life story in an autobiography and researching the biography of a total stranger is the hybrid called a **firsthand biography.** In this type of narrative writing, you record the life of someone you know—a parent, community member, or local celebrity. You may still research for information that falls outside your observation, but you give the biography a personal flavor by including your personal insights.

Use the following writing-process steps to write a firsthand biography:

Prewriting To choose a subject, spend a few minutes making a list of people you know well enough to address in an essay. Review your list to choose a person whose story you think readers should learn. Use a chart like this one to gather information from your own experience, jotting down key events, personality traits, and appearance details. When you complete the chart, narrow your topic to one incident or idea.

▲ **Critical Viewing** What words might the child in this photograph use to describe the older man? **[Describe]**

☑ engineered popular youth service program

☑ local resident since my earliest childhood

☑ leads healthy lifestyle, exercising daily—I see her jogging

Topic: Town Mayor

☑ studied political science at community college where my dad now teaches

Drafting As you draft, refer to your diagram to recall the sequence of events and to highlight interesting details. Include incidents that show your relationship to your subject or that provide insights to make your firsthand biography worthwhile. If you write in the first person—using the pronoun *I*—you can emphasize the personal nature of the biography.

Revising and Editing Have someone who knows the biography subject read your draft. Ask your reviewer to identify characteristics, words, or events that don't seem appropriate to his or her perception of the person. Revise your text or add details to make your subject more believable.

Publishing and Presenting Add photographs to illustrate your firsthand biography. Then, create a booklet to copy and share as a gift with people who know your subject.

Narration

Short Story

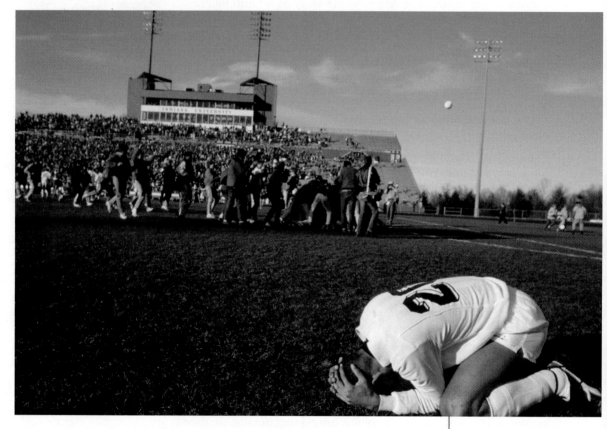

Short Stories in Everyday Life

You tell stories, or narratives, just about every day. For instance, you might tell friends or family about a big soccer game, recounting how a critical play dashed your team's chances at victory. If you were to use your imagination to alter some of the events in the game, you would be creating a short story—a fictional account of a series of events. At times, you have probably entertained friends by creating stories that stray even further from real events. For example, when you were younger, you may have told scary stories at a sleepover party. Whether you knew it or not, you were using elements of storytelling to entertain your friends.

▲ Critical Viewing
What kind of story would you expect this soccer player to tell? **[Hypothesize]**

What Is a Short Story?

As the name suggests, a **short story** is a brief fictional narrative. The American writer Edgar Allan Poe celebrated the unique qualities of short stories and helped to define the genre. He felt that a short story should be brief enough to be read in one sitting. An effective short story

- establishes the setting in time and place.
- presents a main character who takes part in the action as the problem is resolved.
- introduces and develops a conflict, a problem to be resolved.
- weaves a plot, the series of events that make up the action of the story.
- suggests a theme or generalization about life.

To see the criteria against which your short story may be judged, preview the Rubric for Self-Assessment on page 61.

Writers in
ACTION

Native American storyteller N. Scott Momaday finds sources for his writing in his cultural heritage. He taps his own work experience to inspire his writing, as he explains in this quotation:

"When I turn my mind to my early life, it is the imaginative part of it that comes first and irresistibly into reach, and of that part I take hold. This is one way to tell a story."

Types of Short Stories

There are as many types of short stories as there are writers and times. Here are a few examples of types of short stories you may encounter as both a reader and a writer:

- **Historical narratives** illuminate some historic event or moment in time using fictionalized elements, such as dialogue.
- **Mysteries** present a riddle to be solved. These suspenseful pieces often feature a detective who puts clues together to solve a crime.
- **Thrillers** arouse a high level of tension by introducing danger in the conflict they present.
- **Science-fiction stories** are usually based in futuristic settings but address issues of value to today's society.

PREVIEW
Student Work
IN PROGRESS

In this chapter, you will find the work of Ben Spoer, a student at Santa Monica High School in Santa Monica, California. As you will see, Ben used prewriting, drafting, and revising techniques to develop his short story "Too Much Information."

Prewriting

Choosing Your Topic

You can build a story around one strong element. Start with a compelling conflict, an interesting character, or an unusual setting. Use these strategies to help you choose a topic:

Strategies for Generating Topics

1. **Blueprint** Sketch out the setting of a place. This might be a familiar neighborhood, a football stadium, or a completely fictional world. As you draw, consider events that might unfold in the setting you have created. List three or four ideas, and then choose one you'd like to develop.

2. **Song List** Music often sparks memories of people or places. To recall a memory you would like to use as the basis of a short story, list several songs you enjoy. Jot down the ideas the songs bring to mind. Then, review your list, and choose a springboard for your own writing.

3. **Character Sound Off** To generate characters for your story, consider the people you have encountered recently. Make a list of these people, and include a description of each one. Circle the ones who might create an interesting pair. Then, write the dialogue they might have together. Use this dialogue to generate an idea for your story.

Try it out! Use the interactive Blueprint activity in **Section 5.2**, on-line or on CD-ROM.

Student Work IN PROGRESS

Name: _Ben Spoer_
Santa Monica High School
Santa Monica, CA

Creating a Character Sound Off

Ben prepared to write by making a character list. He circled people he'd like to use in a story, and then he created a dialogue between them.

cheerful lunch aide

efficient nurse in doctor's office

(confused patient) — What happened to me?

friendly physics teacher

(busy doctor) — You've had an accident!

mellow bus driver

TOPIC BANK

If you are having difficulty coming up with a topic, consider these possibilities:

1. **"What-If" Story** Choose a recent challenge you have faced, and rewrite it with a different outcome. You could write a story surmising what might have happened if you had lost a key game or had taken a risk you've been afraid to confront.

2. **Story About a Conflict Between Friends** Friendships can be rewarding, harmonious, or tension-filled. In a story, create a conflict between friends who find a way to save their friendship—or decide to call it quits.

Responding to Fine Art

3. The painting *Beach Scene ca. 1935*, at right, might inspire you to imagine an enjoyable day at the beach. Perhaps it suggests a survival story beginning on an ordinary day at the shore. Use one of these suggestions to write a story about a day at the beach.

Beach Scene ca. 1935, Jane Peterson,
The National Museum of Women in the Arts

Responding to Literature

4. Read "The Notorious Jumping Frog of Calaveras County" by Mark Twain. Using the story's exaggerated style as a model, write your own humorous tale. You can find the story in *Prentice Hall Literature, Penguin Edition,* The American Experience.

Timed Writing Prompt

5. When a friend sticks by someone during a tough time, people often say "That's what friends are for." Write a short story about a person who goes the extra mile for a friend. The story should express your vision of what friends are for. **(30 minutes)**

Narrowing Your Topic

To avoid writing a story that goes in all directions, narrow your focus by identifying the major elements of your story. Use the letters in the acronym CASPAR to organize these key items. Following is an example based on Eudora Welty's story "A Worn Path."

Characters	Phoenix Jackson and people she encounters
Adjectives	Old, fragile, determined, weak
Setting	Rural South, bumpy forest path, small town
Problem	Phoenix needs to travel into town to get medicine for her grandson.
Action	hike, struggle, survive, fight
Resolution	Phoenix gets to town and gets medicine.

LITERATURE

To read Eudora Welty's short story "A Worn Path," see *Prentice Hall Literature, Penguin Edition,* The American Experience.

Considering Your Audience and Purpose

Before you begin your draft, identify your audience—the people you expect to read your short story. Knowing the age of your intended audience will help you choose the vocabulary and sentence complexity that is appropriate for your readers.

In addition, consider your purpose in writing your story. You may want to amuse your readers, to frighten them, or to create a character who will confide in them. This chart shows the kinds of details you might use to achieve a specific purpose:

If Your PURPOSE Is — **INCLUDE**

to frighten
- gloomy setting
- description of silences

to amuse
- exaggerated characters
- funny situations

to inspire reflection
- unexpected event
- thoughtful narrator

Gathering Details

As a last step before drafting, take some time to expand your own knowledge of the story you will tell. Gather details on these key elements of narration:

Identify the Conflict Clarify the problem your story will develop. Make notes about the ways the problem will reveal itself and intensify, the ways different characters will react to the problem, and the results of the resolution.

Picture Your Setting Decide on the specific time and place of your story. Then, list details that identify this exact location. Using details of the setting in your narrative will enrich your writing. For example, showing your narrator sitting in rush-hour traffic will convey the setting and possibly raise the conflict level.

Interview Your Character To gather details about the people in your story, devise a questionnaire. Create questions about their personalities, experiences, and the conflict that they face. Then, answer the questions from each character's perspective.

Timed Writing Hint

When writing under a deadline, include at least one vivid detail per paragraph.

Student Work
IN PROGRESS

Name: *Ben Spoer*
Santa Monica High School
Santa Monica, CA

Gathering Details Through Character Interviews
Here is part of the interview Ben created to develop his main character.

How do you like to spend your free time? I enjoy talking to my friends. We go to coffee bars and people-watch. I like to see the way people interact. I think there are a lot of people who talk one way and think another.

How would you describe yourself? I'm very introspective. I think I am an honest person who wants to trust the things people tell me. I want to be liked. I don't think I am part of the "in" crowd.

How would you describe the weeks following your accident? For a brief period, I had the ability to hear people's thoughts. It was interesting but frightening. I wouldn't wish that on anyone.

Drafting

Shaping Your Writing

As you prepare to write, gather all the prewriting you have done. Review your ideas, and sketch out a plan for telling your story.

Review the Elements of Plot

The plot, or sequence of events, in your narrative will probably center on a conflict. Begin with an exposition that establishes the conflict and introduces the setting and characters. In the next part of your draft, called the rising action, build the conflict until it reaches its high point—the story's climax. Next, describe the resolution of the conflict, where the problem is solved. In the falling action of your story, tie up any loose ends of the plot.

Build Toward a Climax Use a plot diagram like the one below to help you plan your plot. To keep the story moving, introduce the problem as soon as you can. Then, add events and details that intensify the problem. Once you know how the climax of your story will play out, add details and events to the rising action to intensify the conflict.

 Challenge

Tell your story as a flashback by starting the action after events have already taken place. The narrator can jump back in time to share the events that have occurred previously.

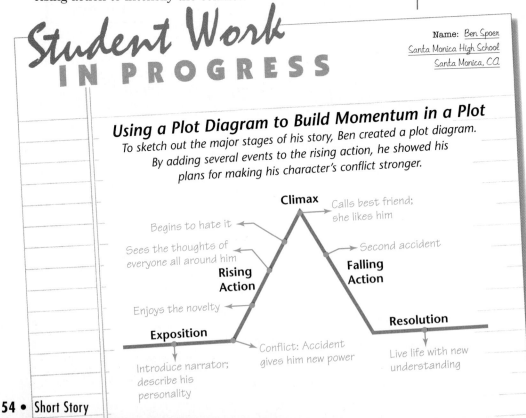

Student Work **IN PROGRESS**

Name: *Ben Spoer*
Santa Monica High School
Santa Monica, CA

Using a Plot Diagram to Build Momentum in a Plot

To sketch out the major stages of his story, Ben created a plot diagram. By adding several events to the rising action, he showed his plans for making his character's conflict stronger.

Climax
Calls best friend; she likes him

Begins to hate it

Sees the thoughts of everyone all around him

Rising Action

Enjoys the novelty

Exposition

Introduce narrator; describe his personality

Conflict: Accident gives him new power

Second accident

Falling Action

Resolution

Live life with new understanding

Providing Elaboration

Once you have developed the frame for your story, fill in the details to create a complete picture for your readers. Remember that you are constructing your story to achieve a specific effect; choose only information that suits your purpose. Knowing what to tell and what to leave out is an important skill of good storytelling.

Show, Don't Tell

To bring a scene to life for readers without dictating what they should think about every character and action, challenge yourself to show more and tell less. Whenever possible, use action to move the story along, use repetition to stress an emotion, and include dialogue to illustrate the characters' personalities. Look at these examples:

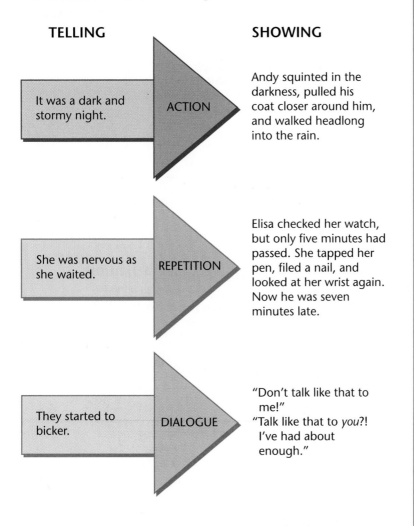

TELLING		SHOWING
It was a dark and stormy night.	ACTION	Andy squinted in the darkness, pulled his coat closer around him, and walked headlong into the rain.
She was nervous as she waited.	REPETITION	Elisa checked her watch, but only five minutes had passed. She tapped her pen, filed a nail, and looked at her wrist again. Now he was seven minutes late.
They started to bicker.	DIALOGUE	"Don't talk like that to me!" "Talk like that to *you*?! I've had about enough."

Revising

Once you have written your first draft, take the time to improve the story. Starting with the big picture and moving in to focus on the smaller details will help you build up your short story.

Revising Your Overall Structure
Get the Reader Involved Early

The first paragraphs of your story should set the mood of your writing, pulling your readers in from the start. Review the exposition of your draft, and consider making the writing more compelling by offering vivid details that make the reader feel part of the scene. Snapshots may help you do this.

▶ **REVISION STRATEGY**
Using Snapshots

Think of each episode in your story as a photograph or a snapshot of a moment in time. Review your exposition, or the beginning of your story, to identify places where the view could be made clearer. Then, add details to make the picture more vivid.

interactive Textbook

Get instant help! To clarify the relationships among events in your narrative, use the Transition Words Revision Checker, accessible from the menu bar, on-line or on CD-ROM.

Student Work
IN PROGRESS

Name: Ben Spoer
Santa Monica High School
Santa Monica, CA

Using Snapshots to Grab the Reader's Attention
When Ben looked at his exposition, he asked questions to bring out more description in his writing. The answers helped him provide a clearer snapshot of the scene.

"I wish I could be normal again. I really do," begin as I stare at the full glass of root beer in front of me. I say to my friend. "But I guess that's impossible since I discovered my power." In the shadows of the dimly lit booth, My listener nods his head silently.

What is the speaker doing? Where is he?

What does the place look like?

Revising Your Paragraphs
Create Stronger Characterization

While characterization can be directly revealed by the narrator of a story, a character's own words and actions reveal a voice and a personality. Look for places where you can develop characters through dialogue and action.

▶ **REVISION STRATEGY**
Adding Dialogue to Reveal Your Characters

Reread your paragraphs one by one. Find places where you can add dialogue to reveal more about your characters. These might be events that you simply described or emotions and attitudes that you explained. In the instances you have found, let the characters speak for themselves.

While a writer may have described the end of an interview with a few brief sentences of narration, notice how the example below shows the character Jeanne to be professional and calm, despite an awkward interview situation.

EVENT NARRATED WITH DIALOGUE:

"So," Jeanne began, wondering how to leave gracefully. "I guess you'll call me when you know who you've chosen."

"Yes, that's right." The manager had already turned her attention to other things.

"Well," again Jeanne kept friendly optimism in her voice, "I enjoyed our meeting, and I look forward to hearing from you soon."

Silence.

"Thanks so much for your time. . . . I'll find my way out." She gathered her things, smiled weakly, and left.

Use Structure to Make Dialogue Realistic To get the feel of the natural way that people talk, listen to a few conversations. Note the rhythms and pacing of conversations and the way the subject affects the way people converse. Then, to achieve that natural effect in your writing, add pauses, use sentence fragments, or let your characters interrupt each other.

Choose the Right Words Just as you use your own diction as you speak, let your characters use the language that is right for them. In your draft, use words that suit the character and the situation. For example, use slang if the character is talking with friends, but use more formal language if the character is talking to someone unfamiliar.

⚙ Grammar and Style Tip

Instead of repeating "said" over and over, choose tag words that show your characters' attitudes. For example, to convey someone's anger, you could write, "'No, I will not!' Amy retorted." To convey her excitement, write "'Yes!' Amy responded enthusiastically."

🕐 Timed Writing Hint

When revising your work, check that dialogue is marked with correct punctuation and that speakers are clearly indicated.

Revising Your Sentences

Vary Sentence Beginnings

Don't fall into the habit of beginning several sentences the same way. To revise this dull pattern in your writing, look at your sentence beginnings and introduce variety where you can.

▶ **REVISION STRATEGY**
Listing Sentence Starters

Make a list of the first words in each sentence of your draft. Challenge yourself to break any pattern that presents itself.

Interactive Textbook

Get instant help! Use the Sentence Openers Variety Revision Checker to evaluate your sentence beginnings. You can find it on the menu bar, on-line or on CD-ROM.

Student Work
IN PROGRESS

Name: Ben Spoer
Santa Monica High School
Santa Monica, CA

Using a Word List to Vary Sentence Beginnings

When Ben looked at the first words in his draft, he noticed that he started several sentences with "I." He made corrections to vary his writing style.

| + Because |
| ~~People~~ There |
| It |
| I |

Because of those experiences,
I believed acting one way and thinking

another was just an adult thing until I got

into middle school. There, People spoke nicely to . . .

Revising Your Word Choice

Use Specific Verbs

Action verbs can provide description without adding too many modifiers. Be sure you have chosen the most efficient verbs.

▶ **REVISION STRATEGY**
Circling Action Verbs

Choose one paragraph, and circle the action verbs it contains. List other verbs that might fit the sentence. Evaluate the meaning each one conveys, and then choose the best verb.

EXAMPLE: The batter *hit* the ball into right field.
The batter *looped* the ball into right field.

Grammar in Your Writing
Action vs. Linking Verbs

Action verbs tell what action someone or something is performing. Action verbs can show both physical and mental action.

Physical action: The bear *swats* the branches away.

Mental action: I *agree* with you.

Linking verbs help one word in a sentence to name or describe the condition of another word in a sentence. The most common linking verb is some form of *be*.

Linking in order to name: The lion *is* the king of the forest.

Linking in order to describe: The argument *was* exhausting.

Find It in Your Reading Reread a short story you have read recently. Identify five action verbs and five linking verbs the writer uses.

Find It in Your Writing Look through your story draft, and find five action verbs and five linking verbs you have used. Challenge yourself to revise sentences that would be improved by a more precise action verb.

For more on action and linking verbs, see Chapter 17.

Peer Review
Group Feedback

Before you make final changes to your draft, get together with a small group of classmates. As writers, share your work, and give each other suggestions for making your short stories better. Listen and participate in the review of each story; you may hear an idea that you can apply to your work.

Read your story aloud to the group twice. The first reading will give your peers a chance to hear the story, meet the characters, and understand the plot. You may ask for initial reactions, but after a second reading, your peers will be more prepared to give you supported responses. Use these questions to guide your peer review:

1. What scene was most vivid?
2. What would you like to know more about?

▲ Critical Viewing How might hearing another student's writing in a group like the one shown here actually improve your writing? **[Support]**

5.5 Editing and Proofreading

Once you have finalized your draft, review it for errors in spelling, punctuation, and grammar. Mechanical mistakes like these pull attention away from the story you have written. Strive to make your final draft error-free.

Focusing on Punctuation

Be sure you have used punctuation correctly.

End marks Check that each sentence has an end mark, such as a period(.), an exclamation point(!), or a question mark(?).

Commas Commas are used to prevent misreading. They can set up relationships among parts of a sentence and make long sentences easier to read. Commas are also critical to punctuating dialogue correctly. Be sure you have not included commas too generously or too sparingly.

Spelling Tip

If you are using a computer word-processing program, use the Spelling and Grammar tool. Then, confirm your draft by asking a classmate to help you identify misspelled words.

Grammar in Your Writing
Punctuating Dialogue Correctly

Punctuate dialogue within quotation marks. Use these conventions to punctuate the exact words of conversation correctly:

• Begin a new paragraph each time the speaker changes.

• Use a comma inside the closing quotation mark when a remark comes before the speaker tag, the narrative identifying the speaker:

"It looks as if it will be a gorgeous day," he said.

• Use a comma after the speaker tag when the speaker tag precedes a quoted statement:

She smiled and replied, "I had hoped it would be."

• When a speaker tag interrupts a direct quotation, use commas to set off the two parts of the quotation:

"Come on," he shouted to the people upstairs, "let's get going!"

Find It in Your Writing As you proofread your short story, check the punctuation of any dialogue you have used.

For more on the conventions of punctuating dialogue, see Chapter 27.

5.6 *Publishing and Presenting*

Building Your Portfolio

Use these suggestions to share your short story with others:

1. **Submit Your Story to a Literary Magazine** Many schools publish student works in a newspaper or magazine. Submit your story to your school's literary magazine. To reach a wider audience, contact a national magazine.

2. **Make a Class Anthology** Form an editorial committee, and ask classmates to submit their papers for a collection of short stories. Add photographs or illustrations to enhance the writing. Design a cover, compose a table of contents, and include an "About the Authors" section, if you like. Then, make copies for your classmates.

Reflecting on Your Writing

Once you've finished your story, use these questions to reflect on the process. Add your response to your portfolio.

- What did you learn about the techniques of professional fiction writers?

- Which strategy worked best for you? How did it help you improve your writing?

 Internet Tip

To see model essays scored with this rubric, go on-line:
PHSchool.com
Enter Web Code:
efk-1101

Rubric for Self-Assessment

Use the following criteria to assess your short story:

	Score 4	Score 3	Score 2	Score 1
Audience and Purpose	Presents an unusual perspective on a conflict	Presents a series of events leading to a clear conflict	Presents little conflict or narrative	Contains no conflict or narrative
Organization	Presents a clear sequence of events in a logical order	Presents a clear sequence of events with some inconsistencies in organization	Presents a weak or unclear connection between ideas or events	Presents no connections between ideas or events
Elaboration	Provides rich details and/or illuminating illustrations; incorporates apt, striking word choice; makes effective use of dialogue	Provides many details but some vague words; includes good use of dialogue	Provides some details through limited word choice; includes some use of dialogue	Provides no details; includes limited dialogue
Use of Language	Demonstrates overall clarity and fluency; presents very few errors in spelling, capitalization, punctuation, and/or usage	Demonstrates good sentence variety; presents some errors in spelling, capitalization, punctuation, and/or usage	Uses awkward or overly simple sentence structures; presents many errors in spelling, usage, and punctuation	Includes incomplete thoughts; creates confusion through errors in spelling, usage, and punctuation

Description

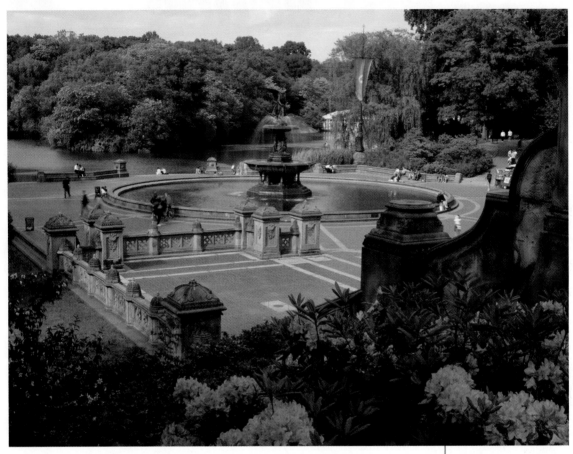

Description in Everyday Life

Imagine returning from a vacation without a single photograph or postcard. Try making a story scary without adding details to bring a scene to life. Challenge yourself to provide a radio-style play-by-play account to audiences who can't see the game. In each case, descriptive language that communicates sights, sounds, and other sensory details can enrich the way you communicate. We give and receive descriptive messages all day long. Advertisements describe products, your social studies text describes places and people, you and your friends describe favorite songs or movies. On the pages that follow, you'll learn how to improve your descriptive writing skills to use description for a variety of purposes.

▲ **Critical Viewing**
What words would you use to convey the sights and sounds suggested by this photograph? **[Describe]**

What Is Description?

Description is writing that uses vivid details to capture a scene, setting, person, or moment. Effective descriptive writing includes

- sensory details—sights, sounds, smells, tastes, and physical sensations.
- vivid, precise language.
- figurative language or comparisons.
- adjectives and adverbs that paint a word picture.
- an organization suited to the subject.

To see the criteria on which your descriptive writing may be evaluated, preview the Rubric for Self-Assessment on page 74.

Writers in

ACTION

Rita Dove uses vivid language to add life to her writing. Here's the challenge she sets for herself and others:

"When we can feel the breeze that sweeps through a valley—that's the kind of descriptive writing that comes alive."

Types of Description

Description can be useful in other forms of writing, but it can also stand alone. Here are some examples of descriptive writing:

- **Physical descriptions** may focus on the appearance of a person, place, or thing, as well as on its significance.
- **Descriptions of ideas** use concrete images or analogies to help readers understand abstract or complicated concepts.
- **Functional descriptions** describe the component parts of a whole for a practical purpose, such as fixing a bicycle.
- **Remembrances** illustrate memorable parts of the writer's past by describing a person, place, thing, or event.
- **Character sketches** illustrate the appearance and personality of a real or fictional character.

PREVIEW
Student Work
IN PROGRESS

Cheryl Boudreau, a student at Boone County High School in Florence, Kentucky, wrote a description entitled "An Autumn Memory." In the following pages, you'll see how Cheryl used the stages of the writing process to plan and write her essay. You can see her final draft at the end of the chapter.

Prewriting

Choosing Your Topic

To choose a subject that you want to describe, begin by looking at your surroundings or looking within yourself. You might describe something in your immediate environment or a person or place from memory. Use one of the following strategies to help you choose a topic:

Strategies for Generating Topics

1. **Blueprint** Draw the floor plan for a place you remember well—such as your home, your school, or a park. Label each part of your blueprint with words that identify each area of the map. Using the labels as column heads, jot down words, phrases, sentences, or names that you associate with each label. Look for connections among your items. Then, choose an idea or a memory that your blueprint inspired.

2. **Magazine Review** Flip through a magazine to find compelling images or articles that inspire ideas for description. As you scan the pages, note ideas that come to mind. Review your list to choose a topic for description.

3. **Personal Experience Timeline** Construct a timeline that highlights important events in your life. Focus your timeline on a specific event; for example, the experience of getting an after-school job or the events leading up to a personal victory. Review your timeline to choose a moment, person, or place as the topic of your description.

Try it out! Use the interactive Personal Experience Timeline in **Section 6.2**, on-line or on CD-ROM.

Student Work
IN PROGRESS

Name: *Cheryl Boudreau*
Boone County High School
Florence, KY

Creating a Personal Experience Timeline

Cheryl analyzed the important events in her high-school career. She decided to focus a descriptive essay on a championship football game.

| My first day of freshman year. | I meet my friend Denise for the first time. | I make the cheerleading team. | I go to my first prom. | I receive my high-school ring. | I cheer for the championship football game. |

TOPIC BANK

If you are having trouble choosing a topic, consider one of these suggestions:

1. **Description of an Artist at Work** Observe and describe a painter, dancer, singer, or other artist working at his or her craft. Use figurative language and comparisons to create a colorful description.

2. **Time-Lapse Description** Choose one location—such as a supermarket or the main lobby at your school—and visit it at three or four different times of day. Note the mood, people, and activity as you witness the location during each of your visits. Then, write a description showing the changes over time.

Responding to Fine Art

3. *Messenger on 42nd* conveys the fast pace and excitement of a city street. Consider another setting that communicates an emotion. For example, in a description you might show the calm of a beach at sunset or the anxiety of a rush-hour crowd waiting for a train.

Responding to Literature

Messenger on 42nd, Tom Christopher, Courtesy of The David Findlay Galleries

4. Read a descriptive portion of John Hersey's book *Hiroshima.* Use it as a model to write your own vivid description of a historic or fictional event as a participant would experience it. You can find an excerpt from *Hiroshima* in *Prentice Hall Literature, Penguin Edition,* The American Experience.

🕐 Timed Writing Prompt

5. Describe a remarkable event you witnessed, such as a winning touchdown or a historic flood. Write a vivid description as a participant would experience it. Use sensory details to make the event come alive for the reader. **(35 minutes)**

Narrowing Your Topic

As you plan your description, narrow your topic into one you can cover in the time and space you have. For example, you would not be able to describe the entire state of Washington in a short essay, but you might successfully describe a single natural feature, such as Mount Saint Helens.

Use Categorizing to Narrow a Topic

To narrow your topic, jot down all the ideas that your broad topic suggests to you. Review your list with the goal of making categories to organize your random ideas. Highlight words that seem similar or related. When you reorder your list into the groups you have identified, you can choose one of these focused topics to develop in your descriptive writing. Look at this example:

Broad topic: Last winter's blizzard

3 feet of snow
drifts to 10 feet
kids sled the next day
5 degrees below zero
-25 degrees wind chill
roads closed
people stranded
snowmen appear the next day

temperature
  5 degrees below zero
  -25 degrees wind chill

snow
  3 feet deep
  drifts to 10 feet

problems
  roads closed
  people stranded

fun
  kids sled the next day
  snowmen appear the next day

Narrowed topic: Kids have fun after a big blizzard.

Considering Your Audience and Purpose

Take a moment to identify the people you hope your writing will reach and the purposes you expect your writing to achieve.

Identify Your Audience Whether they are young children with a limited knowledge or people who share similar experiences with you, knowing your audience will help you choose the level of language and detail to use in your description.

Clarify Your Purpose You may want to describe in order to inspire awe or reflection. In contrast, you may want to describe to amuse or inform. Whatever your purpose, provide details that suit your specific writing goal.

Try it out! Use the interactive Use Categorizing to Narrow a Topic activity in **Section 6.2**, on-line or on CD-ROM.

Timed Writing Hint

Pay careful attention to the wording of the writing prompt. Identify the prompt's topic, purpose, and audience.

Gathering Details

Gathering details before you begin writing will give you the raw materials you need to make your description vivid. Take time to identify details that will help you show your subject.

Use Cubing to Gather Details

Cubing lets you examine a topic from six different angles. Review these instructions for cubing, and then use the strategy to collect information about your topic.

1. **Describe it** by noting its physical characteristics. As you do this, challenge yourself to address all five senses—sight, sound, smell, texture, and taste.
2. **Associate it** by explaining how it reminds you of something else.
3. **Apply it** by considering the ways your topic can be used.
4. **Analyze it** by breaking it into smaller parts.
5. **Compare and contrast it** by showing how your topic is similar to or different from other items.
6. **Argue for or against it** by evaluating your topic's worth.

Collaborative Writing Tip

You may generate more creative ideas when you work with others. If several classmates are writing about the same topic, complete the cubing activity together.

Student Work
IN PROGRESS

Name: Cheryl Boudreau
Boone County High School
Florence, KY

Cubing to Gather Details

Cheryl looked at the football game from six different angles. When she was finished, she decided to generate more sensory details to capture the experience.

SUBJECT: Championship Game

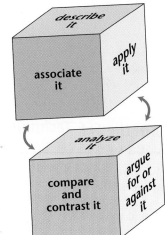

Describe:
• a brisk evening
• expectant faces in the crowd

Associate:
• like my family, our school sticks together during the low times, too

Apply:
• generates pride for our team and devoted fans

Analyze:
• even through defeat, school spirit is strengthened

Compare and contrast:
• team losing was like balloons slowly deflating

Argue for or against:
• fan support should be evident in both good and bad times

6.3 Drafting

Shaping Your Writing

Before you begin drafting, select a method for organizing your description. Consider these two organizational plans:

Plan an Organization

Organizing Details Spatially This organization is useful for physical or functional descriptions. Describe your topic as the eye might see it, moving from top to bottom, left to right, front to back, or outward from the most prominent feature. To make the arrangement of details clear, include directional terms, such as *to the right, on the top,* or *in the center.*

Organizing by Order of Importance This organization is effective in description that conveys an experience, shows a personality, or addresses an idea. Grab your readers' interest with your second-most important point. Then, cover your less important points, and build to your strongest one.

Providing Elaboration

To make your description full, include details that build the impression you want to convey.

Use the SEE Technique to Add Details

The step-by-step approach of the SEE method can help you develop your ideas. Here's what the labels mean:

S   Statement—Write a sentence to convey a main idea.

E   Extension—Restate or develop the main idea.

E   Elaboration—Provide further information to amplify or expand on the main idea.

Try it out! Use the interactive Adding Details With the SEE Technique activity in **Section 6.3**, on-line or on CD-ROM.

Student Work
IN PROGRESS

Name: *Cheryl Boudreau*
Boone County High School
Florence, KY

Adding Details With the SEE Technique
Here's how Cheryl used SEE to develop a paragraph.

[Statement] I felt an overwhelming sense of pride as I looked up into the sea of expectant faces. [Extension] I saw cheering teachers, students, parents, and alumni. [Elaboration] Not only had they all come, but they had made banners, painted their faces in our school's colors, and were on their feet.

6.4 Revising

Once you've written your first draft, take the time to review your description. First review the structure of the writing, and then move into an analysis of paragraphs, sentences, and word choice.

Revising Your Overall Structure

Focus Your Description

Just as a painting or photograph is enhanced by the right frame, your writing can be enhanced by the right words to begin and end it. Frame your description to help the readers focus on your description.

- Your **introduction** should establish the topic of your writing, give readers the general impression you want to convey, and indicate the purpose of your description.
- **Body paragraphs** describe your topic in depth.
- A **conclusion** should return your discussion back to a general level, adding some insight or leaving readers with a new way to see your topic.

▶ **REVISION STRATEGY**
Evaluating Your Frame

Review the opening and closing paragraphs of your writing. As you read each section, decide whether it provides context for your readers. Consider the following suggestions for revision:

Lead With a Comparison Revise your introduction by strengthening the opening two sentences. Create a striking comparison or a particularly dramatic image.

EXAMPLE: The Sequoias, as tall as any skyscraper, are majestic examples of nature's architecture.

Conclude With Figurative Language
Strengthen your conclusion by adding a *metaphor* that synthesizes the details you have presented. To write a metaphor, set your topic equal to another whose qualities you want to stress. In the example below, trees are set equal to towering giants.

EXAMPLE: These towering giants continue to impress visitors with the sheer improbability of their size.

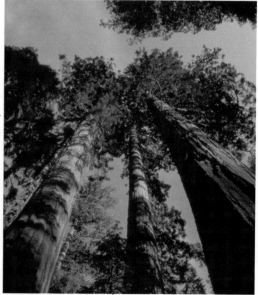

▼ Critical Viewing
How does the unusual angle of this photograph change your perspective of the trees it shows? **[Evaluate]**

Revising Your Paragraphs

Focus on Unity in Paragraphs

Body paragraphs focus on a central idea that is usually expressed in a topic sentence. In a unified paragraph, every other sentence supports, illustrates, or develops this idea. Review your body paragraphs to evaluate paragraph unity.

▶ **REVISION STRATEGY**
Color-Coding to Evaluate Paragraph Unity

Highlight the topic sentence of each topical or body paragraph in your draft. Use another color to underline the supporting details. Then, use these tips to evaluate and revise your writing:

Evaluate

- Does each paragraph have a topic sentence?

- Does each paragraph have enough specific details?
- Is each detail clearly related to the topic sentence?

Revise

- In some cases, your topic may be implied. Consider adding a topic sentence to focus your writing.
- Consider adding elaboration to develop your point.
- Eliminate details that are not related to the topic.

Interactive Textbook

Get instant help! For assistance revising body paragraphs, use the interactive Checking Paragraph Unity activity in **Section 6.4,** on-line or on CD-ROM.

Student Work
IN PROGRESS

Name: *Cheryl Boudreau*
Boone County High School
Florence, KY

Checking Paragraph Unity

When Cheryl evaluated this body paragraph, she decided to add more elaboration to support the main idea.

First, we were up by a touchdown, but two minutes later, the other team had rallied to tie the score.

The game proved to be a close one. ^

Topic sentence needs more support.

Back and forth it went. This exhausting process continued throughout the entire game, but not once did the crowd so much as sit down. They could not stop supporting the team with their enthusiastic spirit.

Revising Your Sentences

Eliminate Dull Sentence Patterns

To improve the rhythm of your writing, review the sentences in your first draft, focusing on sentence length. Challenge yourself to make your final draft more sophisticated by including a variety of sentence lengths.

▶**REVISION STRATEGY**
Combining Short Sentences

As you evaluate sentence lengths in your draft, identify places where you have created a series of short sentences. If you find that you have two or three short sentences in sequence, consider combining some to create longer sentences. When you rewrite two short sentences into one, you can stress the ways the information or ideas are related.

Grammar in Your Writing
Combining Sentences

Short sentences can be combined in a variety of ways.

- Join two independent clauses with a comma and a coordinating conjunction such as *and, but, or, nor,* or *for* to create a compound sentence:

Simple Sentences:	The canyon colors were beautiful. I was most impressed by the rock formations.
Compound Sentence:	The canyon colors were beautiful, and I was most impressed by the rock formations.

- When ideas are very closely related, join two independent clauses with a semicolon to create a compound sentence:

Simple Sentences:	The sunset was gorgeous. We stood in awe.
Compound Sentence:	The sunset was gorgeous; we stood in awe.

- Create a complex sentence by changing one of the sentences into a subordinate clause:

Simple Sentences:	We spent all day there. There was so much to see.
Complex Sentence:	We spent all day there because there was so much to see.

Find It in Your Reading Review a descriptive article. Identify examples of compound and complex sentences that the author uses to combine related ideas.

Find It in Your Writing Identify places in your draft where you have used compound or complex sentences to combine related ideas. Challenge yourself to improve your writing by combining sentences where appropriate.

For more on sentence combining, see Chapter 20.

Revising Your Word Choice

Vague and empty words can make your description longer, but they do not make it more vivid. To make your description powerful and evocative, make every word count.

▶ **REVISION STRATEGY**
Circling Vague Words

Review your draft to circle any vague or empty words in your description that do not add meaning. Then, decide whether to replace or eliminate each one you find.

Student Work
IN PROGRESS

Name: *Cheryl Boudreau*
Boone County High School
Florence, KY

Replacing Vague Words

In this passage, Cheryl replaced several vague words with specific, concrete words.

As I absorbed the many emotions surrounding me, I felt a

wave of pride *wash* come over me; we had done our best and had

valiantly really fought until the end, never once doubting or giving up.

phenomenal
Our fan support had been great, and although we had lost,

filed
everyone came out of the bleachers with their heads held high

warm
and a good feeling in their hearts.

Peer Review
Analytic Talk

Read your description to a small group. Focus a discussion around these revision suggestions:

- Ask your reviewers to identify the main impression that your description conveys. If their response does not match your original plan, you may want to extend the conversation. Ask your reviewers to tell you which images and details contributed to the central impression they identified.

- As you read your essay a second time, ask your reviewers to jot down the words that seemed most powerful to them. Your classmates might also note areas of description that could be sharpened. In a discussion, note their ideas and consider making revisions to your draft.

6.5 Editing and Proofreading

When you have revised the content of your description, you are ready to edit it, proofread it, and create a final draft. Review your paper for errors in grammar, usage, mechanics, and spelling. Strive to make your description error-free.

Focusing on Complete Sentences

When you are writing to convey an impression, it may be easy to fall into the trap of adding a detail that is not expressed as a complete thought. Review your paper to check that every group of words that is punctuated as a sentence can stand alone. Use this tip to guide your analysis:

Read each sentence aloud. Listen as you read to be sure that each sentence conveys a complete idea. To focus on this task, pause between sentences to avoid being distracted by the content.

 Timed Writing Hint

Adapt this strategy of checking for complete sentences by reading each sentence slowly but silently during exam conditions.

Grammar in Your Writing
Avoiding Fragments

While all clauses contain both a subject and a verb, subordinate clauses do not express a complete thought and therefore cannot be punctuated as sentences. There are two ways to correct fragments that begin with a subordinating conjunction.

1. **Eliminate the subordinating conjunction:**

Fragment: As the final seconds of the game approached.

Sentence: The final seconds of the game approached.

2. **Connect the subordinate clause to a main clause:**

Fragment: As the final seconds of the game approached.

Sentence: As the final seconds of the game approached, our team needed one touchdown to clinch the victory.

Find It in Your Writing Look through your draft to catch fragments that have crept into your writing. Correct any fragments that you find.

For additional instruction on sentence fragments, see Chapter 20.

Publishing and Presenting

When you finish writing your description, consider these ideas for sharing it with others:

Building Your Portfolio

Present a Dramatic Reading Working with a group of classmates who have written descriptions on a common theme, prepare a presentation. Select music, develop a sequence of readings, and present an introduction that connects the works. Then, share your work with an audience.

Publish a Literary Magazine Collect the finished descriptions, and publish them in a classroom magazine. As a group, split the tasks of designing the magazine's format, creating a cover and illustrations, and typing and proofreading the descriptions. Print copies of the magazine for your classroom library.

Reflecting on Your Writing

Consider the experience of writing your descriptive essay.

- How did your understanding of your subject change as a result of writing about it?
- What did you discover about the power of specific words that you can apply to your next writing assignment?

📖 Internet Tip

To see model essays scored with this rubric, go on-line:
PHSchool.com
Enter Web Code:
efk-1101

Rubric for Self-Assessment

Use the following criteria to evaluate your description.

	Score 4	Score 3	Score 2	Score 1
Audience and Purpose	Contains details that work together to create a single, dominant impression of the topic	Contains details that create a main impression of the topic	Contains extraneous details that detract from the main impression	Contains details that are unfocused and create no dominant impression
Organization	Consistently presents a logical and effective organization	Presents most details in a suitable organization	Presents some details in an illogical organization	Presents a confusing organization
Elaboration	Contains creative use of figurative language, creating interesting comparisons	Contains figurative language that creates comparisons	Contains figurative language, but the comparisons are not fresh	Contains no figurative language
Use of Language	Contains sensory language that appeals to the five senses; contains no errors in grammar, punctuation, or spelling	Contains some sensory language; contains few errors in grammar, punctuation, and spelling	Contains some sensory language, but it appeals to only one or two of the senses; contains some errors in grammar, punctuation, and spelling	Contains no sensory language; contains many errors in grammar, punctuation, and spelling

Connected Assignment *Poem*

If you saw a descriptive essay rewritten as a poem, you would notice some similarities and differences between the two pieces. Both descriptive prose and poetry focus on creating mental images for readers. **Poems,** however, express ideas in special formats, focus on how words sound, and may strive more intensely to create a particular mood.

These tips can help you write your own poem:

Prewriting To choose a topic for your poem, consider a natural object, an event, or an abstract idea. Make a few poetic choices: Consider whether you will use rhyme, rhythm, or a set line length. Then, gather words to create images for your writing. As you do this, plan the mood you want to convey.

In this model, the poet uses descriptive language to create an image for her readers.

▲ **Critical Viewing**
Why do you think nature is a common topic for poetry and fine art? **[Hypothesize]**

from **Suppose**
Siv Cedering

It could be
that the place my words are looking for
will turn out to be so small
that there will be room for nothing
but silence
—or an ocean so large
some waves will never reach
the sound of the shore

Drafting With poetry that has a set rhyme, rhythm, or line length, work from form to content. With free verse, you can work from content to form. Either way, keep the mood in mind as you draft and choose words that help you achieve it,

Revising and Editing Read your poem aloud, listening for the flow and sound of the words. Revise your word choice by replacing words that don't support the poem's mood.

Publishing and Presenting Share your poetry with classmates in an organized "poetry reading" day.

⚙ **Grammar and Style Tip**

Create alliteration by starting successive words with the same consonant sound. You may also take advantage of onomatopoeia by using words like *crackle* and *buzz* that suggest the sound they name.

Persuasion
Persuasive Essay

Abraham Lincoln–Stephen Douglas Debate at Charleston, Illinois – September 18, 1858, Robert Marshall Root,
Courtesy of the Illinois State Historical Library

Persuasion in Everyday Life

To present your best ideas and defend your unique opinions, you probably use persuasive skills every day. **Persuasion** is writing or speaking that tries to convince others to agree with you or to take an action that they might not take on their own. You use persuasive skills when you convince your friends to read a book you enjoyed, when you argue about whether your school should adopt a controversial new rule, or when you debate an issue in the news. When used effectively, persuasion can be powerful. It can influence election results, gain or lose a job opportunity, even decide whether a great idea is accepted at all.

▲ **Critical Viewing**
This painting depicts a famous debate between Abraham Lincoln and Stephen Douglas. What similarities and differences can you identify between the debate pictured in the painting and today's political debates? **[Compare and Contrast]**

What Is a Persuasive Essay?

As a student, you will often be asked to write persuasively. A **persuasive essay** presents your position on an issue, urges your readers to accept that position, and may encourage them to take an action. An effective persuasive essay

- explores an issue of importance to the writer.

- addresses an issue that is arguable.

- uses facts, examples, statistics, or personal experiences to support a position.

- tries to influence its audience through appeals to the readers' knowledge, experiences, or emotions.

- uses clear organization to present a logical argument.

To see the criteria on which your final persuasive essay may be judged, preview the Rubric for Self-Assessment on page 91 of this lesson.

Writers in
ACTION

Persuasion played a pivotal role in America's struggle for independence. In a memorable persuasive speech, Patrick Henry said:

"I know not what course others may take; but as for me, give me liberty or give me death."

Types of Persuasion

Persuasion can take many forms, ranging from the notes you write to friends asking them to join you in a difficult project to the President's formalized, scripted State of the Union address. Following is a list of a few forms of persuasion accompanied by explanations of the unique purpose of each form:

- **Editorials** are published by the editors of newspapers to share their opinions of events in the news.

- **Position papers** are written to influence policy decisions or to present a stand on a current issue.

- **Persuasive speeches** are presented aloud to an audience.

- **Debates** pit speakers against each other to present opposing sides of controversial issues.

PREVIEW
Student Work
IN PROGRESS

In this chapter, you will follow the work of Joseph Dangelmaier, a student at Archbishop Ryan High School in Philadelphia, Pennsylvania. Notice how he uses prewriting, drafting, and revising techniques to develop his essay "Life in the Fast Lane Just Got Faster."

7.2 **Prewriting**

Choosing Your Topic

To write a persuasive essay that convinces others to accept your views, select a topic that affects you personally. To be sure the issue you select could provoke argument, check that the subject has at least two sides. Consider these strategies:

Strategies for Generating Topics

1. **"News" Notebook** You can find many topics for a persuasive argument in the daily news. Watch television, scan newspapers, and listen to the issues that your friends are discussing now. Record the topics in a news notebook. Circle those that provoke strong feelings in you. Then, select one that you'd like to develop into a persuasive essay.

2. **Round-Table Discussion** Meet with a group of classmates to discuss issues that you consider important. Generate a list of topics, and for each idea, develop opposing statements. Star the ones that create the sharpest controversy or disagreement. On your own, choose a subject and a position that you could defend in a persuasive essay.

Interactive Textbook

Try it out! Use the Collaborating in a Round-Table Discussion activity in **Section 7.2**, on-line or on CD-ROM.

Student Work IN PROGRESS

Name: Joseph Dangelmaier
Archbishop Ryan High School
Philadelphia, PA

Collaborating in a Round-Table Discussion

When Joseph met with a group, he and his classmates outlined these general categories and created "pro" and "con" statements for each. Joseph decided to write a persuasive essay on technology's benefits.

Access to information outweighs the risks.

PRO **Technology** **CON**

Individual privacy is threatened.

Shorter opportunity keeps politicians focused on working for the public good.

PRO **Term limits for politicians** **CON**

Limits would take away leaders with experience.

TOPIC BANK

If you haven't found a topic that inspires you, consider these possibilities:

1. **A Letter to the Editor About Resource Use** The struggle between land developers and environmentalists pits the two sides against each other. Find out about such a controversy in your area. Write a letter to the editor of your local paper to express your position on the conflict.

2. **Persuasive Essay on Dress Codes** High schools often have rules that prohibit short skirts, torn jeans, or T-shirts with slogans. In a persuasive essay, argue the benefits or disadvantages of a school dress code.

Responding to Fine Art

3. This painting of people joining hands might prompt you to think of issues that bring people together. For example, an election can inspire a grass-roots effort to influence voting, or a flood might bring neighbors together to help those in need. Write a persuasive essay about such an occurrence. In your essay, convince others to contribute time, money, or energy to the issue.

Repeat Again, I Do Believe, Phoebe Beasley, Courtesy of the artist

Responding to Literature

4. Read "Civil Disobedience" by Henry David Thoreau. In a persuasive essay, argue for or against Thoreau's philosophy of government. You can find an excerpt from this essay in *Prentice Hall Literature, Penguin Edition,* The American Experience.

🕐 Timed Writing Prompt

5. Many schools have banned students from using cell phones on campus, or even bringing them to school. Write a persuasive essay to the school board explaining your position on this issue. Convince the school board that your position is correct and wise. Support your argument with examples. **(35 minutes)**

Narrowing Your Topic

After you have decided on a topic, consider the arguments that you will need to make in order to convince your audience. For example, if you plan to argue that people should eat nutritious foods, you will have to discuss many kinds of diets and explain why each one is beneficial or harmful. That is probably too broad a topic for the length of your essay. In contrast, a narrower topic such as "Improve Your Health: Eat More Vegetables" can be covered in the space you have. Looping is one strategy for narrowing a topic.

Use Looping to Narrow a Topic

To help you focus on a topic, use these steps in the process of looping: Write freely on your topic for about five minutes. Read what you have written. Circle the most important idea. Write for five minutes on the idea that you circled. Repeat the process until you reveal a topic that is narrow enough to cover well in a persuasive essay.

Student Work
IN PROGRESS

Name: Joseph Dangelmaier
Archbishop Ryan High School
Philadelphia, PA

Looping

Here is how Joseph used looping to narrow his topic:

Broad topic: Technology is both good and bad.

Technology is a mixed bag. On the one hand, technology has always been around. Humans wouldn't have gotten anywhere without it. This goes for everything from making fire to transplanting organs. There are so many (powerful benefits of technology,) in medicine, education, and communication. Naturally, there are drawbacks, too.

Powerful benefits of technology:
The powerful benefits of technology far outweigh the challenges and risks involved in adopting new things. Improvements in medicine, education, and especially communication make the point convincingly that (people should embrace new technologies.)

Narrow topic: People should embrace new technologies.

Considering Your Audience and Purpose

While the purpose of all persuasive writing is to sway readers, the specific audience you expect to address will affect the way you persuade them. Therefore, the first step in convincing your audience is knowing your audience.

Analyze Your Audience

Knowing such characteristics as the age, occupation, values, and prior knowledge of your readers will help you appeal to them effectively. For example, if you were writing to promote research into blue-laser DVDs, which have a higher storage capacity than conventional CDs, you could use a variety of details to support your position. The graph below shows the different appeals that you might make to specific groups of people.

TARGET YOUR APPEAL
TO DIFFERENT AUDIENCES

Business executives

Artists and filmmakers

Students
want to have greater convenience while having fun.

wish to broaden the audience for their work.

look for innovative ways to create products.

Writers in
ACTION

As vice president of communications for the National Urban League, M. Gasby Greely creates letters, essays, and speeches to persuade. She sees each specific audience as an engine that directs her power to persuade. Here she explains how an analysis of each audience can drive her writing:

"The best way I can focus my writing is to keep the audience in mind . . . what is going to get them to understand my point of view?"

Gathering Evidence

To write a strong persuasive essay, support your position with convincing examples. One of the most effective ways to make your examples convincing is to address both sides of your topic.

Get Information on Both Sides of the Issue

In addition to providing arguments and examples that support your position, you should know and address arguments that can be used to attack your ideas. Use the strategies below to marshal the arguments for and against your position. Then, collect the evidence that will lead readers to accept your ideas or to take the action that you recommend.

Make a T-Chart Write your position at the top of a sheet of paper. Then, draw a line down the middle of the page to create two columns. In one column, jot down facts and ideas that support your position. In the other, note arguments and evidence that might be used to attack your position. Use your T-chart to guide further collection of evidence.

SAMPLE T-CHART

The Driving Age Should Be Lowered to Fifteen

Pro	Con
Many teens at 15 have adult responsibilities, so they should have adult privileges like driving.	Many speeding tickets and car accidents involve teenagers.

Conduct Interviews You can gather valuable information by asking the right questions. Consider setting up the following data-collection interviews:

- **Survey Your Audience** To tailor your appeal to your intended readers, find out what they believe about your topic. Talk to classmates, family, or friends and take notes about people's concerns relative to your position.

- **Question the Experts** To strengthen your argument, find out what the experts say. Interview people who study or work in an area related to your topic. Jot down evidence that supports your position and that your readers may not typically know.

💻 Internet Tip

The Internet often has the most up-to-date information on many subjects. As you research your topic, consider going on-line to find arguments for and against your position.

7.3 *Drafting*

Shaping Your Writing

Develop a Thesis Statement

An effective persuasive essay is built around a clearly worded **thesis statement,** a statement of the position you will prove.

SAMPLE THESIS STATEMENTS

- Televised trials often weaken the defendants' ability to gain a fair hearing because lawyers and judges play to the camera.
- Broadcasting trials improves our legal system by exposing general audiences to the everyday workings of the court system.

Organize to Emphasize the Strongest Support

In your draft, introduce your topic and state your thesis. In the body of your essay, make the arguments that support and prove your thesis statement. Follow the organization below:

- Use your second-best argument for a good start.
- Show and argue against the opposing views.
- Organize your details to lead up to your conclusion.
- Save your best argument for a strong finish.

Get instant help! Use the interactive Organizing an Essay Diagram in **Section 7.3,** on-line or on CD-ROM.

Student Work
IN PROGRESS

Name: Joseph Dangelmaier
Archbishop Ryan High School
Philadelphia, PA

Organizing an Essay Diagram

Joseph made a diagram to show the order in which he planned to present his ideas for maximum effect.

```
INTRODUCTION → THESIS STATEMENT → BENEFITS OF TECHNOLOGY
ACKNOWLEDGE OPPOSITION
BEST BENEFIT OF TECHNOLOGY
REFUTE OPPOSITION → CONCLUSION
```

Drafting • **83**

Providing Elaboration
Consider a Variety of Points for Illumination

Build a strong case for your position by choosing the best methods of elaboration. Consider these strategies to support your position:

- **Give the Facts** Include information that is objective and that can be proved. Insert names, dates, and other data that provide background for your topic.

- **Provide Statistics** Strengthen your argument by citing numbers that prove your position. Give information that shows *how many* or *what percentage*.

- **Make a Comparison** Show your readers how your topic matches others they may already know.

- **Share a Personal Experience** Explain how the topic you are addressing has personal meaning for you.

- **Include Details to Fill Out Your Ideas** Details are the specifics that clarify the points you are making. Show the pieces of the larger position you are arguing.

As the chart below indicates, you can elaborate using each of these techniques:

Timed Writing Hint

Read the prompt to determine the types of details or examples it calls for in an essay.

Thesis: The admission price at sporting events should be lowered.

Details:
Admission is expensive. Add it to the cost of programs, souvenirs, and food, and the cost skyrockets.

Comparisons:
Game tickets are more expensive than museum and movie admissions.

Thesis:
The admission price of professional sporting events should be lowered.

Facts:
Most league stadiums can hold more than 50,000 people per game. Teams make money on television rights and advertising revenue, too.

Personal Experience:
I am a die-hard fan, but my family can't afford to go to all the games I want to see.

Statistics:
The price of these tickets has more than tripled in fifteen years. In 1980, a box seat was $8; now, it is $25.

7.4 *Revising*

After you have drafted your persuasive essay, look for ways to make it better. Check to make sure that your argument is clear and your essay well organized. Then, review the details, such as the types of sentences you have used and your choice of words. Revisions that come from such analysis will make your essay more persuasive.

Revising Your Overall Structure

Strengthen Your Introduction

In addition to presenting your thesis statement, the introduction is your first and greatest chance to grab the reader's interest in your topic. The first few sentences of your draft are your lead; they are your chance to build interest in your topic. Review and revise your introduction to take full advantage of this once-in-an-essay opportunity.

▶**REVISION STRATEGY**
Adding Information to Build Interest

Evaluate your lead to see whether added details might help to generate more interest in your topic. Make notes to suggest areas for further development, and jot down ideas that will make the introduction more appealing.

🔋 Research Tip

Consult reference materials to obtain additional information that you need to strengthen your introduction. You can find facts, statistics, and useful details in sources like *InfoTrac* and *Facts on File.*

Student Work
IN PROGRESS

Name: *Joseph Dangelmaier*
Archbishop Ryan High School
Philadelphia, PA

Adding Information to Build Interest

Here is Joseph's first version of the lead in his introduction. When he looked at it again, he decided to perk it up by adding information to it.

Technology, like life, evolves to meet new challenges. People wanted a faster tool for making mathematical calculations, so they developed the processor—then the microprocessor. The need for a more efficient way to transport data inspired the networking technology that we know as the Internet.

What other example of technology can I show? Fire. Ships. Airplanes.

Revising Your Paragraphs

Eliminate Faulty Logic

The more critical your audience, the more important it is for you to draw reasonable conclusions based on adequate evidence that supports your position. A discerning audience will quickly see through errors in logic. Review your draft to eliminate the following patterns of weak arguments:

Circular Reasoning A writer thinks he or she is advancing an argument but is simply restating ideas instead of defending them.

EXAMPLE: The mall is losing business because nobody shops there.

REVISION: The mall is losing business because people are shopping on-line.

Either/Or Argument A writer oversimplifies the issue by offering only two extremes, when in fact there are other possibilities.

EXAMPLE: If store owners don't have more sales, the mall will go out of business.

REVISION: If store owners don't have more sales, provide more conveniences, and improve security, shopping revenue will continue to drop.

▲ Critical Viewing
If you were developing an advertisement for the mall pictured here, how might you attract customers? **[Hypothesize]**

▶**REVISION STRATEGY**
Looking for Logic

You can avoid exasperating your readers by finding and eliminating faulty logic. Review your draft, evaluating each sentence. Bracket any sentences that make logical appeals to your readers, and revise any that contain faulty logic or unreasonable appeals.

Revising Your Sentences

Use Transitions

Adding words that make your reasoning more obvious to your readers can enhance the power of your writing. Consider adding these transitions to improve your sentence clarity.

- **To show a contrast:** however, although, despite
- **To point to a reason:** since, because, if
- **To signal a conclusion:** therefore, consequently, so, then

▶**REVISION STRATEGY**
Color-Coding to Check Connections

Circle any transitions in your paper. Then, read each paragraph of your essay. Underline in green the places where you set up contrasts, underline in blue where you provide reasons, and underline in red where you have drawn conclusions. In each case, decide whether the transition you have used is a strong one. Revise or add transitions as needed.

Grammar in Your Writing
Adverb Clauses

Adverb clauses are groups of words that show the relationship between ideas by telling more about the action of a sentence. Although they contain both a subject and a verb, adverb clauses cannot stand alone. Instead, they can tell *where, when, how, why, to what extent,* or *under what condition* the action of the rest of the sentence occurred.

- Time relationship (when): After the tornado touched down
- Cause-and-effect relationship (why): Because the university has such a wonderful library
- Opposing relationship (under what condition): Although the deputy said that the evidence was insufficient

When an adverb clause introduces a sentence, use a comma to separate it from the rest of the sentence. Note, however, that it is usually not necessary to use a comma before an adverb clause at the end of a sentence.

Find It in Your Reading Review a newspaper article you have read recently. Identify two adverb clauses.

Find It in Your Writing Circle all of the adverb clauses in your draft. Check that you have punctuated them correctly. If you discover you haven't used at least two adverb clauses, challenge yourself to add one.

For more on adverb clauses, see Chapter 19.

Revising Your Word Choice
Consider the Power of Words

The words that you choose can strongly influence your readers' responses to your argument. In making word choices, distinguish between a word's denotations and its connotations.

Check the Denotation The **denotation** of a word is its direct, explicit meaning. By referring to a dictionary, you can see a word's denotation. For example, when you compare the words *mandatory* and *optional*, you will see that they have contrasting denotations.

Measure the Connotation A word's **connotation** is the informal meaning a reader or listener attaches to a word. Each time you choose a word, make sure you know how its connotation will affect your audience. The chart below illustrates how words with similar denotations can have opposite connotations.

Words With Strong Connotations

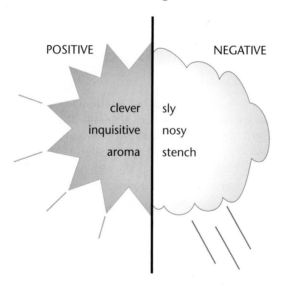

POSITIVE	NEGATIVE
clever	sly
inquisitive	nosy
aroma	stench

▶ **REVISION STRATEGY**
Using a Thesaurus

Look for places in your draft where you criticize your opposition, defend your ideas, or appeal to your readers' emotions. In each case, circle key nouns or verbs. Consult a thesaurus to find synonyms. Then, decide whether words with stronger connotations might sway your readers even more. Revise to achieve this goal.

⏱ Timed Writing Hint

As you revise your essay, replace a repeated adjective with a synonym.

Get instant help! For assistance revising word choice, use the interactive Using a Thesaurus activity in **Section 7.4,** on-line or on CD-ROM.

Peer Review

Analytic Flags

Share your revised draft with a partner. Ask your reviewer to use self-sticking flags or paper clips and small squares of colored paper. Your reviewer can jot down suggestions, comments, or questions for improving your draft and attach each idea to appropriate places in your essay. Ask your partner to consider questions like these:

- Do I create enough interest in my topic?

- Is there any more background information a reader would need to know?

- Do you notice any errors in logic?

- Where can I add more persuasive language?

◄ **Critical Viewing**
What are some good ways to evaluate the feedback you receive in a peer conference like the one shown here? **[Speculate]**

Get instant help! Use the interactive Using Analytic Flags for Peer Review activity in **Section 7.4,** online or on CD-ROM.

Student Work
IN PROGRESS

Name: *Joseph Dangelmaier*
Archbishop Ryan High School
Philadelphia, PA

Using Analytic Flags for Peer Review

Notice the suggestions that Joseph's partner made on his flags. Joseph evaluated each idea and then accepted one and rejected the other.

Students respond more enthusiastically to the colors, interesting sounds, and entertaining animation of a computer program than to a static chalkboard.

Use adjectives to increase appeal.

Add info about computer labels.

Joseph felt this suggestion would pull readers away from the point he was making. He chose not to make the change.

Editing and Proofreading

Errors in writing can confuse your audience and weaken your credibility as an author. To eliminate errors in your writing, double-check spelling, punctuation, and grammar before writing your final draft.

Focusing on Commas

Commas can make your persuasive essay easier to understand by showing the reader when to pause. However, when commas are used incorrectly, your writing can be confusing. One of the most common uses of commas is to set off the following introductory material:

- **Prepositional phrases:** After the coming attractions, the feature will start.

- **Participial phrases:** Packed to the doors, the theater could hold no more patrons.

- **Infinitive phrases:** To be sure we got a seat, we arrived at the theater an hour early.

Review your draft, and add commas where necessary.

> **Learn More**
>
> For more on commas separating introductory elements, see Chapter 27.

Grammar in Your Writing
Serial Commas

In addition to their function of separating introductory elements of a sentence, commas are also used to separate items in a series. Use commas to separate three or more words, phrases, or clauses in a list.

- **Separating words:** Maria paints, sings, and dances.
- **Separating phrases:** Maria paints in art class, sings in the choir, and dances after school.
- **Separating clauses:** Maria learned that painting is challenging, that singing provides an outlet for tension, and that dancing develops coordination.

Find It in Your Reading Find one example of serial commas in a story you have read.

Find It in Your Writing As you proofread your persuasive essay, check to make sure that you have used serial commas correctly.

For more information on serial commas, see Chapter 27.

7.6 Publishing and Presenting

Building Your Portfolio

Sharing your persuasive essay might just achieve results—your ideas could inspire a positive change in behavior, open minds to a fresh perspective, or help to change an unfair policy. Consider these ideas for publishing and presenting your work:

1. **Send Class Letters** Ask your classmates to join you in writing persuasive letters on your topic, if it is appropriate to the purpose, and mail them to a state or federal congressional representative.

2. **Publish in a Newspaper** Send your essay as an opinion piece, or condense it into a letter to the editor of your school or community newspaper.

Reflecting on Your Writing

Take a moment to learn from your writing experience. In a journal, jot down your reflections on the persuasive writing process. Use these questions to get you started:

- What techniques of persuasion can you apply in future writing situations?

- How might persuasive writing affect the way you are influenced?

🖥 Internet Tip

To see model essays scored with this rubric, go on-line:
PHSchool.com
Enter Web Code:
efk-1101

Rubric for Self-Assessment

Use this rubric to evaluate your persuasive essay.

	Score 4	Score 3	Score 2	Score 1
Audience and Purpose	Demonstrates highly effective word choice; clearly states focus on persuasive task	Demonstrates good word choice; states focus on persuasive task	Shows some good word choices; minimally states focus on persuasive task	Shows lack of attention to persuasive task
Organization	Uses clear, consistent organizational strategy	Uses clear organizational strategy with occasional inconsistencies	Uses inconsistent organizational strategy; presentation is not logical	Demonstrates lack of organizational strategy
Elaboration	Provides convincing, well-elaborated reasons to support the writer's position; includes no examples of faulty logic	Provides two or more moderately elaborated reasons to support the writer's position; includes few examples of faulty logic	Provides several reasons but only one is elaborated; includes several examples of faulty logic	Provides no specific reasons or does not elaborate; most ideas indicate faulty logic
Use of Language	Incorporates many transitions to create clarity of expression; includes very few mechanical errors	Incorporates some transitions to help flow of ideas; includes few mechanical errors	Incorporates few transitions; does not connect ideas well; includes many mechanical errors	Does not connect ideas; includes many mechanical errors

Persuasion
Advertisement

Battle of Big Horns, 1988, Phoebe Beasley, Courtesy of the artist

Advertisements in Everyday Life

Newspapers and magazines boast page after page of sales announcements. During most half-hour television programs, eight minutes are devoted to commercials touting new products or services. Imprints on the walls of big-league stadiums—and even the names of many of these arenas—are linked to products. In addition, the layout of many Internet pages makes room for catchy ads to distract Web surfers. In today's commercial environment, you can't go far without seeing an advertisement. As a category of persuasion, advertising seeks to convince an audience to accept a point of view. However, advertising usually has a more focused purpose—to influence what and how much consumers buy.

▲ **Critical Viewing**
In your opinion, what product or service is this artwork suited to advertise? **[Hypothesize]**

What Is an Advertisement?

An **advertisement** is a planned communication meant to be seen, heard, or read. It attempts to persuade an audience to buy a product or service, accept an idea, or support a cause. Advertisements may appear in printed form—in newspapers and magazines, on billboards, or as posters or flyers. They may appear on radio or television, as either commercials or public-service announcements. An effective advertisement includes

- a memorable slogan to grab the audience's attention.

- a call to action, which tries to rally the audience to do something.

- details that provide such information as price, location, date, and time.

To see the criteria by which your final advertisement may be judged, preview the Rubric for Self-Assessment on page 104.

Types of Advertisements

From public-service announcements to billboards to product packing, written advertisements come in a variety of types and styles. Several common types of advertisements are described below:

- **Public-service announcements** provide persuasive information to educate audiences about issues of social concern.

- **Billboards** are posted on highways and in train stations where people have limited time to see the ad.

- **Product packaging** involves the use of an item's container to persuade consumers to buy the product.

- **Political campaign literature** presents a candidate and his or her record to educate and persuade voters.

Writers in **ACTION**

Entrepreneur and author David Ogilvy founded one of the world's largest advertising agencies, known today as Ogilvy and Mather. His firm creates ads for a wide range of products and services, including airlines, credit cards, and luxury cars. Ogilvy sounds a cautionary note to the aspiring copywriter:

"You cannot bore people into buying your product, you can only interest them in buying it."

PREVIEW
Student Work
IN PROGRESS

In this chapter, you'll see how Catherine Johns, a student at Bel Air High School in El Paso, Texas, used the stages of the writing process to create an advertisement for a fictional business.

This magazine advertisement introduces audiences to a new Web site called **Wemedia.com**

LITERATURE

To find an advertisement the U.S. Navy used to attract recruits during World War I, see the Introduction to Unit 5 in *Prentice Hall Literature, Penguin Edition,* The American Experience.

I'M STANDING UP FOR YOU.

Wemedia.com is a web site mobilizing the collective voice of the 54 million Americans with disabilities and over $1 trillion in buying power. The bottom line is access. Access to education, healthcare, financial services and employment. Access to the ear of corporate America and Washington D.C. Access to quality of life. Nothing more, nothing less.

Cary Fields, President/CEO

we media.com

Set in the largest type size on the page, a compelling slogan, "I'm standing up for you," sets up a contradiction with the photograph.

Copy in a smaller size beneath the photograph provides details to introduce the purpose and content of the new Web site.

The Web address at the end of the ad gives readers the practical information they need to visit the Web site.

Reading Writing Connection

Writing Application: Evaluate Word Choice
Like the creators of this ad, choose your words carefully to convey a specific impression.

8.2 *Prewriting*

Choosing Your Topic

Good advertising conveys enthusiasm. To write a persuasive ad, choose a product, service, or political campaign that excites you. The strategies that follow can help.

Strategies for Generating Topics

1. **Product Survey** With a group, identify the products and services that people in your school enjoy. Develop a questionnaire to identify specific product categories and the most popular brand names. Review the survey results, and choose a product or service to promote in an ad.

2. **Twenty-four Hour List** Pay attention to the products and services you use in a typical day. In a list that breaks the time into hour-long blocks, jot down two or three items you use regularly during each interval. Look over your chart to choose a topic for your advertisement.

Interactive Textbook

Try it out! Use the interactive Twenty-four Hour List in **Section 8.2**, on-line or on CD-ROM.

TOPIC BANK

If you're having trouble coming up with your own topic, consider these possibilities:

1. **Advertisement for a Wilderness Adventure** For a print media ad, develop a catchy slogan and text that includes specific details about a trip with an adventure travel company. For example, consider writing an ad to promote backpacking, canoeing, or kayaking trips.

Responding to Literature

2. Read "The Rockpile," by James Baldwin. Create a flyer announcing the start-up of a block association for Roy's block. You can find the story in *Prentice Hall Literature, Penguin Edition,* The American Experience.

🕐 Timed Writing Prompt

3. Suppose a foreign student is selecting a high school in the United States to attend. Write an essay to convince the foreign student that he or she should attend your school. Include examples that highlight your school's positive features and qualities. **(35 minutes)**

Narrowing Your Topic

The real work of advertising is not in choosing a topic, but in deciding which part of the product will appeal to an audience. After you have decided on a topic, identify what your ad will convey about it. The cubing strategy allows you to examine a topic from several angles.

Use Cubing to Narrow a Topic

Study your topic using these six methods:

1. **Describe It** Explain the physical attributes of your topic to an audience who has never seen it.

2. **Associate It** Show how your topic relates to something else or how it reminds you of something else.

3. **Apply It** Tell how your topic can be used.

4. **Analyze It** Separate your topic into smaller parts.

5. **Compare and Contrast It** Explain how other items are similar and different from yours.

6. **Argue for It** While traditional cubing lets you provide reasons to promote or reject an idea, narrow this cubing angle to collect only positive reasons to sell your product or service.

🕐 **Timed Writing Hint**

If you are given thirty-five minutes to write an essay, you should spend about five minutes prewriting.

Student Work IN PROGRESS

Name: Catherine Johns
Bel Air High School
El Paso, TX

Cubing to Narrow a Topic

Catherine chose to promote a company that offers classes in foreign language instruction. When she addressed the "Apply" angle of cubing, she narrowed her topic to focus on this service's usefulness to business professionals.

Describe:

Associate:

Apply: You can do many things with a foreign language, including travel more easily and communicate with people in different cultures. The latter is very important in today's global economy. International business is expanding at a rapid pace. To succeed in the international arena, corporate executives need to know the language spoken in countries where they do business.

Considering Your Audience and Purpose

Remember that the purpose of advertising is to convince people to buy a product or service or to support a candidate for office. The content and appearance of your advertisement must be directed to convince a specific audience.

Identify the Target Audience

There are many ways to sell a product. To be most effective, take the time to figure out whom your advertisement will reach. For example, you may want to reach classmates, parents, or a group of experts. The chart below shows how knowing your target audience will allow you to include details and use language that will appeal to them.

Get instant help! To find language that will appeal to your target audience, use the interactive Word Bins, accessible from the menu bar, on-line or on CD-ROM.

Audience	Appeal	Details to Emphasize
Classmates	Show them it's FUN	exciting, cool, relaxing, interesting
Parents	Show them it has VALUE	money-saving, time-saving, safe, educational
Experts	Show them it has QUALITY	tested, well-built, top-of-the-line

Gathering Details

Before you begin writing your advertisement, gather lively and powerful words to describe your product. Then, identify the product features that deserve these words.

Build a Parts-of-Speech Word Web

In a Word Web like the one shown here, gather details about your topic. Write your main idea or topic in the center of it. Then, identify the nouns, verbs, adverbs, adjectives, and interjections you might use to describe your subject. To make your Word Web even more useful, use a thesaurus to find exactly the right words for each category.

Try it out! Use the interactive Build a Parts-of-Speech Word Web activity in **Section 8.2**, on-line or on CD-ROM.

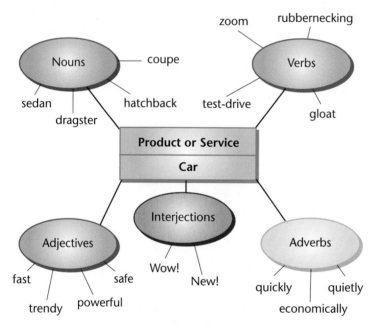

Identify the Features to Promote

Whether you've decided to announce that your topic is sporty or practical, high-fashion or high-tech, you need to back up that assertion with specific references. For each concept you want to convey, jot down the features of your topic that support your idea. Use these suggestions to guide your prewriting:

- **To show a product is practical:** Gather details that address cost and ease of use. Show that the product is necessary, not frivolous.

- **To show a product is fun:** Collect the specific information to show what makes the product exciting or enjoyable.

8.3 *Drafting*

Shaping Your Writing

Create a Slogan

Draft a slogan to shape the details you'll include in your advertisement. Your slogan should grab the audience's attention and make them want to learn more about the product.

SAMPLE SLOGANS

"There are a zillion things to do at the Seattle Street Fair."

"All Over the Map Bookstore—your first stop in travel."

Providing Elaboration

Once you have created an attention-grabbing slogan, it is time to select points to illuminate in your advertisement.

Use a Pentad to Identify Key Points

Because every word in an advertisement counts, you must identify the essential points to illuminate in a limited space. Use a pentad like the one below to develop your elaboration.

Collaborative Writing Tip

Share your lists of slogans with a group. In exchange for a quick first response to your ideas, help the others in your group decide what slogan strategies are most successful and which need more refining.

Student Work IN PROGRESS

Name: *Catherine Johns*
Bel Air High School
El Paso, TX

Using a Pentad

Catherine used a pentad to identify the information she will use to elaborate her slogan: "Everyone can learn another language."

Actors:
Who does the action?
business owners, executives

Acts:
What is done?
learn languages through intensive training

Purposes:
Why is it done?
ensure success in foreign markets

Scenes:
When or where is it done?
on site, anywhere in the United States

Agencies:
How is it done?
training in five sessions

Revising

After drafting your advertisement, begin looking for ways to improve it. In the revising stage, check to make sure that your slogan is catchy and your information persuasive. From the big picture of an overall concept, move toward the small details, such as sentence structure and word choice. Your reward will be an ad that prompts your audience to answer your call to action with a resounding "Yes!"

Revising Your Overall Structure

Review Visual Layout

Before you polish the copy in your ad, devote attention to its visual layout. Remember that visual appeal and persuasive copy work together to create a positive audience response.

▶ **REVISION STRATEGY**
Color-Coding to Improve Layout

Review the text of your advertisement. Use a highlighter to mark the strongest points you want to convey. Make sure that the reader notices these points by making them stand out in some way. Consider placement or font size. Alternatively, use color or bullets to call readers' attention to these key points.

Technology Tip

Explore the wide range of fonts, point sizes, and design styles available in your word-processing program. Select those that will increase the persuasive power of your ad.

Student Work
IN PROGRESS

Name: *Catherine Johns*
Bel Air High School
El Paso, TX

Improving Layout Through Color-Coding
Catherine color-coded her main ideas to evaluate the layout of her ad.

I can make this a leaner bulleted list.

ILTC benefits include a teacher-student ratio of one to five: that's three language and culture experts for every 15 students; 30 instructional days of intensive language and cultural awareness training; and on-site instruction, anywhere in the United States.

When she saw key ideas buried in a paragraph, Catherine decided to try another approach.

Revising Your Paragraphs and Sentences

Use Parallel Structure

Once you are satisfied with the layout of your ad, return to the copy. Check it for clarity and ease of reading. Consider using parallel structures—expressing similar details using similar grammatical structures—to make the information you have presented easier for your readers to absorb.

PARALLEL ADJECTIVES: This drink is *nutritious, refreshing,* and *economical.*

PARALLEL VERBS: Enjoy it while you are *relaxing, talking,* and *laughing.*

PARALLEL PHRASES: Take it with you *to the gym, to the park, on the go*!

▶ **REVISION STRATEGY**
Identifying Sentence Types to Create Parallelism

Identify the sentence types you have used in your advertisement. In a list, indicate the function of each sentence—declarative, imperative, interrogative, or exclamatory. Evaluate this list to see whether you have used parallel structure. Make corrections if necessary. In this example, highlighted material shows a problem in parallelism and its solution.

EXAMPLE: Cool off with Freddie's Fruit Smoothie. Choose black raspberry, strawberry, or lemon-lime. You may wish to add a dollop of whipped cream for even more enjoyment.

ANALYSIS: The first two sentences in this paragraph are imperatives. As a declarative, the last sentence is not parallel with the others. Revising it strengthens the impact of the ad.

REVISION: Cool off with Freddie's Fruit Smoothie. Choose black raspberry, strawberry, or lemon-lime. Add a dollop of whipped cream for even more enjoyment.

▶ **Critical Viewing** What features of these fruitful concoctions would you emphasize in an advertisement? **[Synthesize]**

🕐 **Timed Writing Hint**

If you are given thirty-five minutes to write an essay, you should spend five minutes revising.

🔎 **Learn More**

For more on the four functions of sentences, see Chapter 20.

Revising Your Word Choice

Add Modifiers to Sell

You've probably realized by now that using vivid modifiers is the key to writing a persuasive advertisement. Lively adjectives, in particular, can make your ad more successful.

▶ **REVISION STRATEGY**
Underlining Nouns to Assess Adjectives

Underline all the nouns in your draft. Check each noun to see if it is modified by an adjective or adjective phrase. Then, add modifiers where you think they will increase the power of your advertisement. Alternatively, consider choosing a stronger noun to convey your idea.

Interactive Textbook

Get instant help! For more on using modifiers, use the interactive Adding Modifiers to Strengthen Audience Appeal activity in **Section 8.4**, on-line or on CD-ROM.

Student Work
IN PROGRESS

Name: *Catherine Johns*
Bel Air High School
El Paso, TX

Adding Modifiers to Strengthen Audience Appeal

Catherine added modifiers to strengthen the appeal of her advertisement. Notice that she used adverbs as well as adjectives.

of the fastest growing and most profitable

ILTC <u>clients</u> include many ∧<u>companies</u> in <u>North America</u>.

Peer Review

Focus Groups

When people in the advertising industry create product campaigns, they often test their concepts before launching the ads. Try one of their techniques: the focus group. Show your revised ad to a group of classmates, and listen as they comment on its effects. To get feedback on specific points of concern, formalize the review with these discussion questions:

- What do you think the product is?
- Would you buy the product based on this advertisement?
- What aspect of the advertisement stands out most?

8.5 *Editing and Proofreading*

Errors in grammar, usage, or mechanics can undermine your audience's trust in the product or service your advertisement promotes. To make your advertisement error-free, check your work carefully before creating a final draft.

Focusing on Spelling

Check that each word in your advertisement is spelled correctly. To be sure that you read each word, check the advertisement from the last word to the first. Be especially careful with the spelling of names and addresses.

✔ Spelling Tip

Beware of errors that a spell-check function will not catch, such as homophones like *their* and *there* and proper nouns.

Grammar in Your Writing
Conventions for Providing Practical Information

As you proofread, make sure you have used commonly accepted conventions for writing addresses, telephone numbers, dates, and times.

Addresses Use one line for the street address and another one for city and state. Use a comma to separate the city and state, but do not use one to separate the state from the ZIP Code.

Example: 1000 Maple Avenue
Dallas, Texas 75205

Web addresses Write the exact wording of the address, showing the specific punctuation and spacing of the domain name.

Examples: www.phschool.com   www.senate.gov

Telephone numbers Use parentheses, a hyphen, or a slash to separate the area code from the main number. Use a hyphen before the last four digits.

Examples: (847) 555-4704 or 847-555-4704 or 847/555-4704

Dates Capitalize the month. Place a comma between the day of the month and the year.

Example: January 30, 2003

Find It in Your Reading Review the ad for **Wemedia.com** on page 94. Identify the conventions used in the ad for providing practical information.

Find It in Your Writing Proofread your advertisement to make sure that you have correctly written addresses, telephone numbers, dates, and times.

For more on postal abbreviations to be used in addresses, see the Abbreviations Guide.

Publishing and Presenting

Building Your Portfolio

Advertisements are meant to be shared. Consider these ideas for publishing and presenting your ad:

1. **Create a Newsletter** Prepare a newsletter that reports issues and activities in your class or school. Incorporate the advertisements that you and your classmates have prepared. To avoid confusion, include an article or note informing readers that the ads promote fictional products and services.

2. **Design a Display** Post your advertisements on a bulletin board entitled "Copywriters in Our Class." Add a note to each ad that explains how the writer developed the ad.

Reflecting on Your Writing

Write a reflection on your writing process. Use these questions to get your ideas started:

- How did your understanding of persuasive writing change or develop as a result of writing an advertisement?
- Having written an ad yourself, what strategies for evaluating claims in advertisements would you recommend to a friend?

 Internet Tip

To see model ads scored according to this rubric, go on-line: PHSchool.com
Enter Web Code: efk-1101

Rubric for Self-Assessment

Use the following criteria to evaluate your persuasive advertisement.

	Score 4	Score 3	Score 2	Score 1
Audience and Purpose	Presents effective slogan; clearly addresses persuasive task	Presents good slogan; addresses persuasive task	Presents slogan; minimally addresses persuasive task	Does not present slogan; shows lack of attention to persuasive task
Organization	Uses layout and design to show clear, consistent organizational strategy	Uses layout and design to show clear organizational strategy with few inconsistencies	Uses inconsistent organizational strategy; creates illogical presentation	Demonstrates lack of organizational strategy; creates confusing presentation
Elaboration	Successfully combines words and images to provide convincing, unified support for a position	Combines words and images to provide unified support for a position	Includes some words or images that detract from a position	Uses words and images that do not support a position
Use of Language	Successfully communicates an idea through clever use of language and parallelism; includes very few mechanical errors	Conveys an idea through adequate use of language and parallelism; includes few mechanical errors	Misuses language and lessens impact of ideas; includes many mechanical errors	Demonstrates poor use of language and confuses meaning; includes many mechanical errors

9.4 *Revising*

Revising Your Overall Structure

Once your first draft is complete, review it by checking the structure, paragraphs, sentences, and word choice. The changes you make can make your essay more effective.

Be Sure Your Draft Reflects Your Purpose

Make sure that your essay does what you set out to do. Check that the points of comparison and contrast that you present and the elaboration you provide reflect your original purpose in writing. To verify this, identify sentences that connect to your purpose.

▶ **REVISION STRATEGY**
Bracketing Sentences That Address Your Purpose

Write your specific purpose on a self-sticking note, and attach it to your draft for easy reference. Then, go through your draft to bracket sentences that address your purpose. If you can't identify at least one sentence in each paragraph, consider adding or revising a sentence to clarify how the details in the paragraph support your purpose.

Student Work
IN PROGRESS

Name: *Vanessa Serna*
Bel Air High School
El Paso, TX

Bracketing Sentences That Address Your Purpose
To review her essay's ability to achieve her writing purpose, Vanessa bracketed sentences that helped her prove her point.

One of the major differences between the two forms of Mexican food is in its preparation. Because many Mexican families work on farms, they grow most of their own ingredients. [As a result, authentic Mexican food is juicier and tastier.] . . . Because there is not a vegetable garden outside of every Mexican restaurant . . . most restaurants' ingredients are canned or frozen. *TexMex food lacks the freshness of authentic Mexican food.*

Purpose: To show that authentic Mexican food is better than TexMex food.

Vanessa found one sentence in her paragraph that addressed her purpose. She decided to add another sentence to connect the points in this paragraph more strongly with her writing goal.

Revising Your Paragraphs

After you have reviewed the structure of your draft, take a look at each paragraph of your draft. Make sure that the sentences within each paragraph work together to call attention to the points of comparison and contrast between your subjects. Transitions can help you stress the points you want to make.

▶ **REVISION STRATEGY**
Color-Coding to Evaluate Transitions

Read your draft, and identify the places where you address each subject. Use one color to underline every instance in which you refer to one subject, and use a second color to underline every reference to the other subject. To evaluate your writing in places where the colors meet, judge the connection between the two subjects. Add transitions like the ones below to make the shift clearer.

- **Transitions that show similarities:** *all, similarly, both, in the same way, closely related, equally.*

- **Transitions that show differences:** *on the other hand, in contrast, however, instead, yet.*

Get instant help! For assistance in revising your paragraphs, use the interactive Evaluating Transitions activity in **Section 9.4,** on-line or on CD-ROM.

Student Work
IN PROGRESS

Name: *Vanessa Serna*
Bel Air High School
El Paso, TX

Evaluating Transitions

When she color-coded her paper, Vanessa realized that most of her points of comparison and contrast might not be obvious to readers. She added transitions to make the relationships clear.

Another difference between the two cuisines is in the use of spices and side dishes. For example, chili has an important role
Chili is not included in most TexMex meals.
in almost every Mexican meal, including breakfast. In most of the United States, the term "chili" refers to a mild mixture. In Mexican culture, "chile" refers to a wide variety of peppers, sauces, and mixtures.

Revising Your Sentences

Once you have added transitions to sharpen your points of comparison and contrast within paragraphs, examine your essay on the sentence level. Check that you have used the correct verb tense in each sentence to indicate the time that an action occurred.

Make Verb Tense Work for You

The tenses of verbs allow you to express time by showing when events occurred in a sequence. Unless you want to show action in the past, present, or future, you should be sure that the verb tense of your writing is consistent. For example, if you're writing about two subjects that still exist, use the present tense consistently. However, if you are comparing items in different time periods, you may need to make use of the past tense. Evaluating the verbs in each sentence can help you to avoid unnecessary shifts in verb tense.

▲ **Critical Viewing**
What comparison and contrast can you draw between this truck and a family station wagon? [**Compare and Contrast**]

▶**REVISION STRATEGY**
Identifying the Verb Tense of Each Paragraph

Circle all the verbs in your draft; then, analyze your use of verbs. For each paragraph, confirm that all the verbs fit the same general tense. If they do not, make sure that the verb shift is necessary to indicate a time shift. Look at this example:

EXAMPLE:	The drivers *became* tired after the long interstate trip. They *are driving* for days!
ANALYSIS:	*Became* expresses action that happened in the past. *Are driving* expresses action that is still happening.
EVALUATION:	This unnecessary shift in tense causes confusion. Change the verb to indicate that the second action happened before the first action and does not continue into the present.
REVISION:	The drivers *became* tired after the long interstate trip. They *had been driving* for days!

Grammar in Your Writing
Six Tenses of Verbs

By expressing time through tense, **verbs** can clarify the sequence of events in your writing. The basic forms of the six tenses show the time of an action or condition in the present, past, or future. Each verb form shows the time of an action and whether it is still happening. Use the following as a guide to the correct use of six tenses of verbs.

- **Present** indicates an action that happens regularly or a general truth:
  My family visits Chicago every year.

- **Past** indicates an action that has already happened:
  We visited Chicago last year.

- **Future** indicates an action will happen:
  We will visit Chicago again next year.

- **Present perfect** indicates an action that happened at some indefinite time in the past or an action that happened in the past and is still happening now:
  We have visited Chicago every year for the last three years.

- **Past perfect** indicates an action that has happened before another action in the past:
  We had visited Chicago before we heard about the art exhibit.

- **Future perfect** indicates an action that will have been completed by a specified time in the future:
  We will have visited eight museums by the time we get home.

Use the six tenses of verbs to show a sequence of events. However, be careful not to shift verb tenses unnecessarily within a sentence or as you move from one sentence or paragraph to another.

INCORRECT: We speed into the house and grabbed a drink in the kitchen.

CORRECT: We sped into the house and grabbed a drink in the kitchen.

Find It in Your Reading Choose an essay you have read recently. Identify the verb tenses in at least two paragraphs. If you discover a change in tense, explain why that shift is necessary to meaning.

Find It in Your Writing Identify any shifts in verb tense in your draft. Make sure that each one is necessary to indicate correctly the time when an action happened.

For more on verb tenses, see Chapter 21.

Revising Your Word Choice

Stress the Opposites

The words that you use to describe your subjects can sharpen points of comparison and contrast just as much as transitions can. As you evaluate your word choice, you may find that you can strengthen your points of contrast by adding opposite or nearly opposite words to describe differences. Use a T-chart to examine your word choice for points of contrast.

▶ **REVISION STRATEGY**

Charting Opposites

In a T-chart like the one shown below, identify the words you've used to create contrast in describing your subjects. In one column, write the strongest words you've used to describe one topic. In the other, jot down the words that describe the other topic. Review your chart to see whether opposites are strongly expressed. Revise some of these words in your draft to make your comparison and contrast stronger.

Research Tip

Use a thesaurus to find the most precise words to convey the contrasts you make.

Student Work
IN PROGRESS

Name: *Vanessa Serna*
Bel Air High School
El Paso, TX

Charting to Stress Opposites

Vanessa charted opposite points to improve her word choice and describe the features of both authentic Mexican and Americanized Mexican food more vividly. See her final draft to see how she used opposite words to describe the features of the two types of food.

Mexican Food	TexMex Food
Ripe, fresh	Canned, frozen, processed
From mild to burning hot, spicy	Mildly hot, tomatolike mixture
Fresh avocados and slow-cooked beans	Ready-made from a container
Colorful, bright colors	Colorless

Vanessa decided to use the words "processed" and "spicy" to make her contrasts more clear.

Peer Review

Sharing your revised draft with a small group can help you to look more objectively at your work. Peer reviewers can help you see whether your points of comparison are well developed, clear, and purposeful.

Ask Reviewers to Offer Suggestions

Give a copy of your essay to each member of a group of classmates. Ask each reviewer to read your essay and consider the following questions:

- Is the purpose of comparing and contrasting the two subjects clearly addressed?

- Are both subjects covered equally well?

Your reviewers can attach self-sticking notes with their comments to any areas of your essay that they think could be improved.

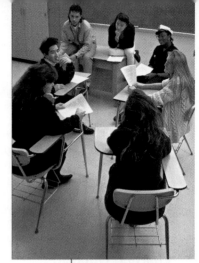

▲ **Critical Viewing**
In what ways can a classmate be a good sounding board for your writing?
[Relate]

Student Work
IN PROGRESS

Name: *Vanessa Serna*
Bel Air High School
El Paso, TX

Asking Reviewers to Respond to Questions
Vanessa asked her peer reviewers to respond to her essay in specific ways. She used her reviewers' comments about this paragraph to develop it more fully.

The look of authentic Mexican food as opposed to TexMex food is also very different. Authentic corn and flour tortillas, for example, look much different from those served at American restaurants. Authentic corn and flour tortillas are a shade of creamy white and have a much softer texture than those served in American restaurants. Another difference in the appearance of the two types of Mexican food is color. Combinations of different fresh ingredients make Mexican food very colorful.

> Add a sentence telling how American tortillas look.

> You could give some concrete examples of the ingredients that make Mexican food colorful.

9.5 Editing and Proofreading

Errors in grammar or mechanics can distract readers from seeing your ideas. Proofread to make your writing error-free.

Focusing on Sentences

Sentences should express a complete thought. Use these tips to review the mechanics of each sentence in your draft:

Avoid Fragments Be sure that each sentence contains a subject and a verb. Revise fragments—those that don't meet these criteria—to create complete sentences.

Avoid Run-on Sentences Run-on sentences are two or more complete sentences written as if they were a single sentence. Revise them to create separate sentences.

Learn More

To study the criteria for effective sentences, see Chapter 20.

Timed Writing Hint

When editing under timed conditions, read your essay to yourself silently. Pause after each sentence and check that it is complete.

Grammar in Your Writing
Comma Splices

A **comma splice** is an error in which a comma by itself joins two independent clauses.

COMMA SPLICE: He loves math, he wants to learn more.

To revise a comma splice, use one of these strategies:

Add a coordinating conjunction such as *and, but, or, nor, for, so,* **or** *yet:*
He loves math, and he wants to learn more.

Use a period or a semicolon between the clauses: He loves math; he wants to learn more. [or] He loves math. He wants to learn more.

Revise one independent clause into a dependent clause: *Because* he loves math, he wants to learn more.

Find It in Your Reading Review Stephen Kuusisto's essay on pages 168–171. Find two sentences in which the writer uses a semicolon or a coordinating conjunction to combine independent clauses.

Find It in Your Writing Read your draft to find and revise any comma splices you have included.

For more on comma splices, see Chapter 20.

Publishing and Presenting

Building Your Portfolio

Consider the following ways to publish or present your final comparison-and-contrast essay for an audience:

1. **Give a Presentation to the Class** Collect photos, maps, or other visuals to enhance your writing. Use the information in your essay along with visual support to make a formal presentation to the class.

2. **Publish Your Essay On-line** Share your essay with others who are interested in your subject by posting it on an Internet site that offers student writing. If you're not sure of the procedures for publishing on-line, ask an experienced Internet user for help.

Reflecting on Your Writing

When your comparison-and-contrast essay is complete, jot down your ideas about the writing process. Use these questions to get started. Add your comments to your writing portfolio.

- What new insight into your subjects did you gain?
- Which strategy for prewriting, drafting, revising, or editing will be most useful to you in future writing projects?

▣ Internet Tip

To see model essays scored with this rubric, go on-line:
PHSchool.com
Enter Web Code:
efk-1101

Rubric for Self-Assessment

Use these criteria to evaluate your comparison-and-contrast essay.

	Score 4	Score 3	Score 2	Score 1
Audience and Purpose	Clearly provides a reason for a comparison-contrast analysis	Adequately provides a reason for a comparison-contrast analysis	Provides a reason for a comparison-contrast analysis	Does not provide a reason for a comparison-contrast analysis
Organization	Clearly presents information in a consistent organization best suited to the topic	Presents information using an organization suited to the topic	Chooses an organization not suited to comparison and contrast	Shows a lack of organizational strategy
Elaboration	Elaborates most ideas with facts, details, or examples; links all information to comparison and contrast	Elaborates many ideas with facts, details, or examples; links most information to comparison and contrast	Does not elaborate all ideas; does not link some details to comparison and contrast	Does not provide facts or examples to support a comparison and contrast
Use of Language	Demonstrates excellent sentence and vocabulary variety; includes very few mechanical errors	Demonstrates adequate sentence and vocabulary variety; includes few mechanical errors	Demonstrates repetitive use of sentence structure and vocabulary; includes many mechanical errors	Demonstrates poor use of language; generates confusion; includes many mechanical errors

TOPIC BANK

If you are having trouble choosing a topic, consider one of the following ideas:

1. **Report on Effects of the Internet** Surfing the Web has helped people to learn more about their favorite actors, to understand health issues, and to meet new people in discussion groups. In an essay, show how the Internet has changed the way people find up-to-date information on almost any subject.

2. **Essay About Causes and Effects in History** Choose a historical event, such as a declaration of war, the signing of a treaty, or the election of a leader. In an essay, analyze the causes and effects of the topic you've chosen.

Responding to Fine Art

3. *The Dow Is Up!* shows the stock market in action. While you may not follow the ups and downs of the stock market, you probably see the effects of increased or decreased prices of gas, clothing, or the food you buy. In a cause-and-effect essay, analyze the causes and effects of economic changes like these.

The Dow Is Up!, Jane Wooster Scott, Private Collection

Responding to Literature

4. Read John F. Kennedy's inaugural speech. Use his comments as a springboard for a cause-and-effect essay discussing the legacy of Kennedy's presidency on volunteer programs such as the Peace Corps. You can find the speech in *Prentice Hall Literature, Penguin Edition,* The American Experience.

 Timed Writing Prompt

5. We remember anything that took hard work to accomplish. All that effort makes us proud of what we are capable of doing. Write an essay about a time when you had to work hard to accomplish something. Explain what caused you to persevere. Discuss the effects, or results, of your diligence. **(40 minutes)**

Narrowing Your Topic

When you have selected a topic, consider its scope. To limit your topic to a subject you can address effectively in your essay, consider all the connections your subject suggests. For example, if you have chosen the effects of the NASA space program on science, you might find this topic too broad. NASA professionals are involved in research, publicity, and space launches, so writing a paper on all of the effects of their work would be too involved for your purposes. You can narrow a topic by pinpointing your interests.

Pinpoint to Narrow Your Topic

Begin by writing your topic at the top of a triangle like the one shown here. To focus your subject, use this first idea to generate a more specific subtopic. Continue this process until you arrive at a cause-and-effect relationship narrow enough to address in your essay.

NARROWING A TOPIC

NASA's Research and Development

Satellite technology

Benefits to average citizen

Improvements in long-distance telephone service

Considering Your Audience and Purpose

Identify an Audience Before you begin to draft, spend a moment identifying your audience. When you know your intended audience, you can tailor the information you include to reach them. For example, you may need to define more terms for a younger audience.

Clarify a Purpose When you write to explain something, your purpose should be to make the information clear to readers. However, you may also want to show your readers how the topic affects them, why they should be interested in it, or how they can create change. Clarify your reason for writing, and choose language and details to suit this refined purpose.

Technology Tip

Some Internet search engines allow you to narrow your research by conducting a second-stage search using the results of your first key word inquiry as a starting set.

Gathering Details

When you are satisfied that your topic is appropriate for your audience, begin to assemble the details to create your draft. In order to establish a sound cause-and-effect relationship, find evidence to prove your point.

Use a Cause-and-Effect Organizer

To find the links you'll describe, use a cause-and-effect organizer like the one below. Above your topic, identify the causes; below it, identify the effects. List as many as you find through research or experience. You can weed out the weaker details as you prepare to draft.

Consider Causes Identify the reasons that produced the topic you will address, and don't limit your information gathering to just one cause. For example, if you are analyzing a flood, heavy rains might be the obvious cause, but don't rule out poor drainage as you list ideas.

List Effects While you look for the effects your topic has produced, consider changes both large and small. When you think small, you might cite a minor inconvenience a flood can cause, but when you look for bigger issues, you may discover that a flood ruined a farmer's entire crop.

 Timed Writing Hint

When writing under timed conditions, use a graphic organizer to outline your essay before you begin to write.

Student Work
IN PROGRESS

Name: *Hilary Odom*
Athens High School
Athens, TX

Completing an Organizer to Gather Details

Here is the bottom half of the cause-and-effect organizer that Hilary constructed to show the effects she wanted to include in her essay.

MY PARTICIPATION IN HIGH-SCHOOL DRAMA

- Recognition I've Received
  - Parents
  - Fans
- Friendships I've Made
  - Cast and Crew
- Personal Growth
  - Commitment
  - Cooperation
  - Responsibility

Drafting

Shaping Your Writing

Choose an Organization

Once you have gathered enough details to establish a clear cause-and-effect link, select an organization that suits your needs. Here are two strategies for presenting information:

Chronological Order This organizational strategy presents events as they occurred. For example, you could use this plan to explain how one historic event had an impact on a subsequent event. You might indicate the order by indicating the time of day, the day of the week, or the month of the year. Transitional words like *first* or *second* can also help establish sequence.

Order of Importance This organizational strategy presents events in a sequence based on the relative importance of each idea to the purpose of the essay. For example, if you are arguing that there are several effects of a stressful environment, you might organize your paper by starting with the annoying nuisances stress generates and building up to the most important effects—the damage stress inflicts on a healthy heart.

Student Work
IN PROGRESS

Name: Hilary Odom
Athens High School
Athens, TX

Organizing According to Order of Importance

Hilary identified three main effects, wrote them on self-sticking notes, and tried several different orders. She finally arrived at this sequence—and decided to present her ideas from least to most important.

LEAST IMPORTANT
①The friendships I've made

②People's reactions to my performances

MOST IMPORTANT
③My personal growth

Providing Elaboration

As you draft your cause-and-effect essay, provide details that show a strong relationship between effects and their causes.

Prove the Connection

To convince your audience that the topics you connect are not just mere coincidence, elaborate the link you are showing.

WEAK CONNECTION:	Many college graduates earn higher salaries than those who are not college graduates.
ANALYSIS:	Without an explanation that proves a cause and an effect, the relationship may just be a coincidence.
CAUSE-AND-EFFECT CONNECTION:	Because their education provides them with marketable skills, many college graduates earn higher salaries than those who are not college graduates.

Specific Facts To prove that the cause-and-effect relationship you describe actually exists, provide supporting evidence that backs up your claim. For example, to prove your belief that a college education translates to higher salaries in the work force, provide the facts that make the connection. You can include facts that show how a college graduate brings specific problem-solving skills, planning abilities, and a focused, professional attitude to a job based on years of academic training.

Personal Testimonies Interview your classmates or other people who have experience related to your subject. Use their comments to help illustrate your ideas. Their stories can provide an interesting human slant to statistics or scientific studies you may cite from other sources. For example, to elaborate the connection between a college education and a future salary, use quotations from an interview with a recent college graduate, a guidance counselor, or a human resources representative.

Writers in ACTION

In addition to his work as an inventor and statesman, Benjamin Franklin wrote many aphorisms that provided his readers with practical wisdom. Notice how he elaborates one such idea through a cause-and-effect chain:

"A little neglect may breed mischief: for want of a nail the shoe was lost; for want of a shoe the horse was lost; and for want of a horse the rider was lost."

▼ Critical Viewing
What do you think is the most important effect of a college education?
[Evaluate]

Revising

When your first draft is finished, take the time to review your cause-and-effect essay. The time you spend polishing your writing will strengthen your ability to convey your ideas.

Revising Your Overall Structure

Clarify the Cause-and-Effect Relationship

Review your introduction and conclusion to check that these paragraphs identify the cause-and-effect relationship you are addressing. Then, to make sure your readers can understand the cause-and-effect relationship you describe throughout your paper, provide more background or definition where necessary. Since a cause-and-effect essay may contain many new terms, make sure that your audience understands all of them.

▶ **REVISION STRATEGY**
Circling Unfamiliar Terms

Reread your essay, circling any terms that may not be familiar to your audience. Challenge yourself to include the definition of these terms in your essay.

Interactive Textbook

Get instant help! For assistance revising, use the interactive Defining Unfamiliar Terms activity in **Section 10.4,** on-line or on CD-ROM.

Student Work
IN PROGRESS

Name: Hilary Odom
Athens High School
Athens, TX

Defining Unfamiliar Terms

When Hilary reviewed her draft, she realized that anyone who had not participated in a drama production might not know what an audition *is and how it proceeds. Therefore, she added the following text to her second paragraph.*

> The first day of auditions lasted four-and-a-half hours. This was nearly half a day of hopeful actors rereading their audition scenes in successive waves, trying to prove themselves completely worthy.

The theatrical experience begins with a nerve-racking (audition). . . . After that obstacle, we were forced home to wait until the posting of the cast list. Some people would shriek with joy; others would weep with disappointment. . . .

Revising Your Paragraphs

Review Body Paragraphs

To support the cause-and-effect relationship you are addressing, review each body paragraph of your essay. Be sure the main idea of each paragraph explains, develops, or supports the cause-and-effect relationship you identify. Review your writing to determine whether you have provided enough support for your ideas, and add transitions to clarify connections.

Adding Additional Support Review each body paragraph to identify the main idea you want to develop. Then, evaluate whether you need to add more support for your ideas. If so, return to your prewriting notes or conduct further research to support the cause-and-effect relationship you describe.

Using Transitions to Show Connections Transition words can help you to make sure the relationship between cause and effect is obvious to your readers. Transition words and phrases signal a connection between ideas and assist the reader in following your line of thinking. Use transitional words and phrases to clarify connections.

Cause-and-Effect Transitions

Introducing Causes	Introducing Effects
Since	Therefore
If	Consequently
Because	As a result
As soon as	Subsequently
Until	Then

 Challenge

Read your paper with a skeptical eye. If you imagine the doubtful attitude your audience may have, you can anticipate their hesitancy and make your argument more convincing.

▶ **REVISION STRATEGY**

Color-Coding to Identify Transitions

Use two different colors to identify places in your draft in which transitions could strengthen the writing. Underline any discussion of cause in one color; underline any discussion of effect in another. Look for areas where the two colors meet, and evaluate your writing.

Evaluate
- Are there places in your draft in which the connections from cause to effect might not be clear to the reader?

Revise
- Add transition words in your draft where they are needed.

Revising Your Sentences

Combine Short Sentences

Short, choppy sentences interrupt the flow of your writing. Read your draft to see where you can combine short sentences into longer ones that smooth the flow of ideas.

EXAMPLE: Satellites are useful because they relay television signals. We use satellites to communicate by telephone as well. Satellites also help us to study weather conditions.

REVISED: Satellites allow us to relay telephone messages, communicate by telephone, and study weather conditions.

▶ **REVISION STRATEGY**
Tracking Sentence Length

To determine whether too many of your sentences are short and choppy, count the words in each sentence and note the results in the margin. If a majority of your sentences are ten words or less, consider combining some short sentences.

> **Technology Tip**
>
> The word-processing software you use probably has a word-count tool that can be used to count the words in a sentence.

Grammar in Your Writing
Using Gerunds to Combine Sentences

When a verb ending in *-ing* functions as a noun, it is called a **gerund.**

Direct Object: I like skiing.

Subject: Skiing has captured the hearts of many.

Object of a Preposition: I have read several books about skiing.

By transforming the action of a short sentence into a gerund, this verb form can be used to combine sentences.

Verbs: Some people swim to exercise. Others run. Some also dance.

Gerunds: Popular forms of exercise are swimming, running, and dancing.

Find It in Your Reading Look for three gerunds in a short story you have read. For each, identify the function it serves.

Find It in Your Writing Review your draft to see whether you have used any gerunds. If not, combine sentences to include at least one gerund in your writing.

For more information on gerunds, see Chapter 19.

Revising Your Word Choice

Delete Empty and Vague Words

An effective writer is careful to make every word count. To tighten your essay, review it for empty words—such as *really* and *very*—that do not add to your writing. Also, look for vague words that can be replaced with more precise language.

▶ **REVISION STRATEGY**
Color-Coding Empty and Vague Words

Draw a red deletion line through all of the empty words you find. Draw a red circle around vague words, such as *good, nice, weird,* or *thing.* Replace the words you've circled with others that convey exactly what you mean.

Student Work
IN PROGRESS

Name: *Hilary Odom*
Athens High School
Athens, TX

Identifying Empty and Vague Words

In this section of her draft, Hilary found several empty words to delete. She also revised some vague words to make her writing more accurate.

One ~~really~~ positive effect of being involved in the productions is the (wonderful) *familial* bond that is created between the cast and crew members. . . . I have also found a (nice friend) *confidante* in my director. . . . I find it ~~very~~ reassuring that age does not ~~really~~ seem to matter to any of us. Each year, there is ~~always~~ another group of freshmen. They are ~~easily~~ recognizable by their (weird) *wide-eyed* expressions and timid whispers.

Peer Review

Pointing

Read your essay twice to a small group of classmates. Ask them to listen the first time. The second time, ask them to point out the strengths of your paper.

To get more critical feedback, ask your peers to jot down places in which they did not clearly perceive the cause-and-effect connections you intended to make. Consider using their suggestions to clarify your writing.

Editing and Proofreading

Make corrections in grammar, usage, and mechanics to ensure that your final draft is error-free.

Focusing on Sentence Clarity

Read each sentence in your draft to make sure it communicates effectively. Be especially careful of the placement of modifiers, those words or phrases that provide more information about another word in a sentence. Misplaced modifiers may cause confusion. In the example below, a misplaced phrase suggests a famous painting was created by a student. Notice how the revision clarifies the writer's meaning.

EXAMPLE: The essay describes a famous painting *by Steven*.

REVISION: The essay *by Steven* describes a famous painting.

Timed Writing Hint

If you are given forty minutes to complete an essay, spend five minutes carefully editing and proofreading.

Grammar in Your Writing
Placement of Adverbs

For clarity, an adverb should be placed near the verb it modifies. On occasion, it may be placed elsewhere in the sentence to emphasize a point, create a dramatic effect, or vary a sentence. Here are examples:

Conventional placement before verb: I **usually** drive down Main Street.

Placement for emphasis: Suddenly, a boy ran in front of my car.

Sometimes, the placement of an adverb changes the meaning of a sentence. Be sure that the placement of adverbs accurately reflects your meaning.

I **only** hope Beth skates. (Writer worries whether Beth skates.)

I hope **only** Beth skates. (Writer hopes Beth—and no one else—skates.)

Find It in Your Reading Find three adverbs in an essay you have read, and note where they appear in relation to the verbs they modify.

Find It in Your Writing Circle all the adverbs in your essay. Check that each one is placed where it is most effective. If your essay includes no adverbs, add at least two.

For more about adverbs, see Chapter 17.

10.6 Publishing and Presenting

Building Your Portfolio

By sharing your cause-and-effect essay, you may help your readers plan for the future or understand the past. Following are some ideas for presenting your work:

1. **Present a Speech** If your essay addresses a situation that other people in your school face, you might offer to speak to classes or clubs that can benefit from your work.

2. **Publish a Feature Article** Submit your essay to your local or high-school newspaper. In a letter accompanying your essay, explain to the editor why the issue you address is important to the newspaper's readership.

Reflecting on Your Writing

After you have completed your essay, use the following questions to begin reflecting on your writing experience. Include your comments, along with the essay, in your portfolio.

- Did learning about the causes and effects of your topic motivate you to take any action?
- What strategy included in this lesson will help you improve your writing in other assignments?

Internet Tip

To see model essays scored with this rubric, go on-line:
PHSchool.com
Enter Web Code:
efk-1101

Rubric for Self-Assessment

Use these criteria to assess your cause-and-effect essay:

	Score 4	Score 3	Score 2	Score 1
Audience and Purpose	Consistently targets an audience; clearly identifies purpose in thesis statement	Targets an audience; identifies purpose in thesis statement	Misses a target audience by including a wide range of word choice and details; presents no clear purpose	Addresses no specific audience or purpose
Organization	Presents a clear, consistent organizational strategy to show cause and effect	Presents a clear organizational strategy with occasional inconsistencies; shows cause and effect	Presents an inconsistent organizational strategy; creates illogical presentation of causes and effects	Demonstrates a lack of organizational strategy; creates a confusing presentation
Elaboration	Successfully links causes with effects; fully elaborates connections among ideas	Links causes with effects; elaborates connections among most ideas	Links some causes with some effects; elaborates connections among most ideas	Develops and elaborates no links between causes and effects
Use of Language	Frequently combines sentences to show relationships and ideas; presents very few mechanical errors	Combines sentences to show relationships and ideas; presents few mechanical errors	Misses some opportunities to combine sentences; presents many mechanical errors	Demonstrates poor use of language; presents many mechanical errors

Exposition
Problem-and-Solution Essay

Problems and Solutions in Everyday Life

When you live in a world as fast-paced as ours, you confront problems every day. You may hear your parents complain about traffic or taxes; you may hear your classmates gripe over new school rules. Even celebrities can find some issue that riles them. Everyone can find something to protest. The challenge is to get beyond the complaining stage and make a difference. For example, people who want to find solutions might insist that a new traffic light be installed, that the way a tax is computed be changed, or that students be invited to join a committee to review new policies. By offering practical solutions to the problems they face, people can call attention to the matters that concern them and may even change a process.

▲ **Critical Viewing**
How do the activities shown in this photo-graph demonstrate effective problem-and-solution skills? **[Analyze]**

What Is a Problem-and-Solution Essay?

Since problem-and-solution essays are generally meant to explain a subject, they are part of the larger category of expository writing. However, a **problem-and-solution essay** goes further than just identifying an issue: It offers an idea for changing it. An effective problem-and-solution essay includes

- a clear statement of the problem, with its causes and effects summarized for the reader.
- a proposal of at least one realistic solution.
- facts, statistics, data, or expert testimony to support the solution.
- language appropriate to the audience's knowledge and ability levels.
- a clear organization that makes the relationship between problem and solution obvious.

To preview the criteria upon which your final problem-and-solution essay may be evaluated, see the Self-Assessment Rubric on page 152.

Writers in
ACTION

Bob Vila, the old-house renovation expert, has solved more than his share of problems. In this quotation, he explains how careful observation along with firsthand experience have helped him analyze problems and find workable solutions:

"I had been lucky in that my father was a carpenter. . . . After all those years of asking questions, at last I was in the position of passing along the information to others."

Types of Problem-and-Solution Essays

Following are some of the types of issues you might address in a problem-and-solution essay:

- **Consumer issues:** quality control and price control
- **Time-management issues:** finding a balance between work, school, and leisure time
- **Local issues:** neighborhood and community concerns

PREVIEW
Student Work
IN PROGRESS

In this chapter, you'll see how Jennifer Tufts, a student at Broken Arrow High School in Broken Arrow, Oklahoma, used writing process techniques to develop an essay that addresses a problem affecting many students.

Choosing Your Topic

If you have a personal interest in a problem and its solution, your essay will be easier to develop. Think of a problem you'd like to solve. Alternatively, you can use these strategies to help you find a problem that needs a solution:

Strategies for Generating Topics

1. **News Journal** Watch the nightly news, and jot down the problems reported. After a few evenings, review your list to choose a problem for which you can offer a solution.
2. **Blueprint** Draw a simple map of a familiar place. Consider blueprinting your neighborhood, your house, or your school. As you sketch, label points of interest or importance and add the names of people where appropriate. As you "travel" along the map, identify problems that may need attention. When you have a good number of problems on your blueprint, review them to see which one grabs your attention. Then, use it as a basis for your writing.

Try it out! Use the interactive Blueprinting to Choose a Topic activity in **Section 11.2**, on-line or on CD-ROM.

Student Work
IN PROGRESS

Name: *Jennifer Tufts*
Broken Arrow High School
Broken Arrow, OK

Blueprinting to Choose a Topic

Jennifer drew a map of her high school. She labeled the classes that she took and identified problems related to each class. When she wrote "I feel like a zombie by lunch time," she knew she had found a problem she wanted to solve.

CAFETERIA
I feel like a zombie by lunch time.
Why am I so tired?

History
How can I study better?

Biology
Are rain forests something I can save?

Math
Why don't we have any group projects?

Literature
Why don't we read more poetry?

TOPIC BANK

If you're having trouble choosing a topic, consider the following possibilities:

1. **Report on Preventing Storm Damage** Each year, hurricanes, tornadoes, and floods destroy people's homes and lives. In an essay, offer tips on how to prepare for such violent weather and prevent the most severe damage.

2. **Problem-and-Solution Essay on Pet Ownership** While cats and dogs are often revered members of a family, some family pets can create trouble. Write an essay explaining how to address a pet's disobedience, hyperactivity, or other unwanted behavior.

Responding to Fine Art

3. *Road of Steel*, showing the installation of railroad track, brings to mind several problems that are suitable for a problem-and-solution essay. Consider the ways a railroad can influence communication or transportation needs, or consider the difficulties of completing such a strenuous job. Alternatively, use your response to this painting to address other problems technology poses. Identify one problem to develop into an essay.

Road of Steel, 1944, Carlos Anderson, Courtesy of Springfield Museum of Art, Springfield, Utah

Responding to Literature

4. Read "A Wagner Matinée," by Willa Cather. In the story, a woman who has moved to the frontier realizes how much she misses the culture of the city. In an essay, offer solutions to this problem. You can find this story in *Prentice Hall Literature, Penguin Edition,* The American Experience.

🕐 **Timed Writing Prompt**

5. Perhaps your community could use a larger library, a new community center, or a skating park. Think of a facility that would fill a need in your community. Write a letter to your mayor to identify this community need and your proposed plan for meeting that need. Give examples of how your proposed facility will help the community. **(40 minutes)**

Narrowing Your Topic

Complex problems often require a whole network of solutions to remedy them—if the solution were easy, the problem
might not exist. Narrow your topic to a problem you can
address effectively in an essay. To help you do this, use the
focus point strategy.

Use Focus Points

After drawing an oval large enough in which to write only
one sentence, summarize the problem you want to develop.
Circle the most important word or phrase in that sentence. In
a second oval, use the key word you've circled to generate a
more narrowed topic. Challenge yourself to continue this
process until you have identified a topic narrow enough to
develop in your essay.

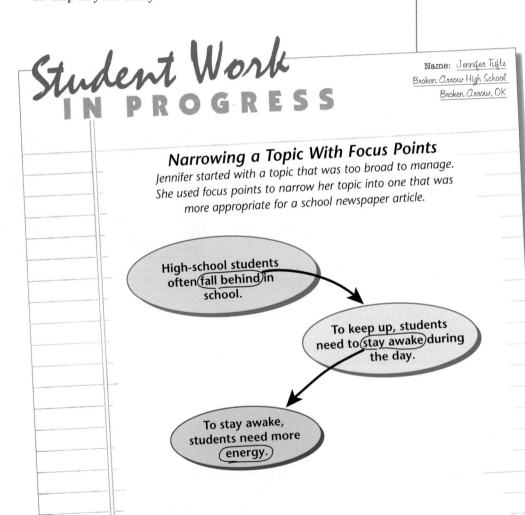

Student Work
IN PROGRESS

Name: _Jennifer Tufts_
Broken Arrow High School
Broken Arrow, OK

Narrowing a Topic With Focus Points

*Jennifer started with a topic that was too broad to manage.
She used focus points to narrow her topic into one that was
more appropriate for a school newspaper article.*

High-school students
often (fall behind) in
school.

To keep up, students
need to (stay awake) during
the day.

To stay awake,
students need more
(energy.)

Considering Your Audience and Purpose

Most commonly, your purpose will be to persuade readers. However, knowing your audience is crucial to writing a strong problem-and-solution essay that will get results. Use the following chart to help you customize your essay to your audience's needs:

ANALYZE YOUR AUDIENCE

Questions	Answers
Who is my audience?	
What does my audience already know about my topic? What information do I need to give them?	
How can I make my audience care about the problem?	
Is my solution one that my audience will be able to implement?	

Gathering Details

To best present your ideas, give your readers a definition of the problem and clarify the specifics of your solution. Take time to gather details that will make your ideas clear to your readers.

Define the Problem Make a list of details, facts, and examples that prove there is a problem. To gather further information, conduct interviews with people who have been frustrated by the situation you'll address.

Clarify Your Solution Conduct research to learn about previously failed solutions. Then, identify the specific parts of your solution. Consider cost, implementation, and the potential new problems your solution might cause. Before you begin to draft, list several reasons to confirm that your solution is valuable.

🔲 Research Tip

To gather more concrete information, conduct interviews, consult media coverage, and go on-line.

11.3 **Drafting**

Shaping Your Writing

In some of the writing you do, you have probably found that it takes more than one paragraph to explain and support an idea you want to develop. In that case, you use *paragraph blocks,* two or more paragraphs that explain and develop a complex key idea.

Organize in Paragraph Blocks

Paragraph blocks are especially useful in problem-and-solution essays because they allow a writer to explain a problem at great length and then identify the many components of a solution. As you plan your draft, identify the ideas that may be best served by a paragraph block plan. Then, use transitional sentences to keep the connections between your ideas clear. Look at this example:

▲ **Critical Viewing**
What are some of the problems young people face as they learn to play a musical instrument? **[Analyze]**

SAMPLE PARAGRAPH BLOCK

Practicing a musical instrument can sometimes be frustrating, but many consider the rewards to be well worth it. At the beginning of my cello lessons, I } *Topic Sentence*

felt angry when I couldn't play a piece well.

However, through weeks of practice, I found my self-confidence and patience level increasing. I } *First Subtopic*

knew that I could eventually master those passages.

I also knew the pride I felt when I finally did hit

those notes right.

Transitional Sentence ∧ My personal reward was not limited to a sense of

self-confidence. I also began to hear the complexity in other music I enjoyed. Since the cello often } *Second Subtopic*

provides the bass notes to balance out the melodies

played by other instruments, I looked for this

balance in the popular music I heard on the radio.

Use paragraph blocks to keep your paragraphs focused, so that your writing will not be too cumbersome for the reader to understand.

144 • *Problem-and-Solution Essay*

Providing Elaboration

Just presenting your opinion of a problem or solution is not sufficient to convince readers. You must support your statements with facts, statistics, personal experiences, expert testimonies, and other documentation that will sway your audience to accept your position.

Extend Your Argument by Depth-Charging

An effective strategy for providing elaboration is *depth-charging*. Using this strategy, begin by making a statement. To elaborate the idea, challenge yourself to provide a fact, statistic, or personal testimony that proves the statement. Then, challenge yourself to provide another type of evidence. Because this strategy encourages you to cite more evidence than you might include otherwise, depth-charging will strengthen your position.

🔋 Research Tip

Professional journals are good sources of expert testimony. Law, psychology, and most other fields publish journals from which you can quote material reliably in your essays. Visit a college library or search on-line to get the information you need.

Student Work
IN PROGRESS

Name: *Jennifer Tufts*
Broken Arrow High School
Broken Arrow, OK

Using Depth-Charging to Provide Elaboration

Jennifer used the depth-charging strategy convincingly in her essay. As she identified the statements to develop, she jotted down notes to herself about how to include facts, testimony, and personal experience to support the ideas.

Topic sentence: One way to fight fatigue is exercise.

Scientific facts: Prove the energizing effect of exercise on the body.

Peer testimonial: Ask Danny how he feels after his daily workouts.

Personal experience: Share benefits of my daily walks.

Revising

Revise your first draft by reviewing the overall structure, paragraphs, sentences, and word choice. The goal of revising is to make your essay as convincing as possible; every sentence and every word must be powerful.

Revising Your Overall Structure

The organization of paragraphs in an effective problem-and-solution essay should proceed in a logical order so that readers can understand the solution you propose.

▶ **REVISION STRATEGY**
Using Note Cards to Reorder Paragraphs

To be sure you have presented your ideas in the clearest way possible, jot down the subject of each supporting paragraph on a separate note card. Then, rearrange the cards to see which order serves your essay best. Choose the sequence you believe will be most convincing, and make revisions to your draft as necessary.

Student Work
IN PROGRESS

Name: *Jennifer Tufts*
Broken Arrow High School
Broken Arrow, OK

Ordering Paragraphs With Note Cards
Jennifer used note cards to arrive at the paragraph order she wanted.

Healthy diet

Water

Exercise (paragraph block)

Natural supplements

Unique solutions

Jennifer's sequence worked best when the cards were arranged in order from most important to least important.

To end with an interesting idea, Jennifer moved "unique solutions" to the end of her paper.

Revising Your Paragraphs

Evaluate Body Paragraphs

Each topical paragraph in your essay should support your proposal by providing enough information to prove that your problem is serious or by elaborating to show that your solution is valid. Check the content of your body paragraphs by reading your essay as if you were opposed to its ideas.

People who oppose new processes often argue that a change will be difficult, too costly, too hard to learn, or just not necessary. Adopt this viewpoint as you review the body paragraphs of your essay.

▶ **REVISION STRATEGY**
Strengthening Content by Taking the Opposing View

As you read your essay, look for places where someone might disagree with your ideas. For each paragraph, generate a question that such a critic might ask you. Use this chart to add new information to paragraphs that exist. Alternatively, you might want to add a single paragraph dedicated to anticipating the negative reactions an audience might have to your ideas. Look at these common points for skepticism:

Try it out! For help in revising your paragraphs, use the interactive Strengthening Content by Taking the Opposing View activity in **Section 11.4**, on-line or on CD-ROM.

Timed Writing Hint

Even if a prompt does not ask you to, address an opposing view at least once in a persuasive essay.

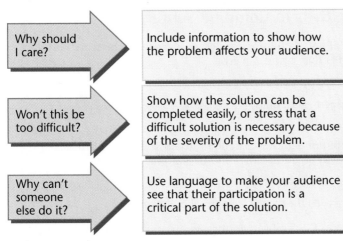

Opposing View   **Strategies for Revision**

Why should I care? → Include information to show how the problem affects your audience.

Won't this be too difficult? → Show how the solution can be completed easily, or stress that a difficult solution is necessary because of the severity of the problem.

Why can't someone else do it? → Use language to make your audience see that their participation is a critical part of the solution.

Revising Your Sentences

Reduce the Frequency of Simple Sentences

The repeated use of simple sentences will make your writing style dull. Use sentence-combining techniques to add variety, sophistication, and vitality to your written work.

▶REVISION STRATEGY
Combining Sentences

Simple sentences contain a single main clause consisting of a subject, a verb, and their modifiers. To make your writing more sophisticated, look for ways to combine simple sentences. First, identify the simple sentences in your essay. When possible, introduce coordinating conjunctions to combine two or more sentences or use a subordinating conjunction to show the relationship between two ideas.

⊘ Learn More

For more on sentence combining, see Chapter 20.

EXAMPLE:	They prepared the document. They stand by its accuracy.
COORDINATING CONJUNCTION:	They prepared the document, *and* they stand by its accuracy.
SUBORDINATING CONJUNCTION:	*Because* they prepared the document, they stand by its accuracy.

Grammar in Your Writing
Using Infinitives to Combine Sentences

An **infinitive** is a form of a verb that generally appears with the word *to* and acts as a noun, an adjective, or an adverb.

Noun: The juniors were asked to participate.

Adjective: They showed an eagerness to help.

Adverb: They were sorry to leave.

By turning the content of one simple sentence into an infinitive phrase, you can use this grammatical structure to combine simple sentences.

Simple Sentences: He researched the debate. He learned about the issues.

Combined Sentence: He researched the debate to learn about the issues.

Find It in Your Reading Find infinitive phrases in a short story you have read. (Don't confuse them with prepositional phrases beginning with *to*.)

Find It in Your Writing As you revise your draft, use infinitives to combine simple sentences.

For more on infinitives and infinitive phrases, see Chapter 19.

Revising Your Word Choice

Evaluate Technical Language

Your choice of words should match the knowledge and expectations of your audience. However, when you are providing an educated discussion of a topic, you may have to include technical words that your audience might not know. Review your draft to identify the words that may need definition or further explanation.

▶ **REVISION STRATEGY**
Color-Coding Technical Language

Review your essay, and highlight words and phrases that your audience might not know. For each, decide whether you should replace a word with a simpler term or provide a definition to make the writing more accessible.

☑ **Collaborative Writing Tip**

If your classmates represent the type of audience you want to address, share your work with a partner. Ask your reader to identify language that needs definition.

Student Work
IN PROGRESS

Name: *Jennifer Tufts*
Broken Arrow High School
Broken Arrow, OK

Highlighting Technical Words

When Jennifer identified scientific and technical language in her original draft, she revised to make the writing more clear for her audience—the classmates who would be reading her article in Tiger Eye, *the high-school newspaper.*

First draft: "Another way to raise low levels of blood sugar is to get more exercise. Exercise increases venous and arterial circulation, releases hormones, and stimulates the nervous system to produce endorphins."

Revised draft: "Another way to fight fatigue is, simply, exercise. Exercise increases blood flow to the muscles and the brain, releases energizing hormones, and stimulates the nervous system to produce chemicals, called endorphins, that elevate mood and produce feelings of well-being."

Since she could convey information without the high-level language, Jennifer deleted references to blood-sugar levels and the types of circulation.

Jennifer added a definition of "endorphin."

Peer Review

Group Feedback

Before you finalize your essay, get the feedback of your peers. As a sneak-preview audience, these readers can tell you what works in your essay and what may need further attention. Read your essay aloud, and ask reviewers to offer concrete responses to help you address any difficulties they perceive.

Set a Task Provide an outline of your essay for each member of the group. Ask reviewers to write one question, comment, or statement next to each idea you present. Reviewers can also place a check next to the points they feel have been addressed effectively. Once reviewers have completed this task, ask them to share their ideas.

▲ **Critical Viewing** How can a peer's opinions help you fine-tune your essay? **[Evaluate]**

Get Specific As you discuss your essay, get the most useful information from your reviewers. If necessary, ask follow-up questions to make vague comments more specific. Look at this sample conference prompted by a problem-and-solution paper about museum funding:

VAGUE RESPONSE:	I liked the paragraph that showed the history of the transit museum.
FOLLOW-UP QUESTION:	What exactly did you like about it?
SPECIFIC RESPONSE:	I didn't know that the museum was created by former conductors and rail-car engineers.
FOLLOW-UP QUESTION:	What else might you want to know?
SPECIFIC RESPONSE:	I'd want to know why the city doesn't offer funding to help the museum develop exhibits.

11.5 Editing and Proofreading

Errors in spelling, punctuation, and grammar may not destroy your essay's ability to convince, but they will distract your audience from your message and cast doubt on your credibility. Always check spelling, punctuation, and grammar to ensure that your final draft is error-free.

Focusing on Complete Sentences

Review your writing to be sure that you have left no fragments in the essay. A fragment is an incomplete thought punctuated as a sentence. If you should find any fragments, revise each one by supplying information to complete the idea. Then, review your essay once more to be certain that all sentences are complete.

 Timed Writing Hint

If you are given forty minutes to complete an essay, spend five minutes editing and proofreading. Check that every sentence contains a complete thought.

Grammar in Your Writing
Avoiding Subordinate Clauses as Sentence Fragments

Although a **subordinate clause** contains both a subject and a verb, it does not express a complete thought. The subordinating conjunction sets up a dependent relationship; without more information, the subordinate clause is incomplete. Look at these examples:

Incorrect: After we spoke to the doctor.

Incorrect: Although we understood the diagnosis.

To correct the sentence fragments created by punctuating subordinate clauses as sentences, add information that completes each idea.

Revised: After we spoke to the doctor, we wanted more information.

Revised: Although we understood the diagnosis, we needed more advice.

Find It in Your Reading Review a short story. Identify two sentences that include subordinating clauses as part of complete sentences.

Find It in Your Writing Review your essay to be certain you have completed all sentences that include subordinate clauses.

For more on sentence fragments, see Chapter 20.

Publishing
and Presenting

Building Your Portfolio

Consider submitting your problem-and-solution essay to a person or group that could benefit from your suggestions. You might try the following options:

1. **Send Your Essay to a Newspaper** By publishing your idea locally, you may win supporters who have the power to implement it. Even if your solution is not adopted, your essay may convince others to tackle the problem.

2. **Mail Your Essay to an Elected Official** Government leaders usually welcome input from the people they represent. Determine whether a local, state, or national leader has the authority to turn your idea into reality, and send a copy of your final draft to the official you identify.

Reflecting on Your Writing

Consider what you have learned from your writing experience. Use these questions to spark your reflection:

• What insight did you gain about the problem you addressed by writing a problem-and-solution essay?

• Which writing process strategy would you use again? Why?

Internet Tip

To see model essays scored with this rubric, go on-line: PHSchool.com
Enter Web Code: efk-1101

Rubric for Self-Assessment

Use the following criteria to evaluate your problem-and-solution essay.

	Score 4	Score 3	Score 2	Score 1
Audience and Purpose	Contains language and details to engage audience and accomplish purpose	Contains language and details appropriate for audience and that help contribute to overall effect	Contains some language and details not suited for audience; contains some details that detract from purpose	Contains language and details that are not geared for a particular audience; has an unclear purpose
Organization	Consistently presents information in a plan suited to problem and solution	Presents information in a plan suited to problem and solution	Introduces some inconsistencies into organizational plan	Presents no clear organization
Elaboration	Clearly defines problem and solution; elaborates all key points	Defines problem and solution; elaborates many points	States problem and solution with little elaboration	Presents no clear problem or solution; provides no elaboration
Use of Language	Demonstrates excellent word choice; contains no errors in grammar, punctuation, or mechanics	Demonstrates good word choice; contains few errors in grammar, punctuation, or mechanics	Demonstrates fair word choice; contains some errors in grammar, punctuation, or mechanics	Demonstrates poor word choice; contains many errors in grammar, punctuation, or mechanics

Connected Assignment

Question-and-Answer Column

In a problem-and-solution essay, you address both a problem and a solution. In real life, however, you might provide only half of the equation. For example, in a **question-and-answer column** such as those published in a magazine or on an on-line source, people send in questions and an expert provides an answer. The question includes a clearly presented request for information or advice along with background information. The answer proposes solutions and explains how they might help.

Using the letter format, present a frequently asked question about a subject you know well. Then, create a responding letter to propose solutions. The writing process skills discussed below will help you develop your letter.

▲ **Critical Viewing**
How might talking with someone else help you overcome some problems? **[Relate]**

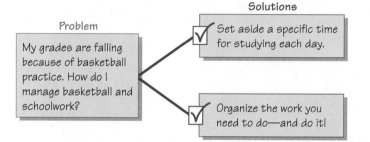

Problem

My grades are falling because of basketball practice. How do I manage basketball and schoolwork?

Solutions

☑ Set aside a specific time for studying each day.

☑ Organize the work you need to do—and do it!

Prewriting Consider the areas you know especially well. For example, you might be a computer whiz, a pro at dealing with younger siblings, or a cooking expert. Devise a common question or an unusual problem related to the area you've chosen. Then, use a chart like the one above to gather possible solutions.

Drafting Follow an informal format as you draft your letter. In your question, present the problem and provide background to explain the situation. Then, write the answer letter, adjusting the tone to reflect your expertise. Propose at least one solution, and explain how it will solve or at least minimize the problem. When appropriate, cite your own experience.

Revising and Editing Ask a peer to read your solution letter to identify the question. If he or she cannot determine what the question was based on your response, rework your letter to more clearly address the problem.

Publishing and Presenting Use your writing as a model for a question-and-answer column for your school newspaper.

Chapter
12 *Research*
Documented Essay

Miracle of Life, 1996, Christian Pierre, Private Collection

Documentation in Everyday Life

We live in an age of information explosion. Journalists, business people, scientists, and other professional analysts spend an increasing part of their time identifying, categorizing, predicting, and reporting new trends. For example, magazine articles quote experts, news programs use interviews to elaborate the stories they cover, and commentators in round-table discussions provide support for their opinions. In these cases, professionals use documentation—proof gathered from other sources—to back up the analyses they provide.

▲ Critical Viewing
How do the details of this painting suggest the joy of research? **[Support]**

What Is a Documented Essay?

A **documented essay** uses research gathered from outside sources to support an idea. What distinguishes this essay from other categories of research is the level and intensity of the research. In a documented essay, the writer consults a limited number of sources to elaborate an idea. In contrast, a formal research paper may include many more research sources. An effective documented essay includes

- a well-defined thesis that can be fully discussed in a brief essay.
- facts and details to support each main point.
- expert or informed ideas gathered from interviews and other sources.
- a clear, coherent method of organization.
- full internal documentation to show sources of information.

To see the criteria on which your final documented essay may be judged, preview the Rubric for Self-Assessment on page 168.

Writers in ACTION

Annie Dillard's insights into human nature and the writing process have made her a "writer's writer." Here, she tells how research influences the work of writing:

"Your freedom as a writer is not freedom of expression in the sense of wild blurting; you may not let rip. It is life at its most free, if you are fortunate enough to be able to try it, because you select your materials, invent your task, and pace yourself."

Types of Documented Essays

Documentation can strengthen the body of most writing. Subjects especially well suited to the documented essay format include the following:

- **Health issues:** The benefits of exercise can be documented.
- **Current events:** The effects of a law on a community can be collected.
- **Cultural trends:** A rising interest in animated films can be shown.

PREVIEW Student Work IN PROGRESS

Shira Pinsker, a student at Miami Palmetto High School in Pinecrest, Florida, wrote a documented essay about high-school graduates joining the armed forces. In this chapter, you will see Shira's work in progress, including the strategies she used to choose a topic, conduct interviews, develop a thesis statement, and present information clearly.

Prewriting

Choosing Your Topic

When you choose a topic for a documented essay, keep two guidelines in mind: Your topic should interest you, and the sources to support your main idea should be readily available. Consider selecting topics that are more contemporary than the ones you might pursue in a formal research paper. The following strategies will help you find a topic:

Strategies for Generating a Topic

1. **Brainstorm for Trends** In a group, identify the new trends you spot in music, clothes, food, and the media. After you generate several ideas, review the list and choose a topic you'd like to develop into a documented essay.

2. **Portfolio Review** Scan the items in your writing portfolio—perhaps a piece of expository or descriptive writing might be strengthened by further research. For example, you might be able to expand a sports article into a documented essay by interviewing the players, the coaches, or some fans. Choose one piece of writing from your portfolio, and develop it into a documented essay.

Try it out! Use the interactive Scanning a Portfolio to Choose a Topic activity in **Section 12.2**, on-line or on CD-ROM.

Student Work
IN PROGRESS

Name: *Shira Pinsker*
Miami Palmetto High School
Pinecrest, FL

Scanning a Portfolio to Choose a Topic

Shira reviewed the work in her writing portfolio to look for topics that might be well suited to a documented-essay format. She decided to build on an interview she'd had with a classmate about joining the armed forces.

Oct 10	Narration	Short story about a race
Oct 18	Persuasion	School should offer a course in visual culture/critical viewing
Nov 1	News Article	Interview with student about joining the army

TOPIC BANK

If you're having trouble finding a topic, consider the following ideas:

1. **Performing Arts Essay** Many people celebrate the challenges and rewards they experience through participating in theater, dance, or music. Make a list of people you know who are active in the arts. Use the sources to develop a documented essay on the benefits of such participation.

2. **Technology Update** Creative computer engineers often tackle new problems with each software advance. Write a documented essay about the problems they encounter, the methods they use to solve them, and the practical applications of their work for the average computer user.

Responding to Fine Art

3. *Les Coureurs (The Runners)* at right, may inspire you to wonder about the effects of competition or the value of exercising with a group. Use one of these suggestions—or another idea the image suggests—to develop into a documented essay.

Les Coureurs (The Runners), Robert Delaunay, Museum of Modern Art, Troyes, France/Lauros-Giraudon, Paris

Responding to Literature

4. Read "The First Seven Years" by Bernard Malamud. Using the story as a springboard, learn more about career development opportunities such as internships or mentoring. You can find the story in *Prentice Hall Literature, Penguin Edition,* The American Experience.

🕐 Timed Writing Prompt

5. Write a documented essay about another person's life. Select a person you admire and already know a lot about. You may choose to write about a friend, a family member, or someone famous. Present the main events in this person's life in chronological order. Include as many facts as possible and discuss his or her many accomplishments. **(45 minutes)**

Narrowing Your Topic

Some topics are too broad to be handled in a few pages. Review your topic to decide whether you can split the subject into specific aspects. If so, you may need to narrow your topic. Another way to sharpen the focus of your topic is to conduct some preliminary research. The expertise you accumulate may help you identify subtopics. Use the listing and itemizing strategy to record what you learn and to focus your topic.

Listing and Itemizing to Narrow a Topic

As you become more familiar with your subject, list each main idea or issue you discover. Then, itemize each entry on your list, generating specific details about it. Consider using one of these narrowed lists to develop your writing. If you find your itemized lists are becoming too lengthy or unmanageable, evaluate whether your topic is still too broad or whether you are including more details than your audience needs.

Try it out! Use the interactive Listing and Itemizing to Narrow a Topic activity in **Section 12.2**, on-line or on CD-ROM.

News Anchor
- High-profile job
- Represent network in on-air performance

Street Reporter
- Entry-level job
- Travel to different locations
- Think on your feet
- Write your own reports

Program Director
- Manage filming and timing of nightly broadcast
- Choose filming angles
- Make clean transitions from live reports to tape

Considering Your Audience and Purpose

If your **audience** for an essay is a group of younger students, you will shape your writing differently from the way you would write for an audience of adult readers. Before you draft your essay, identify the specific audience you will address. Then, include the language and details they will need to understand your topic.

Your **purpose** in a documented essay is generally to inform, to describe, or to persuade. Some essays combine two or three purposes. Considering your exact goal before you write will help you to choose the information that supports your purpose.

Gathering Details

Write What You Already Know

Because you have chosen a topic in which you have a lively interest, you may already know more about it than you realize. Jot down what you already know, adding as many details as you can. Then, collect documentation to fill in any holes you can detect, gathering details that support the main idea of your essay.

Identify Sources of Further Information

Review your notes to identify who and what might help you get more information about the topic. Make a list of questions you'd like to answer, and then find the facts you need. You can refer to magazine articles, television news shows, and Web sites. For more customized information, consider interviewing classmates, friends, relatives, or local experts.

Review Library Sources Depending on your topic, you may be able to find the concrete facts you need at the library. Consider using the following sources:

- **Public records** for population growth or decline rates

- **Almanacs** for statistics

- ***Current Biography*** for information about professional entertainers or athletes

Use the **card catalog**, **on-line catalog,** available **databases**, Internet **search engines,** as well as such reference tools as the *Readers' Guide to Periodical Literature.*

Take notes, recording any relevant information from the sources you find, just as you would for a research report. In all cases, note the titles and authors of sources as well as publication information such as city, publisher, publication date, and the numbers of the pages you referenced.

Conduct Interviews In some cases, you may be able to contact an expert to explain your topic. In others, an average person's experience may support your main idea best. If you want to show how art students can improve their skill through workshop-based courses, interview a teacher or a student who has been involved in such classes.

To make the most of an interview, make sure you have a goal in mind. Develop focused questions in advance, and be sure to record the responses accurately. You may want to bring a tape recorder to make the job easier. For documentation purposes, note the date of all interviews you conduct.

⟳ Learn More

For more on conducting library research, see Chapter 13 and Chapter 31.

▼ **Critical Viewing**
For the topic you are pursuing, identify two facts you could develop through library research. **[Apply]**

Drafting

Shaping Your Writing

After you have gathered details for your essay, you need to organize your information effectively. Before you draft, write a thesis statement and plan an organization for your writing.

Write a Thesis Statement

In a single sentence, write the main idea of your essay.

EXAMPLE: Green is making a fashion comeback.

Organize to Suit Your Topic

Choose an organization that will help you communicate your ideas to your audience. Consider these organizational strategies:

- **Chronological order** presents events in time order. Start at the earliest event and move toward the latest.

- **Cause-and-effect order** shows the relationships between events or trends and their causes or results. Start with a cause, and then investigate the effects it has produced. Alternatively, explain the causes behind a particular effect.

- **Part-to-whole organization** presents information in logical categories that make up the whole topic. Use this method to explain the individual elements of a broad topic.

⏰ Timed Writing Hint

Before you draft your timed essay, formulate a thesis statement that directly addresses the essay prompt.

Student Work
IN PROGRESS

Name: *Shira Pinsker*
Miami Palmetto High School
Pinecrest, FL

Using a Part-to-Whole Organization

Shira grouped details using a part-to-whole organization. She decided to include subheads for each major section in her essay.

Requirements
- diploma
- testing
- English/math

Rewards
- learn skills
- earn money for college
- grow in pride and discipline

Personal Choices
- examine hopes and dreams
- get more information

Providing Elaboration

Let Quotations Tell the Story

Support your thesis with information from your research. Use statistics, facts, examples, details, and expert opinions to support the ideas in your essay. For example, if you want to say that neighborhood safety is a key factor in a family's decision to purchase a home, include a quotation that backs up that claim.

Attribute Information

When you use a quotation to back up an idea, you should provide formal citations that indicate author and page number. Challenge yourself to incorporate references smoothly into your draft. Follow these suggestions for building attribution into your writing:

▲ **Critical Viewing**
How might a real estate agent use the documented essay format to attract clients?
[Hypothesize]

Name Your Source When providing information gathered through research, introduce your sources in your essay. Use phrases like "according to . . . ," "in an interview," or "on the Web site" to prepare readers for the information you will quote next. Then, include full documentation in parentheses.

EXAMPLE: *According to Elaine Rothman,* director of the Realtors for Community Action, prospective home buyers frequently ask about crime rates in the communities where they plan to live. [Elaine Rothman, personal interview with the author, 10 January 2000]

Build the Source's Authority Whatever phrase you use to attribute the ideas, be sure to provide the background to explain why the person or source quoted can provide useful input. Give the person's title, explain his or her experiences, or show how your source is an authority on your subject.

EXAMPLE: Amy Adler, *a first-time buyer,* explained her decision to live in Rockville: "I want to be able to walk my dogs at night without fear." [Amy Adler, personal interview with the author, 1 May 2000]

EXAMPLE: In last year's annual summary *published by town officials,* Rockville reported increased home sales. [Rockville. *Year in Review.* Rockville, Tennessee: Office of Public Information, 1999.]

Revising

After you have completed a first draft, analyze your essay to see whether you have achieved the best possible results. Evaluate the content and style of the essay, and make revisions to improve your work.

Revising Your Overall Structure

Confirm Coherence

To be sure your essay presents information clearly, make sure every main idea supports your thesis statement. Then, decide whether a reader who is unfamiliar with your topic would have trouble following your treatment of it in the essay.

▶ **REVISION STRATEGY**
Bracketing to Identify Paragraph Topics

As you review your draft, identify the focus of each paragraph by bracketing a key word or sentence and numbering each body paragraph. To evaluate the flow of your essay, review the order of ideas you have marked. Consider changing the order of paragraphs or making other revisions to make the progression more logical.

Writers in
ACTION

Revision can be a tricky part of the writing process, especially when a writer knows what's wrong but not how to fix it. While revising his novel The World According to Garp, *John Irving tried the final paragraph several times before an interruption gave him the ideas he needed. In a letter, he wrote:*

"Of course, all the time I was losing the Monopoly game, I was thinking of the last paragraph, and I believe that the time away from my desk was a valuable part of that last paragraph, which I might have written too quickly without the sizeable interruption."

Evaluate	Revise
• Does the order make sense?	• Group closely related paragraphs together. Insert subheads to make these blocks, or sections, of your essay more obvious to readers.
• Does every paragraph contribute to the thesis statement?	• Cut paragraphs that don't support the thesis statement. If you want to keep the information in your draft, revise to make the connection clear.
• Does the information flow smoothly?	• Add transitional paragraphs to connect ideas smoothly. Use brief paragraphs to summarize the previous information or to prepare readers for what will follow.

Revising Your Paragraphs
Smooth Transitions to Quotations

When you quote an interviewee, an expert's ideas, or a research source, you need to ensure that your text is both informative and clear.

▶ **REVISION STRATEGY**
Color-Coding to Evaluate Links to Quoted Material

Review the first draft of your essay, and highlight direct quotations that provide a speaker's exact words. Also, underline passages where you have paraphrased, or quoted a source indirectly. Examine the way in which you have introduced this material and identified its source. Consider adding phrases such as "he/she said" or "according to." During this evaluation, double-check that you introduce the speaker's authority or the background of the source when you are referring to this source for the first time.

Challenge

To improve the content of your paragraph, return to your prewriting notes and add more information to support your ideas.

Student Work
IN PROGRESS

Name: *Shira Pinsker*
Miami Palmetto High School
Pinecrest, FL

Polishing Transitions

When she reviewed her essay, Shira found that she could improve the integration of quoted material into the text: She added words to attribute the information.

Raoul Fuentes , guidance counselor at Palmetto High School, discussed these requirements in an interview. He says He is happy with the diploma requirements and believes many students will benefit from service in the military. "You must have a high-school diploma to be in the military. ," according to Fuentes, " It didn't used to be like that, but it's all technical now." (Raoul Fuentes, personal interview with author, 29 November 1999.)

Revising Your Sentences

Evaluate Sentence Patterns

For your reader, seeing the same type of sentence over and over can be monotonous. Boring writing may not be effective in its aim to persuade, inform, or entertain. To make your writing lively, use a variety of patterns in your sentences.

▶ **REVISION STRATEGY**
Identifying Sentence Patterns

In the example *Penguins eat a diet of crustaceans, fish, and squid*, the subject is the first word of the sentence. Beginning a sentence in this way is one of the most common habits of writers. When you identify your sentence habits, you may see a monotonous pattern that you can revise.

In a list, analyze the beginning words of the sentences in your draft. You may find subjects, verbs, phrases, or clauses. To create variety, add introductory material. Use these tips:

- Start with a prepositional phrase:
  In the Antarctic environment, penguins eat a varied diet.

- Start with an adverb:
  Surprisingly, penguins eat a varied diet.

- Start with a subordinate clause:
  Unless food is scarce, penguins eat a varied diet.

Get instant help! Use the interactive Breaking Up Sentence Patterns activity in **Section 12.4**, on-line or on CD-ROM.

Student Work IN PROGRESS

Name: *Shira Pinsker*
Miami Palmetto High School
Pinecrest, FL

Breaking Up Sentence Patterns

Shira's list showed she began many of her sentences with subjects. To vary her sentences, she added phrases to some of them.

Prepositional phrase ⟶ subject
subject
Infinitive phrase ⟶ subject

subject

For high-school students like Booker,
The armed forces are an alternative ~~for the high-school students like Booker.~~ The requirements are rigorous. *To join the armed forces,* One must have a high-school diploma, a clean police record, and passing scores on a variety of mental and physical tests. Potential recruits must also take the ASVAB, . . .

Grammar in Your Writing
Prepositional Phrases

Prepositions such as *at, over,* and *without* can help you add information to your writing without adding more sentences.

COMMON PREPOSITIONS

about	behind	during	of	through
above	beneath	from	off	under
after	between	in	on	up
before	down	near	over	with

Most **prepositional phrases** include two or three words, but some can be much longer. No matter how long, a prepositional phrase never includes a verb. Prepositional phrases include a preposition and its object, the noun or pronoun that completes the information the preposition provides. In these sample prepositional phrases, the prepositions are indicated in italics and objects are indicated in blue.

SAMPLE PREPOSITIONAL PHRASES

under investigation   *after* further review
in the manila folder   *up* the long and winding staircase

Prepositional phrases can serve as adjectives or adverbs, depending on the words they modify.

Adjective phrases describe nouns. In this example, the prepositional phrase modifies the noun *mammal:*

We noticed a sea mammal with a long tusk.

Adverb phrases describe verbs. In this example, the first prepositional phrase tells *when* the action of the verb took place:

During the cool morning hours, we took a mountain hike.

Find It in Your Reading Choose an essay you have read recently. Find four prepositional phrases and analyze their functions. Which phrases serve as adjectives and which serve as adverbs?

Find It in Your Writing Identify prepositional phrases in your documented essay. If you can't find an example of both a prepositional phrase serving as an adjective and one acting as an adverb, consider revising your sentences to get more informational mileage from them. Challenge yourself to sophisticate your writing by adding two of each type of prepositional phrase.

To learn more about prepositional phrases, see Chapter 19.

Revising Your Word Choice

Evaluate "to Be" Verbs

Just as varied sentence patterns make your writing more lively, vivid verbs can add impact to an essay. While it may be convenient to use forms of the verb *be*, that choice may make your writing dull. The verb *be* and its forms usually link the subject of a sentence with a word that renames or describes it. Replace *be* verbs—including *is, am, are, was, were, be, being,* and *been*—with action verbs that communicate ideas with more power.

▶ **REVISION STRATEGY**
Circling Forms of the Verb *Be*

Circle "to be" verbs in your writing. Challenge yourself to make your writing more powerful by replacing these verbs with action verbs wherever you can. Your verb changes may require further revision of the sentence.

▲ **Critical Viewing**
What action verbs could you use to describe this photograph? **[Connect]**

| "TO BE" VERB: | Jean *was* serious about gardening. |
| ACTION VERB: | Jean *gardened* with flair and commitment. |

"TO BE" VERB:	The garden *is* beautiful.
ACTION VERB:	The flowers in the garden *bloom* beautifully.
ACTION VERB:	The flowers in the garden *burst* with color.

Peer Review

Summarizing

To find the strengths in your writing, ask a group of your classmates to respond to your essay by summarizing its main points.

Read your draft to the group, and then pause. Before you read it a second time, give your listeners a focus: Ask them to tell you what they remember best. Their responses will reveal the ideas you have conveyed most clearly. As you listen to what they tell you, compare their feedback with your intentions. If what you think you communicated doesn't match what they heard, ask your peers for advice on making your thesis and development clearer.

Use the summaries and comments of the group to guide you in making a final revision of your essay.

12.5 *Editing and Proofreading*

Once you are satisfied with the content of your draft, review it for mistakes in spelling, mechanics, and usage. You should strive to produce a final draft that is error-free.

Focusing on Accuracy

Proofread to confirm that your essay is factually correct.

Check the Titles Review your notes or other information you have gathered to confirm the correct names of sources.

Review the Facts Review your notes to see that dates and statistics are correct. To be certain, find a second source to back up your report.

Timed Writing Hint

When editing a timed essay, check that all facts and dates are accurate and correctly punctuated.

Grammar in Your Writing
Providing Internal Documentation

When you cite sources without providing a full reference list at the end of your writing, include all the source information parenthetically. The following models demonstrate conventions set by *The Chicago Manual of Style*.

For a book:
(W.P. Kinsella, *Shoeless Joe* [New York: Ballantine Books, 1982] 103.)

For a magazine article:
(Philip Weiss, "Off the Grid, " *The New York Times Magazine*, 14 April 1996, 159.)

For an interview:
(Samuel Lawrence, personal interview with author, 19 October 1998.)

When you cite a source for the second time, provide a shorter reference. Note these examples:

(Kinsella, *Shoeless*, 167.)   (Weiss, "Grid," 159.)   (Lawrence, 19 October 1998.)

Find It in Your Reading Review the internal documentation style in a magazine article you have read.

Find It in Your Writing As you prepare your final draft, check that you followed the conventions of internal citation accurately.

For further instruction, see *Citing Sources and Preparing Manuscript* on pages 720–726.

12.6 Publishing and Presenting

Building Your Portfolio

The purpose of your documented essay may be to inform, describe, or persuade. Decide how you want to publish your essay and present it to your audience. Consider these ideas:

1. **Develop a Class Magazine** With classmates, use your writing to create a magazine. Organize essays into categories, prepare a table of contents, and choose illustrations. Share the magazine with the school community.

2. **Organize a Presentation Day** Invite members of the community to hear you and your classmates present your research. To avoid reading your paper word for word, prepare note cards and highlight your key points. Use visual aids such as charts or photographs where appropriate.

Reflecting on Your Writing

Consider your experiences in writing your essay. In a note to include in your portfolio, address questions such as these:

- In the process of writing, what did you learn about the topic you chose?

- In what ways did attributing your sources change the way you felt about your writing?

Internet Tip

To see model essays scored according to this rubric, go on-line: PHSchool.com Enter Web Code: efk-1101

Rubric for Self-Assessment

Use these criteria to evaluate your documented essay:

	Score 4	Score 3	Score 2	Score 1
Audience and Purpose	Consistently targets a unique audience; clearly identifies purpose in thesis statement	Targets a specific audience; identifies purpose in thesis statement	Misses target audience by including too many details; presents no clear thesis	Addresses no specific audience or purpose
Organization	Presents a clear, consistent organizational strategy	Presents a clear organizational strategy with few inconsistencies	Presents an inconsistent organizational strategy; creates illogical presentation	Demonstrates a lack of organization; creates confusing presentation
Elaboration	Supports thesis statement with several documented sources; elaborates all main points	Supports thesis statement with some documented sources; elaborates most points	Supports the thesis statement with one documented source; elaborates some points	Provides no documented sources; does not provide thesis
Use of Language	Clearly integrates researched information into the writing; presents very few mechanical errors	Integrates most researched information into the writing; presents very few mechanical errors	Does not integrate researched information into the writing; presents many mechanical errors	Demonstrates poor use of language; presents many mechanical errors

Connected Assignment *Statistical Report*

When you rely heavily on numbers, percentages, and ratios to support a thesis, you are creating a **statistical report.** The paper's topic need not be related to numbers—it could be the history of westward expansion—but by citing data such as percentages and sheer quantity, statistics tell the story.

Use the writing process steps below to write your own statistical report:

Prewriting Choose a topic that can be developed through references to statistics. For example, sports lend themselves to numerical analyses, as do surveys on any topic. Explore your topic by listing what you know and need to learn about it—a K-W-L chart like the one shown below might help.

K - Know	W - Want to Know	L - Learned
Career opportunities have opened up for women over the last 40 years.	What has been the progression, in numbers, of women working outside the home since the 1960's?	In the last decade, we have seen the largest number of women working outside the home.

Use specialized encyclopedias, almanacs, and on-line research to gather your statistics. Then, generate a thesis or main idea from the information you've found.

Drafting Follow these suggestions for drafting:
1. State your thesis in the opening paragraph.
2. Present supporting evidence in a series of paragraphs, incorporating statistics as appropriate.
3. Interpret any charts, tables, or graphs that you include.
4. Finish with a strong conclusion.

Revising and Editing Reread your report, and revise language that is overly opinionated or emotional. Let the facts speak for themselves. Make sure to include only pertinent statistics, and double-check that your statistics are accurately typed.

Publishing and Presenting Share your report with classmates.

Untitled, John Martin

Research Writing in Everyday Life

Whenever you want to learn more about a person, an issue, a product, or an event, you use research skills. Whenever you turn on a television news program, read an article in the newspaper, or type in a key word on an Internet search engine, you are conducting informal research and accessing the results of someone's investigation. You may have already used more formal research skills for a writing assignment in school. As you move into adulthood, research writing skills can serve you well in the workplace, in the marketplace, and in your intellectual life.

▲ **Critical Viewing** What does this painting suggest about the nature of research? **[Analyze]**

What Is a Research Paper?

A **research paper** presents and interprets information gathered through an extensive study of a subject. An effective research paper has

- a clearly stated thesis statement.
- convincing factual support from a variety of outside sources, including direct quotations whose sources are credited.
- a clear organization that includes an introduction, body, and conclusion.
- a bibliography, or works-cited list, that provides a complete listing of research sources.

To preview the criteria on which your research may be judged, see the Rubric for Self-Assessment on page 188.

Types of Research Papers

There are as many types of research papers as purposes for research. Here are some of the research formats you may encounter:

- **Lab reports** present the purposes, processes, and results of an experiment.
- **Annotated bibliographies** provide a list of materials about a specific topic. In addition to source information, such as titles and authors, these bibliographies summarize and evaluate each entry.
- **Multigenre research papers** present research using a variety of genres. For example, a multigenre approach might include an essay, a short story, poetry, letters, and new articles to convey the information gathered through research.

Writers in ACTION

Music writer and editor Gillian Gaar incorporates research into many of the projects she undertakes. While she reviews bands and live concerts, she also uses the material she finds through library research and interviews:

"Research is really the backbone of my writing because it gives me access to information I wouldn't have otherwise. You probably wouldn't put everything you learned about your subject in one article—or even one book. But it gives you an overall familiarity with the subject. . . . [I]f I'm interested in a subject, I like to learn . . . as much as I can about it."

PREVIEW Student Work IN PROGRESS

In her research paper, Rebecca Potter, a student at Central High School, Omaha, Nebraska, examines the legacy and influence of an African American sculptor. As you will see, Rebecca used prewriting, drafting, and revising techniques to develop her essay "Augusta Savage: Artist of the Harlem Renaissance." Her final draft appears at the end of the chapter.

Prewriting

Choosing Your Topic

Because your study will be extensive, two key issues should drive your choice of a research topic. First, you should have a commitment to the topic and an interest in learning more. Second, your topic should be one for which you can find enough information to present it well.

Strategies for Generating Topics

1. **Dewey Decimal Brainstorm** The Dewey Decimal System is a classification system used by some libraries to organize books by topic. You can find a chart of the major categories in Chapter 31, "Study, Reference, and Test-Taking Skills." Refer to this chart, and use the general categories to spark ideas for topics. Jot down one idea or question per category. Select one on which to write a research paper.

2. **Reviewing Notebooks, Journals, and Textbooks** As you flip through school notebooks, textbooks, and your writing journal, make a list of topics you may be able to pursue in a research paper. Consider the development of the theorems you've studied in math, a specific event in history that interests you, or a writer whose work you enjoy. Review your list, and choose a topic for research.

Get instant help! For additional assistance finding a topic, use the interactive Topic Generators, accessible from the menu bar, on-line or on CD-ROM.

Student Work
IN PROGRESS

Name: Rebecca Potter
Central High School
Omaha, NE

Reviewing Notebooks, Journals, and Textbooks

In looking for a topic, Rebecca began with the table of contents of her literature textbook. By listing the main periods of American literature, she identified a period she wanted to research.

- Beginnings to 1750
- A Nation Is Born (1750–1800)
- A Growing Nation (1800–1870)
- Division, Reconciliation, and Expansion (1850–1914)
- Disillusion, Defiance, and Discontent (1914–1946) ← *Harlem Renaissance*
- Prosperity and Protest (1946–Present)

TOPIC BANK

1. **Report on the Uses of Music** From formal symphonic concerts to pervasive elevator melodies, some form of music can be found in most aspects of modern life. Research the power of music to fulfill a specific function, and present your findings in a research paper.

2. **Analysis of the Origins of Basketball** Dr. James Naismith has traditionally been credited as the inventor of basketball. More recently, some claim that the game originated elsewhere. Research this question, and write a research paper to report your conclusions.

Responding to Fine Art

3. The painting *Tourists*, at right, might inspire you to ask several questions about tourism. You might wonder about the history of the national parks, the geological causes of the Grand Canyon, or the ways in which such natural wonders have inspired writers and artists. Use one of these issues as the basis of a research paper.

Tourists, Woody Gwyn, Courtesy of the artist

Responding to Literature

4. Use William Faulkner's "Nobel Prize Acceptance Speech" as a springboard for your research topic. You might explore the work of other winners or categorize the themes that prize-winning authors have addressed. You can find the speech in *Prentice Hall Literature, Penguin Edition, The American Experience.*

⏱ Timed Writing Prompt

5. Think about a topic you enjoy. Perhaps it is basketball history, nanotechnology, or current events. Identify a research question that you would like to pursue within this topic. Then, write a proposal for a research paper. Explain why your research question is important and how you would research it. Discuss the resources that you would use. **(45 minutes)**

Narrowing Your Topic

Browse through the library's reference section, and surf the Internet to see what has been written on your general topic. Make sure there are solid references to support your topic. Once you have determined that there is enough information available, narrow your subject into a suitably focused topic.

To make your research project manageable, be sure your topic is narrow enough to be presented thoroughly. For example, the Civil War is too broad to address effectively in a short research paper. To focus that subject, you might research only the role of women in the war or the effects of Sherman's march through Atlanta. Use webbing to narrow your topic.

Complete a Topic Web to Narrow Your Topic

As you begin your preliminary research, complete a topic web to help you narrow the subject of your research paper. Write your broad subject in the middle of a circle. Identify subtopics by writing them in circles radiating off the main topic. For each of these categories, identify the ideas that you have found. Use these categories to generate even more specific ideas until you find a topic that is narrow enough to cover in a research paper.

⏱ Timed Writing Hint

Most prompts provide very specific topics to write about. Be sure to structure your essay to address the prompt directly.

Student Work IN PROGRESS

Name: Rebecca Potter
Central High School
Omaha, NE

Webbing to Narrow a Topic

Rebecca used webbing to narrow her topic. Her preliminary research provided her with several artists and writers to pursue. She chose to focus on one: Augusta Savage.

Considering Your Audience and Purpose

When you research, you'll probably find more information than you can use in your report. A knowledge of your audience and purpose will help you clarify which information to include and how to present it.

Analyze Your Audience

How much your audience knows about your subject will influence the amount of detail you include. If your audience has little knowledge of your topic, you should provide background, context, and a definition of each unfamiliar term you use. As the chart below suggests, identifying a specific audience can help you determine the degree of detail to include.

BUILDING AN INFORMATION BASE

Statement: One major reason for the rise in baseball's popularity is the introduction of inter-league play.

Expert audiences know what inter-league play is and why it makes the game exciting.

Intermediate audiences may need to know how inter-league play is different from championship games.

Novice audiences need to have even more elaboration.

Refine Your Purpose

You can use the results of research to achieve a variety of purposes. You might want to describe, explain, or persuade. Refine your purpose, and then use language and details that support it. Following are three common research purposes:

- **To praise your subject:** Include words and details that show your subject's positive qualities.

- **To persuade your readers to adopt your position:** Include facts and examples that support your ideas.

- **To explain a complex cause-and-effect relationship:** Include facts and details that show the connection.

> **Research Tip**
>
> To understand the knowledge level of your audience, interview the people you think will read your paper. Take notes about ideas and questions they may have about your subject.

Gathering Details

Your sources give you the data you need to write an effective research piece. Begin with the goal of learning as much as possible about your topic. Then, explore a wide range of sources. Knowing where to look for facts about a specific topic will save a lot of time and energy. Use these tips to make your research more effective:

Use Library Resources

Reference Books You might begin with a good general reference article in an encyclopedia to give you introductory information and to suggest subtopics. Other reference books— such as collections of biographies, atlases, and almanacs—might provide additional information.

Nonfiction Books Locate good nonfiction books about your topic to give you necessary background information and general knowledge. Books with bibliographies are particularly useful because these can lead you to further sources of information.

Newspaper and Magazine Articles Use these to focus on specific aspects of the topic. You can locate articles by using an index called *Readers' Guide to Periodical Literature.*

Databases A library reference section may have databases, or on-line reference lists, for larger topics such as language. For example, the Modern Language Association has articles about different aspects of the English language and humanities. Educational Resources Information Center (ERIC) has an extensive list of sources relating to anything about education.

Internet Using the Web, you can access the holdings of most major libraries to find sources. Once located, you can request these through an interlibrary loan. While there is much information directly available on the Internet, choose Web sites wisely. Internet sources should not represent the bulk of your research because they are not always reliable.

Interviews If you cannot find printed matter to cover an aspect of your topic, consider interviewing people with expert knowledge. Professionals become an important source of information when you are researching new areas or when you wish to provide interpretation of a survey you have conducted.

▲ **Critical Viewing**
How can investigation lead you to refine your research topic? **[Hypothesize]**

🖥 **Internet Tip**

Some browsers have a tab called "What's Related." If you have found a site that provides useful information, click on this link to view other sites related to your subject.

Take Notes

Make your work efficient by establishing a system for collecting information as you conduct your research. Creating both source cards and note cards will save you time later when you'll need to reference this information.

Source Cards On a separate card for each source, include all the information that you'll need in order to reference the material you use; note title, author, publisher, and the city and date of publication. Jot down information that would help you find the source if you need to locate it again. Assign a number to each source. Write this number on the card and on any note card you create using this source.

Note Cards Use note cards to record specific information. Place only one item on a card, and include a categorizing label to identify the contents. When copying a direct quotation, record the words accurately. In addition to any notes, indicate the source number you assigned, and note the exact page numbers to indicate where you found the information.

High-Tech Options Print out information you find on-line, or photocopy articles that address your topic. Copy the publishing information found on the copyright page; you will need it when you reference the material. Then, circle or highlight the key facts or details you find.

Research Tip

Avoid plagiarism, the dangerous practice of presenting someone else's work as your own. When using another writer's words, quote your source directly. If you summarize or rephrase, be sure the words are your own and be sure you give credit.

Student Work
IN PROGRESS

Name: Rebecca Potter
Central High School
Omaha, NE

Creating Source Cards and Note Cards

Here is an example of the notes that Rebecca prepared while she was researching her paper. Note that she assigned this source the number 2 and used the categorizing word TEACHING on the note card to make her note-taking system more efficient.

2

Anderson, Jervis. This Was
Harlem. New York:
Farrar Straus Giroux, 1982.

Central High School library

2

TEACHING
Savage felt her teaching was
an important part of
her legacy.

Drafting

Shaping Your Writing

How you shape your writing depends on your audience, your purpose, and the data you have researched. Begin the drafting process with a thesis statement.

Propose a Thesis Statement

Whether you developed a thesis statement before you began your research or you are proposing one now, review your research to formalize your idea. Your thesis statement summarizes the main idea of your paper. It should express an idea that can be defended or refuted.

One way to write a thesis statement is to look for one idea that can be supported by a majority of the information you have found in your research. To do this

- Put your notes in front of you, and read through them.
- Find the relationships, and decide on the idea that best summarizes your research notes. Write a sentence that sums up the main idea.
- Confirm that your thesis is narrow enough to be addressed clearly in your writing.

🔋 Research Tip

In drafting your paper, you may notice your ideas shifting or the focus of your paper changing. Be open to the idea that your thesis statement may need to be revised later.

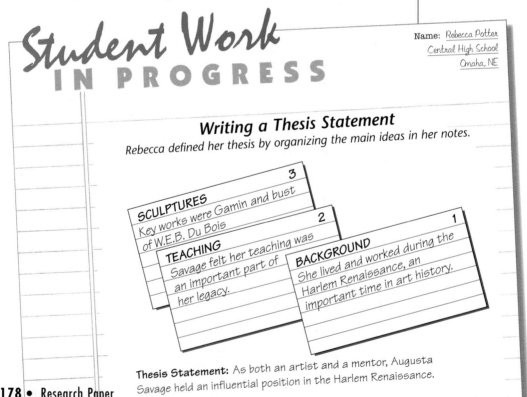

Student Work
IN PROGRESS

Name: Rebecca Potter
Central High School
Omaha, NE

Writing a Thesis Statement
Rebecca defined her thesis by organizing the main ideas in her notes.

3
SCULPTURES
Key works were Gamin and bust of W.E.B. Du Bois

2
TEACHING
Savage felt her teaching was an important part of her legacy.

1
BACKGROUND
She lived and worked during the Harlem Renaissance, an important time in art history.

Thesis Statement: As both an artist and a mentor, Augusta Savage held an influential position in the Harlem Renaissance.

Develop an Organizational Plan

After you have decided on your thesis statement, choose an organizational plan for your paper. Consider the strategies in the chart below, and identify one that suits your topic.

Types of Organization	Examples
Chronological Order • Presents events in order in which they occurred • Ideal for reporting the history of a subject	Explaining the events leading up to the launch of the space shuttle
Order of Importance • Presents details in order of increasing or decreasing importance • Ideal for writing persuasively or for building an argument	Defending or opposing an amendment to the Constitution
Comparison and Contrast • Presents similarities and differences • Ideal for addressing two or more subjects	Discussing the writing style of two best-selling authors
Parts to Whole • Presents information in categories that make up a whole • Ideal for analyzing elements of a large topic	Categorizing the instruments in a symphony

 Challenge

Consider organizing your paper using inductive reasoning. Using this strategy, cite specific examples and build to a general conclusion. In contrast, an argument based on deductive reasoning starts with a general claim and concludes with a specific statement.

Writing a Formal Outline An outline will help you to implement the organizational plan you've chosen. Next to each Roman numeral, list the main points you'll cover. Next to the capital letters, write the topics that fall under the main points. Finally, next to the numbers, list details about each topic.

OUTLINE FOR A PART-TO-WHOLE ORGANIZATION

   I. Edgar Allan Poe's Fiction
      A. Horror Stories
         (1) "The Cask of Amontillado"
         (2) "The Fall of the House of Usher"
      B. Detective Stories
         (1) "The Murders in the Rue Morgue"
         (2) "The Purloined Letter"
  II. Edgar Allan Poe's Poetry
      A. Love poem
      B. Narrative poem

Writing a Sentence Outline To expand your ideas before writing the final draft, use a sentence outline. For each part of your essay, identify a topic sentence you'll develop.

Providing Elaboration

Include a Variety of Outside Sources

As you draft, make use of the information you've collected. Review all your research notes, and choose the quotations or visuals that best prove your point.

Choosing Material to Support Your Thesis Your research has provided information that you may want to include in your draft as elaboration. Consider these options:

- **Direct Quotations and Paraphrases** When you refer to another writer's work, you have two options: You can either include direct quotations or paraphrase by restating another writer's ideas in your own words. In either case, you need to cite your source and make the relationship between your thesis and the researched information clear.

- **Visuals** If a visual will make your topic more accessible, take the opportunity to include one. For example, when appropriate consider these formats for conveying information visually:

  Charts can provide information concisely.

  Graphs can show a growth or decline over time.

  Maps can illustrate geography, climate, or population.

Rural and Urban Population in the United States, 1890–1920

Year	Rural	Urban
1890	65%	35%
1900	60%	40%
1910	54%	46%
1920	49%	51%

☐ Rural Population   ☐ Urban Population

▲ Critical Viewing How could this chart support a research paper on the growth of cities in the United States? **[Support]**

Integrating References by Framing Just as you write an introduction and conclusion to frame the body of your draft, you need to provide context for the quotations or visuals that you include in your research paper. For each quotation, follow a simple strategy. First, introduce the quotation by naming the writer or linking the quotation to the material it follows. Then, give the quoted material. Finally, explain the quotation by showing how it supports the point you are presenting.

Prepare to Credit Your Sources

When you include a direct quotation, present an original idea that is not your own, or report a fact that is available from only one source, you must include documentation. In writing your first draft, circle all ideas and words that are not your own. At this stage, for each circled item, use parentheses to note the author's last name and the page numbers of the material used. Later, you can use this record to create the necessary formal citations your research paper requires.

13.4 Revising

Your research paper reflects an extensive amount of time, commitment, and effort. To polish your draft, read it over several times, each time focusing on a different aspect of the writing.

Revising Your Overall Structure

Check Coherence

You want your readers to be able to identify your thesis statement and to follow your organizational plan. To achieve this level of coherence, be sure that each paragraph has a manageable topic sentence that is covered by the content of the paragraph. When you track coherence, you may find that some paragraphs actually comprise several topic sentences.

▶ **REVISION STRATEGY**
Bracketing to Track Coherence

Use a separate color to bracket sentences that introduce your discussion of each main idea in your outline. Review the marked items to see whether the ideas support the thesis statement and connect logically. If you have two or more colors in the same paragraph, break the paragraph into separate ones. Create appropriate topic sentences, and then decide whether you provide enough support for each idea.

Get instant help! For assistance in revising structure, use the interactive Improving Coherence by Restructuring Paragraphs activity in **Section 13.4**, on-line or on CD-ROM.

Student Work
IN PROGRESS

Name: *Rebecca Potter*
Central High School
Omaha, NE

Improving Coherence by Restructuring Paragraphs

Rebecca had written one long paragraph about Augusta Savage's background. When she listed the points she had included, she saw that she was trying to cover too much in a single paragraph.

- born in Florida in 1892
- traveled to Harlem
- attended Cooper Union

- life-changing opportunity - bust of W.E.B. Du Bois
- busts of other prominent people

- recognition grew
- sculpts *Gamin*

- leading artist
- teaching art to children most important achievement

By bracketing ideas that she could group into single paragraphs, she created a plan for revision.

Revising Your Paragraphs
Add Transitions to Improve the Flow of Ideas

Review your paragraphs to be sure that the connection you make between ideas is clear. Transitional words and phrases like *because, as a result, if, therefore, in addition, despite,* and *recently* can clarify the connections you want to stress.

▶ **REVISION STRATEGY**
Transition Boxes

To evaluate your use of transitions, use this strategy in several paragraphs of your research paper:
1. Draw a box between the end punctuation of each sentence and the first word of the next sentence.
2. Identify the relationship that connects the sentences on either side of the box.
3. Evaluate the writing as it exists. Place a check in a box if the relationship between the sentences it connects is clear.
4. If the relationship is not clear, add a transition. Place the new word or phrase at the point where the box is located. As an alternative, you might draw a line from the box to a space where the transition makes the most sense.

Challenge yourself to apply this strategy to other paragraphs in your essay.

Get instant help! For assistance with revising, use the interactive Using Transition Boxes activity in **Section 13.4**, on-line or on CD-ROM.

Student Work
IN PROGRESS

Name: *Rebecca Potter*
Central High School
Omaha, NE

Using Transition Boxes
Rebecca added transitions to make her ideas flow more smoothly.

Savage showed talent at the school and a *While at the school* special interest in African art.☐She received what would be a life-changing opportunity...

A transition is needed to clarify the life-changing opportunity occurring while at the school.

The NAACP believed the bust of Du Bois that Savage created to be one of the finest of him ever made.☐Savage was *Consequently,* asked to make busts of other prominent people. . . .

"Consequently" needs to be added to show that the second sentence is a result of the first.

TOPIC BANK

If you are having trouble choosing a topic, consider the following suggestions:

1. **Response to a Children's Book** Scan your childhood memories to find a book that was a particular favorite of yours. Visit the public library to find a copy. Then, write a response to the book, explaining why a child might cherish it. In addition, provide your responses to the book from the new perspective you bring to it as a young adult.

2. **Review of a Novel** Whether bestsellers or classics, novels allow readers to meet fascinating characters and embark on adventures they might never experience. In a response to a favorite novel, share your judgment and explain why the book was successful.

Responding to Fine Art

3. *The White Mantel,* right, conveys a wintry scene. Like fine art, literature can give readers a glimpse of a vivid setting. For example, Edgar Allan Poe's writing often creates an eerie setting, and William Faulkner's work reflects a unique image of the rural South. Choose a piece of literature that features a wintry or snowy setting, and write a response to address it.

Responding to Literature

The White Mantel 1927–1929, Frank Harmon Myers, National Museum of American Art, Washington, DC

4. Robert Frost's harrowing poem "Out, Out—" evokes a different response in each reader. In an essay, analyze the poem's effect on you. You can find the poem in *Prentice Hall Literature, Penguin Edition,* The American Experience.

Timed Writing Prompt

5. The English novelist E. M. Forster once said "The novel tells a story." Write an essay in which you agree or disagree with that statement. Use examples from novels that you have read to support your argument. **(45 minutes)**

Narrowing Your Topic

Each piece of writing includes so many facets—plot, characters, theme, setting, writing style, elaboration, and evidence—that an essay addressing each of these elements could not discuss any of them well. Instead, a focused response treats one issue thoroughly. Hexagonal writing can help you narrow a topic.

Use Hexagonal Writing to Narrow a Topic

When you use hexagonal writing, you look at a piece of literature from a variety of angles. Complete each angle in a hexagon according to the directions that follow. When you have completed your hexagon, review the notes and narrow your topic.

Plot Summarize or paraphrase the writing you have chosen.
Personal Allusions Jot down people, places, situations, or events from your own life that the selection suggests to you.
Theme Briefly state the generalization or message about life that the selection conveys to you.
Analysis Cite evidence from the text to support the theme you have identified.
Literary Allusions Consider other literature that the selection suggests to you.
Evaluation Decide whether you liked the work.

Challenge

Find a partner who has chosen the same piece of literature as you have. After you each complete a hexagon, compare your results. It may surprise you, but the finished charts will probably be unexpectedly different!

Student Work
IN PROGRESS

Name: J. B. Nelson
Hart High School
Newhall, CA

Using Hexagonal Writing to Narrow a Topic

After J. B. completed his hexagon, he decided to address an issue that presented itself: Sandra Cisneros's ability to overcome obstacles.

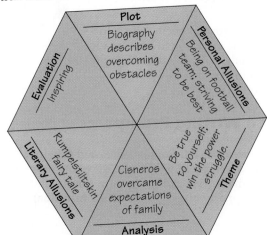

Considering Your Audience and Purpose

Once you have narrowed your topic, consider the format your response will take. A reader's response to Emily Dickinson's poetry would include personal reactions; a literary analysis of the same work for an audience of classmates who have studied Dickinson would include a more formal examination of her writing. Before you draft, take the time to identify your intended audience and your specific purpose.

Develop an Audience Profile

Your intended audience will affect the length, vocabulary, and level of detail you will use in writing your response to the literature you've chosen. To be sure your draft will address your target audience, complete a profile like the one shown here. Then, use your responses to shape your draft.

AUDIENCE PROFILE	
Age and background	16 and 17 year olds, urban, fairly sophisticated
Interest, biases	Enjoy good stories; are not impressed by especially formal diction
Vocabulary level	average to above average
What they know about the topic	have read several works by this author; know her style and common themes
Literature features of interest	conflict

interactive Textbook

Get instant help! To find language that will appeal to your intended audience, use the interactive Word Bins, accessible from the menu bar, on-line or on CD-ROM.

Clarify Your Purpose

Whether you are sharing your enthusiasm for a new writer, expressing your interpretation of a well-known short story, or writing to achieve another purpose, include details that support your writing goal. Consider these tips:

- **To praise,** include concrete details about what you liked.
- **To analyze,** back up your ideas with evidence from the text.
- **To explain a personal response,** show how the writing connects to the experience, ideas, or situation you describe.

Gathering Details

Once you have a clear idea of your audience and purpose, generate a list of the kinds of details you need. To do this, summarize your purpose in one sentence. Then, review the literature to find the details to back it up. Here's a sample:

What I Want to Show:

- James Thurber's "The Night the Ghost Got In"
- Uses exaggeration to create comedy

What Details I Need to Include:

- Characters whose behavior is unusually quirky
- Reactions that are overblown
- Language that creates overstatement

Use these tips to gather details on specific literary elements:

Character If you are planning to discuss a specific character, review the literature to make notes about the character's actions, ideas, appearance, and motivation. Note any changes the character undergoes. Look for any information provided by the narrator, and study the other characters' reactions to the character you'll describe.

Setting To write a response that focuses on setting, clarify the time and place in which the work unfolds. Note the mood or atmosphere that the setting helps to convey, and assemble details that add to it.

Diction When discussing a writer's word choice, back up your ideas with specific examples. Consider the vocabulary level and both the denotations (or dictionary meanings) and the connotations (or emotional meanings) of the words that the writer has used.

Sound Devices If you want to focus on sound devices in poetry, collect examples of rhythm, rhyme, alliteration, or assonance to support your ideas. Look for patterns in rhyme and rhythm, or look for the imagery the poet creates in the writing.

Theme To analyze the message of an author's writing, look at the way a conflict is resolved, examine the attitudes and actions and statements of the characters, and study the expository parts of the writing. Use these details to draw conclusions about the author's generalization about life.

Research Tip

Treat this stage of the writing process as research. Consider photocopying the selection you'll analyze. Then, use a highlighter or a red pen to identify the elements that support your response.

14.3 Drafting

Shaping Your Writing
Organize to Support a Response

Introduction Start with an interesting lead that connects to the ideas you will present. Consider drafting a description, presenting a problem, or creating context. To keep the momentum going, identify the title and author of the selection, and present the main idea of your essay in a thesis statement.

Summary Before jumping into an analysis of the literature, summarize or paraphrase the work. Limit your summary to a sentence or two, but inform your readers of key elements in the text.

Body Use the body of your essay to develop your thesis statement. Use details, paraphrases, or direct quotations from the work to support the points you make. Strive for analysis; avoid retelling the plot or describing characters in detail.

Conclusion Restate your thesis and summarize your main points, but take your conclusion beyond the basics. Use your conclusion as an opportunity to make a personal recommendation, ask a question, or make a prediction.

Timed Writing Hint

Remember the letters ISBC: I = Introduction, S = Structure, B = Body, C = Conclusion. This hint will help structure your response to a literature prompt.

Student Work
IN PROGRESS

Name: J. B. Nelson
Hart High School
Newhall, CA

Organizing With a Sentence Outline

To organize his essay, J. B. used a sentence outline to present his drafting plan.

Introduction	Describe fairy tale "Rumpelstiltskin" and link to Cisneros's life.
Thesis Statement	The struggle for control over her own future has been a big part of Cisneros's life.
Body Paragraph 1	Analyze "My name." To the narrator, a name represents personality.
Body Paragraph 2	Analyze "A House of My Own." To the narrator, a house represents success.
Summary Paragraph	Connect back to Rumpelstiltskin.
Conclusion	Make a connection to my own experiences.

Providing Elaboration

For each main idea you develop, include a specific example from the text that illustrates your point.

Incorporate References From the Text

Instead of asking your readers to trust your interpretation, add the proof you need by incorporating references from the text. You can include direct quotations or paraphrases using your own words to summarize the information. In both cases, make sure you incorporate the material by introducing the reference, giving the reference, and then explaining how it supports your ideas.

SAMPLE DIRECT QUOTATION:

In "The Story of an Hour," the reader is presented with an unsettling opening line that sets the stage for a surprising story. The writer begins with this sentence: "Knowing that Mrs. Mallard was afflicted with a heart trouble, great care was taken to break to her as gently as possible the news of her husband's death." From the start, readers can anticipate that Mrs. Mallard's reaction to this news may be dramatic.

Student Work
IN PROGRESS

Name: J. B. Nelson
Hart High School
Newhall, CA

Incorporating References From the Text

To develop the narrator's desire for a modern name, J. B. quotes Cisneros's text. Showing which names might be considered modern makes the point more clear.

She was given her grandmother's name, Esperanza. That name is Spanish, and the narrator feels it is too traditional. In the story, she says she wants a more modern name, citing the more imaginative "Lisandra or Maritza, or Zeze the X." (Cisneros, *The House on Mango Street*, 13.) Instead of inheriting her grandmother's name, and potentially her life, she wants to live her own life, follow her own rules, and have her own name. To the narrator, a name clearly represents who she is. In her mind, people must earn a name much as they earn respect.

14.4 *Revising*

Once your draft is written, make the effort to improve your writing. Analyze your response to literature on four levels: overall structure, paragraphs, sentences, and word choice.

Revising Your Overall Structure

Present a United Front

While you may have a mixed response to the literature you've chosen to discuss, avoid confusing your reader. Present a concise, unified opinion, and back it up with support. Unless you can relate the discussion of other elements to the thesis statement, eliminate paragraphs or details that do not support the main impression your response addresses.

▶ **REVISION STRATEGY**
Identifying Contradictory Information

Write your thesis statement on a small piece of paper to move along the side of your draft. As you read your essay, slide your thesis statement down the page, confirming that each paragraph contains information that supports it. If you notice paragraphs, details, or examples that contradict your main idea, circle them. When you have reviewed your entire draft, evaluate the circled information.

Evaluate

- Are there several circled items that can be connected in some way?

- Are there some circled items you can delete?

Revise

- If the information is important enough to your analysis, add a single paragraph to address this group of details. Use a transitional sentence to acknowledge this paragraph as a contrast to your thesis.
- Eliminate items that seem random or that cannot be connected to your thesis.

Writers in
ACTION

Theresa Park, literary agent, takes as much care analyzing her own writing as she does reviewing that of her clients. Because her response guides their success, she needs to provide concrete details to support her evaluation. She explains here:

"I think it's really important to be as specific about your criticism as possible. It's not enough to say that the writing is bad, or that it's weak. Why is it bad? Why is it weak?"

Revising Your Paragraphs

Review each paragraph in your draft to be sure it logically contributes to your thesis statement. Pay special attention to your conclusion; what you include there should leave your reader with something to consider long after reading your essay.

Strengthen Your Conclusion

In revising your conclusion, check that you have restated your thesis and reminded readers of the evidence you used to support it. To take your conclusion beyond the basics, find a way to make your last paragraphs memorable, personal, or provocative. Consider making a recommendation to your readers or linking the literary selection to a larger historical or contemporary context.

▶ **REVISION STRATEGY**
Personalizing Your Response

Review your prewriting work to recall how you found a topic that appealed to you. Review the draft to evaluate whether a personal reflection could improve your conclusion. Make revisions by adding information that links the literature to your life and experiences.

Student Work
IN PROGRESS

Name: J. B. Nelson
Hart High School
Newhall, CA

Personalizing the Conclusion

J. B. found a quotation from Cisneros's writing in the body of his essay that he could relate back to his own life.
These are the notes he made to create a more personal conclusion.

| J. B. models Cisneros's deliberate use of sentence fragments. |

Cisneros's quotation: "Not a man's. Not Daddy's. A house all my own. . . . a space for myself to go, clean as paper before a poem."

Conclusion: To paraphrase the writer, here is the lesson I can take from her: "Not for daddy, not for the coaches, not for your friends, but for yourself. Life, clean as paper before a poem. Don't write what you're told; write what you want."

Revising Your Sentences

Review Sentence Clarity

As you read your draft, look for sentences that may be incomplete, those that lack a subject or verb, or those that are run-ons. Such sentences can be confusing to your readers.

▶ **REVISION STRATEGY**
Bracketing Complete Sentences

Bracket each sentence of your draft. Evaluate each group of words you've marked by confirming that it expresses a complete thought. When you come across a fragment or a run-on punctuated as a sentence, revise it to correct the error.

Try it out! Use the interactive Bracketing Complete Sentences activity in **Section 14.4,** on-line or on CD-ROM.

Grammar in Your Writing

Sentence Fragments, Fused Sentences, and Comma Splices

Although they are incorrectly punctuated as sentences, **sentence fragments** do not express complete thoughts. Subordinate clauses beginning with conjunctions such as *after*, *although*, *despite*, *because*, and *since* are common targets for such errors.

Fragment: When we go to the fiesta in April.
Sentence: When we go to the fiesta in April, we'll enjoy the food.

One type of run-on sentence, a **fused sentence,** consists of two or more sentences that are neither separated nor joined by any punctuation at all.

Fused Sentence: We love the music we never get to hear it enough.
Correct: We love the music; however, we never get to hear it enough.

A second type of run-on sentence is the **comma splice.** A comma splice is created when two or more main clauses are separated only by commas instead of by commas and conjunctions or by semicolons.

Comma Splice: They brought plenty of supplies, nothing was left over.
Correct: They brought plenty of supplies; nothing was left over.

Find It in Your Reading Except for a deliberate use for effect, most professionally published writing does not include errors such as accidental sentence fragments, fused sentences, or comma splices. Review an essay by your favorite author to see how he or she uses punctuation and subordination to generate correct and sophisticated sentences.

Find It in Your Writing Review your draft to find any sentence fragments, fused sentences, and comma splices. Correct fragments by providing what is missing, and punctuate run-on sentences correctly.

For more on sentence fragments, fused sentences, and comma splices, see Chapter 20.

Revising Your Word Choice

Review Evaluative Modifiers

The adjectives and adverbs that convey appraisal or judgment in your draft should be words that are precise. These modifiers convey the strength of your response and the depth of your assessment of the literature you address.

▶**REVISION STRATEGY**
Circling Words of Praise or Criticism

Review your draft, and circle any words that convey either a positive or negative response. Then, evaluate your draft on three levels. First, decide whether your writing includes enough evaluative modifiers. Second, note whether you repeat the same ones too frequently. Finally, decide whether your evaluative modifiers precisely convey your response. Consider adding words like these to improve your draft:

- **Mild Praise:** *appealing, readable, factual, intelligent, solid, accurate, expressive, comprehensive*

- **High Praise:** *imaginative, refreshing, inspired, lively, brilliant, beautiful, entertaining, honest, original*

- **Mild Disapproval:** *dull, predictable, silly, inaccurate, vague, confusing, repetitious, unfocused*

- **Strong Disapproval:** *insulting, biased, pretentious, trivial, pointless, false, awful*

Get instant help! For assistance in revising word choice, use the interactive Evaluative Words Word Bin, accessible under Word Bins on the menu bar, on-line or on CD-ROM.

Student Work IN PROGRESS

Name: J. B. Nelson
Hart High School
Newhall, CA

Revising Evaluative Modifiers

When J. B. circled words that conveyed praise in his draft, he saw the opportunity to make his writing stronger.

These same concerns are ⟨evident⟩ in *The House on Mango Street,* the ⟨poetic⟩ novel that helped Cisneros break away from
and inspired
other people's plans for her. With this ∧ novel, she spun straw,
engaging
the low expectations held for her, into gold, her own success.

Peer Review

Plus and Minus Scoring

In a small group, share your revised draft. Using the criteria in the chart below, ask your readers to evaluate your work on specific elements. You may want to alter the chart to target your draft more closely.

As you read the criteria in each category, ask your reviewers to give you a plus or minus score. Record their responses, and ask your reviewers to explain their evaluations. Take notes when necessary. Then, use your classmates' responses to revise your draft.

▲ Critical Viewing
How can a peer review discussion spark debate over a literary selection? **[Hypothesize]**

PLUS AND MINUS CHART

CRITERIA	Group Members			COMMENTS
	1	2	3	
Interesting introduction: first two sentences hook reader				
Identifiable thesis				
Identifiable title and author				
First idea clearly stated and elaborated				
Second idea clearly stated and elaborated				
Successful conclusion				
Overall evaluation				

14.5 *Editing and Proofreading*

Errors in spelling, punctuation, and grammar can undermine your credibility or make your draft difficult to read. Proofread your writing several times, looking for different kinds of mistakes with each reading. If you leave a few minutes between each session, your review will be more accurate. When you return to your draft each time with a fresh perspective, you will see errors that you didn't notice before.

Focusing on Spelling

Check the spelling of each word in your draft. To keep your focus on this task, consider looking at each word, starting with the last word in each paragraph and moving toward the first.

Confirm Names If your writing contains many references to literary places or characters, go back to the original works to confirm the correct spelling of the names. Check the spelling of the title and authors of the works you discuss, too.

Collaborative Writing Tip

Trade papers with a classmate. Another editor may find errors you missed.

Grammar in Your Writing
Common Homophones

A common spelling error stems from confusion over homophones. A **homophone** is a word that sounds the same as another word but has a different meaning and a different spelling. Here are some common homophones:

allot/a lot: *Allot* is usually a verb that means "to give out in shares"; *a lot* is an informal expression meaning "a great amount." Although you should avoid using *a lot* in formal writing, note that the phrase is two words and is never spelled *alot*.

principal/principle: *Principal* can be a noun that means "the person who has controlling authority." It is also used an adjective meaning "most important." *Principle* is always used as a noun meaning "a fundamental law."

your/you're: *Your* is generally used as a possessive adjective; *you're* is a contraction of the words *you* and *are*.

Use a dictionary to clarify the meaning and spelling of any homophone pairs that present difficulty.

Find It in Your Writing As you proofread your draft, check that you have not introduced confusion by including a homophone for a word you intended.

For more on common homophones, see Chapter 25.

14.6 Publishing and Presenting

Building Your Portfolio

Here are some ways to share your response to literature with a wider audience:

1. **Post an On-line Response** Booksellers on the Web often invite readers to post reviews. In an on-line response, you can share your reactions with potential book buyers. You can also compare ideas with those of other reviewers.

2. **Mail Your Response** You may have a friend or relative who would enjoy the piece of literature you've chosen. You may even want to share your ideas with the author. Send a copy of your essay. Then, keep in your portfolio any responses your mailing generates.

Reflecting on Your Writing

In a brief reflection, jot down your thoughts on the process of writing your response to literature. Use these questions to start your writing:

- In what ways did writing your response to literature deepen your understanding of the work?

- Which prewriting strategy did you find most useful? Explain.

 Internet Tip

To see model essays scored with this rubric, go on-line: PHSchool.com
Enter Web Code: efk-1101

Rubric for Self-Assessment

Use these criteria to evaluate your response to literature.

	Score 4	Score 3	Score 2	Score 1
Audience and Purpose	Presents sufficient background on the work(s); presents the writer's reactions forcefully	Presents background on the work(s); presents the writer's reactions clearly	Presents some background on the work(s); presents the writer's reactions at points	Presents little or no background on the work(s); presents few of the writer's reactions
Organization	Presents points in logical order, smoothly connecting them to the overall focus	Presents points in logical order and connects them to the overall focus	Organizes points poorly in places; connects some points to an overall focus	Presents information in a scattered, disorganized manner
Elaboration	Supports reactions and evaluations with elaborated reasons and well-chosen examples	Supports reactions and evaluations with specific reasons and examples	Supports some reactions and evaluations with reasons and examples	Offers little support for reactions and evaluations
Use of Language	Shows overall clarity and fluency; uses precise, evaluative words; makes few mechanical errors	Shows good sentence variety; uses some precise evaluative terms; makes some mechanical errors	Uses awkward or overly simple sentence structures and vague evaluative terms; makes many mechanical errors	Presents incomplete thoughts; makes mechanical errors that create confusion

Writing for Assessment

Assessment in School

School assessment comes in many forms. Whether it's a lab report, a group discussion, a writing portfolio, or a standardized test, you are often asked to demonstrate your understanding of a topic or your mastery of a body of academic material. This periodic check or assessment helps you and your teachers to identify strengths and weaknesses and to maximize your educational achievement.

When you are prepared, tests are challenges that you can meet with confidence. They offer you the chance to show what you know and to earn good grades. In this chapter, you will sharpen your performance skills for one of the most common types of assessment in school: the essay test.

▲ **Critical Viewing**
How is writing in a test situation different from writing an assigned essay?
[Contrast]

What Is Assessment?

One of the most common types of school assessment is the written test. Most often, a written test is announced in advance, allowing you time to study and prepare. When a test includes an essay, you are expected to write a response that includes

- a clearly stated and well-supported thesis or main idea.
- specific information about the topic, derived from your reading or from class discussion.
- a clear organization.

To see the criteria on which an essay test may be evaluated, preview the Rubric for Self-Assessment on page 217.

Types of Assessment

While an essay test may be written on any number of topics, the format it takes might be limited to a handful of familiar writing tasks. In your school career, you will probably encounter questions that ask you to address each of the following types of writing:

- **Explain a process** (how a bill becomes a law).
- **Defend a position** (why a character in literature took a certain action).
- **Compare, contrast, or categorize** (the similarities and differences among mammals, reptiles, and amphibians).
- **Show cause and effect** (how the Industrial Revolution changed city life).

Writers in ACTION

In the United States, the value of an educated mind has been close to the hearts of teachers and political leaders for centuries. In fact, in a 1936 speech then-candidate Franklin D. Roosevelt extolled the value of learning this way:

"The gains of education are never really lost. Books may be burned and cities sacked, but truth, like the yearning for freedom, lives in the hearts of humble men."

PREVIEW Student Work IN PROGRESS

Margaret Boehme, a student at Buena High School in Ventura, California, wrote an essay test response about the factors causing the American Revolution. In this chapter, you will see her work in progress, including strategies she used to write and revise the essay.

15.1 **Prewriting**

Choosing Your Topic

In an essay test, the writing topic is generally assigned. Occasionally, however, you will be given a choice of topics. Since an essay test often involves the pressure of time limitations, choosing a suitable topic will help you to make the most of the time available. Read all the prompts or questions before deciding which one to complete. Follow these guidelines:

Match Task With Time Examine each question to determine which will take the least time. Ask yourself how many specific details spring to mind about each one without much effort. As you evaluate the prompts, consider the topics you feel most confident in developing, remember which subjects you have reviewed most recently, and choose a prompt.

Identify Your Strengths Review each prompt to decide whether you can write about the subject in the way the questions require. For example, you may feel comfortable providing the history of an event, but you may not feel as secure in analyzing the aftereffects of the same subject. As you read each prompt, jot down two or three ideas that help you evaluate your potential success. Review your notes to choose a prompt.

Frame a Focus Choose a topic for which you can identify a focus or main idea. With open-ended questions—such as those that ask you to identify and discuss a significant theme, event, or trend—choose a prompt for which you will be able to present a thesis supported by relevant details and examples.

Interactive Textbook

Get instant help! To time your work, use the Timer button available with Essay Builder, accessible from the menu bar, on-line or on CD-ROM.

TOPIC BANK

Following are some essay test questions. If you plan to practice writing for assessment, choose one of these or ask your teacher to provide you with one.

1. **Vitamins and Nutrition** Explain how a balanced diet can contribute to a healthy body. Choose three essential vitamins, identify the foods in which they are most commonly found, and explain their influence on the body.

2. **Bravery in the Face of Danger** Characters in literature often display intense courage when they face a difficult or dangerous situation. Choose a character from a work of literature that you have recently read. Summarize the character's situation, and explain how unusual bravery helped resolve the problem.

Narrowing Your Response

To answer an essay test question effectively, plan your response by narrowing your focus to provide only what the question requires. Take a moment to analyze the prompt you've chosen. To do this successfully, review the key words and identify your purpose.

Circle Key Words to Identify Your Purpose

Read the prompt and circle verbs, nouns, and other key phrases in the question that provide directions about the type of information the response requires. The chart below shows common key words to expect.

Key Words	Essay Objectives
analyze	examine how elements contribute to the whole
compare/contrast	stress how subjects are alike/different
define	give examples to explain meaning
discuss	support generalizations with facts and examples
evaluate, judge	assign a value or explain an opinion
interpret	support thesis with examples from text

Challenge

While you might feel pressured to start writing right away, take the time to plan your response. Every minute you devote to planning your essay and gathering details will give you a stronger structure and provide you with more content to include in your essay.

Student Work IN PROGRESS

Name: *Margaret Boehme*
Buena High School
Ventura, CA

Circling Key Words in Test Prompts

Margaret reviewed the prompt she chose, circling the words that would focus her writing. To help shape her answer, she noted her own interpretation of key words.

judgment, opinion   *ranked*

#1. Evaluate the relative importance of the following as factors

prompting the Americans to rebel in 1776:

4 factors
- parliamentary taxation
- restriction of civil liberties
- the legacy of colonial religious and political ideas
- British military methods

15.2 Drafting

Shaping Your Writing

Find a Focus

Once you have chosen your topic, identify a focus for your essay. Consider the type of writing you are creating, and draft a simple statement to direct your writing.

- **Exposition** Develop a thesis statement that directly responds to the question presented. For problem-and-solution, cause-and-effect, or comparison-and-contrast essays, follow the expectations of those types of writing.

- **Persuasion** Choose a position to argue, and identify the support you'll use to defend it.

- **Response to Literature** Identify a focus for writing. It might be an analysis of one or more literary elements in a work; for example, conflict in a short story, dialogue in a play, imagery and sound effects in a poem, or theme in a novel.

▲ Critical Viewing
What parts of a test-taking situation might challenge a student's ability to concentrate? [Relate]

Plan a Structure

Before you draft your essay, sketch an outline to organize your material. This will keep you on track and help you address all the points you want to discuss in your response. Because your outline is part of your planning and not part of your grade, do not spend time creating an elaborate structure of Roman numerals. For an essay test, strive to get the ideas down and to leave yourself enough time to develop a strong essay.

Introduction, Body, and Conclusion When you sketch an outline for your essay, divide it into three parts: introduction, body, and conclusion. The **introduction** should address the question and state your thesis. The **body** of the essay should present at least two main points to support your thesis. The **conclusion** should restate the answer expressed in the thesis and sum up the main points in the body.

Memory Aids For each section of your outline, note the main ideas you want to convey. If ideas are flowing quickly as you create the outline, jot down key words to remind you of the main points or details you'll want to include as you draft.

Providing Elaboration

A critical part of an essay test response is its level of detail. As you write, include the specific information that supports your main idea or thesis. Whenever you can, refer to ideas that you have learned in class discussions and assigned readings.

Back Up Your Thesis With Support

Whether your purpose in an essay test is to inform, to persuade, to compare and contrast, or to explain cause and effect, you need to include specific evidence supporting your answer. Unless you're taking an "open-book test," these details must come from your memory or personal experience. Here are some types of details you can use in an essay:

- **Facts, Incidents, or Trends** Provide precise information to prove you know your subject. In an essay about a battle during the American Revolution, identify the location, the date, the leaders on both sides, and the outcome.

- **Specific Examples** Often, the best way to prove a point is to include examples that support the point for you. For example, in an essay about the music of Mozart, include specific discussions of at least two of his major works.

- **Descriptive Details** In an essay comparing and contrasting lions and tigers, include specific descriptions of the habitat and social organization of the two species.

Get instant help! For assistance with elaboration, use the interactive Including Support activity in **Section 15.2**, on-line or on CD-ROM.

Student Work
IN PROGRESS

Name: Margaret Boehme
Buena High School
Ventura, CA

Including Support

In her essay, Margaret had to evaluate the four factors identified in the prompt. In this passage about taxation, she used insert marks to make her examples and details more specific.

Opposition to the Tea Tax imposed by the British was largely in
—even with the three-cent tax—
principle. British tea was often the cheapest tea available, but many

colonists chose to purchase the more expensive (and illegal under the

Navigation Laws) Dutch-imported tea, for it was the notion of being

taxed that they disliked.

Revising

Don't allow the pressure of a test situation to cause you to hand in your essay before you check it for form and content.

Revising Your Overall Structure
Get the Big Picture

Your essay will be judged mainly on how effectively and accurately you answer the test question. Take the time to check your answer against the prompt the test presented.

▶ **REVISION STRATEGY**
Comparing the Question With the Answer

Check to see that you have followed the instructions in the question. Use these tips to guide your evaluation:

- **Check the Numbers** If the question has asked you to provide a specific number of examples, be sure you address the correct number in your response.

- **Review the Tasks** Some questions provide a list of tasks. For example, you might need to summarize an event, critique the people involved, and then make a prediction. Be sure you have completed each segment of the assignment.

Revising Your Paragraphs
Confirm Coherence

Taking a single page from draft to final copy can pose a problem if you change your thesis while you write. To be sure you present one idea coherently without changing direction in the middle, compare your introduction with your conclusion.

▶ **REVISION STRATEGY**
Checking the Introduction Against the Conclusion

The first paragraph of your essay should state your focus or thesis in response to the essay question. Your conclusion should tie the threads of your essay together, explaining how each point you've made supports the thesis.

Evaluate

- Do the main points in the introduction and conclusion match?

Revise

- Revise either paragraph to make your draft more unified. If necessary, revise the body paragraphs or add transitional sentences to bring the essay together.

Learn More

For specific strategies for taking state and national standardized tests, see the Standardized Test Preparation Workshops at the end of each chapter.

What Is Workplace Writing?

Workplace writing is probably the format you'll use most after you finish school. It is used in offices, factories, and by workers on the road. Workplace writing includes a variety of formats that share common features. In general, workplace writing is fact-based writing that communicates specific information to readers in a structured format. Effective workplace writing

- communicates information concisely to make the best use of both the writer's and the reader's time.
- includes a level of detail that provides necessary information and anticipates potential questions.
- reflects the writer's care if it is error-free and neatly presented.

Types of Workplace Writing

From the form you fill out to sign up for computer time at school to a memo to Cabinet members from the President of the United States, workplace writing is something we all do. There are many types of business communication—both electronic and print—and each type addresses a specific purpose:

- **Business letters** are written to formally address and communicate issues of concern to both writers and readers.
- **Memos** are prepared to share information within a company, club, organization, or other group.
- **Résumés** are created by job-seekers to summarize job, educational, and life experiences for potential employers.
- **Forms and applications** are completed to provide specific, factual information necessary for an identified purpose, such as opening a bank account or joining a gym.

Writers in
ACTION

Whether or not you have read Lucy Maud Montgomery's popular Anne of Green Gables *books, you'll probably enjoy her writing advice. Keep it in mind, particularly when writing for the workplace, where people often feel pressed for time:*

"The point of good writing is knowing when to stop."

Take her words to heart when you write in a work environment. Strive to limit business writing to one page.

PREVIEW

Chapter Contents

In the following pages, you'll see several examples of real-life workplace writing—a letter of complaint about a defective product, a memo welcoming a new employee, the résumé of a student seeking summer employment, an application for a learner's permit, and the forms typically used to cover faxes and transmit phone messages. As you'll see, using the stages of the writing process can make these formal pieces of writing more effective.

Business Letter

What Is a Business Letter?

Business letters can serve a number of purposes. One letter might request an interview, another might express dissatisfaction with a product, a third might pledge support for an idea. Whatever the subject, an effective business letter

- includes six parts: the heading, the inside address, the salutation or greeting, the body, the closing, and the signature.

- follows one of several acceptable formats—in *block format*, each part of the letter begins at the left margin; in *modified block format*, the heading, the closing, and the signature are indented to the center of the page.

- uses formal language to communicate courteously, regardless of the letter's content.

A business letter includes two addresses. The **heading** indicates where the letter originates and the date it was written. The **inside address** shows where the letter will be sent.

Model Business Letter

In this letter, the writer used a modified block format to outline the problems she encountered with an audio-cassette.

A **salutation** allows for a polite greeting and is punctuated by a colon.

The **body** of the letter identifies the writer's purpose. In this case, the writer politely expresses a complaint.

Here the writer specifies the actions she wants the company to take in response to her complaint.

The **closing** *Sincerely* is common, but *Respectfully yours* or *Yours truly* are also acceptable. To end the letter, the writer includes a **signature** and types her name.

---

200 Oak Street, Apt. G4
Cedar Rapids, IA 52402

March 9th, 20- -

Grant McLaughlin, Manager
Customer Service Department
Audioscope Recordings
4300 Corporate Drive
Herndon, VA 22071

Dear Mr. McLaughlin:

I purchased a tape entitled *The Life and Times of Sherlock Holmes* just two weeks ago at my local bookstore. To my disappointment, the cassette would not play. On closer examination, I noticed that the cassette contained no actual tape—the spools were empty!

I have written to you directly for two reasons. First, the bookstore where I purchased this tape no longer has copies of the audiocassette and, therefore, cannot replace my purchase. Second, I wish to communicate my surprise at this carelessness. Your products always seem produced and packaged with great care. How could a cassette leave your factory without any tape on it?

Please replace the enclosed audiocassette with a functioning copy of *The Life and Times of Sherlock Holmes*. You may send it to me at the address listed above.

Thank you in advance for your prompt attention to this matter.

Sincerely,

Jeannette DuPres

Jeannette DuPres

TOPIC BANK

To write a business letter that communicates effectively, choose an issue or problem that matters to you. If you have trouble coming up with a topic, consider these possibilities:

1. **Letter to a Package Delivery Company** People send packages all around the world for many different reasons. What happens when one gets lost? Write a letter of complaint about the loss of an important package.

2. **Letter to a Local Newspaper** The local newspaper is sponsoring a photography contest for high-school students. Write a cover letter to accompany your contest submission.

Prewriting Make every attempt to identify the name and position of the person who can best respond to your letter. Use a phone book or other resource to identify that person and obtain a correct address. Then, jot down the information you'll need to share with the person you've identified. For example, gather the names, dates, or product numbers you'll need to explain your situation clearly.

Drafting Before you write, list the main points that you wish to address. List your central reason for writing, any background or surrounding events, and any response or action you may be seeking. Prioritize your list, and then draft your letter. For ease of reading, allow about one paragraph for each main point.

Revising Review your letter to evaluate whether the format, situation, and purpose are clear. Check that diction or word choice is appropriately respectful. Consider revising words to better convey your feelings. For example, words like *clearly* and *obviously* communicate a different message from *perhaps* and *maybe*.

Editing and Proofreading Once you are satisfied with the content of your letter, focus on the format. Be sure you've used proper punctuation in the salutation and the closing. Confirm the placement of both addresses. Finally, check the spelling of every word—especially names. Nothing undercuts a letter's purpose more than misspelling the recipient's name.

Publishing and Presenting Fold your letter neatly, and enclose it in a properly addressed business envelope. Include your return address and postage before mailing.

Memo

What Is a Memo?

A memo is a brief, informally structured communication between parties who share an interest in a common issue. It may travel between people who work side by side in an office, or it may reach a more widespread audience, connecting members of a corporate community in several states. An effective memo

- is written in block format, with each new element beginning at the left margin.
- clearly states the sender, audience, date, and topic.
- communicates information briefly, keeping the total memo length under one page whenever possible.
- outlines any actions that the recipient should take.

> The writer includes her title to emphasize her authority in sending the memo.

Model Memo

In this memo, the manager of a key department introduces a new staff member to the rest of the company.

> Capital letters draw readers' attention to the memo topic. The word re: is Latin for "about" and is commonly used in memos.

> The body of the memo elaborates on the topic line, providing information to introduce the new employee.

> The writer assumes her audience shares certain basic knowledge about the subject. For example, she does not elaborate on the function of market research.

> Finally, the memo suggests a course of action: Readers should welcome Perrin.

Memo

TO: All
FROM: Dana Pollero
         Vice President, Market Research
DATE: August 26, 20- -
RE: WELCOME TO PERRIN SAMUELS

 Firefly Multimedia

Please join the Market Research Department in welcoming Perrin Samuels, who is joining our department as Senior Research Consultant, reporting to me.

Perrin has ten years of experience in market research and joins us from Music Markets, a well-known specialty publisher. In her position there as Manager of Market Research, she was involved with secondary research and sales support. She designed and maintained a dozen fact books on the music recording and publication industries for use by fourteen different sales teams.

Prior to Music Markets, Perrin worked for more than six years conducting research for advertisers, publishers, and producers of music-related products and services. She has experience with different information-gathering methods, including questionnaires and focus testing, and has successfully managed several projects. Perrin has directed a wide variety of research projects from start-up to final outcome. She has experience with new-product development, advertising campaigns, and sales analysis.

Perrin holds Bachelor degrees in Business Administration and in Music History from Adelphi University and a Master of Business Administration from the University of Bridgeport.

Please join the Market Research Department in welcoming Perrin to Firefly Multimedia. She will be in office 2K33, opposite Andy Graziano.

TOPIC BANK

To write a memo that gets the message across quickly and efficiently, choose information that the recipient needs to know. If you're having trouble coming up with your own topic, consider these possibilities:

1. **Memo About a School Dance** Students in many schools are taking charge of planning dances. Write a memo to your classmates or to a faculty advisor in which you outline an idea for a dance at your school.

2. **Memo to Members of a Club** When organized groups, such as the yearbook staff or the computer club, welcome new members, they often provide basic information about schedules, policies, and financial matters. Write a memo to a new club member in which you briefly explain the function of a club that you enjoy.

Prewriting Define your topic narrowly to keep your memo brief. To avoid unnecessary words, remember that the information you and your audience already share does not need to be included. For example, in a memo to teachers about a school dance, you probably won't need to explain the age of students you expect will attend.

Drafting Organize your memo in order of priority, placing the most important information first. Add one or two body paragraphs explaining the issue. Consider using bulleted or numbered lists for your readers' ease.

Revising Compare the language of your memo against your intended audience. For example, if you are enlisting the help of a group, you'll probably want to use *we* more than *I*. In addition, make sure that your language is appropriately formal.

Editing and Proofreading Check content by verifying the accuracy of facts. Then, review mechanics by confirming that sentences are correctly punctuated. Finally, look at the layout and be sure the spacing between paragraphs is consistent.

Publishing and Presenting Photocopy your memo, and deliver it in person, use the e-mail function on your computer to send the memo to interested parties, or deposit it in school or home mailboxes.

Résumé

What Is a Résumé?

One workplace writing form that you will probably use and update frequently as you accumulate skills and experience is the résumé. This document, a written summary of your qualifications, is a key part of most career or job searches. An effective résumé

- includes the writer's name, address, and telephone number.
- briefly presents the writer's educational background, work experience, and other qualifying life experiences.
- organizes information logically and in labeled sections.
- uses visual organization to direct a reader's attention.

> A résumé is almost always typed or printed from a computer or word processor.

Model Résumé

With limited formal work experience, high-school student Rebecca Irizarry expanded her résumé to include life skills and experiences.

> The labels Work Experience, Skills, Education, and Awards indicate this résumé is organized by topic.

> Here, the writer focuses information by providing the dates of work experience.

> Résumés should be kept to one page—the goal is to get an interview, not tell an entire life story.

REBECCA IRIZARRY
200 Magnolia Street
Garland, TX 75046
(555) 555-1234
E-mail: RI@address.com

WORK EXPERIENCE

Summer 2001:   Clerical Assistant   BBS Video Productions
Garland, TX
- Handled general office work: typed manuscripts; entered information into database; checked CD-ROMs for correct content; created and maintained manuscript-tracking charts; prepared packages for large mailings; and conducted Internet searches on behalf of supervisors

Summer 2000:   Soccer Trainer   Garland Recreation Department
Garland, TX
- Trained six-to eight-year-olds in soccer techniques and rules; refereed games

August 1999–Present: Staffer   Garland Art Publicity Department
Garland, TX
- Worked on publicity for local cultural organization: put up posters conducted ticket sales; addressed telephone inquiries

SKILLS
- Word processing (Microsoft Word '97), including making charts and graphs; typing; filing; database entry on FileMaker Pro
- Operate latest photocopiers and fax machines

EDUCATION
- Student at Columbia High School, Garland, TX
- College preparatory diploma to be conferred June 2003
- Well-rounded educational experience, including varsity soccer, lacrosse, and tennis; orchestra; science fair projects; yearbook staff; head of holiday spirit committee

AWARDS
- First-prize poster: Foreign Language Week

TOPIC BANK

To write a résumé that propels your application to the top of a pile, create one to fit your job-seeking goals. Include experiences of particular interest to your audience, and highlight the positive. Develop a résumé that conveys your talents and achievements, or practice the format with one of these topics:

1. **Résumé of a Historical Figure** People who have influenced history often have compelling job and life experiences. Consider writers, inventors, government leaders, or professional athletes. Choose a person who interests you, and conduct research in order to write his or her résumé.

2. **Résumé of a Fictional Character** Choose a character who has appeared in literature, film, or television. Use the information you can gather from a close analysis to write a résumé summarizing the character's work and life experiences.

Learn More

To keep your résumé consistent, review the rules of parallelism in Chapter 20.

Prewriting For your own résumé or that of someone else, list highlights from educational and work experiences. Consider life skills that demonstrate responsibility, such as those gained from baby-sitting, extracurricular activities, or community work. Gather key details about dates and locations of these experiences.

Drafting Choose an organization method, and apply it consistently as you draft. Use either sentences or phrases in your experience descriptions, but don't mix the two.

Revising Review the job or experience descriptions you have written. Sharpen the language with action verbs that show what you've done and quantify accomplishments with concrete numbers.

Editing and Proofreading Experiment with layout and typestyles to further highlight important information. Check for mistakes in consistency, and correct any variations in format.

Publishing and Presenting To use the résumé of your talents and skills, print the document on good-quality paper in a neutral color, such as white or ivory. When you hear or read about a job you'd like to pursue, send your résumé along with a cover letter, using standard business-letter format.

Forms and Applications

What Are Forms and Applications?

At times, it may seem as if all you do is fill out forms and applications—at school, to get a job, even for on-line shopping. These documents are preprinted with spaces provided for specific information. Three common workplace forms are fax cover sheets, applications, and phone message logs. To effectively complete a form:

- Write legibly so that readers can read the information easily.
- Give only pertinent information, and be brief, unless asked for more extensive responses.
- Double-check the headings to be sure you have provided the requested information in the appropriate areas.

Model Fax Cover Sheet

Fax cover sheets accompany faxed documents to provide important identifying information to the recipient. They explain who sent the fax and how to contact the sender. Most fax cover sheets allow space for a brief message. Look at this example:

> A company letterhead lets readers quickly recognize the sender of the fax.

> The sender completes this information accurately to make sure his fax reaches the intended person.

> Fax cover sheets typically include a full-page count so recipients can verify successful transmission of all the pages.

> An explanatory note is optional. The level of formality of this note should be dictated by the writer's knowledge of the receiver.

TECHNOLOGY and SYSTEMS CONSULTING
67 Camp Street • San Francisco, CA 94110
phone 415.555.7601 • fax 415.555.3355
e-mail: JeffN@address.network

Fax

FACSIMILE COVER SHEET/TRANSMITTAL

DATE: _9/14/20- -_

TO: _Gabriel Saxe – FutureTech Systems_

FAX NUMBER: _407/555-1001_

FAX SOURCE TRANSMISSION NUMBER: _415/555-3355_

FROM: _Jeff Nelson_

TOTAL NUMBER OF PAGES (including this cover sheet): _5_

REMARKS:

Gabe - As discussed, here is the information you need to finish the software manual. Please call with any questions.

Thanks, Jeff

Model Application

In many states, people over a specified age must obtain a learner's permit in order to pursue driving instruction. In the model below, notice how one student completed the application for a learner's permit.

> Instructions tell applicants what information will be necessary. Read them carefully, and follow them exactly.

APPLICATION FOR A LEARNER'S PERMIT

DEPARTMENT OF MOTOR VEHICLES

Instructions: Complete 1-17, then present items listed below to Cashier
1. Identifications (evidence of identity and date of birth)
2. Address Verification
3. Certification of Parental Consent (*if not properly accompanied by authorized consenter*)
4. $6.00 permit fee

1. APPLICANT'S NAME (Last, First, Middle)	2. SEX	3. DATE OF BIRTH
Mulligan, Jack Michael	☑ M ☐ F	*1/15/1982*

4. MAILING ADDRESS (No., Street, City or Town, State, Zip Code)	5. RESIDENCE ADDRESS (if different)
605 Alex St. Bridgeport, CT 06607	

6. ARE YOU A CITIZEN OF THE UNITED STATES?	7. ARE YOU A RESIDENT OF THIS STATE?
☑ YES ☐ NO	☑ YES ☐ NO

8. NAME OF DRIVING SCHOOL OR LOCATION OF DMV BRANCH OFFICE	9. SOCIAL SECURITY NUMBER (optional)
Bridgeport	*123-45-6789*

QUESTIONS	YES(✓)	NO (✓)		
10. Is your right to operate a motor vehicle suspended here or in any other state?		✓		
11. Do you now, or have you ever previously held a license?		✓		

MEDICAL CERTIFICATION	I hereby certify that I meet the vision and health standards contained in Motor Vehicle Regulations 14-45a-1 et seq., as amended, and that I do not have any health or vision problems or conditions that prevent me from driving safely.	SIGNATURE OF APPLICANT *Jack M. Mulligan*

DO NOT WRITE BELOW THIS LINE – OFFICE USE ONLY

PROOF OF IDENTIFICATION	TYPE OF ACCEPTABLE I.D. SHOWN	PREVIOUS LICENSE INFORMATION	DRIVER LICENSE NUMBER
PARENTAL CONSENT	I hereby request that a learner's permit and/or license be issued to the minor (age 16-17) filing this application.	RELATIONSHIP TO MINOR	SIGNED (Authorized Conse...

> Here, the applicant had to abbreviate *Street* and *Connecticut* in order to fit the required information into the provided space. If you think you won't be able to fit your facts, try to write smaller or create a second line within the allotted space.

> A signature confirms the applicant's agreement to the rules stated in the contract. Read everything on an application before signing your name—especially the fine print.

Grammar, Usage, and Mechanics

The Parts of Speech

City Hall, Alexandria, Virginia

Every English word, depending on its meaning and its use in a sentence, can be identified as one of the eight parts of speech.

THE PARTS OF SPEECH		
nouns	adjectives	prepositions
pronouns	adverbs	conjunctions
verbs		interjections

This chapter provides explanations of, and practice with, the eight parts of speech.

▲ Critical Viewing
What nouns can be used to identify details you see in this picture? What adjectives might describe them? [**Relate**]

Diagnostic Test

Directions: Write all answers on a separate sheet of paper.

Skill Check A. Match each noun with its description.

1. Alexandria Town Hall
2. legislature
3. townhouse
4. self-improvements
5. Europeans

a. concrete, compound, and singular
b. common, compound, and abstract
c. common, singular, and collective
d. proper and plural
e. proper, concrete, and compound

Skill Check B. Identify the pronoun or pronouns in each numbered section of the following paragraph. Then, identify each pronoun's antecedent. Antecedents may appear in previous sentences. The pronoun *I* refers to the person telling the story.

[6] Alexandria, Virginia, was an early colonial settlement. It was founded in 1749. [7] George Washington was one of its trustees and a part-time resident of the town, where he drew early maps of it in 1748 and 1749. [8] I visited Alexandria last year. [9] That was an interesting trip. [10] My brother and I drove to Cameron Street in Old Alexandria. [11] Washington himself had a home there. [12] Residents are proud of their connection to Washington. [13] This is evident in the many buildings named for him. [14] One place you should visit is the Carlyle House. [15] What is a better way to learn about history?

Skill Check C. On your paper, list the pronouns you found in each numbered section in Skill Check B. Then, identify the type of each pronoun. There are fifteen pronouns.

Skill Check D. List the verbs and verb phrases in each sentence. Then, label each *transitive, intransitive,* or *linking.*

16. Nomadic hunters probably first entered what would become Virginia about 10,000 to 12,000 years ago.
17. Native American communities later developed in the East.
18. Almost 20,000 Native Americans were living in Virginia when European explorers and settlers first arrived.
19. Powhatan was the chief of the Powhatan Confederacy of Algonquin tribes when English settlers first built Jamestown.
20. Warfare erupted after colonists had taken lands that belonged to the Powhatan Confederacy.

Skill Check E. Identify the part of speech of each underlined word.

[21] In 1606, King James I granted <u>two</u> <u>companies</u> the right to colonize Virginia. [22] The <u>following</u> year, the <u>Virginia Company of London</u> established a colony called Jamestown. [23] <u>This</u> was the first permanent English settlement <u>in</u> America. [24] The first years <u>of</u> the colony were <u>extremely</u> difficult, as settlers faced an array of problems that included famine, disease, and hostile <u>Native American</u> tribes. [25] Despite these <u>trying</u> times, new settlers moved in <u>almost</u> continually.

Nouns and Pronouns

Nouns and pronouns are an essential part of language. Together, these two parts of speech make it possible for people to label and refer to everything around them. First, you will examine nouns.

Nouns

You probably recall this common definition of a noun:

KEY CONCEPT A **noun** is the part of speech that names a person, place, or thing. ∎

The categories of *person* or *place* are self-evident:

PERSON: Bob, colonist, swimmer, Ms. Yang, Captain Smith

PLACE: kitchen, James River, canyon, Oklahoma

The category *thing*, on the other hand, contains several subcategories: visible things, ideas, actions, conditions, and qualities.

VISIBLE THINGS: duck, daffodil, fort
IDEAS: capitalism, recession, freedom
ACTIONS: competition, exercise, labor
CONDITIONS: joy, health, happiness
QUALITIES: compassion, intelligence, drive

Concrete and Abstract Nouns Nouns can be grouped not only as people, places, or things, but also as concrete or abstract. A **concrete noun** names something you can see, touch, taste, hear, or smell. An **abstract noun** names something you cannot perceive through any of your five senses.

CONCRETE NOUNS: person, cannon, road, city, music
ABSTRACT NOUNS: hope, improvement, independence, desperation, cooperation

Theme: American
Colonial History
....
In this section, you will learn about nouns and pronouns. All the examples and exercises are about historic Virginia.
....
Cross-Curricular Connection: Social Studies

▲ Critical Viewing
What concrete nouns name things you might see or experience on this cobblestone street in Old Alexandria, Virginia? **[Analyze]**

Singular and Plural Nouns A noun can also indicate *number*. A **singular noun** names one person, place, or thing. **Plural nouns** name more than one person, place, or thing. Most plural nouns are formed by adding *-s* or *-es* to their singular forms. The plurals of some nouns, however, are formed in other ways and must be memorized. Notice in the examples below that the plural forms of the last two are both formed in unusual ways.

SINGULAR NOUNS: meal, sickness, knife, alumnus

PLURAL NOUNS: meals, sicknesses, knives, alumni

💡 **Spelling Tip**

To form the plural for most singular nouns ending with *f* or *fe*, change the *f* to *v* and add *-s* or *-es* (*wife, wives; leaf, leaves*).

Collective Nouns A **collective noun** names a *group* of people or things.

COLLECTIVE NOUNS			
army	choir	troop	faculty
cast	class	crew	legislature

Compound Nouns A **compound noun** is a noun made up of two or more words functioning as a single unit. Compound nouns may be written as separate words, hyphenated words, or combined words.

COMPOUND NOUNS	
Separated	life preserver, coffee table, bird dog
Hyphenated	sergeant-at-arms, self-rule, daughter-in-law
Combined	battlefield, dreamland, porthole

Check a dictionary if you are not sure when to write a compound noun as two separate words, a hyphenated word, or as a single combined word.

Common and Proper Nouns Any noun may be categorized as either *common* or *proper*. A **common noun** names any one of a class of people, places, or things. A **proper noun** names a specific person, place, or thing. Proper nouns are capitalized while common nouns are not. (See Chapter 26 for specific rules of capitalization.)

COMMON NOUNS: leader, place, book, war

PROPER NOUNS: Jefferson, Virginia, *Leaves of Grass*, Revolutionary War

◀ **Critical Viewing**
What nouns name things about this picture of rural Virginia that would probably surprise a Jamestown settler? **[Connect]**

▶ **Exercise 1** Identifying Types of Nouns Write the numbered nouns on your paper. Next to each noun, write the correct description from each of these lettered pairs: (A) *concrete* or *abstract*, (B) *singular* or *plural*, (C) *collective* or *not collective*, (D) *compound* or *not compound*, (E) *common* or *proper*.

EXAMPLE: freedom
ANSWER: (A) abstract, (B) singular, (C) not collective, (D) not compound, (E) common

1. colony
2. Jamestown
3. leadership
4. farmer
5. Captain John Smith
6. self-government
7. Pocahontas
8. peace
9. farmland
10. history

▶ **Exercise 2** Recognizing and Classifying Nouns Identify the nouns in the following excerpt from *The General History of Virginia*. Label each as *concrete* or *abstract*, *singular* or *plural*, *common* or *proper*. Then, indicate whether any of the nouns are collective or compound.

He demanding for their captain, they showed him Opechancanough, King of Pamunkee, to whom he gave a round ivory double compass dial. Much they marveled at the playing of the fly and needle, which they could see so plainly and yet not touch it because of the glass that covered them. But when he demonstrated by that globe-like jewel the roundness of the earth and skies, the sphere of the sun, moon, and stars, and how the sun did chase the night round about the world continually, . . . they all stood as amazed with admiration.

More Practice

Grammar Exercise Workbook
• pp. 1–2
On-line Exercise Bank
• Section 17.1
  Go on-line:
  PHSchool.com
  Enter Web Code:
  efk-1102

Get instant feedback! Exercises 1 and 2 are available on-line or on CD-ROM.

Pronouns

To avoid the awkward repetition of a noun, speakers and writers use another part of speech—*pronouns*.

▶**KEY CONCEPT** A **pronoun** is a word that takes the place of a noun, another pronoun, or a group of words functioning as a noun. ■

▶**KEY CONCEPT** An **antecedent** is the noun, pronoun, or group of words functioning as a noun to which a pronoun refers. ■

EXAMPLES: A crowd quickly gathered. Looking at the sea, *they*

saw a schooner inching *its* way into Jamestown harbor.

Losing the crops was frightening; *it* was an

experience the colonist said *she* would never forget.

Most pronouns have specific antecedents, but some do not. The rest of this section describes the different kinds of pronouns and tells whether or not they have antecedents.

Personal Pronouns   Personal pronouns are the pronouns commonly used to refer to particular people, places, and things.

▶**KEY CONCEPT** A personal pronoun is a pronoun that refers to the person speaking (first person), the person spoken to (second person), or the person, place, or thing spoken about (third person). ■

PERSONAL PRONOUNS		
	Singular	Plural
First Person	I, me, my, mine	we, us, our, ours
Second Person	you, your, yours	you, your, yours
Third Person	he, him, his, she, her, hers, it, its	they, them, their, theirs

Reflexive and Intensive Pronouns These two types of pronouns look the same, but they function differently in sentences.

▶ **KEY CONCEPTS** A **reflexive pronoun** ends in *-self* or *-selves* and indicates that someone or something in the sentence acts for or on itself. An **intensive pronoun** ends in *-self* or *-selves* and simply adds emphasis to a noun or pronoun in the same sentence. ■

Grammar and Style Tip

Don't be tempted to use a reflexive pronoun in place of a personal pronoun. For example, it is not correct to say, "Eric and myself like early American history." You should say, "Eric and I like early American history."

REFLEXIVE AND INTENSIVE PRONOUNS	Singular	Plural
First Person	myself	ourselves
Second Person	yourself	yourselves
Third Person	himself, herself, itself	themselves

REFLEXIVE: The settlers prepared *themselves* for the approaching winter.

INTENSIVE: John Smith *himself* wrote an account of the meeting.

GRAMMAR IN LITERATURE

from **A Wagner Matinée**
Willa Cather

In this excerpt, notice that the reflexive pronoun herself *refers to the subject* she *used earlier in the sentence.*

Beneath the soiled linen duster, which on her arrival was the most conspicuous feature of her costume, *she* wore a black stuff dress whose ornamentation showed that *she* had surrendered *herself* unquestioningly into the hands of a country dressmaker. My poor aunt's figure, however, would have presented astonishing difficulties to any dressmaker.

Section 17.2 **Section Review**

GRAMMAR EXERCISES 16–22

▶ **Exercise 16** Identifying Action and Linking Verbs On your paper, write *action verb* or *linking verb* to identify the underlined verb in each sentence.

1. Skiing <u>is</u> the practice of attaching a runner or ski to each foot.
2. Skis <u>enable</u> the skier to glide over snow.
3. In downhill skiing, the skier <u>battles</u> bumpy and steep slopes.
4. Then, the skier <u>takes</u> a lift back up the mountain for another run.
5. Skiers <u>become</u> exhausted by the end of the day.

▶ **Exercise 17** Distinguishing Between Transitive and Intransitive Verbs On your paper, write *transitive* or *intransitive* to identify the underlined verb in each sentence.

1. Ice and snow competitions <u>occur</u> in many parts of the world.
2. A group in Fairbanks, Alaska, <u>sponsors</u> an ice-sculpting competition.
3. The carnival <u>originated</u> in 1934.
4. Originally, the carnival <u>included</u> only one ice sculpture.
5. This ice castle or throne <u>belonged</u> to the king and queen of the carnival.
6. The simple design of the first ice throne <u>drew</u> attention.
7. Each year following, competitors <u>created</u> a more and more elaborate throne.
8. One year, the throne <u>was illuminated</u> by lights.
9. Another year, a transplanted forest <u>surrounded</u> the throne.
10. These early designers <u>set</u> the stage for future ice sculptors and competitions.

▶ **Exercise 18** Identifying Verb Phrases Write the verb phrase in each sentence on your paper. Circle the helping verb. Underline the main verb.

1. Many activities will be happening at the winter carnival.
2. You can always start by viewing the ice and snow sculptures.
3. There have been both amateur and professional sculpting competitions.
4. The snowmobile race has become a popular event.
5. Thrill seekers can try the sledding or tobogganing areas.

▶ **Exercise 19** Revising a Passage by Changing Verbs Revise the following passage by replacing the underlined words with verbs that express more precise actions. You may make other minor changes.

Leanne <u>put on</u> her boots. She knew that when she <u>went</u> outside, the wind would <u>go through</u> her thin coat. Still, someone had to <u>get</u> the snow off the driveway. She <u>walked</u> to the door and went out.

▶ **Exercise 20** Find It in Your Reading On your paper, write two intransitive verbs from "Journal of the First Voyage to America" on page 245. Explain why they are intransitive.

▶ **Exercise 21** Find It in Your Writing Review a piece of writing from your portfolio. Find two transitive verbs, two intransitive verbs, and a verb phrase.

▶ **Exercise 22** Writing Application Write a brief account of a winter event. Then, identify your linking verbs and your action verbs.

Adjectives and Adverbs

Adjectives and **adverbs** are *modifiers*. In other words, they are the parts of speech that slightly change the meaning of other words by adding description or by making them more specific. Adjectives modify nouns and pronouns; adverbs modify verbs, adjectives, and other adverbs.

Adjectives

Without adjectives, much of the color in written and spoken language would be missing. These words allow people to describe in more detail the nouns and pronouns they use.

▶ **KEY CONCEPT** An **adjective** is a word used to describe a noun or pronoun or to give a noun or pronoun a more specific meaning. ■

Adjectives modify nouns and pronouns by providing information that answers any of the following questions about the noun or pronoun: *What kind? Which one? How many? How much?*

EXAMPLES: *big* nests (*What kind* of nests?)
              that bird (*Which* bird?)
              seventeen flocks (*How many* flocks?)
              more bird seed (*How much* bird seed?)

These examples show the usual location of an adjective—preceding a noun. Sometimes, however, the adjective is located after the noun it modifies.

EXAMPLE: The nest looked *old.*

An adjective that modifies a pronoun usually follows the pronoun, but, on occasion, it can precede the pronoun.

AFTER: He was tired after the long flight.

BEFORE: *Tired* after the flight, he rested.

More than one adjective may modify a noun or pronoun.

EXAMPLE: The quick, darting falcon captured its prey.

Nouns Used as Adjectives Occasionally, words that are usually nouns will function as adjectives modifying another noun and answering *what kind* or *which one.*

NOUNS:

    vegetable

    bird

USED AS ADJECTIVES:

    vegetable soup

    bird food

Proper Adjectives Like nouns, some adjectives can be proper. Proper adjectives are proper nouns used as adjectives or adjectives formed from proper nouns. They modify other nouns and begin with a capital letter.

PROPER NOUNS:

    Audubon

    Florida

    North America

    Spain

PROPER ADJECTIVES:

    Audubon paintings

    Florida sunshine

    North American birds

    Spanish language

Compound Adjectives Adjectives can also be compound, or made up of more than one word. Some compound adjectives are hyphenated; some are written as combined words. Compound proper adjectives are usually written as two separate words. Check a dictionary when in doubt.

HYPHENATED: long-term mates, oval-shaped nest

COMBINED: warmblooded animals, lifelong partners

SEPARATED: South American birds

Grammar and Style Tip

Numbers can function as adjectives. In formal writing, most numbers should be spelled out, as in *fifty* eagles or *three* French hens.

▼ Critical Viewing
What compound adjectives apply to this bird? **[Apply]**

Pronouns Used as Adjectives Some pronouns can be used as adjectives, as shown in the chart that follows.

The seven personal pronouns that are listed at the beginning are known either as *possessive adjectives* or as *possessive pronouns*. These words do double duty. They are pronouns because they have antecedents; they are adjectives because they modify nouns by answering *which one*.

The other pronouns in the chart become adjectives instead of pronouns when they stand before a noun and answer *which one*.

Research Tip

Look in a library or bookstore for field guides about birds. These will offer basic information and descriptions of birds, including vivid descriptive adjectives.

PRONOUNS USED AS ADJECTIVES

Possessive Pronouns or Adjectives	
my, your, his, her, its, our, their	ANTECEDENT The bird built *its* nest.
Demonstrative Adjectives	
this, that, these, those	*That* hummingbird flew to the flowers. *Those* roses wilted in the sun.
Interrogative Adjectives	
which, what, whose	*Which* parakeet will you take? *Whose* money is on the table?
Indefinite Adjectives	
Used with singular nouns: another, each, either, little, much, neither, one	Give me *another* chance.
Used with plural nouns: both, few, many, several	*Many* crows raided the garden.
Used with singular or plural nouns: all, any, more, most, other, some	Give me *some* birdseed, please. I received *some* gifts.

Verb Forms Used as Adjectives Verb forms ending in *-ing* or *-ed* can be used as adjectives.

VERBS USED AS ADJECTIVES
The *rippling* water felt refreshing to the herons.
The *washed* clothes were neatly folded.

Remember that nouns, pronouns, and verbs are adjectives only when they modify nouns or pronouns. Notice how their function can change from one sentence to another.

	Regular Function	As an Adjective
Noun	The *blood* coursed through his veins.	His *blood* count was fine.
Pronoun	*That* is my lovebird.	*That* lovebird is beautiful.
Verb	The President *vetoed* the bill.	The *vetoed* bill was reintroduced.

> **Exercise 23** Identifying Adjectives On your paper, write the adjectives you find in each numbered section and tell which words they modify.

[1] Seventeen known species of penguins inhabit the world. [2] They live in coastal areas of the Southern Hemisphere, and they are generally not found north of the equator. [3] The two largest living penguins are the emperor and king penguins, [4] which are found in Antarctic regions. [5] The emperor is the tallest and heaviest of all penguins. [6] While most penguins lay about two eggs, emperor females lay only one egg. [7] Emperor penguins primarily eat squid and fish, as well as occasional small crustaceans.

[8] The king penguin is the second-largest penguin in the world. [9] These birds have more orange coloring, and they have longer bills. [10] Their dietary choices include crustaceans, squid, small fish, and plankton.

[11] Penguins range in height from fifteen inches to four feet. [12] Their thick feathers protect them from the cold. [13] Although they have a wobbling walk, [14] these birds are excellent swimmers. [15] Penguins are a popular attraction at the New England Aquarium.

More Practice

Grammar Exercise Workbook
• pp. 11–12
On-line Exercise Bank
• Section 17.3
  Go on-line:
  PHSchool.com
  Enter Web Code:
  efk-1102

▼ Critical Viewing Describe this penguin with adjectives telling *What kind? Which one? How many?* or *How much?* **[Analyze]**

Adverbs

Like adjectives, adverbs describe or make other words more specific.

▶ **KEY CONCEPT** An **adverb** is a word that modifies a verb, an adjective, or another adverb. ■

An adverb that modifies a verb answers any of four questions: *Where? When? In what way? To what extent?* An adverb that modifies an adjective or another adverb answers the question *To what extent?*

⚙ **Grammar** ⚙ **and Style Tip**

Use adverbs in your writing to make the meanings of your verbs more vivid and precise.

ADVERBS MODIFYING VERBS
Where?
The finch flew *up*.   Her eggs lay *here*.
When?
The flock's migration began *today*.
Now they will fly south for the winter.
In what way?
The falcon *quickly* passed over our heads.
I *was eagerly* awaiting the bird-sighting tour.
To what extent?
We have *just* enough time.
She did *not* warn me it was spicy chicken!
ADVERBS MODIFYING ADJECTIVES
To what extent?
The chicks are *extremely* hungry.
The *overly* excited bird-watcher collapsed.
ADVERBS MODIFYING ADVERBS
To what extent?
She cleans her young chicks *rather* carefully.
The chicken coop was *not* completely clean yet.

Nouns Functioning as Adverbs A few words that usually act as nouns can function as adverbs that answer *where* and *when*. Some of these words are *home, yesterday, today, tomorrow, mornings, afternoons, evenings, week,* and *year*.

EXAMPLES: We raced *home* to see the news of the eagle sighting. (Raced *where?*)

I saw them *yesterday*. (Saw *when?*)

Adverb or Adjective? You can distinguish between adjectives and adverbs by remembering that adverbs modify verbs, adjectives, and adverbs; adjectives modify nouns and pronouns.

ADVERB: Spring arrived *early*. (*Early* modifies a verb.)

ADJECTIVE: The early bird gets the worm. (*Early* modifies a noun.)

ADJECTIVES: *slow* flight, *hasty* decision

ADVERBS: flew *slowly*, decided *hastily*

ADJECTIVES
THAT END
IN *-ly*:   a *lonely* thrush, a *ghostly* wail

GRAMMAR IN
LITERATURE

from **The Raven**
Edgar Allan Poe

In this poem, the speaker encounters a raven who seems to be more than an ordinary bird. The adjectives (other than articles) are highlighted in red italics; the adverbs, in blue italics.

Once upon a midnight *dreary*, while I pondered,
   weak and *weary*,
Over *many* a *quaint* and *curious* volume of *forgotten*
   lore—
While I nodded, *nearly napping*, *suddenly* there came
   a tapping,
As of someone *gently* rapping, rapping at *my*
   chamber door.

▲ **Critical Viewing**
What adverbs could you use to describe the way this raven is perched? **[Apply]**

Exercise 24 Identifying Adverbs Write the sentences, underlining all the adverbs. Then, draw an arrow from each adverb to the word it modifies.

1. Many paleontologists firmly believe that birds are related to dinosaurs.
2. In centuries past, anatomists frequently noted that birds looked very similar to reptiles.
3. Discovered in 1861, *archaeopteryx* remains the oldest known fossil definitely identified as a bird.
4. Although *archaeopteryx* had many reptilelike features, it also had feathers and claws.
5. With its well-developed wings, *archaeopteryx* probably glided easily.

Exercise 25 Revising Sentences by Adding Adverbs Read all the sentences before you begin. Then, revise each sentence by adding one or more adverbs to it. You may make other minor changes as needed.

1. Peregrine falcons fly.
2. They can swoop for prey at a speed of 200 miles per hour.
3. They build nests in cliffs near seacoasts, rivers, and lakes.
4. Peregrine falcons live in many places in the world.
5. They can even be found living in cities.
6. They build nests on the ledges of bridges and skyscrapers.
7. To a falcon, a skyscraper looks like a cliff.
8. A bridge is better, because it is by the water.
9. Time will tell if these new nesting habits are successful.
10. Scientists are monitoring to see if these "city nests" work.

More Practice

Grammar Exercise Workbook
• pp. 13–14
On-line Exercise Bank
• Section 17.3

Go on-line:
PHSchool.com
Enter Web Code:
efk-1102

Interactive Textbook

Get instant feedback! Exercises 24 and 25 are available on-line or on CD-ROM.

▼ Critical Viewing The peregrine falcon, pictured here, is known for its high-speed dives after prey. Use adverbs to tell in what way it might fly and dive. **[Infer]**

Section 17.3 *Section Review*

GRAMMAR EXERCISES 26–31

Exercise 26 Recognizing Adjectives On your paper, write the adjectives in these sentences. Then, write the noun that each adjective modifies.

1. Bald eagles, weighing up to fourteen pounds, are very large birds of prey.
2. Female bald eagles are usually larger than male bald eagles.
3. These North American birds have a dark-brown body, white head, white tail, and sharp yellow beak.
4. An eagle's nest is usually hidden.
5. The cliff towers on which eagles build their homes are safe from predators.
6. Eagles are lifelong partners.
7. If something happens to one eagle, the other eagle may pine for months.
8. The male eagle and female eagle share the eaglet-raising responsibilities.
9. While the male hunts, the female will guard the stick-and-twig nest.
10. When the female hunts, the male takes on guard duty.

Exercise 27 Recognizing Adverbs and Their Uses On your paper, write the adverbs in these sentences. Next to them, write the word each one modifies.

1. Many types of hawks live freely throughout North America.
2. The Cooper's hawk is also known, somewhat derogatorily, as the "chicken hawk."
3. This very powerful bird kills large prey, such as chickens.
4. In the nineteenth century, hawks were frequently shot.
5. All hawks have become completely protected by federal law.
6. Today, we better understand the role birds of prey play in the natural world.
7. The Harris's hawk behaves very socially, which greatly puzzles scientists.

8. It is very common to find several birds happily sharing a nest.
9. It is not surprising to find two Harris's hawks flying home with one catch; the hawks even hunt in pairs.
10. On an early March morning, thousands of red-tailed hawks rise up and continue the annual migration.

Exercise 28 Revising a Passage by Adding Adjectives and Adverbs Look at the picture on the previous page. Then, revise the following passage to describe a peregrine falcon by adding adjectives and adverbs. You may make other minor changes to sentences as needed.

The peregrine falcon is a bird. Feathers cover its body. Eyes fix a stare on anyone who dares to come near. Feathers near the eyes make the eyes seem larger than they are.

Exercise 29 Find It in Your Reading Reread the passage from "The Raven" on p. 253. On your paper, identify the words that are modified by *dreary, weak, weary,* and *suddenly.*

Exercise 30 Find It in Your Writing Review a piece of descriptive writing from your portfolio. Identify three adjectives and three adverbs that you used. Challenge yourself to add at least two more of each modifier.

Exercise 31 Writing Application Write a description of a real or imaginary bird. Use a variety of adjectives and adverbs in your description.

Prepositions, Conjunctions, and Interjections

Prepositions

Prepositions perform the important job of linking words within a sentence. They indicate relationships between separate things. The relationships may involve such things as location, direction, cause, or possession.

▶ **KEY CONCEPT** A **preposition** is a word that relates the noun or pronoun that appears with it to another word in the sentence. ■

Familiarize yourself with the most common prepositions, which are shown in the chart that follows. Notice that some prepositions are composed of more than one word. These are sometimes called *compound prepositions*.

PREPOSITIONS			
aboard	before	in addition to	out
about	behind	in back of	out of
above	below	in front of	over
according to	beneath	in place of	owing to
across	beside	in regard to	past
after	besides	inside	prior to
against	between	in spite of	regarding
ahead of	beyond	instead of	round
along	but	into	through
alongside	by	in view of	throughout
amid	by means of	like	till
among	concerning	near	to
apart from	considering	next to	toward
around	despite	of	under
aside from	down	off	until
as of	during	on	unto
at	except	on account of	up
atop	for	onto	upon
barring	from	on top of	with
because of	in	opposite	within

Theme: African American History

In this section, you will learn about prepositions, conjunctions, and interjections. All the examples and exercises are about significant people and events in African American history.

Cross-Curricular Connection: Social Studies

Prepositional Phrases Prepositions are always part of a group of words called a *prepositional phrase.* A prepositional phrase contains a preposition and a noun or pronoun known as the *object of the preposition.*

In the following examples, the prepositional phrase is in italics. The preposition is underlined, the object of the preposition is circled, and an arrow shows to which word or words the object of the preposition relates.

EXAMPLES: Who is the famous actress *in the movie*?

Shawn checked *under the couch and chair.*

> **Exercise 32** Identifying Prepositions and Prepositional Phrases Copy each sentence onto your paper. Then, underline each preposition, circle each object, and draw an arrow to show the word to which the object relates.

EXAMPLE: Sit beside me, and tell me about Crispus Attucks.

ANSWER: Sit beside me, and tell me about Crispus Attucks.

1. Crispus Attucks was a former slave of African ancestry who probably spent much of his later life aboard whaling ships.
2. To this day, little is known of him aside from a fateful event in 1770.
3. On March 5, in Boston, Massachusetts, British soldiers fired upon a crowd of American colonists.
4. The crowd had gathered outside, opposite the soldiers, and had begun to challenge them.
5. Attucks was killed in the conflict on that day.

Preposition or Adverb? Because many words may be used either as prepositions or as adverbs, you may have difficulty telling them apart. *Around, down, in, off, on, out, over,* and *up* are some of the words that can function either as prepositions or as adverbs. Remember that a preposition must appear with an object of the preposition.

PREPOSITION: Joe Louis sidled *around the ring.*
ADVERB: The boxer slowly looked *around.*

Learn More

For more on prepositions and prepositional phrases, see Chapter 19.

More Practice

Grammar Exercise Workbook
• pp. 15–16
On-line Exercise Bank
• Section 17.4
    Go on-line:
    PHSchool.com
    Enter Web Code:
    efk-1102

Interactive Textbook

Get instant feedback! Exercise 32 is available on-line or on CD-ROM.

▶ **Exercise 33** Distinguishing Between Prepositions and Adverbs Identify each underlined word as either a *preposition* or an *adverb*. If the word is a preposition, write its object.

EXAMPLE: Frederick Douglass is renowned <u>above</u> almost all other abolitionists.

ANSWER: preposition (abolitionists)

1. He went <u>outside</u> to retrieve from the car all of his articles on Frederick Douglass.
2. Douglass was born the son of a slave <u>in</u> Maryland in 1817.
3. He yearned <u>over</u> and over to become a free man.
4. <u>Around</u> this time, in secret, he learned to read.
5. He soon crossed <u>over</u> the northern borders into freedom.

Conjunctions

Unlike prepositions, which simply relate words, conjunctions join words into a single unit.

▶ **KEY CONCEPT** A **conjunction** is a word used to connect other words or groups of words. ■

There are three kinds of conjunctions: *coordinating, correlative,* and *subordinating* conjunctions. A special kind of adverb, called a *conjunctive adverb,* is often considered a conjunction.

Coordinating Conjunctions These conjunctions connect words or groups of words.

In the following examples, the coordinating conjunctions are in italics. The connected words are underlined.

EXAMPLES: <u>She</u> *and* <u>Grandmother</u> once went to see Bessie Smith.
Turning <u>to the left</u> *or* <u>to the right</u>, all Bessie could see was a throng of admiring fans.
<u>They climbed aboard the midnight train</u>, *for* <u>the tour was just beginning</u>.

COORDINATING CONJUNCTIONS			
and	for	or	yet
but	nor	so	

▲ Critical Viewing Use prepositional phrases to describe the appearance of Frederick Douglass in this portrait. **[Describe]**

Correlative Conjunctions These conjunctions also join equal elements in sentences, but they always work in pairs.

CORRELATIVE CONJUCTIONS		
both . . . and	either . . . or	neither . . . nor
not only . . . but also	whether . . . or	

Here are some of the ways these conjunctions may be used. The conjunctions are shown in italics. The words they connect are underlined.

EXAMPLES: *Neither* Lola *nor* he knows about Paul Robeson.

He was *not only* intelligent *but also* charismatic.

He excelled *both* during college *and* in life.

His choice after college was *either* athletics *or* law.

Subordinating Conjunctions Subordinating conjunctions join two complete ideas by making one of the ideas subordinate—that is, dependent—on the other. (See Chapter 19 for more information about subordinate clauses.)

SUBORDINATING CONJUNCTIONS			
after	because	lest	till
although	before	now that	unless
as	even if	provided that	until
as if	even though	since	when
as long as	how	so that	whenever
as much as	if	than	where
as soon as	inasmuch as	that	wherever
as though	in order that	though	while

EXAMPLES:

main idea   subordinate idea
I watch Robeson's films *whenever I can.*

subordinate idea
Now that the new video store is open,

main idea
we probably will watch videos more often.

Conjunctive Adverbs Conjunctive adverbs are used as conjunctions to connect complete ideas. They are often used as transitions, creating bridges between different ideas by showing comparisons, contrasts, or results.

CONJUNCTIVE ADVERBS		
accordingly	finally	nevertheless
again	furthermore	otherwise
also	however	then
besides	indeed	therefore
consequently	instead	thus
	moreover	

Notice the punctuation that is used before and after the conjunctive adverbs in the following examples. (See Chapter 27 for more about punctuation with conjunctive adverbs.)

EXAMPLES: The film was great; *nevertheless,* I prefer *Show Boat.*
Show Boat starts at 8:00 P.M.; we should, *therefore,* leave soon.

▶ **Exercise 34** **Identifying Conjunctions in Sentences** Write the conjunctions used in the following sentences. Then, identify each as *coordinating, correlative,* or *subordinating.*

EXAMPLE: I looked for *The Proud Valley,* but I couldn't find it.
ANSWER: but (coordinating)

1. Paul Robeson became neither a lawyer nor an athlete after his academic career.
2. He did not become a lawyer because there were few opportunities for African Americans at law firms in 1923.
3. He began his celebrated acting career while he was earning his law degree.
4. *The Emperor Jones* was both a critical and a commercial success.
5. Theater audiences hailed Robeson in the title role, yet they knew little of his terrific singing talent.

▼ **Critical Viewing**
Use a subordinating conjunction and a subordinate clause in a sentence that describes the emotions shown on Paul Robeson's face. **[Analyze]**

Exercise 35 Using Conjunctive Adverbs Rewrite each pair of sentences, inserting an appropriate conjunctive adverb to connect the related ideas. Punctuate the new sentence correctly.

EXAMPLE: Jackie Robinson faced many difficult challenges in his life. He soldiered on with dignity and grace.

ANSWER: Jackie Robinson faced many difficult challenges in his life; nevertheless, he soldiered on with dignity and grace.

1. Jackie Robinson was a spectacular all-around athlete during college. He is most famous for his baseball career.
2. Robinson next became an officer in the army. He still harbored dreams of playing professional sports.
3. When Robinson started playing professional baseball, there were many talented African American players. African Americans did not play in the major leagues.
4. Branch Rickey wanted to integrate major league baseball. He was interested in signing Jackie Robinson.
5. Rickey wanted to sign Robinson because Robinson was a talented and fast player. He had courage and dignity.
6. Robinson joined the Brooklyn Dodgers in 1947. He played all ten years of his major league career with the Dodgers.
7. At first, both fans and opposing players taunted and threatened him. Robinson endured this treatment in silence and dignity.
8. In 1947, Robinson was named Rookie of the Year. In 1949, he was named the National League's Most Valuable Player.
9. Robinson was an outstanding fielder and hitter. He was a superior runner and base stealer.
10. Robinson's skills and achievements were many. He was elected to the Baseball Hall of Fame in 1962.

Exercise 36 Writing Sentences With Conjunctions and Conjunctive Adverbs Follow the directions to write sentences. You may need to draw on details and information you've learned in this section.
1. Write two sentences about Branch Rickey's feelings about Jackie Robinson's baseball skills. Use *consequently* in the second sentence.
2. Use *yet* in a sentence about Robinson's behavior when reacting to the opposition he faced.
3. Use *and* in a sentence describing Robinson's personality.
4. Write two or three sentences about Branch Rickey's plan to integrate major league baseball. Use *nevertheless* in one of the sentences.
5. Write three sentences about Robinson's qualifications for the Hall of Fame. Use *furthermore* in one of the sentences.

More Practice

Grammar Exercise Workbook
• pp. 17–18
On-line Exercise Bank
• Section 17.4
  Go on-line:
  PHSchool.com
  Enter Web Code:
  efk-1102

Complete the exercises on-line! Exercises 34, 35, and 36 are available on-line or on CD-ROM.

Internet Tip

Conjunctions are essential in limiting advanced searches. Use AND (as in *Thurgood Marshall* AND *Brown* v. *Board of Education*) to match all of the words in your search string, and use OR to match any of the words.

Interjections

Unlike other parts of speech, interjections never have a grammatical connection to other words in a sentence.

▶ **KEY CONCEPT** An **interjection** is a word that expresses feeling or emotion and functions independently of a sentence. ■

Interjections can express a variety of feelings, such as joy, fear, anger, surprise, exhaustion, dismay, or sorrow.

SOME COMMON INTERJECTIONS				
ah	dear	hey	ouch	well
aha	goodness	hurrah	psst	whew
alas	gracious	oh	tsk	wow

Interjections are set off from the rest of the sentence by either an exclamation mark or a comma.

EXAMPLES: *Whew!* That was a close one.
Hey, wait a minute!

▶ **Exercise 37** Using Interjections Write five sentences using an appropriate interjection to express the emotion or feeling indicated. Then, underline each interjection.
1. joy
2. pain
3. hesitation
4. surprise
5. impatience

▶ **More Practice**

Grammar Exercise Workbook
• pp. 19–20
On-line Exercise Bank
• Section 17.4
  Go on-line:
  PHSchool.com
  Enter Web Code:
  efk-1102

interactive Textbook

Complete the exercises on-line! Exercise 37 is available on-line or on CD-ROM.

◀ Critical Viewing What interjections might each player use to express his feelings? **[Deduce]**

Section Review

GRAMMAR EXERCISES 38–43

Exercise 38 Classifying
Conjunctions On your paper, write the conjunction in each sentence. Then, identify each as *coordinating, correlative,* or *subordinating.*

1. Charlie Parker and Dizzy Gillespie are two of the founders of bebop.
2. Parker played alto saxophone, and Gillespie played trumpet.
3. Both Parker and Gillespie composed music and led bands.
4. After they played with many bands in the 1930's and 1940's, Gillespie began to jam in Harlem with Parker and others.
5. The recordings they made together are timeless, but many young people have never heard their music.

Exercise 39 Identifying
Prepositions, Conjunctions, and Interjections In the following sentences, identify and label the words that are *prepositions, conjunctions,* or *interjections.*

1. Duke Ellington played piano, wrote songs, and led one of the greatest big bands ever.
2. In fact, Ellington, with others, founded big-band music, which greatly influenced swing music.
3. Don Redman and Fletcher Henderson were also great, even though they were not as famous.
4. Ellington wrote not only big-band music but also opera!
5. Wow! Did you hear that set?

Exercise 40 Supplying
Prepositions Add an appropriate preposition to complete each sentence.

1. Richard Wright was born ___?___

1908 near a small Mississippi town.
2. He made his way to the North ___?___ working as an unskilled laborer.
3. During the Great Depression, he was the editor ___?___ a newspaper ___?___ New York City.
4. He wrote books that were ahead ___?___ their time.
5. ___?___ many critics, *Native Son* is the best of all his works.

Exercise 41 Find It in Your
Reading On your paper, copy the following excerpt from *My Bondage and My Freedom* by Frederick Douglass. Underline prepositional phrases once. Underline prepositions twice. Then, circle conjunctions.

Seized with a determination to learn to read, at any cost, I hit upon many expedients to accomplish the desired end. . . . I used to carry, almost constantly, a copy of Webster's spelling book in my pocket; and, when sent on errands, or when play time was allowed me, I would step, with my young friends, aside, and take a lesson in spelling.

Exercise 42 Find It in Your
Writing Review a piece of writing from your portfolio. Identify conjunctions and prepositions you have used. Then, challenge yourself to combine sentences by using conjunctions.

Exercise 43 Writing Application
Write an anecdote about a person you admire. Use prepositional phrases to elaborate your points. Use conjunctions to combine thoughts where appropriate.

Words as Different Parts of Speech

Many words change from one part of speech to another depending on their function in a sentence.

Identifying Parts of Speech

To *function* means to "serve in a particular capacity." The function of a word may change from one sentence to another.

> **KEY CONCEPT** The way a word is used in a sentence determines its part of speech. ■

Look, for example, at the roles played by the word *well* in the following sentences.

AS A NOUN:	Our *well* ran dry.
AS A VERB:	After a scolding, tears *well* in the child's eyes.
AS AN ADJECTIVE:	She does not feel *well* today.

Following is a quick review of the definition of each part of speech. The column of questions in each chart shows you what to ask to determine how a word is being used.

Nouns, Pronouns, and Verbs A **noun** names a person, place, or thing. A **pronoun** stands for a noun. A **verb** shows action, condition, or existence.

Parts of Speech	Questions to Ask Yourself	Examples
Noun	Does the word name a person, place, or thing?	Our *visit* to the *Grand Canyon* delighted *Rosa*.
Pronoun	Does the word stand for a noun?	*They* gave *some* to *him*.
Verb	Does the word tell what someone or something did?	We *played* baseball.
	Does the word link one word with another word that identifies or describes it?	The woman *was* a lawyer. Mother *appeared* happy.
	Does the word merely show that something exists?	The family *is* here.

Theme: Gardening

In this section, you will learn about words as different parts of speech. The exercises and examples are about gardening.

Cross-Curricular Connection: Science

The Other Parts of Speech An **adjective** modifies a noun or pronoun. An **adverb** modifies a verb, an adjective, or another adverb. A **preposition** relates a noun or pronoun that appears with it to another word. A **conjunction** connects words or groups of words. An **interjection** expresses emotion.

Parts of Speech	Questions to Ask Yourself	Examples
Adjective	Does the word tell *what kind, which one, how many,* or *how much?*	*Those three* apples are an *unusual* color.
Adverb	Does the word tell *where, when, in what way,* or *to what extent?*	Go *home.* Leave *now.* Drive *very slowly.* I am *thoroughly* tired.
Preposition	Is the word part of a phrase that includes a noun or pronoun?	*Near* our house, the carnival was *in* full swing.
Conjunction	Does the word connect other words in the sentence or connect clauses?	*Both* you *and* I will go *because* they need more people; *besides,* it will be fun.
Interjection	Does the word express feeling or emotion and function independently of the sentence?	*Hey,* give me that! *Ouch,* that hurt!

More Practice

Grammar Exercise Workbook
• pp. 21–22
On-line Exercise Bank
• Section 17.5
Go on-line:
PHSchool.com
Enter Web Code:
efk-1102

Interactive Textbook

Get instant feedback! Exercise 44 is available on-line or on CD-ROM.

▼ Critical Viewing
Tulips are common spring flowers. Use the words *spring* and *flowers* as verbs in sentences about tulips. [Apply]

Exercise 44 Identifying All Parts of Speech Identify the part of speech of the underlined word in each pair of sentences.

EXAMPLE: (a) The garden hose was left out.
            (b) The hose was left out in the garden.
ANSWER: (a) adjective (b) noun

1. (a) Please <u>run</u> the water into the bucket.
   (b) The dog <u>run</u> is next to the garden.
2. (a) I don't like <u>either</u> flower.
   (b) <u>Either</u> is equally fragrant.
3. (a) The stalks tipped <u>over</u>.
   (b) We put a protective cover <u>over</u> the delicate bloom.
4. (a) We worked <u>hard</u> during harvest.
   (b) That was <u>hard</u> work.
5. (a) The harvest took place <u>late</u> in the summer.
   (b) We didn't start until <u>late</u> summer.

Hands-on Grammar

Parts-of-Speech Notch Book

Explore how a single word can function as many parts of speech by creating a notch book. Use four colors of construction paper to make the pages.

Cut the pages as indicated on the drawing, so that each section can turn independently. Label the "notch" of each section as shown.

Use the sentences shown in the example as the first ones in your notch book. Add other words that can be used as more than one part of speech, such as *well, opposite, stop,* or *play.* You will not always be able to use a word in every section. Over time, add more sentences to the book.

Find It in Your Reading Choose a simple sentence from a work you are reading. Use two of the words as examples in your parts-of-speech book. Challenge yourself to use two of the words in the sentence as examples of other parts of speech in the other sections of the book.

Find It in Your Writing Choose a simple sentence from a piece of your own writing. Look for a place in the rest of your piece where you have used one of the words in your sentence as a different part of speech. If you cannot find the word used differently elsewhere, challenge yourself to add a sentence that does use it differently.

Section Review

GRAMMAR EXERCISES 45–50

▶ **Exercise 45** Identifying Nouns and Verbs Identify the underlined word as a *noun* or a *verb*.

1. (a) Special <u>lights</u> help the plants grow.
   (b) The sun <u>lights</u> the greenhouse.
2. (a) <u>Show</u> the judge the roses.
   (b) They won first prize in the <u>show</u>.
3. (a) The <u>rain</u> will help the plants.
   (b) It might <u>rain</u> tomorrow.
4. (a) We won't <u>wait</u> long.
   (b) They had a long <u>wait</u> between shows.
5. (a) They had a <u>feeling</u> they would win.
   (b) Still, they were <u>feeling</u> nervous.

▶ **Exercise 46** Identifying Adjectives and Adverbs Identify the underlined word as an *adverb* or an *adjective*. Then, tell which word is modified.

1. This is a <u>hardy</u> variety.
2. It blooms <u>early</u> in the spring.
3. This bag is <u>light</u>.
4. This daisy grows <u>fast</u>.
5. The garden is reflected in the <u>still</u> water.

▶ **Exercise 47** Identifying All the Parts of Speech Identify the parts of speech of the underlined words in each sentence.

1. We have a <u>garden</u> <u>near</u> my house.
2. <u>We</u> go out to relax.
3. <u>In</u> the <u>early</u> morning, it is quiet and peaceful.
4. The flowers <u>turn</u> their <u>blossoms</u> up toward the sun.
5. <u>Gardening</u> does not always <u>cost</u> much.
6. Several plants <u>can be started</u> from <u>cuttings</u>.
7. The <u>place</u> you choose is important.
8. Taller plants can be loosely tied to <u>supporting</u> stakes.

9. The correct amount of <u>water</u> is crucial.
10. You can <u>question</u> experts <u>about</u> problem plants.
11. There is a <u>commercial</u> greenhouse <u>nearby</u>.
12. <u>There</u>, the <u>cost</u> of plants is reasonable.
13. The gardener will tell you <u>where</u> you should <u>place</u> each variety you buy.
14. He will <u>correct</u> gardening errors.
15. He knows the answer to almost any gardening <u>question</u>.

▶ **Exercise 48** Find It in Your Reading Read the following excerpt from "The Corn Planting" by Sherwood Anderson. Identify the part of speech of each underlined word.

The farmers who come <u>to</u> our <u>town</u> to trade are a <u>part</u> of the <u>town</u> life. Saturday is the big day. Often the children <u>come</u> to the high school in town. <u>It</u> is so with <u>Hatch</u> Hutchenson. Although his <u>farm</u>, some <u>three</u> miles from town, is small, it is known to be <u>one</u> of the best-kept and best-worked places in all our section.

▶ **Exercise 49** Find It in Your Writing Review a piece of writing from your portfolio. Identify at least one example of each part of speech. Find one example of a word that is used as two different parts of speech.

▶ **Exercise 50** Writing Application Write an explanation of how to care for a plant. Identify one example of each part of speech. Challenge yourself to use a word, such as *water* or *flower*, for two different functions.

Basic Sentence Parts

A Doubtfire Handshake, Charles M. Russell

▲ **Critical Viewing**
What is the subject of this picture ? What verb would you use to complete a sentence about the picture? [**Connect**]

Throughout history, language has been the tool people use to shape their ideas and communicate with others. During the days of the western frontier, the only way to communicate over long distances was via mail. Pony express riders braved many hardships and dangers to carry messages and packages to the West.

Because today we have many means of communication, the importance of language has not diminished. For communication to be meaningful, a speaker or writer must choose appropriate words and put them in an order that the listener or reader can follow. This chapter will focus on ways in which words are combined to form basic sentence parts.

Diagnostic Test

Directions: Write all answers on a separate sheet of paper.

Skill Check A. Write the sentences, drawing a vertical line between the complete subject and the complete predicate. Then, underline each subject once and each verb twice.

1. Stories of the Wild West tell about many heroes and outlaws.
2. Wild Bill Hickok left home at an early age and tried several careers.
3. He worked as a scout and stagecoach driver.
4. Farm work and law enforcement were also among his jobs.
5. This American frontiersman survived a bear attack.
6. He served as a Union spy in Missouri during the Civil War.
7. This famous figure of the Wild West was appointed Deputy United States Marshal at Fort Riley, Kansas.
8. His courage and his skill as a marksman brought order to this tough town.
9. In Abilene, Kansas, Hickok shot and killed a police officer by accident.
10. Hickok's adventures and escapades made him a legend in his own time.

Skill Check B. Write the subject and verb in each sentence. Underline the subjects once and the verbs twice. Write understood words (those implied, not directly stated) in parentheses.

11. Have you heard of Wild Bill Hickok?
12. In the biography section of the library are several books on this interesting character.
13. There is also a video about him.
14. Did he tour with the Wild West show?
15. See the librarian to find out more information about him.

Skill Check C. Write the complement(s) in each sentence, and label them *DO* (direct object), *IO* (indirect object), *OC* (object complement), *PA* (predicate adjective), or *PN* (predicate nominative). Write *none* if the sentence contains no complements.

16. At a young age, Wyatt Earp drove stagecoaches.
17. He also surveyed land in parts of Kansas.
18. The government named him Chief Deputy Marshal of Dodge City.
19. Within a year, he brought the city peace.
20. Then, he moved to a new town.
21. He had finally received a promotion!
22. Soon, he was named Deputy United States Marshal for the whole Arizona territory.
23. The famous OK Corral gunfight made him a legend.
24. Were the arrested cattle rustlers criminals?
25. He sounds brave!

Subjects and Predicates

In any language, the basic unit of thought that expresses meaning is the sentence. In English, every sentence has two essential parts, a complete subject and a complete predicate. These parts may be either clearly stated or implied.

▶ **KEY CONCEPT** A **sentence** is a group of words with two main parts: a complete subject and a complete predicate. Together, these parts express a complete thought. ■

A *complete subject* is the noun, pronoun, or group of words acting as a noun, plus any modifiers, that tells *who* or *what* the sentence is about. The *complete predicate* is the verb or verb phrase, plus any modifiers and complements, that tells what the complete subject of the sentence does or is. (See Section 18.3 for a definition of complements.) As the following examples show, complete subjects and complete predicates can vary in length.

Complete Subjects	Complete Predicates
Cowboys	roamed.
Buffalo Bill	delivered mail.
Pony express riders	carried packages more than 2,000 miles.
The service	lasted for only eighteen months.

Although the complete subject usually comes first, occasionally part of a complete predicate will be found at the beginning of a sentence with the rest at the end. In the first example below, the adverb *yesterday* modifies *visited*. In the second example, the prepositional phrase *At the exhibit* modifies *saw*. The complete subject is underlined once and the complete predicate, twice.

EXAMPLES: Yesterday my social studies class visited a Wild West exhibit.

At the exhibit, we saw a collection of Wild West memorabilia.

Theme: Wild West
· ·
In this section, you will learn about subjects and predicates. The examples and exercises in this section are about the Wild West.
· ·
Cross-Curricular Connection: Social Studies

Exercise 1 Recognizing Complete Subjects and Predicates

Make two columns as shown in the example. Then, write each complete subject in the first column and each complete predicate in the second column.

EXAMPLE: The tall cowboy tipped his hat politely.

ANSWER:

Complete Subject	Complete Predicate
The tall cowboy	tipped his hat politely.

1. Frederic Sackrider Remington was a famous American artist.
2. He painted scenes of the Wild West.
3. The New York native also sculpted many cowboys and Native Americans.
4. More than 2,700 pieces were created by him.
5. At Yale University, he studied art.
6. Early in his career, he traveled to the West.
7. Later, the artist settled in New Rochelle, New York.
8. Remington's sculptures were influenced by the famous artist Fredrick Ruckstull.
9. Remington's work helped create the myth of the Wild West.
10. The sculpture *Coming Through the Rye* was created in 1902.
11. This famous sculpture is featured in many art books.
12. Remington's action-filled style made him popular.
13. His early works were full of detail.
14. The Metropolitan Museum of Art in New York City contains some of Remington's work.
15. His story is just one of many from the Wild West.

More Practice

Grammar Exercise Workbook
• pp. 23–24
On-line Exercise Bank
• Section 18.1
  Go on-line:
  PHSchool.com
  Enter Web Code:
  efk-1102

interactive Textbook

Get instant feedback! Exercise 1 is available on-line or on CD-ROM.

Partners, Charles M. Russell

◄ **Critical Viewing** Suggest a predicate that tells what the man in this photo may be doing. **[Analyze]**

Simple Subjects and Predicates

Each complete subject and complete predicate contains a word or group of words that is essential to the sentence. Without these elements, known as the *simple subject* and *simple predicate*, a sentence is considered incomplete.

> **KEY CONCEPTS** The **simple subject** is the essential noun, pronoun, or group of words acting as a noun that cannot be left out of the complete subject. ■

The **simple predicate** is the essential verb or verb phrase that cannot be left out of the complete predicate. ■

In the following chart, the simple subjects are underlined once, and the simple predicates are underlined twice. Notice the other words in the sentences: They either modify the simple subject or the simple predicate of the sentence, or they help the simple predicate complete the meaning of the sentence.

In the last example, notice that the simple subject is *nation*, not *San Marino*. The object of a preposition is never a simple subject. Notice also that the simple predicate is a verb phrase, *has received*, that is interrupted by an adverb.

🌞 Grammar and Style Tip

Examine complete subjects and complete predicates to evaluate whether groups of words could be replaced with a more precise noun or verb.

SIMPLE SUBJECTS AND SIMPLE PREDICATES	
Complete Subjects	**Complete Predicates**
<u>Tickets</u> for the rodeo	<u>sold</u> quickly.
The writer's <u>children</u>	<u>published</u> all of his early poetry in 1868 but none of his sketches.
The tiny <u>nation</u> of San Marino	<u>has</u> always <u>received</u> most of its income from the sale of postage stamps.

Note About *Terminology:* From this point on in this book, the term *subject* will be used to refer to a simple subject and the term *verb* will be used to refer to a simple predicate. Whenever subjects and verbs need to be indicated in examples, subjects will be underlined once and verbs will be underlined twice.

Locating Subjects and Verbs Knowing a method for locating subjects and verbs in sentences will help you express complete thoughts in your own writing.

To find the subject, ask, "What word tells what this sentence is about?" Then ask, "What did the subject do?" The answer gives you the verb.

To find the verb, first ask, "What word expresses action or state of being in this sentence?" Then ask, "Who or what?" before the verb. The answer will be the subject of the verb.

Notice how these methods work with the following sentence:

EXAMPLE: The train whistle signaled a warning.

To find the subject, first ask, "What word tells what this sentence is about?"

ANSWER: train whistle (*Train whistle* is the subject.)

Then, to find the verb, ask, "What did the train whistle do?"

ANSWER: signaled (*Signaled* is the verb.)

To find the verb, first ask, "What word expresses action or state of being in this sentence?"

ANSWER: signaled (*Signaled* is the verb.)

Then, to find the subject, ask, "Who or what signaled?"

ANSWER: train whistle (*Train whistle* is the subject.)

▼ Critical Viewing
Write a complete sentence describing one difficulty of traveling across the country in a wagon train.
[Draw Conclusions]

George Ives, *Road Agent*, Olaf Seltzer

▲ **Critical Viewing** Use a compound verb to tell two or more actions you might take if you were a passenger in this stagecoach. **[Relate]**

▶ **Exercise 2** Identifying Subjects and Verbs Write the sentences, drawing a vertical line between the complete subject and the complete predicate. Then, underline each subject once and each verb twice.

EXAMPLE: Cattle <u>farmers</u> | <u>sent</u> their herds to market.

1. Cattle herders worked up to twenty hours a day.
2. They drove cattle up and down the Chisholm Trail.
3. Sources of water were sometimes not easily found.
4. Natural predators hunted the cattle.
5. Wild buffalo stampedes often occurred at night.
6. Cowboys on the plains earned only about seven dollars a week.
7. The cowboy era finally ended around 1890.
8. The remaining cattle farmers put fences around their ranges.
9. The famous Transcontinental Railroad connected the two coasts.
10. The need for long cattle drives was over.

More Practice

Grammar Exercise
Workbook
• pp. 27–28
On-line Exercise Bank
• Section 18.1

Go on-line:
PHSchool.com
Enter Web Code:
efk-1102

*i*nteractive
Textbook

Get instant feedback!
Exercise 2 is available
on-line or on CD-ROM.

Recognizing More Than One Subject or Verb

Sometimes, a sentence may contain a compound subject or compound verb.

▶ **KEY CONCEPT** A **compound subject** is two or more subjects that have the same verb and are joined by a conjunction such as *and* or *or*. ■

In the following example, the parts of the compound subject are underlined once. The verb is underlined twice.

EXAMPLE: Neither the horse nor the driver looked tired.

▶ **KEY CONCEPT** A **compound verb** is two or more verbs that have the same subject and are joined by a conjunction such as *and* or *or*. ■

Notice in the second example that it is not necessary to repeat the same helping verb twice. Some sentence constructions may contain both compound subjects and compound verbs.

EXAMPLES: She sneezed and coughed throughout the trip.
We will load the wagon and leave soon.
The dog and cat eyed each other, circled warily, and then advanced into combat.

GRAMMAR IN LITERATURE

from **Bidwell Ghost**
Louise Erdrich

In this excerpt, using the compound verbs bowed *and* complained *avoids repeating the subject* orchard. *Using the compound verbs* cracked *and* fell *avoids repeating the subject* branches.

First the orchard *bowed* low and *complained*
of the unpicked fruit,
then the branches *cracked* apart and *fell*.

⊚ Technology Tip

When editing your work, use the copy, cut, and paste functions rather than retyping sentences or paragraphs.

◔ Learn More

To find additional information about nouns, pronouns, and verbs, see Chapter 17.

> **Exercise 3** Locating Compound Subjects and Verbs Write the words that make up the subject and verb in each sentence. Label them *compound subject* and *compound verb.*
> 1. Dogs and wolves are closely related to the coyote.
> 2. A howling coyote and cowboys around a campfire bring to mind a picture of the Wild West.
> 3. Coyotes in desert climates escape the heat and sleep in caves during the daytime.
> 4. Farmers and ranchers sometimes call coyotes prairie wolves.
> 5. Coyotes roam the range and look for food.

> **Exercise 4** Combining Sentences With Compound Subjects and Verbs Combine the two sentences into one sentence with a compound subject or a compound verb.
> 1. Settlers traveled under difficult conditions. Settlers faced many dangers.
> 2. Horses were used to pull covered wagons. Mules were used to pull covered wagons.
> 3. The settlers moved into the unknown. They left the familiar behind.
> 4. The wide open spaces appealed to many. The opportunities for independence also appealed to many.
> 5. The settlers traveled during the day. They camped at night.

> **More Practice**
>
> Grammar Exercise Workbook
> • pp. 27–28
> On-line Exercise Bank
> • Section 18.1
> *Go on-line:*
> PHSchool.com
> *Enter Web Code:*
> efk-1102

Get instant feedback! Exercises 3 and 4 are available on-line or on CD-ROM.

▼ **Critical Viewing** Use a compound subject to describe an advantage of camping for the night in this formation. [**Assess**]

Section Review

GRAMMAR EXERCISES 5–10

▶ **Exercise 5** Recognizing Complete Subjects and Predicates Make two columns. Label one *complete subject* and the other, *complete predicate*. Then, write each complete subject in the first column and each complete predicate in the second column.

1. Jesse James was born in Missouri on September 5, 1847.
2. He was a soldier at the age of seventeen.
3. This infamous outlaw formed a gang with his brother and cousins after the Civil War.
4. They attacked stagecoaches, banks, and railroads.
5. Railroad companies offered rewards for James's capture.
6. In 1876, the gang attempted a robbery of two banks at once in Northfield, Minnesota.
7. All except for Jesse and his brother were captured.
8. The brothers formed another gang.
9. Members of the new gang later turned against the brothers.
10. For Jesse, his brother, and their gangs, crime did not pay.

▶ **Exercise 6** Identifying Subjects and Verbs Write the sentences, drawing a vertical line between the complete subject and the complete predicate. Underline each subject once and each verb twice.

1. Outlaws of the Wild West often ended their careers badly.
2. Billy the Kid died at the young age of twenty-two.
3. Sheriff Pat Garrett captured the young outlaw.
4. John Wesley Harding, Sam Bass, Black Bart, Butch Cassidy, and others ended their careers in gunfights.

5. Emmett Dalton was badly wounded during a holdup.

▶ **Exercise 7** Revision Practice: Sentence Combining Revise the following paragraph by combining sentences in places where combining would improve the flow of the writing. Use compound subects or verbs as needed.

A cattle drive was hot, dirty, tiring work. Cowboys learned to live with discomfort. They learned to live with danger. Stampedes were one hazard cowboys faced. Thunder could set off a herd of cattle. A gunshot could, too. Cow towns such as Abilene prospered. Dodge City, a cow town, prospered. After months on the trail, cowboys were ready for a good meal and a soft bed. Dance halls catered to cowboys. Hotels catered to cowboys, too.

▶ **Exercise 8** Find It in Your Reading Identify the compound verb in this sentence from "Pecos Bill Becomes a Coyote."

The mother and eight or ten of the older children hurried back to the river and hunted everywhere, but they could find no trace of the lost boy.

▶ **Exercise 9** Find It in Your Writing Look through your portfolio to find at least one example of a compound subject and one example of a compound verb.

▶ **Exercise 10** Writing Application Write a brief narrative about the travels of an imaginary group of explorers. In each sentence, underline the subject(s) once and the verb(s) twice.

Hard-to-Find Subjects

Most sentences have subjects that can easily be found; some, however, contain subjects that are more elusive. Each of the four sentence functions (declarative, interrogative, imperative, and exclamatory) deserves individual examination.

Subjects in Declarative Sentences Beginning With *Here* or *There*   When *there* or *here* is found at the beginning of a declarative sentence, it is often mistaken for the subject.

▶ **KEY CONCEPT**   The subject of a sentence is never *there* or *here*. ■

In normal use, *there* and *here* are usually adverbs that modify the verb by pointing out *where*. Occasionally, *there* may be used merely to start the sentence and will have no adverbial function at all. In this case, *there* is called an *expletive*.

Many sentences beginning with *here* or *there* are inverted: The subject follows the verb. Rearrange such a sentence in subject-verb order to more easily identify the subject.

INVERTED: There <u>are</u> the <u>buses</u>.
REARRANGED: The <u>buses</u> <u>are</u> there.

Sentences Beginning With *There* or *Here*	Sentences Rearranged With Subject Before Verb
There <u>are</u> the downtown <u>buildings</u>.	The downtown <u>buildings</u> <u>are</u> there.
Here <u>is</u> the <u>ticket</u> for your trip.	The <u>ticket</u> for your trip <u>is</u> here.
There <u>is</u> <u>money</u> available.	<u>Money</u> <u>is</u> available.

Occasionally, sentences beginning with *there* or *here* are in normal word order with the subject before the verb.

EXAMPLE: There <u>she</u> <u>is</u>.

Theme: Chicago
In this section, you will learn to locate hard-to-find subjects. The examples and exercises in this section are about Chicago.

Cross-Curricular Connection: Social Studies

▼ **Critical Viewing** Comment on the lights of Chicago in a sentence beginning with *There is* or *There are*. **[Relate]**

KEY CONCEPT In some declarative sentences, the subject follows the verb in order to receive greater emphasis. ■

By deliberately placing the subject at the end, these sentences put special emphasis on it. Such inverted sentences usually begin with prepositional phrases.

Sentences Inverted for Emphasis	Sentences Rephrased With Subject Before Verb
Toward the elevated train rushed the evening commuters.	The evening commuters rushed toward the elevated train.
Around the corner careened the speeding car.	The speeding car careened around the corner.

Subjects in Interrogative Sentences In some interrogative sentences, the subject comes before the verb in a normal sequence and, thus, is easily identified.

EXAMPLE: Which car gets the best mileage?

Often, however, the sequence is inverted.

KEY CONCEPT In interrogative sentences, the subject often follows the verb. ■

An inverted interrogative sentence can begin with a verb, a helping verb, or one of the following words: *how, what, when, where, which, who, whose,* or *why.* To locate the subject, mentally rephrase the sentence in normal order.

Questions	Rephrased as Statements
Is the Chicago Zoo open in the morning?	The Chicago Zoo is open in the morning.
Do they own that house?	They do own that house.
When will the coffee be done?	The coffee will be done when.

 Internet Tip

You can sometimes target a search more precisely by using the word *NOT* fully capitalized. For example: "Chicago NOT Fire" would eliminate Chicago listings that include the Great Chicago Fire.

Subjects in Imperative Sentences The subject of an imperative sentence is usually implied rather than specifically stated.

KEY CONCEPT In imperative sentences, the subject is understood to be *you*. ■

Notice in the following chart that the subjects of the imperative sentences on the left are not directly expressed. The examples on the right illustrate where the subjects are understood to occur in the sentences.

Imperative Sentences	With Understood *You* Added
First <u>visit</u> the Sears Tower.	First [<u>you</u>] <u>visit</u> the Sears Tower.
After the tour, <u>come</u> home right away.	After the tour, [<u>you</u>] <u>come</u> home right away.
Sue, <u>show</u> me the map.	Sue, [<u>you</u>] <u>show</u> me the map.

In the last example in the chart, notice that *Sue*, the name of the person being addressed, is not the subject of the sentence. The subject is still understood to be *you*.

Subjects in Exclamatory Sentences Some exclamatory sentences have the subject before the verb, but some do not.

KEY CONCEPT In an exclamatory sentence, the subject may come after the verb or may be understood. ■

To find the subject in many exclamatory sentences, simply follow the same techniques that you would for finding subjects in interrogative sentences.

EXAMPLES: How <u>could</u> <u>I</u> have <u>known</u>! (<u>I</u> <u>could have known</u> how.)
What <u>does</u> <u>he</u> <u>know</u>! (<u>He</u> <u>does know</u> what.)

Other exclamatory sentences may be so elliptical that both their subject and verb may be understood.

EXAMPLES: Fire! [You <u>put</u> out the) fire!]
Let's go! [<u>We</u> <u>demand</u> to] go!]

More Practice

Grammar Exercise Workbook
• pp. 29–30
On-line Exercise Bank
• Section 18.2

Go on-line:
PHSchool.com
Enter Web Code:
efk-1102

GRAMMAR IN LITERATURE

from **Chicago**
Carl Sandburg

The first sentence in these lines from the poem is imperative. The subject of Come *and* show *is understood to be* you. *In the inverted second sentence, the subject is* slugger.

Come and *show* me another city with lifted head singing so proud to be alive and coarse and strong and cunning. . . . [H]ere is a tall bold *slugger* set vivid against the little soft cities;

▶ **Exercise 11** Locating Hard-to-Find Subjects Write the subject and verb in each sentence, underlining subjects once and verbs twice. Put any understood words in parentheses.

EXAMPLE: Where is the meeting?

ANSWER: <u>meeting</u> <u>is</u>

1. On the shores of Lake Michigan sits Chicago.
2. There are few buildings in Chicago taller than the John Hancock building.
3. At its top is an observatory offering a spectacular view of the city.
4. How could you miss it!
5. Go there between 9:00 A.M. and midnight.
6. Listen to the talking telescopes with sound effects.
7. There are four languages offered.
8. Where could you have more fun?
9. Tallest of all Chicago's buildings is the Sears Tower.
10. Did you walk along the lakefront?
11. Also, visit Chicago's famous Navy Pier.
12. What does it offer?
13. Go and see!
14. Does the elevated train go to the zoo?
15. Here is a ticket for the el.

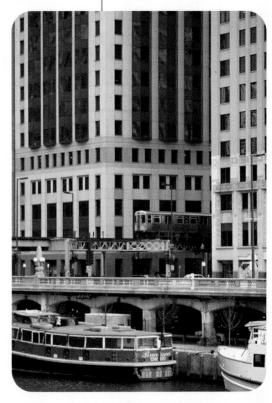

▼ **Critical Viewing** Using question words (*what, which, why, how,* etc.), ask two questions about the modes of transportation depicted in this photograph of a Chicago waterfront area. **[Analyze]**

Hands-on Grammar

Where's the Subject?

Take a sheet of construction paper and fold a pocket in it as shown in the illustration below. Draw a line down the middle of the pocket, and label the left side *Subject* and the right side *Predicate.* Write the following sentences on strips of paper.

1. Go home!
2. Where is that dog?
3. There is a new restaurant in town.
4. Over there is where you register.
5. Put your name at the top of the page.

Tape a pile of the strips on the paper, as shown, to make a flip book. Write each of the words from the sentences on cards that will fit in the pocket with the words showing.

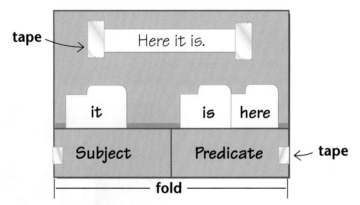

The object of this project is to find the subject of the sentence. As you know from reading the section, the subject is not always easy to find. Put all the words that pertain to the subject on the Subject side of the pocket. Put all the words that pertain to the predicate on the Predicate side of the pocket. Then, when you have correctly identified the subject, flip the sentence over and do the same thing with the next one. Remember that some sentences don't have a written subject, so have a *you* card handy to put into the subject side for those cases.

Find It in Your Reading Do this activity with sentences that you find in your reading. These may be interrogatives, imperatives, exclamations, those beginning with *here* or *there,* or those with inverted word order.

Find It in Your Writing Review some of the writing in your portfolio. Find examples of sentences with hard-to-find subjects. If you can't find any, challenge yourself to write sentences with more variety.

Section 18.2 *Section Review*

GRAMMAR EXERCISES 12–16

Exercise 12 Locating Hard-to-Find Subjects Write the subject and verb in each sentence, underlining subjects once and verbs twice. Put any understood words in parentheses.

1. There are so many great sights in Chicago!
2. Have you heard of Frank Lloyd Wright?
3. Was he an architect?
4. Read the travel guide!
5. Here is a section on architecture.
6. There is also a short history of the city.
7. In October 1971, there was a special fireworks display in Chicago.
8. The event commemorated the Great Chicago Fire one hundred years earlier.
9. At the center of the fire was Patrick O'Leary's barn.
10. How did the fire start?
11. There was panic everywhere.
12. Extinguish the fire!
13. Finally helping to douse the fire was a heavy rainstorm.
14. Did you know about the casualties at the zoo?
15. Can you imagine the property damage?

Exercise 13 Writing Questions Rewrite each of the following as a question. Then, locate the subject of each sentence.

1. There was a famous fire in Chicago in 1903.
2. The fire was at the Iroquois Theater.
3. The staff was unprepared for a fire.
4. The lead actor controlled the situation.
5. Many people suffered from smoke inhalation.

Exercise 14 Find It in Your Reading On a separate sheet of paper, copy the following lines from Carl Sandburg's "Grass." Underline the subject of each sentence or clause once. Underline the verb twice. If a subject is understood, write it in parentheses.

> Two years, ten years, and passengers
> ask the conductor:
> What place is this?
> Where are we now?
>
> I am grass.
> Let me work.

Exercise 15 Find It in Your Writing Look through your writing portfolio. Find examples of a declarative sentence with the subject following the verb, an interrogative sentence, an imperative sentence, and an exclamatory sentence. Identify the subject of each sentence. If you cannot find all types of examples, challenge yourself to add those types of sentences for variety.

Exercise 16 Writing Application Prepare the text of a travel brochure for a city in your state. Use inverted sentences, interrogative sentences, and imperative sentences as headings. In each heading you write, identify the subject and the verb.

Complements

The meaning of some sentences is complete when they contain no more than a subject and a verb with perhaps some modifiers, as in *I laughed* or *I laughed wholeheartedly.* In other sentences, however, the verbs need more than modifiers to complete the meaning, as in *The U.S. government established . . .* or *The astronauts are . . .* These sentences require *complements,* such as *NASA* and *courageous,* to finish the meaning of the verbs: *The U.S. government established NASA* and *The astronauts are courageous.*

▷ **KEY CONCEPT** A **complement** is a word or group of words that completes the meaning of the predicate of a sentence. ■

Five different kinds of complements can be found in English sentences:

• *direct objects*

• *indirect objects*

• *objective complements*

• *predicate nominatives*

• *predicate adjectives*

The last two, which are often grouped together, are called *subject complements.*

This section will explain how each complement works to complete the meaning of a sentence.

◀ **Critical Viewing** Describe the figure in this photograph by adding complements to these sentences: "The astronaut is wearing . . ." "The suit protects . . ." "He feels . . ." **[Infer]**

Direct Objects

Found only with transitive verbs, direct objects complete the meaning of verbs by receiving action from them.

> **KEY CONCEPT** A **direct object** is a noun, pronoun, or group of words acting as a noun that receives the action of a transitive verb. ∎

EXAMPLES: We <u>watched</u> the liftoff.
          ^{DO}

          I <u>invited</u> her to our outer-space party.
          ^{DO}

To find a direct object in a sentence, ask *Whom?* or *What?* after an action verb. If you find no answer, the verb is intransitive and has no direct object. (See Chapter 17 for more about transitive and intransitive verbs.)

EXAMPLES: I was watching the show until midnight. (Was watching *what? Answer:* show)
          It taught me about gravity. (taught *whom? Answer:* me)
          The meteor crashed into a planet. (Crashed *what? Answer:* none; the verb is intransitive)

In some inverted questions, the direct object will appear near the beginning of the sentence, before the verb. To locate the direct object in this type of question, rephrase the question in normal word order.

INVERTED QUESTION: Which shuttle <u>did you visit</u>?
                     ^{DO}

REWORDED: <u>You did visit</u> which shuttle?
            ^{DO}

Also, remember that a verb may have more than one direct object, called a *compound direct object*. If a sentence contains a compound direct object, asking *Whom?* or *What?* after the action verb will give you two or more answers.

EXAMPLES: Buzz Aldrin explored the moon and outer space.
                         ^{DO}   ^{DO}

          He copiloted *Gemini 12* and *Apollo 11* in space.
                        ^{DO}   ^{DO}

In the second example, *space* is the object of the preposition *in.* It is not a direct object. You should keep in mind that an object of a preposition can never be a direct object in a sentence.

 Internet Tip

To learn more about space exploration, visit NASA's Web site at **www.NASA.gov**

▲ Critical Viewing
What missions
might these astro-
nauts have accom-
plished? Use direct
objects in your
answer.
[Speculate]

▶ **Exercise 17** Recognizing Direct Objects Write the direct objects in the following sentences, including all parts of any compound direct objects. If a sentence has no direct object, write *none*.

1. In college, Sally Ride studied physics and English.
2. Then, she applied to the astronaut-training program.
3. Ride earned a pilot's license during training.
4. For her first flight, she rode in the shuttle *Challenger.*
5. On that mission, she launched two satellites.
6. She also launched and retrieved a test satellite.
7. Which shuttle mission did Ride fly for NASA?
8. Sally Ride earned the title First American Woman in Space.
9. While at NASA, she established the Office of Exploration.
10. Later, she produced a report on the future of the space program.

▶ **Exercise 18** Writing Sentences With Direct Objects Use each of the following as a direct object in a sentence.

1. her students
2. the movie
3. the space shuttle
4. astronaut
5. NASA

▶ **More Practice**

Grammar Exercise
Workbook
• pp. 31–32
On-line Exercise Bank
• Section 18.3

Go on-line:
PHSchool.com
Enter Web Code:
efk-1102

Complete the exer-
cises on-line! Exercises
17 and 18 are avail-
able on-line or on
CD-ROM.

Indirect Objects

Indirect objects are found in sentences that already contain direct objects.

▶ **KEY CONCEPT** An **indirect object** is a noun or pronoun that appears with a direct object and names the person or thing that something is given to or done for. ■

Indirect objects appear only with transitive action verbs. They are usually found after such verbs as *ask, bring, buy, give, lend, make, promise, show, teach, tell,* and *write.* Examples of sentences with indirect objects follow.

✓ Spelling Tip

Words like *NASA* are acronyms, or words formed from the first letters of a series of words. They do not require periods after the letters. NASA is an acronym for National Aeronautics and Space Administration.

	IO	DO

EXAMPLES: I showed Randy the book.

They gave the space shuttle a thorough cleaning.

To find the indirect object in a sentence, first make certain that the sentence contains a direct object. Then ask *To or for whom?* or *To or for what?* after the verb and direct object.

EXAMPLES: I took her the slides. (Took slides *to or for whom? Answer:* her)

We sent NASA the letters. (Sent letters *to or for what? Answer:* NASA)

Like direct objects, indirect objects may be compound.

EXAMPLES: I lent Richard and Tom my videotape of the launch.

It is important to remember that an indirect object is never the object of the preposition *to* or *for.*

EXAMPLES: She took the NASA souvenir for her sister.

She took her sister a NASA souvenir.

In the first of the examples you just read, *sister* is not an indirect object. Only when the word *sister* is placed before the direct object and when the preposition *for* is dropped from the sentence does the word *sister* become an indirect object, as you see in the second example.

Exercise 19 Recognizing Indirect Objects Write each underlined item, and identify it as a *direct object, indirect object*, or *object of a preposition*.

EXAMPLE: Frank gave his <u>friends</u> <u>gifts</u> from his trip.

ANSWER: friends (indirect object)   gifts (direct object)

1. The tour guide told <u>him</u> <u>facts</u> about NASA.
2. The U.S. government established <u>NASA</u> in 1958.
3. NASA has launched manned <u>space shuttles</u>, <u>satellites</u>, and <u>space probes</u>.
4. NASA does not oversee military <u>developments</u>.
5. The President appoints an <u>administrator</u> for <u>NASA</u>.
6. This person gives the <u>government</u> and the scientific com- munity <u>plans</u> for cooperation.
7. He or she also develops <u>programs</u> with other countries.
8. Space exploration brings new <u>developments</u> to the whole <u>world</u>.
9. The space shuttle program promises continued <u>success</u>.
10. Frank brought <u>me</u> a <u>guidebook</u> for further reading.

Objective Complements

An objective complement completes the meaning of the direct object in a sentence. It occurs, therefore, only in sen- tences that already contain a direct object.

▶ **KEY CONCEPT** An **objective complement** is an adjective or noun that appears with a direct object and describes or renames it. ■

Objective complements are found only after such verbs as *appoint, call, consider, elect, label, make, name,* or *think.*

EXAMPLES: The President <u>named</u> her admin- istrator of NASA.
            (DO: named, OC: administrator)

            I <u>consider</u> her the best candidate for the job.
            (DO: consider, OC: candidate)

▼ Critical Viewing What feelings might watching a rocket launch give you? Use an indirect object in your answer. **[Relate]**

Exercise 20 Identifying Objective Complements Identify the objective complement in each sentence. Then, write the object that is renamed or described.

EXAMPLE: The Soviet Union called the satellite *Sputnik*.

ANSWER: *Sputnik* renames *satellite*.

1. The scientists thought it wonderful.
2. Critics called the mission unnecessary and wasteful.
3. The officials appointed the dog Laika the passenger.
4. She was the first dog in space, and we consider her a hero.
5. Now, people call *Sputnik* historic and inspiring.

Subject Complements

Direct objects, indirect objects, and objective complements appear with action verbs. Subject complements appear with linking verbs.

KEY CONCEPT A **subject complement** is a noun, a pronoun, or an adjective that appears with a linking verb and tells something about the subject. ■

There are two kinds of subject complements: *predicate nominatives* and *predicate adjectives*.

KEY CONCEPT A **predicate nominative** is a noun or pronoun that appears with a linking verb and renames, identifies, or explains the subject. ■

EXAMPLES: Neil Armstrong <u>became</u> an astronaut.
              PN

              John Glenn <u>is</u> a former astronaut and senator.
              PN   PN

KEY CONCEPT A **predicate adjective** is an adjective that appears with a linking verb and describes the subject of the sentence. ■

Notice that the predicate adjective in the second example is compound.

EXAMPLES: The <u>surface</u> of the planet <u>looked</u> hilly.
              PA

              Today, space <u>travel</u> <u>seems</u> plausible and exciting.
              PA   PA

More Practice

Grammar Exercise Workbook
• pp. 35–36
On-line Exercise Bank
• Section 18.3
 Go on-line:
 PHSchool.com
 Enter Web Code:
 efk-1102

Interactive Textbook

Get instant feedback! Exercises 19 and 20 are available on-line or on CD-ROM.

Learn More

For information about linking verbs, see Chapter 17.

18.3

Exercise 21 Identifying Subject Complements Write the subject complement in each sentence, including all parts of any compound subject complements. Then, identify each as a *predicate nominative* or *predicate adjective*.

EXAMPLE: After the mission, the crew looked exhausted.
ANSWER: exhausted (predicate adjective)

1. For thousands of years, spaceflight seemed a dream.
2. The desire to fly remained distant and elusive.
3. Nicolaus Copernicus was a Polish astronomer in the sixteenth century.
4. His observations of the universe were quite insightful.
5. Other contributors to the study of astronautics were physicists, mathematicians, and astronomers.
6. The information quickly became very advanced.
7. Poor technology was the obstacle.
8. In the early twentieth century, the study of rocket propulsion was promising.
9. The development of new inventions seemed rapid.
10. The dream of space travel became a reality.

▼ Critical Viewing How dramatic is this photograph? Describe it in several sentences, using subject complements. [Evaluate]

Exercise 22 Supplying Subject Complements On your paper, complete each sentence with either a predicate adjective *(PA)* or predicate nominative *(PN)*, according to the instructions.

EXAMPLE: One of America's greatest achievements is ___?___. *(PN)*
ANSWER: One of America's greatest achievements is its space program.

1. The organization responsible for our space program is ___?___. *(PN)*
2. America's investment in the space program seems ___?___. *(PA)*
3. For astronauts, going into space to repair orbiting equipment becomes ___?___. *(PN)*
4. Films of astronauts walking in space are ___?___. *(PA)*
5. From the astronauts' radio reports, space missions sound ___?___. *(PA)*

More Practice

Grammar Exercise Workbook
• pp. 37–38
On-line Exercise Bank
• Section 18.3
Go on-line:
PHSchool.com
Enter Web Code:
efk-1102

Complete the exercises on-line! Exercises 21 and 22 are available on-line or on CD-ROM.

Section 18.3 *Section Review*

GRAMMAR EXERCISES 23–27

Exercise 23 Recognizing Direct and Indirect Objects Identify the underlined items as a *direct object, indirect object,* or *object of a preposition.*

1. Satellites carry scientific measuring <u>devices</u> to outer <u>space</u>.
2. They obtain <u>data</u> for scientists and make accurate <u>studies</u> of the planets.
3. Since 1962, Orbiting Solar Observatories have studied solar <u>radiation</u>.
4. Pioneer satellites bring <u>information</u> about space to <u>scientists</u> on Earth.
5. Other types of orbiting observatories send <u>astronomers</u> stellar <u>observations</u>.
6. Scientists expect even greater astronomical <u>discoveries</u> from the Hubble Space Telescope, launched in 1990.
7. Astronauts repaired a <u>flaw</u> in the main mirror of the telescope in 1993.
8. Its observations of a black hole provided much <u>information</u> for <u>study</u>.
9. In 1996, a telescope sent <u>scientists</u> the first <u>images</u> of Pluto's surface.
10. Cameras on many satellites send <u>us</u> <u>photographs</u> of the discoveries.

Exercise 24 Identifying All Types of Complements Write all complements in the following sentences. Then label each one *direct object, indirect object, objective complement, predicate nominative,* or *predicate adjective.*

1. Unmanned spacecraft perform many functions.
2. Communications satellites provide companies and the government extensive communication abilities.
3. These satellites transmit television signals, telephone conversations, and digital data.
4. People consider this technology a necessity.

5. Weather satellites observe temperatures and cloud patterns.
6. Other environmental satellites use multispectral optical scanners.
7. Color enhancement makes these images informative and valuable.
8. They show environmentalists soil characteristics and pollution levels.
9. For geologists, images of the Earth's crust become maps of oil deposits.
10. Modern satellite images grow more and more detailed and exact.

Exercise 25 Find It in Your Reading Identify the complements in these lines from Archibald MacLeish's "Ars Poetica." Tell what kind of complement each is.

A poem should be palpable and mute
As a globed fruit. . . .

A poem should be wordless
As the flight of birds.

A poem should be motionless in time
As the moon climbs, . . .

Exercise 26 Find It in Your Writing Review your portfolio to find examples of at least three kinds of complements. Challenge yourself to add detail to your writing by adding complements to sentences.

Exercise 27 Writing Application Write a summary of a science-fiction story, television show, or movie. Identify any complements you use.

Phrases and *Clauses*

Good writers need to venture beyond the comfortable routine of using only basic sentence patterns when they write. Varying sentence structure with well-placed phrases and clauses adds clarity and style to any good piece of prose. Effective use of phrases and clauses allows writers to personalize their writing, making it distinct from everyone else's. For example, with varied, sophisticated sentences, writers have for centuries given voice to their convictions and offered their unique perspectives on the world.

This chapter describes the various kinds of phrases and clauses that you can use to expand the basic patterns of the sentences you write. Learning to expand the basic patterns of your sentences will help you to express your ideas clearly and to improve the style of your writing.

Diagnostic Test

Directions: Write all answers on a separate sheet of paper.

Skill Check A. Write the prepositional phrases and appositive phrases in the following items. Label each phrase *prep* or *app*.

1. Carol Shields, a Canadian American novelist, writes about simple people and their emotional crises.
2. Her novel *The Stone Diaries* won her the Pulitzer Prize for Fiction.
3. Born in Illinois, Shields moved to Canada with her husband in 1957.
4. Her first novel, *Small Ceremonies*, is about a woman who is writing a biography about a nineteenth-century Canadian author.
5. *The Stone Diaries* is a detailed fictional account of the life of a Canadian woman born in 1905.

Skill Check B. Write the verbal or verbal phrase in the following sentences, and label it *participial, gerund,* or *infinitive.*

6. Having written 270 books in her lifetime, Louisa May Alcott is among America's most prolific authors.
7. She is best remembered for writing the novel *Little Women.*
8. Alcott drew largely on personal experience to write *Little Women.*
9. Writing was the way she supported her poor family.
10. Though her writing fed her family, Alcott's true passion was fighting for women's rights.

Skill Check C. Write the subordinate clause in each item, and identify it as *adjective, adverb,* or *noun.*

11. Maya Angelou, whose powerful writing has inspired a generation of women, has defied social norms all her life.
12. Her literary talents emerged after her grandmother introduced her to literature.
13. Angelou worked as an actor, streetcar conductor, and fund-raiser before she began focusing on her writing in the 1960's.
14. Her autobiographical works and poetry, which offer insight into the experience of black women in the twentieth century, have won numerous awards.
15. Angelou's words will continue to move whoever reads them.

Skill Check D. Label each sentence *simple, compound, complex,* or *compound-complex.*

16. Gwendolyn Brooks was introverted and shy as a child.
17. She grew up reading the classics, and she wrote prolifically.
18. Brooks published her first poem at age thirteen; some thought her a prodigy.
19. Though she worked for a while as a housekeeper and a secretary, Brooks continued writing in her spare time.
20. Eventually, her poems gained recognition, and Brooks, who is considered a very fine writer, has achieved the fame she deserves.

Appositive Phrases

Phrases can often help the writer overcome the inadequacies of one-word modifiers.

> **KEY CONCEPT** A **phrase** is a group of words without a subject or verb that functions as one part of speech. ■

Two types of phrases frequently used to add detail to sentences are *prepositional phrases* and *appositive phrases.*

Prepositional Phrases

A **prepositional phrase** consists of a preposition accompanied by a noun or pronoun called the object of the preposition. The object may be compound and may have modifiers.

EXAMPLES:

PREP   OBJ   OBJ
near the table and chairs

PREP   OBJ
after a cool, refreshing swim

Prepositional phrases may function as either adjectives or adverbs within sentences.

Adjective Phrases A prepositional phrase that describes a noun or pronoun is an *adjective phrase.*

> **KEY CONCEPT** An **adjective phrase** is a prepositional phrase that modifies a noun or pronoun by telling *what kind* or *which one.* ■

EXAMPLES: The book *on the table* is green. (*Which* book?)
She wrote a novel *about a large family.* (*What kind* of novel?)
I sent my cousin *in Detroit* some books by Isabel Allende. (*Which* cousin?)
She is a writer *with many books to her credit.* (*What kind* of writer? *Which* books?)

More than one adjective phrase may modify the same word.

EXAMPLE: The book by Swanson about women writers is mine.

Theme: Women Writers

In this section, you will learn to identify and use prepositional phrases and appositive phrases. The examples and exercises in this section are about notable women writers.

Cross-Curricular Connection: Social Studies

▲ **Critical Viewing** "My life closed twice before its close—" and "Success is counted sweetest" are two of Emily Dickinson's well-known poems. Use adjective phrases to describe the probable theme of each poem. **[Infer]**

Adverb Phrases A prepositional phrase that acts as an adverb is an *adverb phrase*.

> **KEY CONCEPT** An **adverb phrase** is a prepositional phrase that modifies a verb, an adjective, or an adverb by pointing out *where, when, in what way,* or *to what extent.* ■

In the following examples, notice how adverb phrases answer any one of the four questions for adverbs.

MODIFYING A VERB:
Elizabeth Bishop was born *in 1911.* (Was born *when?*)

He talked *with me.* (Talked *in what way?*)

Except for the conclusion, the book was finished. (Was finished *to what extent?*)

Beloved is regarded *by many* as Toni Morrison's most successful novel. (Is regarded *to what extent?*)

MODIFYING AN ADJECTIVE:
She is helpful *to everyone.* (Helpful *to what extent?*)

MODIFYING AN ADVERB:
I read early *in the morning.* (Early *to what extent?*)

Sentences can contain more than one adverb phrase, and all of them can modify the same word.

EXAMPLE:
At Howard University, Toni Morrison wrote *about compelling characters.* (Wrote *where?* Wrote *in what way?*)

▲ **Critical Viewing**
What adverb phrase would you use to describe the way in which Toni Morrison is smiling? **[Infer]**

⊙ **Technology Tip**

Do not rely too heavily on the spell-check feature in your word-processing program. If you type the word *form* instead of the preposition *from,* the spell-check feature will not catch the error. Always proofread your work!

▶ **Exercise 1** Identifying Adjective and Adverb Phrases

Write the prepositional phrase or phrases in each sentence below. Then, identify each phrase as an *adjective* or *adverb*.

EXAMPLE: The study of writers is fascinating.

ANSWER: of writers (adjective)

1. Harriet Beecher was born in 1811, the seventh child of a famous Protestant preacher.
2. She worked as a teacher with her sister Catherine.
3. Harriet's only book about the geography of the United States was published in 1833.
4. The book, written for children, was published under her sister's name.
5. After her brief teaching career, Harriet married the professor and clergyman Calvin Stowe.
6. To supplement Calvin's teaching salary, she wrote stories about domestic life for local and religious periodicals.
7. When Congress passed the Fugitive Slave Law in 1850, she started a serial novel denouncing slavery.
8. *Uncle Tom's Cabin* was first published in serial form in the *National Era.*
9. The nation quickly became fascinated by the story line.
10. *Uncle Tom's Cabin* was first published in book form in 1852, and it was the first novel with an African American hero.

▲ **Critical Viewing** Include at least one appositive phrase in a sentence about this picture of Harriet Beecher Stowe. **[Analyze]**

▶ **Exercise 2** Supplying Adjective and Adverb Phrases

Supply prepositional phrases to complete the following sentences. Then, indicate whether each prepositional phrase is functioning as an *adjective* or an *adverb*.

1. I think I do my best writing ___?___.
2. These days, I'm working on a story ___?___.
3. The two main characters ___?___ are in conflict ___?___.
4. The winner ___?___ will receive an inheritance.
5. I hope to be able to finish the story ___?___.

▶ **More Practice**

Grammar Exercise Workbook
• pp. 43–44
On-line Exercise Bank
• Section 19.1
Go on-line:
PHSchool.com
Enter Web Code:
efk-1102

Appositives and Appositive Phrases

Although they are not modifiers, appositives and appositive phrases are similar to adjective phrases in that they add detail to nouns and pronouns.

Appositives The word *appositive* comes from a Latin verb meaning "to put near or next to."

KEY CONCEPT An **appositive** is a noun or pronoun placed next to another noun or pronoun to identify, rename, or explain it. ■

EXAMPLES: Margaret Atwood's specialty, *the historical novel,* can be very entertaining.

His favorite writer, *Annie Dillard,* will read from her work tonight.

Be alert when punctuating appositives. If an appositive contains *nonessential* material (material that can be removed from the sentence without altering its meaning), set the appositive off from the rest of the sentence with commas or other appropriate punctuation, as in the examples above. If, on the other hand, the material is *essential* to the meaning of the sentence, no punctuation is necessary. Below is an example of essential material.

EXAMPLE: The short story *"Fire and Ice"* has a sad ending.

Note also that the terms *restrictive* and *nonrestrictive* are sometimes used instead of *essential* and *nonessential.* (See Chapter 27 for more about punctuating appositives.)

Appositive Phrases An *appositive phrase* is simply an appositive with one or more modifiers.

KEY CONCEPT An **appositive phrase** is a noun or pronoun with modifiers that is placed next to a noun or pronoun to add information and details. ■

The modifiers in an appositive phrase can be adjectives, adjective phrases, or other words that function as adjectives.

EXAMPLE: That desk, *the roll-top oak one,* is where I write.

▶ **KEY CONCEPT** Appositives and appositive phrases can add information to almost any noun or pronoun in a sentence. ■

WITH A SUBJECT:	Beverly Cleary, *winner of many awards for children's fiction*, writes insightfully about the lives of young people.
WITH A DIRECT OBJECT:	E. Annie Proulx won a prestigious commendation, *the Pulitzer Prize for Fiction.*
WITH AN INDIRECT OBJECT:	I gave Dean, *my younger brother*, my old desk.
WITH AN OBJECTIVE COMPLEMENT:	We stained it walnut—*a dark shade.*
WITH A PREDICATE NOMINATIVE:	Her new book is a mystery—*a real page-turner.*
WITH AN OBJECT OF A PREPOSITION:	The stack of books—*all mysteries*—looked inviting.

Appositives and appositive phrases can be compound.

EXAMPLES: Her writing—*novels and stories*—is acclaimed.

Elizabeth Bowen, *an Irish novelist and short-story writer*, was a perceptive observer of middle-class life.

Be alert for opportunities to use appositives and appositive phrases to rid your writing of unnecessary words. Often, two sentences can be combined into one by condensing the information from one sentence into an appositive.

TWO SENTENCES:	The professor is a world-renowned expert on medieval history. She lectured on the construction of castles during this period.
SENTENCE WITH APPOSITIVE PHRASE:	The professor, a world-renowned expert on medieval history, lectured on the construction of castles during this period.

⚙ Grammar and Style Tip

A nonrestrictive appositive can be set off with one or two dashes, especially when it is internally punctuated. Dashes give the information in apposition greater emphasis than commas do.

GRAMMAR IN
LITERATURE

from **The Story of an Hour**
Kate Chopin

Notice how the appositive phrase the unsolved mystery *adds information to explain the noun* love *in this paragraph.*

And yet she had loved him—sometimes. Often she had not. What did it matter! What could love, *the unsolved mystery,* count for in face of this possession of self-assertion which she suddenly recognized as the strongest impulse of her being!

▶ **Exercise 3** Identifying Appositives and Appositive Phrases
Write each appositive or appositive phrase. Write *none* if a sentence has no appositives.

EXAMPLE: My friends Jean and Bob are going with me.
ANSWER: Jean and Bob

1. Lillian Hellman, an American dramatist, was born in New Orleans.
2. In New York, Hellman attended two schools—New York and Columbia universities.
3. Her character development, a notable quality of her work, is world renowned.
4. Her subject matter—a condemnation of personal and social evils—is timeless.
5. She adapted two of her plays—*The Lark* and *Candide*—from French works.
6. She received the New York Drama Critic's Circle Award, a prestigious accolade, twice.
7. Most of her plays—thought-provoking dramas—have been made into movies.
8. Hellman, a playwright first, also wrote nonfiction.
9. Her autobiography, *An Unfinished Woman*, won her the National Book Award.
10. The second part of her autobiography, *Pentimento,* is a collection of prose portraits of herself and those whose lives influenced hers.

▶ **More Practice**

Grammar Exercise Workbook
• pp. 45–46
On-line Exercise Bank
• Section 19.1
  Go on-line:
  PHSchool.com
  Enter Web Code:
  efk-1102

interactive
Textbook

Get instant feedback! Exercise 3 is available on-line or on CD-ROM.

Exercise 4 Using Appositives and Appositive Phrases to Combine Sentences Turn each pair of sentences into a single sentence with an appositive or appositive phrase.

EXAMPLE: I will ask Beth. She is an excellent student.

ANSWER: I will ask Beth, an excellent student.

1. Margaret Mead is widely known for her studies of primitive societies. She was an American anthropologist.
2. Mead was born in Philadelphia and went to Barnard College. It is a school in New York City.
3. At Barnard, Mead was introduced to a new science devoted to the study of human culture. The science was anthropology.
4. She conducted studies in New Guinea, Samoa, and Bali. This was notable research.
5. The result of her field work was a tremendously successful book. It was *Coming of Age in Samoa.*
6. Her other interests were topics of several publications. They included child care and American character and culture.
7. In her analysis of American society, she focused on a particular issue. It was the problems of young people.
8. Most anthropologists spend their lives studying one primitive society, but Margaret Mead studied half a dozen. She was a brilliant anthropologist.
9. In addition to her books, Mead is known for her contributions to various government committees. Her books include *New Lives for Old, Male and Female,* and others.
10. Her clear style of writing and public speaking brought advanced ideas to the general public. The ideas were insights into our culture.

Exercise 5 Revising a Passage With Appositives Revise the following passage by combining sentences where appropriate, using appositives and appositive phrases.

     Diana Chang was born in 1934. She is an Asian poet, novelist, and translator. Although not born in China, she spent most of her childhood there. She returned to her birthplace after World War II. Her birthplace was the United States. She attended Barnard College. Barnard College is a college in New York City. Her works include *The Frontiers of Love* and *What Matisse Is After. The Frontiers of Love* is a novel. *What Matisse Is After* is a collection of poetry. Her poetry is spare and introspective. It shows the influence of traditional Asian verse forms. She also translated Asian writings into English.

More Practice

Grammar Exercise Workbook
• pp. 45–46
On-line Exercise Bank
• Section 19.1
  Go on-line:
  PHSchool.com
  Enter Web Code:
  efk-1102

interactive Textbook

Complete the exercises on-line! Exercises 4 and 5 are available on-line or on CD-ROM.

Gerund Phrases Gerunds accompanied by modifiers or complements are called *gerund phrases.*

▶ **KEY CONCEPT** A **gerund phrase** is a gerund with modifiers or a complement, all acting together as a noun. ■

EXAMPLES: *Low-priced, excellent boating* is available on Yellowstone Lake.

I suggested *lending her my boat.*

▶ **Exercise 15**   Identifying Gerunds and Gerund Phrases
Write each gerund or gerund phrase. Then, identify its function as a *subject, direct object, indirect object, object of a preposition, predicate nominative,* or *appositive.*
1. Preserving Yosemite National Park became a priority in the 1850's.
2. Because of Yosemite's sheer granite cliffs, climbing has become a favorite activity of the park's visitors.
3. Many consider rising before the sun to attack the cliffs.
4. Rock climbers enjoy ascending the monolith El Capitan.
5. Glacier Point is popular for providing spectacular views.
6. Walking along the Mercer River makes one feel at peace.
7. An impressive sight is the cascading of water over cliffs.
8. Giant sequoias invite a favorite tourist activity, taking photographs.
9. The eastern and western parts of the park were connected by rebuilding the Tioga Pass Road.
10. The original road facilitated mining in the area.

▶ **More Practice**

Grammar Exercise Workbook
• pp. 49–50
On-line Exercise Bank
• Section 19.2
  Go on-line:
  PHSchool.com
  Enter Web Code:
  efk-1102

Get instant feedback! Exercise 15 is available on-line or on CD-ROM.

◀ Critical Viewing Using at least one gerund phrase, explain why you think so many tourists are drawn to the Petrified Forest. **[Connect]**

Infinitives and Infinitive Phrases

A third type of verbal is the *infinitive*. Infinitives can function as three parts of speech.

▶ **KEY CONCEPT** An **infinitive** is a form of a verb that generally appears with the word *to* and acts as a noun, an adjective, or an adverb. ■

EXAMPLE: *To go* to Yellowstone is my dream. (noun)
I made the decision *to go.* (adjective)
I was excited *to go.* (adverb)

Remember that an infinitive is made up of *to* plus a verb. A prepositional phrase beginning with *to*, on the other hand, is made up of *to* plus a noun or pronoun.

INFINITIVES: to swim, to hike
PREPOSITIONAL PHRASES: to me, to the park

Sometimes, infinitives do not include the word *to*. After the verbs *dare, hear, help, let, make, please, see,* and *watch,* the *to* in an infinitive is usually understood rather than stated.

EXAMPLE: He didn't dare *move.*
I have never seen an eagle *soar.*

The Function of Infinitives in Sentences As the following chart shows, infinitives have many uses in sentences:

INFINITIVES USED AS NOUNS	
As a Subject:	*To move* his arm may cause further injury.
As a Direct Object:	With two weeks off, Nina planned *to relax.*
As a Predicate Nominative:	This summer, Joel's plan was *to travel.*
As an Appositive:	The suggestion, *to return,* was rejected.
INFINITIVES USED AS MODIFIERS	
As an Adjective:	The whole group displayed an ardent desire *to ski.*
As an Adverb:	Everyone thought the reef was beautiful *to see.*

Grammar and Style Tip

Many infinitive phrases and participial phrases can be moved around within a sentence as long as it is clear which word they modify. Place them in your sentences where you think they create the most desirable effects.

GRAMMAR IN
LITERATURE

from **Walden**
Henry David Thoreau

In the following passage, notice how the use of infinitive phrases (highlighted in blue) helps the writer express ideas clearly and adds variety to his sentences.

I went to the woods because I wished *to live deliberately, to front only the essential facts of life,* and see if I could not learn what it had *to teach,* and not, when I came to die, discover that I had not lived. I did not wish *to live what was not life,* living is so dear; nor did I wish *to practice resignation,* unless it was quite necessary.

Infinitive Phrases Like other verbals, infinitives can be expanded into phrases.

▶ **KEY CONCEPT** An **infinitive phrase** is an infinitive with modifiers, a complement, or a subject, all acting together as a single part of speech. ■

EXAMPLE: Mr. Wilkins decided *to walk briskly.*
We started *to pack our equipment.*
Dr. Rose left *to buy her son a mountain bike.*

▼ Critical Viewing
What would being in this scene inspire you to do? Use at least three infinitive phrases in your answer. **[Relate]**

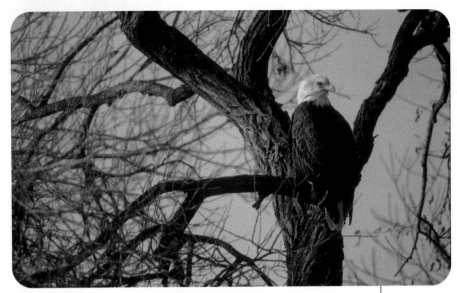

Exercise 16 Identifying Infinitives and Infinitive Phrases
Write each infinitive or infinitive phrase. Then, label each *subject, direct object, predicate nominative, appositive, adjective,* or *adverb.*

EXAMPLE: The bird is ready to fly.
ANSWER: to fly (adverb)

1. The goal of the National Park Service is to conserve natural scenery and wildlife.
2. National parks are designated by Congress to provide public recreation areas.
3. To maintain the parks takes a great deal of money.
4. Guides are happy to meet the needs of visitors.
5. Yellowstone was the first area to become a national park.
6. To hunt in the park is a serious offense.
7. We need to monitor fishing and mining carefully.
8. The name "Yellowstone" is thought to come from the Native Americans who named the area for its yellow cliffs.
9. Mount Washburn is a beautiful sight to see.
10. The Yellowstone River flows north to cross the valley.

Exercise 17 Writing With Infinitives Write five sentences about a local park or recreation area. Include in each sentence one of the following infinitives. Use at least one as a noun, one as an adjective, and one as an adverb.
1. to picnic
2. to climb
3. to hike
4. to play
5. to swim

▲ **Critical Viewing**
Which of the eagle's capabilities make it a fearsome bird of prey? Use infinitive phrases in your answer. **[Evaluate]**

▶ **More Practice**

Grammar Exercise Workbook
• pp. 51–52
On-line Exercise Bank
• Section 19.2
Go on-line:
PHSchool.com
Enter Web Code:
efk-1102

Complete the exercises on-line! Exercises 16 and 17 are available on-line or on CD-ROM.

Hands-on Grammar

Sentence Revision Cube

Practice using verbal phrases to expand and improve sentences by making and using a sentence revision cube. Using construction paper and a ruler, measure equal squares to create the shape below. Cut only the solid lines of the outside shape. Do not cut where the diagram shows dotted lines. Label your cube outline as shown. Fold on the dotted lines to form a cube. Use tape or glue to fasten the tabs to the inside of the cube and hold it together.

Begin with a simple sentence, such as *The eagle flies.* Toss the cube. Revise the sentence to include the type of verbal that is shown on the top of the cube. You may need to add other words so that the sentence makes sense.

For example, *The eagle flies* might become *The flying eagle soars above the trees.* Toss the cube again, revising the sentences with the type of verbal shown on top. Then, start with a new sentence.

Find It in Your Reading Toss the cube. Look through a short story to find a sentence containing the type of verbal shown. Continue tossing the cube until you have found at least one example of each type of verbal.

Find It in Your Writing Choose several sentences from a piece of writing in your portfolio. Toss the cube, and revise one of the sentences to include the type of verbal shown. Continue until you have used a verbal in each of the sentences.

Section Review

GRAMMAR EXERCISES 18–26

▶ **Exercise 18** Identifying Participles and Participial Phrases
Identify each participle or participial phrase. Then, label it *present, past,* or *perfect.*

1. Operating as a part of the U.S. Department of the Interior, the National Park Service administers more than twenty types of areas.
2. These areas are divided into three categories, indicating the main purpose of each area.
3. Forests, rivers, and wildlife preserves, protected for their natural splendor, fall under the "natural" category.
4. Areas preserved for their historic significance include battlefields and memorials.
5. Having determined a need to offer opportunities for sports and leisure activities, the National Park Service created several recreation areas.

▶ **Exercise 19** Punctuating Participial Phrases
Write the sentences, underlining each participial phrase. Set off any nonessential participial phrases with commas.

1. Glacier Bay having been established as a monument in 1925 was redesignated as a national park in 1980.
2. The park located in Alaska is noted for its tidewater glaciers and mountainous peaks.
3. Glaciers rising 200 feet above sea level form a skyline.
4. Named for the American explorer who first sighted it Muir Glacier is the most famous ice floe in the bay.
5. We learned that the glacier is fed by a stream of ice flowing down the slopes of Mount Fairweather.

6. Forming a barrier across the head of the bay Muir Glacier ranges from 135 to 210 feet high.
7. Most of the glacier extending 760 feet below the water's surface is not visible.
8. Towering above the glaciers Mount Fairweather's peak reaches an altitude of 15,300 feet.
9. This peak forming part of the St. Elias range is also the highest point in the Canadian province of British Columbia.
10. Scientists researching the formation and movement of glaciers consider Glacier Bay an important resource.

▶ **Exercise 20** Identifying Gerunds and Gerund Phrases
Write each gerund or gerund phrase. Then, identify its function as a *subject, direct object, indirect object, object of a preposition, predicate nominative,* or *appositive.*

1. A difficult problem in Death Valley is finding water.
2. Many settlers struggled with crossing the valley's vast desert.
3. Searching for gold caused only one miner to perish in Death Valley.
4. The valley later became a center of mining for borax.
5. Hiking is now Death Valley's greatest tourist activity.
6. Disturbing the delicate valley flora and fauna is not allowed under park rules.
7. Death Valley is unique for containing the lowest, driest, and hottest point in the Western Hemisphere.
8. In 1913, the valley's temperature made history by climbing to 134 degrees Fahrenheit.
9. When you visit, avoid hiking in the midday sun.
10. Because of the heat, frequent resting is advised.

▶ **Exercise 21** Identifying Infinitives and Infinitive Phrases Write each infinitive or infinitive phrase. Then, label it *subject, direct object, predicate nominative, appositive, adjective,* or *adverb.*

1. In 1933, legislation was passed to establish the Civilian Conservation Corps.
2. The corps hired unemployed young men to labor on national lands.
3. Because of the Depression, these men needed to work.
4. Many were sent to Death Valley to prepare the park for the American public.
5. Some 1,200 men worked to finish the Death Valley Monument.
6. Their first task was to build barracks and other permanent structures.
7. Next, they began to install water and telephone lines.
8. These men helped make the park what it is today.
9. Many of the men in the corps were the first to go to war in 1942.
10. To see their work, visit the campgrounds in Death Valley.

▶ **Exercise 22** Identifying All Kinds of Verbal Phrases Identify each participial phrase, gerund phrase, or infinitive phrase in the following sentences.

1. A preserve in South Florida containing marine, terrestrial, and amphibious life is Biscayne National Park.
2. Covering 95 percent of the park's area, water is everywhere.
3. Consequently, many of the area's activities include boating.
4. Most visitors like to engage in these activities before the heat of midday.
5. Embracing 180,000 acres, Biscayne is a protectorate for living coral reefs.
6. The park has the simple beauty of a child's drawing.
7. Biscayne National Park shows America's commitment to protecting rare subtropical environments.

8. The waters, teeming with life, are clear.
9. The coral reef provides a colorful habitat for tropical fish to populate.
10. A snorkler can spend hours drifting lazily in the waters above the reef.

▶ **Exercise 23** Using Verbal Phrases to Combine Sentences Using infinitive, gerund, and participial phrases, combine each pair of sentences into one.

1. Ghost towns were once boom towns. Now they are deserted.
2. There are a number of ghost towns in Death Valley. All were built around the mining industry.
3. When you visit these ghost towns, treat them like museums. Do not disturb anything.
4. Ballarat was named after an Australian gold camp. It was home to 400 people in 1898.
5. Water was carried into the town of Greenwater. Water sold for fifteen dollars a barrel.

▶ **Exercise 24** Find It in Your Reading Find an example of a gerund in the excerpt from *Walden* on page 309.

▶ **Exercise 25** Find It in Your Writing In a piece of writing from your portfolio, find one example of a participle, a gerund, and an infinitive. If you cannot find one, challenge yourself to add at least one of each type of verbal to your writing.

▶ **Exercise 26** Writing Application Write a description of your favorite vacation spot for a travel magazine. Be sure to vary your sentences with at least one participial phrase, one gerund or gerund phrase, and one infinitive or infinitive phrase. Underline and label each.

Clauses

Whereas a phrase is a group of words without a subject and a verb, a clause does include a subject and a verb.

▶ **KEY CONCEPT** A **clause** is a group of words with its own subject and verb. ■

There are two basic kinds of clauses: *independent clauses* and *subordinate clauses*.

Independent and Subordinate Clauses

▶ **KEY CONCEPTS** An **independent clause** can stand by itself as a complete sentence. A **subordinate clause**, although it has a subject and a verb, cannot stand by itself as a complete sentence; it can only be part of a sentence. ■

Every complete sentence must contain an independent clause. The clause can either stand by itself or be connected to one or more other independent clauses or subordinate clauses.

INDEPENDENT CLAUSE:	Robert E. Peary was an explorer.
TWO INDEPENDENT CLAUSES:	Peary reached the North Pole in 1909, but this claim is still in dispute.
INDEPENDENT CLAUSE:	He reached the pole on a sled
SUBORDINATE CLAUSE:	that was pulled by dogs.

Like phrases, subordinate clauses function in sentences as single parts of speech: as adjectives, as adverbs, or as nouns. This section will describe these three uses of subordinate clauses.

▶ **Exercise 27** Distinguishing Clauses Identify each of the following clauses as *independent* or *subordinate*.
1. Icy winds blew.
2. He shivered.
3. Because night was falling as was the temperature.
4. Which caused him to make his way to shelter.
5. Please stay warm and dry!

Theme: Arctic Regions

In this section, you will learn how to recognize and use adjective, adverb, and noun clauses. The examples and exercises in this section are about Arctic regions.

Cross-Curricular Connection: Social Studies

▶ Critical Viewing Even an independent person needs to be dependent on someone else when exploring frozen wastelands. Explain this statement, using sentences with more than one clause. [**Make a Judgment**]

Adjective Clauses

One way to describe, limit, or qualify any noun or pronoun in a sentence is to use an *adjective clause.*

KEY CONCEPT An **adjective clause** is a subordinate clause that modifies a noun or pronoun by telling *what kind* or *which one.* ■

An adjective clause is usually connected to the word it modifies by one of the relative pronouns (*that, which, who, whom,* or *whose*). Sometimes, it is connected by a relative adverb (such as *after, before, since, when, where,* or *why*).

EXAMPLES: Arctic winters, *which are long and cold,* are severe.

The Arctic is a region *where life is difficult.*

Essential and Nonessential Adjective Clauses Like participial and appositive phrases, adjective clauses are set off by punctuation only when they are not essential to the meaning of a sentence.

KEY CONCEPTS An adjective clause that is not essential to the basic meaning of a sentence is set off by commas. An essential adjective clause is not set off by commas. ■

NONESSENTIAL ADJECTIVE CLAUSE: The ship, *which was a nuclear submarine,* became the first vessel to pass beneath the North Pole.

ESSENTIAL ADJECTIVE CLAUSE: The first vessel *that passed beneath the North Pole* was a nuclear submarine.

By using either a nonessential or an essential adjective clause, you can often combine the ideas from two sentences into one, thus showing the relationship between the ideas.

TWO SENTENCES: The *Arktika* was the first surface ship to crack through the Arctic ice pack. It was a Soviet icebreaker.

COMBINED WITH ADJECTIVE CLAUSE: The *Arktika, which was a Soviet icebreaker,* was the first surface ship to crack the Arctic ice pack.

Introductory Words in Adjective Clauses Relative pronouns and relative adverbs not only introduce adjective clauses, but also function within the subordinate clause.

> **KEY CONCEPT** A **relative pronoun** or **relative adverb** (1) connects the adjective clause to the modified word and (2) acts within the clause as a subject, direct object, or other sentence part. ■

The following chart shows the various roles of relative pronouns in adjective clauses.

THE USES OF RELATIVE PRONOUNS WITHIN THE CLAUSE

As a Subject

Sentence: The part of Alaska *that is within the Arctic Circle* is cold most of the year.

Clause: that is within the Arctic Circle

As a Direct Object

Sentence: The explorer *whom I met last year* has never been to the North Pole.
Reworded clause: I met whom last year

As the Object of a Preposition

Sentence: The climate is one *in which little foliage can grow.*

Reworded clause: little foliage can grow in which

As an Adjective

Sentence: I saw a dog *whose sled left without him.*

Clause: whose sled left without him

Note About Understood Relative Pronouns: Sometimes, a relative pronoun is understood rather than expressed. It, nevertheless, still functions in the sentence.

EXAMPLES: The dog sled [*that*] Ted *drove* won the race.

Few Arctic explorers [*whom*] I *know* live in warm climates.

Relative adverbs can act only as adverbs within a clause.

Grammar and Style Tip

The relative pronouns *who, which,* and *that* do not have different singular and plural forms. When one of these pronouns serves as a subject, its verb should agree with the noun or other pronoun to which the relative pronoun refers (its antecedent).

THE USE OF RELATIVE ADVERBS WITHIN THE CLAUSE

Sentence: The temperature will plummet in the hours *after the sun sets.*

Reworded clause: the <u>sun</u> <u>sets</u> after

Exercise 28 Identifying Adjective Clauses Write the adjective clause in each sentence, circling the relative pronoun or relative adverb. Then, label the use of the circled word within the clause *subject, direct object, object of a preposition, adjective,* or *adverb.*

EXAMPLE: Arctic winds batter ships that sail the Northwest Passage.

ANSWER: (that) sail the Northwest Passage (subject)

1. The severe cold for which the Arctic is known does not drive away all plant and animal life.
2. Coastal regions, where climate is moderated by warmer ocean waters, have abundant flora and fauna.
3. Spring brings a resurgence of life to the Arctic, which is home to more than 400 species of plants.
4. A multitude of animals, whose names may be familiar to you, also survive in the Arctic region.
5. These animals have extra insulation that keeps them warm in colder months.

More Practice

Grammar Exercise Workbook
• pp. 53–54
On-line Exercise Bank
• Section 19.3
  Go on-line:
  PHSchool.com
  Enter Web Code:
  efk-1102

interactive Textbook

Get instant feedback! Exercise 28 is available on-line or on CD-ROM.

◄ Critical Viewing
Use a sentence containing an adjective clause to explain for whom or what this dog might be waiting. **[Infer]**

Adverb Clauses

Subordinate clauses may also serve as adverbs in sentences.

> **KEY CONCEPT** **Adverb clauses** modify verbs, adjectives, adverbs, or verbals by telling *where, when, in what way, to what extent, under what condition,* or *why.* ■

Each adverb clause contains a subject and a verb and is introduced by a subordinating conjunction, such as *although, because, if, where,* or *while.* (See Chapter 17 for a more complete list.) An adverb clause can modify any word that an adverb can modify.

Spelling Tip

In formal writing, always spell out the word *because.* The shortened form *'cause* is only used in informal situations.

ADVERB CLAUSES	
Modified Words	**Examples**
Verb:	The Yukon entered Canada's confederation *after a gold rush brought 100,000 people to the territory.*
Adjective:	The miner's children were nervous *whenever he entered a tunnel.*
Adverb:	Today's dig lasted longer *than the one yesterday.*
Participle:	The miners, cheering *whenever someone made a strike,* were excited.
Gerund:	Digging *wherever miners thought there was gold* has left the Yukon full of old mines.
Infinitive:	The tired miners wanted to relax *after the workday ended.*

Some adverb clauses are *elliptical,* especially those beginning with *as* or *than.* In an elliptical adverb clause, the verb or both the subject and verb are not stated but are understood. Nevertheless, they still function to make the clause complete.

VERB UNDERSTOOD: I am taller *than he* [is].

SUBJECT AND   The Yukon has almost as many rural
VERB UNDERSTOOD: inhabitants *as* [it has] *urban inhabitants.*

GRAMMAR IN LITERATURE

from **To Build a Fire**
Jack London

In the following selection, Jack London uses subordinate clauses to add details and to show the relationship between ideas in his sentences. The adverb clause is shown in blue; the adjective clause is shown in red.

Day had broken cold and gray, exceedingly cold and gray, when the man turned aside from the main Yukon trail and climbed the high earth-bank, where a dim and little-traveled trail led eastward through the fat spruce timberland.

Exercise 29 Identifying Adverb Clauses Identify the adverb clause in each sentence. Then, indicate whether it modifies a *verb*, an *adjective*, an *adverb*, or a *verbal*.

EXAMPLE: The Yukon was called Rupert's Land until its name was changed to the Northwest Territories in 1868.

ANSWER: until its name was changed to the Northwest Territories in 1868 (verb)

1. The Yukon is located in Canada's northwest corner, where Canada borders Alaska.
2. Before the territory was known as the Yukon, it had two other names.
3. Changing its name again as the nineteenth century ended, the Yukon officially became part of Canada in 1898.
4. Whereas the vast majority of the area is landlocked, its northernmost point borders on the Beaufort Sea.
5. The territory's emblematic stone, blue lazulite, looks bluer than the sky does on a clear summer day.
6. The capital city, Whitehorse, sits near the Yukon River, where the river becomes navigable.
7. Whitehorse replaced Dawson City as the capital after the Gold Rush began.
8. While it is the highest point in Canada, Yukon's Mt. Logan is only the second-highest peak in North America.
9. Although we find permafrost in many areas of the Yukon, it appears mostly in its northern regions.
10. To visit the Yukon after winter has set in is a frigid experience.

More Practice

Grammar Exercise Workbook
• pp. 55–56
On-line Exercise Bank
• Section 19.3
  Go on-line:
  PHSchool.com
  Enter Web Code:
  efk-1102

Get instant feedback! Exercise 29 is available on-line or on CD-ROM.

► **Exercise 30** Recognizing Elliptical Clauses Write the elliptical adverb clause in each sentence, adding the understood words, in parentheses, where they belong.

EXAMPLE: The city of Whitehorse has many more people than Dawson City.

ANSWER: than Dawson City (does)

1. The Yukon has a smaller land area than most other Canadian provinces.
2. The territory has as many forested areas as unforested.
3. The Yukon has a lower population density than the rest of Canada.
4. Its native peoples make up a greater percentage of the Yukon's population than in other provinces.
5. Its population under age nineteen is ten times larger than its over-sixty-five population.

Noun Clauses

Noun clauses can perform any function in a sentence that a single-word noun can.

► **KEY CONCEPT** A **noun clause** is a subordinate clause that acts as a noun. ■

The following chart shows the various functions of noun clauses.

USES OF NOUN CLAUSES IN SENTENCES	
Functions in Sentences	**Examples**
Subject:	*Whoever travels the Pelly River* follows in the footsteps of the explorer Robert Campbell.
Direct Object:	You must pack *whatever you will need.*
Indirect Object:	You should give *whoever waits at the camp* a copy of your route.
Object of a Preposition:	Robert Campbell settled trading camps in *whatever regions the Hudson's Bay Company sent him.*
Predicate Nominative:	At 40, Campbell's most notable achievement was *that he established Fort Selkirk.*

KEY CONCEPTS Noun clauses frequently begin with *that,
which, who, whom,* or *whose*. Other words that can begin
noun clauses are *how, if, what, whatever, when, where,
whether, whichever, whoever,* or *whomever*. In addition to introducing a noun clause, these words generally serve a function
within the clause. ■

**Grammar
and Style Tip**

That and *which* are
frequently confused.
An easy way to know
when to use each one
properly is to remem-
ber this distinction:
That is not preceded
by a comma when it
begins a clause; *which*
is **always** preceded by
a comma when it
begins a clause.

SOME USES OF INTRODUCTORY WORDS IN NOUN CLAUSES	
Functions in Sentences	**Examples**
Adjective:	John Bell chose *which tributary to explore.*
Adverb:	We want to know *how we should dress.*
Subject:	I want the recipe from *whoever* [S] *made that delicious casserole.*
Direct Object:	McGill University's Redpath Museum, *which* [DO] *Sir John William Dawson founded,* specializes in botany and geology.
No Function:	The doctor determined *that she had the measles.*

When *that* has no function in the noun clause other than as
an introductory word, it is often omitted.

EXAMPLE: I know [*that*] *you tried your best.*

Because some of the words that introduce noun clauses
also introduce adjective and adverb clauses, check the function of the clause in the sentence to determine its type. You
can also try substituting the words *it,
you, fact,* or *thing* for the clause. If the
sentence retains its smoothness, you
probably replaced a noun clause.

NOUN CLAUSE: I knew *that this would
                    happen.*

SUBSTITUTION: I knew it.

▼ Critical Viewing
What do you think
of the work of the
photographer who
took this picture? In
your answer, use at
least one noun
clause beginning
with *whoever.*
[Evaluate]

Exercise 31 Identifying Noun Clauses Write the noun clause in each sentence, indicating whether the clause is functioning as a *subject, direct object, indirect object, object of a preposition, predicate nominative,* or *appositive.*

EXAMPLE: Explorers discovered where the Klondike River flows into the Yukon River.

ANSWER: where the Klondike River flows into the Yukon River (direct object)

1. Whoever travels on the Yukon River in winter must account for the cold temperatures.
2. The miners believed that they could find gold quickly.
3. A frenzy of interest was caused by whoever found gold in Bonanza Creek.
4. Hopeful miners occupied whatever claims they could find.
5. Whoever heard of the Klondike gold strike traveled north, hoping to become rich.
6. Many American miners were unprepared for how difficult the Klondike's rugged terrain would be for them.
7. Whoever used the Yukon River as the main access route in the winter was caught in the ice and had to be rescued.
8. Among the thousands of miners who went to the Klondike, a large percentage were disappointed by how little gold they found.
9. Dreams of gold along the Yukon River gave whoever had a good imagination a reason to travel.
10. Often, their only possessions were whatever they could carry on their backs.

▲ **Critical Viewing** Use the noun clause *what I wouldn't like* in a sentence about this picture. **[Relate]**

Exercise 32 Classifying Subordinate Clauses Identify each underlined clause as *adjective, adverb,* or *noun.*

EXAMPLE:　　Sled dogs love to run, <u>which they have been bred for thousands of years to do.</u> (adverb)

1. The indigenous peoples <u>who live in the far north</u> adapted sled dogs for use as transportation.
2. They used dogs <u>whenever they traveled.</u>
3. Early expeditions <u>that settled colder northern regions</u> would have been impossible without sled dogs.
4. <u>Even though modes of travel have advanced,</u> sled dogs still offer reliable transportation in subzero climes.
5. Sled-dog racing has evolved into a sport <u>that is popular in colder parts of the world.</u>
6. <u>Although small local races were held in the nineteenth century,</u> a major sled-dog race was not staged until 1908.
7. <u>Whoever wants to enter a sled-dog race today</u> has a choice of more than 3,000 competitions.
8. The number of competitions has increased every year <u>since sled dog-racing was organized.</u>
9. The International Federation of Sled Dog Sports, <u>which governs racing,</u> was formed in 1986 to promote the sport.
10. <u>Because its efforts were effective,</u> sled-dog racing is being considered for inclusion in winter athletic festivals.

Exercise 33 Using Subordinate Clauses to Combine Sentences Combine each pair of sentences by changing one of the sentences into the type of clause indicated. Underline each subordinate clause.

EXAMPLE:　　*Combine using an adjective clause:* We saw the landscape. It was breathtaking.

ANSWER:　　The landscape <u>that we saw</u> was breathtaking.

1. *Combine using an adjective clause:* Whitehorse was a terminal on the White Pass and Yukon Railway. The city is on the Alaska Highway.
2. *Combine using an adverb clause:* Whitehorse was a center of copper mining and fur trapping. Then, it became the capital of the Yukon Territory.
3. *Combine using a noun clause:* Whitehorse was important in the Yukon's history. Many people don't know this.
4. *Combine using an adjective clause:* The city numbers approximately 23,000 people. It is large for the territory.
5. *Combine using an adverb clause:* An economic lull hit Whitehorse in the mid-1980's. The discovery of the world's largest tungsten reserve at Mae Pass revitalized the city.

More Practice

Grammar Exercise Workbook
• pp. 57–58
On-line Exercise Bank
• Section 19.3
　Go on-line:
　PHSchool.com
　Enter Web Code:
　efk-1102

Complete the exercises on-line! Exercises 31, 32, and 33 are available on-line or on CD-ROM.

Section Review

GRAMMAR EXERCISES 34–42

Exercise 34 Identifying Adjective Clauses Write the adjective clause in each sentence, and circle the relative pronoun or relative adverb. Then, label the use of the circled word within the clause *subject, direct object, object of a preposition, adjective,* or *adverb.*

1. Europeans who were interested in mapping new regions first explored the Arctic in the sixteenth century.
2. The Englishman John Davis, after whom the Davis Strait is named, trekked to Sanderson's Hope in 1587.
3. Britain, whose explorers were among the most persistent, continued to explore the Arctic for the next 400 years.
4. In Russia, where the Arctic covers the northern part of the country, exploration began in earnest in the 1700's.
5. Much of the Arctic had a scattered, indigenous population, whom explorers sometimes encountered.

Exercise 35 Identifying Adverb Clauses Write the adverb clause in each sentence. Then, indicate whether it modifies a verb, an adjective, an adverb, or a verbal.

1. Although people live in the Arctic, they are still limited by its harsh climate.
2. Food cultivation and animal husbandry are more difficult there than they are in warmer climates.
3. However, reindeer herding is widespread because the animal tolerates cold well.
4. Sheep are raised in southwestern Greenland and in Iceland because the climate is not as frigid.
5. Wherever the environment will allow it, dairy farming supplies milk products to nearby communities.

Exercise 36 Recognizing Elliptical Clauses Write the elliptical adverb clause in each sentence, adding the understood words, in parentheses, where they belong.

1. Sled dogs, such as Alaskan huskies, have much thicker coats than most dogs.
2. In fact, the fur of Alaskan huskies is twice as thick as that of breeds from warmer climates.
3. Their dense fur allows them to endure weather as cold as the Arctic's for long periods.
4. As a breed, sled dogs also tend to have broader feet than those of most other breeds.
5. Their broader feet help them bound through the snow as quickly as a snowshoe hare.

Exercise 37 Recognizing and Identifying Noun Clauses Write the noun clause or clauses in each of the following sentences. Then, indicate whether the clause is functioning as a *subject, direct object, indirect object, object of a preposition, predicate nominative,* or *appositive.*

1. The question of how you should train a sled dog is a difficult one.
2. Whoever trains a sled dog should have experience.
3. Adequate knowledge of how one should handle the animal comes from years of experience.
4. Veteran trainers offer a great deal of love and discipline to whatever dogs they train.
5. These experts say that the best time to begin a sled dog's training is when the dog is still a puppy.

Exercise 38 Identifying and Classifying Subordinate Clauses Write the subordinate clause in each sentence, and indicate whether the clause is functioning as an *adjective*, an *adverb*, or a *noun*.

1. White Pass, which is a hazardous mountain trail, was blazed by gold prospectors going to the Klondike in 1897.
2. When news of gold spread, the prospectors sought and established an alternative route to the heavily traveled Chilkoot Pass.
3. To visit White Pass, one must travel to where Alaska and the Canadian province of British Columbia meet.
4. Whoever took the new, treacherous trail had to be prepared for the worst.
5. Many prospectors perished even though they were prepared.
6. Between 1898 and 1900, the White Pass and Yukon Railway was built to traverse the route, which is at an altitude of nearly 3,000 feet.
7. After it was completed, the railway provided safe transportation from the Pacific tidewater to the Yukon Valley.
8. Travel from Skagway to White Horse, the two towns between which the railway ran, was made much more comfortable, too.
9. The railway, which lasted more than eighty years, suspended full-time service in 1982.
10. Even though it no longer runs, the railroad is remembered as an important part of the settlement of the Yukon region.

Exercise 39 Using Subordinate Clauses to Combine Sentences Combine each pair of sentences by changing one of the sentences into the type of clause indicated.

1. *Combine using an adjective clause:* Mushers are individuals. They drive and lead sled-dog racing teams.

2. *Combine using an adverb clause:* Some mushers compete using a sled, and others use skis. There are two racing classes.
3. *Combine using an adverb clause:* Mushers have to maintain control of their team. Dogs are swift animals.
4. *Combine using an adjective clause:* The best mushers are excellent dog handlers. These mushers win races often.
5. *Combine using a noun clause:* What is the best way to keep control of a team? This is an important question for mushers.

Exercise 40 Find It in Your Reading Identify the word modified by each subordinate clause in the excerpt from "To Build a Fire" on page 319.

Exercise 41 Find It in Your Writing Look through your writing portfolio. Find one example of an adjective clause and one of an adverb clause. If you cannot find one, challenge yourself to improve your writing by adding one of each.

Exercise 42 Writing Application Write five original sentences about winter weather in your area of the country using the type of clause indicated. Underline all clauses.
1. Write a sentence using a nonessential adjective clause.
2. Write a sentence using an essential adjective clause.
3. Write a sentence using an adverb clause that modifies a verb.
4. Write a sentence using an elliptical adverb clause.
5. Write a sentence using a noun clause that functions in a sentence as the subject.

Sentences Classified by Structure

Sentences are often classified according to the kind and number of clauses they contain.

The Four Structures of Sentences

The structure of a sentence depends on the kind and number of clauses it contains. The following rules define the four different sentence structures:

KEY CONCEPTS A **simple sentence** consists of a single independent clause. ■

A **compound sentence** consists of two or more independent clauses joined by a comma and a coordinating conjunction or by a semicolon. ■

A **complex sentence** consists of one independent—or main—clause and one or more subordinate clauses. ■

A **compound-complex sentence** consists of two or more independent clauses and one or more subordinate clauses. ■

As you study the examples in the chart on the next page, notice that simple sentences can contain compound subjects, compound verbs, or both. Notice also that a subordinate clause may fall between the parts of another clause or even within another clause.

FOUR STRUCTURES OF SENTENCES	
Functions in Sentences	**Examples**
Simple Sentences:	Ellis Island <u>was</u> the first stop for many immigrants to America. Ed and I <u>checked</u> and <u>rechecked</u> our answer.
Compound Sentences:	My <u>brother</u> <u>bought</u> some stamps yesterday, and <u>he</u> <u>mounted</u> them in his stamp collection. The <u>Statue of Liberty</u> and <u>Ellis Island</u> <u>were</u> the subject of a border dispute between New York and New Jersey; both <u>monuments</u> <u>rest</u> on islands between the two states.
Complex Sentences:	main clause The <u>Statue of Liberty–Ellis Island Foundation</u> subordinate clause <u>is</u> a nonprofit organization <u>that</u> <u>was founded</u> in 1982. main subordinate clause main clause Our <u>band</u>, <u>which</u> <u>won</u> the trophy, <u>will perform</u> subordinate clause after the <u>game</u> <u>is</u> over. main clause The largest historic <u>restoration</u> in the United main clause subordinate clause States <u>was performed</u> by <u>whoever</u> <u>restored</u> subordinate clause the main <u>building</u> on Ellis Island.
Compound-Complex Sentences:	independent clause <u>I</u> <u>ran</u> down the path to the spot subordinate clause independent clause where <u>it</u> <u>divides</u>, and then <u>I</u> <u>turned</u> back. subordinate clause independent clause After <u>it</u> <u>was restored</u>, <u>Ellis Island</u> <u>received</u> independent clause a $20 million endowment, but charitable independent subordinate clause <u>contributions</u>, <u>which</u> <u>come</u> from many independent clause sources, <u>are</u> still <u>being accepted</u>.

💡 **Spelling Tip**

The adjectives *historic* and *historical* are used differently. *Historic* always modifies something that is important in history. *Historical* always modifies something that occurred in the past, whether or not it was important.

💿 **Technology Tip**

The grammar checker on most of the word-processing programs may flag perfectly correct compound-complex sentences as run-ons because they are long. Rely on your own sense of grammar to revise and correct your writing.

▶ **KEY CONCEPT** Analyzing the structure of sentences can help you to understand long, involved sentences when you read. It can also help you check the logic and flow of your own ideas when you write. ■

As you could see in the preceding chart, independent clauses in complex sentences are often called *main clauses* to distinguish them from subordinate clauses. The subject and verb of a main clause, in turn, are usually called the *subject of the sentence* and the *main verb* to distinguish them from other subjects and verbs.

▶ **Exercise 43** **Identifying the Four Structures of Sentences** Identify each sentence as *simple, compound, complex,* or *compound-complex.*

EXAMPLE: People have emigrated from their original homelands.

ANSWER: simple

1. Angel Island is the largest island in San Francisco Bay.
2. In 1905, an immigration station was constructed in the China Cove area of the island.
3. Although it was the subject of some public controversy, the station officially opened in 1910.
4. A flood of European immigrants was expected in California when the Panama Canal opened, but the outbreak of World War I curtailed the expected rush of Europeans.
5. Instead, the majority of foreigners who immigrated to America through Angel Island came from Asia.
6. Like many immigrants, the Asians were trying to escape the hardships of their native lands, but they faced further difficulties at Angel Island.
7. The Europeans who arrived in the United States through Ellis Island were processed within a matter of hours or days; on Angel Island, Asian immigrants were detained for weeks or even months.
8. Laws, such as the Chinese Exclusion Act of 1882, restricted Asian immigration to America, and Angel Island effectively became a detention center.
9. Although these laws had an impact on all Asians, those most affected were the Chinese, who comprised more than 70 percent of the immigrants detained on Angel Island.
10. The island was a U.S. Army base from 1863 to 1946, but it became a missile radar site in 1952.

▶ **More Practice**

Grammar Exercise Workbook
• pp. 59–60
On-line Exercise Bank
• Section 19.4
  Go on-line:
  PHSchool.com
  Enter Web Code:
  efk-1102

Get instant feedback! Exercise 43 is available on-line or on CD-ROM.

✓ **Spelling Tip**

The nouns *emigrant* and *immigrant* are often confused, but they are not interchangeable. An *emigrant* is one who moves *from* a country. An *immigrant* is one who moves *to* a country.

Section Review

GRAMMAR EXERCISES 44–49

Exercise 44 **Identifying the Four Structures of Sentences** Identify each sentence as *simple, compound, complex,* or *compound-complex.*

1. Beginning with the Immigration Act of 1891, the United States federal government assumed the responsibility of immigration.
2. Prior to the Immigration Act, America encouraged open immigration because new immigrants strengthened the young, relatively unpopulated nation.
3. However, certain states began to pass their own immigration laws after the Civil War, and the Supreme Court was forced to step in.
4. In 1875, the Court ruled that the regulation of immigration is the responsibility of the federal government.
5. Enforcing immigration laws, which included processing all immigrants seeking admission to America, was a new legal concept, and it would take the Immigration Service a decade to implement its national policy.

Exercise 45 **Revising Sentences With Subordinate Clauses** Create complex sentences by adding a subordinate clause to the following independent clauses.

1. My friend's grandparents were not born in the United States.
2. They immigrated to America in 1920.
3. They settled in New York.
4. My friend's parents were raised in the United States.
5. Both my friend and I would enjoy visiting Ellis Island.

Exercise 46 **Revising a Passage by Varying Sentence Structure** Revise the following passage to use a variety of sentence structures.

The Immigration and Naturalization Service has altered its focus in recent years. It has also undergone tremendous growth. World migration patterns have changed. Travel has been made easier for business and pleasure by the airplane. Controlling illegal immigration became a primary concern. The Immigration and Naturalization Service (INS) needed more employees. The INS work force numbered approximately 8,000 from World War II through the late 1970's. The INS now includes more than 30,000 employees. There are thirty-six INS districts at home and abroad.

Exercise 47 **Find It in Your Reading** Examine a newspaper or magazine article to find examples of all four sentence structures.

Exercise 48 **Find It in Your Writing** Review one of your own compositions. Revise and improve the work by varying your sentence structure and using subordinate clauses. Be sure that all four types of sentence structure are represented.

Exercise 49 **Writing Application** Write a brief description of a historic landmark in your area. Use each type of sentence structure at least once.

▲ **Critical Viewing**
What types of words connect sentences in the same way that this bridge connects Philadelphia to towns on the other side of the Delaware River? **[Connect]**

When you first begin to write, one of the first things you learn is how to write a complete sentence. As you develop as a writer, it is essential to continue to improve your use of sentences by learning how to vary them and how to avoid sentence errors. This chapter looks at the different types of sentences and provides a variety of strategies to help you use sentences more effectively and avoid problems in your writing.

Exercise 10 Combining Sentences Using Subordinate Clauses Using the subordinating conjunction given in parentheses, combine the following pairs of sentences. Sentences should also be revised for clarity.

EXAMPLE: The nation won its independence. Then, it had to establish its own financial system. (after)

ANSWER: After the nation won its independence, it had to establish its own financial system.

1. The establishment of one unified currency and financial system was necessary. The nation was in debt, and some states were even bankrupt. (because)
2. One group of people greatly opposed establishing a federal bank. The First Bank of the United States was established in 1791 in Philadelphia. (although)
3. The bank had a twenty-year charter. It could act as a commercial and central bank during this time. (while)
4. The bank was built as a symbol of democracy. Its neoclassical design recalls the democracy of ancient Greece. (because)
5. The First Bank functioned successfully. The charter was not renewed in 1811. (even though)

▲ **Critical Viewing**
Write a sentence with a subordinate clause in which you compare the First Bank (shown here) with a bank with which you are familiar. **[Compare]**

Exercise 11 Combining Sentences Using Subordinating Conjunctions Combine each pair of sentences using a subordinating conjunction. Sentences should also be revised for clarity.

EXAMPLE: Pennsylvania's economy is greatly dependent on service industries. Agriculture also plays a role.

ANSWER: Although Pennsylvania's economy is greatly dependent on service industries, agriculture is also important.

1. Pennsylvania ranks fourth in national coal production. Mining comprises one percent of its gross national product.
2. Pennsylvania is rich in natural resources. It has many mining communities.
3. You are using sand, gravel, limestone, or natural gas. Remember that they may have come from Pennsylvania.
4. Milk is the state's leading agricultural product. Dairy farms flourish in eastern Pennsylvania.
5. The leading crops are corn and hay. Much of it is not sold but used to feed the state's beef and dairy cattle.

▶ **KEY CONCEPT** Sentences can be combined by changing one of them into a phrase. ■

When you are combining sentences in which one of the sentences just adds detail, change one of the sentences into a phrase.

EXAMPLE: The Pittsburgh Pirates play tomorrow. They play the Philadelphia Phillies.

COMBINED BY The Pittsburgh Pirates play against the
USING A PHRASE: Philadelphia Phillies tomorrow.

▶ **Exercise 12** Combining Sentences Using Phrases
Combine the following pairs of sentences by changing one into a phrase. Sentences should also be revised for clarity.

1. Native Americans lived in the Pennsylvania region for hundreds of years before European explorers came. These Native Americans, such as the Algonquian and Iroquoian tribes, lived in the Pennsylvania region.
2. In 1609, Henry Hudson sailed into the Delaware Bay. He was an English explorer.
3. Hudson was trying to find a trade route to the Far East. He was trying to find it for the Dutch East India Company.
4. After Hudson left the area, the Dutch sent someone else. They sent explorer Cornelius Hendricksen.
5. Hendricksen sailed farther up the Delaware River. He sailed all the way to what is now Philadelphia.
6. In 1643, the Swedes made the first permanent settlement in the region. They called it New Sweden.
7. In 1655, Peter Stuyvesant, leading Dutch troops, captured New Sweden. He was the last Dutch governor of New Netherland.
8. The English captured the region. They captured it in 1664.
9. A nobleman controlled the region until 1681, when it was granted to William Penn. The Duke of York controlled it.
10. The region derived its name from two sources. The sources were *Penn*, in honor of William Penn's father, and *sylvania*, which means "woods."

▶ **More Practice**
Grammar Exercise
Workbook
• pp. 63–64
On-line Exercise Bank
• Section 20.2
Go on-line:
PHSchool.com
Enter Web Code:
efk-1102

ínteractive Textbook

Complete the exercise on-line! Exercise 12 is available on-line or on CD-ROM.

▼ **Critical Viewing**
In what time period do you think this artwork of the Delaware River and Philadelphia was created? Why? **[Speculate]**

Hands-on Grammar

Clip-on Sentence Combiner

Practice using phrases to combine sentences by using a sentence combining clip-on activity. Write each of the following sentences on a strip of colored paper.

> The trip to Philadelphia was fun.

> The trip was on Saturday.

> Philadelphia is in Pennsylvania.

> Pennsylvania was one of the first states.

In the second sentence of each pair, locate the words that give more information about a word in the first sentence. Cut away the words that are not part of the phrase. Then, use a paper clip to clip the phrase to the first sentence in the pair in the place that it makes the most sense. (Usually, one or more of the words you have cut away will also be part of the first sentence. You will often find that you should clip the phrase near these words from the first sentence.)

Find It in Your Reading Look for phrases in sentences from your science or social studies textbook. Create clip-ons to show how the phrase fits into the sentence.

Find It in Your Writing Choose a piece of writing from your portfolio. Look for sentences that give more information about a word in the preceding or following sentence. Create a clip-on to see whether these sentences could be combined by turning one of them into a phrase. Revise your work where appropriate.

> on Saturday.
> The trip to Philadelphia was fun.

> one of the first states.
> Philadelphia is in Pennsylvania.

GRAMMAR EXERCISES 13–18

Exercise 13 Combining Sentences Using Compound Subjects, Verbs, Objects, and Sentences Combine each of the following pairs of sentences. Revise as necessary for clarity.

1. King Charles II granted Pennsylvania to William Penn. The king believed it would repay a debt to Penn's father.
2. Penn wanted a place of religious freedom. Other Quakers also wanted to worship freely.
3. Penn also wanted others to have religious freedom. He supported religious freedom for all people.
4. Penn gave people personal and property rights. He gave them the right to self-government.
5. Penn was the governor of Pennsylvania. He wrote a constitution and established a legislative body.

Exercise 14 Combining Sentences Using Subordinating Conjunctions Combine each of the following pairs of sentences by making one of the sentences into a subordinate clause. Revise as necessary for clarity.

1. The Amish are also Pennsylvania Dutch. All Pennsylvania Dutch are not Amish.
2. The common background of the Pennsylvania Dutch is German. Some also have French backgrounds.
3. The Amish settled in the Pennsylvania region. William Penn made it a place of religious tolerance.
4. At home, the Amish speak a dialect of German. When they are at school, they speak English.
5. The Amish receive their education in a one-room school. There are children of many ages in one classroom.

Exercise 15 Combining Sentences Using Phrases Combine the sentences by making one a phrase. Also, revise the sentences for clarity.

1. For fun in Lancaster, see the Amazing Maize Maze. The maze is made of corn.
2. The maze covers ten acres. The maze is located in a cornfield.
3. I'd like to visit this maze. It is located on a farm called Cherry-Crest Farm.
4. I would like to solve the maze. I want to figure it out without help.
5. I have never solved this type of maze. It is such a large size.

Exercise 16 Find It in Your Reading Look through newspapers, magazines, and textbooks to identify at least five pairs of sentences that could be combined into single sentences. Combine each pair. Then, explain whether you think that each combined sentence is or is not more effective than the original pair.

Exercise 17 Find It in Your Writing Choose a piece of writing from your portfolio. Identify at least five pairs of sentences that you can combine into single sentences. Then, combine these pairs using at least three different sentence-combining methods.

Exercise 18 Writing Application Write an essay about the history of your hometown. After completing the rough draft, review it and mark places where you can combine ideas. Then, revise it, combining at least five pairs of sentences into single sentences. Provide an explanation of why you combined each.

Section 20.3 *Varying Sentences*

Varying Sentence Length

If you use too many short sentences, your writing will sound choppy. On the other hand, too many long sentences will make your writing dull. Vary your sentence length to create a rhythm and to emphasize key ideas. For example, insert short, direct sentences to interrupt a string of long sentences. Doing so is an excellent way to drive home a main point.

EXAMPLE: In 1787, Pennsylvania became the second state to ratify the Constitution, but important political events took place there before this date. For example, the First and Second Continental Congresses met in Philadelphia, and Congress adopted the Declaration of Independence there. *Pennsylvania played a vital role in the birth of the nation.*

> **Exercise 19** Revising to Improve Variety of Sentence Length Revise the following passage to establish a greater variety of sentence lengths. Where appropriate, divide long sentences into two or more shorter ones, or rework long sentences to state the ideas more simply and directly.

The women of Pennsylvania contributed greatly to both the American Revolution and the Civil War, providing many different types of support to the soldiers fighting the battles. Female patriots from Pennsylvania include Catherine Smith, who manufactured musket barrels; battle heroine Molly Pitcher; and Sara Franklin Bache and Ester De Berdt Reed, who organized 2,200 women to help soldiers.

Pennsylvanian women also contributed to the abolitionist movement and fought for women's rights. They worked for many reforms, including women's rights, during the 1700's and 1800's; although rights for women changed little during this time, their efforts laid the groundwork for future reforms. Lucretia Mott was one of four women to take part in the formation of the American Anti-Slavery Society in Philadelphia in 1833, and she later became the president of the Female Anti-Slavery Society. Jane Grey Swisshelm, abolitionist and advocate of women's rights, launched an abolitionist paper, *The Saturday Visit[o]r*, which featured arguments against slavery and information on women's rights. Swisshelm's newspapers, essays, and lectures influenced the state legislature to grant married women the right to own property, and in 1848, they also helped to change people's views on women's role in society.

Theme: The History of Pennsylvania

In this section, you will learn about varying your sentences. The examples and exercises are about the history of Pennsylvania.

Cross-Curricular Connection: Social Studies

> **More Practice**

Grammar Exercise Workbook
• pp. 65–70
On-line Exercise Bank
• Section 20.3

Go on-line:
PHSchool.com
Enter Web Code:
efk-1102

Complete the exercise on-line! Exercise 19 is available on-line or on CD-ROM.

▶ **Exercise 20** Revising to Vary Sentence Lengths Revise the following paragraph. Break long sentences into two or more sentences or restate the ideas in a simpler way.

(1) During the Civil War, Pennsylvania played an important role in the Union war effort, shielding northeastern states when southern forces attempted to move north through the Shenandoah Valley, a natural highway leading from Virginia to the North. (2) Pennsylvania aided the economic strength of the North with its industrial enterprises, such as the railroads, and with its natural resources, such as steel and iron, which were vital to the war effort. (3) The state governor during the Civil War, Andrew Curtin, was very active in supporting the Union and created the Pennsylvania Reserve Corps, which consisted of fifteen regiments enlisted for three years of service. (4) After the first Battle of Bull Run, these men joined the Army of the Potomac, and thousands of other Pennsylvanians joined them; in all, 350,000 Pennsylvanians served in the Union army, including 8,600 African American volunteers. (5) Camp Curtin was one of the main troop concentration centers during the war, and the state turned out many important officers, including George B. McClellan.

▼ Critical Viewing
What does this painting reveal about the nature of combat during the Civil War? [Analyze]

Varying Sentence Beginnings

Another way to create sentence variety is to begin your sentences with different parts of speech.

STARTING SENTENCES WITH DIFFERENT PARTS OF SPEECH	
Start with a noun	The natural resources of Pennsylvania were of great use during World War I.
Start with an adverb	Fortunately, Pennsylvania's many natural resources were available to the war effort during World War I.
Start with a participle	Having many important natural resources, Pennsylvania was able to contribute greatly to the war effort.
Start with a prepositional phrase	During World War I, Pennsylvania's natural resources were of great use.

▶ **Exercise 21** Revising to Vary Sentence Beginnings Revise the following sentences so that they begin with the part of speech indicated in parentheses.

1. In 1861, the first school for nurses opened in Pennsylvania. (noun)
2. The state then played an important role in the suffrage movement. (prepositional phrase)
3. Women in Philadelphia boldly organized the Women's Suffrage Association in 1868. (adverb)
4. The General Assembly of Pennsylvania, having seen the need for change, approved the women's suffrage amendment in 1913 and again in 1915. (participial phrase)
5. Both times, unfortunately, the state's male voters rejected the amendment. (adverb)
6. The United States approved the Nineteenth Amendment to the Constitution on June 4, 1919. (prepositional phrase)
7. Pennsylvania, ratifying it just days later, became the seventh state to accept the amendment. (participial phrase)
8. By August 1920, women in Pennsylvania who wanted to vote were protected by the law. (noun)
9. Mary Cassatt, born in Allegheny City, was the only woman whose work was exhibited in a show of the ten greatest American painters. (participial phrase)
10. She received her training at the Pennsylvania Academy of Fine Arts and was awarded a gold Medal of Honor in 1914. (prepositional phrase)

▶ **More Practice**

Grammar Exercise Workbook
• pp. 65–70
On-line Exercise Bank
• Section 20.3
 Go on-line:
 PHSchool.com
 Enter Web Code:
 efk-1102

Complete the exercises on-line! Exercises 20 and 21 are available on-line or on CD-ROM.

Using Inverted Word Order

You can also vary sentences by reversing the traditional subject-verb order.

EXAMPLE:

SUBJECT–LINKING VERB–COMPLEMENT: The train is here.
COMPLEMENT–LINKING VERB–SUBJECT: Here is the train.
SUBJECT–VERB–PREPOSITIONAL PHRASE: The ship sailed on the Delaware River.

PREPOSITIONAL PHRASE–VERB–SUBJECT: On the Delaware River sailed the ship.

More Practice

Grammar Exercise Workbook
• pp. 65–70
On-line Exercise Bank
• Section 20.3

Go on-line:
PHSchool.com
Enter Web Code:
efk-1102

▶ **Exercise 22** Varying Sentences Using Inverted Word Order Revise the following sentences by inverting them or reversing the traditional order of the words.

1. The manufacturing of steel and iron products was at one time Pennsylvania's largest industry.
2. The fortunes of men such as Andrew Carnegie, Charles M. Schwab, and Eugene Grace were made from these resources.
3. The steel industry furnished the rails for the nation's vast rail network, the steel for rapidly expanding cities, and the arms for national defense.
4. Andrew Carnegie was a Scotch immigrant who started his career as a telegrapher for the Pennsylvania Railroad.
5. He also handled messages for the army during the Civil War before he entered railroad management.
6. Carnegie began to build new steel mills in 1873.
7. His success was great, making him a very rich man.
8. Andrew Carnegie balanced his good fortune with a pledge to pay the world back by distributing his wealth.
9. He sold Carnegie Steel Company to U.S. Steel in 1901.
10. He spent the rest of his life managing his enormous charitable foundation.

▼ **Critical Viewing** Write a series of sentences describing this picture of steel being manufactured. Vary the length and structure of the sentences. [Describe]

Section 20.3 Section Review

GRAMMAR EXERCISES 23–28

> **Exercise 23** Revising Sentence
Length Revise the paragraph by breaking long sentences into shorter sentences or by making long sentences clearer.

During the 1800's, Pennsylvania was a leader in many science-related fields, including practical inventions, scientific applications in industry and daily life, and precision instruments for astronomy. In medicine, Philadelphia was one of the leading centers for medical advancement in the world, with Hahnemann Medical College, Jefferson Medical College, and the University of Pennsylvania all within its boundaries. Medical colleges were established at the University of Pittsburgh in 1885 and at Temple University in 1901, and these institutions made noteworthy contributions to medicine. Pennsylvanians who made contributions to science included the four Rogers brothers of Philadelphia: James and Robert were noted chemists, William was the state geologist of Virginia and later the president of the Massachusetts Institute of Technology, and Henry directed the first geological survey of Pennsylvania. John A. Roebling, who spent most of his active life in Pennsylvania, led the way in the development of steel-wire rope and bridges, and his son continued his engineering works.

> **Exercise 24** Revising Sentence
Beginnings Revise the sentences as indicated in the directions in parentheses.

1. Pennsylvania pioneered the development of railroads in the nineteenth century. (prepositional phrase)
2. The Pennsylvania Railroad, chartered in 1846, reached Pittsburgh in 1852. (participial phrase)
3. After 1865, Pennsylvania extended its lines to several major cities. (noun)

4. The Reading and Lehigh Valley systems were to join in the expansion soon. (adverb)
5. Certain trains only transported ore to steel mills. (adverb)

> **Exercise 25** Inverting Sentences
to Vary Beginnings Revise these sentences, reversing the traditional word order. Also, revise the sentences for clarity.

1. H. J. Heinz, Inc., known as the "good provider," was incorporated in 1905.
2. Food processing at the time had become an important industry.
3. Heinz had a model factory, providing workers a clean, pleasant workplace.
4. Having a job in his factory also provided the opportunity for workers to advance.
5. Heinz was also an activist for consumer rights.

> **Exercise 26** Find It in Your
Reading Find a news article that demonstrates sentence variety. Make a photocopy. Then, use different-colored highlighters to indicate long and short sentences and varied sentence openers.

> **Exercise 27** Find It in Your
Writing Rework a piece of writing from your portfolio to improve the variety of your sentences. Where possible, use shorter sentences to emphasize key points.

> **Exercise 28** Writing Application
Write an article about a recent local or national event. As you write, focus on varying sentence length, structure, and openers. Try to end each paragraph with a short sentence that reinforces the main point.

Avoiding Fragments and Run-ons

When you speak to your friends, you don't have to follow rules. You can express incomplete thoughts, or let one thought flow right into another. When you write sentences, on the other hand, you have to follow a set of rules. Sentence errors occur when these rules aren't followed. Two of the most common types of sentence errors are fragments and run-ons.

Recognizing Fragments

A fragment is a group of words with end punctuation that either does not have a subject or a verb or does not express a complete thought. While fragments are considered acceptable in written dialogue and are sometimes used for effect in today's fiction, they are generally not considered acceptable in formal compositions.

▶ **KEY CONCEPT** When you write, avoid fragments by making sure that each of your sentences has a subject and a verb and expresses a complete thought. ■

Most fragments are phrases, subordinate clauses, or words in a series. The following are strategies for correcting each of these types of fragments.

Correcting Phrase Fragments Many phrase fragments can be corrected simply by linking them to words that come before or after them. For example, a noun and its modifiers (a noun phrase) may be meant as an appositive but become detached from the sentence in which it belongs. Similarly, other phrases may be detached from the words they should modify.

FRAGMENT:	*A chair built by my father.*
ADDED TO NEARBY SENTENCE:	Our neighbor asked about a piece of furniture, *a chair built by my father.*
FRAGMENT:	*On top of my dresser.*
ADDED TO NEARBY SENTENCE:	I bought a vase that I keep *on top of my dresser.*

A fragment with a pronoun and a participial phrase can often be added to a nearby sentence if you drop the pronoun.

FRAGMENT:	*One stuffed with down.*
ADDED TO NEARBY SENTENCE:	I bought a pillow *stuffed with down*

Theme: Hobbies and Crafts

In this section, you will learn how to recognize and correct fragments and run-ons. Most of the examples and exercises are about hobbies and crafts.

Cross-Curricular Connection: Art

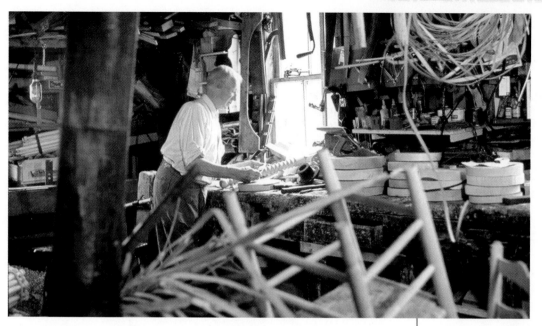

In some situations, you will need to add missing sentence parts to make a phrase fragment into a complete sentence.

A noun fragment will need a verb if the fragment is used as a subject. A noun fragment will need both a subject and a verb if it is used as a complement, an object of a preposition, or an appositive.

FRAGMENT:	*The embroidered tapestry.*
COMPLETED SENTENCES:	*The embroidered tapestry* hung on the wall. We stopped to admire *the embroidered tapestry.* There are unicorns and goats on *the embroidered tapestry.* The museum paid a hefty sum for a family heirloom, *the embroidered tapestry.*

If a noun fragment contains a noun modified by a participial phrase, you may be able to complete the sentence by adding a helping verb to change the participle into a verb.

FRAGMENT:	*The weaver making a rug.*
COMPLETED SENTENCE:	*The weaver* is *making a rug.*

▲ **Critical Viewing**
What similarities can you identify between making furniture and writing complete sentences? **[Compare]**

⚙ **Grammar
and Style Tip**

Two main clauses cannot be linked with a comma unless they are joined by a coordinating conjunction such as *and, but, or, nor, for, so,* or *yet.*

Correcting Clause Fragments Subordinate clauses cannot stand alone as sentences. Either connect them to nearby independent clauses or add the missing sentence parts.

FRAGMENT: *Because we wanted to avoid crowds.*

COMPLETED   *Because we wanted to avoid crowds, we arrived*
SENTENCE: *at the crafts fair early.*

FRAGMENT: *Whatever the artists produce.*

COMPLETED   *People seem to like whatever the artists produce.*
SENTENCE:

Correcting Series Fragments Always check to see that a series of words has both a subject and a verb.

FRAGMENT: *Tulips bursting out of the ground, daffodils beginning to fade, and violets pushing through the grass.*

COMPLETED   *Tulips bursting out of the ground, daffodils*
SENTENCE: *beginning to fade, and violets pushing through the grass* were all captured in the painting.

▶ **Exercise 29** Identifying and Correcting Fragments
Rewrite the following groups of words to eliminate fragments.

EXAMPLE: All types of artists are drawn to our town. To attend the crafts fair held every summer.

ANSWER: All types of artists are drawn to our town to attend the crafts fair held every summer.

1. By displaying and selling their work at crafts fairs. Artisans give people across the country a chance to admire and purchase their works.
2. There are many different types of crafts. Ceramics, weaving, knitting, and painting.
3. One of my favorite crafts fairs is held every summer. In the Berkshire Mountains in Massachusetts.
4. Glassware, rugs, tapestries, vases, colorful prints. There are so many types of works from which you can choose.
5. Displaying paintings based on nursery rhymes. One of the artists had the perfect gift for my youngest brother.

Exercise 30 Proofreading to Correct Fragments Revise this paragraph, eliminating all fragments.

Crafts are decorative or functional objects. Often made by hand. Crafts can come in many forms. For use and enjoyment. Papier-mâché, the craft of fashioning objects from any kind of absorbent paper soaked in water and glue. Bookbinding requires dexterity. It is not difficult to learn. Weaving a method of creating fabric by interlacing two sets of yarn threads. Weaving, plaiting, and coiling techniques to make baskets, mats, and rugs. Wall hangings, bags, and containers made from macramé or ornamental knotting. In embroidery, a needle and thread are used to create designs on fabric. Inserting thin strips of wool through a heavy base fabric with a hand hook. Rug hooking requires patience. In quilting, three layers of fabric are stitched or tied together. A decorative top layer, filler, and a liner.

More Practice

Grammar Exercise Workbook
• pp. 71–74
On-line Exercise Bank
• Section 20.4

Go on-line:
PHSchool.com
Enter Web Code:
efk-1102

interactive Textbook

Complete the exercises on-line! Exercises 29 and 30 are available on-line or on CD-ROM.

◀ Critical Viewing Come up with a fragment that might be used in describing this weaver at work. Explain how you could correct this fragment. **[Connect]**

Recognizing Run-ons

A *run-on sentence* is two or more complete sentences incorrectly punctuated as if they were one.

KEY CONCEPT Use punctuation, conjunctions, or other methods to join or separate the parts of a run-on sentence. ■

The following chart shows four different ways of correcting run-on sentences.

FOUR WAYS TO CORRECT RUN-ONS	
With End Marks and Capitals	
Run-on	**Sentence**
Elizabeth turned at the sudden noise a bird had crashed into the picture window.	Elizabeth turned at the sudden noise. A bird had crashed into the picture window.
With Commas and Conjunctions	
Run-on	**Sentence**
I baked the cake this morning, I have not frosted it yet.	I baked the cake this morning, but I have not frosted it yet.
With Semicolons	
Run-on	**Sentence**
The novice potter kept trying to make a vase, however he failed each time.	The novice potter kept trying to make a vase; however, he failed each time.
By Rewriting	
Run-on	**Sentence**
My aunt stayed with us for a week, my cousins came too.	My aunt and cousins stayed with us for a week. (Simple sentence with compound subject) When my aunt stayed with us for a week, my cousins came too. (Complex sentence beginning with subordinate clause)

More Practice

Grammar Exercise Workbook
• pp. 73–74
On-line Exercise Bank
• Section 20.4

Go on-line:
PHSchool.com
Enter Web Code:
efk-1102

Fused Sentences and Comma Splices When you edit your work, be on the lookout for two specific types of run-ons: fused sentences and comma splices. A *fused sentence* consists of two or more sentences not separated or joined by any punctuation. A *comma splice* is two or more sentences separated by a comma instead of by a comma and a conjunction.

FUSED SENTENCE: *The quiltmaker put on a demonstration the crowds came to see her at work.*

COMMA SPLICE: *The potter displayed his vases, the painter showed her portraits.*

Exercise 31 Identifying and Correcting Run-on Sentences
If a sentence is correct as written, write *correct.* If it is a run-on, rewrite it.

1. My grandmother taught me about quilting I really enjoy this craft.
2. When I was little it was difficult but now it is easier.
3. On Saturdays, I visit her, and we spend time working together.
4. Sometimes we follow a traditional pattern and sometimes we make scenes that tell a story.
5. Last year, my sister started learning to quilt, she enjoys it almost as much as I do.
6. We all sit together for a long time, we have many interesting conversations.
7. My grandmother tells us about her life as a little girl, we are often surprised that it is, in some ways, very similar to our lives.
8. We are making a quilt that shows the generations of our family it has figures representing my grandmother, my mother, and my sister and me as well as our birthdays embroidered on the figures.
9. When it is finished, it will be a work of art we will hang it on the wall in my grandmother's house.
10. I love the time I spend with my grandmother, I love the beautiful quilts we make.

▼ Critical Viewing
Why would a craft like quiltmaking be passed on from generation to generation? **[Draw Conclusions]**

▶ **Exercise 32** Revising a Passage to Eliminate Run-on Sentences Copy the following passage on a separate sheet of paper. Revise to eliminate run-on sentences. Use each of the four methods for correcting run-ons at least once.

Both knitted and crocheted fabrics are made from a single strand of thread the fabric is composed of loops chained together to form a continuous textile. Knitting the loops of thread are usually formed by means of a pair of rods called needles. Thread of contrasting colors may be introduced to form patterns the more colors introduced, the more intricate the pattern.

In weft knitting, a hand-knitting process that can also be done by machine, the work progresses back and forth. Each row of stitches is called a course each chain of loops hanging vertically from the needles is called a wale.

Knitting developed as a folk craft with traditional regional designs Ireland, Scandinavia, and the Shetland Islands were distinguished by different patterns.

Knitting and crocheting are similar, however, crocheting is a method of working interlocking loops of thread into a chain by means of a slender rod hooked at one end. A single chain of loops is formed, catching the yarn and drawing it through the previous loop. The chain is made to the planned width of the finished piece, the yarn is turned at the end of the chain, and a second chain is crocheted, each new stitch being looped through a stitch in the previous row. Little is known about the early history of crocheting some ancient cords may have been made by finger crocheting.

▶ **Exercise 33** Avoiding Run-on Sentences in Writing Write a description of the picture on the previous page. In your description, include each of the following pairs of features in a single sentence. Be sure you write the sentence without creating a run-on sentence.

EXAMPLE: girl is speaking: grandmother is listening.

ANSWER: The girl is speaking, and the grandmother is listening.

1. quilt in progress is traditional pattern: quilt on wall tells a story
2. they enjoy quilting: they are smiling
3. girl is speaking: girl is looking at her work
4. grandmother is pausing: she is listening to the girl speak
5. quilt is colorful: quilt uses many patches of fabric

Section 20.4 *Section Review*

GRAMMAR EXERCISES 34–39

> **Exercise 34** Proofreading to Eliminate Fragments Revise this paragraph, eliminating all fragments.

Crafts are as old as human history. Most crafts practiced today can be traced back many hundreds of years. Basketry, weaving, and pottery among the earliest basic crafts. Originally fulfilling useful purposes. Crafts are now primarily decorative. Craftwork forming the basis of city economies in Europe up to the Industrial Revolution in the 1800's. Once items could be mass-produced. Artisans were no longer needed.

> **Exercise 35** Proofreading to Eliminate Run-ons Revise the following paragraph, correcting all run-ons.

The top layer of a quilt bears a design, generally produced in one of three ways, the fabric may be left plain, so that the quilting stitches form the design. More commonly, the top is made from a process called appliqué pieces are cut from various cloths and stitched onto a background fabric, making pictures and patterns. Tops of quilts may also be pieced or patched in a process known as patchwork units of cloth are sewn together to form geometric patterns. In the final stage of assembly the quilt's three layers are stretched on a frame then, are sewn together. With short running stitches called quilting stitches. This final step is more than mechanical however the design of the top is artfully thrown into relief, allowing the play of light and shadow on the surface.

> **Exercise 36** Proofreading to Correct Fragments and Run-ons Revise this passage, eliminating fragments and run-ons.

Gardens come in many different types of designs, styles, and techniques. Including, among others, rock gardens, herb gardens, wildflower gardens, water gardens, and Japanese gardens.

A rock garden duplicating the natural environmental conditions in which rock and mountain plants thrive. It is somewhat easier to cultivate than an ordinary garden, the plants are hardier and more resistant to drought and cold and require far less fertilizer than plants that succeed in other types of gardens. Slightly sloping ground is the best location. That is well drained. The most suitable plants for rock gardens are flowering, hardy perennials, in addition, rock gardens are often planted with dwarf trees and shrubs.

> **Exercise 37** Find It in Your Reading Choose a passage from a magazine article. Type out the passage, introducing at least two fragments and two run-ons. Exchange papers with a classmate, and correct the errors that your partner has introduced.

> **Exercise 38** Find It in Your Writing Choose a piece of writing from your portfolio to review for fragments and run-ons. Mark any instances of these errors. Then, revise your writing to correct these problems.

> **Exercise 39** Writing Application Write a brief description of a hobby or craft that you enjoy. Include at least five fragments and five run-ons in your first draft. Then, revise your work, correcting the fragments and run-ons.

Misplaced and Dangling Modifiers

As a general rule, a modifier should be placed as close as possible to the word it modifies. If a modifier is misplaced or left dangling in a sentence, it will seem to modify the wrong word or no word at all. This section will examine both of these sentence errors and show you how to correct them.

Misplaced Modifiers

When a modifier is placed too far from the word it should modify, the meaning of the sentence can become unclear.

▶ **KEY CONCEPT** A misplaced modifier seems to modify the wrong word in the sentence. ■

Any phrase or clause that acts as an adjective or adverb can unintentionally be misplaced in a sentence.

MISPLACED MODIFIERS:	George Washington borrowed money to attend his first inauguration *deep in debt*.
	The first inaugural ball was held in the New York State Assembly *attended by many foreign ministers*.

In the first example, the misplaced prepositional phrase seems to modify *inauguration* rather than *George Washington*. In the second example, the misplaced participial phrase seems to modify *New York State Assembly* rather than *ball*.

To correct such sentence errors, simply move the phrase or clause that is misplaced closer to the word that it should logically modify. Some additional rewording may be necessary.

CORRECTED SENTENCES:	*Deep in debt*, George Washington borrowed money to attend his first inauguration.
	Attended by many foreign ministers, the first inaugural ball was held in the New York State Assembly.

Theme: The Presidency

In this section, you will learn how to avoid misplaced and dangling modifiers. The examples and exercises are about the United States presidency.

Cross-Curricular Connection: Social Studies

💿 Technology Tip

Often, a misplaced modifier needs only to be moved closer to the word it is intended to describe. Use the Cut, Copy, and Paste functions in your word-processing program to experiment with different word arrangements until you find the correct one.

Exercise 40 Identifying and Correcting Misplaced
Modifiers Rewrite each sentence, correcting the misplaced
modifiers.

EXAMPLE: The President receives guests in the Blue Room
during state dinners at the White House.

ANSWER: During state dinners, the President receives
guests in the Blue Room of the White House.

1. The White House is constructed of Virginia sandstone built
in a classical style.
2. Numerous trees grow on the White House property of historical interest.
3. The White House occupies eighteen acres of manicured
lawns and gardens constructed before 1800.
4. The architect James Hoban designed the White House who
won a public architecture contest.
5. The low-lying terraces were added while Thomas Jefferson
was president to the main building.
6. The third floor of the White House is closed to the public
consisting primarily of guest rooms.
7. The East Room is the largest room in the White House
used mainly for state receptions and balls.
8. The White House has retained its simple character subject
to many renovations.
9. Destroying the interior British troops burned the structure
during the War of 1812.
10. The White House has been the home of every president
except George Washington in American history.

More Practice

Grammar Exercise
Workbook
• pp. 75–78
On-line Exercise Bank
• Section 20.5
Go on-line:
PHSchool.com
Enter Web Code:
efk-1102

Interactive Textbook

Complete the exercise
on-line! Exercise 40 is
available on-line or on
CD-ROM.

▼ Critical Viewing
Write a sentence with
a misplaced modifier
describing this view
of the White House.
How can you correct
the misplaced modifier? [Describe]

Dangling Modifiers

▶ **KEY CONCEPT** A dangling modifier seems to modify the wrong word or no word at all because the word it should modify has been omitted from the sentence. ■

DANGLING MODIFIER:	*Shortly after his inauguration,* President Kennedy's wife began refurbishing the White House.
CORRECTED SENTENCE:	*Shortly after President Kennedy's inauguration,* his wife began refurbishing the White House.
DANGLING MODIFIER:	*While touring the White House,* shoes must be worn.
CORRECTED SENTENCE:	*While touring the White House,* visitors must wear shoes.
DANGLING MODIFIER:	*Importing French furniture,* the White House was decorated.
CORRECTED SENTENCE:	*Importing French furniture,* Thomas Jefferson decorated the White House.

▶ **Exercise 41** **Identifying and Correcting Dangling Modifiers** If a sentence is correct, write *correct*. If a sentence contains a dangling modifier, rewrite it to make it correct.

1. While the sailors were rowing George Washington to his inauguration, white was worn.
2. On the way to his inauguration, Washington's boat took him up the Hudson River.
3. After walking to the Capitol, Thomas Jefferson's inauguration began.
4. When he was inaugurated, Jefferson's predecessor refused to attend.
5. Stormy early, Lincoln's inauguration cleared by afternoon.
6. Snowing heavily, Grant's inaugural parade was delayed.
7. While being inaugurated, Franklin Roosevelt's mother was present.
8. The first of such ceremonies to be televised, Harry Truman was inaugurated on January 20, 1949.
9. After clearing away eight inches of snow, John Kennedy's inaugural parade proceeded.
10. At his inauguration, Bill Clinton thanked George Bush for his years of service.

▶ **More Practice**

Grammar Exercise Workbook
• pp. 75–78
On-line Exercise Bank
• Section 20.5

Go on-line:
PHSchool.com
Enter Web Code:
efk-1102

Complete the exercise on-line! Exercise 41 is available on-line or on CD-ROM.

Section
20.5 **Section Review**

GRAMMAR EXERCISES 42–47

▶ **Exercise 42** Identifying and
Correcting Misplaced Modifiers
Rewrite each sentence, correcting all
misplaced modifiers.

1. The Map Room in the White House
   during World War II was used
   by Franklin Roosevelt to follow
   developments.
2. Entertaining guests, the room now
   serves as a private meeting area for
   the President or First Lady.
3. The room has been visited by many
   dignitaries decorated in the
   Chippendale style.
4. A rare French version of a colonial
   map hangs on the east wall, covering
   a case of world maps.
5. The sandstone mantel is simple but
   large, resting under a map made for
   Franklin Roosevelt.

▶ **Exercise 43** Identifying and
Correcting Dangling Modifiers If a
sentence is correct, write *correct*. If a sentence contains a dangling modifier, rewrite
it to correct it.

1. After George Washington was elected
   by a unanimous vote, the trip was
   made to New York.
2. Having accepted the presidency, prece-
   dents would be set by Washington in
   his administration.
3. To take the oath of office, Article II of
   the new federal Constitution was followed by Washington.
4. When he was inaugurated, the
   speech by Washington was short but
   important.
5. Consulting the members of his newly
   appointed Cabinet, day-to-day duties
   were outlined by the President.

▶ **Exercise 44** Revising to Correct
Misplaced and Dangling Modifiers
Rewrite the following paragraph, correcting
any misplaced or dangling modifiers.

(1) To defeat his rivals, the House of
Representatives was needed by Thomas
Jefferson to vote for him. (2) Listed in
Article II, Section 1 of the Constitution,
the House has the power to break a tie in
the electoral college. (3) After his election,
an inauguration with few of the elaborate
trappings of the past Federalist adminis-
trations was planned. (4) Wanting to
appear as an average citizen, Jefferson
walked along Pennsylvania Avenue from
his boardinghouse for his inauguration.
(5) Still under construction, Jefferson was
the first President to take the oath of
office at the Capitol.

▶ **Exercise 45** Find It in Your
Reading Flip through magazines to see
whether you can find an example of either
a misplaced or a dangling modifier in a
print advertisement.

▶ **Exercise 46** Find It in Your
Writing Choose a piece of writing from
your portfolio to review for misplaced and
dangling modifiers. Mark any instances of
these errors that you find. Then, revise
your writing to correct these problems.

▶ **Exercise 47** Writing Application
Imagine that you are running for president of your class at school. Write a
speech in which you try to persuade your
classmates to vote for you. As you revise,
check carefully for misplaced or dangling
modifiers. Revise your speech to correct
any that you find.

Faulty Parallelism

Recognizing the Correct Use of Parallelism

Parallel grammatical structures can be two or more words of the same part of speech, two or more phrases of the same type, two or more clauses of the same type, or two or more sentences with the same pattern.

▶ **KEY CONCEPT** **Parallelism** is the placement of equal ideas in words, phrases, clauses, or sentences of similar types. ∎

PARALLEL WORDS:
Philadelphia is home to many *universities, museums,* and *libraries.*

PARALLEL PHRASES:
Philadelphia is famous for *hosting the First Continental Congress, housing the Liberty Bell,* and *publishing the country's first newspaper.*

PARALLEL CLAUSES:
Because we were hot and because we were tired, we stopped to rest in Fairmount Park.

PARALLEL SENTENCES: *I came. I saw. I conquered.*

Use parallelism to create a rhythm and emphasize key ideas in your writing. The following excerpt is from a speech delivered by Winston Churchill during World War II. Notice how the use of parallel structures creates repetition that builds up to the powerful concluding statement:

EFFECTIVE USE
OF PARALLELISM:
We shall not flag nor fail. We shall go on to the end. We shall fight in France, we shall fight on the seas and oceans, we shall fight with growing confidence and growing strength in the air, we shall defend our island, whatever the cost may be, we shall fight on the beaches, we shall fight on the landing grounds, we shall fight in the fields and in the streets, we shall fight in the hills; we shall never surrender.

After the first item in a series, sometimes a word is omitted in parallel structures. The word is understood to be part of the phrase or clause because it is in the first item. Churchill, for example, did not repeat *with* in the series *with growing confidence and growing strength in the air.*

In this section, you will learn how to use parallelism in your writing and how to avoid faulty parallelism. The examples and exercises provide information about the history of Philadelphia and about its role as the birthplace of liberty.

Cross-Curricular Connection: Social Studies

> **Exercise 48** Recognizing Parallel Structures Write the parallel structures in each sentence. Then, identify the composition of each as *words, phrases,* or *clauses.*

EXAMPLE: Philadelphia is the birthplace of the United States, the home of the Liberty Bell, and the City of Brotherly Love.
the birthplace of the United States, the home of the Liberty Bell, and the City of Brotherly Love (phrases)

1. The Delaware Indians once hunted, farmed, and fished in the area that is now Philadelphia.
2. Dutch sailors visited the area; Swedish families settled there.
3. The Dutch, English, and Swedes fought over the land until the English won control in 1674.
4. In the 1680's, William Penn received a charter, founded the Pennsylvania Colony, and planned the city of Philadelphia.
5. Penn chose Philadelphia as the capital of the colony because of its resources, size, and location.
6. The new colonists who joined Penn were seeking adventure, fleeing poverty, or escaping persecution.
7. Philadelphia grew, the people prospered, and the colony thrived.
8. Benjamin Franklin's newspaper, almanac, and pamphlets helped to establish Philadelphia as a major publishing center.
9. The founding fathers signed the Declaration of Independence and adopted the United States Constitution in Philadelphia.
10. Philadelphia was the capital of Pennsylvania from 1683 to 1799 and was the United States capital from 1790 to 1800.

More Practice

Grammar Exercise Workbook
• pp. 79–82
On-line Exercise Bank
• Section 20.6
Go on-line:
PHSchool.com
Enter Web Code:
efk-1102

interactive **Textbook**

Get instant feedback! Exercise 48 is available on-line or on CD-ROM.

▼ Critical Viewing
For what effect might the writers of official documents such as the Declaration of Independence have used parallel phrases? **[Apply]**

Faulty Parallelism

Faulty parallelism occurs when equal grammatical structures are not used to express equal or related ideas. Faulty parallelism can involve words, phrases, and clauses in series as well as in comparisons.

> **KEY CONCEPT** Correct a sentence containing faulty parallelism by rewriting it so that each parallel idea is expressed in the same grammatical structure. ■

Nonparallel Words, Phrases, and Clauses in Series

When you write, check every series of ideas for parallelism. If you write a description using a series of one-word adjectives, for example, make sure the series does not include a prepositional phrase instead of a suitable one-word adjective.

Notice how nonparallel structures not only interrupt the natural flow of the sentences but also cloud their meanings.

Grammar and Style Tip

Parallelism not only ensures similarity of form but also enhances coherence by clearly relating paired or opposite units. Effective parallelism will enable you to combine related ideas in a single, well-ordered sentence that you might have otherwise expressed in separate sentences.

| CORRECTING FAULTY PARALLELISM IN SERIES ||
Nonparallel Structures	Corrected Sentences
NOUN NOUN *Museums, theaters,* and GERUND PHRASE *listening to live music* make Philadelphia an exciting destination.	NOUN NOUN *Museums, theaters,* and NOUN *live music* make Philadelphia an exciting destination.
PREP PHRASE We rowed *past the boathouse,* PREP PHRASE *under the bridge,* and INDEPENDENT CLAUSE *the boat crossed the finish line.*	PREP PHRASE We rowed *past the boathouse,* PREP PHRASE *under the bridge,* and PREP PHRASE *through the finish line.*
My voice teacher says *that I* NOUN CLAUSE *have a very strong voice,* INDEPENDENT CLAUSE but *I sing off key.*	My voice teacher says *that I* NOUN CLAUSE *have a very strong voice* NOUN CLAUSE but *that I sing off key.*

Coordinating conjunctions such as *and, but,* and *or* often connect items in a series. When you proofread your work, use them as a signal to check the items they connect for parallelism.

Section
20.7

Section Review

GRAMMAR EXERCISES 58–63

▶ **Exercise 58** Identifying Faulty Coordination For the sentences in which coordination is used correctly, write *correct*. For the others, write *faulty*.

1. Philadelphia is a leading center of commerce in the United States and was once one of the world's leading manufacturing cities.
2. Manufacturing has declined in the city since 1950, but it is still an integral part of the city's economy.
3. The service industries have begun to play a greater role in Philadelphia, and the city's economy is more complex.
4. The Port of Philadelphia handles more than 30 million tons of cargo each year and is host to some 5,000 ships.
5. Grain and coal are the city's main exports, and petroleum is imported for processing at the waterfront refineries.

▶ **Exercise 59** Revising to Correct Faulty Coordination Write each sentence, correcting the faulty coordination.

1. In the early 1800's, coal mines west of Philadelphia provided a huge fuel supply, and industries thrived in the city.
2. Manufacturing industries moved to Philadelphia, and trade was increased by canals, roads, and railroads.
3. Rapid industrialization drew thousands of immigrants to Philadelphia in the mid-1800's, and they competed fiercely for work.
4. The Pennsylvania State Legislature merged the city and Philadelphia County in 1854, and eleven towns became part of Philadelphia.
5. With that act, Philadelphia grew by leaps and bounds, and it had a population of more than 500,000.

▶ **Exercise 60** Avoiding Faulty Coordination in Sentence Combining Combine each pair of sentences, avoiding faulty coordination.

1. Culture plays a major role in Philadelphia. Theater, music, and the visual arts are all well represented.
2. Philadelphia has a large, active theater district. The Walnut Street Theatre is one of several in the downtown area.
3. The Walnut Street Theatre is the oldest active theater in the United States. It opened in 1809.
4. The Marionette Theater features plays for children. It is located in Fairmount Park.
5. The University of Pennsylvania also has a theater group. The troupe specializes in experimental plays.

▶ **Exercise 61** Find It in Your Reading Find a travel article about a place that interests you. Then, rework a passage from the article to introduce five examples of faulty coordination. Exchange papers with a partner. Then, identify and correct each instance of faulty coordination your partner has introduced.

▶ **Exercise 62** Find It in Your Writing Review a piece of writing from your portfolio for faulty coordination. Mark any instances of these errors. Revise your writing to correct these problems.

▶ **Exercise 63** Writing Application Create a one-page print advertisement to attract visitors to your town. Highlight all the key attractions. Carefully check your advertisement for faulty coordination.

Verb Usage

Action can happen at any time in the past, the present, or the future. The following sentences, for example, describe actions taking place at different times in Texas.

—Years ago, Texas <u>fought</u> for its independence from Mexico.

—Today, Texans <u>are constructing</u> new homes and other buildings in their growing cities.

The underlined words are verbs, which show both time and action. When you consider the numerous forms and uses of verbs, the many words that can act as verbs, and the likelihood that a sentence will have more than one verb, the chances of misusing verbs are very great. To avoid errors, it is important to know the rules that govern verb usage.

This chapter will show how verbs are formed and the ways in which verbs indicate time. It will also explain how verbs help to express facts, commands, and wishes or possibilities, as well as how verbs can show whether subjects perform or receive action.

▲ **Critical Viewing**
What occurred at this old mission that gave rise to the expression "Remember the Alamo"? Respond with verbs denoting the past. **[Speculate]**

Diagnostic Test

Directions: Write all answers on a separate sheet of paper.

Skill Check A. Write whether each verb is a *basic form*, a *progressive form*, or an *emphatic form*. Then, identify the verb's tense.

1. My mother drove her car to El Paso.
2. Mike certainly does like Texas sports teams.
3. Near the museum, a performer was singing Mexican songs.
4. Yes, my father did bring me a souvenir from his trip to Dallas.
5. Miguel will be visiting his aunt in Corpus Christi next month.

Skill Check B. Write the appropriate past or past participle for each verb in parentheses.

6. Last summer, my family (drive) to San Antonio.
7. We had never (go) there before.
8. We (see) many interesting sights along the way.
9. Have you ever (eat) Tex-Mex food?
10. My mother has (speak) about a trip to Austin next year.

Skill Check C. Rewrite the sentences, correcting any unnecessary shift in tense. Then, write whether the events are *simultaneous* or *sequential*.

11. People know that cowboys and clowns still performed at rodeos.
12. Thousands will be flocking to rodeos because they are so exciting.
13. Cowboys are roping calves when we arrived.
14. I had come to the rodeo because I hope to see the best riders.
15. Often, riders will practice their act until they get it right.

Skill Check D. Where necessary, change the verbs in the following sentences to the subjunctive mood. If the subjunctive is not needed, write *correct*.

16. I wish that I was able to see more of my cousin in Houston.
17. If there was enough room in our house for his snake collection, he would visit us more often.
18. When I told my mother that Frank could keep his snakes in our kitchen, she stared at me as if I was crazy.
19. She prefers that he leaves his snakes at home.
20. However, I noticed that if my mother was home when Frank arrived, she would always invite him in.

Skill Check E. Write whether the following sentences are in the *active* or *passive voice*.

21. Texas has been embraced by musicians.
22. Numerous bluegrass bands have been seen by Texas fans.
23. Many rock-and-roll artists of the 1950's got their start in Texas.
24. A legacy of innovative guitar pickers, piano players, fiddlers, and songwriters is held by West Texas.
25. In fact, a variety of music that the world had never heard was produced by the West Texas Panhandle.

Verb Tenses

The *tense* of a verb indicates whether something is happening now, was happening at some time in the past, or will be happening at some time in the future.

▶ **KEY CONCEPT** A **tense** is a form of a verb that shows the time of an action or a condition. ■

The Six Verb Tenses

Verbs have six tenses to show the time of an action or condition. Each tense has at least two forms; the present and past tenses have a third form.

▶ **KEY CONCEPT** Each verb tense has a *basic* form and a *progressive* form. The present and past tenses also have the *emphatic*, formed with the helping verb *do, does,* or *did.*

THE BASIC FORMS OF THE SIX TENSES	
Present:	I *learn* more about Texas every day.
Past:	I *learned* something new yesterday.
Future:	I *will learn* more tomorrow.
Present Perfect:	I *have learned* about Texas cities.
Past Perfect:	I *had learned* about the senator before I read her book.
Future Perfect:	I *will have learned* more by year's end.

THE PROGRESSIVE FORMS OF THE SIX TENSES	
Present Progressive:	I *am reading* about Texas's many cities now.
Past Progressive:	I *was reading* about Dallas last night.
Future Progressive:	I *will be reading* about Houston sometime next week.
Present Perfect Progressive:	I *have been reading* about colleges in Texas.
Past Perfect Progressive:	I *had been reading* about Texas cuisine when the lights went out.
Future Perfect Progressive:	I *will have been reading* for an hour when the alarm goes off.

Theme: Texas
....
In this section, you will learn about six verb tenses and the progressive and emphatic forms. The examples and exercises in this section are about Texas.
....
Cross-Curricular Connection: Social Studies

⊘ **Learn More**

For more information about verbs, see Chapter 17.

THE EMPHATIC FORMS OF THE PRESENT AND THE PAST	
Present Emphatic:	I *do talk* to Grandmother quite frequently.
Past Emphatic:	I *did talk* to David about his tardiness.

Exercise 1 Recognizing Basic, Progressive, and Emphatic Forms Identify the tense and form of each verb.

EXAMPLE: Texans have been enjoying chili for years.
ANSWER: present perfect progressive

1. Texas comprises a large part of the western Southcentral region of the United States.
2. Certainly, Texas did derive its name from a Native American word meaning "friends" or "allies."
3. Native Americans had been living in the vast regions of Texas before the arrival of Spaniards and other Europeans.
4. On December 19, 1845, Texas became the twenty-eighth state in the Union.
5. Residents of Texas have been commemorating that occasion for more than 150 years.
6. In the year 2045, Texas will have been a state for 200 years.
7. The state flower is the bluebonnet.
8. Mexico has been influencing Texas culture for centuries.
9. Different cultures and traditions will coexist in Texas for many more years.
10. Texans do cherish their unique culture and history.

Exercise 2 Using the Progressive and Emphatic Forms Write the progressive or emphatic form of each verb, following the instructions given in parentheses.

EXAMPLE: By 1839, a hill in Austin (past perfect progressive of *choose*) as the site for the capitol.
ANSWER: had been chosen

1. Visitors (present emphatic of *admire*) the Texas capitol.
2. Even before 1888, when it was completed, the capitol (past perfect progressive of *attract*) much attention.
3. The dome (present perfect of *win*) praise for its impressive architectural details.
4. Every day, visitors (present progressive of *climb*) to the galleries around the legislative chambers.
5. Often, from the gallery, spectators (present emphatic of *watch*) the lawmakers at work.

More Practice

Grammar Exercise Workbook
• pp. 87–88
On-line Exercise Bank
• Section 21.1
Go on-line:
PHSchool.com
Enter Web Code:
efk-1102

Interactive Textbook

Get instant feedback! Exercises 1 and 2 are available on-line or on CD-ROM.

The Four Principal Parts of Verbs

Every verb has four principal parts. It is from these four principal parts that all of the tenses are formed.

▶**KEY CONCEPT** A verb has four principal parts: the *present*, the *present participle*, the *past*, and the *past participle*.

THE FOUR PRINCIPAL PARTS			
Present	Present Participle	Past	Past Participle
listen speak	listening speaking	listened spoke	listened spoken

These examples show how each principal part is used.

PRESENT: The Texas governor *lives* in Austin.
PRESENT PARTICIPLE: Lawmakers are *debating* in the capitol.
PAST: The city *wanted* to build a new airport.
PAST PARTICIPLE: Austin's hills, tall trees, and historic architecture have *delighted* visitors.

▶**Exercise 3** Recognizing Principal Parts Identify the principal part used to form each verb in Exercise 1 on page 371.

EXAMPLE: People have been admiring the capitol.
ANSWER: present participle (admiring)

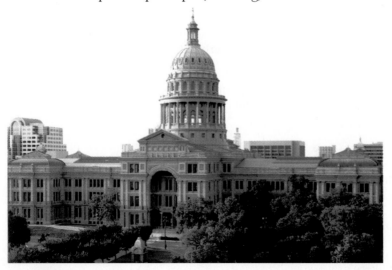

◀ Critical Viewing In what way do you think the Texas capitol building was inspired by the Capitol in Washington, D.C.? Use at least two principal parts of verbs in your response. **[Compare]**

Regular and Irregular Verbs

The changes that occur in the past and past participle forms of a verb determine whether the verb is classified as *regular* or *irregular*.

Regular Verbs The past and past participle of regular verbs are formed according to a predictable pattern.

▶ **KEY CONCEPT** A **regular verb** is one in which the past and past participle are formed by adding *-ed* or *-d* to the present form. ■

PRINCIPAL PARTS OF REGULAR VERBS			
Present	Present Participle	Past	Past Participle
laugh	laughing	laughed	(have) laughed
hop	hopping	hopped	(have) hopped
wave	waving	waved	(have) waved

Irregular Verbs The past and past participle of irregular verbs are not formed according to a predictable pattern.

▶ **KEY CONCEPT** An **irregular verb** is one in which the past and past participle are not formed by adding *-ed* or *-d* to the present form.

You need to know the principal parts of irregular verbs because they often cause usage problems. One common problem is treating an irregular verb as if it were a regular verb (for example, *teached* instead of *taught*). A second problem is confusing the past and past participle when they are different (saying, for example, "I seen" instead of "I saw"). A third problem is spelling. As you read through the charts on the following pages, notice that a final consonant is sometimes doubled to form both the present participle (*getting*) and the past participle (*gotten*). A final *-e* may also be dropped to form the present participle (*arising*).

If you are in doubt about the principal parts of an irregular verb, consult a dictionary. The principal parts are usually listed immediately after the part-of-speech label.

📓 Journal Tip

This section contains a variety of information about Texas. In your journal, take notes on some of the facts that interest you, and review them later to find a topic for an essay or a research report.

⚙ Grammar and Style Tip

Never write *snuck*. The correct past or past participle of *sneak* is *sneaked*.

IRREGULAR VERBS WITH THE SAME PAST AND PAST PARTICIPLE

Present	Present Participle	Past	Past Participle
bind	binding	bound	(have) bound
bring	bringing	brought	(have) brought
build	building	built	(have) built
buy	buying	bought	(have) bought
catch	catching	caught	(have) caught
creep	creeping	crept	(have) crept
fight	fighting	fought	(have) fought
find	finding	found	(have) found
fling	flinging	flung	(have) flung
get	getting	got	(have) got or (have) gotten
grind	grinding	ground	(have) ground
hang	hanging	hung	(have) hung
hold	holding	held	(have) held
keep	keeping	kept	(have) kept
lay	laying	laid	(have) laid
lead	leading	led	(have) led
leave	leaving	left	(have) left
lend	lending	lent	(have) lent
lose	losing	lost	(have) lost
pay	paying	paid	(have) paid
say	saying	said	(have) said
seek	seeking	sought	(have) sought
sell	selling	sold	(have) sold
send	sending	sent	(have) sent
shine	shining	shone or shined	(have) shone or (have) shined
sit	sitting	sat	(have) sat
sleep	sleeping	slept	(have) slept
spend	spending	spent	(have) spent
spin	spinning	spun	(have) spun
stand	standing	stood	(have) stood
stick	sticking	stuck	(have) stuck
sting	stinging	stung	(have) stung
strike	striking	struck	(have) struck
swing	swinging	swung	(have) swung
teach	teaching	taught	(have) taught
win	winning	won	(have) won
wind	winding	wound	(have) wound
wring	wringing	wrung	(have) wrung

▶ **Exercise 4** Supplying the Correct Forms of Irregular
Verbs Write the appropriate past or past participle for each
verb in parentheses.

EXAMPLE: The Rio Grande has (hold) the imagination of
            Texans.

ANSWER: held

1. Since the early days of Texas's history, the Rio Grande has
   (stand) as a boundary between much of Texas and Mexico.
2. Residents of Texas have often (seek) out the state's many
   lakes and rivers.
3. They may also have (catch) fish in them.
4. Some may even have (build) cabins near Texas's streams.
5. Texas also has numerous state and national parks, where
   people have (seek) to escape the cities.
6. Many Texans have (find) peace of mind near these natural
   resources.
7. Visitors have been (teach) to
   ride horses and ponies on Texas
   ranches.
8. In recent times, urban growth
   (creep) up in Texas, as it did in
   other parts of the country.
9. Modern skyscrapers (bring)
   changes to the look of such places
   as Dallas.
10. Developers have (build) large sub-
    urban communities outside the
    cities.
11. Texas also has thousands of miles
    of highways through areas where
    people once could not have (find)
    a road.
12. The financing of the changes began
    when oil was (strike) in the early
    part of the twentieth century.
13. Texans' ancestors would not have
    (think) that such cities would
    spring up.
14. Giant metropolises now occupy the
    land where small farms once
    (stand).
15. Despite the rapid growth of the
    cities, Texans have not (lose) sight
    of their vast and varied culture.

▶ **More Practice**

Grammar Exercise
Workbook
• pp. 89–90
On-line Exercise Bank
• Section 21.1
  Go on-line:
  PHSchool.com
  Enter Web Code:
  efk-1102

▼ **Critical Viewing**
What verbs tell the
actions of the artist
who created this sculp-
ture? Are they regular
or irregular? **[Relate]**

Sculpture in Houston by French artist Jean Dubuffet

IRREGULAR VERBS THAT CHANGE IN OTHER WAYS			
Present	Present Participle	Past	Past Participle
become	becoming	became	(have) become
begin	beginning	began	(have) begun
break	breaking	broke	(have) broken
choose	choosing	chose	(have) chosen
come	coming	came	(have) come
do	doing	did	(have) done
draw	drawing	drew	(have) drawn
drink	drinking	drank	(have) drunk
drive	driving	drove	(have) driven
eat	eating	ate	(have) eaten
fall	falling	fell	(have) fallen
fly	flying	flew	(have) flown
forget	forgetting	forgot	(have) forgotten *or* forgot
freeze	freezing	froze	(have) frozen
give	giving	gave	(have) given
go	going	went	(have) gone
grow	growing	grew	(have) grown
know	knowing	knew	(have) known
lie	lying	lay	(have) lain
ride	riding	rode	(have) ridden
ring	ringing	rang	(have) rung
rise	rising	rose	(have) risen
run	running	ran	(have) run
see	seeing	saw	(have) seen
shake	shaking	shook	(have) shaken
shrink	shrinking	shrank	(have) shrunk
sing	singing	sang	(have) sung
sink	sinking	sank	(have) sunk
speak	speaking	spoke	(have) spoken
spring	springing	sprang	(have) sprung
strive	striving	strove	(have) striven
swear	swearing	swore	(have) sworn
swim	swimming	swam	(have) swum
take	taking	took	(have) taken
tear	tearing	tore	(have) torn
throw	throwing	threw	(have) thrown
wear	wearing	wore	(have) worn
weave	weaving	wove	(have) woven *or* (have) wove
write	writing	wrote	(have) written

 Internet Tip

You can use an on-line dictionary not only to access definitions of words, but also to find the principal parts of irregular verbs. Simply type "on-line dictionaries" in the query field of your search engine. The first or second result should be a convenient dictionary that you can bookmark for easy use.

▶ **Exercise 5** Learning the Principal Parts of Irregular Verbs

Write the *present participle*, the *past*, and the *past participle* of each verb.

EXAMPLE: swim

ANSWER: swimming, swam, swum

1. win	6. stand	11. sing	16. drive
2. shake	7. keep	12. go	17. get
3. become	8. draw	13. steal	18. sit
4. build	9. break	14. rise	19. pay
5. fight	10. drink	15. swing	20. weave

▶ **Exercise 6** Revising to Correct Forms of Irregular Verbs

Revise these sentences, correcting irregular verb forms.

EXAMPLE: Which armies fighted at the Alamo?

ANSWER: fought

1. Because Texas and Mexico share a border, many Texans have went to Mexico.
2. Also, numerous Texans have came from Mexico.
3. These immigrants have choosed to work for better wages in the United States.
4. Many Texans who live near the border of Mexico have grew up speaking both English and Spanish.
5. By the early 1500's, Alonso Alvarez de Pineda, a Spanish explorer, had drawed maps of the Texas coast.
6. He reported to Spain on what he seen.
7. He sung the praises of a beautiful country.
8. His exploration begun the Spanish settlement of Texas.
9. In 1528, a Spanish ship sunk off the Texas coast.
10. Members of the expedition had striked out to explore the area.

More Practice

Grammar Exercise Workbook
• pp. 89–90
On-line Exercise Bank
• Section 21.1
  Go on-line:
  PHSchool.com
  Enter Web Code:
  efk-1102

Interactive Textbook

Get instant feedback! Exercises 5 and 6 are available on-line or on CD-ROM.

◀ Critical Viewing Using past tense forms of irregular verbs, explain the ways in which this ancient mission in San Antonio reflects Spanish influence in Texas. **[Analyze]**

Verb Conjugation

One way to learn the forms of a verb is through *conjugation*.

> ◢ **KEY CONCEPT** A **conjugation** is a complete list of the singular and plural forms of a verb in a particular tense. ■

The singular forms of a verb correspond to the singular personal pronouns (*I, you, he, she, it*), and the plural forms correspond to the plural personal pronouns (*we, you, they*).

The chart that follows conjugates the irregular verb *run*. To conjugate a verb, you need to use the principal parts: the present (*run*), the past (*ran*), and the past participle (*run*). You also need to use various helping verbs, such as *has, have, had*, and *will*.

Note that if you were to add the progressive and emphatic tenses to this conjugation, you would also need to use the present participle *running* and forms of *be* and *do* as helping verbs.

CONJUGATION OF THE BASIC FORMS OF *RUN*		
Present	**Singular**	**Plural**
First Person Second Person Third Person	I run you run he, she, it runs	we run you run they run
Past	**Singular**	**Plural**
First Person Second Person Third Person	I ran you ran he, she, it ran	we ran you ran they ran
Future	**Singular**	**Plural**
First Person Second Person Third Person	I will run you will run he, she, it will run	we will run you will run they will run
Present Perfect	**Singular**	**Plural**
First Person Second Person Third Person	I have run you have run he, she, it has run	we have run you have run they have run
Past Perfect	**Singular**	**Plural**
First Person Second Person Third Person	I had run you had run he, she, it had run	we had run you had run they had run
Future Perfect	**Singular**	**Plural**
First Person Second Person Third Person	I will have run you will have run he, she, it will have run	we will have run you will have run they will have run

Note About *Be:* *Be* is one of the most irregular verbs in its principal parts. The present participle is *being.* The past participle is *been.* The present and the past, however, vary depending on the subject.

PRESENT:	I am	we are
	you are	you are
	he, she, it is	they are
PAST:	I was	we were
	you were	you were
	he, she, it was	they were
FUTURE:	I will be	we will be
	you will be	you will be
	he, she, it will be	they will be

GRAMMAR IN
LITERATURE

from **A Journey Through Texas**
Alvar Núñez Cabeza de Vaca

The highlighted verbs in this excerpt are all past forms. Which verbs are regular, and which are irregular?

The same Indians *led* us to a plain beyond the chain of mountains, where people *came* to meet us from a long distance. By those we were treated in the same manner as before, and they *made* so many presents to the Indians who *came* with us that, unable to carry all, they *left* half of it. . . . We *told* these people our route *was* towards sunset, and they *replied* that in that direction people *lived* very far away. So we *ordered* them to send there and inform the inhabitants that we were coming and how. From this they *begged* to be excused, because the others *were* their enemies, and they did not want us to go to them.

▼ **Critical Viewing** Besides the obvious inconveniences of traveling long distances with only horses or donkeys and wagons, what might have been some of the advantages? Respond using past tense verbs. **[Infer]**

▶ **Exercise 7** Conjugating Verbs Conjugate the verbs below in the form specified.
1. become (basic)
2. go (progressive)
3. bring (emphatic)
4. give (basic)
5. know (progressive)

▶ **Exercise 8** Practicing Verb Tenses Write short sentences, using the form indicated for each verb.

EXAMPLE: spend—past perfect, first-person plural
ANSWER: We had spent.

1. *stand*—past perfect, second-person singular
2. *build*—past, third-person singular
3. *forget*—past progressive, second-person plural
4. *eat*—present perfect, second-person singular
5. *speak*—present perfect progressive, third-person plural
6. *swear*—present emphatic, second-person plural
7. *shrink*—past perfect, first-person singular
8. *drive*—future progressive, third-person singular
9. *give*—past perfect progressive, first-person plural
10. *pay*—future perfect, second-person singular
11. *know*—past emphatic, third-person plural
12. *sleep*—future perfect progressive, second-person plural
13. *seen*—present perfect, third-person singular
14. *grow*—past progressive, first-person singular
15. *shake*—present perfect progressive, second-person plural
16. *do*—future progressive, third-person plural
17. *choose*—past perfect, first-person plural
18. *swim*—past perfect progressive, first-person singular
19. *rise*—past emphatic, third-person singular
20. *write*—future perfect progressive, first-person plural

▲ Critical Viewing
Using "The lights of Dallas" as a subject, conjugate the verb *shine* in the third-person plural. [Relate]

▶ **More Practice**

Grammar Exercise Workbook
• pp. 91–92
On-line Exercise Bank
• Section 21.1

Go on-line:
PHSchool.com
Enter Web Code:
efk-1102

Complete the exercises on-line! Exercises 7 and 8 are available on-line or on CD-ROM.

(interactive) Interactive Textbook

Section 21.1 Section Review

GRAMMAR EXERCISES 9–15

Exercise 9 Identifying Verb Forms
Identify the form of each verb as *basic*, *progressive*, or *emphatic*.

1. Texas has been growing rapidly.
2. Now, it ranks as one of the most populous states in the United States.
3. Thousands of Texans will be moving into urban centers.
4. Twenty percent do live in rural areas.
5. Texans will remain near cities.
6. My grandmother really enjoys art.
7. Texas does boast numerous museums.
8. I have been planning a trip to the Dallas Museum of Fine Arts.
9. We will see many famous paintings.
10. I do hope to visit her again soon.

Exercise 10 Writing Sentences
With Irregular Verbs Write two sentences for each verb, one in the present perfect tense, and the other in the present progressive.

1. strive
2. fight
3. fall
4. ring
5. shake

Exercise 11 Revising to Correct
Verb Forms Revise these sentences, correcting the form of the verb as necessary. If no change is needed, write *correct*.

1. In 1924, Texans choosed Miriam A. Ferguson as their governor.
2. Texas had become the second state to elect a female governor.
3. She was knowed as "Ma Ferguson."
4. Then, in 1990, Ann Richards begun a term as governor.
5. It had took nearly seventy years for another woman to hold the office.
6. Many other women have led the way in Texas.

7. Barbara Bush, President Bush's wife, has builded her literacy campaign.
8. Barbara Jordan rised as the first African American congresswoman from the South.
9. She also teached politics and ethics at the University of Texas.
10. Lady Bird Johnson, wife of President Lyndon Johnson, done much to beautify the state.

Exercise 12 Revising to Change
Verb Tenses Change the verb in each of these sentences to either the present perfect, past perfect, or future perfect tense.

1. Texas shows great diversity.
2. Its rich soil produces many crops.
3. Many people, however, associate Texas with its oil industry.
4. By 1866, drillers discovered oil.
5. We will learn about the state by next week.

Exercise 13 Find It in Your
Reading Go back to the excerpt from "A Journey Through Texas" on page 379, and identify one progressive and one emphatic verb form.

Exercise 14 Find It in Your
Writing Choose a paper from your portfolio containing verbs written in the perfect tenses. Review it to make sure all the past participles are formed correctly.

Exercise 15 Writing Application
Briefly describe a historical event that took place in your state. Include verbs in the past, present perfect, and past perfect tenses.

The Correct Use of Tenses

The tenses of verbs allow you to express time within one of three main categories: the present, the past, and the future. Within each of these main categories, the time of an action or a condition can be expressed in slightly different ways.

As you will learn in this section, each verb form has particular uses that make it different from the other forms.

Present, Past, and Future Time

A clear understanding of the way verbs are used within the three categories of time is important for correct usage.

Uses of Tense in Present Time Present time can be expressed with a basic, a progressive, and an emphatic form.

▶ **KEY CONCEPT** The three forms of the present tense show present actions or conditions, as well as various continuing actions or conditions. ■

The chart below gives an example of each of the three forms.

FORMS EXPRESSING PRESENT TIME	
Present:	I surf.
Present Progressive:	I am surfing.
Present Emphatic:	I do surf.

The next chart shows the main uses of the present tense.

USES OF THE PRESENT	
Present action:	I *paddle* a raft down the river.
Present condition:	Barbara *is* very upset that the beach is closed.
Regularly occurring action:	Tourists *travel* to Hawaii in the summer.
Regularly occurring condition:	I *am* usually punctual.
Constant action:	The earth *rotates* on its axis.
Constant condition:	People *are* not infallible.

Theme: Water Sports

In this section, you will learn how to use verb tenses and forms. The examples and exercises in this section are about water sports.

Cross-Curricular Connection: Physical Education

When the present tense is used to relate historical events, it is called the *historical present*. Writers sometimes use the historical present to bring to life past actions or conditions.

THE HISTORICAL PRESENT	
Past action expressed in the historical present:	A confident soldier *marches* through France during World War II.
Past condition expressed in the historical present:	For the surfers of the 1940's, Hawaii's gigantic waves *are* very intimidating.

Another use of the present is called the *critical present*. It is frequently used in discussions of deceased authors and their literary works.

THE CRITICAL PRESENT	
Action expressed in the critical present:	Ernest Hemingway *shows* his genius even in his early novels.
Condition expressed in the critical present	Emily Dickinson *is* a famous nineteenth-century poet.

The uses of the present progressive are shown in the next chart. Notice that the continuing actions can be of a long or short duration.

USES OF THE PRESENT PROGRESSIVE	
Long continuing action:	She *is writing* a novel.
Short continuing action:	Samantha *is fixing* the sail.
Continuing condition:	The weather *is being* very unpredictable.

The four main uses of the present emphatic are shown in the chart on the next page.

Grammar and Style Tip

If you begin using the critical present to relate the events of a story, it is important to stay with the present tense and not shift back and forth between the present and the past.

USES OF THE PRESENT EMPHATIC

Emphasizing a statement:	Windsurfing *does require* much practice.
Denying a contrary assertion:	No, I *do* not *like* raw oysters.
Asking a question:	Do you *play* water polo?
Making a sentence negative:	She *does* not *own* a boat.

Exercise 16 Revising Sentences to Change From Past Tense to Present Tense Verbs Revise these sentences, changing the verbs to the present tense. Then, indicate the present tense use of each verb.

1. To prepare for the competition, Alexi swam every day.
2. She did not want to miss her chance to stand out.
3. She was thinking of a famous swimmer-turned-movie star.
4. Esther Williams was a swimmer-actress of the 1940's and 1950's.
5. In her autobiography, *The Million Dollar Mermaid,* she described her glamourous life.

Uses of Tense in Past Time Seven verb forms express actions and conditions that took place some time before the present.

KEY CONCEPT The seven forms that express past time show actions and conditions beginning in the past. ■

FORMS EXPRESSING PAST TIME	
Past:	I paddled.
Present Perfect:	I have paddled.
Past Perfect:	I had paddled.
Past Progressive:	I was paddling.
Present Perfect Progressive:	I have been paddling.
Past Perfect Progressive:	I had been paddling.
Past Emphatic:	I did paddle.

More Practice

Grammar Exercise Workbook
• pp. 93–94
On-line Exercise Bank
• Section 21.2
  Go on-line:
  PHSchool.com
  Enter Web Code:
  efk-1102

Complete the exercise on-line! Exercise 16 is available on-line or on CD-ROM.

Exercise 22 Revising to Add the Correct Forms of Participles and Infinitives Revise each sentence, following the instructions in parentheses.

EXAMPLE: I'm sure you played very well. (Add a phrase with the perfect participle of *watch*.)

ANSWER: Having watched your games before, I'm sure you played very well.

1. Have you ever tried playing water polo? (Change *playing* to a present infinitive.)
2. People seemed to play it in the late 1800's. (Change *to play* to a perfect infinitive.)
3. These early swimmers were reputed to model their game after soccer. (Change *to model* to a perfect infinitive.)
4. We tried the game ourselves last summer. (Add a phrase using the perfect participle of *study*.)
5. We were glad to learn the rules of the game ahead of time. (Change *to learn* to a perfect infinitive.)

Modifiers That Help Clarify Tense

Adverbs such as *often* or *sometimes* and phrases such as *once in a while* or *within a week* are often used to help clarify the time expressed by a verb.

KEY CONCEPT Use modifiers when they can help clarify the tense of a verb. ■

EXAMPLES: *Occasionally,* I enjoy playing volleyball at the beach.
Susan *always* swam with her goggles on.
By next year, Walter will have fished in every river in Colorado.
I swim laps *once a week.*

Exercise 23 Adding Modifiers to Improve Meaning Revise each sentence by adding a modifier that indicates time.

1. Water-skiing is one of the most popular water sports in the world.
2. It was considered a sport for daredevils.
3. It is considered a recreational activity that can be enjoyed by almost everyone.
4. Thousands of water-skiers rush to lakes and oceans with their equipment in tow.
5. These places became the site of one of the world's most thrilling pastimes.

Learn More

To review adverbs and adverb phrases, see Chapter 17 and Chapter 19.

Hands-on Grammar

The Perfect Booklet!

Use a "perfect" two-way booklet to keep track of the perfect tenses.

Begin with a 6" X 8-1/2" sheet of paper. Fold it in half the short way and in half again; then, unfold it. The paper will have three parallel creases. Then, fold the paper in half on the middle crease. With a pair of scissors, cut three slits through the folded edge of the paper at 1-1/2" intervals. Cut *only* as far as the next crease. (See illustration.) Then, unfold and flatten the paper.

Next, cut two 6" X 1-3/4" strips of paper in a color different from that of the full sheet of paper. Weave each strip through the slits in the full sheet, forming a checkerboard pattern. Now, refold the paper on the creases, making a narrow booklet. Notice that opening the booklet on the middle fold on one side gives you two checkered pages; opening the middle fold on the other side gives you four checkered pages—for a total of six.

Now, in the top "square" of each checkered page, print a different perfect tense: Present Perfect, Past Perfect, Future Perfect, Present Perfect Progressive, Past Perfect Progressive, Future Perfect Progressive. Then, choose six verbs, and with two per square, write their perfect tenses on the appropriate pages. When you have finished, you will have a booklet with which to review the perfect tenses.

Find It in Your Reading Look through several pages of a history book, and identify the perfect tenses. Note how many you find in the progressive form.

Find It in Your Writing Review a piece of writing from your portfolio. Identify three verbs in a perfect tense. See if there are any places where you might use a perfect progressive.

THE VERB *CHOOSE* IN THE PASSIVE VOICE	
Present:	she is chosen
Past:	she was chosen
Future:	she will be chosen
Present Perfect:	she has been chosen
Past Perfect:	she had been chosen
Future Perfect:	she will have been chosen
Present Progressive:	she is being chosen
Past Progressive:	she was chosen

▼ **Critical Viewing**
What do the pictures in this montage say about the activities of an inventor? Answer with one sentence in the active voice and one in the passive voice. **[Draw Conclusions]**

Exercise 36 Identifying and Revising Active and Passive Voice Identify each verb as *active* or *passive*. Then, revise those that are passive to active, adding or changing words as needed.

EXAMPLE: Peanut butter was invented by G. W. Carver.

ANSWER: (passive) G. W. Carver invented peanut butter.

1. George Washington Carver earned his bachelor's degree in science from Iowa State College in 1894.
2. Following his graduation, he was hired by Iowa State College as a faculty member to teach agriculture.
3. Later, an idle field at a school in Tuskegee, Alabama, was transformed by Carver into a prosperous farm.
4. Peanuts were championed by Carver as a good crop for Alabama soil, and he developed more than three hundred different products—including oil, paint, ink, and butter—from the simple peanut.
5. By the time of his death in 1943, Carver had been recognized by numerous organizations and scientists.

George Washington Carver, agriculturist and inventor

Exercise 37 Forming the Tenses of Passive Verbs
Conjugate each verb in the passive voice, using the chart above.
1. drive   2. invent   3. write   4. grow   5. own

More Practice

Grammar Exercise Workbook
• pp. 99–102
On-line Exercise Bank
• Section 21.4

Go on-line:
PHSchool.com
Enter Web Code:
efk-1102

Using Active and Passive Voice

Once you are able to distinguish between the active and passive voice, you can apply this knowledge to your own writing. The active voice is generally more forceful than the passive voice.

▶ **KEY CONCEPT** Use the active voice whenever possible because it is usually more direct and economical. ■

ACTIVE VOICE: Carver *invented* many products.
PASSIVE VOICE: Many products *were* invented by Carver.

The passive voice has two important uses in English.

▶ **KEY CONCEPTS** Use the passive voice to emphasize the receiver of an action, rather than the performer of an action. Use the passive voice to point out the receiver of an action when the performer is not important or not easily identified. ■

RECEIVER EMPHASIZED: Wood *was carried* by Harriet Tubman.

PERFORMER UNKNOWN: A child *was helped* across the river.

PERFORMER UNIMPORTANT: The runaways *were saved.*

▶ **Exercise 38** Revising to Correct Unnecessary Use of the Passive Voice Revise the following passage, changing unnecessary uses of the passive voice to the active voice. Not every use of the passive voice will need to change.

A hard life was had by Harriet Tubman because of the prejudices and injustices of the early 1800's. She was born into slavery in Dorchester County, Maryland, around 1819. She was forced by plantation owners to labor in the fields. In 1849, Tubman was sold by her masters to a distant plantation. Traveling to the new plantation, she was overcome by a desire to escape. She slipped into the woods and stealthily made her way north toward states where slavery had been outlawed. Tubman was helped during her trip by people sympathetic to runaway slaves. She traveled more than one hundred miles and eventually reached Philadelphia, a free city. Later, a significant role was played by Tubman in the Underground Railroad. She was called the "Moses" of her people.

▼ Critical Viewing
One could say that Harriet Tubman lived her life "in the active voice." What aspect of this photograph suggests Tubman's strength? Answer in the active voice. **[Analyze]**

Section 21.4 *Section Review*

GRAMMAR EXERCISES 39–43

▶ **Exercise 39** Identifying Active and Passive Voice Identify each verb as *active* or *passive*.

1. In addition to his skills as a scientist, George Washington Carver enjoyed music.
2. While working in Winterset, Iowa, Carver was given piano lessons by Mrs. Millholland, a gifted musician.
3. His skills as a musician helped him later in life.
4. In his early days at Tuskegee, Carver played a series of recitals to raise money for the school's agriculture program.
5. Enough money was raised from those concerts for the purchase of much-needed farm equipment.
6. Carver also enjoyed the visual arts.
7. While at Simpson College, he was coached in painting by Etta Budd.
8. Carver's creativity was nurtured by Budd.
9. Fueled by her encouragement, Carver painted numerous pictures while at Simpson College.
10. Some of Carver's paintings were exhibited by art experts at an exposition in 1893.

▶ **Exercise 40** Revising to Change Verbs to the Active Voice Rewrite the following sentences using the active voice. Change or add words as necessary in order to put each verb into the active voice.

1. George Washington Carver is remembered by historians as a pioneer African American scientist.
2. Great sacrifices were made by Carver throughout his professional life.
3. Forty-five years were spent by Carver at Tuskegee.

4. During that time, his services were sought by numerous prestigious institutions.
5. Carver was invited by Thomas A. Edison to join the staff of the famous Edison Laboratories in New Jersey.
6. A large salary was offered to Carver by Edison.
7. That offer, and many other similar offers, were turned down by Carver.
8. Carver was driven by a love of research and the desire to help African Americans.
9. In 1923, an honorary doctor of science degree was given to him by the University of Rochester.
10. A second honorary doctor of science degree was awarded to him by Simpson College.

▶ **Exercise 41** Find It in Your Reading Look through a social studies textbook to find examples of the passive voice being used because the performer of an action is unknown or not specific.

▶ **Exercise 42** Find It in Your Writing In your own writing, find at least three examples of verbs in the passive voice. If any example contains an unnecessary use of the passive voice, rewrite it in the active voice.

▶ **Exercise 43** Writing Application Write an account of an incident you experienced that illustrates the positive value of friendship. Include two appropriate sentences using the passive voice correctly.

Benjamin Franklin opening the first subscription library in Philadelphia, Charles E. Mills

In the English language, some words may change form according to the way they are used in sentences. This occurs frequently with pronouns. For instance, the form of a pronoun used as a subject may be different from its form as a direct object.

This quality of pronouns helps writers to express simple and complicated ideas effectively. Indeed, writers, editors, and printers all pay special attention to the way pronouns are used in sentences.

In this chapter, you will study the various forms of pronouns and their uses.

▲ **Critical Viewing** Choose two people in this picture, and describe their actions using such pronouns as *he, she, him, her, his, hers, they, them,* and *their.* **[Analyze]**

Diagnostic Test

Directions: Write all answers on a separate sheet of paper.

Skill Check A. Identify the pronoun, and tell whether its case is *nominative, objective,* or *possessive.*

1. her biography
2. dedicated the book to him
3. found it in nonfiction
4. they published
5. my favorite author

Skill Check B. Identify the case of each underlined pronoun, and tell how it is used in the sentence.

6. <u>Our</u> eleventh-grade English class used the library extensively to study American authors.
7. <u>I</u>, for one, read a biography of Samuel L. Clemens, who wrote under the pen name Mark Twain.
8. *"The Notorious Jumping Frog of Calaveras County" and Other Sketches* was <u>his</u> first work, and it was considered a financial failure.
9. It was not until one hundred years later that <u>it</u> was reprinted.
10. *The Adventures of Tom Sawyer,* one of Twain's works, was read to <u>me</u> by my grandfather.
11. I read <u>it</u> again myself to relive Tom's adventures.
12. My friend, on the other hand, researched the life of Louisa May Alcott and <u>her</u> literary career.
13. It was <u>she</u> who wrote the *Little Women* series.
14. Abe's and Peter's friend introduced <u>them</u> to many of the works of Jack London, including his boxing stories and his war correspondence.
15. London's interest in the Yukon, California, and the South Pacific inspired <u>him</u> to write extensively about those places.

Skill Check C. Choose the correct pronoun in each sentence.

16. (Who, Whom) wrote *The Sea-Wolf*?
17. From (whom, who) did we receive such works as *Flower Fables* and *Hospital Sketches*?
18. Was it Huck Finn (who, whom) grew up along the Mississippi River?
19. I'm curious about (whoever, whomever) published her first work under the pseudonym Flora Fairfield.
20. I will read (whoever, whomever) the librarian recommends.

Skill Check D. Choose the correct pronoun to complete the elliptical clause.

21. Jack London was as prolific as (he, him).
22. Louisa May Alcott is known to my friends as well as (I, me).
23. They like Twain's works more than (me, I).
24. No authors are more widely known than (them, they).
25. This book is dearer to me than (he, him).

Case

Case is characteristic of only two parts of speech: nouns and pronouns.

▶ **KEY CONCEPT** **Case** is the form of a noun or a pronoun that indicates its use in a sentence. ■

The Three Cases

Both nouns and pronouns have three cases—*nominative, objective,* and *possessive.* Nouns, however, usually present no problem because their form changes only in the possessive case.

NOMINATIVE: The *library* opens in one hour.
OBJECTIVE: There are many resources available in the *library.*
POSSESSIVE: The *library's* collection of periodicals is extensive.

In the first example, *library* is nominative because it is the subject of the verb *opens;* in the second, *library* is objective because it is the object of the preposition *in.* The form changes only in the possessive case. An apostrophe and *s* are added for the singular possessive, and just an apostrophe is added for the plural possessive.

In contrast to nouns, personal pronouns have different forms for all three cases.

▶ **KEY CONCEPT** The three cases of personal pronouns are nominative, objective, and possessive. The pronoun forms are different in each case. ■

Nominative	Objective	Possessive
I	me	my, mine
you	you	your, yours
he, she, it	him, her, it	his, her, hers, its
we	us	our, ours
they	them	their, theirs

▶ **Exercise 1** Writing Sentences With Pronouns Write sentences using pronouns according to the instructions below.
1. Use *he* or *she* and *his* or *hers* in a sentence about a librarian.
2. Use *I, me,* and *mine* in a sentence about a library book.
3. Use *they, them,* and *their* in a sentence about two students.
4. Use *we, our,* and *ours* in a sentence about a presentation.
5. Use *you, your,* and *yours* in a sentence about a Web site.

Theme: Books and Libraries

In this chapter, you will learn about pronoun usage. The examples and exercises in this section are about books and libraries.

✿ Spelling Tip

Notice that the possessive pronouns *yours, his, hers, its, ours,* and *theirs* end in *s* but never take an apostrophe.

▶ **Exercise 2** Identifying Case On a separate sheet of paper, write the case of each underlined pronoun.

EXAMPLE: Sheila gave <u>him</u> two books for the report.

ANSWER: objective

1. Our libraries provide <u>us</u> with a wealth of information and literary enjoyment.
2. It is important that you know how to use a library in order to make the most of <u>your</u> visit.
3. Librarians are very knowledgeable and can guide <u>us</u> in our search for material.
4. Card and computer catalogs allow you and <u>me</u> to access information about subjects, titles, and authors.
5. <u>They</u> also provide call numbers that will enable you to find the book in the library.
6. The Dewey Decimal System is used by many libraries to allow <u>them</u> to divide and catalog nonfiction books into ten main categories.
7. <u>They</u> are general topics, philosophy, religion, social science, language, pure science, technology, the arts, language and rhetoric, and geography and history.
8. Fiction books are shelved by the first three letters of <u>their</u> authors' last names.
9. Biographies and autobiographies are assigned the call number 921 and are arranged by <u>their</u> subjects' last names.
10. You will find many reference resources to help <u>you</u> with information about a specific topic.

More Practice

Grammar Exercise Workbook
• pp. 103–104
On-line Exercise Bank
• Section 22.1
Go on-line:
PHSchool.com
Enter Web Code:
efk-1102

interactive Textbook

Get instant feedback! Exercises 1 and 2 are available on-line or on CD-ROM.

▶ Critical Viewing To what degree do you think these readers are enjoying the book? Answer this question using at least three pronouns—one in each case. [Analyze]

The Nominative Case

The nominative case is used when a personal pronoun acts in one of three ways:

> **KEY CONCEPT** Use the nominative case for the *subject* of a verb, for a *predicate nominative*, and for the pronoun in a *nominative absolute*. ■

These uses are illustrated in the following chart:

NOMINATIVE PRONOUNS	
As the subject of a verb:	*They* are going to the library.
As a predicate nominative:	The only one left is *he*.
In a nominative absolute:	*She* having finished her lecture, the students left quietly.

Informal Use of the Predicate Nominative Although formal usage requires a nominative pronoun after a linking verb, people often use the objective case in informal situations. For essays and other formal writing, however, you should make a point to use the nominative case.

INFORMAL: It was me who answered the telephone.
FORMAL: It was I who answered the telephone.

Nominative Pronouns in Compounds When you use a pronoun in a compound subject or predicate nominative, check the case by mentally removing the other part of the compound or by mentally inverting the sentence.

COMPOUND SUBJECT: Joanne and *I* prepared the report.
(*I* prepared the report.)
Doug and *she* solved the problem.
(*She* solved the problem.)

COMPOUND PREDICATE NOMINATIVE: The contestants are Fran and *I*.
(Fran and *I* are the contestants.)
The guilty ones are Ethel and *he*.
(Ethel and *he* are the guilty ones.)

Nominative Pronouns With Appositives When an appositive follows a pronoun used as a subject or predicate nominative, the pronoun should stay in the nominative case.

SUBJECT: *We* New Yorkers are proud of our city's library system.

PREDICATE NOMINATIVE: The only ones invited are *we* juniors.

Speaking and Listening Tip

Together with one or two of your classmates, take turns reading aloud Exercises 3 and 4 on the next page in order to accustom yourselves to using nominative pronouns correctly.

► **Exercise 3** Identifying Pronouns in the Nominative Case
Choose the pronoun in the nominative case to complete each sentence. Then, identify the use of the pronoun.

EXAMPLE: Amy and (he, him) collaborated on that book.
ANSWER: he (subject)

1. Paul and (me, I) decided to compose a mystery novel.
2. Charlene and (he, him) deserve credit for the initial idea.
3. The ones who decided the plot structure were (we, us) authors.
4. (I, Me) having finished the outline, Paul began to write.
5. (He, Him) and Amy collaborated on the illustrations.
6. Harold and (they, them) helped the effort by gathering further reference materials.
7. However, it was Carla and (I, me) who carefully edited the finished manuscript.
8. I could not find Paul, (he, him) having left for the publisher's office.
9. The very first readers of the manuscript were (we, us) friends.
10. Both Marc and (her, she) are excellent at handling all aspects of publicity.

► **Exercise 4** Using Pronouns in the Nominative Case Write a nominative pronoun to complete each sentence. Then, identify the use of the pronoun.

1. You and ___?___ will study the role of illustration in comic books.
2. It is ___?___ who is most talented at drawing cartoons for these types of books.
3. The model for our new cartoon character will be ___?___.
4. The new representatives at the cartoon convention will be Jack and ___?___.
5. Esther and ___?___ will teach us how to create an interesting sketch that matches the character description in the book.
6. The eager participants and ___?___ plan to listen carefully to Esther's instructions.
7. ___?___ having given the instructions, the participants began their sketches.
8. Karl and ___?___ used their thumb prints on a stamp pad as outlines for their sketches.
9. As a result, ___?___ learned unusual techniques for illustrating characters.
10. "The winner of the prize for the cartoon with the best personality is ___?___!" cried Karl's mother.

► **More Practice**
Grammar Exercise Workbook
• pp. 105–106
On-line Exercise Bank
• Section 22.1
Go on-line:
PHSchool.com
Enter Web Code:
efk-1102

Complete the exercises on-line! Exercises 3 and 4 are available on-line or on CD-ROM.

The Objective Case

Objective pronouns are used for any kind of object in a sentence as well as for subjects of infinitives.

> **KEY CONCEPT** Use the objective case for the object of any verb, verbal, or preposition, as well as for the object or subject of an infinitive. ■

The chart below illustrates the uses of objective pronouns.

OBJECTIVE PRONOUNS	
Direct Object	The ending of the novel greatly surprised *me*.
Indirect Object	Reading the tiny print gave *her* a headache.
Object of Participle	The problems bothering *him* remained a secret.
Object of Gerund	Solving *them* will not be easy.
Object of Infinitive	Graham wanted to show *us* his new book club membership.
Object of Preposition	The mail carrier said that the package was for *her*.
Subject of Infinitive	Carol wants Harry and *me* to help organize the author's study group.

Objective Pronouns in Compounds As with the nominative case, most usage problems in the objective case occur with pronouns in compounds. To check your usage, mentally remove the other part of the compound.

EXAMPLES: Al sent Carol and *me* tickets to the dramatic reading.
(Al sent *me* tickets to the dramatic reading.)
The hero rescued Bill and *her* in the second act.
(The hero rescued *her* in the second act.)

You should take special care to use the objective case after the preposition *between*.

INCORRECT: The intermission snacks will be split between you and *I*.

CORRECT: The intermission snacks will be split between you and *me*.

⌕ Learn More

For more information about pronouns, see Chapter 17.

✦ Grammar and Style Tip

In some situations where the nominative case is correct, it may sound too formal for your purpose. Consider revising the sentence so that you may correctly use the objective case.

Objective Pronouns With Appositives

When a pronoun used as an object or as the subject of an infinitive has an appositive, make sure you use the objective case.

EXAMPLES: The professor encouraged *us* budding playwrights.

The professor gave *us* students some scenes to rewrite.

Our classmates asked *us* stragglers to hurry up.

▲ **Critical Viewing** Describe the effect of this imposing structure on a boy, a girl, and you. Use objective pronouns to refer to each person. **[Analyze]**

> **Exercise 5** Identifying Pronouns in the Objective Case

Choose the pronoun in the objective case to complete each sentence. Then, write the use of the pronoun.

1. My father took (I, me) to the Library of Congress on our recent trip to Washington, D.C.
2. The Library of Congress is the largest research library available to (us, we) in the United States.
3. The Library of Congress is the center of all libraries in our nation and provides (them, they) with catalogs of all new publications.
4. One of the library's goals is to make its extensive collections easily accessible to the government and (you, your), the general public.
5. The Library of Congress will allow (we, us) use of its facilities if we are over the appropriate age.
6. A guide was happy to show (they, them) how to obtain special permission to use the library.
7. All researchers intending to use the public reading rooms are required to have reader identification cards issued to (them, they) by the library.
8. A reader identification card is valid for two years, and one must renew (it, its) when it expires.
9. The Office of the Librarian of Congress is solely responsible for making the institution's rules and regulations, enforcing (they, them), and appointing its staff.
10. The reader registration system was initiated by (they, them) to protect the library's collection.

> **More Practice**

Grammar Exercise Workbook
• pp. 105–106
On-line Exercise Bank
• Section 22.1

Go on-line:
PHSchool.com
Enter Web Code:
efk-1102

Get instant feedback! Exercise 5 is available on-line or on CD-ROM.

> **Exercise 6** Using Pronouns in the Objective Case Write an objective pronoun that will complete each sentence.

1. Our cousins were coming, so we decided to assemble a family photo album for ___?___.
2. Between my sister and ___?___, we came up with some great photo choices.
3. We considered ___?___ and then made our selections.
4. Because Grandmother was looking on, we asked ___?___ for suggestions.
5. Because our brother is artistic, we decided to ask ___?___ to monogram the album.

Errors to Avoid With Possessive Pronouns

Although errors are less common with the possessive case than with the two other cases, mistakes are sometimes made when pronouns are used before gerunds.

> **KEY CONCEPT** Use the possessive case before gerunds. ■

EXAMPLES: *His* objecting to the research caused an uproar.
I respect *your* maintaining an optimistic outlook.
Tad resents *my* using his writing desk.

Another error to avoid is using an apostrophe with possessive pronouns, which already indicate ownership. Spellings such as *our's, their's,* and *your's* are incorrect. In addition, do not confuse a possessive pronoun with a contraction.

POSSESSIVE PRONOUN: The vivid print had retained *its* clarity.
CONTRACTION: *It's* wise to proofread your report.

> **Exercise 7** Using Pronouns in the Possessive Case Choose the correct word in each set of parentheses.

An event that happened 500 years ago has been discussed ever since. (1) (Its, It's) the origin of printing as we know it today. (2) (It's, Its) inventor is thought to have been Johann Gutenberg. (3) (He's, He) responsible for the art of printing with movable type. Of course, the work was done much more slowly than (4) (it's, its) done today. Ink was rolled over the raised surfaces of handset letters within a frame and pressed against a sheet of paper. (5) (Us, Our) learning about Gutenberg has led me to explore further the history of printing.

Spelling Tip

The three forms of *their* sound similar. Remember: *There* refers to place, *their* shows ownership, and *they're* means "they are."

More Practice

Grammar Exercise Workbook
• pp. 107–108
On-line Exercise Bank
• Section 22.1

Go on-line:
PHSchool.com
Enter Web Code:
efk-1102

Interactive Textbook

Complete the exercises on-line! Exercises 6 and 7 are available on-line or on CD-ROM.

Hands-on Grammar

Pronoun Case Triangle

Create a pronoun case triangle to help you remember the uses of the three cases of pronouns. First, cut out a large triangle with three equal sides from colored paper. Next, fold one point of the triangle so that it touches the opposite side. Then, unfold it, leaving the crease. Fold the other two points of the triangle as well. After folding each point, your triangle should look like the diagram at right. (The dotted lines indicate creases.)

Write the name of each pronoun case on a crease. In the point (shown as a shaded small triangle in the diagram), write the uses of the case.

Turn the triangle over, and write the pronouns of the case on the back of the point that contains the uses.

Reverse side
me, you, him, her, it, us, them

Does the action or renames the subject
Nominative

Is acted on or acted toward

Objective

Possessive

Shows ownership and is used with gerunds

Paper-clip your triangle to a sheet of notebook paper, and keep it in your folder to record examples as you find them.

Find It in Your Reading As you encounter uses of each pronoun case in your reading, record on your notebook paper the sentence in which the pronoun is used.

Find It in Your Writing Look through your portfolio to find examples of each pronoun case. On the paper, write the sentences in which you use the pronouns.

Section Review

GRAMMAR EXERCISES 8–15

Exercise 8 Identifying Cases of Pronouns On a separate sheet of paper, write the personal pronouns you find in each sentence. Identify the case of each personal pronoun.

1. To write a research report, you must first list topics of interest to you.
2. Talk about them with a friend.
3. He or she can help you choose a topic.
4. Write three questions about your topic.
5. Find facts that answer them.
6. Use your notes as supporting details.
7. When your report is ready, read it to friends.
8. Ask them for their reactions.
9. They can edit it with you.
10. Proofread the final result, and check it for capitalization and punctuation.

Exercise 9 Choosing Pronouns in the Nominative Case Choose the pronoun in the nominative case to complete each sentence. Then, identify the use of the pronoun.

1. My friends and (me, I) went to a book-signing event at our local bookstore.
2. (We, Us) waited for more than an hour to meet our favorite author.
3. (Her, She) being a prolific author, millions have read her novels.
4. A press agent was on hand, and it was (he, him) who directed us to the author.
5. "The illustrator is (him, he)!" cried the exultant author.
6. (He, Him) having been highly recommended, we turned to him for help.
7. Billy and (her, she) discovered that a copyright page tells when the copyright of the book was issued.
8. It was (they, them), who reminded us about the copyright laws.

9. Kristin and (me, I) blushed when the author said she would acknowledge our help in the introduction to her book.
10. (We, Us) having praised her work, the author smiled and signed our copies of her book.

Exercise 10 Choosing Pronouns in the Objective Case Choose the pronoun in the objective case to complete each sentence. Then, identify the use of the pronoun.

1. The graphic charts displayed in the book's appendix were drawn by Julie and (I, me).
2. The additional maps were photocopied and delivered to Caroline and (he, him).
3. Give (us, we) students a chance to figure out the definition of the difficult word by looking at the glossary.
4. A kind of miniature dictionary, a glossary supplies (us, we) with meanings of words.
5. The definition of *millennium* was found by (her, she).
6. The bibliography will help Suzie and (her, she) locate additional information on their research topic.
7. Exciting (us, we) most was the variety of information about new computer technology.
8. This list of related books will benefit (they, them) also.
9. The man helping (us, we) with the alphabetized index was the reference librarian.
10. He also reminded (they, them) about the important parts of a book.

▶ **Exercise 11** Classifying Pronouns and Their Uses On a separate sheet of paper, write the case of each personal pronoun and its use.

1. The printing press and its development depended on the refinement of paper in China over several centuries.
2. Did you know Chinese "rag" paper was a cheap cloth and plant-fiber substitute for precious silk paper?
3. Chinese prisoners passed the technology on to their Arab captors in the eighth century.
4. The secrets of the craft were revealed by them to Europeans.
5. They were the same techniques the Chinese had given to the Arabs.
6. Long before Gutenberg and his invention of the printing press, Chinese block printing and movable clay type fed the push toward expanding the range of written material.
7. Although the European innovations came much later, they certainly reached a wider audience.
8. Because their alphabet employs ideograms, the use of movable type was much harder for the Chinese.
9. Consequently, movable type did not change production for the Chinese as dramatically as it did for Europeans.
10. Some historians also assert that the sequential, linear, and standardized character of the printed word especially suited us in the Western world.

▶ **Exercise 12** Correcting Errors in Pronoun Usage Rewrite each sentence, correcting any mistakes in pronoun usage. Write *correct* if the sentence contains no errors.

1. Lee and me attended a poetry reading at the community library.
2. The poets read they're poetry.
3. Bentley sent them and I to the meeting room to inspect the seating plan.
4. Lee informed Philip and she that formal reservations were not necessary.
5. The special events coordinator signaled to Lee and I from behind the podium.
6. Please give her and me a chance before you begin the program.
7. The man seating we students in the front row was Bentley's father.
8. Jules decided to sit between Cynthia and I.
9. After hearing Ben's reading, we thought his' interpretation was best.
10. The entire gathering applauded the authors and there poetic genius.

▶ **Exercise 13** Find It in Your Reading In the following sentence from "The First Seven Years," identify at least one pronoun in each of the three cases and tell how each is used.

He had begged her to go, pointing out how many fathers could not afford to send their children to college. But she said she wanted to be independent.

▶ **Exercise 14** Find It in Your Writing In your portfolio, find two examples of pronouns in each of the three cases. Check to make sure that each is used correctly. Then, write down each pronoun, its case, and its use in the sentence.

▶ **Exercise 15** Writing Application Write a paragraph on the subject of books or libraries. Use at least five of the nouns listed below. For each noun, include a pronoun that refers to it. Try to include pronouns in all three cases. Then, circle each pronoun.

1. author
2. book
3. print
4. publisher
5. librarian
6. idea
7. Gutenberg
8. libraries
9. readers
10. pages

Special Problems With Pronouns

The incorrect form of a pronoun may sometimes sound correct. For example, would it be correct to say, "Darlene is more qualified than *me*"? Though the sentence may sound correct to you, it is incorrect because an objective pronoun has been used when a nominative pronoun is needed. This section discusses the proper uses of *who* and *whom* and the use of pronouns in clauses where some of the words are omitted but understood.

Using *Who* and *Whom* Correctly

Deciding which form of *who* and *whom* to use is often a problem. In order to use the correct form, you must understand how the pronoun is used and what case is appropriate.

▷ **KEY CONCEPT** Learn to recognize the cases of *who* and *whom* and to use them correctly in sentences. ■

The following chart shows the forms of these pronouns and their uses in sentences.

Case	Pronoun	Use in Sentence
Nominative	who, whoever	Subject of a verb Predicate nominative
Objective	whom, whomever	Direct object Object of a preposition
Possessive	whose, whosever	To show ownership

Note about *whose:* The possessive case rarely causes problems, but you should be careful not to confuse the contraction *who's*, meaning "who is," with the pronoun *whose*.

POSSESSIVE PRONOUN: *Whose* car will we take to the job interview?

CONTRACTION: *Who's* going to drive us to the job interview?

Theme: Careers

In this section, you will learn about *who* and *whom* and the correct use of pronouns in elliptical clauses. The examples and exercises in this section are about careers.

Cross-Curricular Connection: Social Studies

 Spelling Tip

Remember that *whoever* and *whomever* are compound words.

The nominative pronouns *who* and *whoever* often serve as the subject in questions. They can also serve as predicate nominatives, but this use of *whoever* is rare.

SUBJECT: *Who* wrote the career guide?
Whoever undertakes such a challenging job will work hard.

PREDICATE NOMINATIVE: The news commentator was *who*?

The main usage problems with *who* and *whoever* occur when they are used in complex sentences to begin a subordinate clause. It is important to remember that the pronoun's role within the subordinate clause determines the proper case.

```
              ┌──── subord. clause ────┐
              S
EXAMPLE:   Assign this task to whoever will accept it.
```

In this example, the pronoun seems to be the object of the preposition *to*, but *whoever* is the subject of the clause. The entire subordinate clause acts as the object of the preposition.

The objective pronouns *whom* and *whomever* are also used in questions as either direct objects or objects of prepositions. If you are in doubt about the use of the pronoun, reword the question as a statement with a pronoun. Use the case of the pronoun as a clue to whether you should use *who* or *whom*.

DIRECT OBJECT: *Whom* did you consult?
You did consult *her*. [not *she*]

OBJECT OF PREPOSITION: To *whom* are you writing?
You are writing to *him*. [not *he*]

It is especially important to examine the pronoun's use in a complex sentence. Begin by isolating the subordinate clause. If necessary, reword the clause (a clause correctly beginning with *whom* or *whomever* will always be inverted). Finally, determine the use of the pronoun and the appropriate case.

EXAMPLES: This waiter is an unpleasant fellow *whom* I dislike.
Subordinate clause: whom I dislike
Reworded clause: I dislike *him*. [not *he*]
Use of pronoun: direct object of *dislike*
Case for direct object: objective

John charmed *whomever* he spoke with.
Subordinate clause: whomever he spoke with
Reworded clause: he spoke with *them* [not *they*]
Use of pronoun: object of preposition *with*
Case for object of preposition: objective

Technology Tip

Sometimes your spell-check feature will try to separate *who* and *ever* or *whom* and *ever*. Put them back together.

▲ **Critical Viewing**
Explain this scene, using *who* to describe the teacher and *whom* to describe the students. **[Connect]**

Determining Case in Subordinate Clauses With Parenthetical Expressions

Ignore expressions such as *they say* or *I suppose* when choosing between *who* and *whom*, because they do not affect the rest of the clause.

EXAMPLES: He is the one *who*, I think, will get the job.

He is the one *whom*, I think, the board will hire.

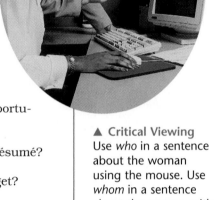

▶ **Exercise 16** Using Forms of *Who* Correctly in Questions Choose the correct pronoun in each sentence:

1. (Who, Whom) would like to learn about career opportunities in the world of business?
2. (Who, Whom) has the skills to apply for this job?
3. From (who, whom) did you receive this excellent résumé?
4. This report will be (who's, whose) responsibility?
5. (Who, Whom) is most adept at balancing the budget?

▲ **Critical Viewing**
Use *who* in a sentence about the woman using the mouse. Use *whom* in a sentence about the woman with the pencil. **[Draw Conclusions]**

▶ **Exercise 17** Using Forms of *Who* Correctly in Clauses Choose the correct form of *who* and *whom*. Then, on a separate sheet of paper, write the subordinate clause.

EXAMPLE: I want to know (who, whom) wrote this.
ANSWER: *who* wrote this

1. An animator is a person (who, whom) creates the illusion of life by generating computer images, drawings, or models.
2. An animator should be someone (who, whom) has experience in drawing, cartooning, or graphic design.
3. Animators are graphic artists (who, whom) use traditional animation, computer graphics animation, or claymation.
4. Part of an animator's job may be to design animation, hand draw or paint characters, and meet with (whoever, whomever) commissions his or her work.
5. (Whoever, Whomever) chooses a career as an animator needs to keep him- or herself up to date with new techniques and computer programs.

▶ **More Practice**

Grammar Exercise Workbook
• pp. 109–110
On-line Exercise Bank
• Section 22.2

Go on-line:
PHSchool.com
Enter Web Code:
efk-1102

Get instant feedback! Exercises 16 and 17 are available on-line or on CD-ROM.

Pronouns in Elliptical Clauses

Another problem with pronoun usage occurs in complex sentences containing an *elliptical clause*—that is, a clause in which some words are understood rather than stated. Such clauses generally make a comparison and begin with *than* or *as*.

> **KEY CONCEPT** In elliptical clauses beginning with *than* or *as*, use the form of the pronoun that you would use if the clause were fully stated. ■

The case of the pronoun depends on whether the omitted words belong after or before the pronoun. In the examples below, the omitted words are supplied in brackets.

WORDS LEFT OUT
AFTER PRONOUN: Amanda is as capable as *he* [is].

WORDS LEFT OUT
BEFORE PRONOUN: Betty sent Karen more applicants than [she sent] *me*.

When you choose a pronoun for an elliptical clause, mentally complete the clause. If the understood words come *after* the pronoun, use a nominative pronoun. If the understood words come *before* the pronoun, use an objective pronoun.

In some sentences, the case of the pronoun completely changes the meaning of the sentence.

NOMINATIVE PRONOUN: I liked his career counselor more than *he*.
I liked his career counselor more than *he* [did].

OBJECTIVE PRONOUN: I liked his career counselor more than *him*.
I liked his career counselor more than [I liked] *him*.

In choosing a pronoun for an elliptical clause, follow the steps outlined below:

STEPS FOR CHOOSING A PRONOUN IN ELLIPTICAL CLAUSES
1. Consider the choices of pronouns: nominative or objective.
2. Mentally complete the elliptical clause.
3. Base your choice on what you find.

GRAMMAR IN
LITERATURE

from **The First Seven Years**
Bernard Malamud

In the following passage, the objective case whom *is used.*

Neither the shifting white blur outside, nor the sudden deep remembrance of the snowy Polish village where he had wasted his youth could turn his thoughts from Max the college boy, (a constant visitor in the mind since early that morning when Feld saw him trudging through the snowdrifts on his way to school) *whom* he so much respected because of the sacrifices he had made. . . .

▶ **Exercise 18** Identifying the Correct Pronoun in Elliptical Clauses Rewrite each sentence, choosing the correct pronoun in parentheses and completing the elliptical clause.

EXAMPLE: She has as many years of experience as (he, him).
ANSWER: She has as many years of experience as *he* does.

1. Your guidance counselor can help you learn more about a career in music therapy than (I, me).
2. In some ways, music therapists are like doctors and can spend as much time with patients as (they, them).
3. The challenge of helping others is more difficult for him than (she, her).
4. Music often has a deeper effect on patients than (we, us).
5. Our therapist can develop John's coordination as well as (she, her).

▶ **Exercise 19** Using the Correct Pronoun in Elliptical Clauses Use a pronoun to complete each elliptical clause correctly. Write the word(s) that complete each elliptical clause.

EXAMPLE: Joy is taller than ___?___ .
ANSWER: he (is)

1. The meteorologist knows more about weather than ___?___ .
2. A meteorologist knows the atmosphere better than ___?___ .
3. No other meteorologist is as accurate as ___?___ .
4. His weather forecaster is more knowledgeable than ___?___ .
5. Clouds are more interesting to Joe than ___?___ .

▶ **More Practice**

Grammar Exercise Workbook
• pp. 109–110
On-line Exercise Bank
• Section 22.2

Go on-line:
PHSchool.com
Enter Web Code:
efk-1102

Complete the exercises on-line! Exercises 18 and 19 are available on-line or on CD-ROM.

Section
22.2 *Section Review*

GRAMMAR EXERCISES 20–25

▶ **Exercise 20** Using *Who* and
Whom in Questions On a separate
sheet of paper, write the pronoun that
completes each question.

1. (Who, Whom) would like to help people
   learn by working in a museum?
2. From (who, whom) did you acquire
   your interest in museum employment?
3. (Who, Whom) would be interested in
   volunteering at a museum to gain
   work experience?
4. Would a tour guide be a good entry-
   level position for (whoever, whomever) is
   interested in a museum career?
5. (Who, Whom) can I contact at the
   Smithsonian Institution regarding possible internships?

▶ **Exercise 21** Recognizing Uses of
Who and *Whom* On a separate sheet of
paper, write the subordinate clause found
in each sentence. Then, indicate how the
form of *who* or *whom* is used.

1. We applauded the woman who conducted the magnificent symphony
   orchestra.
2. Coincidentally, she is the same person
   whom I once saw in a rock band.
3. Whoever aims for a performing career
   in classical music may aspire to be an
   orchestral player.
4. That orchestral player is the one to
   whom she gave lessons.
5. It is wise to give a position in the symphony to whoever has technical
   expertise in music.

▶ **Exercise 22** Using Pronouns in
Elliptical Structures Add a pronoun to
each sentence that completes the elliptical
structure. Then, write out the full elliptical
structure.

1. Because she was extremely well prepared and organized, Vivian interviewed better than ___?___.
2. She dressed as professionally as
   ___?___ for her interview.
3. Vivian had more experience and better
   job skills than ___?___.
4. No one else in the waiting room was as
   confident as ___?___.
5. The interview was more important to
   Vivian than ___?___.

▶ **Exercise 23** Find It in Your
Reading Determine the use and the
case of the pronoun *whom* in the passage
from "The First Seven Years" on the previous page. Begin by isolating the subordinate clause to determine how the pronoun
is used.

▶ **Exercise 24** Find It in Your
Writing Deciding when to use *who* or
whom is often a problem. Look through
your portfolio for examples of the pronouns
who and *whom* in your writing. Using this
section as a guide, make sure each example is used correctly.

▶ **Exercise 25** Writing Application
Think of a family member or friend
whose career you admire. Write ten interview questions to learn more about this
person's career or place of business. Use
each of the following words at least once.

Who   Whoever
Whom   Whomever

Agreement

The bodies in our solar system maintain special relation-ships. Planets revolve around the sun, and moons revolve around planets. The laws of the universe keep the stars and planets in harmony with each other.

Similarly, subjects and verbs as well as pronouns and their antecedents form special relationships within sentences. For instance, subjects and verbs must always agree in number. Pronouns and their antecedents must also agree in number.

The laws of grammar keep subjects and verbs as well as pronouns and their antecedents in harmony with each other also. For instance, when a subject and its verb work together properly, they are said to agree with each other. In this chapter, you will study the grammatical agreement of subjects and verbs as well as that of pronouns and their antecedents.

▲ Critical Viewing
Think of a sentence that tells two things the sun appears to do. How does the subject agree with the verb? [**Classify, Distinguish**]

Diagnostic Test

Directions: Write all answers on a separate sheet of paper.

Skill Check A. Choose the verb in parentheses that agrees with the subject in each sentence.

1. The planets (has, have) always captured people's imaginations.
2. There (is, are) nine planets in our solar system.
3. Astronomers (has, have) studied the planets for centuries.
4. A beautiful sight in the night sky (is, are) the stars.
5. The sun, which is surrounded by the planets, (shines, shine) brightly in the sky.
6. The sun and the moon (is, are) heavenly bodies that observers easily (sees, see).
7. During a solar eclipse, the moon (blocks, block) the sun.
8. Lunar eclipses, which (occurs, occur) from time to time, (is, are) not as dramatic as solar eclipses.
9. The class (is, are) making their own special viewers.
10. (There's, There are) times when observation is more valuable than traditional research.
11. Following the solar eclipse (is, are) discussion groups on planetary motion.
12. Interplanetary physics (is, are) one of my favorite subjects.
13. Each of the planets (has, have) its own orbit around the sun.
14. Some of the planets (is, are) visible without a telescope.
15. Neither my brother nor my friends (has, have) a good telescope.

Skill Check B. Choose the correct pronoun in each sentence.

16. Neither my friend John nor my brother lets me use (his, their) telescope.
17. Sam is going to a store where (you, he) can buy a good telescope.
18. Sam's telescope may need (its, their) magnification adjusted.
19. Both of the models he looked at had (its, their) appealing features.
20. Sam and (myself, I) will study the planets.

Skill Check C. Rewrite the following sentences, correcting the vague, ambiguous, or distant pronoun references.

21. You can see many planets and moons, and it starts with a good telescope.
22. On the news, it talked about a comet coming close to Earth.
23. Marion showed Janet that her telescope was pointed toward the portion of the sky that the comet will cross.
24. My parents were going to give me some books about comets, but they haven't arrived yet.
25. Many stars have disappeared by the time we see them, which not many people realize.

Subject and Verb Agreement

Singular and Plural Subjects

There are two basic rules of subject and verb agreement that govern all of the other rules:

KEY CONCEPT A singular subject must have a singular verb. A plural subject must have a plural verb. ■

In the examples below and on the next page, the subjects are underlined once and the verbs, twice.

SINGULAR SUBJECT AND VERB:	He looks through the telescope. This large telescope is powerful. Elizabeth has been studying the solar system.
PLURAL SUBJECT AND VERB:	They look through the telescope. These large telescopes are powerful. We have been studying the solar system.

Exercise 1 Making Verbs Agree With Their Subjects
Choose the verb in parentheses that agrees with the subject of each sentence.
1. The Milky Way (is, are) the Earth's home galaxy.
2. Our sun's nine planets (is, are) located in the Milky Way.
3. The sun (travels, travel) through space.
4. The planets (revolves, revolve) around the sun.
5. The solar system constantly (moves, move) through space toward the constellation Hercules.

◀ Critical Viewing
Use *sun* and *moon* in a sentence about an eclipse. Is the verb singular or plural? **[Connect, Draw Conclusions]**

GRAMMAR IN LITERATURE

More Practice

Grammar Exercise
Workbook
• pp. 111–112
On-line Exercise Bank
• Section 23.1

Go on-line:
PHSchool.com
Enter Web Code:
efk-1102

from **To His Excellency, General Washington**

Phillis Wheatley

Notice that the singular subject she *agrees with the singular verb* flashes. *The plural subject* nations *agrees with the plural verb* gaze. *The subjects are shown in red, and the verbs are shown in blue. The subject* you *is understood in the second-to-last line.*

Celestial choir! enthron'd in realms of light,
   Columbia's scenes of glorious toils I write.
While freedom's cause her anxious breast alarms,
She flashes dreadful in refulgent arms.
See mother earth her offspring's fate bemoan,
And nations gaze at scenes before unknown!

Intervening Phrases and Clauses

A verb must agree with its subject even if a phrase or clause comes between them.

▷ **KEY CONCEPT** A phrase or clause that comes between a subject and its verb does not affect subject-verb agreement. ■

In the first example below, a prepositional phrase separates a singular subject and its singular verb. In the second example, a clause interrupts a plural subject and its plural verb.

EXAMPLES: <u>Sam</u>, with several of his friends, <u>observes</u> the sky.
The <u>astronomers</u>, who have a large chart, <u>observe</u> the sky.

Pay particular attention to parenthetical expressions interrupting a subject and its verb. These expressions are usually set off by commas and begin with such words as *along with, as well as,* or *including.* They do not affect the agreement of the subject and its verb.

EXAMPLES: Your <u>theory</u>, as well as his ideas, <u>lacks</u> support.
The nine <u>planets</u>, along with their moons, <u>revolve</u> around our sun.

Subject and Verb Agreement • **427**

> **Exercise 2** Making Separated Subjects and Verbs Agree
Choose the verb in parentheses that agrees with the subject of each sentence.

1. Saturn, along with Jupiter and Uranus, (has, have) rings that encircle the planet.
2. Scientists who study the universe (has, have) several theories about the rings around planets.
3. Saturn, which is the sixth planet from the sun, (rotates, rotate) every 10 hours and 14 minutes.
4. The rings of Saturn, unlike those of Jupiter, (contains, contain) mostly ice and rock.
5. One of Jupiter's moons (has, have) a great deal of volcanic activity.

Relative Pronouns as Subjects

When *who, which,* or *that* acts as a subject of a subordinate clause, its verb is singular or plural, depending on the number of its antecedent.

> **KEY CONCEPT** The antecedent of a relative pronoun determines its agreement with a verb. ∎

In the first example, the antecedent of *who* is *one;* therefore, a singular verb is required. In the next example, the antecedent of *who* is *trainees;* therefore, a plural verb is needed.

EXAMPLES: Sam is the only one of the trainees who has applied.
Sam is the only qualified person among the

astronaut trainees who have applied.

> **Exercise 3** Making Relative Pronouns Agree With Their
Verbs Choose the verb in parentheses that agrees with the subject of each subordinate clause.

1. The sun, which (supports, support) life on Earth, is not a very big star in the Milky Way.
2. Stars are glowing balls of gas that (erupts, erupt) at times.
3. The sun has a gigantic atmosphere that (contains, contain) winds of electrically charged particles.
4. Hydrogen is one of the main gases that (makes, make) up the sun.
5. Our science teacher is someone who (knows, know) many facts about the sun and the solar system.

> **More Practice**

Grammar Exercise Workbook
• pp. 111–112
On-line Exercise Bank
• Section 23.1

Go on-line:
PHSchool.com
Enter Web Code:
efk-1102

Get instant feedback! Exercises 2 and 3 are available on-line or on CD-ROM.

Compound Subjects

Four different rules of agreement apply to compound subjects joined by *or, nor,* or *and:*

> **KEY CONCEPT** A compound subject joined by *and* is generally plural and must have a plural verb. ■

The conjunction *and* acts as a plus sign. Whether the parts of the compound are all singular, all plural, or mixed in number, they add up to a plural compound subject and therefore require a plural verb.

EXAMPLES: Wind and rain exist on Earth.
Winds and rainstorms exist on Earth.
Winds and rain exist on Earth.

Exceptions to this rule occur when the parts of the compound subject equal one thing and when the word *each* or *every* is used before a compound subject. Each of these situations requires a singular verb.

EXAMPLES: Macaroni and cheese is an easy dish to make.
Each man and woman was waving a flag.

> **KEY CONCEPT** Two or more singular subjects joined by *or* or *nor* must have a singular verb. ■

EXAMPLE: Either Jupiter or Saturn makes a fascinating topic of study.

> **KEY CONCEPT** Two or more plural subjects joined by *or* or *nor* must have a plural verb. ■

EXAMPLE: Space probes or space shuttles provide information about space.

> **KEY CONCEPT** If one or more singular subjects are joined to one or more plural subjects by *or* or *nor,* the subject closest to the verb determines agreement. ■

EXAMPLES: Neither atmosphere nor clouds exist on Mercury.
Neither clouds nor atmosphere exists on Mercury.

⚙ Grammar and Style Tip

Use compound subjects to combine sentences and streamline your writing.

23.1

Exercise 4 Making Compound Subjects Agree With Their Verbs Choose the verb in parentheses that agrees with the subject in each sentence.

1. Mercury and Venus (is, are) closer to the sun than Earth is.
2. Neither Venus nor Mars (appears, appear) to support life.
3. Neither plants nor animals (lives, live) on these planets.
4. Earth and Venus (seems, seem) nearly the same size.
5. Saturn and Jupiter (has, have) many moons.
6. Titan and several other moons (revolves, revolve) around Saturn.
7. The planet's moons, or its three rings, (is, are) visible through a telescope.
8. Either Jupiter's moons or its single ring (was, were) the subject of a recent study.
9. Phobos and Deimos (is, are) the two moons of Mars.
10. Neither Rick nor his classmates (knows, know) much about Mars.

Exercise 5 Writing Sentences With Compound Subjects
Use each of these compound subjects in a sentence.

1. The Earth and the moon
2. Mars and Venus
3. A telescope or binoculars
4. Neither the sun nor the moon
5. The stars and planets

Exercise 6 Revising to Correct Errors in Subject-Verb Agreement Revise these sentences where necessary to correct errors in agreement. If the sentence has no agreement error, write *correct.*

1. Either Neptune or Pluto make a good topic for a report.
2. Every planet and satellite rotates constantly.
3. Mars and Jupiter is visible to the unaided eye.
4. Neither Uranus nor the other two outer planets is visible without a telescope.
5. Every boy and girl learn about the solar system in school.
6. Either Kim or Barry is creating a model of the solar system for the science fair.
7. Mr. Thomas and Ms. Jassey teaches earth science.
8. Neither Marcia nor her sisters is ready for the science test.
9. Every tenth grader and eleventh grader knows that Earth is the third planet from the sun.
10. Freeze-dried spaghetti and meatballs are a meal available to astronauts.

More Practice

Grammar Exercise Workbook
• pp. 113–114
On-line Exercise Bank
• Section 23.1
Go on-line:
PHSchool.com
Enter Web Code:
efk-1102

Interactive Textbook

Complete the exercises on-line! Exercises 4, 5, and 6 are available on-line or on CD-ROM.

Confusing Subjects

Some subjects—hard-to-find subjects, subjects of linking verbs, collective nouns, nouns that look like plurals, indefinite pronouns, titles, amounts, and measurements—require special attention.

Hard-to-Find Subjects If a subject comes after its verb, you must still make sure the subject and verb agree in number.

▷ **KEY CONCEPT** When a subject comes after its verb, the verb must still agree with the subject in number. ∎

A sentence in which the subject comes after its verb is said to be inverted. You can check the subject-verb agreement by mentally putting the sentence in the normal subject-verb order.

EXAMPLES: Beyond our galaxy's stars <u>is</u> another galaxy.
(Another <u>galaxy</u> <u>is</u> beyond our galaxy's stars.)
Which of the science reports <u>has</u> <u>she</u> <u>read</u>?
(<u>She</u> <u>has read</u> which of the science reports?)

The words *here* and *there* at the beginning of a sentence often signal an inverted sentence. When putting the sentence in normal subject-verb order, the word *here* or *there* is no longer necessary.

INVERTED: There <u>is</u> a <u>model</u> of the solar system on the table.
S-V ORDER: A <u>model</u> of the solar system <u>is</u> on the table.

There's and *here's*, contractions for *there is* and *here is,* contain the singular verb *is* and therefore cannot be used with plural subjects.

INCORRECT: Among scientists, there<u>'s</u> some <u>believers</u> in life on other planets.

CORRECT: Among scientists, there <u>are</u> some <u>believers</u> in life on other planets.

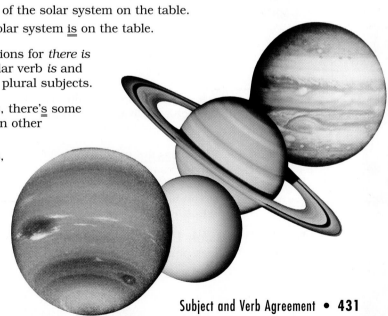

▶ **Critical Viewing** What action verb could you use in a sentence with the subject *planets?* Is it plural or singular in form? **[Analyze]**

Subjects of Linking Verbs

Another problem with agreement involves linking verbs and predicate nominatives.

 KEY CONCEPT A linking verb must agree with its subject, regardless of the number of its predicate nominative—the noun or pronoun that renames, identifies, or explains the subject. ■

In the first example below, the subject *craters* agrees with the plural verb *are* in spite of the singular predicate nominative *sign*. In the second example, the nouns are reversed. The subject *sign* agrees with the singular verb *is*, and *craters* is the predicate nominative.

EXAMPLES: Moon <u>craters</u> <u>are</u> one sign of meteor storms.
One <u>sign</u> of meteor storms <u>is</u> moon craters.

▲ **Critical Viewing** Name a verb you can use with the subject *Mars*. **[Apply]**

Collective Nouns

Collective nouns—such as *audience, team, class,* and *crowd*—name groups of people or things and may be either singular or plural, depending on how they are used.

 KEY CONCEPT A collective noun takes a singular verb when the group it names acts as a single unit. ■

EXAMPLES: The <u>class</u> <u>is</u> excited to be learning about the solar system.
NASA's <u>committee</u> <u>has decided</u> to launch the shuttle.

🔁 **Learn More**

For a review of linking verbs, see Section 18.2.

KEY CONCEPT A collective noun takes a plural verb when the group it names act as individuals with different points of view. ■

EXAMPLES: The <u>class</u> <u>are</u> unable to decide which planets to discuss in their reports.
NASA's <u>committee</u> <u>have been</u> unable to come to an agreement on whether to launch the shuttle.

Nouns That Look Like Plurals Other confusing subjects are nouns that look plural but are singular in meaning.

KEY CONCEPT Nouns that are plural in form but singular in meaning take singular verbs. ■

Some of these nouns are singular names for branches of knowledge: *acoustics, civics, economics, ethics, mathematics, physics, politics, social studies.* Others have singular meanings because they name single units: *confetti* (one mass of paper bits), *measles* (one disease), *news* (one set of information).

SINGULAR: Physics <u>is</u> a challenging subject.
                    The <u>news was</u> not very interesting yesterday.

Some of these words can be difficult to use correctly. When words such as *acoustics* and *ethics* do not name branches of knowledge but rather indicate characteristics, their meanings are plural. Similarly, words such as *eyeglasses, pliers,* and *scissors,* though they name single items, take plural verbs.

PLURAL: The <u>acoustics</u> in the theater <u>are</u> excellent.
                My lost <u>eyeglasses were</u> behind the sofa.

Indefinite Pronouns

Some indefinite pronouns are always singular *(anybody, everyone, each,* and so on). Others are always plural *(both, many,* and so on). Two simple rules apply to these indefinite pronouns:

KEY CONCEPT Singular indefinite pronouns take singular verbs. ■

Notice in the examples below that an interrupting phrase does not affect the subject-verb agreement.

EXAMPLES: <u>Each</u> of the planets <u>is rotating</u> at all times.
                <u>Everyone</u> in the class <u>wants</u> to travel in space someday.

KEY CONCEPT Plural indefinite pronouns take plural verbs. ■

EXAMPLES: <u>Both</u> of these planets <u>were formed</u> at about the same time.
                <u>Several</u> of these space probes <u>require</u> further investigation.

For those indefinite pronouns that can be either singular or plural, agreement depends on the number of the antecedent.

▶ **KEY CONCEPT** The pronouns *all, any, more, most, none,* and *some* usually take a singular verb if the antecedent is singular and a plural verb if the antecedent is plural. ■

In the first example below, the antecedent of *most* is *planet*, a singular noun. In the second example, the antecedent of *most* is *planets*, a plural noun.

SINGULAR: <u>Most</u> of our planet <u>is</u> water.
PLURAL: <u>Most</u> of the planets <u>are</u> large.

Titles The titles of books or works of art may be misleading if they sound plural or consist of many words.

▶ **KEY CONCEPT** A title is singular and therefore takes a singular verb. ■

EXAMPLES: <u>*Space*</u> <u>is</u> a novel by James A. Michener.
              <u>*The Merry Wives of Windsor*</u> <u>is</u> a Shakespearean play.

Amounts and Measurements

Most amounts and measurements, although appearing plural, express single units.

▶ **KEY CONCEPT** A noun expressing an amount or measurement is usually singular and requires a singular verb. ■

In the first three examples, the subjects agree with singular verbs. *Twelve dollars* equals one sum of money; *thirty miles* equals one measurement; and *two thirds* is one part of a whole. In the last example, *half* refers to individual items and is plural.

EXAMPLES: <u>Twelve dollars</u> <u>is</u> the price of the ticket.
              <u>Thirty miles</u> <u>was</u> a long distance to travel.
              <u>Two thirds</u> of the produce <u>has spoiled</u>.
              <u>Half</u> of the invitations <u>were mailed</u> today.

Technology Tip

If your computer's grammar-check tool highlights a large part of a sentence, check to see whether the subject and verb agree.

▼ **Critical Viewing** On a clear, dark night, approximately 3,000 stars can be seen. Would you say 3,000 *is* a large number or 3,000 *are* a large number? **[Distinguish]**

▶ **Exercise 7** Making Verbs Agree With Confusing Subjects
Choose the verb in parentheses that agrees with the subject of
each sentence.
1. *2001: A Space Odyssey* (is, are) a novel written by Arthur
   C. Clarke.
2. Physics (is, are) a subject that Clarke studied when he
   attended the University of London.
3. *Fountains of Paradise* (was, were) also written by Clarke.
4. (Was, Were) both Clarke and director Stanley Kubrick
   involved with producing the movie version of *2001*?
5. The subject of the movie (is, are) human ventures into space.
6. Our class (has, have) their favorite characters.
7. (There's, There are) many themes in this story.
8. Some (believes, believe) that the book is better than the
   movie.
9. Some of Clarke's fans (thinks, think) that the movie is the
   best ever made.
10. Most of the fans also (enjoys, enjoy) other science-fiction
    movies, such as *Aliens* and *Star Wars*.
11. *Star Wars* (is, are) my all-time favorite science-fiction movie.
12. Following the first movie (was, were) several sequels.
13. NASA's team (is, are) planning a mission to Mars.
14. Many in the agency (hopes, hope) that NASA will send
    astronauts to Mars.
15. There (is, are) a model of Mars on the cabinet.

▶ **Exercise 8** Revising to Correct Errors in Agreement With
Confusing Subjects Revise these sentences where necessary to
correct errors in agreement. If there are no errors in agreement, write *correct*.
1. Some in the scientific community believes that conditions
   on Mars could support life.
2. Do the presence of water in the form of ice indicate that
   life could have existed on Mars?
3. Everyone sees that the planet's polar icecaps grows and
   shrinks in a predictable way.
4. Higher than Earth's mountains are Mars' 17-mile-high
   Olympus Mons.
5. Where was the information about Mars and its moons?
6. About $265 million was the cost of the Mars *Pathfinder*
   mission.
7. Many in the government considers that cost to be low relative to the cost of other space missions.
8. A billion dollars have been spent on some missions!
9. Everyone were interested in what *Sojourner*, *Pathfinder's*
   roving component, would find.
10. A group of students plans to follow the flight of the *Mars
    Polar Lander*, launched in January 1999.

Section Review

Grammar Exercises 9–17

Exercise 9 Making Verbs Agree With Their Subjects Choose the verb in parentheses that agrees with the subject of each sentence.

1. Nine known planets (rotates, rotate) around the sun.
2. Percival Lowell, along with many other scientists, (has, have) studied the skies.
3. Space probes that travel the solar system (has, have) taken photographs of the sun, moon, and planets.
4. Photographs from space probes (shows, show) a planet with many craters.
5. Every age (has, have) had scientists who studied planetary motion.
6. The word *planet*, which (derives, derive) from the Greek word for *wanderer*, describes the nine large bodies rotating around the sun.
7. A planet with worn-down craters (appears, appear) to be older than one with sharp craters.
8. The planets (is, are) named for mythical Roman and Greek gods.
9. Mercury (is, are) the planet closest to the sun.
10. We (observes, observe) Mercury through our telescope just before sunrise or just after sunset.
11. A year on Mercury (lasts, last) 88 Earth days.
12. Mercury, which is one of the hottest planets, (is, are) named for the Roman god of commerce and quick wit.
13. Scientists who study Mercury (agrees, agree) that the side of the planet facing the sun becomes extremely hot.
14. Mercury, because of its low gravitational forces, (does, do) not have an atmosphere.
15. One of the reasons that Mercury's atmosphere escapes (is, are) lack of gravity.

Exercise 10 Making Verbs Agree With Compound Subjects Choose the verb in parentheses that agrees with the subject of the sentence.

1. Carl Sagan and other scientists (has, have) studied these bodies.
2. Either the moons or the planets (provides, provide) fascinating topics of study for most scientists.
3. Either asteroids or a comet (appears, appear) in this photograph.
4. The comet Halley and the comet Hale-Bopp (orbits, orbit) the sun in regular and predictable cycles.
5. NASA and the United States government (promotes, promote) public support for the space program.
6. Every man and woman in the space program (hopes, hope) to become an astronaut.
7. Neil Armstrong and Buzz Aldrin (was, were) the first astronauts to walk on the moon.
8. Each astronaut and astronomer (studies, study) gravitational forces in space.
9. Bacon and eggs (is, are) a dish too high in cholesterol for astronauts to eat on a regular basis.
10. A camera and other instruments (enables, enable) further exploration of planets that future astronauts may visit.

Exercise 11 Revising to Correct Errors in Agreement With Compound Subjects Revise these sentences, correcting errors in agreement.

1. Our nine planets and our sun rotates constantly.
2. Mercury and Venus is closest to the sun.
3. Neither Mercury nor Venus have moons.

4. Either Saturn or Uranus have the greatest number of moons.
5. Ganymede and Europa is two moons of Jupiter that may contain water.

Exercise 12 Making Verbs Agree With Confusing Subjects Choose the verb in parentheses that agrees with the subject of the sentence.

1. (There's, There are) only one moon orbiting the Earth.
2. One of NASA's plans to map the moon (includes, include) the *Lunar Prospector.*
3. Various investigations of the moon's gravity and composition (was, were) the mission of *Prospector.*
4. About $70 million (has, have) been spent on the *Lunar Prospector.*
5. Everyone of those involved in the program (believes, believe) that the money was well spent.
6. Some of the scientists (has, have) the idea that the *Prospector* could determine if water exists on the moon.
7. The committee of scientists (agrees, agree) on how to use *Prospector* to such an end.
8. (There's, There are) plans to crash-land the *Prospector* on the moon.
9. Many of the observers (looks, look) forward to studying the dust cloud that will result from the crash landing.
10. Our science class (has, have) been unable to decide which moon to study.

Exercise 13 Supplying Verbs That Agree With Confusing Subjects Copy each sentence onto a separate sheet of paper. Then, write *is* or *are* in the blank to complete each sentence.

1. There ___?___ many reasons to send spacecraft into orbit.
2. Here ___?___ one rationale for spending money on the space program.
3. Now ___?___ the time to find out whether life exists on other planets.

4. Why ___?___ these questions hard to answer?
5. Beyond our galaxy ___?___ mysteries that may astound us.

Exercise 14 Revising for Subject-Verb Agreement On a separate sheet of paper, revise the following paragraph. Be sure to correct all errors in subject and verb agreement.

(1) Many of today's scientists believes that some moons in our solar system contains water. (2) Does any of these moons hold the answers to a researcher's perplexing questions? (3) There's several questions researchers might ask. (4) Could moons that have water give scientists hints about Earth's resources? (5) Perhaps, the answers to these questions lies in the near future.

Exercise 15 Find It in Your Reading Identify two subjects and verbs in the excerpt from "To His Excellency, General Washington" on page 427. Tell whether each verb is singular or plural.

Exercise 16 Find It in Your Writing Choose a paragraph from a recent piece of writing. Underline each subject once and each verb twice. Check to make sure that each subject and verb agree.

Exercise 17 Writing Application Write a brief factual account of one of the nine planets or a moon in our solar system. After you have completed the paragraph, draw a single line under the subject of each sentence. Draw a double line under each verb. Then, tell whether each verb is singular or plural.

Pronoun and Antecedent Agreement

Antecedents are the nouns (or the words that take the place of nouns) for which pronouns stand. This section will show that just as a subject and verb must agree, so must a pronoun and its antecedent agree.

Agreement Between Personal Pronouns and Antecedents

One rule of pronoun and antecedent agreement governs almost all of the other rules:

▶ **KEY CONCEPT** A personal pronoun must agree with its antecedent in number, person, and gender. ■

You have already learned that the *number* of a pronoun indicates whether it is singular or plural. *Person* indicates whether the pronoun is first person, second person, or third person—that is, if the pronoun refers to the one speaking, the one spoken to, or the one spoken about.

Some nouns and pronouns can also indicate one of three *genders*: *masculine*, for words referring to males; *feminine*, for words referring to females; and *neuter*, for words referring to neither males nor females.

The only pronouns that indicate gender are third-person singular personal pronouns.

GENDER OF THIRD-PERSON SINGULAR PRONOUNS		
Masculine	Feminine	Neuter
he, him, his	she, her, hers	it, its

▲ **Critical Viewing** Using two feminine pronouns, describe what this musician is doing. **[Connect]**

In the following example, the pronoun *her* agrees with its antecedent, *Claire*, in number (both are singular), in person (both are third person), and in gender (both are feminine):

EXAMPLE: *Claire* expressed *her* doubts about joining the band.

GRAMMAR IN
LITERATURE

from **I Hear America Singing**
Walt Whitman

Notice that the pronouns his *and* he *agree with the
antecedents* carpenter *and* mason *in number, person, and
gender in the following lines:*

The carpenter singing his as he measures his plank or
  beam,
The mason singing his as he makes ready for work, or
  leaves off work,

Agreement in Number

Pronoun-antecedent agreement is sometimes a problem
when the antecedent is a compound.

▶ **KEY CONCEPT** Use a singular personal pronoun with two
or more singular antecedents joined by *or* or *nor.* ∎

EXAMPLE: Neither *Tom* nor *Ken* brought *his* equipment.

▶ **KEY CONCEPT** Use a plural personal pronoun with two
or more antecedents joined by *and.* ∎

EXAMPLE: *Sue* and *Stan* have chosen *their* instruments.

An exception to these two rules occurs when it is necessary
to distinguish between individual and joint ownership. In the
examples below, changing from a singular pronoun to a plural
pronoun changes the ownership from individual to joint.

SINGULAR: Neither *Linda* nor *Maria* let me play *her* guitar.
             (Linda and Maria each own a guitar.)

PLURAL: Neither *Linda* nor *Maria* let me play *their* guitar.
             (Linda and Maria own the guitar together.)

SINGULAR: My *mother* and *father* discovered that *his* old vio-
             lin is a valuable antique. (Father owns the violin.)

PLURAL: My *mother* and *father* discovered that *their* old
             violin is a valuable antique. (Both parents own
             the violin.)

▶ **KEY CONCEPT** Use a plural personal pronoun if any part of a compound antecedent joined by *or* or *nor* is plural. ■

EXAMPLE: If my *sisters* or *Carol* arrives, ask *them* to wait.

Agreement in Person and Gender Other errors in agreement with personal pronouns occur when there is an unnecessary shift in person or gender.

▶ **KEY CONCEPT** When dealing with pronoun-antecedent agreement, take care not to shift either person or gender. ■

SHIFT IN PERSON:	*Kris* is going to New York City, where *you* can attend a fine music school.
CORRECT:	*Kris* is going to New York City, where *he* can attend a fine music school.
SHIFT IN GENDER:	The *ship* came loose from *her* moorings, and *it* gently drifted out to sea.
CORRECT:	The *ship* came loose from *its* moorings, and *it* gently drifted out to sea.

Traditionally, a masculine pronoun has been used in reference to a singular antecedent whose gender is unknown. Such use of the masculine pronoun is said to be *generic*, meaning it covers both masculine and feminine genders. Although use of the generic pronoun is still accepted, it is preferable to use *his* or *her* or to rewrite the sentence.

▶ **KEY CONCEPT** When gender is not specified, use *his or her* or rewrite the sentence. ■

EXAMPLES: Each *member* of the band must practice *his or her* music daily.

Each *member* of the band must practice daily.

All *members* of the band must practice *their* music daily.

▼ **Critical Viewing** Write a sentence about these band members containing at least one pronoun and its antecedent. Identify the pronouns and antecedents you have used. [**Relate, Distinguish**]

Exercise 18 Avoiding Shifts in Person and Gender

Choose the correct pronoun in parentheses to complete each sentence.

1. Many people are discovering that (you, they) can enjoy different forms of music, such as the blues.
2. New York City attracts many blues musicians because of its large number of nightclubs and (her, its) concert halls.
3. Men and women who have worked hard all day are finding that (you, they) can unwind by listening to Bessie Smith sing the blues.
4. Sue likes to listen to Bessie Smith because (you, she) can relate to the feelings expressed.
5. This club has become very popular since it introduced the blues to (her, its) customers.

Exercise 19 Making Personal Pronouns Agree With Their Antecedents Choose an appropriate personal pronoun to complete each sentence.

1. Neither my sisters nor Sue bought ___?___ tickets.
2. My aunt and uncle expressed ___?___ gratitude for the concert tickets.
3. Zubin Mehta and ___?___ orchestra gave an outstanding performance.
4. Every orchestra has ___?___ own unique sound.
5. If Luciano Pavarotti or Placido Domingo decides to give concerts this year, tickets for ___?___ shows will sell out.
6. We purchased the piano even though ___?___ keys were stained.
7. Piano students should take ___?___ lessons seriously.
8. Laura and Alyssa are working hard to prepare for ___?___ recital.
9. David and ___?___ brothers are thinking of starting a band.
10. Did the girls or their brother practice before ___?___ performed?

Exercise 20 Revising to Eliminate Shifts in Person and Gender Revise these sentences where necessary to correct errors in pronoun-antecedent agreement.

1. Many blues fans are finding that you enjoy the music of Ethel Waters.
2. We know that we will need to arrive early to get a good seat at the concert.
3. Henry wants to study music because it will broaden your background.
4. Typical of my friends and me is their interest in music.
5. After jazz musicians have performed in a concert, you need to rest.

> **More Practice**
>
> Grammar Exercise Workbook
> • pp. 117–118
> On-line Exercise Bank
> • Section 23.2
>
> *Go on-line:*
> PHSchool.com
> *Enter Web Code:*
> efk-1102

Get instant feedback! Exercises 18, 19, and 20 are available on-line or on CD-ROM.

Agreement With Indefinite Pronouns

When an indefinite pronoun (such as *each*, *all*, or *most*) is used with a personal pronoun, both pronouns must agree. Usage problems are rare when both pronouns are plural.

▶ **KEY CONCEPT** Use a plural personal pronoun when the antecedent is a plural indefinite pronoun. ■

EXAMPLE: *Many* of the children were excited about *their* music lessons.

When both pronouns are singular, a similar rule applies:

▶ **KEY CONCEPT** Use a singular personal pronoun when the antecedent is a singular indefinite pronoun. ■

In the following example, the personal pronoun *his* agrees in number with the singular indefinite pronoun *one*. The gender (masculine) is determined by the word *boys*.

EXAMPLE: Only *one* of the boys practiced *his* trumpet.

If other words in the sentence do not indicate a gender, you may use *him or her*, *he or she*, *his or hers*, or rephrase the sentence.

EXAMPLES: Each of the musicians wore *his or her* uniform.

The musicians wore *their* uniforms.

For indefinite pronouns that can be either singular or plural (*all*, *any*, *more*, *most*, *none*, and *some*), agreement depends on the antecedent of the indefinite pronoun. In the first example below, *its* is used because the antecedent of *most* is the singular noun *music*. In the second example, *their* is used because the antecedent of *most* is the plural noun *listeners*.

EXAMPLES: *Most* of the music had lost *its* appeal.

Most of the listeners wanted *their* money back.

In some situations, strict grammatical agreement may be illogical. In these situations, you should let the meaning of the sentence determine the number of the personal pronoun.

ILLOGICAL: When *each* of the telephones rang simultaneously, I answered *it* as quickly as possible.

CORRECT: When *each* of the telephones rang simultaneously, I answered *them* as quickly as possible.

▶ **Exercise 21** Making Personal Pronouns Agree With Indefinite Pronouns Choose the correct pronoun to complete each sentence.

1. Most of my friends rent (his, their) instruments for music lessons.
2. Each of us band members has (his or her, our) own favorite kind of music.
3. Not all see (his or her, their) future in music.
4. However, each enjoys (his or her, their) time in the band.
5. One of my friends has in (her, their) collection a book about musical careers.

▶ **Exercise 22** Revising to Correct Agreement Errors Revise these sentences where necessary to correct errrors in pronoun-antecedent agreement. If there are no errors in agreement, write *correct*.

1. Most of the careers have special training associated with it.
2. None guarantees that a person will be successful in them.
3. Some are interesting; I will investigate them further.
4. Each of the band members has their favorite musical group.
5. When anyone in my band goes to a concert, they shares stories with the rest of us.

▶ **More Practice**

Grammar Exercise Workbook
• pp. 119–120
On-line Exercise Bank
• Section 23.2
Go on-line:
PHSchool.com
Enter Web Code:
efk-1102

▼ **Critical Viewing** What indefinite pronouns and personal pronouns could you use in a sentence describing this rock band? [Analyze, Identify]

Agreement With Reflexive Pronouns

Reflexive pronouns end in *-self* or *-selves* and are used correctly only when they refer to a word earlier in the same sentence, as in "*Frank* made dinner for *himself.*"

▶ **KEY CONCEPT** A reflexive pronoun must agree with an antecedent that is clearly stated. ■

INCORRECT: Our parents listen to my sister and *myself.*
CORRECT: Our parents listen to my sister and *me.*

▶ **Exercise 23** Using Reflexive Pronouns Correctly Rewrite each sentence, correcting the misused reflexive pronoun.
1. Rachel and <u>myself</u> enjoy listening to country music.
2. All of the country music CDs in our collection were paid for by <u>ourselves</u>.
3. I said to my mother, "Who but <u>yourself</u> would have bought us tickets to a Garth Brooks concert?"
4. My father said that he will drive <u>myself</u> to the concert.
5. When you pick up the tickets for the concert, ask for Rachel or <u>himself</u>.
6. You'll find the tickets for yourself and <u>ourselves</u> in the envelope.
7. They said that country music did not interest <u>themselves</u>.
8. Who besides <u>ourselves</u> enjoys listening to the music of Loretta Lynn and Tammy Wynette?
9. On television last night, my brother and <u>myself</u> watched the country music special.
10. All of our favorite performers entertained <u>ourselves</u>.

▶ **Exercise 24** Supplying Correct Pronouns On your paper, write the reflexive or personal pronoun that correctly completes each sentence.
1. Even on short drives, my friend and ___?___ like listening to the car radio.
2. However, there's occasionally an argument between ___?___ concerning which station to tune in.
3. She prefers country music, but as for ___?___, I like the latest popular music.
4. Often, both of us enjoy ___?___ singing along to oldies from the sixties and seventies.
5. Did you say that you sing along with the radio to keep ___?___ from getting bored on long car trips?

▶ **More Practice**

Grammar Exercise Workbook
• pp. 119–120
On-line Exercise Bank
• Section 23.2
   Go on-line:
   PHSchool.com
   Enter Web Code:
   efk-1102

Interactive Textbook

Get instant feedback! Exercises 23 and 24 are available on-line or on CD-ROM.

Section 23.2 *Section Review*

GRAMMAR EXERCISES 25–30

▶ **Exercise 25**   Making Personal Pronouns Agree With Their Antecedents
Write an appropriate personal pronoun to complete each sentence.

1. Latin music has __?__ roots in African, Spanish, and Latin American music.
2. Celia Cruz is a compelling performer. __?__ is also known by __?__ title the "Queen of Salsa."
3. Cruz's fans enjoy seeing __?__ favorite performer put on a show.
4. Carlos Santana and __?__ band pioneered "Latin rock" when __?__ added a Caribbean beat to rock-and-roll music.
5. Neither Santana nor __?__ band could have imagined the fame that would come to __?__ .

▶ **Exercise 26**   Choosing Correct Personal Pronouns Write the correct pronoun to complete each sentence.

1. My brother and two other students are studying music because of (his, their) vocal talent.
2. Rikki believes that it is important to study Italian to improve (your, her) chances of becoming an opera singer.
3. Many female opera singers are finding out that (they, you) can compete in salary with male singers.
4. After a person has been to the opera, (he or she, they) may feel inspired.
5. *The Magic Flute* is a masterpiece because of (its, their) brilliant score.
6. Both of my teachers brought (his, their) classical music CDs to class.
7. Each of the students reacted to the music in (his or her, their) own way.
8. Some of the music we heard gained (its, their) popularity in the 1800's.

9. Neither of the classical pieces he wrote has (its, their) melody completed.
10. Both of these other pieces have (its, their) merits.

▶ **Exercise 27**   Revising to Correct Errors in Reflexive Pronouns Revise the sentences below to correct any misuse of reflexive pronouns. If the reflexive pronoun is used correctly, write *correct*.

1. My brother bought himself a guitar.
2. My mother and myself encouraged him to practice.
3. Who but himself could make such a racket?
4. Our mother told me to keep my opinions to myself.
5. Still, Mom bought earplugs for myself.

▶ **Exercise 28**   Find It in Your Reading Identify the indefinite and personal pronouns in this line from Walt Whitman's "I Hear America Singing," and tell why they agree.

"Each singing what belongs to him or her and to none else, . . ."

▶ **Exercise 29**   Find It in Your Writing Go through your portfolio to find examples of pronouns, especially indefinite pronouns. Make sure that you have used the correct personal pronoun to agree with each indefinite pronoun.

▶ **Exercise 30**   Writing Application Write a paragraph about your favorite musical group. Use at least four personal pronouns and two indefinite pronouns. Check your pronoun agreement.

Special Problems With Pronoun Agreement

Once you are familiar with the basic rules of pronoun and antecedent agreement, you can refine your skills in this area. This section will show you how to avoid some common errors that can obscure the meaning of your sentences.

◀ **Critical Viewing** What pronoun would you use to refer to the man? What pronoun would you use to refer to the man and the whale? **[Compare and Contrast]**

Vague Pronoun References

One basic rule governs the other, more specific rules of clear pronoun reference:

▶ **KEY CONCEPT** A pronoun requires an antecedent that is either stated or clearly understood to avoid confusion. ■

The pronouns *which, this, that,* and *these* should not be used to refer to a vague or overly general idea.

In the following example, it is impossible to determine exactly what the pronoun *these* stands for because it refers to three different groups of words.

VAGUE REFERENCE: Jay was carsick, the dog was restless, and the air conditioner was broken. *These* made our trip to the aquarium unpleasant.

The vague reference can be corrected in two ways. One way is to change the pronoun to an adjective that modifies a specific noun. The second way is to revise the sentence so that the pronoun *these* is eliminated.

CORRECT: Jay was carsick, the dog was restless, and the air conditioner was broken. *These misfortunes* made our trip to the aquarium unpleasant.

Jay's carsickness, the dog's restlessness, and the air conditioner's breakdown made our trip to the aquarium unpleasant.

▶ **KEY CONCEPT** The personal pronouns *it*, *they*, and *you* should always have a clear antecedent. ■

In the next example, the pronoun *it* has no clearly stated antecedent.

VAGUE
REFERENCE: Marge is studying marine mammals next year. *It* should be very educational.

Again, there are two methods of correction. The first method is to replace the personal pronoun with a specific noun. The second method is to revise the sentence entirely in order to make the whole idea clear.

CORRECT: Marge is studying marine mammals next year. *The experience* should be very educational.
Marge's study of marine mammals next year should be very educational.

In the next example, the pronoun *they* is used without an accurate antecedent.

VAGUE
REFERENCE: I enjoyed reading *Moby-Dick,* but *they* never explained what the whale symbolized.

CORRECT: I enjoyed reading *Moby-Dick,* but *the author* never explained what the whale symbolized.
I enjoyed reading *Moby-Dick* by Melville, but *he* never explained what the whale symbolized.

VAGUE
REFERENCE: When we arrived at the aquarium, they told us that the whale show was about to start.

CORRECT: When we arrived at the aquarium, the ticket-taker told us that the whale show was about to start.
When we arrived at the aquarium, we were told that the whale show was about to start.

KEY CONCEPT Use *you* only when the reference is truly to the reader or listener. ■

VAGUE REFERENCE:	*You* couldn't understand a word Jim said.
CORRECT:	*We* couldn't understand a word Jim said.
VAGUE REFERENCE:	In the school my great-aunt attended, *you* were expected to stand up when addressed.
CORRECT:	In the school my great-aunt attended, *students* were expected to stand up when addressed.

Note About *It*: In many idiomatic expressions, the personal pronoun *it* has no specific antecedent. In statements such as "It is late," "It is raining," and "It is true," the idiomatic use of *it* is accepted as standard English.

Exercise 31 Revising to Correct Vague Pronoun References Rewrite the sentences below, correcting the vague pronouns.

EXAMPLE:	The whale is a fascinating mammal living in the sea, which has long interested people.
CORRECT:	The whale, a fascinating mammal that lives in the sea, has long interested people.

1. Whales are warmblooded mammals that breathe with lungs, which not everyone knows.
2. There are two kinds of whales—toothed whales and baleen whales. This was explained by our teacher.
3. Baleen whales eat krill, which I learned in science class.
4. We learned about the eating habits of whales. It was very interesting.
5. Giant baleen whales need many pounds of food to fill their bellies, which didn't surprise me.
6. Baleen whales have baleen plates that hang down from their upper jaw. From the outside, these look like half-closed vertical blinds.
7. From the inside, baleen plates look like thick, white hair. This helps the whale filter water out and keep food in.
8. The bottlenose whale has teeth, which means it has a different diet.
9. Orcas hunt with each other. This makes them communal animals.
10. The orca's diet consists of sea birds, fish, turtles, and seals. They showed them in a television documentary.

More Practice

Grammar Exercise Workbook
• pp. 121–122
On-line Exercise Bank
• Section 23.3

Go on-line:
PHSchool.com
Enter Web Code:
efk-1102

Complete the exercise on-line! Exercise 31 is available on-line or on CD-ROM.

Ambiguous Pronoun References

A pronoun is *ambiguous* if it can refer to more than one antecedent. When a pronoun has more than one possible antecedent, the sentence is unclear and difficult to understand.

KEY CONCEPTS A pronoun should never refer to more than one antecedent. ■

A personal pronoun should always be tied to a single, obvious antecedent. ■

In the following sentence, *he* is confusing because it can refer to either *Joe* or *Walt*. Revise such a sentence by changing the pronoun to a noun or revising the sentence entirely.

AMBIGUOUS REFERENCE:	Joe told Walt about the whales *he* wanted to observe.
CORRECT:	Joe told Walt about the whales *Walt* wanted to observe.

KEY CONCEPT Do not repeat a personal pronoun in a sentence if it can refer to a different antecedent each time. ■

AMBIGUOUS REPETITION:	When Jon asked his father if *he* could borrow the car, *he* said *he* needed it to go to work.
CLEAR:	Jon asked his father if *he* could borrow the car, because *he* needed it to go to work.
	When Jon asked his father if *he* could borrow the car, his *father* said *he* needed it himself to go to work.

In the example, the second and third uses of *he* are unclear. To eliminate the confusion, one of the repeated pronouns was replaced. Notice in the second correction that the pronoun *himself* helps to clarify the meaning.

▲ **Critical Viewing** In what way is this photograph of a whale like a sentence containing an ambiguous pronoun reference? **[Compare]**

> **Exercise 32** Revising to Correct Ambiguous Pronoun References Rewrite the following sentences, correcting the ambiguous pronoun references.

1. Marine biologists study undersea animals and plants. They are my favorite topic.
2. Steven hopes to be a marine biologist like his father. He studies the behavior of dolphins.
3. When Steven told his brother Mark about his plans, he said that he would have to go to a school near the ocean to study marine biology.
4. There was an article about dolphins in a magazine, but I couldn't find it.
5. The trainer of a dolphin named Brenda reported that she had invented a new game.
6. Dolphins have been known to befriend humans because they are so playful.
7. Donald, a dolphin who lived off the coast of England, would interact with a local diver. Sometimes, his antics were annoying.
8. Several times, Donald tried to carry off a diver. He was just trying to be friendly, but the experience was frightening.
9. Scientists want to conduct research on the sounds dolphins make. The question is, how do they do it?
10. Because dolphins lack vocal cords, they are not sure how they emit sounds.

> **More Practice**

Grammar Exercise Workbook
• pp. 123–124
On-line Exercise Bank
• Section 23.3

Go on-line:
PHSchool.com
Enter Web Code:
efk-1102

Interactive Textbook

Complete the exercise on-line! Exercise 32 is available on-line or on CD-ROM.

◀ Critical Viewing In two or three sentences, describe the actions of these dolphins. Use the pronouns *it* and *they* at least once, making sure the antecedents are clear. **[Connect]**

GRAMMAR IN LITERATURE

from **When I Heard the Learn'd Astronomer**
Walt Whitman

Notice that the author repeats the noun astronomer *rather than using the pronoun* he, *since there are a number of words of text between the two uses.*

When I heard the learn'd *astronomer*,
When the proofs, the figures, were ranged in columns
    before me,
When I was shown the charts and diagrams, to add, divide
    and measure them,
When I sitting heard the *astronomer* where he lectured
    with much applause in the lecture room,
How soon unaccountable I became tired and sick, . . .

Avoiding Distant Pronoun References

A pronoun too far away from its antecedent will cause confusion.

KEY CONCEPT A personal pronoun should always be close enough to its antecedent to prevent confusion. ■

A distant pronoun reference can be corrected by moving the pronoun closer to its antecedent or by changing the pronoun to a noun. In the example below, *it* is too far from the antecedent *leg*.

DISTANT REFERENCE:	Molly shifted her weight from her injured leg. Two days ago, she had fallen, cutting herself on the glass that littered the street. Now *it* was swathed in bandages.
CORRECT:	Molly shifted her weight from her injured leg. Now *it* was swathed in bandages. Two days ago, she had fallen, cutting herself on the glass that littered the street.
	Molly shifted her weight from her injured leg. Two days ago, she had fallen, cutting herself on the glass that littered the street. Now her *leg* was swathed in bandages.

Internet Tip

Find out more about marine mammals by searching for words such as *whales, dolphins, porpoises, seals, walruses,* and *manatees.*

▶ **Exercise 33** Revising to Correct Distant Pronoun
References Rewrite the following sentences, correcting the distant pronoun references.

1. At the helm of the ship stood the captain, gazing at the horizon. The passengers stood at the edge of the deck. Suddenly, he saw a whale's fluke rising from the water.
2. The waves lapped the sides of the ship. Birds circled overhead. It rose and fell with the swell of the waves.
3. The scientist wanted to see how whales behaved in the deep sea. The ship sailed far out into the ocean. In their natural habitat, their behavior might be quite different from those in captivity.
4. Imagine the problems of studying the lives of whales. A scientist needs to be patient. They spend so little time at the surface and travel far from shore.
5. Researchers can attach a small transmitter to a whale's back. The researchers track the movement and habits of the whale. It uses satellite technology.
6. The U.S. Navy has allowed researchers to use special water microphones, called hydrophones. Whale researchers wish to find out about the sounds made by whales. They allow the researchers to listen to underwater sounds made by whales.
7. A team of whale researchers wanted to find out why humpback whales blow bubbles. The researchers observed the humpbacks off the Alaskan coast. They might be a clue to how the animals hunt.
8. The bubbles emit a special feeding sound. Because fish are trapped by the bubbles, they move toward the surface when they hear it.
9. Barnacles live on the throat, chin, fins, and tail of humpbacks. The barnacles form whitish patterns on the whales. Some researchers recognize them by their "barnacle neckties."
10. On our field trip, we were fortunate to see a pod of humpback whales. In spite of rough seas, we found the trip inspiring. They broke the surface of the water several times.

▶ **More Practice**
Grammar Exercise Workbook
• pp. 123–124
On-line Exercise Bank
• Section 23.3

Go on-line:
PHSchool.com
Enter Web Code:
efk-1102

▲ **Critical Viewing**
In this photograph, how does the closeness of the whale to the ship help to clarify the size relationship between them? **[Analyze]**

Hands-on Grammar

Cutting Out Vague Pronoun Reference

Write the following sentence on a strip of paper. Make sure that you begin or end a line with the pronoun *they*.

When we arrived at the aquarium, they told us that the show was starting.

Cut the corner of the paper so that you have a small rectangle with the pronoun *they* written on it. Slide it along the sentence, looking for the noun or pronoun to which *they* refers. (You will not be able to find it!) Correct the vague pronoun reference by turning over the small rectangle and writing a noun that makes sense. Place the noun in the sentence where the pronoun *they* once was. Read the new sentence aloud.

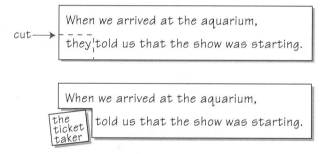

Identify the vague pronoun references in each of the following sentences. Write each sentence on a strip of paper, making sure that the vague pronoun begins or ends a line so that you can easily cut it out. Replace the pronoun with a noun. You might replace some pronouns with more than one word. Read the new sentence or sentences aloud.

Long ago, sailors believed that manatees were mermaids, which not everyone knows.

They say that from a distance, the manatee looks like a human.

The manatee has very big eyes, but this is not enough to convince me.

Find It in Your Reading Find examples of clear pronoun references in a short story.

Find It in Your Writing Choose a piece of narrative writing from your portfolio and check it for vague pronoun references. Revise as needed.

Section Review

GRAMMAR EXERCISES 34–38

Exercise 34 Revising to Correct Vague and Ambiguous Pronoun References Rewrite the sentences below to correct the problems with agreement. Make sure that all antecedents are clear.

1. Grays and humpbacks are both baleen whales. This explains why they have so many similarities.
2. In college, she studied whales and other marine mammals. That was difficult.
3. Whale researchers sometimes think that they cannot be hurt while boating out in the open sea. This leads them to take great risks.
4. You can't always expect to see a whale during a whale-watch trip.
5. Researchers who study the gray whales have found that they do not seem to sleep at night.
6. The whales seem to migrate during the night, which takes a great deal of energy.
7. If you study whales, you must have patience.
8. Sometimes the whales will not come to the surface for long periods of time, and this can be frustrating.
9. When the whales do surface, they often raise their tail flukes as they dive down again. That is a beautiful sight.
10. Many whales use their voices to communicate, which we refer to as songs.

Exercise 35 Revising to Correct Distant Pronoun References Rewrite the following sentences, correcting the distant pronoun references.

1. Using small transmitters, a British research team devised a clever way to track beluga whales. The researchers hoped to follow the whales' movements. They are attached to the whales' backs.
2. Belugas seem to be able to find holes for breathing even when traveling under thick arctic ice. They dive deep into the water. Then, they use either eyesight or sonar abilities to find them.
3. Other researchers have found that belugas are great imitators of sounds. Belugas can make bird sounds, whistling sounds, and even train sounds. They are trying to find out about other sounds, too.
4. One researcher published a paper on whale songs. The researcher had observed whales for several years. It described the different tones that whales emit.
5. The size of belugas is discussed in this article. Belugas are relatively small whales, whose young are only about five feet long. It was published in a scientific journal.

Exercise 36 Find It in Your Reading Identify the pronouns and their antecedents in the following excerpt from *Moby-Dick*. Then, tell whether each is singular or plural.

> Soon his steady, ivory stride was heard,
> as to and fro he paced his old rounds,
> upon planks so familiar to his tread,
> that they were all over dented, like geological stones, with the peculiar mark of his walk.

Exercise 37 Find It in Your Writing Look through your writing portfolio. Find three examples of personal pronouns. Revise if necessary to make sure the pronouns agree with their antecedents.

Exercise 38 Writing Application Write a brief description of a body of water you have visited. Check that all your personal pronouns have clear antecedents.

Chapter Review

GRAMMAR EXERCISES 39–41

▶ **Exercise 39** **Making Verbs Agree With Their Subjects** Choose the verb in parentheses that agrees with the subject of each sentence.

1. Killer whales (is, are) carnivores.
2. They (has, have) very large appetites.
3. A killer whale (spends, spend) about half its time hunting for food.
4. Seals, dolphins, sea lions, and other creatures (makes, make) up this whale's diet.
5. The killer whale (hunts, hunt) its prey near shore and in the sea.
6. This mammal, like many others, (excels, excel) at hunting.
7. Sometimes, two or more killer whales (cooperates, cooperate) to hunt.
8. The largest member of a family of whales known as *Delphinidea* (is, are) the killer whale.
9. Killer whales, whose scientific name is *Orcinus orca*, (is, are) also called *orcas*.
10. The orca, compared to the blue whale, (is, are) small.
11. Orcas, which can be found in all the waters of the ocean, (seems, seem) to prefer cold waters.
12. The killer whale's flippers, which (is, are) large rounded fins, can be as long as six feet or more.
13. The dorsal fin on the whale's back contains a gray patch that (helps, help) researchers distinguish one whale from another.
14. The killer whale is an animal that (appears, appear) to be quite intelligent.
15. Each pod has specific calls that only the whales of that pod (makes, make).

▶ **Exercise 40** **Supplying Verbs That Agree With Subjects** Supply a verb to complete each sentence.

1. Dolphins, porpoises, and whales

____?____ to a group of mammals called the cetaceans.
2. Neither a dolphin nor a porpoise ____?____ able to breathe in the water.
3. Every dolphin, porpoise, and whale ____?____ warmblooded.
4. Sea turtles and sharks ____?____ examples of coldblooded animals.
5. Porpoises ____?____ short snouts.
6. A squid or a few fish ____?____ a good meal for a dolphin.
7. The harbor porpoise and the Dall's porpoise ____?____ two of the six kinds of porpoises.
8. Neither the harbor porpoise nor Dall's porpoise ____?____ in the Southern Hemisphere.
9. The Northern Hemisphere and the Southern Hemisphere ____?____ their own porpoises.
10. Both dolphins and porpoises ____?____ able to survive in aquariums.

▶ **Exercise 41** **Revising to Eliminate Agreement Errors** Revise these sentences as necessary to correct agreement errors.

1. Everyone knows that mermaids do not exist.
2. Yet, there's stories that tell of sailors spying creatures that appeared to be half woman, half fish.
3. Some of the leading biologists believes that the sailors were really seeing manatees.
4. Manatees is part of a group of marine mammals called *Sirenia.*
5. Ten thousand dollars was spent on the research project that studied manatees.
6. The news about manatees was very interesting.
7. Some of the manatees' habitats is being destroyed.

The Arrival of Winthrop's Ships in Boston Harbor, 1630, W. F. Halsall

Adjectives and **adverbs,** also known as modifiers, are important tools in the effective use of language. Well-chosen modifiers can transform dull sentences into interesting ones. They can provide contrast, emphasis, and shades of meaning.

An important use of modifiers is to make comparisons. For example, when writing about another society, you might use modifiers in this way. If you were studying Puritans of seventeenth-century New England, you would use adjectives and adverbs to highlight the differences between today's society and Puritan life. You would also use modifiers to clearly describe the many elements of Puritan society that were instrumental in shaping our society. This chapter will show you how to use adjectives and adverbs to make comparisons and how to avoid some common usage problems involving comparisons.

▲ Critical Viewing
What adjectives and adverbs can you use to compare and contrast the ships in this picture? [**Analyze, Compare**]

Diagnostic Test

Directions: Write all answers on a separate sheet of paper.

Skill Check A. Identify the degree of each underlined modifier as *positive, comparative,* or *superlative.*

1. Puritans in England made the <u>difficult</u> choice to leave their country.
2. They wanted a <u>better</u> life for themselves and their families.
3. They sailed across the Atlantic to establish <u>new</u> colonies in America.
4. Though life was difficult in the new land, Puritans were <u>freer</u> to practice their religion here than they were in England.
5. Their <u>most successful</u> colonies were in New England.

Skill Check B. Write the appropriate comparative or superlative degree of the modifier in parentheses.

6. Which colony was (far) away, New England or Virginia?
7. Of all the factors, which was (important) in the Puritans' decision to come to America?
8. Freedom to practice their religion was their (great) concern.
9. The climate and terrain were (harsh) than the Puritans had anticipated.
10. Their will to succeed was (strong) than the obstacles they had to overcome.

Skill Check C. Write the correct form of the irregular modifier in parentheses.

11. The Puritans often fared (bad) in the new colonies than they had expected.
12. Still, they felt that their choice was the (good) one they could have made.
13. They believed they had (much) opportunity here than in England.
14. There had been (little) religious freedom for the Puritans in England than there was in America.
15. They had to travel (far) than they had expected, but freedom was worth the effort.

Skill Check D. Rewrite the following sentences to make the comparisons logical.

16. Partly because of the Puritans' success in New England, more people in the world speak English than any language.
17. Life was much different for the Puritans than today.
18. The most unique aspect of their immigration was that they came to New England in family groups.
19. Religion was more important to them than anything.
20. The Puritans had more freedom of religion in America than England.

Degrees of Comparison

English has three *degrees*, or forms, of adjectives and adverbs that are used to make comparisons. To recognize the different degrees of comparison, you need to know the name of each degree. They are the positive, the comparative, and the superlative.

> **KEY CONCEPT** The three degrees of comparison are the *positive*, the *comparative*, and the *superlative*. ■

There are three different ways that a word may change form to indicate the comparative and superlative degrees:

(1) *-er* or *-est* may be added at the end of the word.

(2) *more* or *most* may be added before the word.

(3) the word may assume an entirely different form.

DEGREES OF ADJECTIVES		
Positive	**Comparative**	**Superlative**
quick	quicker	quickest
pleasant	more pleasant	most pleasant
bad	worse	worst
DEGREES OF ADVERBS		
slow	slower	slowest
pleasantly	more pleasantly	most pleasantly
badly	worse	worst

> **Exercise 1** Recognizing Positive, Comparative, and Superlative Degrees Identify the degree of each underlined modifier.

EXAMPLE: Life in New England was <u>more difficult</u> than the Puritans had expected.

ANSWER: comparative

1. The Puritans wanted to be <u>free</u> to practice their religion.
2. They sought what they believed to be a <u>purer</u> form of religion than that practiced by the Anglican Church.
3. The Bible was their <u>most important</u> book.
4. They established the Massachusetts Bay Colony in 1629, but other colonies were founded <u>earlier</u> than that.
5. Puritans in New England were <u>more strict</u> than their English counterparts.

Theme: Puritan Life

In this section, you will learn about degrees of comparison. The examples and exercises in this section are about Puritan life.

Cross-Curricular Connection: Social Studies

More Practice

Grammar Exercise Workbook
• pp. 125–126
On-line Exercise Bank
• Section 24.1
  Go on-line:
  PHSchool.com
  Enter Web Code:
  efk-1102

Interactive Textbook

Get instant feedback! Exercise 1 is available on-line or on CD-ROM.

Using Regular Forms

Adjectives and adverbs can be either regular or irregular, depending on how their comparative and superlative degrees are formed. The comparative and superlative degrees of most adjectives and adverbs are formed regularly. Two rules govern the formation of regular modifiers. The first concerns modifiers of one or two syllables; the second concerns modifiers of three or more syllables:

▶ **KEY CONCEPT** Use *-er* or *more* to form the comparative degree and *-est* or *most* to form the superlative degree of most one- and two-syllable modifiers. ■

The more commonly used method of forming the comparative and superlative degrees of one- and two-syllable modifiers is to add *-er* and *-est* rather than *more* and *most*. Though English often allows the use of either method, *more* and *most* should be avoided when the construction sounds awkward. For example, "Life was *more hard* than they thought" sounds much more awkward than "Life was *harder* than they thought."

The examples below show one- and two-syllable modifiers formed regularly with *-er* and *-est*.

EXAMPLES:
bright	brighter	brightest
crafty	craftier	craftiest
subtle	subtler	subtlest

More and *most* are used with a number of one- and two-syllable modifiers when *-er* and *-est* would sound awkward. Rely on your ear to determine which words sound awkward with *-er* and *-est*.

EXAMPLES:
just	more just	most just
pleasing	more pleasing	most pleasing
devout	more devout	most devout

All adverbs that end in *-ly*, regardless of the number of syllables, form their comparative and superlative degrees with *more* and *most*.

EXAMPLES:
freely	more freely	most freely
happily	more happily	most happily
abruptly	more abruptly	most abruptly

Spelling Tip

When comparing two things, add the word *more* or the suffix *-er*, but never both together!

GRAMMAR IN LITERATURE

from **Sinners in the Hands of an Angry God**
Jonathan Edwards

The author has used the comparative form greater *and the superlative forms* stoutest *and* sturdiest *to make comparisons in this excerpt. These modifiers are shown in blue italics.*

"If God should only withdraw his hand from the floodgate, it would immediately fly open, and the fiery floods of the fierceness and wrath of God, would rush forth with inconceivable fury, and would come upon you with omnipotent power; and if your strength were ten thousand times *greater* than it is, yea, ten thousand times greater than the strength of the *stoutest, sturdiest* devil in Hell, it would be nothing to withstand or endure it."

When a modifier consists of three or more syllables, the comparative and superlative degrees are easily formed.

▶ **KEY CONCEPT** Use *more* and *most* to form the comparative and superlative degrees of all modifiers with three or more syllables. ■

EXAMPLES:		
delicate	more delicate	most delicate
dependable	more dependable	most dependable
ambitious	more ambitious	most ambitious
generous	more generous	most generous

Note About *Comparisons With* Less *and* Least: *Less* and *least* mean the opposite of *more* and *most* and can be used to form the comparative and superlative degrees of most modifiers.

EXAMPLES:		
smooth	less smooth	least smooth
acceptable	less acceptable	least acceptable
explicitly	less explicitly	least explicitly

💡 **Spelling Tip**

When comparing three or more things, add the word *most* or the suffix *-est,* but never both together!

Exercise 2 Forming Comparative and Superlative
Degrees Write the comparative and the superlative form of
each modifier.

1. pure
2. simple
3. religious
4. brave
5. important
6. strong
7. democratic
8. smart
9. excited
10. virtuously
11. successfully
12. instrumental
13. early
14. strict
15. restrictive
16. harsh
17. powerful
18. exclusive
19. severe
20. hard

More Practice

Grammar Exercise
Workbook
• pp. 125–126
On-line Exercise Bank
• Section 24.1

Go on-line:
PHSchool.com
Enter Web Code:
efk-1102

Exercise 3 Supplying Comparative and Superlative
Degrees Write the appropriate comparative or superlative
degree of the underlined modifier by following the instructions
in parentheses.

EXAMPLE: The Puritans placed <u>strong</u> emphasis on
           religion than on trade. (comparative)

ANSWER: stronger

1. Many Puritans found their new lives <u>hard</u> than the
   ones they had left behind. (comparative)
2. The climate was <u>severe</u> than in England. (comparative)
3. The first winter was the <u>difficult</u>. (superlative)
4. Still, they worshiped <u>freely</u> than before. (comparative)
5. Many Puritans found life got <u>easy</u> as more people settled
   in the colony. (comparative)
6. Not many groups were <u>industrious</u> than the Puritans.
   (comparative)
7. They were among the <u>rigid</u> thinkers of all. (superlative)
8. Native Americans lived even <u>simply</u> than the Puritans.
   (comparative)
9. The Puritans formed a government that was <u>democratic</u>
   than that of England. (comparative)
10. The Massachusetts Bay Colony became the <u>successful</u> of
    all the New England colonies. (superlative)

▲ Critical Viewing
What does this seal of
the Massachusetts
Bay Colony suggest
about how the
Puritans regarded the
Native Americans?
**[Infer, Interpret,
Draw Conclusions]**

Exercise 4 Writing Sentences With Comparative and
Superlative Modifiers Write a sentence correctly using each
modifier.

1. more resilient
2. coldest
3. most intelligent
4. more prosperous
5. more devout
6. most sacred
7. more intolerant
8. severest
9. sturdiest
10. bleaker

Using Irregular Forms

The comparative and superlative degrees of a few adjectives and adverbs are not formed according to any predictable pattern; they must be memorized.

KEY CONCEPT The irregular comparative and superlative forms of certain adjectives and adverbs must be memorized. ■

The chart below lists the three degrees of these irregular modifiers. Study the chart, and make a mental note of the irregular modifiers that you are likely to misuse. Notice that some modifiers differ only in the positive degree. Both *good* and *well*, for example, have the same comparative and superlative degrees (*better, best*).

DEGREES OF ADJECTIVES		
Positive	Comparative	Superlative
bad	worse	worst
badly	worse	worst
far (distance)	farther	farthest
far (extent)	further	furthest
good	better	best
late	later	last or latest
little (amount)	less	least
many	more	most
much	more	most
well	better	best

◄ Critical Viewing How is this colonial house similar to and different from homes in your neighborhood? **[Compare and Contrast]**

Note About *Bad* and *Badly*: *Bad* is an adjective that can be used after a linking verb. It *cannot* be used as an adverb after an action verb.

INCORRECT: Puritans fared *bad* in English society.

CORRECT: Puritans felt *bad* about English society.

Badly is an adverb that can be used after an action verb. It *cannot* be used as an adjective after a linking verb.

INCORRECT: They felt *badly* about leaving their homes.

CORRECT: The government treated them *badly*.

Note About *Good* and *Well*: Like *bad, good* is an adjective that can be used after a linking verb. It cannot be used as an adverb after an action verb.

INCORRECT: They acted *good* in choosing new lives.

CORRECT: They felt *good* about their new lives.

Well is usually an adverb and, like *badly,* can be used after an action verb.

CORRECT: Some Puritans did *well* in the new colony.

Well is an adjective when it is used to mean "healthy." Thus, it can sometimes be used after a linking verb.

CORRECT: After landing, they soon felt *well* again.

▶ **Exercise 5** Revising to Correct Errors in Irregular Modifiers
Rewrite each sentence, correcting the underlined irregular modifier by following the instructions in parentheses.
1. The harsh New England winters were <u>more bad</u> than the first Puritan settlers had imagined. (comparative)
2. <u>Much</u> settlers died during the first winter in the new land. (positive)
3. In addition to the cold weather, the settlers were <u>farther</u> challenged by disease and other hardships. (comparative)
4. Despite facing <u>most</u> challenges, the settlers endured and established thriving communities. (positive)
5. Today, the Puritan settlers remain one of the <u>most good</u> examples of the human ability to endure and to overcome obstacles. (superlative)

▶ **More Practice**
Grammar Exercise Workbook
• pp. 127–128
On-line Exercise Bank
• Section 24.1
Go on-line:
PHSchool.com
Enter Web Code:
efk-1102

Get instant feedback! Exercise 5 is available on-line or on CD-ROM.

Degrees of Comparison • **463**

► **Exercise 6** Forming Irregular Comparative and Superlative Degrees Write the appropriate form of the underlined modifier to complete each sentence.

EXAMPLE   Living conditions may be <u>bad</u> in some ways now, but they were ___?___ for the Puritans.

ANSWER: worse

1. Conditions were not <u>good</u> for the Puritans in England, so they came to New England to find a ___?___ life.
2. They traveled <u>far</u> to get to New England, but those who went south traveled even ___?___ .
3. Some felt <u>bad</u> during the long sea voyage, but many more felt ___?___ during their first winter here.
4. The Puritans were <u>much</u> concerned about government, but they were even ___?___ concerned about religion.
5. They attached <u>little</u> importance to the traditions of the Church of England and ___?___ to those of Roman Catholicism.
6. English Puritans emphasized the literal interpretation of the Bible <u>more</u> than other Protestants did, but American Puritans emphasized it the ___?___ .
7. They had <u>little</u> tolerance for dissenting opinion and still ___?___ for dissenting behavior.
8. They placed <u>much</u> emphasis on public order, but even ___?___ on religious and moral order.
9. Many Puritans who farmed eventually did <u>well</u>, but those who became involved in trade did even ___?___ .
10. Among the <u>good</u> qualities the Puritans passed on to their descendants, their industriousness may have been the ___?___ .

► **Exercise 7** Revising Sentences to Correct Irregular Comparative and Superlative Degrees Rewrite each sentence with the correct form of the irregular modifier.

1. The Puritans often treated bad anyone with other religious beliefs.
2. While the Puritans eventually did good in New England, it took years after they first arrived for life to get better.
3. She felt badly that she knew so little about her Puritan ancestors.
4. When she asked her parents, they had less information about her heritage, but they encouraged her to learn more.
5. She learned little during her first visit to the library, but the furthest she dug into the material, the more success she had.

► **More Practice**

Grammar Exercise Workbook
• pp. 127–128
On-line Exercise Bank
• Section 24.1
  Go on-line:
  PHSchool.com
  Enter Web Code:
  efk-1102

▼ **Critical Viewing** Compare and contrast the attire of John Winthrop (pictured here) with the clothes worn by you and your classmates. **[Compare and Contrast]**

Section 24.1 Section Review

GRAMMAR EXERCISES 8–13

Exercise 8 Recognizing Positive, Comparative, and Superlative Degrees
Identify the degree of each underlined modifier.

1. The Massachusetts Bay Company was granted a <u>small</u> tract of land.
2. Puritans wanted to be one of the <u>most powerful</u> forces in the company.
3. As a result, the Puritans gained <u>greater</u> control of their charter.
4. This development was <u>most unusual</u> in the British Empire at the time.
5. Puritans were <u>wealthier</u> than many other settlers.
6. Their society was <u>more democratic</u> than is usually thought.
7. They believed tax-paying was a duty, and they paid <u>cheerfully</u>.
8. They took <u>better</u> care of the poor than many other societies did.
9. The importance of Bible reading made New England one of the <u>most literate</u> societies in the world.
10. The Puritans founded a college <u>sooner</u> than people in the other colonies did.

Exercise 9 Forming Comparative and Superlative Degrees Write the appropriate comparative or superlative degree of the underlined modifier by following the instructions in parentheses.

1. Puritans were <u>little</u> tolerant of different beliefs than others were. (comparative)
2. The <u>strange</u> punishment for sinners was to shame them. (superlative)
3. The <u>well</u>-known fictional example of shaming is in Nathaniel Hawthorne's novel *The Scarlet Letter*. (superlative)
4. Banishment was often a <u>effective</u> way of dealing with offenders. (comparative)
5. Anne M. Hutchinson was the <u>famous</u> person to be banished. (superlative)

6. The Puritans thought this punishment would cause the <u>little</u> damage. (superlative)
7. She was <u>lucky</u> than other dissenters. (comparative)
8. The Puritans often used <u>violent</u> methods of correction. (comparative)
9. One of the <u>extreme</u> punishments was hanging. (superlative)
10. Roger Williams founded the <u>tolerant</u> colony, Rhode Island. (superlative)

Exercise 10 Writing Sentences to Revise Degrees of Comparison Rewrite ten sentences from Exercises 8 and 9. Change the degree of comparison in each.

Exercise 11 Find It in Your Reading Find two examples of comparative adverbs in this excerpt from "Sinners in the Hands of an Angry God." Identify the degree of comparison of each example.

The wrath of God is like great waters that are dammed for the present; they increase more and more, and rise higher and higher, till an outlet is given. . . .

Exercise 12 Find It in Your Writing Review a piece of your writing, and identify three or more examples of comparative and superlative modifiers. If you cannot find at least three, revise your work to add one example of each form.

Exercise 13 Writing Application Write a brief comparison of two or more people, places, or things. Be sure to use the correct comparative and superlative forms of adjectives and adverbs.

Making Clear Comparisons

Once you have mastered the forms of regular and irregular modifiers, you can learn how to use these forms to make clear comparisons. In this section, you will learn how to use the comparative and superlative degrees correctly, how to make logical comparisons, and how to recognize modifiers that should not be used in comparisons.

Using Comparative and Superlative Degrees

One basic rule covers the correct use of comparative and superlative forms:

▶ **KEY CONCEPT** Use the comparative degree to compare two persons, places, or things. Use the superlative degree to compare three or more persons, places, or things. ■

It is not necessary to mention specific numbers when making a comparison. The context of the sentence should indicate whether two items or more than two items are being compared.

COMPARATIVE: My broker is *more* dependable than Florence's.
                        My portfolio is *larger* than his.
                        He requires *less* money than she does.

SUPERLATIVE: That is the *most* dependable broker I know.
                        This is the *largest* portfolio I have ever had.
                        He requires the *least* possible number of
                        material things to make him happy.

Occasionally, the superlative degree is used just for emphasis, without any specific comparison. This usage is more acceptable in informal writing than in formal writing.

EXAMPLES: He is the *greatest*!
                     She was *most treacherously* betrayed.

Note About *Double Comparisons:* A *double comparison* is an error in usage caused by using both *-er* and *more* or both *-est* and *most* to form a regular modifier. A double comparison can also be caused by adding *-er, -est, more,* or *most* to a modifier that is irregular.

INCORRECT: Your workload is *more heavier* than mine.
                     That stock is performing *worser* than ever.

CORRECT: Your workload is *heavier* than mine.
                     That stock is performing *worse* than ever.

Theme: New York Stock Exchange

In this section, you will learn about using logical comparisons and avoiding absolute modifiers. The examples and exercises in this section are about the New York Stock Exchange.

Cross-Curricular Connection: Social Studies

▶ **Exercise 14** Supplying the Comparative and Superlative **Degrees** Write the appropriate comparative or superlative degree of the modifier in parentheses.

1. Many people think stocks are (good) than bonds.
2. Some investments are (risky) than others.
3. Stocks often have the (big) financial yield.
4. The (safe) way to invest is to choose low-risk investments.
5. The number of companies selling stocks on the New York Stock Exchange is continually growing (large).
6. Investors who believe stock prices will soar (high) than current levels are called bulls.
7. On the other hand, investors called bears think prices will fall (low).
8. Investors are (confident) during a bull market than during a bear market.
9. The (important) feature of any stock exchange is the trading floor.
10. Visitors to the New York Stock Exchange may think the activity on the floor is (confusing) than it actually is.

▶ **Exercise 15** Revising Sentences to Correct **Errors in Modifier Usage** Rewrite each sentence, correcting any errors in the usage of comparative modifiers.

1. Each worker on the floor seems to be trying to shout more louder than the others.
2. However, the activity is most organized than it appears.
3. The loud shouting allows more wide participation in trades than one might think.
4. It is the fairer way to determine stock prices competitively.
5. Because of the high volume of trading done, it is essential that the New York Stock Exchange have the advanced technology available.
6. The mostest money ever paid for a seat on the Exchange was almost $1.5 million.
7. The more famous instance of falling stock prices was the Wall Street crash of 1929.
8. The long shutdown in the history of the Exchange was in 1914.
9. Founded in 1792, the New York Stock Exchange is sixteen years youngest than our nation.
10. It is the largest stock market in the world.

▶ **More Practice**

Grammar Exercise Workbook
• pp. 129–130
On-line Exercise Bank
• Section 24.2

Go on-line:
PHSchool.com
Enter Web Code:
efk-1102

▲ **Critical Viewing** Use comparative modifiers to connect the architecture of the New York Stock Exchange building with the architecture of ancient Greek temples. **[Connect]**

Using Logical Comparisons

Two common usage problems involving comparisons are the comparison of unrelated items and the comparison of something with itself.

Balanced Comparisons When you write a comparison, be certain that the two or more things being compared are properly balanced. Otherwise, the comparison may be illogical and even ridiculous.

▶ **KEY CONCEPT** Make sure that your sentences compare only items of a similar kind. ■

In the following unbalanced sentences, the sentences illogically compare dissimilar things.

UNBALANCED:	*Jim's portfolio* is better balanced than *Ray.*
BALANCED:	*Jim's portfolio* is better balanced than *Ray's.*
UNBALANCED:	The *yield from this stock* is higher than *a bond.*
BALANCED:	The *yield from this stock* is higher than the *yield from a bond.*
UNBALANCED:	The *damage* from the panic of 1907 was less than the *one* in 1929.
BALANCED:	The *damage* from the panic of 1907 was less than *that* from the crash of 1929.

As you can see, *portfolio* cannot be compared to *Ray*, a stock's *yield* cannot be compared to a whole *bond*, and *damage* from a panic cannot be compared to a *panic*. In the last set of examples, note the use of pronouns. The first sentence is incorrect because *one* refers to *panic* rather than to *damage*.

▶ Critical Viewing
Use logical comparisons to describe the skills required to perform the tasks shown in this photograph. [Analyze, Draw Conclusions]

> **Exercise 16** Revising Unbalanced Comparisons Rewrite each sentence, correcting the unbalanced comparison.

EXAMPLE: Emily's stock was more profitable than Luke.

ANSWER: Emily's stock was more profitable than Luke's.

1. The New York Stock Exchange is larger than London.
2. The stock market crash of 1929 was more severe than 1907.
3. The New York Stock Exchange became more important in 1918 than 1914.
4. The number of companies listed on the Exchange now is greater than 1970.
5. We have more advanced technology today than twenty years ago.
6. Information on the stock market is more accessible today than the past.
7. The value of my stock is higher than your stock.
8. The dividends on this stock are lower than that one.
9. Today's investor has greater awareness of the workings of the Exchange than yesterday.
10. Ellen's investments are less risky than Michael.

Other and *Else* in Comparisons Another illogical comparison, which is similar to an unbalanced comparison, results when something is inadvertently compared with itself.

> **KEY CONCEPT** When comparing one of a group with the rest of the group, make sure that your sentence contains the word *other* or the word *else*. ■

Adding *other* or *else* in such situations will make the comparison clear.

ILLOGICAL: John was *busier than any* broker on the floor.

LOGICAL: John was *busier than any other* broker on the floor.

ILLOGICAL: Ruth worked *harder than anyone* in the office.

LOGICAL: Ruth worked *harder than anyone else* in the office.

In the first set of examples, because *John* is one of the brokers on the floor, he cannot logically be compared to all of the brokers, as that group includes himself. The addition of *other* excludes John from the rest of the brokers. In the second set, *Ruth* cannot be compared to all the workers in the office because she herself is one of those workers. The addition of *else* excludes her from the rest of the group.

> **More Practice**

Grammar Exercise Workbook
• pp. 131–132
On-line Exercise Bank
• Section 24.2
  Go on-line:
  PHSchool.com
  Enter Web Code:
  efk-1102

interactive
Textbook

Complete the exercise on-line! Exercise 16 is available on-line or on CD-ROM.

 Learn More

To review adjectives and adverbs, see Section 17.3, Adjectives and Adverbs.

> **Exercise 17** Revising Sentences Using *Other* and *Else*
> **Correctly in Comparisons** Rewrite each sentence, using *other*
> or *else* to correct the illogical comparison.

EXAMPLE: The New York Stock Exchange is larger than any exchange.

ANSWER: The New York Stock Exchange is larger than any other exchange.

1. Establishing a stock exchange is fairer than any way to set stock prices.
2. The New York Stock Exchange is more famous than any exchange.
3. There are more stock trades there than anywhere.
4. New York City has a greater impact on the nation's economy than any city has.
5. A secure investment is better than any kind.
6. An industry analyst is often better informed about a certain stock than anyone.
7. There is greater public participation in the market now than at any time.
8. One of the principles of the New York Stock Exchange is to ensure that small investors are treated the same as everyone.
9. The corporate stock of one New York City bank is older than that of any bank.
10. Information on the Exchange travels faster now than at any time.

▲ **Critical Viewing**
Based on this picture, how do you imagine working on the New York Stock Exchange compares with any jobs you have had?
[Compare and Contrast]

> **More Practice**

Grammar Exercise Workbook
• pp. 131–132
On-line Exercise Bank
• Section 24.2

Go on-line:
PHSchool.com
Enter Web Code:
efk-1102

Avoiding Comparisons With Absolute Modifiers

Some modifiers cannot be used logically to make comparisons because their meanings are *absolute*—that is, their meanings are entirely contained in the positive degree. For example, if a line is *vertical*, another line cannot be *more* vertical. Either a line is vertical or it is not; there are no degrees of verticality. Some other common absolute modifiers are *dead, entirely, fatal, final, identical, opposite, perfect,* and *unique*.

Often, it is not only the word *more* or *most* that makes an absolute modifier illogical; sometimes an absolute modifier alone is illogical in the context of a sentence. In such cases, it is best to replace the absolute modifier with one that expresses the intended meaning more precisely.

> **KEY CONCEPT** Avoid using absolute modifiers illogically in comparisons. ■

ILLOGICAL: Of all the stock market panics, that one was *the most fatal.*

CORRECT: Of all the stock market panics, that one was the *most severe.*

In the preceding example, *the most fatal* is illogical because something is either fatal or it is not. However, even *fatal* by itself would be an illogical overstatement. *Most severe* better conveys the intended meaning.

> **Exercise 18** Revising Sentences to Avoid Comparisons Using Absolute Modifiers Correct the illogical comparison in each sentence by replacing the absolute modifier with one or more other words.

1. Some people believe that the stock exchange is the most perfect method of setting prices.
2. It is one of the most unique expressions of capitalism.
3. The most dead time on Wall Street is after the Stock Exchange closes.
4. The American Exchange is identical to the New York Stock Exchange.
5. The Hong Kong Exchange is on the most opposite side of the world from New York City.
6. Specialists are entirely knowledgeable about their particular stocks.
7. They usually have more complete company information than other brokers.
8. Making a profit is the more ultimate desire of investors.
9. One final answer to a robust economy is a strong stock exchange.
10. The crash of 1929 was most fatal to the U.S. economy.

⚙ Grammar and Style Tip

An absolute modifier can never be more or less absolute than it is. Never use the suffix *-er* or *-est* or the words *more* or *most* with an absolute modifier.

> **More Practice**

Grammar Exercise Workbook
• pp. 133–134
On-line Exercise Bank
• Section 24.2

Go on-line:
PHSchool.com
Enter Web Code:
efk-1102

Complete the exercises on-line! Exercises 17 and 18 are available on-line or on CD-ROM.

Hands-on Grammar

Adjective and Adverb Window Shutters

Practice forming the comparative and superlative forms by doing the following activity:

Cut out a piece of paper approximately 3" x 7". Fold two sides in to form shutters, as shown in the illustration, leaving a space in the middle. Cut two slots about 1" wide, as shown. Under the left shutter, write *more* and *most*. Under the right shutter, write *-er* and *-est*.

On a strip of paper about 1" wide, list adjectives and adverbs, such as *clear, precious, just, incredible, arbitrarily, slow, meaningful, dirty, strict, clever.* Feed the strip of paper through the slots as shown, making sure that a word shows in the window.

Now, decide whether the modifier forms its comparative and superlative degrees with *more* and *most* or with *-er* and *-est*. First, close the right shutter to cover up *-er* and *-est*, and say the word with *more* and with *most*. Then, close the left shutter, and try the word with *-er* and *-est*. By always closing one shutter, you will avoid forming a double comparison. Decide how the comparative and superlative degrees are formed. If you are unsure, consult a dictionary.

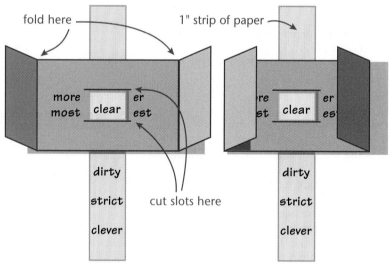

Find It in Your Reading Choose modifiers from a short story you are reading. Create a new strip to use with the window shutters.

Find It in Your Writing Review a piece of writing in your portfolio. Check to see that you have correctly used the comparative and superlative forms of adjectives and adverbs. If you have not used the comparative or superlative of at least two modifiers, challenge yourself to add at least two comparisons to your writing.

Section Review

GRAMMAR EXERCISES 19–24

Exercise 19 Using Comparative and Superlative Forms Correctly Write the appropriate comparative or superlative degree of the modifier in parentheses.

1. The 1929 Wall Street crash was the (devastating) financial crisis ever.
2. The (sad) outcome of the crash was the Great Depression.
3. The New York Stock Exchange is one of the (great) examples of capitalism.
4. Brokers who work there are some of the (busy) people in New York City.
5. Most businesses open at 9:00 A.M., but the Exchange opens (late) than that.
6. The fast pace of trading is (stressful) than some jobs.
7. Nonetheless, many brokers are (happy) in this occupation than they would be in another.
8. At six and a half hours, the trading day is (short) than most working days.
9. The (wise) thing you can do before investing is to consult an expert.
10. It is (easy) to lose money in the stock market than to make it.

Exercise 20 Revising Illogical Comparisons Rewrite each sentence, correcting the illogical comparison.

1. Is money in a bank safer than the market?
2. Investing in the market can be riskier than the bank.
3. The profits from that company are larger than last year.
4. Your broker's picks have performed better than my broker.
5. He is more cautious than anyone.
6. As a result, there is less risk with his picks than with any broker.
7. Investing in overseas companies can be riskier than in the United States.
8. Some believe that emerging markets

abroad are more risky than anywhere.
9. You can get more return on these companies than on any investments.
10. With care, you can make more money than anyone with this type of trading.

Exercise 21 Revising to Avoid Absolute Modifiers Rewrite each sentence, replacing the absolute modifier to correct the illogical comparison.

1. What is the most ultimate price you will pay for that stock?
2. If it does not do well, it will be pretty fatal to your finances.
3. It would be more perfect if the price went up.
4. Do you have absolute complete confidence in your broker?
5. Please confirm that selling those stocks is your most final decision.

Exercise 22 Find It in Your Reading Reread the excerpt from "Sinners in the Hands of an Angry God" on page 460. Find one adjective in the comparative and one in the positive degree. Write the other comparative forms for each word.

Exercise 23 Find It in Your Writing Look through your writing portfolio for several examples of adjectives in the comparative and in the superlative degrees. Make sure that your comparisons are logical.

Exercise 24 Writing Application Write a comparison of two businesses that you patronize. Use modifiers in the comparative degree, and make sure that your comparisons are clear and logical.

Miscellaneous Problems in Usage

The bright lights and cacophony of sounds at a carnival can easily distract a visitor, just as usage problems can distract a reader and spoil the clarity of one's writing. Many of these problems do not fall into any of the broad categories of usage covered in preceding chapters. Some problems arise from a conflict between standard and nonstandard usage. Some words can cause problems merely because they have similar meanings or spellings. In this chapter, you will learn how to form negative sentences correctly, and you will study a list of troublesome words and expressions.

▲ Critical Viewing
Use a negative sentence to indicate what this scene is *not*. [Describe]

Diagnostic Test

Directions: Write all answers on a separate sheet of paper.

Skill Check A. Choose the word in parentheses that best completes each sentence.

1. There isn't (anything, nothing) new about festivals.
2. In very ancient times, people gave thanks for harvests so that they wouldn't anger (no, any) gods.
3. The early Pilgrims (were, weren't) here but one year when they held the first Thanksgiving.
4. Today, people (can, can't) hardly wait for their Thanksgiving feasts.
5. We enjoy many other festivals now because of the many immigrants who didn't like to leave (none, any) of their cultural celebrations behind.

Skill Check B. Identify whether each of these sentences does or does not use understatement.

6. Street fairs are not uncommon in the summer months.
7. They are popular in my town.
8. Frequently, I find something of interest.
9. My friends are happy when I invite them.
10. We do not dislike street fairs.

Skill Check C. Choose the word in parentheses that best completes each sentence.

11. The first celebrations took place more (than, then) two thousand years ago.
12. The first float to (proceed, precede) down a parade route was made in Athens in the sixth century.
13. When people immigrate to a new country, they often underestimate the (affect, effect) of the move.
14. They (adopted, adapted) some old customs to a new culture.
15. For example, because cities don't have much open space, they don't have (nowhere, anywhere) to put large outdoor carnivals.
16. Nevertheless, (a lot, alot) of people do go to them.
17. Street fairs are (different from, different than) carnivals.
18. However, at both you can choose (among, between) a wide variety of food and entertainment.
19. On Independence Day, thousands turn out to celebrate the (principals, principles) on which this country was founded.
20. The parades and music have an emotional (affect, effect).
21. You can often see fireworks, (too, to).
22. My brother likes everything (accept, except) the noise.
23. (Regardless, Irregardless) of their tastes, most people enjoy these community festivities.
24. The celebrations for these holidays (teach, learn) us lessons about our cultural history.
25. We are always (anxious, eager) to attend.

Negative Sentences

Recognizing Double Negatives

The use of two negative words when one is sufficient is called a *double negative*.

▶ **KEY CONCEPT** Do not write sentences with double negatives. ∎

Notice in the examples in the chart below that double negatives can be corrected in two ways.

CORRECTING DOUBLE NEGATIVES	
Double Negatives	**Corrections**
Tom *doesn't* like *no* carnival rides.	Tom *doesn't* like any carnival rides. Tom likes *no* carnival rides.
Nobody can't march in the parade.	*Nobody* can march in the parade. They *can't* march in the parade.
The band *never* played *none*.	The band played *none*. The band *never* played any marches.

Some sentences can correctly contain more than one negative word. Notice in the example below, however, that each clause contains only one negative word.

EXAMPLE: The girls *didn't* go to the fair because they had *no* money.

▶ **Exercise 1** Avoiding Double Negatives Choose the word that correctly makes each sentence negative.
1. Don't (ever, never) go to a county fair without a lot of energy.
2. I almost (did, didn't) last the whole day.
3. There wasn't (anything, nothing) I couldn't do there.
4. Without a map, I (did, didn't) know where to start.
5. At first, I couldn't find (any, no) carnival rides.
6. They weren't (anywhere, nowhere) near the food tents.
7. I didn't ask (no one, anyone) for directions.
8. My family couldn't find me (nowhere, anywhere).
9. I was (never, ever) more lost in my life.
10. Still, I didn't leave without winning (nothing, anything).

Theme: Festivals

In this section, you will learn how to form negatives correctly, including how to avoid using double negatives. The examples and exercises in this section are about carnivals and festivals.

Cross-Curricular Connection: Social Studies

▶ **More Practice**

Grammar Exercise Workbook
• pp. 135–136
On-line Exercise Bank
• Section 25.1
Go on-line:
PHSchool.com
Enter Web Code:
efk-1102

Get instant feedback! Exercise 1 is available on-line or on CD-ROM.

Forming Negative Sentences Correctly

There are three ways of making a sentence negative.

Using One Negative Word The most common method of writing negative sentences is to use a single negative word, such as *never, no, nobody, nothing, nowhere, not,* or the contraction *-n't* added to a helping verb.

▶**KEY CONCEPT** Do not use two negative words in the same clause. ■

DOUBLE NEGATIVE:	The cotton candy <u>wasn't no</u> good.
CORRECT:	The cotton candy <u>wasn't</u> any good.
	The cotton candy was <u>bad</u>.

Using *But* in a Negative Sense *But* used negatively means *only* and should not be used with another negative word.

▶**KEY CONCEPT** Do not use *but* in its negative sense with another negative. ■

DOUBLE NEGATIVE:	The circus <u>doesn't</u> have <u>but</u> one big top.
CORRECT:	The circus has <u>but</u> one big top.
	The circus has <u>only</u> one big top.

Using *Barely, Hardly,* and *Scarcely* Do not use these words with another negative word.

▶**KEY CONCEPT** Do not use *barely, hardly,* or *scarcely* with another negative. ■

DOUBLE NEGATIVE:	We <u>didn't barely</u> make the minimum height requirement for the ride.
CORRECT:	We barely made the minimum height requirement for the ride.
DOUBLE NEGATIVE:	My family <u>doesn't hardly</u> celebrate New Year's Eve.
CORRECT:	My family <u>hardly</u> celebrates New Year's Eve.
DOUBLE NEGATIVE:	They <u>hadn't scarcely</u> seen everything before they went home.
CORRECT:	They had <u>scarcely</u> seen everything before they went home.

🖥 Internet Tip

The word *not* can be used to help narrow a search on the Internet. For example, on many search engines, the search phrase "sports NOT basketball" will return only those entries that do not pertain to basketball.

Exercise 2 Avoiding Problems With Negatives Choose the word in parentheses that makes each sentence negative without creating a double negative.

1. Thanksgiving (doesn't come, comes) but once a year.
2. The first settlers in Jamestown, Virginia, (had, hadn't) barely survived to celebrate Thanksgiving that first year.
3. They had (no, any) feasts to celebrate.
4. Without a good harvest, which gave hope to the Plymouth colonists, there may (never, ever) have been a feast for Thanksgiving.
5. There (wasn't, was) but one crop that survived that first year: corn.
6. (Nobody, Anybody) failed to rejoice at surviving the harsh New England winter.
7. Abraham Lincoln (wasn't, was) hardly the first American after the colonists to give thanks, but he named Thanksgiving a national holiday.
8. The United States (isn't, is) hardly the only country to celebrate a day of thanks.
9. Canadians don't (never, ever) observe the Thanksgiving Day of the United States because they have their own Thanksgiving Day.
10. Hardly (no one, anyone) in the Virgin Islands fails to celebrate their Thanksgiving Day in honor of the end of the hurricane season.

Exercise 3 Proofreading to Correct Double Negatives Proofread each sentence. Then, rewrite each sentence, correcting the double negative.

1. Many festivals and celebrations don't have no rides and games.
2. Some cultural festivals don't celebrate but a single art form.
3. Is there nobody who hasn't heard of festivals for music, art, or literature?
4. There is no classical music enthusiast who doesn't know nothing about the Salzburg festival in Austria.
5. In Copenhagen, one can't scarcely be ignorant of the jazz festival held there each summer.
6. No art lover doesn't want to miss the big art show held in Venice, Italy, every other year.
7. I didn't never see it but once.
8. I couldn't hardly take in all the beautiful works by international artists.
9. The yearly art show on the streets of New York City doesn't feature but local artists.
10. If you don't have nothing to do on Saturday, let's go down to Greenwich Village and take a look at the arts and crafts.

Grammar and Style Tip

Although double negatives are used by writers for characterization in dialogue, double negatives are nonstandard and should never be used in formal writing.

More Practice

Grammar Exercise Workbook
• pp. 135–136
On-line Exercise Bank
• Section 25.1
Go on-line:
PHSchool.com
Enter Web Code:
efk-1102

Interactive Textbook

Complete the exercises on-line! Exercises 2, 3, and 4 are available on-line or on CD-ROM.

Using Negatives to Achieve Understatement

Sometimes a writer wishes to express an idea indirectly, either to minimize the importance of the idea or to draw attention to it. One such technique is called *understatement*.

KEY CONCEPT Understatement can be achieved by using a negative word and a word with a negative prefix, such as *un-, in-, im-, dis-,* and *under-* ■

EXAMPLES: She was <u>hardly inexperienced</u> at judging contests.
Maria does <u>not dislike</u> the Ferris wheel.

Exercise 4 Writing Sentences With Understatement
Rewrite each sentence, using understatement.

EXAMPLE: The boys estimated they would have a lot of fun at the parade.
The boys <u>did not underestimate</u> the fun they would have at the parade.

1. Street fairs are a common sight in most major U.S. cities in the summer.
2. Raoul appreciated the time he had at the fair last weekend.
3. The band stationed at the east end was talented.
4. The goods for sale were expensive.
5. Raoul attends street fairs frequently.

⊛**Technology Tip**

In formal writing, it is better to write out the negative than to use a contraction. Use the search feature to find *-n't,* and change it to *not.* Be careful with the words *can't* and *won't.*

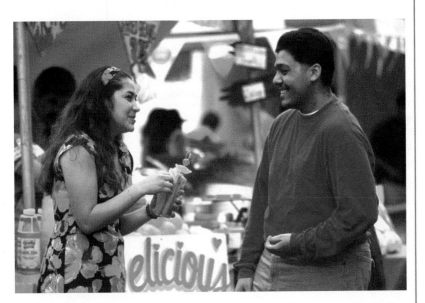

◀ **Critical Viewing**
Use understatement to describe how these two people are probably feeling. **[Describe]**

Hands-on Grammar

Strip Out Double Negatives

Fan-fold a long, narrow strip of paper to create at least fifteen sections. Leave the first, or top, section blank. In each following section of the strip, write a negative word. (See the example on this page.) You may choose to use *-n't* on the "not" section to remind you that contractions formed with *not* are negative words, or you may list each negative contraction on its own section. When you are finished listing negative words, fold the strip and label the front "Negative Words." Use the strip to help you check for double negatives when you proofread.

One strategy you can use when proofreading is to put an *x* on each negative word you find in your writing. If you see two words with an *x* in any sentence, evaluate whether both negative words are needed.

There is hardly no time left to finish the project.

There is hardly *any* time left to finish the project.

Notice that two words on the list are crossed out of the sentence. To restore the intended meaning of the sentence, *no* is replaced with *any*.

Find It in Your Reading Read a short story or a nonfiction article or essay. List all the negative words you find. Compare the list from your reading to the original list you made. If you have missed any negative words, add them to your list. (You do not need to start over; you can tape an additional strip of paper to the first one.)

Find It in Your Writing Use your Negative Words list to proofread a piece of writing from your portfolio.

Section Review

GRAMMAR EXERCISES 5–11

▶ **Exercise 5** Avoiding Double Negatives Choose the word in parentheses that best completes each sentence.

(1) Carnivals today don't look (nothing, anything) like they did hundreds of years ago. (2) There (were, weren't) no flashing lights or mechanized rides. (3) That doesn't mean people long ago (did, didn't) have fun. (4) Because they didn't have (any, no) electricity for fancy equipment, they played games and music and sold their wares. (5) That's not to say that modern carnivals and their ancient counterparts don't have (no, any) similarities.

▶ **Exercise 6** Identifying and Correcting Double Negatives Rewrite the following sentences to eliminate double negatives. If the sentence contains no double negative, write *correct*.

(1) You shouldn't hardly be surprised to see costumed people in parades at modern carnivals. (2) Some masquerade costumes are so good, you will not be able to tell who is inside. (3) Some modern carnivals don't never stop traveling. (4) Permanent amusement parks don't have none of the travel problems that carnivals face. (5) We don't live nowhere near an amusement park, so we wait for the carnivals.

▶ **Exercise 7** Writing Sentences With Understatement Rewrite the following sentences to achieve understatement.

1. We were pleased with the carnival.
2. It was like the one we went to last year.
3. The weather was pleasant.
4. My friends and I were happy.
5. The fireworks were expected.

▶ **Exercise 8** Proofreading Practice: Negative Sentences Revise the following paragraph. Correct any errors in double negatives that you find.

Mardi Gras didn't begin nowhere near the United States. For hundreds of years, people in Europe celebrated feast days with games and food because they weren't permitted to eat nothing during the fast days that followed. Mardi Gras isn't but one of many feast days they celebrated. French colonists introduced Mardi Gras to America in the 1700's.

▶ **Exercise 9** Find It in Your Reading Read the following excerpt from Patrick Henry's speech before the Virginia Convention. Identify the words in each sentence that make it a negative sentence.

I have but one lamp by which my feet are guided, and that is the lamp of experience. I know of no way of judging of the future but by the past.

▶ **Exercise 10** Find It in Your Writing Choose a piece of persuasive writing from your portfolio. Identify the negative sentences you have used. If you have not used any, add one to elaborate on your position.

▶ **Exercise 11** Writing Application Write a brief description of a celebration, street fair, or carnival you have attended or heard about. Use at least two examples of understatement in your description.

Common Usage Problems

(1) a, an The article *a* is used before consonant sounds; *an* is used before vowel sounds. Words beginning with *ho, o,* or *u* may have either a vowel sound or a consonant sound.

EXAMPLES: Rain forests are <u>a</u> universal concern.
They have become <u>an</u> issue of international importance.
The rain forest is <u>a</u> habitat for many species of animals and plants.
We need <u>an</u> honest appraisal of the situation.

(2) accept, except *Accept,* a verb, means "to receive." *Except,* a preposition, means "leaving out" or "other than."

VERB: We must *accept* responsibility for preserving the rain forest.

PREPOSITION: If we don't, nothing will be left *except* scrub.

(3) adapt, adopt *Adapt,* a verb, means "to change." *Adopt,* also a verb, means "to take as one's own."

EXAMPLES: Companies must *adapt* to conform to environmental regulations.
More and more companies are *adopting* policies geared toward preservation.

(4) affect, effect *Affect* is almost always a verb meaning "to influence." *Effect* is usually a noun meaning "result." Occasionally, *effect* is a verb meaning "to bring about" or "to cause."

VERB: It is not clear how much the destruction of the rain forests *affects* the world's climate.

NOUN: One *effect* may be global warming.

VERB: Concern over this situation has *effected* some change in attitudes toward rain forests.

(5) aggravate *Aggravate* means "to make worse." Avoid using this word to mean "to annoy."

LESS
ACCEPTABLE: Some people are *aggravated* by disregard for the environment.

PREFERRED: Continued deforestation will *aggravate* climatic changes.

(6) ain't *Ain't,* originally a contraction of *am not,* is not considered acceptable standard English. Avoid using it in all writing and speaking.

(7) all ready, already *All ready* is an expression meaning

Theme: Rain Forests

In this section, you will learn about a number of common usage problems. The examples and exercises in this section are about the rain forests.

Cross-Curricular Connection: Science

▶ **More Practice**

Grammar Exercise Workbook
• pp. 139–140
On-line Exercise Bank
• Section 25.2
   Go on-line:
   PHSchool.com
   Enter Web Code:
   efk-1102

"ready." The expression functions as an adjective. *Already* is an adverb meaning "by or before this time" or "even now."

ADJECTIVE: Are people all ready to help preserve the rain forest?

ADVERB: Much destruction has already been done.

(8) all right, alright *Alright* is a nonstandard spelling. Always use the two-word form in your writing.

NONSTANDARD: With help, the rain forest may still be *alright.*

CORRECT: With help, the rain forest may still be *all right.*

(9) all together, altogether These two adverbs have different meanings. *All together* means "all at once." *Altogether* means "completely" or "in all."

EXAMPLES: The monkeys sat in the trees *all together.*
               A rain forest is not *altogether* the same as a jungle.

(10) among, between *Among* and *between* are both prepositions. *Among* always implies three or more. *Between* is usually properly used with just two items.

EXAMPLES: Orchids may be found *among* the many different plants of the rain forest.
               Vines called *lianas* are found in the layers *between* the upper canopy and the forest floor.

> **Exercise 12** Avoiding Usage Problems Choose the correct expression to complete each sentence.
> 1. Our class has (adapted, adopted) a new research project policy.
> 2. The way we find our information (affects, effects) our grade.
> 3. He is (annoyed, aggravated) by the lack of information on his topic.
> 4. He cannot find (a, an) useful Internet site related to his topic.
> 5. Our group divided the research tasks (among, between) the group members.
> 6. The rain forest topic was (already, all ready) taken.
> 7. (Ain't, Aren't) you going to choose another topic?
> 8. Is this outline (all right, alright) with the group?
> 9. Some think it is (all together, altogether) too difficult.
> 10. By now, most of the group has (accepted, excepted) it.

▲ **Critical Viewing**
In one sentence, tell what factors affect the growth of plants. In another sentence, tell the effect of rain and sunshine on plant growth. **[Distinguish]**

(11) *anxious* *Anxious* means "worried," "uneasy," or "fearful." Do not use it as a substitute for *eager.*

AMBIGUOUS: Environmentalists are *anxious* for change.

CLEAR: Environmentalists are *anxious* about the results of deforestation and *eager* for change.

(12) *anyone, any one, everyone, every one* *Anyone* and *everyone* mean "any person" and "every person," respectively. *Any one* means "any single person (or thing)," and *every one* means "every single person (or thing)."

EXAMPLES: *Anyone* may take an interest in preservation.
Any one of the rain forest plants could provide a life-saving drug.
Everyone should be concerned about the environment.
Every one of the rain forests' plants and animals plays a role in maintaining the ecosystem.

(13) *anyway, anywhere, everywhere, nowhere, somewhere* These adverbs should never end in *-s.*

NONSTANDARD: There are unknown species *somewheres* in the rain forest.

CORRECT: There are unknown species *somewhere* in the rain forest.

(14) *as* Do not use the conjunction *as* to mean "because."

LESS ACCEPTABLE: There are few plants on the forest floor *as there* is very little sunlight.

PREFERRED: There are few plants on the forest floor *because* there is very little sunlight.

(15) *as to* *As to* is awkward. Replace it with *about.*

NONSTANDARD: There is some doubt *as to* whether the rain forests will survive.

CORRECT: There is some doubt *about* the rain forests' survival.

(16) *at* Do not use *at* after *where.* Simply eliminate it.

NONSTANDARD: Where in the world are rain forests *at?*

CORRECT: Where in the world *are* rain forests?

(17) *at about* Avoid using *at about.* Use *at, around,* or *near.*

LESS ACCEPTABLE: Many rain forests are found *at about* the equator.

PREFERRED: Many rain forests are found *near* the equator.

> **More Practice**
>
> Grammar Exercise Workbook
> • pp. 139–140
> On-line Exercise Bank
> • Section 25.2
>   *Go on-line:*
>   PHSchool.com
>   *Enter Web Code:*
>   efk-1102

(18) awful, awfully *Awful* is used informally to mean "extremely bad." *Awfully* is used informally to mean "very." Better writers replace both with more descriptive words. In formal writing, use *awful* only to mean "inspiring fear."

INFORMAL: The heat is *awful.*

BETTER: The heat is debilitating.

INFORMAL: It can get *awfully* hot in the rain forest.

BETTER: It can get *extremely* hot in the rain forest.

FORMAL: There may be *awful* viruses as yet undiscovered in the rain forests.

(19) awhile, a while *Awhile* is an adverb, which in itself means "for a while." *A while* is an article and a noun usually used after the preposition *for.*

ADVERB: Vines live off trees *awhile,* but they eventually strangle them.

NOUN: Concern about the rain forest has been growing for *a while.*

▲ **Critical Viewing**
Revise this sentence about the frog in the picture: "The frog is awfully small."
[Describe]

(20) beat, win *Beat* means "to overcome (an opponent)." *Win* means "to achieve victory in."

NONSTANDARD: A successful plant has *won* the others in competition for resources.

CORRECT: A successful plant has *beaten* the others in competition for resources.

▶ **Exercise 13** Avoiding Usage Problems Choose the correct expression to complete each sentence.

1. There are rain forests (somewhere, somewheres) in Brazil.
2. Gliding is a useful adaptation of animals (as, because) it allows them to move about freely.
3. Countries are concerned (as to, about) how to balance industrial growth and the preservation of rain forests.
4. Where do ants (live, live at) in the rain forest?
5. Pharmaceutical companies are (anxious, eager) to find new medicines.
6. We saw a frog sitting (near, at about) the edge of the stream.
7. We got (awfully, very) wet.
8. A snake could be hiding under (anyone, any one) of these leaves.
9. The detrimental effects of a venomous snakebite last for (awhile, a while).
10. Pharmaceutical companies are trying to (beat, win) one another to develop valuable medicines.

(21) because Do not use *because* after *the reason*. Say "The reason is . . . that" or reword the sentence.

NONSTANDARD: *One reason* to preserve the environment is because it will benefit humans.

CORRECT: We try to preserve the environment *because* it will benefit humans.

(22) being as, being that Avoid using either expression. Use *because* instead.

NONSTANDARD: *Being as* (or *that*) the ecosystem is so fragile, competition among plants and animals is fierce.

CORRECT: *Because* the ecosystem is so fragile, competition among plants and animals is fierce.

(23) beside, besides *Beside* means "at the side of" or "close to." *Besides* means "in addition to."

EXAMPLES: Mangrove forests are often found *beside* rain forests near the coastline.
There are other kinds of rain forests *besides* the equatorial kind.

(24) bring, take *Bring* means "to carry from a distant place to a nearer one." *Take* means the opposite: "to carry from a near place to a more distant place."

EXAMPLES: I saw a movie about a man who *brings* a diseased monkey to the United States.
Birds and bats *take* seeds from plants and disperse them throughout the forest.

(25) can, may *Can* means "has the ability to." *May* means "has permission to" or "possible or likely to."

ABILITY: Some rain forest animals *can* climb trees.
PERMISSION: Everyone *may* join our effort to preserve the environment.
POSSIBILITY: There *may* be a solution that pleases everyone.

(26) clipped words Avoid using clipped or shortened words—such as *gym, phone,* or *photo* in formal writing.

INFORMAL: There are no *phones* deep in the rain forest.
FORMAL: There are no *telephones* deep in the rain forest.

Grammar and Style Tip

Avoid using wordy expressions such as "being as" to sound formal or academic. Choose the most direct way of expressing your point.

(27) *different from, different than* Use *from.*

LESS ACCEPTABLE:	The rain forest of the Amazon Basin is *different than* that of the northwestern United States.
PREFERRED:	The rain forest of the Amazon Basin is *different from* that of the northwestern United States.

(28) *doesn't, don't* Do not use *don't* with third-person singular subjects. Use *doesn't* instead.

NONSTANDARD:	A rain forest *don't* have a dry season.
CORRECT:	A rain forest *doesn't* have a dry season.

(29) *done* *Done*, the past participle of *do*, should always follow a helping verb.

NONSTANDARD:	We *done* what we could to help.
CORRECT:	We *have done* what we could to help.

(30) *due to* *Due to* means "caused by" and should be used only when the words "caused by" can logically be substituted.

NONSTANDARD:	Few plants live on the forest floor *due to* lack of sunlight.
CORRECT:	The scarcity of plants on the forest floor is *due to* lack of sunlight.

▶ **Exercise 14** Proofreading to Correct Usage Problems
Proofread each of the following sentences. On a separate sheet of paper, correctly write any sentences that contain errors or nonstandard usage. If a sentence contains no errors, write "correct as is."

1. A successful cure will take a great deal of money to the company that discovers it.
2. They may even discover a drug to cure cancer.
3. Many magazines feature photos of the rain forest.
4. Some species are found no place on Earth beside the rain forest.
5. Being as there is little change in temperature, there is great biological diversity.
6. Another reason for this diversity is that there is little distinction among the seasons.
7. The vine done much damage to the trees.
8. The tree will soon die due to the fact that the vine is strangling it.
9. She says that she don't know much about the rain forest.
10. Nocturnal animals are different than those that come out during the day.

▶ **More Practice**

Grammar Exercise Workbook
• pp. 139–140
On-line Exercise Bank
• Section 25.2
  Go on-line:
  PHSchool.com
  Enter Web Code:
  efk-1102

Interactive Textbook

Complete the exercise on-line! Exercise 14 is available on-line or on CD-ROM.

(31) each other, one another Each other and one another are usually interchangeable. At times, however, each other is more logically used in reference to only two; one another, in reference to more than two.

EXAMPLES:　　Animals and plants in the rain forest often benefit *each other* (or *one another*).
In a symbiotic relationship, both organisms involved benefit *each other.*
Ideally, we should care for the rain forest as we care for *one another.*

(32) farther, further Farther refers to distance. Further means "additional" or "to a greater degree or extent."

EXAMPLES:　　The African rain forests are *farther* from here than those of South America.
Further study is being done to ascertain the effects of humans on the rain forest.

(33) fewer, less Use *fewer* with objects that can be counted. Use *less* with quantities and qualities that cannot be counted.

EXAMPLES:　　*fewer* animals, *fewer* resources, *fewer* acres
less rainfall, *less* diversity, *less* acreage

(34) get, got, gotten These forms of the verb *to get* are acceptable in standard usage, but, whenever possible, it is best to use a more specific word.

INFORMAL:　　*get* water, *got* more fragile, have *gotten* encouragement

BETTER:　　*obtain* water, *became* more fragile, have *received* encouragement

(35) gone, went Gone is the past participle of *go* and should be used as a verb only with a helping verb. *Went* is the past tense of *go* and is never used with a helping verb.

NONSTANDARD:　　The bird *gone* away, but the monkeys remain.
The bird *should never have went* near the snake.

CORRECT:　　The bird went away, but the monkeys remain.
The bird *should never have gone* near the snake.

(36) good, lovely, nice These three adjectives are weak and overused. Try to use a more specific adjective.

WEAK:　　*good* example, *lovely* green leaves, *nice* aroma

BETTER:　　*useful* example, *lush* green leaves, *pleasing* aroma

▼ Critical Viewing
Revise the following sentence about the parrot in the picture: "The parrot has nice colors." [Describe]

(37) in, into *In* refers to position. *Into* suggests motion.

EXAMPLES: Many insect species live *in* the rain forest.
Plants take nutrients from the soil *into* their roots.

(38) irregardless Avoid this word. Use *regardless*.

(39) kind of, sort of Do not use *kind of* or *sort of* to mean "rather" or "somewhat."

(40) lay, lie *Lay* means "to put or set (something) down." Its principal parts—*lay, laying, laid,* and *laid*—are usually followed by a direct object. *Lie* means "to recline." Its principal parts—*lie, lying, lay,* and *lain*—are never followed by a direct object.

LAY: That fungus is poisonous; *lay* it down at once.
New legislation *is laying* the foundation for the future.
He *laid* the camera aside after he took the picture.
The ant queen *has laid* her eggs in that hollow branch.

LIE: *Lie* on the grass, and watch the clouds drift by.
The root of that tree *is lying* above ground.
The snake *lay* on the branch.
These seeds *have lain* on the ground a long time.

Get instant feedback! Exercise 15 is available on-line or on CD-ROM.

> **Exercise 15** Avoiding Usage Problems Choose the correct expression to complete each sentence.
> 1. He had (got, gotten) a thorough medical examination when he returned from the tropics.
> 2. She gave a(n) (good, effective) speech.
> 3. Scientists travel (in, into) the rain forest to look for new species.
> 4. We enjoyed the speech, (irregardless, regardless).
> 5. Rain forest trees and the fungi that grow in their roots help (each other, one another) to obtain nourishment.
> 6. The tree will not die because it has (fewer, less) vines than it did before.
> 7. Scientists are (kind of, somewhat) concerned about global warming.
> 8. Scientists will explore the issue (farther, further).
> 9. Some of these logs have (laid, lain) here for years.
> 10. The scientists (gone, went) home when they finished their research.
> 11. Global warming is partly (due to, because of) increased levels of carbon dioxide in the Earth's atmosphere.
> 12. He took many (photos, photographs) while he was in Brazil.
> 13. Nocturnal animals are different (from, than) those that come out during the day.
> 14. That animal (don't, doesn't) look too friendly.
> 15. She is going to the equator (irregardless, regardless) of the hot weather.

More Practice

Grammar Exercise Workbook
• pp. 139–140
On-line Exercise Bank
• Section 25.2
  Go on-line:
  PHSchool.com
  Enter Web Code:
  efk-1102

▶ **Speaking and Listening Tip**

Read the correct version of each sentence aloud to a partner to develop the habits of standard usage in speaking as well as in writing.

Common Usage Problems • **489**

(41) learn, teach *Learn* means "to acquire knowledge." *Teach* means "to give knowledge to."

EXAMPLES: You can *learn* much about the rain forest from that documentary.
   Experience has *taught* us that the rain forest is beneficial to us.

(42) leave, let *Leave* means "to allow to remain." *Let* means "to permit."

NONSTANDARD: *Let* the snake alone, and it won't trouble you.

CORRECT: *Leave* the snake alone, and it won't trouble you.

(43) like *Like* is a preposition and should not be used in place of the subordinating conjunction *as*.

NONSTANDARD: That exhibit looks *like* a rain forest should look.

CORRECT: That exhibit looks as a rain forest should look.
   That exhibit looks *like* a rain forest.

(44) loose, lose *Loose* is usually an adjective or a part of such idioms as *cut loose, turn loose,* or *break loose. Lose* is always a verb, generally meaning "to miss from one's possession."

EXAMPLES: The branch is *loose,* and it may fall.
   Without our help, these animals will *lose* their habitat.

(45) maybe, may be *Maybe* is an adverb meaning "perhaps." *May be* is a helping verb and a verb.

ADVERB: *Maybe* we can preserve the rain forest if we all work together.

VERB: It *may be* too late to save it.

(46) of Do not use the preposition *of* in place of the verb *have.* Moreover, do not use *of* after *outside, inside, off,* and *atop.* Simply eliminate it.

NONSTANDARD: We *should of* tried to stop the damage <u>inside of</u> the rain forest.

CORRECT: We *should have* tried to stop the damage <u>inside</u> the rain forest.

More Practice

Grammar Exercise Workbook
• pp. 139–140
On-line Exercise Bank
• Section 25.2
  Go on-line:
  PHSchool.com
  Enter Web Code:
  efk-1102

(47) ***OK, O.K., okay*** In informal writing, *OK, O.K.,* and *okay* are acceptably used to mean "all right." In formal writing, however, do not use either the abbreviations or *okay.*

(48) ***only*** *Only* should be placed in front of the word it logically modifies.

EXAMPLES:
Only people can protect the environment.
(No one else can protect it.)
People can protect *only* the environment.
(They can protect nothing else.)

(49) ***ought*** Never use *ought* with *have* or *had.* Simply eliminate *have* or *had.*

NONSTANDARD:
We hadn't *ought* to have cut down so many trees.

CORRECT:
We *ought* not to have cut down so many trees.

(50) ***outside of*** Do not use this expression to mean "besides" or "except."

NONSTANDARD:
Many species are found nowhere else *outside of* the rain forest.

CORRECT:
Many species are found nowhere else *except* the rain forest.

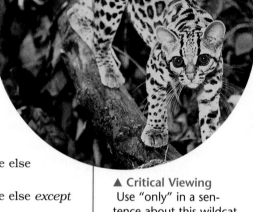

▲ Critical Viewing
Use "only" in a sentence about this wildcat called a margay.
[Describe]

▶ **Exercise 16** Avoiding Usage Problems Choose the correct expression to complete each sentence.
1. Scientists hope to (teach, learn) other people about exotic animals.
2. That animal (maybe, may be) looking for food.
3. The soil is not very (loose, lose) where it is mostly clay.
4. Gorillas are not playful (as, like) the chimps are.
5. The roots are not very deep (inside, inside of) the ground.
6. Some insect species are (found only, only found) in the rain forest.
7. It is best to (let, leave) animals alone while they are eating.
8. (Outside of, Except for) seedlings, little grows there.
9. Rain forest plants and animals have adapted (okay, well) to the hot, humid environment.
10. You (had ought, ought) to read more about it.

Spelling Tip

To distinguish between the spelling of *loose* and *lose,* remember that *lose* has "lost" an o.

▶ **Exercise 17** Writing Sentences With Correct Usage
Write a sentence correctly using each word.
1. loose   2. learn   3. like   4. lose   5. teach

(51) plurals that do not end in -s The plurals of certain nouns from Greek and Latin are formed as they were in their original language. Words such as *criteria, media,* and *phenomena* are plural and should not be treated as if they were singular (*criterion, medium, phenomenon*).

INCORRECT: The *media is* instrumental in raising environmental awareness.

CORRECT: The *media* are instrumental in raising environmental awareness.

(52) precede, proceed *Precede* means "to go before." *Proceed* means "to move or go forward."

EXAMPLES: Dr. Scott's research *preceded* Dr. Fagle's.
Will you *proceed* with your research?

(53) principal, principle As an adjective, *principal* means "most important" or "chief." As a noun, it means "a person who has controlling authority." *Principle*, always a noun, means "a fundamental law."

ADJECTIVE: Broadleaf evergreens are the *principal* trees of the equatorial rain forests.

NOUN: The school's *principal* encourages environmental awareness.

NOUN: Life in the rain forest operates according to fundamental biological *principles*.

(54) real *Real* means "authentic." The use of *real* to mean "very" or "really" should be avoided in formal writing.

INFORMAL: Lianas are *real* tight around the trees.
FORMAL: Lianas are *very* tight around the trees.

(55) says *Says* should not be used as a substitute for *said*.

NONSTANDARD: Yesterday an environmentalist *says* that less than two percent of the original coastal rain forest of Brazil is left.

CORRECT: Yesterday an environmentalist *said* that less than two percent of the original coastal rain forest of Brazil was left.

(56) than, then *Than* is used in comparisons. Do not confuse it with the adverb *then*, which usually refers to time.

EXAMPLES: Temperate rain forests have a greater temperature range *than* equatorial rain forests.
Read this book, and *then* decide whether you want to help the rain forest.

(57) *that, which, who* *That* refers to people or things; *which* refers only to things; *who* refers only to people.

EXAMPLES: Plants have several ways to capture the nutrients *that* they need.

He is a man *that* (or *who*) cares about the environment.

(58) *their, there, they're* *Their*, a possessive pronoun, always modifies a noun. *There* can be used either as an expletive at the beginning of a sentence or as an adverb. *They're* is a contraction for *they are*.

PRONOUN: Many trees get *their* nutrients with the help of fungi that live among the roots.

EXPLETIVE: *There* is little we can do to repair the damage already done.

ADVERB: I've never been to Africa, but I'd like to go *there* someday.

CONTRACTION: From what I've heard of the rain forests, *they're* very hot.

(59) *to, too, two* *To*, a preposition, begins a prepositional phrase or an infinitive. *Too*, an adverb, modifies adjectives and other adverbs. *Two* is a number.

PREPOSITION: *to* the tropics, *to* Brazil
INFINITIVE: *to* grow, *to* survive
ADVERB: *too* hot, *too* densely populated
NUMBER: *two* species, *two* types

(60) *when, where* Do not use *when* or *where* directly after a linking verb. Also, do not use *where* in place of *that*.

NONSTANDARD: The annual flood is *when* fish enter the rain forest in large numbers.

The rain forest is *where* the greatest biological diversity on Earth is found.

I heard the other day *where* destruction is proceeding at an alarming rate.

CORRECT: During the annual flood, fish enter the rain forest in large numbers.

The greatest biological diversity on Earth is found in the rain forest.

I heard the other day that destruction is proceeding at an alarming rate.

💡 Spelling Tip

Remember that spell checkers on word-processing programs will accept *their*, *there*, and *they're* as correctly spelled. Proofread to check correct spellings of homophones such as these.

Exercise 18 Avoiding Usage Problems Choose the correct expression to complete each sentence.

1. Some of the timber from the temperate forests is (really, extremely) valuable.
2. The valuable timber is the (principle, principal) reason for industry to enter the area.
3. Many people believe that protection of the rain forests should be a guiding (principle, principal).
4. They think it's wiser to prevent damage (then, than) to observe the results.
5. Studies are (preceding, proceeding) with the help of research teams.
6. Yesterday, he (says, said) that he had watched a program about the rain forest.
7. Some criteria for judging a rain forest (includes, include) latitude, temperature, and rainfall.
8. The temperature never falls (to, too, two) low in the rain forest.
9. The summer is (when, the season when) the temperature is hottest.
10. Very heavy rainfall is a striking (phenomenon, phenomena) of a rain forest.

Exercise 19 Proofreading to Correct Usage Problems
On a separate sheet of paper, revise the following paragraph to eliminate awkward or problematic usage. You may need to reorder words.

The trees are generally taller in the temperate forests then they are in the tropical ones. The floor of a rain forest is a place of very little light. Most animals have special abilities that help them survive in there habitat. Some animals who are common to rain forests include monkeys, parrots, hummingbirds, bats, tree frogs, snakes, and beetles. Scientists which study these species of animals find the variety of species astounding.

More Practice

Grammar Exercise Workbook
• pp. 139–140
On-line Exercise Bank
• Section 25.2
  Go on-line:
  PHSchool.com
  Enter Web Code:
  efk-1102

interactive Textbook

Complete the exercises on-line! Exercises 18 and 19 are available on-line or on CD-ROM.

▶ Critical Viewing
Compare these flowers with flowers in your area. Use the word *than* in your comparison. **[Compare]**

Section 25.2 Section Review

GRAMMAR EXERCISES 20–25

Exercise 20 Using *a* and *an*
Complete each expression with *a* or *an*.

1. ___?___ unusual amount of rain
2. ___?___ unique environment
3. ___?___ arboreal species
4. ___?___ excellent source
5. ___?___ uniform layer
6. ___?___ honest living
7. ___?___ hot climate
8. ___?___ one-sided relationship
9. ___?___ herbivorous mammal
10. ___?___ insectivore

Exercise 21 Avoiding Usage
Problems Choose the correct expression to complete each sentence.

1. If we (accept, except) the idea that rain forests are essential to the environment, we must search for alternatives to deforestation.
2. Ants have (adapted, adopted) all the layers of the forest in which to make their homes.
3. Some diseases (affect, effect) the nervous system.
4. Others are less serious; they are simply (aggravating, annoying).
5. Whatever the time of year, the rain forests (ain't, aren't) going to be dry.
6. Many new species have (already, all ready) been discovered.
7. It is never (alright, all right) to do nothing.
8. If nobody does anything, there will be no (farther, further) progress.
9. There are (fewer, less) insect species in the temperate forests than in other types of forests.
10. The rain forest has (gotten to be, become) a major concern since the 1970's.

Exercise 22 Proofreading to
Correct Usage Problems Rewrite each sentence, correcting the error in usage.

(1) The rain forest of the Amazon Basin may contain more than ten million species of plants and animals all together. (2) Between these millions of species are found large numbers of insects. (3) Are you anxious to see the rain forest? (4) Everyone of the millions of species is necessary. (5) Ants live everywheres in the rain forest. (6) Anacondas constrict their prey, which makes these snakes awfully dangerous. (7) As to length, they can grow to more than thirty feet. (8) It is a good thing those snakes live at the rain forest and not here. (9) The tree is still laying where it fell. (10) Some mammals are learned survival techniques by their parents.

Exercise 23 Find It in Your
Reading Review a newspaper or magazine article to find examples of correct usage for at least four of the usage issues identified in this chapter.

Exercise 24 Find It in Your
Writing Choose one piece of writing in your portfolio. Check it carefully for the usage problems discussed in this chapter. Identify examples of correct usage. Correct any usage errors that you find.

Exercise 25 Writing Application
Write a brief description of the climate in your area. Check your work for the usage errors discussed in this chapter.

Capitalization

The process of writing existed long before capital letters; the first examples of capital letters are seen in writing from around the fifth century B.C. At that time, capital letters were straight, sharp-cornered letters used for inscriptions in stone or metal. Although the straight lines were easier to carve, rounded lowercase letters were preferred for most handwriting. Capital letters were saved for important things, such as a person's name or the beginning of a new thought. Today, the conventions of written English call for capitals to be used in similar ways.

▲ **Critical Viewing**
Looking at the remains of this town, what sentence would you write about the intensity of the Civil War? Which words in your sentence should begin with a capital letter? [**Draw Conclusions**]

Diagnostic Test

Directions: Write all answers on a separate sheet of paper.

Skill Check A. Copy each of the underlined items, and tell whether it is a proper noun or proper adjective.

1. Stephen Douglas
2. Confederate cavalry
3. Veterans Day
4. American soldier
5. Lincoln Memorial

Skill Check B. Write the words that should be capitalized in the following sentences.

6. at the outset of the civil war, most northerners thought that the south would be defeated within a few months.
7. after the battle of bull run in april 1861, however, it became clear that the war would last much longer.
8. during the coming years, tens of thousands of men would participate in hundreds of battles all across america.
9. the confederacy, which consisted of eleven states—including south carolina, alabama, georgia, and louisiana—was led by president jefferson davis.
10. the northern states, known as the union, were led by men such as abraham lincoln and secretary of state william seward.

Skill Check C. Copy the following paragraph, using capital letters as needed.

(11) most of the fighting took place in southern states, (12) but battles were also fought in the west and along the atlantic coast. (13) for instance, the first ironclad ships, the *monitor* and the *merrimack,* (14) battled each other near the mouth of the james river off the coast of virginia. (15) small towns—such as murfreesboro, tennessee, and perryville, kentucky, (16) became the sites of ferocious battles. after more than four years (17) of bitter fighting, the war ended with the surrender of general robert e. lee to general ulysses s. grant. (18) today, the civil war era is kept alive (19) by books, such as *the red badge of courage,* and (20) historic landmarks, such as kennesaw mountain battlefield.

Skill Check D. Correct the capitalization in each underlined group of words. If no correction is needed, write *correct.*

21. We enjoyed the Shakespearean Play that we saw at the theater.
22. The theater is located on the corner of Saddle and West streets.
23. The british actors stayed after the performance to answer questions.
24. My grandmother knew one of the actors.
25. He signed grandma's program with a flourish.

Just as road signs help to guide people through a town, capital letters help to guide readers through their reading. Capitalization signals the start of a new sentence or points out certain words within a sentence to give readers visual clues that aid in their understanding.

> **KEY CONCEPT** To **capitalize** means to begin a word with a capital letter. ■

Using Capitals to Begin a Sentence

Always signal the start of a new idea by capitalizing the first word in a sentence.

> **KEY CONCEPT** Capitalize the first word in declarative, interrogative, imperative, and exclamatory sentences. ■

DECLARATIVE:	The war was long and costly.
INTERROGATIVE:	Where was the battle fought?
IMPERATIVE:	Watch for enemy soldiers.
EXCLAMATORY:	What an astounding turn of events!

> **KEY CONCEPT** Capitalize the first word in interjections and incomplete questions. ■

INTERJECTIONS:	Oh! Wonderful!
INCOMPLETE QUESTIONS:	What? How many?

> **KEY CONCEPT** Capitalize the first word of a quotation. Do not capitalize the first word of a continuing quotation interrupted by identifying words or a quotation that is the continuation of the writer's thought. ■

EXAMPLES: Joe exclaimed, "The enemy is in the field!" (speaker's words follow the introductory words)

"As the ship came plowing through the water," he said, "she cut the waves like a sword cutting through silk." (speaker's words interrupted by identifying words)

At the end of the battle, Grant remarked that it was "the saddest affair I have witnessed in war." (speaker's words are a continuation of the writer's thought)

Theme: The Civil War
In this chapter, you will learn about capitalizing proper nouns, adjectives, titles, and the first words of sentences. The examples and exercises in this chapter are about the Civil War.

Cross-Curricular Connection: Social Studies

▶ **KEY CONCEPT** Capitalize the first word after a colon only if the word begins a complete sentence. Do not capitalize the word if it begins a list of words or phrases. ■

SENTENCE FOLLOWING A COLON:	He repeated his statement emphatically: He was unable to continue marching.
LIST FOLLOWING A COLON:	The soldiers were issued the following equipment: backpacks, uniforms, canteens, and blankets.

▶ **KEY CONCEPT** Capitalize the first word in each line of traditional poetry, even if the line does not start a new sentence. ■

EXAMPLE: I think that I shall never see
            A poem lovely as a tree. — Joyce Kilmer

▶ **Exercise 1** Capitalizing First Words Copy the following items, adding capitals where necessary.

EXAMPLE: patriots lined up at recruitment centers.
ANSWER: Patriots lined up at recruitment centers.

1. the American Civil War was fought from 1861 until 1865.
2. despite the terrible consequences that he knew war would bring, President Lincoln made his decision: the Union would be preserved.
3. one senator from Kansas said that he would be willing to do battle for his principles.
4. "it is well that war is so terrible," said Robert E. Lee, "lest we grow too fond of it."
5. in his inaugural address, President Lincoln said that peace would be achieved "with malice toward none, with charity for all."
6. both armies consisted of three main elements: infantry, cavalry, and artillery.
7. how many families would lose fathers, sons, and brothers in the fighting to come?
8. more Americans perished in the Civil War than in all other wars in which Americans fought.
9. "exult, O shores, and ring, O bells!
         but I with mournful tread,
            walk the deck my captain lies,
                fallen cold and dead."—Walt Whitman
10. hurrah! the war is finally over!

▼ **Critical Viewing** General Robert E. Lee was commander of the Confederate forces. What details in this photo reveal something of his character? Begin your answer with "These details represent Lee's character:" and capitalize the words following the colon correctly. **[Analyze]**

▶ **More Practice**

Grammar Exercise Workbook
• pp. 141–142
On-line Exercise Bank
• Chapter 26
Go on-line:
PHSchool.com
Enter Web Code:
efk-1102

Using Capitals for Proper Nouns

Nouns, as you may remember, are either common or proper. Common nouns identify classes of people, places, or things.

EXAMPLES: sailor, brother, leader
street, city, country
cannon, ship, magazine

Proper nouns, on the other hand, name specific examples of each class and should be capitalized.

KEY CONCEPT Capitalize all proper nouns. ■

EXAMPLES: Jennifer, Professor Wilkens, Governor Percy,
Main Street, Halloran House, Chicago,
The Red Badge of Courage, U.S.S. *Monitor, The Cliffside News*

Names Each part of a person's name—the given name, the middle name, and the surname—should be capitalized.

KEY CONCEPT Capitalize each part of a person's name even when the full name is not used—Bill, John, Sarah. ■

EXAMPLES: Jean Grogan, R. R. Brighton, Ernesto H. Sanchez

Capitalize the proper names that are given to animals.

EXAMPLES: Flipper, Traveler, Rin Tin Tin

Exercise 2 Writing Sentences With Capital Letters On your paper, write a sentence for each numbered item. Supply capital letters wherever necessary.

EXAMPLE: civil war battlefield
ANSWER: We visited a Civil War battlefield.

1. jefferson davis
2. confederate soldiers
3. *north & south* magazine
4. president abraham lincoln
5. troops stationed in north carolina

More Practice

Grammar Exercise Workbook
• pp. 141–142
On-line Exercise Bank
• Chapter 26
  Go on-line:
  PHSchool.com
  Enter Web Code:
  efk-1102

Complete the exercise on-line! Exercise 2 is available on-line or on CD-ROM.

Geographical and Place Names Although there is a wide variety of categories of geographical and place names, a single general rule for capitalization applies:

> **KEY CONCEPT** Capitalize geographical and place names. ■

Examples of different kinds of geographical and place names are listed in the following chart. Each item should serve as a model for similar names.

GEOGRAPHICAL AND PLACE NAMES	
Streets	Madison Avenue, First Street, Chicken Valley Road
Boroughs, Towns, and Cities	Brooklyn, Oakdale, Michigan City
Counties, States, and Provinces	Champlain County, New Mexico, Quebec
Nations and Continents	Austria, Kenya, the United States of America, the Union, Asia, the Confederate States of America
Mountains	the Adirondacks, Mount Washington
Valleys and Deserts	the San Fernando Valley, the Mojave Desert, the Gobi Desert
Islands and Peninsulas	Aruba, the Faroe Islands, Cape York Peninsula
Sections of a Country	the Northeast, Siberia, the Great Plains
Scenic Spots	Gateway National Park, Carlsbad Caverns
Rivers and Falls	the Missouri River, Victoria Falls
Lakes and Bays	Lake Cayuga, Green Bay, the Bay of Biscayne
Seas and Oceans	the Sargasso Sea, the Indian Ocean
Celestial Bodies	the Milky Way, Mars, the Big Dipper
Monuments and Memorials	the Tomb of the Unknown Soldier, Kennedy Memorial Library, the Soldiers and Sailors Monument
Buildings	Madison Square Garden, the Cleveland Museum of Art, Fort Hood, the Astrodome, the White House
School and Meeting Rooms	Room 6, Laboratory 3B, the Red Room, Conference Room C

■ Internet Tip

It is important to use proper capitalization in your writing; however, when you are conducting an Internet search, it is not necessary to capitalize proper nouns. Search engines will look for all instances of a word or phrase whether or not it is capitalized.

Note About *Capitalizing Directions:* Words indicating direction can be used in two ways: (1) to name a section of a larger geographical area or (2) simply to give or indicate direction. Words indicating direction are capitalized only when they refer to a section of a larger geographical area.

EXAMPLES: The courier made his way through the *South*.
I will meet you at the park.
The train stops two miles *east* of the city.

Note About *Capitalizing Names of Celestial Bodies:* Two celestial bodies whose names are not capitalized are *moon* and *sun*. They are exceptions to the rule.

EXAMPLE: When the *moon* passes between the *sun* and the *Earth*, a solar eclipse occurs.

Note About *Capitalizing* **theater, hotel, university,** *and* **similar words:** Do not capitalize words such as *theater, hotel, university, park*, and so forth unless the word is part of a proper name.

EXAMPLES: We visited Stone Mountain Park.
I will meet you at the park.

▼ Critical Viewing
If you had background information about this picture, what details might be capitalized? For example, you would capitalize the names of the people who live in the houses. Give at least three other examples of words that would be capitalized. **[Analyze]**

Events and Times Capitalize references to historic events, periods, and documents as well as dates and holidays.

▷ **KEY CONCEPT** Capitalize the names of specific events and periods in history. ■

SPECIAL EVENTS AND TIMES	
Historic Events	the Siege of Vicksburg, the Black Plague, the Battle of Chickamauga, World War I, Strategic Arms Limitations Talks (SALT)
Historical Periods	the Enlightenment, the Age of Napoleon, Reconstruction, the Great Depression
Documents	the Bill of Rights, the Gettysburg Address, the Constitution of the United States
Days and Months Holidays Religious Holidays	Monday, June 22, the third week in May Labor Day, Memorial Day, Veterans Day Rosh Hashanah, Christmas, Easter
Special Events	the Riverhead High School Clambake, the World Series, the Civil War Antiques Show, Tanglewood Music Festival

Internet Tip

Use the Internet to learn more about the Civil War. Search key words, such as *Civil War, Confederacy,* or *secession.* For narrowly defined topics, try more specific words, such as *Fort Sumter* or *Abraham Lincoln.*

Most college dictionaries and general encyclopedias include extensive listings of historic events and periods that can be consulted if you are unsure about their capitalization.

Note About *Capitalizing Seasons* Although days and months are capitalized, you should not capitalize seasons unless the name of the season is being used as a proper noun or adjective.

EXAMPLES: The soldiers were particularly uncomfortable during the *summer* because of their wool uniforms.

The *Autumn* Harvest Dance is next week.

▶**KEY CONCEPT** Capitalize the names of organizations, government bodies, political parties, races, nationalities, languages, and religions. ■

VARIOUS GROUPS	
Clubs	Rotary, Knights of Columbus, San Francisco Athletic Club
Organizations	the Red Cross, American Association of University Women, the Urban League
Institutions	the Metropolitan Museum of Art, the Chicago Symphony, the Mayo Clinic
Schools	John F. Kennedy High School, Exeter Academy, Michigan State University, Colby College, United States Naval Academy
Businesses	General Motors, R.J. Whipple and Sons, Prentice Hall
Government Bodies and Organizations	Department of State, Federal Trade Commission, House of Representatives, Parliament (United Kingdom), North Atlantic Treaty Organization (NATO), the United States Army
Political Parties	Republicans, the Democratic party
Nationalities	American, Mexican, Chinese, Israeli, Canadian, Swiss
Languages	English, Italian, Polish, Swahili
Religions and Religious References	*Christianity:* God, the Lord, the Father, the Holy Spirit, the Bible, the New Testament, the Holy Father *Judaism:* God, the Lord, the Prophets, the Torah, the Talmud *Islam:* Allah, the Prophets, the Koran, Mohammed, Muslims *Hinduism:* Brahma, the Bhagavad Gita, the Vedas *Buddhism:* the Buddha, Mahayana, Hinayana

Note About *Capitalizing References to Mythological Gods:*
When referring to ancient mythology, do not capitalize the
word *god.*

EXAMPLES: the *gods* of Olympus
the Greek *goddess* Athena

KEY CONCEPT Capitalize the names of awards; the
names of specific types of air, sea, space, and land craft; and
brand names. ■

OTHER IMPORTANT PROPER NOUNS	
Awards	the Pulitzer Prize, Phi Beta Kappa, the Medal of Honor
Specific Air, Sea, Space, and Land Craft	Condorjet 898, the U.S.S. *Kearsarge, Apollo V*, Road Ranger 4x4
Brand Names	Biska Treats, Dento-White

Exercise 3 Capitalizing Proper Nouns On a separate
sheet of paper, rewrite the words in the following sentences
that should be capitalized.

EXAMPLE: Jefferson davis was president of the confederacy.
ANSWER: Davis, Confederacy

1. Ulysses s. grant, who would become a general in the union
army, began his career inauspiciously.
2. He was born the son of a farmer in point pleasant, ohio, in a
small cabin near the ohio river.
3. When he was old enough, grant studied such subjects as
latin and english at both the maysville seminary and the
presbyterian academy in ripley, ohio.
4. He continued his education at the united states military academy, which is located on the hudson river in west point, new
york.
5. Upon his graduation, grant was sent to the west, where he
fought in the mexican war.

More Practice

Grammar Exercise
Workbook
• pp. 141–142
On-line Exercise Bank
• Chapter 26
Go on-line:
PHSchool.com
Enter Web Code:
efk-1102

Get instant feedback!
Exercise 3 is available
on-line or on CD-ROM.

◀ **Critical Viewing**
Imagine what these two Civil War soldiers would have to say to each other. What proper nouns might enter their conversation? **[Speculate]**

▶ **Exercise 4** Proofreading for Capitalization of Proper Nouns On a separate sheet of paper, write the following paragraph, adding the missing capitals.

EXAMPLE: For his bravery during the battle of shiloh, the young lieutenant was awarded the medal of honor.

ANSWER: For his bravery during the Battle of Shiloh, the young lieutenant was awarded the Medal of Honor.

Fought near washington, d.c., the first battle of manassas was the first pitched battle between the north and south. The north hoped to capture the confederate capital at richmond, virginia, and bring an early end to the war. Union forces attacked confederate positions along a small creek called bull run on july 18, 1861. Early in the morning, yankee troops charged toward a dusty road known as the warrenton turnpike. Confederate forces retreated toward henry house hill. More than 11,000 confederate reinforcements were brought in from the shenandoah valley. Men and women from washington, d.c., crossed the potomac river into virginia so they could watch the battle. Albert ely, a member of congress, was captured by southern troops during the fighting. After losing the battle, the weary union soldiers staggered down pennsylvania avenue, past the unfinished washington monument, and on toward the white house. Educated at west point, general george mcclellan took command of the union forces following the battle.

More Practice

Grammar Exercise Workbook
• pp. 141–142
On-line Exercise Bank
• Chapter 26
  Go on-line:
  PHSchool.com
  Enter Web Code:
  efk-1102

Get instant feedback! Exercise 4 is available on-line or on CD-ROM.

 Learn More

For more information on proper nouns, see Chapter 17.

Using Capitals for Proper Adjectives

A proper adjective is either an adjective formed from a proper noun or a proper noun used as an adjective.

 KEY CONCEPT Capitalize most proper adjectives. ∎

PROPER ADJECTIVES FORMED FROM PROPER NOUNS:	Australian kangaroo, Shakespearean play, Afghan hound, European settlers, Spanish ambassador
PROPER NOUNS USED AS ADJECTIVES:	the Senate floor, the Stevenson speeches, Shakespeare festival, a Bible class

Care must be taken in a number of cases to use proper adjectives correctly. Some proper adjectives have become so commonly used that they are no longer capitalized.

EXAMPLES: herculean effort, french fries, pasteurized milk, quixotic hope, venetian blinds

Brand names are often used as proper adjectives.

 KEY CONCEPT Capitalize a brand name when it is used as an adjective, but do not capitalize the common noun it modifies. ∎

EXAMPLES: Timo watches, Switzles chocolate

 KEY CONCEPT Do not capitalize a common noun used with two proper adjectives. ∎

One Proper Adjective	Two Proper Adjectives
Mississippi River	Ohio and Mississippi rivers
Washington Street	Washington and Madison streets
Suez Canal	Suez and Panama canals

💡 Spelling Tip

Sometimes a brand name used as an adjective will also show ownership and will need an apostrophe: *Mr. Nutty's* peanuts, *Pico's* spices.

Prefixes used with proper adjectives should be capitalized only if they refer to a nationality.

Learn More

For more information on using hyphens to clarify the meaning of words, see Chapter 27.

KEY CONCEPT Do not capitalize prefixes attached to proper adjectives unless the prefix refers to a nationality. ■

EXAMPLES: all-American   Anglo-American

KEY CONCEPT In a hyphenated adjective, capitalize only the proper adjective. ■

EXAMPLE: Chinese-speaking American

Exercise 5 Capitalizing Proper Nouns and Proper Adjectives Copy each of the following items onto a separate sheet of paper, making the necessary corrections.

EXAMPLE: Missouri and Savannah Rivers
ANSWER: Missouri and Savannah rivers

1. pennsylvania avenue
2. pro-union states
3. soldiers of the confederacy
4. mississippi river valley
5. Chesapeake bay
6. northwest tennessee
7. European Influences
8. the bill of rights
9. british diplomats
10. ulysses s. grant
11. native american
12. blue ridge mountains
13. santa fe, new mexico
14. irish accent
15. French-Speaking advisors

More Practice

Grammar Exercise Workbook
• pp. 141–142
On-line Exercise Bank
• Chapter 26
 Go on-line:
 PHSchool.com
 Enter Web Code:
 efk-1102

► Critical Viewing Which letters would be capitalized in a sentence about this picture? [Connect]

Using Capitals for Titles

Capitals are used for titles of people and titles of literary and artistic works. The charts and rules on the following pages will guide you in capitalizing titles correctly.

> ▶ **KEY CONCEPT** Capitalize a person's title only when it is used with the person's name or when it is used as a proper name. ■

WITH A PROPER NAME: At dusk, Sergeant Mason gave the order to attack.

AS A PROPER NAME: Here is your sword, General.

IN A GENERAL REFERENCE: The senator followed the progress of the debate.

The following chart illustrates the correct form for a variety of titles. Study the chart, paying particular attention to compound titles and titles with prefixes or suffixes.

SOCIAL, BUSINESS, RELIGIOUS, MILITARY, AND GOVERNMENT TITLES	
Commonly Used Titles	Sir, Madam, Miss, Professor, Doctor, Reverend, Bishop, Sister, Father, Rabbi, Corporal, Major, Admiral, Mayor, Governor, Ambassador
Abbreviated Titles	*Before names:* Mr., Mrs., Ms., Dr., Hon. *After names:* Jr., Sr., Ph.D., M.D., D.D.S., Esq.
Compound Titles	Vice President, Secretary of State, Lieutenant Governor, Commander in Chief
Titles With Prefixes or Suffixes	ex-Congressman Randolph, Governor-elect Loughman

GRAMMAR IN
LITERATURE

from A Confederate Account of the Battle of Gettysburg

Randolph McKim

In the following passage, names of people, places, and battalions are capitalized.

Then came <u>General Ewell's</u> order to assume the offensive and assail the crest of <u>Culp's Hill</u>, on our right. . . .

On swept the gallant little brigade, the <u>Third North Carolina</u> on the right of the line, next the <u>Second Maryland</u>, then the three <u>Virginia</u> regiments (10th, 23d, and 37th), with the <u>First North Carolina</u> on the extreme left.

Titles for heads of state, high-ranking officials, and some members of royalty are capitalized. For example, the incumbent President, Vice President, and Chief Justice of the United States Supreme Court, the Queen of England, the Prince of Wales, or the Sultan of Brunei.

▶**KEY CONCEPT** Capitalize the titles of certain high government officials even when the titles are not followed by a proper name. ■

EXAMPLE: The Senate approved the *President's* choice for *Chief Justice*.

Occasionally, the titles of other government officials may be capitalized as a sign of respect when referring to a specific person whose name is not given.

EXAMPLE: The *Governor* dedicated the monument to the fallen soldiers.

▶**KEY CONCEPT** Relatives are often referred to by titles. These references should be capitalized when used with or as the person's name. ■

WITH THE PERSON'S NAME: In the summer, Uncle Ted enjoys gardening.

AS A NAME: He says that Grandmother enjoys gardening, too.

KEY CONCEPT Do not capitalize titles showing family relationships when they are preceded by a possessive noun or pronoun. ■

EXAMPLES: my aunt, her father, Jeff's mother

KEY CONCEPT Capitalize the first word and all other key words in the titles of books, periodicals, poems, stories, plays, paintings, and other works of art. ■

The following chart lists examples to guide you in capitalizing titles and subtitles of various works. Note that the articles (a, an, and the) are not capitalized unless they are used as the first word of a title or subtitle. Conjunctions and prepositions are also left uncapitalized unless they are the first or last word in a title or subtitle or contain four letters or more. Note also that verbs, no matter how short, are always capitalized.

TITLES OF WORKS	
Books	*The Red Badge of Courage* *Battle Cry of Freedom: The Civil War Era*
Periodicals	*International Wildlife* *The Saturday Review of Literature*
Poems	"The Raven" "The Rime of the Ancient Mariner"
Stories and Articles	"Editha" "The Fall of the House of Usher" "Here Is New York"
Plays	*Our American Cousin* *Our Town*
Paintings	*Starry Night* *The Mona Lisa*
Music	*The Unfinished Symphony* "Heartbreak Hotel"

✿ Grammar and Style Tip

When you title your own written works, consider using a short, interest-catching title followed by a colon and a longer explanatory subtitle. Remember to follow the rules for capitalizing words in titles.

> **KEY CONCEPT** Capitalize titles of educational courses when they are language courses or when they are followed by a number or preceded by a proper noun or adjective. ∎

WITH CAPITALS: Latin, Honors Biology, History 105
WITHOUT CAPITALS: geology, psychology, woodworking

> **Exercise 6** Capitalizing Titles of People and Things Copy each of the following sentences, adding any necessary capitals. Underline words that are printed in italics.

EXAMPLE: After operating on the man for several hours, dr. Roberts was able to save his life.

ANSWER: After operating on the man for several hours, Dr. Roberts was able to save his life.

1. Many people recognize president lincoln's gettysburg address from the civil war era, but many other great works derive from this period.
2. For example, *harper's weekly* was an immensely popular periodical that was probably read by such notables as vice president johnson and chief justice taney.
3. Also widely read were *the new york times,* the *boston herald,* and a host of other newspapers that also reported the progress of the war.
4. A newspaper called *the liberator,* published by mr. William Lloyd Garrison, helped to propel the cause of abolition.
5. Perhaps inspired by *the new york tribune*'s cry of "Forward to Richmond!" brigadier general McDowell marched his troops into virginia.
6. Other newspapers, such as *leslie's weekly* and the *augusta chronicle,* relied on battlefield artists to illustrate their articles.
7. Battlefield artist Winslow Homer published many works during the war, but he is best known for his painting *the sharpshooter.*
8. During the war, Confederate soldiers adopted the song "dixie" as their anthem, while northern soldiers preferred "the battle hymn of the republic."
9. Many songs were popular during the civil war, including "when johnny comes marching home again" and "yankee doodle," which are still known today.
10. Even some diaries of the period, such as Emma Simpson's *when will this cruel war be over?,* remain available.

▼ **Critical Viewing**
What titles apply to Abraham Lincoln himself? What book, poem, or movie titles do you know that pertain to Lincoln or the Civil War era? How are they capitalized? **[Connect]**

> **More Practice**

Grammar Exercise Workbook
• pp. 143–144
On-line Exercise Bank
• Chapter 26
Go on-line:
PHSchool.com
Enter Web Code:
efk-1102

Hands-on Grammar

Capitalization Rules Reference

Create a capitalization reference tool to keep in your notebook. Choose four different colors of notebook-size paper. Divide the top one inch of each page into four equal sections. From the first page, cut away the three sections closest to the right side of the page. From the second page, cut away two sections. From the third page, cut away only one section. Do not cut any sections from the last page. Stack the pages in order, with the first cut page on top. Staple them, or fasten the pages with clips. Then, label the top strips as shown. The notches and colors will make it easy for you to select the category you need. On each page, write abbreviated versions of the rules. (See the example page for proper nouns below.) Make a cover for your reference pages, and keep the booklet in your folder.

Proper Nouns Proper Adjectives	Titles	First Words	Exceptions Special Problems

People's Name—Betsy

Place Names—Cincinnati, Los Angeles

Geographic Areas— the Midwest

Celestial Bodies—Saturn

Groups—Drama Club

Brand Names—Readi ravioli

After attaching the cover, use paper fasteners to bind the pages together.

Find It in Your Reading As you read for pleasure or for school assignments, look for words that illustrate each of the capitalization rules. Add them to your reference pages as examples.

Find It in Your Writing Look through selected pieces of writing from your portfolio for words you have capitalized. Add them to the appropriate page in your reference. (Do not add numerous words that illustrate the same rule. Look for a range of words that illustrate a variety of rules.)

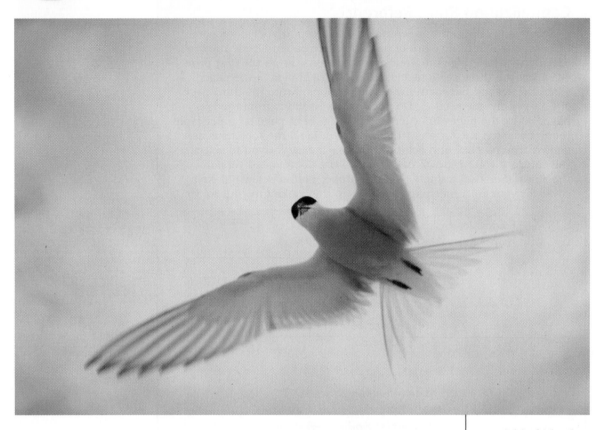

To punctuate correctly requires a knowledge of the parts of a sentence and their relationships to each other. It also requires an understanding of different types of sentences and the punctuation marks used either to separate or to join them.

Punctuation marks are so important that sentence meaning is easily affected by them. Observe how a simple change in punctuation results in very different meanings:

The Arctic tern's head is black. (statement of fact)
The Arctic tern's head is black? (question)
Did you see Ann? (Did someone see Ann?)
Did you see, Ann? (Did Ann see something?)

An effort to master the rules in this chapter will help you greatly in your writing. Study the rules carefully, and refer to this chapter whenever you are uncertain about a particular problem in punctuation.

▲ **Critical Viewing**
Make an observation about the breadth of the tern's wingspan. Can you then change the statement to a question simply by raising your voice at the end? **[Analyze]**

Diagnostic Test

Directions: Write all answers on a separate sheet of paper.

Skill Check A. Write the following sentences, using proper end marks to punctuate them.

1. Most species of penguins live in the frigid Antarctic
2. Have you ever seen one
3. Wow Temperatures in the Antarctic can reach 62° below zero
4. Really That is absolutely remarkable
5. There are penguins at the zoo Do you want to go see them

Skill Check B. Write the following sentences, inserting commas where necessary.

6. Aside from living in Antarctica penguins live in other places.
7. Penguins inhabit Australia South Africa and South America.
8. The largest species is the emperor penguin which can reach a height of four feet.
9. Incidentally the little blue penguin is the smallest.
10. Both have blue-gray patches on their soft warm feathers.

Skill Check C. Write the following sentences, inserting colons and semicolons where necessary.

11. The emperor penguin has another distinguishing feature a bright red patch on the side of its face.
12. Not all penguins look alike for example, the yellow-eyed penguin has two crests of feathers on its face.
13. The six other species that have crests live in a variety of places New Zealand, Tasmania, and Argentina.
14. Two species of penguins even live in the tropics a current of icy water makes this possible.
15. Penguins cannot fly however, they are excellent swimmers.

Skill Check D. Write the following sentences, inserting quotation marks where necessary.

16. Do you know how penguin feathers are shaped? he asked.
17. I replied, No, I don't.
18. Most birds have a variety of long and short feathers, he said.
19. If you look at the feathers on a penguin, he explained, you will see that they are short.
20. Most birds shed their feathers gradually, he said.

Skill Check E. Write the following sentences, inserting apostrophes and dashes where necessary.

21. The penguins body is designed to withstand extreme cold.
22. The penguins small features help to conserve body heat.
23. Its true that a penguin has a thick layer of fat under its skin.
24. The feathers waterproofing effect helps keep the penguin warm.
25. Small features, a layer of fat, and a waterproof coat of feathers all of these things help the penguin survive in the cold.

End Marks

The three end marks are the period (.), the question mark (?), and the exclamation mark (!). They have a number of basic uses as well as a few more specialized uses.

Basic Uses of End Marks

Most of the basic uses of end marks are for full sentences. A few, as you will see, are for words and phrases.

The Period The period is the most common end mark.

▶ **KEY CONCEPT** Use a period to end a declarative sentence, a mild imperative, and an indirect question. ■

A **declarative statement** is a statement of fact or opinion.

STATEMENT OF FACT:	There are more than 10,000 species of birds.
STATEMENT OF OPINION:	The veterinarian believes my parrot will recover from its illness.

Some declarative sentences include an indirect question.

INDIRECT QUESTION:	My father asked whether we saw the bald eagle.

An **imperative sentence** gives a direction or a command. Often, the first word of an imperative sentence is a verb.

DIRECTION:	Fill the birdfeeder first, and then hang it in the tree.
COMMAND:	Clean the bird cage.

▶ **Exercise 1** Writing Declarative and Imperative Sentences
Write declarative and imperative sentences with end punctuation, following the instructions below.

EXAMPLE:	command about pigeons
ANSWER:	Feed these breadcrumbs to the pigeons.

1. statement of fact about a bird
2. direction for finding pet store listings in the Yellow Pages
3. indirect question about a bird
4. statement of opinion about pet birds
5. command about studying for a science test

The Question Mark Use a question mark with a direct question.

KEY CONCEPT Use a question mark to end an interrogative sentence, an incomplete question, or a statement intended as a question. ■

Often, the word order as well as the punctuation of an interrogative sentence is different from that of a declarative sentence.

EXAMPLES: Why are there so many birds in our yard**?**
Are bats considered birds or mammals**?**

A question mark is also used with one or more interrogative words when a complete sentence is not necessary.

EXAMPLE: Penguins have lost the ability to fly. Why**?**

Occasionally, a question mark is used at the end of a statement that asks a question.

EXAMPLE: Birds eat grasshoppers**?**

Use care, however, in ending statements with question marks. It is better to rephrase the statement as a direct question.

STATEMENT WITH A
QUESTION MARK: The geese haven't migrated yet**?**

REVISED INTO A
DIRECT QUESTION: Haven't the geese migrated yet**?**

The Exclamation Mark An exclamation mark signals an exclamatory sentence, an imperative sentence, or an interjection. It indicates strong emotion and should be used sparingly.

KEY CONCEPT Use an exclamation mark to end an exclamatory sentence, a forceful imperative sentence, or an interjection expressing strong emotion. ■

EXCLAMATORY   This new information changes nothing**!**
SENTENCES: That vulture is frightening**!**

IMPERATIVE   Don't let the bird out of the cage this time**!**
SENTENCES: Remember to feed my parrot**!**

Depending on emphasis, an exclamation mark or a comma can be used with an interjection.

WITH AN
EXCLAMATION MARK: Oh**!** What an enormous bird!

WITH A COMMA: Oh**,** it is only an owl.

▲ Critical Viewing
Write three questions you would try to answer in a research project about this bird. Make sure to punctuate each one correctly. **[Question]**

End Marks • **517**

Other Uses of End Marks

> **KEY CONCEPT** Most abbreviations end with a period. ∎

ABBREVIATIONS
WITH PERIODS: in., Dr., etc., Sr., A.M.
                 D.D.S., Ave., Mrs., Tex., Co., B.C.

ABBREVIATIONS
WITHOUT PERIODS: FBI, NASA, TX, COD

When an abbreviation ending with a period is found at the end of a sentence, do not add another period as an end mark.

INCORRECT: The speaker will be Adam Martin, Jr..
CORRECT: The speaker will be Adam Martin, Jr.

If an end mark other than a period is required, however, you must add the end mark.

EXAMPLE: Is the speaker Adam Martin, Jr.?

> **KEY CONCEPT** Use a period after numbers and letters in outlines. ∎

EXAMPLE: I. Maintaining your pet's health
              A. Diet
                1. For a puppy
                2. For a mature dog
              B. Exercise
              C. Cleanliness
              D. Preventing accidents

> **Exercise 2** Using End Marks Copy the following items, punctuating each of them correctly.

EXAMPLE: The hawk flew high above the rocks
ANSWER: The hawk flew high above the rocks.

1. Have you ever visited the bird sanctuary
2. I went there with my class last month
3. It was so much fun
4. We had a very knowledgeable tour guide who told us many interesting facts
5. For instance, did you know that birds are the only animals that have feathers

---

📟 Internet Tip

When entering World Wide Web addresses, be sure to include the proper end marks. For example, in the address **www.chess.com**, you must always place a period after **www** and before **com** This same rule applies to the suffixes **edu, net, org,** and **gov**

> **More Practice**
> Grammar Exercise Workbook
> • pp. 145–146
> On-line Exercise Bank
> • Section 27.1
>   Go on-line:
>   PHSchool.com
>   Enter Web Code:
>   efk-1102

Get instant feedback! Exercise 2 is available on-line or on CD-ROM.

Section 27.1 Section Review

GRAMMAR EXERCISES 3–9

Exercise 3 Using End Marks
Rewrite the following sentences, adding the proper end marks.

1. I asked if all birds had the ability to fly
2. No, not all of them
3. Is the ostrich a flightless bird
4. Did you know that the ostrich is the largest bird in the world
5. Wow Ostriches can run as fast as 40 miles per hour

Exercise 4 Using Periods in
Special Situations Copy the following items, adding any necessary periods. Not every item will need punctuation.

1. 9:37 PM
2. Stephanie Davis, MS
3. Blue Ridge Canoe Co
4. Flagstaff, Ariz
5. http://www xyxco edu
6. Dear Mr Jackson:
7. 3 tsp cinnamon
8. ASPCA
9. 125 BC to AD 560
10. 1423 21st St

Exercise 5 Using All Kinds of End
Marks Rewrite the following items, adding periods, question marks, and exclamation points as needed.

1. He asked what kind of hawk was soaring above us
2. Dr Smith began the program to reestablish the owl population
3. This label is on the carton: 1 doz Grade A eggs
4. Astounding Did you see that eagle grab the fish out of the lake
5. Mom reminded us to be sure to set up the birdbath before Apr 18

Exercise 6 Proofreading for End
Marks Revise the following paragraph, adding or correcting end marks as needed.

Yesterday, we heard a lecture on exotic birds by Dr Alan Lee, Jr.. The lecture was scheduled for 10 AM, but it was delayed an hour! Dr. Lee was coming from Fresno, Calif, and his flight was late. He began by asking if anyone in the audience had an exotic bird as a pet? Several had finches or cockatoos Dr Lee then talked about toucans, macaws, and the speckled mousebird. How stunning his slides were.

Exercise 7 Find It in Your Reading
Read this excerpt from Carl Sandburg's "Grass." Explain why the author used a period rather than an exclamation point after the word *work* in the last line.

Pile the bodies high at Austerlitz and
    Waterloo.
Shovel them under and let me work—
    I am the grass; I cover all.
    . . .
    I am grass.
    Let me work.

Exercise 8 Find It in Your Writing
Look through your portfolio for at least three examples of an abbreviation. Write these down, and then exchange lists with a partner to make sure the abbreviations are properly punctuated.

Exercise 9 Writing Application
Write a short anecdote about an animal —either imaginary or real. In it, use at least one period, one question mark, and one exclamation mark. Also, use at least one abbreviation that contains a period.

Commas

The comma is used to separate a number of basic elements and to set off many different kinds of added elements within sentences. As you learn the rules for the correct use of the comma, you will at the same time reinforce your understanding of sentence structure. Study the rules, making certain you understand each relationship described within them.

Commas With Compound Sentences

A single independent clause expresses a complete thought and often stands alone as a simple sentence. Two independent clauses, correctly joined and punctuated, form a compound sentence. The conjunctions used to connect independent clauses are called *coordinating conjunctions.* The seven coordinating conjunctions are *and, but, for, nor, or, so,* and *yet.*

▶ **KEY CONCEPT** Use a comma before the conjunction to separate two independent clauses in a compound sentence. ■

EXAMPLES: I had a meeting with my guidance counselor, and then I applied to several schools in New York.
My mother loves the country, but my father prefers the city.
She might go to a museum, or she might go to the opera.

As you can see, the ideas in the independent clauses in a compound sentence are clearly related to each other. Compound sentences should not be formed unless there exists some type of relationship between the independent clauses.

Although a comma and a coordinating conjunction are used to separate two independent clauses in a compound sentence, a comma is not used to separate a compound verb in a simple sentence. Compare the following two examples.

COMPOUND
SENTENCE: Leslie went to Broadway, and she saw a play.
SIMPLE
SENTENCE: Leslie went to Broadway and saw a play.

The second sentence has only one subject, *Leslie.* Before placing a comma before a conjunction, you should always make sure that you have a complete sentence on both sides of the conjunction, not just a compound verb.

⚙ **Grammar
and Style Tip**

Do not join two sentences with only a comma. Place a comma between two sentences when they are linked by the coordinating conjunctions *for, and, nor, but, or, yet,* or *so.*

▶ **Exercise 10** Using Commas to Separate Independent Clauses Copy each of the following sentences, adding commas as needed.

EXAMPLE: I wanted to go to the concert in Central Park but it was sold out.

ANSWER: I wanted to go to the concert in Central Park, but it was sold out.

More Practice
Grammar Exercise Workbook
• pp. 147–148
On-line Exercise Bank
• Section 27.2
Go on-line:
PHSchool.com
Enter Web Code:
efk-1102

1. New York City was founded by the Dutch in 1626 but it was called New Amsterdam.
2. The British seized the city in 1664 and renamed it New York City.
3. A fleet of British ships was sent to capture the city but the ships did not attack.
4. The governor of New Amsterdam was told to surrender peacefully or the city would be attacked.
5. The city was surrendered so no one was injured.
6. The Dutch did not want to lose control of the city yet they could not defend it against the British fleet.
7. It quickly expanded for many people chose to settle there.
8. In 1700, the first library was opened and construction on the city hall was completed.
9. Henry Hudson was not the first explorer to discover what would become New York City nor was he the first to view the river that bears his name.
10. In New York City, many people became dissatisfied with British rule and rebelled.

▲ **Critical Viewing** Using a compound sentence, compare the relative positions of New York City and Liberty Island as shown in this photograph. Where in your sentence would you use a comma? [Compare]

▶ **Exercise 11** Proofreading for Comma Usage in Compounds Rewrite the following sentences, adding or deleting commas as necessary.

EXAMPLE: I want to see the Statue of Liberty and I will!

ANSWER: I want to see the Statue of Liberty, and I will!

1. The Statue of Liberty was built in France, and then shipped to New York.
2. Frédéric-Auguste Bartholdi designed the statue and Alexandre Gustave Eiffel devised the interior framework.
3. It was originally named Liberty Enlightening the World but is now known as the Statue of Liberty.
4. The French people paid for the construction of the statue and Americans donated the money to build the pedestal.
5. It was completed in 1886 and dedicated on October 28.

Commas • **521**

Commas With Series and Adjectives

Like independent clauses, items in a series and certain kinds of adjectives should be separated by commas.

Series A series consists of three or more words, phrases, or subordinate clauses of a similar kind. A series can occur in any part of a sentence.

Learn More

To learn more about phrases and clauses, see Chapter 19.

▶ **KEY CONCEPT** Use commas to separate three or more words, phrases, or clauses in a series. ■

WORDS:	The subway car was crowded, noisy, and fast. I like to put ham, pepperoni, turkey, and cheese on my deli sandwiches.
PHRASES:	We explored the city by bus, by train, and by car.
CLAUSES:	The survey revealed that many New Yorkers were satisfied with the mayor, that they supported the new laws, and that they wanted the fiscal policy to continue.

As you may know, in a variant style for using commas in a series, the last comma before the conjunction is dropped. You are likely to find the full use of commas easier to follow, however. This is especially true when the omission of the final comma leads to confusion, as it does in the following example. By always using a comma after all but the final item in a series, you can avoid this problem.

CONFUSING:	The crowds, the aromas from the hot dog carts and the talkative taxi drivers made the trip memorable.
ALWAYS CLEAR:	The crowds, the aromas from the hotdog carts, and the talkative taxi drivers made the trip memorable.

When conjunctions are used to separate all of the items in a series, no commas are needed.

EXAMPLE:	We wanted to watch the game and eat hot dogs and then see the fireworks.

Do not use commas between items that are paired so often that they are thought of as one item. In the following example, *peanut butter and jelly* are considered a single item.

EXAMPLE:	We ate grilled cheese sandwiches, baloney sandwiches, and peanut butter and jelly sandwiches.

Adjectives When two or more adjectives precede a noun, they sometimes will need to be separated with commas.

KEY CONCEPT Use commas to separate adjectives of equal rank. ■

Adjectives are equal in rank if you can insert the word *and* between them without changing the meaning of the sentence. Another way to determine whether adjectives are of equal rank is to reverse the order in which they appear. If the sentence still sounds correct, the adjectives are of equal rank. Adjectives of equal rank are called *coordinate adjectives.*

EXAMPLES: A tall, majestic building rose above the skyline.
               The bright, bold sign was posted above the door.

If you cannot place the word *and* between the adjectives or reverse their order without changing the meaning of the sentence, do not use commas between them. Adjectives that must remain in a specific order are called *cumulative adjectives.*

KEY CONCEPT Do not use commas to separate adjectives that must stay in a specific order. ■

EXAMPLES: The second-oldest building in the city was renovated.
               The long ticket line is moving faster than the shorter reservations line.

Exercise 12 Supplying Commas to Separate Items in a Series Copy each of the following sentences, inserting commas to separate items as needed.

EXAMPLE: Buses cars and trucks crowded the city streets.
ANSWER: Buses, cars, and trucks crowded the city streets.

1. New York City is an enormous place with many things to do much to see and lots of places to go.
2. The city is divided into five boroughs: Manhattan the Bronx Queens Brooklyn and Staten Island.
3. Some of the famous buildings that dominate the city skyline are the Empire State Building the Chrysler Building and Trump Tower.
4. You can go to the top of the Empire State Building walk onto the observation deck and look out across the entire city.
5. The Metropolitan Museum of Art exhibits paintings by famous artists such as Gauguin Monet van Gogh and Cézanne.

More Practice

Grammar Exercise Workbook
• pp. 147–148
On-line Exercise Bank
• Section 27.2
   Go on-line:
   PHSchool.com
   Enter Web Code:
   efk-1102

Get instant feedback! Exercise 12 is available on-line or on CD-ROM.

More Practice

Grammar Exercise
Workbook
• pp. 147–148
On-line Exercise Bank
• Section 27.2
Go on-line:
PHSchool.com
Enter Web Code:
efk-1102

Exercise 13 Distinguishing Between Coordinate and Cumulative Adjectives Copy each sentence with coordinate adjectives, inserting a comma between them. For sentences with cumulative adjectives, just write *cumulative*.

EXAMPLE: The large European ship entered the harbor. (cumulative)

1. I visited New York City during the hot humid month of August.
2. My grandfather took me to see some of the many fascinating sites.
3. We traveled on the noisy crowded subway.
4. It took us right into the heart of the city in just forty short minutes.
5. We walked up the long steep stairway to the street.
6. The city was bustling with throngs of busy impatient people.
7. My grandfather hailed a bright yellow taxi.
8. We drove past the tall impressive skyscrapers.
9. Rockefeller Center was the first of many interesting stops.
10. Our long exciting day finally ended after we stopped at Central Park.

Exercise 14 Revising to Correct Commas in a Series and With Adjectives Revise this paragraph, inserting or deleting commas as necessary.

New York is a city of festivals conventions and parades. Every year, on a blustery, mid-March afternoon, you can see a long steady stream of colorful, marching bands and floats moving up Fifth Avenue. The green white, and orange flags and the bright, green stripe painted on the avenue tell you it's Saint Patrick's day. The Easter Parade also takes place on Fifth Avenue; however, instead of formal organized marchers, masses of ordinary New Yorkers promenade in their finery. The splendor of the day is the great array of extraordinary eye-catching "Easter bonnets." Some of the most exciting, New York parades take place on lower Broadway in the Canyon of Heroes. Here is where astronauts champion ball teams, and war heroes have been honored by admiring crowds politicians and blizzards of paper thrown from skyscraper windows.

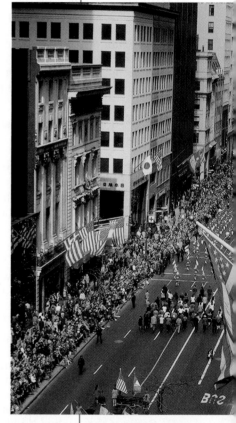

▲ Critical Viewing How are words in an unpunctuated sentence like people in a crowd? **[Relate]**

Commas After Introductory Material

Most introductory material is set off with a comma.

▶ **KEY CONCEPT** Use a comma after an introductory word, phrase, or clause. ■

Study the following examples to see what types of introductory material should be set off with commas.

INTRODUCTORY WORDS:	Well, I find it difficult to decide. Yes, Charles agrees with our plan to visit Central Park. Oh, did he really say that?
COMMON EXPRESSIONS:	Of course, I'll do it for you.
INTRODUCTORY ADVERBS:	Certainly, you may borrow the book about New York. Frantically, they searched for a parking spot.
PREPOSITIONAL PHRASES:	At the very top, my father paused to enjoy the view. In the heart of the city, you will find many skyscrapers.
PARTICIPIAL PHRASES:	Walking slowly, she reached the subway in about ten minutes. Written carefully, the speech was a masterpiece.
INFINITIVE PHRASES:	To get to the train before it left, she ran all the way. To get to Broadway, they rode in a taxi.
ADVERB CLAUSES:	When the team got off the plane, hundreds of onlookers began to cheer. If you intend to travel to New York this summer, you should make your plans now.

It is not absolutely necessary to set off short prepositional phrases. However, you may find that a comma is needed with a two- or three-word phrase in order to avoid confusion.

CLEAR:	At Times Square we met our friends.
CONFUSING:	Inside the house walls began to crumble.
CLEAR:	Inside the house, walls began to crumble.

Exercise 15 Using Commas After Introductory Material

Copy each sentence that needs a comma, inserting the comma where it is needed. If a sentence does not require a comma, write *correct*.

EXAMPLE: Chris have you visited Grand Central Station yet?

ANSWER: Chris, have you visited Grand Central Station yet?

1. Born in December, 1882 Fiorello La Guardia would become one of New York City's best-known mayors.
2. The son of a military man La Guardia was born in New York, but he grew up at an army base in Arizona.
3. After his father left the army the family moved to Trieste, Italy.
4. While living overseas the young La Guardia joined the U.S. consular service.
5. Initially serving as a clerk he would eventually become the consular agent in the city of Fiume.
6. In 1906 La Guardia returned to New York.
7. Attending New York University Law School at night he worked as an interpreter at Ellis Island during the day.
8. Already fluent in German, Croatian, and Italian La Guardia soon mastered Spanish, French, and Yiddish.
9. Upon his graduation from law school he quit his job at Ellis Island and opened a small law practice.
10. Within a few years La Guardia was elected to the U.S. House of Representatives.
11. When the United States entered World War I he left Congress and enlisted in the Army Air Service.
12. Courageously serving the country La Guardia worked as a pilot on the Italian front.
13. Following the war he returned to Congress and served for seven consecutive terms.
14. A Republican La Guardia was eventually swept from office when Democrat Franklin Roosevelt became president in 1932.
15. The following year he was elected New York City's mayor.
16. A fiercely honest and determined man La Guardia reformed the city's government.
17. Of course his policies met with much resistance.
18. From the very beginning of his administration La Guardia appointed highly qualified, nonpartisan people to the city government.
19. To eliminate the influence of organized crime he initiated a campaign against all forms of gambling.
20. Although La Guardia's term as mayor ended in 1945 many of his contributions to New York City are still evident today.

More Practice

Grammar Exercise Workbook
• pp. 149–150
On-line Exercise Bank
• Section 27.2
Go on-line:
PHSchool.com
Enter Web Code:
efk-1102

Get instant feedback!
Exercise 15 is available on-line or on CD-ROM.

Commas With Parenthetical and Nonessential Expressions

Commas are also used to set off two types of expressions that often fall in the middle or at the end of a sentence:

Parenthetical Expressions Parenthetical expressions consist of one or more words that, in a sense, interrupt the flow of a sentence. Such expressions are set off by one or more commas, regardless of where they occur in a sentence.

KEY CONCEPT Use commas to set off parenthetical expressions. ∎

Below are some common types of parenthetical expressions. Notice that a parenthetical expression may fall in the middle or at the end of a sentence. Notice also that each sentence is complete without the parenthetical expression.

NOUNS OF DIRECT ADDRESS:	Please, Ben, could you help me? I'll do it right away, Mother.
CONJUNCTIVE ADVERBS:	The tennis match, therefore, was held after the rain shower. They did their best, however.
COMMON EXPRESSIONS:	I am explaining his theory, I believe, as clearly as I can. You know, of course, that she is ill.
CONTRASTING EXPRESSIONS:	We took the subway, not the bus, to work. New York City, not Chicago, has the Empire State Building.

▼ **Critical Viewing** How do you think it feels to live and work in a "vertical city"? Respond, using at least one parenthetical expression. **[Evaluate]**

Essential and Nonessential Expressions Depending on their importance in a sentence, appositives, participial phrases, and adjective clauses can be either essential or nonessential. (The terms *restrictive* and *nonrestrictive* may also be used.) An essential phrase or clause is necessary to the meaning of the sentence. It helps to describe or identify the person or object the sentence is about.

▶ **KEY CONCEPT** Do not use commas to set off essential expressions. ■

ESSENTIAL APPOSITIVE:	The part was played by the famous actor *Henry Fonda.*
ESSENTIAL PARTICIPIAL PHRASE:	The man *wearing the white cap* is my uncle.
ESSENTIAL ADJECTIVE CLAUSE:	The paragraph *that we propose to add* changes the entire bill.

The preceding examples illustrate three kinds of essential elements. In the first example, the appositive *Henry Fonda* identifies a specific actor. In the next example, the participial phrase *wearing the white cap* identifies a specific man. In the last example, the adjective clause *that we propose to add* indicates which paragraph. The items are all essential because they limit or restrict identification to the person or thing described in the appositive, phrase, or clause. Because they cannot be removed without changing the meaning of the sentence, they require no commas.

Nonessential elements also provide information, but that information is not necessary to the meaning of the rest of the sentence. Because nonessential elements do not alter the meaning, they do require commas.

▶ **KEY CONCEPT** Use commas to set off nonessential expressions. ■

NONESSENTIAL APPOSITIVE:	The part was played by Henry Fonda, *the famous actor.*
NONESSENTIAL PARTICIPIAL PHRASE:	This graceful bridge, *built in the 1800's,* spans a lake in Central Park.
NONESSENTIAL ADJECTIVE CLAUSE:	The lake, *which sometimes freezes in winter,* is lovely for summer boating.

In the first clause, Henry Fonda is clearly identified. The appositive *the famous actor* is not needed to identify a particular person. The same thing is true of the other examples. Although the nonessential material may be interesting, the sentences can be read without them and still make sense.

> **Speaking and Listening Tip**
>
> A comma signals a pause in a sentence. With a partner, take turns reading Exercises 16 and 17 aloud. Accustom yourself to hearing where commas belong to set off parenthetical and other nonessential expressions.

Exercise 16 Using Commas to Set off Parenthetical Expressions Copy the following sentences, inserting commas to set off parenthetical expressions.

EXAMPLE: His reasoning therefore was faulty.

ANSWER: His reasoning, therefore, was faulty.

1. The bitter rivalry between Alexander Hamilton and Aaron Burr is in my opinion one of the most interesting events in New York City's history.
2. Burr was a Republican not a Federalist like Hamilton.
3. Hamilton in fact thwarted Burr's political activities at every turn.
4. It was Hamilton most likely who prevented Burr from becoming president in 1800.
5. He also checked Burr's bid to be governor of New York in 1804 I believe.
6. Burr therefore challenged the reluctant Hamilton to a duel.
7. The duel as you may know took place on July 11, 1804.
8. It was Burr not Hamilton who won the duel.
9. Hamilton was killed; Burr however was discredited, and his political career was finished.
10. If Hamilton had survived, the history of New York would have been much different I suppose.

▶ **More Practice**

Grammar Exercise Workbook
• pp. 149–150
On-line Exercise Bank
• Section 27.2
  Go on-line:
  PHSchool.com
  Enter Web Code:
  efk-1102

▼ Critical Viewing Contrast this peaceful Central Park scene with what you know or believe about the city that surrounds it. Include a parenthetical expression in your response. **[Contrast]**

Exercise 17 Supplying Commas to Set Off Nonessential Expressions Copy the sentences that contain nonessential expressions, inserting one or more commas as needed. If a sentence does not require any commas, write *correct*.

1. Grand Central Terminal which was renovated recently is one of New York City's most famous landmarks.
2. Its history stretches back to 1831 when the first rail line into New York City was established.
3. Between 1831 and 1836, a station that was built for the New York and Harlem lines was located in the heart of the city.
4. Several lines including the New York and New Haven line and the Hudson River line began serving the city shortly thereafter.
5. The shipping magnate Cornelius Vanderbilt eventually purchased both lines and consolidated them.
6. In 1869 he purchased property for a new centralized train depot that would be located at the corner of Madison Avenue and 42nd Street.
7. The renowned architect James B. Snook designed the building.
8. Grand Central Depot as it was called cost Vanderbilt roughly $6.4 million.
9. The new building which would service all of the railroad lines operating in the city was opened in October 1871.
10. The improvements and expansions that led to the rebirth of the depot as Grand Central Terminal were completed by the turn of the century.

More Practice

Grammar Exercise Workbook
• pp. 149–150
On-line Exercise Bank
• Section 27.2
  Go on-line:
  PHSchool.com
  Enter Web Code:
  efk-1102

Get instant feedback! Exercise 17 is available on-line or on CD-ROM.

◀ **Critical Viewing**
Why do you think so few commas appear in signs? What does this tell you about the uses of the comma? **[Deduce]**

NO PARKING DO NOT OBSTRUCT

Other Uses of the Comma

Many other situations also require the use of commas.

Geographical Names Geographical names are often made up of several parts.

> **KEY CONCEPT** When a geographical name is made up of two or more parts, use a comma after each item. ■

EXAMPLES: My uncle in New York, New York, is a lawyer.
We traveled to Niagara Falls, Ontario, Canada, by car.

Dates Commas are also used with dates made up of several parts, such as month, day, and year.

> **KEY CONCEPT** When a date is made up of two or more parts, use a comma after each item except in the case of a month followed by a day. ■

EXAMPLES: Thursday, September 26, is my birthday.
I saw a Broadway play on October 6, 2000.
On April 8, 1999, my brother was born.

If dates contain only months and years, commas are not necessary.

EXAMPLE: November 1989 was the month David Dinkins was elected mayor of New York City.

Titles After a Name Some titles require commas.

> **KEY CONCEPT** When a name is followed by one or more titles, use a comma after the name and after each title. ■

EXAMPLES: Theresa Kelly, M.D., is my doctor.
John Roe, Sr., Ph.D., lectured on Greek drama.
Did Prentice-Hall, Inc., publish this book?

Addresses Commas are used to separate the items in addresses.

▶ **KEY CONCEPT** Use a comma after each item in an address made up of two or more parts. ■

EXAMPLE: We sent the package to Emma Chandee, 1237 Oakland Parkway, Anytown, New York 10583.

In the preceding example, commas are placed after the name, street, and city. Do not use a comma between the state and the ZIP Code.

In an address in a letter or on an envelope, a comma between the city and the state only is needed.

EXAMPLE: Emma Chandee
1237 Oakland Parkway
Anytown, NY 10583

Salutations and Closings Commas are used after the salutation and closing in letters.

▶ **KEY CONCEPT** Use a comma after the salutation in a personal letter and after the closing in all letters. ■

SALUTATIONS: Dear Jimmy, Dear Aunt Harriet,
My dear friend,

CLOSINGS: Your friend, Sincerely, Yours truly,

Large Numbers Commas make large numbers easier to read.

▶ **KEY CONCEPT** When writing numbers of more than three digits, place a comma before every third digit counting from the right. ■

EXAMPLES: 186,000 miles per second
2,527 people
3,625,353 peanuts

Do not, however, use commas in ZIP Codes, telephone numbers, page numbers, serial numbers, years, or house numbers.

ZIP CODE: 07624
TELEPHONE NUMBER: (207) 555-2457
PAGE NUMBER: Page 1127
SERIAL NUMBER: 081 32 5334
YEAR: A.D. 2002
HOUSE NUMBER: 2787

💻 **Internet Tip**

You can use the Internet to find addresses and phone numbers. Go to a search engine, and click once on the hot link to White Pages or Yellow Pages. You can also look up ZIP Codes through the U.S. Postal Service site: **http://www. usps.gov**

Elliptical Sentences In an elliptical sentence, even though words are left out, the meaning is clearly understood. Inserting a comma in an elliptical sentence makes it easier to read.

KEY CONCEPT Use a comma to indicate the words left out of an elliptical sentence. ■

EXAMPLE: Tom read the paper quickly; Rachel, more slowly.

Even though the words *read the paper* have been omitted from the second clause in the preceding elliptical sentence, the meaning is not lost. The comma inserted in place of the missing words helps to make the meaning clear.

Direct Quotations Commas also set off direct quotations.

KEY CONCEPT Use commas to set off a direct quotation from the rest of the sentence. ■

EXAMPLES: "I finished my report on the Empire State Building," Linda stated happily.
Kevin sighed, "I wish mine were done."
"Perhaps," Linda replied, "yours will be better than mine because you've spent more time on it."

For Clarity You may also need to use a comma to prevent readers from misunderstanding a sentence.

KEY CONCEPT Use a comma to prevent a sentence from being misunderstood. ■

UNCLEAR: For New York police horses have been a mode of transportation.
CLEAR: For New York police, horses have been a mode of transportation.

Learn the rules about the use of commas, and apply them in your writing. Take care not to use commas where none are required.

KEY CONCEPT Make certain that you know why you are inserting a comma in a sentence. In this way, you will not overuse them. ■

Because the comma is one of the most frequently used punctuation marks, some people sprinkle commas carelessly throughout their writing.

These examples illustrate some of the ways in which commas are often misused. Avoid these misuses when using prepositional phrases or compound elements in sentences.

MISUSED WITH PREPOSITIONAL PHRASES:	Yesterday, I saw a fluffy, aristocratic-looking poodle, on Park Avenue.
CORRECT:	Yesterday, I saw a fluffy, aristocratic-looking poodle on Park Avenue.
MISUSED WITH COMPOUND SUBJECTS:	I thought the four pizzas, and the two hoagies, would never arrive.
CORRECT:	I thought the four pizzas and the two hoagies would never arrive.
MISUSED WITH COMPOUND VERBS:	I looked at her, and asked her to leave.
CORRECT:	I looked at her and asked her to leave.
MISUSED WITH COMPOUND OBJECTS:	I love the house, and the garden.
CORRECT:	I love the house and the garden.
MISUSED WITH CLAUSES:	She asked what you wanted, and where you were going.
CORRECT:	She asked what you wanted and where you were going.

GRAMMAR IN LITERATURE

from **An Occurrence at Owl Creek Bridge**
Ambrose Bierce

Notice how the author uses commas to separate the three parts of a compound verb.

The soldiers had almost finished reloading; the metal ramrods flashed all at once in the sunshine as they were drawn from the barrels, turned in the air, and thrust into their sockets.

Exercise 18 Using Commas in Other Situations Copy the following sentences, inserting commas where necessary.

EXAMPLE: The speed of light is 186000 miles per second.
ANSWER: The speed of light is 186,000 miles per second.

1. Theodore Roosevelt Jr. was born in New York City in 1858.
2. On May 24 1883 the Brooklyn Bridge was first opened to the public.
3. Grand Central Terminal officially opened at 12:01 A.M. on Sunday February 2 1913.
4. New York New York is a densely populated city in the northeastern United States.
5. The plane took off from John F. Kennedy Airport, bound for Paris France.

Exercise 19 Proofreading a Letter for Comma Errors
Rewrite the following letter, inserting and deleting commas where necessary.

> 2672 Highland Avenue
> Somewhere, Maryland, 33056
> May 4 2000

Dear Austin

Your last letter indicated that you have lined up your summer intern position with Rush Green and Stipe Inc. in New York City. I see your plans are concrete; mine not so.

With high hopes I applied to all the companies you did. I even wrote to Harris Johnson, Jr. for a position at HiTek Corp., but got no response.

I'm very eager to work in a city with more than 8000000 people, and with so many great things to see and do. Although I still haven't heard from any of the companies. I'm not going to give up hope. As my mom said to me last night "Just hang in there." She added if I don't hear something by next week, she will call my Uncle Phil, who has a business in Ridgewood, New Jersey across the Hudson River from New York. He is sure to have a spot for his ambitious talented nephew!

Wish me luck, and write soon.

> Your friend
> Pete

More Practice
Grammar Exercise Workbook
• pp. 151–152
On-line Exercise Bank
• Section 27.2
Go on-line:
PHSchool.com
Enter Web Code:
efk-1102

Interactive Textbook

Get instant feedback! Exercises 18 and 19 are available on-line or on CD-ROM.

▼ Critical Viewing
In a postcard to a friend, how would you describe this view of New York at night? How would you punctuate your salutation and closing? **[Analyze]**

Exercise 20 Using Commas Correctly Copy each of the following sentences, inserting commas where necessary.

EXAMPLE: A trip to the city I think is a good idea.

ANSWER: A trip to the city, I think, is a good idea.

1. Theodore Roosevelt Jr. was one of the most famous people ever to live in New York City.
2. His family roots in New York can be traced back to Klaes Martensen van Roosevelt who came to New Amsterdam in 1649.
3. Roosevelt was born in the city on October 27 1858.
4. His parents lived in Gramercy Park one of the more exclusive neighborhoods in the city.
5. An elegant brownstone building located on East 20th Street was where he grew up.
6. Roosevelt's father Theodore Roosevelt Sr. was a successful businessman in the city.
7. As a young boy Roosevelt suffered from asthma and he was always very sickly.
8. His father hoping to improve Teddy's health installed a gymnasium in the family home.
9. Roosevelt became active in boxing wrestling swimming riding and hunting.
10. In the years that followed Roosevelt's health did in fact improve dramatically.
11. By 1872 he had left New York to travel to such places as Cairo Egypt and Vienna Austria.
12. He lived at the home of a kind generous family in Germany for almost two years.
13. At the age of eighteen Roosevelt enrolled at Harvard University and became an excellent student.
14. During these years he met Alice Hathaway Lee whom he would eventually marry after his graduation.
15. He returned to New York with his wife and they settled into a home in the heart of the city.
16. Roosevelt began taking courses at Columbia University Law School but soon dropped out.
17. He decided that his future was in politics not law.
18. In November of 1881 Roosevelt was elected to the state assembly in Albany New York.
19. He soon won the respect of his colleagues by exposing corruption by resolving tough issues and by working for reform.
20. He would serve one-year terms in the legislature in 1882 1883 and 1884.

More Practice

Grammar Exercise Workbook
• pp. 151–152
On-line Exercise Bank
• Section 27.2
  Go on-line:
  PHSchool.com
  Enter Web Code:
  efk-1102

Get instant feedback! Exercise 20 is available on-line or on CD-ROM.

◄ **Critical Viewing**
Why might this
street in New York
City sometimes be
referred to as a
"canyon"? Answer in
a sentence with
compound elements
that would require at
least two commas.
[Draw Conclusions]

21. Two of the worst tragedies in Roosevelt's life occurred on
    February 14 1884 when both his wife and his mother died.
22. However after spending time in the West and in Washington
    D.C. Roosevelt returned to public service in New York.
23. He was elected police commissioner in 1895 and he immedi-
    ately began reforming the city's police department.
24. He would become the governor of New York just a few short
    years later yet that was merely the start of his dramatic
    career.
25. Roosevelt who would go on to become the Vice President
    President and the recipient of the Nobel Peace Prize eventually
    died at his home on Sagamore Hill in Oyster Bay Long Island
    in 1919.

GRAMMAR EXERCISES 21–29

▶ **Exercise 21** Punctuating Simple and Compound Sentences Copy each sentence that requires punctuation, adding commas where necessary. If no comma is required, write *correct*.

1. In 1928 the Waldorf–Astoria Hotel was demolished and construction of the Empire State Building began in 1930.
2. The architecture of many buildings at that time was ornate but designer William F. Lamb chose a simple design.
3. Lamb had to design the building according to certain specifications or the city would not allow it to be built.
4. Zoning laws in the city required that tall buildings become narrower as they got higher so Lamb incorporated into his design several tiers that were set back from the building's base.
5. Lamb's final design is one of the most striking in modern architecture yet it is said that he based it upon the shape of a pencil.

▶ **Exercise 22** Using Commas to Separate Items in a Series Copy each of the following sentences, inserting commas to separate items as needed.

1. The Empire State Building would rise higher than the Woolworth Building the Bank of Manhattan and the Chrysler Building.
2. The structure was finished ahead of schedule under budget and to the complete satisfaction of its owners.
3. The exterior of the building contains 200,000 cubic feet of limestone and granite 10 million bricks and 730 tons of aluminum and steel.
4. Architect William Lamb was patient clever and meticulous.
5. A glass steel and aluminum tower was mounted on the top of the building.

▶ **Exercise 23** Distinguishing Between Coordinate and Cumulative Adjectives Copy each sentence with coordinate adjectives, inserting a comma where necessary. For sentences with cumulative adjectives, write *cumulative*.

1. More than 60,000 tons of cold hard steel was required to complete the Empire State Building.
2. Marble was quarried from all over Europe for the lavish front entrance.
3. Construction crews worked long difficult hours high above the city.
4. The workers added fourteen floors during one remarkable often-discussed ten-day period.
5. A noisy excited crowd turned out for the grand opening of the building on May 1, 1931.

▶ **Exercise 24** Using Commas After Introductory Material Copy each sentence that needs a comma, inserting the comma where it is needed. If a sentence does not require a comma, write *correct*.

1. Built at the end of the eighteenth century Gracie Mansion is the official residence of the mayor of New York City.
2. When the Revolutionary War ended a Scottish immigrant named Archibald Gracie purchased the land and built a large home on it.
3. As the city expanded it appropriated the mansion and its surrounding land in 1896, turning the area into a park.
4. Unfortunately the building was neglected, and it fell into disrepair.
5. By 1923 preservationists had restored the mansion, and it briefly served as the Museum of New York City.

▶ **Exercise 25** Using Commas to Set Off Parenthetical and Nonessential Expressions Copy the following sentences, inserting commas where necessary to set off parenthetical expressions.

1. Central Park which was one of New York's largest public works projects first opened in 1859.
2. The wealthy citizens who admired the public parks of London and Paris pushed for the development of a large park in New York City.
3. Three years of debate over price and location of the park finally came to an end in 1853 when the state legislature authorized the park's construction.
4. The city therefore acquired more than 700 acres in the center of Manhattan.
5. The land was for the most part undesirable for homes and other private development.

▶ **Exercise 26** Proofreading to Correct Comma Errors Revise each of the following sentences, inserting or deleting commas as necessary.

1. Since the founding of New York City Brooklyn and Manhattan have been important parts of the city.
2. Until the late 1800's people, who wished to travel from one borough to the other, had to rely on ferryboats which would shuttle them back and forth across the East River.
3. In 1867 New York legislators finally agreed to fund a bridge, and chartered the New York Bridge Company to do the job.
4. The company soon chose John A. Roebling a wire manufacturer and engineer to design the bridge, and oversee its construction.
5. His design called for a rail line a walkway for pedestrians and a roadway for horse-drawn carriages.
6. Unfortunately in July, 1869 John A. Roebling died in an accident.
7. His son Washington Roebling succeeded him.
8. Work on the bridge began in January, 1870, but by 1871 Washington Roebling was crippled by disease.
9. His wife took over the job of instructing the engineers while Roebling supervised the work from his Brooklyn bedroom window.
10. The Brooklyn Bridge eventually opened on May 24 1883.
11. During its construction twenty-seven men had died, including its designer John A. Roebling.

▶ **Exercise 27** Find It in Your Reading Read the following excerpt from James Thurber's "The Night the Ghost Got In." Then, explain the rules governing his use of commas.

The police were on hand in a commendably short time: a Ford sedan full of them, two on motorcycles, and a patrol wagon with about eight in it and a few reporters.

▶ **Exercise 28** Find It in Your Writing In your portfolio, look for examples of coordinate and cumulative adjectives. If you can't find any examples, challenge yourself to add one or two. Make sure you have used commas correctly in each example.

▶ **Exercise 29** Writing Application Write a paragraph about the history of an interesting home, building, or other architectural structure near your school. When you finish, review all of the rules for commas, and make sure you have used commas correctly in your paragraph.

Semicolons and Colons

The semicolon (;) and the colon (:) are similar-looking punctuation marks with very different uses. A semicolon can be used to establish a relationship between two or more independent clauses and also to prevent confusion in sentences containing other internal punctuation marks. A colon can be used as an introductory device to point ahead to additional information, for clarification, and in other special situations.

The Semicolon

Semicolons are used to connect two independent clauses containing similar or contrasting ideas. Often, the independent clauses connected by a semicolon are similar to each other in structure as well as in meaning.

> **KEY CONCEPT** Use a semicolon to join independent clauses that are not already joined by the conjunction *and, but, for, not, or, so,* or *yet.* ■

A semicolon is not the most common way to separate independent clauses. In most cases, they are joined with a comma and coordinating conjunction.

EXAMPLE: The First Lady is married to the President, but her role is also very important.

When you write a sentence containing two or more independent clauses and no coordinating conjunction, however, use a semicolon instead of a comma to join them.

The semicolon is a stronger punctuation mark than a comma. It replaces both the comma and the conjunction. Do not capitalize the word following the semicolon unless the word is a proper noun or a proper adjective.

EXAMPLE: Martha Washington was the first First Lady; she was married to George Washington.

Sometimes, the first word of a second independent clause is a conjunctive adverb or a transitional expression.

▼ Critical Viewing A President and a First Lady have many separate and independent roles. In what way are they like a sentence containing a semicolon? **[Compare]**

KEY CONCEPT Use a semicolon to join independent clauses separated by either a conjunctive adverb or a transitional expression. ■

Conjunctive adverbs are adverbs used as conjunctions to connect independent clauses. Common conjunctive adverbs are *accordingly, also, besides, consequently, furthermore, however, indeed, instead, namely, nevertheless, otherwise, similarly, therefore,* and *thus. Transitional expressions* are expressions that connect one independent clause with another. Transitional expressions include *as a result, at this time, first, for instance, in fact, on the other hand, second,* and *that is.*

CONJUNCTIVE ADVERBS:	We think of Washington, D.C., as the nation's capital; *however,* the capital used to be in New York City. Then, the capital moved to Philadelphia; *therefore,* the First Family moved as well.
TRANSITIONAL EXPRESSIONS:	Martha Washington entertained graciously; *in fact,* she set a precedent for First Ladies. She enjoyed her role as hostess; *on the other hand,* there was a great deal of pressure to set a good example.

Another use of the semicolon is with independent clauses or series that already contain a number of commas. The use of a semicolon can help prevent confusion in these sentences.

KEY CONCEPT Use a semicolon to avoid confusion when independent clauses or items in a series already contain commas. ■

INDEPENDENT CLAUSES:	Abigail Adams, who was descended from a prestigious colonial family, had little formal education; still she was an eager reader.
ITEMS IN A SERIES:	She read inspirational works, like the Bible, and philosophy; religious sermons and essays; nonfiction, including historical accounts; and she turned to her husband, John, for further instruction.

In the preceding example, semicolons are used to separate the three major parts of the series. Commas are used within the major parts to set off the modifying participial phrases. When items in a series contain appositives or adjective clauses, semicolons should also be used to separate the major parts of the series.

 Internet Tip

To locate more information about First Ladies of the United States, type "First Ladies" in the query field of your search engine or go directly to "The First Ladies" Web site from **www.whitehouse.gov**

More Practice
Grammar Exercise Workbook
• pp. 153–154
On-line Exercise Bank
• Section 27.3
Go on-line:
PHSchool.com
Enter Web Code:
efk-1102

Exercise 30 Understanding the Use of the Semicolon

Copy the following sentences. Insert semicolons where necessary. Some of the sentences may require only a comma to separate independent clauses.

EXAMPLE: Abigail Adams had great curiosity in fact, she
            was to become one of the most well-read women
            in America.

ANSWER: Abigail Adams had great curiosity; in fact, she
            was to become one of the most well-read women
            in America.

1. Reading was a common interest of Abigail and her husband therefore, it acted as a strong bond between them.
2. John Adams went to Harvard and there he studied for a career in law.
3. They were married in 1764 at this time, Abigail was only nineteen years old.
4. They lived on a small farm outside Boston however, John Adams's law practice was in town.
5. Later, Abigail looked after the children and John traveled as a circuit judge.
6. The couple were frequently apart as a result, Abigail wrote hundreds of letters.
7. Abigail, ahead of her time with many of her ideas, became a trusted and influential political advisor to her husband and he discussed all the politics of the day with her.
8. Living in France was a new experience for the Adamses: John Adams served at his diplomatic post, which was in Paris Abigail lived in Paris with him, observing the manners of the French both of them met social discourtesies bravely.
9. John Adams was the first President to live in Washington, D.C. indeed, the city was still a wilderness.
10. Abigail's letters have left a legacy of a loving marriage furthermore, they help us better understand the history of our nation.

▼ Critical Viewing
Describe Abigail Adams's posture and the expression on her face using two closely related independent clauses that could be joined by a semicolon. [**Connect**]

The Colon

The colon (:) is a distinctive punctuation mark with a number of important uses. One important use of the colon is to introduce a list following an independent clause.

▶ **KEY CONCEPT** Use a colon before a list of items following an independent clause. ■

EXAMPLES: Dolley Madison entertained all kinds of people: politicians, diplomats, and the general public.
Her husband, James Madison, was many things: congressman, President, and writer of the Federalist papers.
The United States government has three branches: the executive, the legislative, and the judicial.

Details may be listed without using a colon. Compare the following examples with the preceding ones.

ALSO CORRECT: Dolley Madison entertained all kinds of people, including politicians, diplomats, and the general public.
The United States government consists of the executive branch, the legislative branch, and the judicial branch.

In each of the examples above, the list is not preceded by an independent clause, so no colon is used. Always make sure that an independent clause precedes the list before you insert a colon. The independent clause before a list often begins or ends in a phrase such as *the following* or *the following items,* signaling the need for a colon.

▶ **KEY CONCEPT** Use a colon to introduce a quotation that is formal or lengthy or a quotation that does not contain a "he said/she said" expression. ■

EXAMPLES: In *The Living White House,* Rosalynn Carter writes about the history of the White House: "I also have found real pleasure in learning the details about the furniture of the Federal period."
Helen Taft said about her husband: "It has always been my ambition to see Mr. Taft President of the United States."

A casual quoted remark or dialogue should be introduced by a comma even if lengthy. Use a colon only for more formal quotations and for those without "he said/she said" expressions.

▶ **KEY CONCEPT** Use a colon to introduce a sentence that summarizes or explains the sentence before it. ■

EXAMPLE: Mary Todd Lincoln was very active during the Civil War: She visited hospitals, read to the soldiers, wrote them letters, and raised money.

As you see in the preceding example, the colon serves as an introductory device for the sentence that amplifies the preceding sentence. Notice that a capital letter follows the colon because the words following make a complete sentence.

▶ **KEY CONCEPT** Use a colon to introduce a formal appositive that follows an independent clause. ■

A colon is a stronger mark than a comma, so using a colon gives more emphasis to the appositive it introduces.

EXAMPLE: Mrs. Lincoln strongly supported the main Union policy: antislavery.

The colon has a number of other uses as well.

SPECIAL SITUATIONS REQUIRING COLONS	
Time expressed in numerals	7:10 P.M. 12:01 A.M.
References to periodicals (volume number: page number)	*Psychology Today;* 24:189 *Science* 169:611–612
Biblical references (chapter number: verse number)	Deuteronomy 4:11
Subtitles of books and magazines	*The Causes of World War I: A Chronology of Events*
Salutations in business letters	Gentlemen: Dear Ms. Wills:
Labels used to signal important ideas	**Warning:** Trespassers will be prosecuted.

Exercise 31 Understanding the Use of the Colon Copy the following items, inserting colons where necessary.

EXAMPLE: Eleanor Roosevelt was sent to boarding school in England when she was young fifteen years old.

ANSWER: Eleanor Roosevelt was sent to boarding school in England when she was young: fifteen years old.

1. Eleanor Roosevelt was the first of the modern First Ladies for one major reason She resolved to have a career of her own.
2. Upon returning home to New York, she married her distant relative Franklin Roosevelt.
3. She became involved in various women's groups the League of Women Voters and the Women's Trade Union League.
4. Dear Mrs. Roosevelt
5. In 1921, Franklin Roosevelt was stricken with a debilitating illness polio.
6. Eleanor Roosevelt championed a wide range of social causes youth employment, civil rights, and women's rights.
7. She believed in the activity of women "Women should not be afraid to soil their hands. Those who are not afraid make the best politicians."
8. Many recent First Ladies have continued to support important causes mental health (Rosalynn Carter); foster grandparents (Nancy Reagan); beautification of the land (Lady Bird Johnson); and literacy (Barbara Bush).
9. Barbara Bush established The Foundation for Family Literacy; this is part of its mission to establish literacy as a value in every family in America.
10. Many of Bush's experiences are chronicled in her book *Barbara Bush A Memoir.*

More Practice

Grammar Exercise Workbook
• pp. 153–154
On-line Exercise Bank
• Section 27.3
 Go on-line:
 PHSchool.com
 Enter Web Code:
 efk-1102

Get instant feedback! Exercise 31 is available on-line or on CD-ROM.

▶ Critical Viewing What is the response of these children to hearing Barbara Bush, former President George Bush's wife, read to them? If the book had a subtitle, what punctuation mark would separate it from the main title? **[Infer]**

27.3

More Practice

Grammar Exercise
Workbook
• pp. 153–154
On-line Exercise Bank
• Section 27.3

Go on-line:
PHSchool.com
Enter Web Code:
efk-1102

Exercise 32 Using Semicolons and Colons Correctly Copy each of the following items, adding semicolons and colons where appropriate.

EXAMPLE: Jacqueline Kennedy was First Lady during the administration of her husband John F. Kennedy.

ANSWER: Jacqueline Kennedy was First Lady during the administration of her husband: John F. Kennedy.

1. While Mrs. Kennedy lived in the White House, she had it restored and redecorated as a result, it was declared a national museum.
2. She wrote a book to raise funds for this project *The White House An Historic Guide.*
3. She searched old government buildings for antiques and worked with antique experts in fact, she even asked citizens to send back White House furnishings or other items that had been sold.
4. Mrs. Kennedy was a patron of the arts it was her clothing that made her an international trendsetter.
5. She helped convince the French government to lend the United States a famous painting the *Mona Lisa.*
6. With her husband, Mrs. Kennedy shared many dreams American space exploration, civil rights, and better education for all citizens.
7. She was riding with President Kennedy when he was assassinated at approximately 12 30 P.M. on November 22, 1963.
8. After this sad event, she made a decision she would move to New York City and live more privately.
9. Books had always been her greatest love therefore, she became an editor.
10. Jackie Kennedy describes her proudest work as First Lady "To call attention to what was finest in America, what should be esteemed and honored."

▲ Critical Viewing
Jacqueline Kennedy worked as an editor after leaving public life. What kind of decisions about punctuation would she have had to make while on the job? [Classify]

Section 27.3 *Section Review*

GRAMMAR EXERCISES 33–37

Exercise 33 Proofreading for Semicolons and Colons Revise the following sentences, adding, deleting, or changing semicolons and colons.

1. While she was just a girl, Betty Ford admired Eleanor Roosevelt "I really liked the idea that a woman was speaking out and expressing herself; rather than just expressing the views of her husband."
2. Ford lived in New York City, where she studied dance with Martha Graham: she also worked as a model.
3. When she moved back to her home in Grand Rapids, Michigan, she made a career decision She would teach modern dance to poor children in the city.
4. She met Gerald Ford when he was a busy young lawyer, in fact, at the time he was running for Congress.
5. The Equal Rights Amendment was an issue while Ford was in Congress it was a bill that Betty Ford strongly supported.
6. In 1973, President Richard Nixon selected her husband to fill an important position Vice President.
7. President Nixon resigned suddenly: Gerald Ford then became president of the United States.
8. Ford, in his inaugural address, acknowledged his wife "I am indebted to no man and only to one woman, my dear wife, Betty."
9. Betty Ford spoke openly about the traditional roles of women wife, mother, and homemaker.
10. In 1976, Jimmy Carter defeated Gerald Ford Carter's wife, Rosalyn, became the new First Lady.

Exercise 34 Proofreading a Letter Read the following letter. Rewrite it, inserting the proper semicolons and colons.

September 1, 1962

Dear Mrs. Kennedy

　I am writing about our visit to the White House at 1 30 P.M. last Tuesday. My daughter and I were greatly looking forward to an interesting visit indeed, all of our expectations were met. My daughter would have liked to see more of the private quarters the kitchen, the bathroom, and the bedrooms. Of course, we saw the sign No visitors beyond this point. We understood that these areas were off limits nevertheless, we were very happy with the visit. The tour guide was friendly and entertaining furthermore, he was extremely knowledgeable about American history. You have a splendid residence we were glad to be able to see it.

Sincerely yours,

Maggie Geiger

Exercise 35 Find It in Your Reading Reread the passage from "An Occurrence at Owl Creek Bridge" on page 534. Explain in writing why the author used a semicolon after the word *reloading*.

Exercise 36 Find It in Your Writing In a piece of your writing, find two related independent clauses that are linked by a comma and coordinating conjunction. Rewrite the sentence so that the clauses are joined by a semicolon instead.

Exercise 37 Writing Application Write a paragraph about packing for a trip. Use a colon to introduce a list of "must haves."

Quotation Marks and Underlining

Direct quotations from other people can support the ideas or arguments of a writer. Direct quotations also enliven short stories, novels, and other works of fiction. When the characters themselves speak, the writing becomes more exciting.

Study the many rules and examples in this section carefully to master the use of quotation marks. This section will also discuss the use of underlining as well as quotation marks to indicate different types of titles, names, and words.

Quotation Marks for Direct Quotations

Before direct quotations can be discussed, it is important to distinguish between *direct* and *indirect quotations.*

▶ **KEY CONCEPTS** A **direct quotation** represents a person's exact speech or thoughts and is enclosed in quotation marks (" "). ■

An **indirect quotation** reports only the general meaning of what a person said or thought and does not require quotation marks. ■

DIRECT QUOTATION:	The journalist said, "I expect to be finished with the article before the deadline."
INDIRECT QUOTATION:	The journalist said that he expected to be finished with the article before the deadline.

An indirect quotation rephrases someone else's words. It does not use the exact words of the speaker. In a direct quotation, the words of the speaker are quoted exactly.

Sometimes, the exact words of the speaker are not available, and the only way to express the speaker's sentiments is to rephrase them in an indirect quotation. If the actual words of the speaker are available, however, they should usually be used in order to achieve dynamic, strong writing.

A sentence that is an uninterrupted direct quotation requires quotation marks around it.

EXAMPLE: "To be a journalist is to have a ringside seat to the unfolding of history." —Wes Gallagher

Notice that the preceding quotation begins with a capital letter and is a complete sentence. Each sentence of quoted material should always begin with a capital letter.

Theme: Journalism

In this section, you will learn about the many uses of quotation marks and underlining. The examples and exercises in this section are about journalism.

Cross-Curricular Connection: Social Studies

▶ **KEY CONCEPT** The first word of a quoted phrase or fragment is capitalized only when it falls at the beginning of a sentence or when it would be capitalized regardless of its position in a sentence. ■

Notice in the following examples that quotation marks are still placed around the quoted words, but the need for capitalization changes.

EXAMPLES: In "Memories of Christmas," Dylan Thomas mentions that one Christmas "was so much like another."

"The song of the people, transformed by the experiences of each generation" is what holds people together, according to Alice Walker.

Many direct quotations contain two parts: the actual words of the speaker (the direct quotation) and a group of words identifying the speaker. The words identifying the speaker are called conversational tags or "he said/she said" expressions. They include such common expressions as *she said, he replied, the professor explained,* and *Gary asked.* The possibilities are almost endless, but they all have one feature in common: Conversational tags are not enclosed in quotation marks.

There are three ways of using a conversational tag in a sentence: as an introductory expression, as a concluding expression, or as an interrupting expression.

▶ **KEY CONCEPT** Use a comma or colon after an introductory expression. ■

EXAMPLE: The tour guide explained, "*The New York Times* was founded in 1851 by Henry J. Raymond."

In the preceding example, the conversational tag comes first and is set off from the direct quotation with a comma. If the introductory expression is more formal in tone or if it contains no conversational tag, use a colon instead of a comma.

EXAMPLE: She gazed at the assembled crowd: "Thank you for the honor you have awarded me."

▲ Critical Viewing
Why do journalists make extensive use of quotation marks? Why don't they just describe the statements of newsmakers? **[Infer]**

Sometimes, a direct quotation comes before a conversational tag.

> **KEY CONCEPT** Use a comma, question mark, or exclamation mark after a quotation followed by a concluding expression. ■

EXAMPLE: "*The New York Times* was founded in 1851 by Henry J. Raymond," the tour guide explained.

In the preceding example, a comma follows the direct quotation, and a period is used after the conversational tag because it ends the sentence. Notice also that the comma comes before the quotation mark.

In addition to preceding or following a quotation, there is a third way of using a conversational tag: The conversational tag can interrupt the direct quotation.

> **KEY CONCEPT** Use a comma after the part of a quoted sentence that is followed by an interrupting expression. Use another comma after the expression. ■

EXAMPLE: "*The New York Times*," the tour guide explained, "was founded in 1851 by Henry J. Raymond."

In this example, the quotation has been interrupted by a conversational tag. Both parts are enclosed in quotation marks, and there are commas before and after the conversational tag. Once again, the first comma comes before the quotation mark.

A final rule must be followed whenever a conversational tag interrupts a quotation that is several sentences long:

> **KEY CONCEPT** Use a comma, question mark, or exclamation mark after a quoted sentence that comes before an interrupting expression. Use a period after the expression. ■

EXAMPLE: "I want to have time to look for my children and see how many I can find. Maybe I shall find them among the dead," said Chief Joseph of the Nez Percé. "Hear me, my chiefs. I am tired; my heart is sick and sad. From where the sun now stands I will fight no more forever."

Writers vary their use of conversational tags in the ways shown in the preceding examples to achieve variety.

▶ **Exercise 38** Using Quotation Marks With Direct Quotations Copy each sentence that needs punctuation, adding whatever punctuation is needed. In one instance, a quoted fragment has been underlined so that you can tell where it begins and ends. If a sentence is not a direct quotation and requires no quotation marks, write *indirect*.

EXAMPLE: His editor explained why he did not agree with him.

ANSWER: indirect

EXAMPLE: We have different ethical standards, he said.

ANSWER: "We have different ethical standards," he said.

1. You're scheduled to cover the city council meeting tonight my editor told me.
2. I'm looking forward to it! I replied, and I was.
3. I went on to tell him that I had a tantalizing lead about a scandal that was about to break.
4. What is it? he wanted to know.
5. I had heard that the mayor might resign this evening, but I didn't completely trust my source. I told my editor this.
6. Interesting, he mused. I think you should take Joe with you.
7. Joe is our best photographer, and I told my editor that I liked his idea.
8. Just last week, our paper had written that the mayor is <u>one of the most honest men in politics today</u>, but in tomorrow's paper, who knows what we'll write?
9. Make sure Joe gets shots of both the council and the audience, he instructed me. We may have a big story here!
10. I told him that I'd catch Joe on my way out of the building.

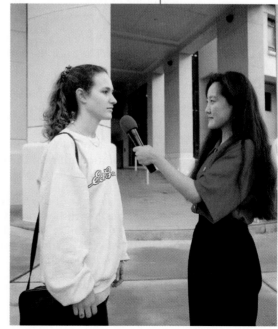

▶ Critical Viewing
Why might a person speaking with a journalist insist upon being quoted directly, with quotation marks around any statements, rather than having the remarks paraphrased by a writer? [Speculate]

▶ **More Practice**

Grammar Exercise Workbook
• pp. 155–156
On-line Exercise Bank
• Section 27.4
Go on-line:
PHSchool.com
Enter Web Code:
efk-1102

Get instant feedback! Exercise 38 is available on-line or on CD-ROM.

Other Punctuation Marks With Quotation Marks

Quotation marks are used in conjunction with many other punctuation marks. Unfortunately, the location of the quotation marks in relation to the other punctuation marks is not always the same. It varies depending on the other punctuation marks and, in some cases, on the meaning of the sentence.

The rule for commas and periods is always the same.

▶ KEY CONCEPT Always place a comma or a period inside the final quotation mark. ■

EXAMPLES: The reporter said, "I'm ready if you are."

"I took several pictures of the candidate," the photographer said.

The rule is the reverse when quotation marks are used with semicolons and colons.

▶ KEY CONCEPT Always place a semicolon or colon outside the final quotation mark. ■

EXAMPLES: I fully understand what she means by a "call for drastic action"; the situation becomes more pressing each day.

We emphatically deny these "nasty accusations": They are ill-founded and not based on fact.

The rules for the use of quotation marks with question marks and exclamation marks are more complicated.

▶ KEY CONCEPT Place a question mark or an exclamation mark inside the final quotation mark if the end mark is part of the quotation. ■

The question mark in the first of the following examples is placed inside the quotation mark because it belongs to the quotation itself. The same is true of the exclamation mark in the second example. It belongs inside the quotation mark because it is part of the quotation itself.

EXAMPLES: Marie asked, "Have the reporters phoned yet?"
The spokesman exclaimed, "We demand our rights!"

Notice the difference when the exclamation mark or question mark refers to the entire sentence.

▲ **Critical Viewing** What makes a reader or viewer choose one newspaper or newscast over another? Does the inclusion of direct quotes have any effect on this decision? **[Evaluate]**

EXAMPLES: Did the editor state, "This is an equal opportunity organization"**?**

Run from anyone who whispers, "I have a deal you can't refuse"**!**

In each example, the end mark goes outside of the puncuation mark because it belongs to the entire sentence, not to the quote. You should also place the end mark outside if both the quote and the entire sentence require a question mark or an exclamation mark.

▶ **Exercise 39** Using Other Punctuation Marks With Direct Quotations Copy each of the following sentences, adding quotation marks as needed. Quoted fragments are underlined.

EXAMPLE: The magazine staff looked up when Jennifer shouted, We must leave *now*!

ANSWER: The magazine staff looked up when Jennifer shouted, "We must leave *now!*"

1. Our journalism professor stated: This business is all about hard-hitting questions, honest answers, and a bit of wisdom.
2. The city editor asked, Do we have any witnesses who will talk to us about the fire?
3. This article is well written, he said. The reporter was fair and accurate.
4. Are you certain? he asked his source. These are explosive allegations you are making.
5. Did your article state: The defendant refused to comment?
6. Quick! I yelled to our photojournalist. Take the picture, and let's get out of here!
7. If that article isn't on my desk by 6 P.M., my editor warned, you better start looking for another job.
8. Moved to the front page, the editorial called for the senator's immediate resignation; other papers expressed similar demands.
9. There is the central and very serious mission of *communicating*—gathering facts, yes; understanding them, yes; but then going that essential step further. —Conrad Fink
10. The world does not want to wait for the assessment of history; it wants the information at the time history is being made. —M. L. Stein

▶ **More Practice**

Grammar Exercise Workbook
• pp. 157–158
On-line Exercise Bank
• Section 27.4
Go on-line:
PHSchool.com
Enter Web Code:
efk-1102

Get instant feedback! Exercise 39 is available on-line or on CD-ROM.

⚙ **Grammar** ⚙ **and Style Tip**

Don't combine commas with other end marks when writing quotations. An exclamation mark, for example, will supersede a comma. For example: *"Look out!" he yelled.*

Quotation Marks in Special Situations

You also need to know how to use quotation marks in dialogues and in quotations of more than one paragraph. In addition, you may want to leave out part of a person's words in a quotation or to include one quotation within another. The following rules will guide you in these special situations.

Dialogue and Long Quotations In many stories and novels, the use of dialogue, or direct conversation between two or more people, plays an important role. Much of what is happening is indicated through the words of the characters.

Each writer develops his or her own style in writing dialogue. The writer must follow the rules for writing quotations, however, so that the reader will know who is speaking.

▶ **KEY CONCEPT** When writing dialogue, begin a new paragraph with each change of speaker. ■

GRAMMAR IN LITERATURE

from **The Woman Warrior**
Maxine Hong Kingston

The structure of this dialogue makes it easy to tell that Brave Orchid is speaking in the first, third, fifth, and seventh paragraphs. She is talking to Moon Orchid, who is speaking in the second, fourth, sixth, and eighth paragraphs.

"You're an old woman," said Brave Orchid.

"Aiaa. *You're* an old woman."

"But *you* are really old. Surely, you can't say that about me. I'm not old the way you're old."

"But you really are old. You're one year older than I am."

"Your hair is white and your face all wrinkled."

"You're so skinny."

"You're so fat."

"Fat women are more beautiful than skinny women."

Another type of quotation consists of several paragraphs in a row. For this type of quotation, quotation marks are placed at the beginning of each paragraph and at the end of the final paragraph.

Sidebar:

💡 **Spelling Tip**

When writing dialogue, you can deliberately misspell words in order to show a character's particular style of pronunciation, such as a regional accent, but be sure you understand what the correct spelling is.

> **KEY CONCEPT** For quotations longer than a paragraph, put quotation marks at the beginning of each paragraph and at the end of the final paragraph. ■

EXAMPLE: "When messages are misunderstood, it is easy to blame the speaker. The listener, however, must share the responsibility for effective communication. It takes a lot of concentration and effort to be a good listener. Statistics show, in fact, that most people are poor listeners. The average person misses about 75 percent of what he or she hears.

"The encouraging fact is that no one has to remain a poor listener. Listening, like speaking, reading, or writing, is a skill that can be learned. Learning to listen does, however, take a lot of self-motivation and practice."

—J. Regis O'Connor

When you are quoting several paragraphs, make certain that you remember to include the final quotation mark.

Ellipsis Marks and Single Quotation Marks There are two other special problems involving the use of quotation marks. The first concerns the use of ellipsis marks (. . .) in a shortened quotation. Frequently, a writer wishes to include only a portion of a long quotation in a piece of writing. In such a situation, ellipsis marks can be used to show that some words have been omitted.

> **KEY CONCEPT** Use three ellipsis marks in a quotation to indicate that words have been omitted. ■

Ellipsis marks can be used at the beginning, in the middle, or at the end of a quotation.

AN ENTIRE
QUOTATION: "Whenever I prepare for a journey I prepare as though for death. Should I never return, all is in order. This is what life has taught me."
—Katherine Mansfield

ELLIPSES AT
THE BEGINNING: Katherine Mansfield speaks of preparing for a trip ". . . as though for death."

ELLIPSES IN
THE MIDDLE: Katherine Mansfield once wrote, "Whenever I prepare for a journey I prepare . . . for death."

ELLIPSES AT
THE END: Walt Whitman once wrote, "I hear America singing. . . ."

Notice that when a period is part of the quotation, as in the last two examples, it is added to the ellipsis marks to conclude the sentence.

The second special problem involving quotation marks concerns a quotation within a quotation. A quotation within a quotation is set off with single quotation marks (' ') instead of the regular double marks (" "). The larger quotation is still set off with double quotation marks.

KEY CONCEPT Use single quotation marks for a quotation within a quotation. ■

EXAMPLE: I can still hear our tenth-grade English teacher reciting the line from Poe: "Quoth the Raven, 'Nevermore.'"

Notice that the single quotation mark goes outside the period, just as a double quotation mark does.

If a quotation within a quotation causes confusion, rephrase the material to eliminate the quotation within a quotation.

Exercise 40 Writing Sentences With Ellipsis Marks and Single Quotation Marks Write five original sentences, each incorporating either part of one of the quotations below (using ellipsis marks) or the whole quotation inside another quotation (using single quotation marks).

EXAMPLE: "We have just begun to fight."
ANSWER: The teacher asked us, "Do you know who said, 'We have just begun to fight'?"

EXAMPLE: "From what we get, we can make a living; what we give, however, makes a life." —Arthur Ashe
ANSWER: I'm going to volunteer because, as Arthur Ashe said, ". . . what we give . . . makes a life."

1. "Not everything that can be counted counts, and not everything that counts can be counted." —*Albert Einstein*
2. "The artist is nothing without the gift, but the gift is nothing without work." —*Emile Zola*
3. "I find that the harder I work, the more luck I seem to have." —*Thomas Jefferson*
4. "In the end, we will remember not the words of our enemies, but the silence of our friends." —*Martin Luther King, Jr.*
5. "Writing only leads to more writing." —*Collette*

Exercise 41 Using Ellipsis Marks and Single Quotation
Marks Copy each of the following sentences, inserting double
quotation marks (" ") and single quotation marks (' ') as needed. Underline any words that are printed in italics. The quoted
fragments are underlined.

EXAMPLE: I asked, Were you serious when you said, I
            won't?

ANSWER: I asked, "Were you serious when you said, 'I
            won't'?"

1. "In his triumphant speech, the lawyer for the newspaper
   said, We have won a victory for freedom of the press, and
   then he smiled broadly."
2. "I refer you to the First Amendment, which states,
   Congress shall make no law . . . abridging the freedom of
   speech, or of the press."
3. "The so called <u>Yellow Press</u> is any newspaper which glows
   with the color of sunshine and throws light into dark
   places." —Ella Wheeler Wilcox
4. The author of the editorial wrote, Our senator has done
   . . . an adequate job representing the district.
5. The court reporter overheard the defendant tell the
   judge, Stone walls do not a prison make. . . .
6. "As a journalist, I was able to get into the locker
   room, where I heard one player grumbling about
   what he called <u>the worst playing field in the history
   of the game</u>."
7. "He kept saying, Would you at least consider me for
   the foreign correspondent position? but the editor
   always refused."
8. The title of Hemingway's book *For Whom the Bell Tolls*
   refers to a line in one of John Donne's meditations,
   which states, . . . never send to know for whom the bell
   tolls; it tolls for thee.
9. The speaker observed: My statement was interrupted by
   a reporter who asked me, Do you think you will run for
   office?
10. When it comes to freedom of the press, most journalists
    agree with Patrick Henry, who said, . . . but as for me,
    give me liberty or give me death.

Exercise 42 Writing Original Dialogue Write approximately one page of original dialogue about two characters
attempting to solve a problem or resolve a dispute. Include
a few lines of description. Enclose the lines of dialogue in
quotation marks. Include enough conversational tags so that
there is no confusion about who is speaking.

More Practice

Grammar Exercise
Workbook
• pp. 157–158
On-line Exercise Bank
• Section 27.4
  Go on-line:
  PHSchool.com
  Enter Web Code:
  efk-1102

▲ **Critical Viewing**
Why might a journal-
ist choose to shorten
a direct quotation?
What should a read-
er be aware of when
he or she sees ellipsis
marks in a quota-
tion? **[Interpret]**

Quotation Marks and Underlining • **557**

Underlining, Italics, and Quotation Marks

There are various ways of indicating titles in writing. In books, periodicals, and other printed publications, italics are used to indicate many types of titles. In handwritten material, the writer underlines items that in print would be italicized. When using a word processor, you may choose to underline or use italic type. Other types of titles require the use of quotation marks. Quotation marks are used in both printed and hand-written materials.

The following rules will help you use underlining and quotation marks correctly in titles and in other situations.

Underlining and Italic The titles of long works are generally indicated by underlining or italic type.

> ▶ **KEY CONCEPT** Underline or italicize the titles of books and other long written works, of publications that are published as a single work, of plays, and of other works of art. ■

BOOKS:	I want to read Nancy Wolcott's <u>Women and the American Experience</u>.
MAGAZINES:	The <u>Atlantic Monthly</u> is a very good magazine.
NEWSPAPERS:	I subscribe to <u>The New York Times</u>.
PAMPHLETS:	Distributed at the start of the Revolutionary War, Thomas Paine's <u>Common Sense</u> helped to turn the tide of public opinion.
LONG POEMS:	<u>The Rime of the Ancient Mariner</u> is one of my favorite poems.
MOVIES:	At the time of its release, <u>Titanic</u> was the most expensive movie ever made.
MUSICALS:	Critics called <u>Oklahoma!</u> a work of genius.
PLAYS (two acts or longer):	<u>The Glass Menagerie</u> is a sad play about the fragile nature of humanity.
WORKS OF ART:	<u>Mona Lisa</u> is a masterful example of Da Vinci's talent.
ALBUMS:	I bought a copy of The Beatles' <u>Abbey Road</u>.
TV PROGRAMS:	Did you watch <u>60 Minutes</u> last night?
OPERAS AND SYMPHONIES:	Mozart's <u>Figaro</u> is my favorite opera.

KEY CONCEPT Underline or italicize the names of individual air, sea, space, and land craft.

EXAMPLE: The President arrived on <u>Air Force One</u>.

KEY CONCEPT Underline or italicize foreign words or phrases not yet accepted into English. ■

EXAMPLES: The famous star signed the letter <u>con amore</u>, "with love."
The French expression <u>mère de famille</u> means "mother of a family."
The composer's notation read <u>con spirito</u>, "with spirit."

Some foreign words and phrases retain their foreign pronunciation but are no longer underlined or italicized because they are now considered part of our language.

NOT UNDERLINED: amour, caveat emptor, cliché, blitzkrieg, gourmet, milieu, siesta, staccato, chauffeur, pizza, dilettante

Individual numbers, letters, and words used to name themselves are underlined or italicized to make them stand out.

KEY CONCEPT Underline or italicize numbers, symbols, letters, and words used as names for themselves. ■

NUMBERS: Is that a <u>3</u> or an <u>8</u>?
SYMBOLS: Use a <u>?</u> after a direct question.
LETTERS: He has a strange way of writing his <u>f</u>'s and <u>t</u>'s.
WORDS: She often uses <u>nevertheless</u> to connect her ideas.

Underlining or italics may also be used to emphasize a particular word or phrase.

KEY CONCEPT Underline or italicize words that you wish to stress. ■

EXAMPLE: Be sure to study the rules <u>carefully</u>.

Do not overuse underlining to emphasize your meaning. Rely instead on a precise choice and arrangement of words.

⊙ Technology Tip

When using a word processor, you can italicize titles rather than underlining them. An icon for italics—as well as for underlining and boldface—appears on the toolbar of most word processors.

Quotation Marks Like underlining, quotation marks are used to indicate certain titles.

▶ **KEY CONCEPT** Use quotation marks around the titles of short written works (including one-act plays and short poems), chapters in a book, episodes in a series (including individual episodes of television programs), songs, and parts of long musical compositions or collections. ■

EXAMPLES: I admire the poem "I Hear America Singing."

"Charles" is one of my favorite short stories.

His favorite song by The Beatles is "Something."

Read Chapter 1, "Dynamic Democracy," in Freedom's Ferment.

Titles Without Underlining or Quotation Marks Two types of titles should not be underlined or enclosed in quotation marks. The first type is made up of religious works.

▶ **KEY CONCEPT** Do not underline, italicize, or place in quotation marks the name of the Bible, its books and divisions or versions or other holy scriptures, such as the Torah and the Koran. ■

EXAMPLE: Will you read from Genesis in the Old Testament?

Other titles that should not be underlined or enclosed in quotation marks are government documents.

▶ **KEY CONCEPT** Do not underline, italicize, or place in quotation marks the titles of government charters, alliances, treaties, acts, statutes, speeches, or reports. ■

EXAMPLES: The Taft-Hartley Labor Act was passed in 1947.

We memorized the Preamble to the Constitution.

▶ **Exercise 43** Writing Sentences Containing Titles Write sentences, following the instructions given below. Be sure to use underlining and quotation marks correctly.

1. Write a sentence about subscribing to a new magazine.
2. Write a question inviting someone to a new movie.
3. Write a sentence about President Lincoln's famous speech at Gettysburg.
4. Write a sentence about a favorite song.
5. Write a sentence recommending a book you like.

Exercise 44 **Revising to Supply Underlining** Revise each of the following sentences, underlining where necessary.

EXAMPLE: The movie Gone With the Wind was made in 1939.

ANSWER: The movie <u>Gone With the Wind</u> was made in 1939.

1. A favorite bon mot among journalists is "Write the things that you have seen."
2. The city's great newspapers sent photographers to take pictures of the Queen Elizabeth 2 as it first docked in New York Harbor.
3. The theater critic for the local paper reviewed the recent performance of Death of a Salesman.
4. It's hard to read that reporter's notes because he never crosses his t's or dots his i's, and he writes a 7 with a line through it.
5. On the news was a photo essay about Vincent van Gogh and his painting Sunflowers.
6. Have you read the book The American Journalist by David Weaver and G. Cleveland Wilhoit?
7. My editor told me never to say the word can't when talking about a story.
8. As they say in Germany, it is verboten to enter the building without a press pass.
9. Woodward and Bernstein were reporters for the Washington Post when they broke the Watergate story.
10. Never use the @ in place of the word at in formal writing.

More Practice

Grammar Exercise Workbook
• pp. 159–160
On-line Exercise Bank
• Section 27.4
  Go on-line:
  PHSchool.com
  Enter Web Code:
  efk-1102

interactive Textbook

Complete the exercises on-line! Exercises 43 and 44 are available on-line or on CD-ROM.

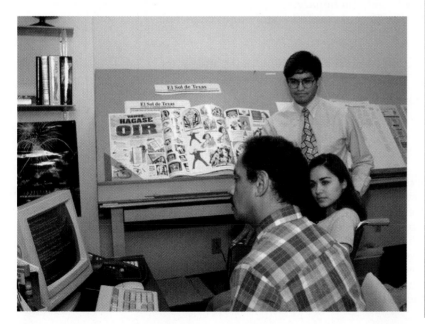

◀ **Critical Viewing** These journalists are collaborating on a news story about their community. Suggest three titles for the article they might be writing, using quotation marks properly. **[Speculate]**

Exercise 45 Using Underlining and Quotation Marks for Titles For each item, either copy it and add needed underlining or quotation marks or write *correct*.

EXAMPLE: Amendment XVI of the Constitution of the United States permits the taxing of income.

ANSWER: correct

1. Novelist John Steinbeck worked as a war correspondent for Newsday in the 1960's.
2. Ernie Pyle, a famous correspondent during World War II, wrote the book Brave Men.
3. USA Today has become one of the most widely read newspapers in the country.
4. When President Lincoln delivered the Gettysburg Address in 1864, newspapers of the day criticized the speech because it was uncharacteristically short.
5. I found that Chapter 4, Public Affairs Reporting, was particularly helpful for this assignment.
6. In 1735, a court case involving John Peter Zenger's newspaper, the New York Weekly Journal, helped establish freedom of the press in this country.
7. My journalism professor handed out a pamphlet called How to Become a Better Writer in Three Easy Steps.
8. Walt Whitman was an occasional journalist who gained fame after he published his book of poems Leaves of Grass, which included his poem Song of Myself.
9. The young journalist was constantly referring to his copy of Webster's New World™ Dictionary.
10. The reporter for The Record covered a story in Uzbekistan.

Exercise 46 Proofreading for Quotation Marks and Underlining Revise each of the following sentences, adding quotation marks and underlining as needed.

EXAMPLE: Read the poem Barbara Frietchie today, Tim said.
ANSWER: "Read the poem 'Barbara Frietchie' today," Tim said.

1. Syndicated columnist Will Rogers summed up Hoover's defeat by Roosevelt by stating, The little fellow felt that he never had a chance. . . .
2. Brad Pitt's character is a reporter for a small Montana newspaper in the movie A River Runs Through It.
3. Never use the word ain't in formal writing.
4. At home, the newspaper costs only a quarter, she said. How much does it cost here?
5. The digits in the phone number are all 9's and 7's.

More Practice

Grammar Exercise Workbook
• pp. 159–160
On-line Exercise Bank
• Section 27.4
  Go on-line:
  PHSchool.com
  Enter Web Code:
  efk-1102

Get instant feedback! Exercises 45, 46, and 47 are available on-line or on CD-ROM.

 Learn More

To learn more about properly punctuating titles, refer to Chapter 26, Capitalization.

> **Exercise 47** More Proofreading for Quotation Marks and Underlining Revise each of the following sentences, adding quotation marks and underlining as needed.

EXAMPLE: When Roberto leaves, he always says, Adios, amigo.

ANSWER: When Roberto leaves, he always says, <u>"Adios, amigo."</u>

1. I recommend that all journalists keep a copy of The World Almanac on their desks.
2. The new version of Our Town received a terrible review in last night's newspaper.
3. Chapter 8, Dateline—The World, explores the international impact of journalism.
4. No, the editor told him, we can't stop the presses.
5. The correspondent recorded the words of the general, who stated, The war will be over by Christmas.
6. We were served coq au vin at the Press Club dinner.
7. The movie All the President's Men tells the true story of two reporters working in Washington, D.C.
8. Ambrose Bierce was a cynical journalist who wrote a mock-dictionary called The Devil's Dictionary.
9. When writing for the magazine, always spell out the number four.
10. Janice heard an announcement on the news today that said Van Gogh's Starry Night sold for more than ten million dollars.
11. Reporters for the Los Angeles Times have won numerous awards for journalistic excellence.
12. Do not, I repeat, do not forget to edit the article before it goes to the printer!
13. What will you write about? my professor asked me.
14. National Public Radio played Beethoven's Fifth Symphony in its entirety.
15. The editor hit the ? key on the keyboard and inserted the necessary end mark into the paragraph.
16. Author and journalist Steven Crane wrote his short story The Open Boat after having been shipwrecked in 1896.
17. Crane's first novel, Maggie: A Girl of the Streets, was published in 1893.
18. She overuses the transition however in her magazine articles.
19. Did you know that one of my favorite columnists writes for Rolling Stone?
20. She said, I always read a chapter or two of a novel before I go to sleep.

 Internet Tip

To find out more about careers in journalism, try searching the Internet with key words such as *journalism, photojournalism, newspapers,* or *the press.* You can also try a more specific search using the names of particular newspapers or magazines.

Section Review

GRAMMAR EXERCISES 48–55

▶ **Exercise 48** Proofreading for Quotation Marks With Direct Quotations Revise each sentence that requires punctuation, adding whatever punctuation is needed. A quoted fragment is underlined so that you can tell where it begins and ends. If no additional punctuation is needed, write *correct.*

1. When a dog bites a man, that is not news editor John B. Bogart once said. When a man bites a dog, that is news.
2. The editor told the new writers that he expected them to be both aggressive and honest in their reporting.
3. A spokesman told reporters that the military base was being shut down because it was no longer needed.
4. In class today, Professor Wilkens said The press plays a crucial watchdog role in our society.
5. As he walked back to his desk, the reporter thought to himself That's how I'll write the lead for this story.

▶ **Exercise 49** Using Other Punctuation Marks With Quotation Marks Copy each of the following sentences, adding quotation marks. Quoted fragments are underlined.

1. Before he submitted his article, the writer asked himself, Am I telling this story honestly, or am I putting a spin on it?
2. I know what he expects, he sighed. If only I can reach those lofty goals.
3. It's hard to write a neutral story when it's obvious who the good guys are.
4. Get in there and get the story! he shouted above the noise.
5. The story is developing as we speak; reporters are on their way to the scene right now.

▶ **Exercise 50** Proofreading for Single Quotation Marks Revise each of the following sentences, inserting single quotation marks (' ') as needed.

1. "Did you read about the president who said, I think that if we can eliminate the bickering, . . . then we will be able to pass the bill?"
2. "His editor constantly encouraged the young writer, telling him I have complete confidence in your ability."
3. "In that case, the court declared: The plaintiff must show actual malice on the part of the journalist. This decision changed the face of journalism."
4. "Make sure you read the first section of our code of ethics, which states: We will not accept any gifts or preferential treatment from a source. Memorize it before you start writing."
5. "In the interview, she told me, I think he is a good candidate for the Senate."

▶ **Exercise 51** Using Underlining, Quotation Marks, and Ellipsis Marks Underline or enclose in quotation marks the titles below. Use part of each quotation (items 9 and 10) in a sentence, with ellipsis marks to indicate missing words.

1. novel: Crime and Punishment
2. song: And I Love Her
3. movie: Remains of the Day
4. musical: Phantom of the Opera
5. chapter: Using Nouns and Verbs
6. painting: Guernica
7. radio series: All Things Considered
8. television series: Happy Days
9. "Be content with your lot; one cannot be first in everything." —*Aesop*
10. "Beware of small expenses; a small leak will sink a great ship." —*Benjamin Franklin*

Exercise 52 Proofreading for Quotation Marks and Underlinings
Revise each of the following sentences, adding quotation marks and underlining as needed. Quoted fragments are underlined. If no additional punctuation is required, write *correct.*

1. I always keep a copy of Bartlett's Familiar Quotations on my desk, and I looked up entries under Journalism.
2. Historian Geoffrey C. Ward once said Journalism is merely history's first draft.
3. I get up in the morning with an idea for a three-volume novel, said humorist Don Marquis, and by nightfall, it's a paragraph in my [newspaper] column.
4. An anonymous journalist once wrote, Doctors bury their mistakes. Lawyers hang them. But journalists put theirs on the front page.
5. Reporter Carl Bernstein wrote that journalism is the <u>lowest form of popular culture.</u>
6. "I think many journalists agree with Alexander Smith, who said, To be quoted is the only fame I care for."
7. That's the nice thing about this job, former President Reagan said. You get to quote yourself shamelessly.
8. A writer who uses quotations to <u>show that he is learned and well read</u> . . . will only gain the contempt of his reader, according to Henry Fowler.
9. British playwright Tom Stoppard stated, . . . I still believe that if you wish to change the world, journalism is a more short-term weapon.
10. The newspaper's lawyer said that the reporter was within his rights according to the Constitution.
11. When writing a formal article, you should never use the & in place of the word and.
12. Cape Canaveral was packed with reporters waiting for the launch of the space shuttle Atlantis.
13. The movie critic said that The Wizard of Oz was great for all ages.
14. How many times during his speech did he say, I am clearly the best man for the job?
15. As they say in France, it is time to put stylo à feuille.

Exercise 53 Find It in Your Reading Find a short magazine or newspaper article that illustrates at least three of the different rules for quotations, ellipsis marks, and underlining. Remember that most words that would be underlined in handwritten material will appear in italics in a printed article. Copy the sentences and write out the rules that are being illustrated.

Exercise 54 Find It in Your Writing Look in your portfolio for a selection that might be made more vivid or interesting by including a direct quotation. For example, if you wrote a piece about your student government, you might include a quotation from your student body president. Obtain a relevant quotation, and add it to your work, making sure to punctuate it correctly.

Exercise 55 Writing Application Choose one of the categories listed in Exercise 51 (novel, song, movie, etc.), and write a paragraph reviewing an item in that category. For example, you might review the movie *Titanic* or the novel *Things Fall Apart*. In your review, use at least two direct quotations. Make sure to follow all the rules for quotations and underlining. If you use only part of a quotation, remember to use ellipsis marks.

Dashes, Parentheses, Brackets, and Hyphens

This section will present some of the less frequently used punctuation marks: dashes (—), parentheses (( )), brackets ([ ]), and hyphens (-). These punctuation marks should not be used indiscriminately. There are special rules for the use of each. Even though you may not be called upon to use them often, it is important to learn the rules that govern their use.

Dashes

The dash, a much stronger mark than a comma, signals a sudden break in the structure or thought of a sentence. A simple, dramatic punctuation mark, the dash should not be used haphazardly in place of the comma and other separators. Overuse of the dash reduces its dramatic effect and indicates a lazy writer, one who has not mastered the rules of punctuation.

There are several rules governing use of the dash, the first of which is the broadest.

▶ **KEY CONCEPT** Use dashes to indicate an abrupt change of thought, a dramatic interrupting idea, or a summary statement. ■

The following chart shows the three basic uses of the dash.

USES OF THE DASH	
To indicate an abrupt change of thought	The article doesn't provide enough information on Japan—by the way, did you find it in the school library?
To set off interrupting ideas dramatically	The pagoda was built—you may find this hard to believe—in one month. The pagoda was built—where did they get the money?—in one month.
To set off a summary statement	A good scholastic record and good political connections—if you have these, you may be able to get a job in a congressional office.

Words such as *all*, *these*, *those*, *this*, and *that* will often be found at or near the beginning of a summary sentence preceded by a dash.

✿ Grammar and Style Tip

Avoid the frequent use of dashes simply to replace commas and periods. Even in informal writing, overuse of dashes will look haphazard and may even confuse your meaning.

> **KEY CONCEPT** Use dashes to set off a nonessential appositive or modifier when it is long, when it is already punctuated, or when you want to be dramatic. ■

Although they are usually set off with commas, nonessential appositives and modifiers may also be set off with dashes.

APPOSITIVES: Two Japanese islands—Honshu and Hokkaido—were the group's destinations.

Yesterday, I met three old neighbors from Osaka—Kenji Oe, his brother Nobuo, and their friend Shizuo Akiyama—and learned about all the changes in the old neighborhood. Some students—for example, Mitsuye, Fran, and Kevin—always do well on tests.

MODIFIERS: Mount Fuji—which is called *Fujiyama* in Japanese—can be seen from many places in Tokyo. Matsushika Hokusai (1760–1849)— who was a master Japanese painter and wood engraver—produced numerous works featuring Mount Fuji.

Dashes may be used to set off one other special type of sentence interrupter—the parenthetical expression.

> **KEY CONCEPT** Use dashes to set off a parenthetical expression when it is long, already punctuated, or especially dramatic. ■

EXAMPLES: The searing heat—it was ninety all last week, and on Monday and Tuesday of this week it was over one hundred—has forced many of the citizens of Tokyo to stay indoors.
The sushi—have you ever seen such an elaborate presentation of food?—was an unusual taste experience.

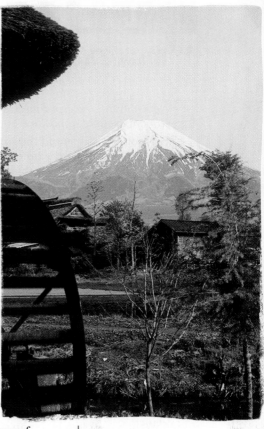

▲ **Critical Viewing** Mt. Fuji's last volcanic eruption was in 1708. What might happen to Tokyo if the volcano were to become active again? Answer in a sentence, using dashes to set off a dramatic parenthetical expression. **[Speculate]**

GRAMMAR IN LITERATURE

from *The Story of an Hour*
Kate Chopin

Notice in this excerpt that Kate Chopin uses a dash to set off a nonessential appositive in the last sentence.

Someone was opening the front door with a latchkey. It was Brently Mallard who entered, a little travel-stained, composedly carrying his gripsack and umbrella. He had been far from the scene of accident, and did not know there had been one. He stood amazed at Josephine's piercing cry; at Richards's quick motion to screen him from the view of his wife.

But Richards was too late.

When the doctors came they said she had died of heart disease—of joy that kills.

▶ **Exercise 56** Revising to Supply Dashes Revise the following sentences, inserting dashes where appropriate.

EXAMPLE: Tokyo is Japan's most populous city more than eighteen million people inhabit it.

ANSWER: Tokyo is Japan's most populous city—more than eighteen million people inhabit it.

1. The history and culture of Japan I could study it for days! is unique and interesting.
2. The Japanese call their country *Dai Nippon* Great Land of the Sun.
3. Japan was founded according to legend in 660 B.C.
4. The country consists of four main islands Honshu, Kyushu, Shikoku, and Hokkaido and hundreds of smaller islands.
5. Of these, Honshu thought of as the mainland is the largest.
6. Fujiyama what a sight! is the tallest mountain in Japan.
7. Tens of thousands of people are drawn to the mountain every year to witness its majesty it is the cultural heart of Japan.
8. Natural disasters especially earthquakes and tsunamis have plagued Japan throughout its history.
9. In 1995, an earthquake which originated north of the cities of Nagasaki and Minamata struck the city of Kobe.
10. Japan is densely populated more than 126 million people live in an area smaller than the state of Texas.

▶ **More Practice**

Grammar Exercise Workbook
• pp. 161–162
On-line Exercise Bank
• Section 27.5
Go on-line:
PHSchool.com
Enter Web Code:
efk-1102

Get instant feedback! Exercises 56 and 57 are available on-line or on CD-ROM.

▶ **Exercise 57** More Revising to Supply Dashes Revise the following sentences, inserting dashes where appropriate.

1. Several cities in Japan Yokohama is one example have populations of well over two million people.
2. Kyoto an ancient, culturally significant city that dates back to the eighth century was the capital of Japan until the 1860's.
3. Today, Tokyo located on the island of Honshu is the country's capital.
4. Tokyo an enormous modern city rivals New York and London.
5. Ethnic Japanese make up the bulk of the country's population more than 99 percent but a small number of other cultures are represented as well.
6. Most Japanese practice the religions of Shinto or Buddhism less than one percent of the population is Christian.
7. Theater in Japan Kabuki, Noh, and Bunraku are the three main types is an important part of Japanese culture.
8. The Japanese are also avid sports fans more than fifteen million people attend baseball games each year.
9. Rice is an essential food in Japan most people eat at least two servings every day.
10. The Japanese are steeped in culture and tradition, yet they are leading the way into the twenty-first century they are on the cutting edge of technology.

Technology Tip

To form a dash when using a word processor, place two hyphens between the words that will be set apart by the dash. Do not include any spacing. Many programs will draw the two hyphens together to form a dash.
You can also go to the Help feature in your word processor to learn how to make dashes by using the keyboard.

◀ Critical Viewing A dash may be used to set off an abrupt change in thought. How might the sights and sounds in a busy city like Tokyo cause many abrupt changes in the thoughts of a person walking down this street? [Connect]

Parentheses

Parentheses are used to enclose material in a sentence or a paragraph. Although commas are generally used for this purpose, parentheses are preferred in certain cases. Parentheses are the strongest separators a writer can use. Because of their strength, they should be used infrequently.

Basic Uses of Parentheses

Parentheses are most often used to set off asides or explanatory information. Even here, caution must be used.

▶ **KEY CONCEPT** Use parentheses to set off asides and explanations only when the material consists of one or more sentences, or when the material is not essential. ■

EXAMPLES: There are many three- and five-story wooden pagodas in the Kansai area of Japan. (In the distant past, there were even seven- and nine-story pagodas.)

Despite many powerful earthquakes (including the disastrous earthquake of 1995), there are almost no records reporting the collapse of these ancient high-rises.

▶ **KEY CONCEPT** Use parentheses to set off numerical explanations such as dates of a person's birth and death and around numbers and letters marking a series. ■

EXAMPLES: Akira Kurosawa (1910–1998) was an internationally celebrated Japanese filmmaker.
The committee can be reached at (607) 555-3001.
My teacher ranks our great presidents in this way: (1) Abraham Lincoln, (2) George Washington, (3) Theodore Roosevelt, (4) Thomas Jefferson, and (5) Franklin D. Roosevelt.
Her report on energy will deal with the use of (a) wood, (b) coal, (c) oil, and (d) solar power.

▲ Critical Viewing This photo suggests a sense of stillness and reflection. Write an example of how parentheses can be used to include an aside or a reflection within a sentence. **[Relate]**

Other Punctuation Marks Used With Parentheses

Sometimes parentheses and other punctuation marks are used together. Several rules govern these uses.

▶ **KEY CONCEPT** When a phrase or declarative sentence interrupts another sentence, do not use an initial capital or end mark inside the parentheses. ■

EXAMPLE: Sarah (she has always loved animals) took in the stray kitten and fed it.

▶ **KEY CONCEPT** When a question or exclamation interrupts another sentence, use both an initial capital and an end mark inside the parentheses. ■

EXAMPLES: The car (Do you think we could be out of gas?) won't start.
On Sunday (What a beautiful day it was!) we climbed to the top of Bald Mountain and had a picnic.

When a sentence in parentheses falls between two other sentences, use the following rule:

▶ **KEY CONCEPT** With any sentence that falls between two complete sentences, use both an initial capital and an end mark inside the parentheses. ■

EXAMPLE: I started working on Saturday morning for a florist. (It was difficult to get up so early.) My duties include arranging flowers and delivering them all over town.

▶ **KEY CONCEPT** In a sentence with a set-off phrase, place any punctuation belonging to the main sentence after the parentheses. ■

EXAMPLES: When I arrived (about two o'clock), he was waiting.

The artist had finally accepted the invitation to exhibit his works (after having been invited twice before); therefore, he spent the summer preparing the material for display.

⚙ **Grammar and Style Tip**

Parentheses should be used sparingly because they interrupt the flow of your writing. In most instances, the information should be worked into the body of your writing.

Exercise 58 Revising to Supply Parentheses Revise the following items, adding parentheses, any other punctuation marks, and capitals where necessary. Underline the words that are in italics.

More Practice

Grammar Exercise Workbook
• pp. 163–164
On-line Exercise Bank
• Section 27.5
Go on-line:
PHSchool.com
Enter Web Code:
efk-1102

EXAMPLE: Tickets for the play are hard to get it is a play I have wanted to see for a long time! we finally were able to get some for next week.

ANSWER: Tickets for the play are hard to get. (It is a play I have wanted to see for a long time!) We finally were able to get some for next week.

1. The Japanese flag called *Hinomaru* depicts the rising sun.
2. General Douglas MacArthur 1880–1964 supervised the occupation of Japan at the end of World War II.
3. The three main types of traditional Japanese theater are a Kabuki, b Noh, and c Bunraku.
4. The worst natural disaster to strike modern Japan was the Great Kanto Earthquake more than 100,000 people were killed in 1923.
5. I believe the phone number for the Japanese consulate is 800 555-0000.
6. The *Kojiki* which means Record of Ancient Matters is the oldest collection of writings in Japan.
7. Learning to read and write Japanese is difficult there are more than three thousand characters to learn!, but learning to speak Japanese is even more difficult.
8. The emperor of Japan Akihito is the emperor I read about is largely a symbolic position today.
9. Japan's enormous population 126 million people lives in an area that is significantly smaller than the state of Texas.
10. Tokyo will it ever stop growing? is one of the most densely populated cities in the world.

▲ Critical Viewing The traditional clothing shown here suggests a different time. How can text within parentheses evoke a different time from the rest of the sentence? **[Infer]**

Brackets

Brackets have one major use: to enclose a word or words inserted by a writer into a quotation from someone else.

KEY CONCEPT Use brackets to enclose a word or words you insert in a quotation when you are quoting someone else. ■

EXAMPLE: Edmund Morris describes an attempt by Theodore Roosevelt to feed his hungry regiment during the Spanish-American War. "On the morning of June 26 [1898], Roosevelt got wind of a stockpile of beans on the beach [in Cuba] and marched a squad of men hastily down to investigate."

Brackets are sometimes also used with the Latin expression *sic* (meaning "thus") in a quotation to show that the original writer misspelled or misused a word or phrase. The expression *sic* calls attention to the original form used by the author.

EXAMPLE: As a recommendation, he wrote, "He don't [sic] lie."

Exercise 59 Using Brackets Copy the following items, adding brackets where you find them most appropriate.

EXAMPLE: "The results of this vote 98–2 indicate overwhelming support for our proposal," he stated.

ANSWER: "The results of this vote [98–2] indicate overwhelming support for our proposal," he stated.

1. The misprinted guide book read, "Tokeo is a fast-paced, ultra-modern city with much to see and do."
2. At a monument in Hiroshima, Japan, the words, "Rest in peace. The mistake nuclear war shall not be made again," are inscribed on a small plaque.
3. "We the Japanese people have resolved to endure the unendurable and suffer what is insufferable." —Emperor Hirohito
4. "People with high ideals don't necessarily make good politicians. If it noble politics is so important, we should leave the job to the scientists and the clergy." —Michio Watanabe
5. "You will find the same label Made in Japan on the back of many computers, stereos, televisions, and cameras."

Grammar and Style Tip

Do not misuse brackets in place of parentheses. Brackets should be used only to insert new words into material that has been directly quoted. They inform the reader that you have added words that will clarify information taken from other sources.

More Practice

Grammar Exercise Workbook
• pp. 165–166
On-line Exercise Bank
• Section 27.5
  Go on-line:
  PHSchool.com
  Enter Web Code:
  efk-1102

Interactive Textbook

Get instant feedback! Exercises 58 and 59 are available on-line or on CD-ROM.

Hyphens

Hyphens are used to join certain numbers and parts of words, to join some compound words, and to divide words at the ends of lines. Although it resembles the dash, the hyphen is distinctly shorter. In handwritten material, be sure to make your hyphens half as long as your dashes. In typewritten material, use one hyphen mark for a hyphen (-) and two hyphen marks for a dash (--).

Hyphens are used with numbers, word parts, and compound words.

Numbers Hyphens help to make the meaning of compound numbers clear.

▶ **KEY CONCEPT** Use a hyphen when writing out the numbers *twenty-one* through *ninety-nine*. ■

EXAMPLES:　thirty-three inches　forty-seven acres

▶ **KEY CONCEPT** Use a hyphen with fractions used as adjectives. ■

EXAMPLES:　one-half inch　three-fifths majority

If a fraction is used as a noun instead of an adjective, the hyphen is not used.

EXAMPLE:　*Three quarters* of the report on Japan is completed.

Word Parts Certain word parts are also joined by hyphens.

Use a hyphen after a prefix that is followed by a proper noun or adjective.

EXAMPLES:　pro-Japanese　all-American　mid-October

Certain prefixes are often found before proper nouns and proper adjectives. They include the following: *ante-, anti-, mid-, post-, pre-, pro-,* and *un-*.

Three other prefixes and one suffix are always used with a hyphen.

▶ **KEY CONCEPT** Use a hyphen in words with the prefixes *all-, ex-,* and *self-* and words with the suffix *-elect.* ■

EXAMPLES:　all-powerful　　　　ex-football player
self-adjusting brakes　president-elect

Compound Words Hyphens are also used to join some compound words.

KEY CONCEPT Use a hyphen to connect two or more words that are used as one word unless the dictionary gives a contrary spelling. ■

Some compound nouns are written as one word, others are written as separate words, and still others are joined by a hyphen. If you are uncertain as to how a compound word should be spelled, consult a dictionary.

EXAMPLES: brother-in-law
             two-year-olds
             secretary-treasurer
             jack-of-all-trades

Compound modifiers, as well as compound nouns, sometimes require hyphens.

▲ **Critical Viewing** Hyphens are used to join certain numbers and words. What common elements— such as history, culture, or interests— join many of the people pictured here? **[Connect]**

KEY CONCEPT Use a hyphen to connect a compound modifier that comes *before* a noun unless it includes a word ending in *-ly* or is a compound proper adjective or compound proper noun acting as an adjective. ■

EXAMPLES   a strong-willed businessman
WITH HYPHENS: an up-to-date design
                  well-attended Japanese festival

EXAMPLES   a highly unlikely suspect
WITHOUT HYPHENS: the North American continent

Although compound adjectives in front of a noun are usually hyphenated, a hyphen is generally not needed when compound adjectives follow a noun.

EXAMPLE: The Japanese festival is *well attended.*

If your dictionary spells a word with hyphens, however, that word always should be hyphenated.

EXAMPLE: That design is *up-to-date.*

For Clarity Another use of hyphens is to prevent the misreading of a word or group of words.

▶**KEY CONCEPT** Use a hyphen within a word when a combination of letters might otherwise be confusing. ■

EXAMPLES: a bell-like sound   a semi-invalid
            a re-served ball   an expensive co-op

▶**KEY CONCEPT** Use a hyphen between words when necessary for clarity. ■

EXAMPLES: The *new-car owner* worried about potholes.
            The *new car-owner* was proud of her acquisition.

▶**Exercise 60** Using Hyphens to Combine Words Copy each item that needs hyphenation, adding hyphens where necessary. If an item does not require a hyphen, write *correct*.

EXAMPLE: Japanese speaking guest
ANSWER: Japanese-speaking guest

1. high scoring player
2. pre Cambrian
3. ex governor
4. little known fact
5. South American continent
6. one tenth of a mile
7. pro American
8. unusually warm summer
9. mother in law
10. post war

Using Hyphens at the Ends of Lines

Although you should try not to divide a word at the end of a line, sometimes it is necessary. Certain rules can help you divide words correctly when you must divide them.

The most important rule involves dividing words between syllables.

▶**KEY CONCEPT** If a word must be divided, always divide it between syllables. ■

Never divide one-syllable words. When you divide a word of more than one syllable, place the hyphen at the end of the first line. Also, take care never to use a hyphen at the end of the last line on a page. If you are unsure of how to divide a word into syllables, consult a dictionary.

EXAMPLE: Did you finish the difficult American history assignment that was due today?

⚙ **Grammar and Style Tip**

Although they look similar, do not confuse hyphens with dashes. Hyphens are used to join words together, and dashes are used to separate different thoughts.

💻 **Internet Tip**

If you cannot reach a Web site that contains a hyphen in its address, check to make sure that you have not added unnecessary spacing. Even one space within a hyphenated word will make the address incorrect.

▶ **KEY CONCEPT** Prefixes and suffixes provide natural places for division. If a word contains word parts, it can almost always be divided between the prefix and the root or the root and the suffix. ■

PREFIX: ex-tract   in-dent
SUFFIX: care-less   play-ful

▶ **KEY CONCEPT** Do not divide a word so that a single letter or the letters *-ed* stand alone. ■

INCORRECT: hast-y   a-round   i-dentity   chas-ed
CORRECT: hasty   around   iden-tity   chased

▶ **KEY CONCEPT** Avoid dividing proper nouns and proper adjectives. ■

INCORRECT: Jeff-rey   Euro-pean
CORRECT: Jeffrey   European

▶ **KEY CONCEPT** Divide a hyphenated word only after the hyphen. ■

INCORRECT: I would like to introduce you to our new ed-itor-in-chief.
CORRECT: I would like to introduce you to our new editor-in-chief.

▶ **Exercise 61** Using Hyphens to Divide Words at the Ends of Lines If a word has been divided as it should be if it appeared at the end of a line, write *correct*. If it has been divided incorrectly, write the word as it should appear.

EXAMPLE: dre-am
ANSWER: dream

1. Japan-ese
2. dolph-in
3. employ-ed
4. in-tellect
5. yel-low
6. mou-se
7. Geor-gia
8. ex-cruciating
9. gre-en
10. com-puter

○ Learn More

Refer to Chapter 26 on capitalization to learn more about using the hyphen with proper nouns.

▶ **More Practice**

Grammar Exercise Workbook
• pp. 167–168
On-line Exercise Bank
• Section 27.5
  Go on-line:
  PHSchool.com
  Enter Web Code:
  efk-1102

Get instant feedback! Exercises 60 and 61 are available on-line or on CD-ROM.

GRAMMAR EXERCISES 62–70

▶ **Exercise 62** Revising to Supply
Dashes Revise the following sentences, adding dashes where appropriate.

1. Tokyo do you know much about it? is the largest city in Japan.
2. In actuality, there is no such place as the city of Tokyo how can that be? because the government has designated it a special administrative unit and not a city.
3. The city's name was changed in the 1800's it used to be called Edo.
4. It became the capital of Japan Kyoto had been the capital in 1868.
5. The Imperial Palace where the emperor of Japan lives is located in the center of the city.
6. Located nearby are many government buildings, including the National Diet Building Japan's legislature.
7. The Kanda Shrine one of the oldest and most highly attended in Tokyo is known for festivals that celebrate the traditions of the city.
8. An important business center for many countries the United States, France, and Great Britain are just a few Tokyo is at the heart of international trade.
9. The city's economy it supports more than eight million workers gains its strength from more than 800,000 businesses.
10. Government buildings, religious sanctuaries, and large corporations all these things make Tokyo a vital city.

▶ **Exercise 63** Revising to Supply
Parentheses Revise the following sentences, adding parentheses where appropriate.

1. Edo which means "Gate of the Inlet" was the original name of Tokyo.

2. The history of Tokyo dates back to the twelfth century and the rise of the first shogun he was Minamoto Yoritomo.
3. Minamoto Yoritomo won a civil war, which gave rise to centuries 700 years of shogun rule.
4. In 1457, General Ota Dokan he was also a shogun built a fortress known as Edo Castle.
5. The Tokugawa clan ruled over Edo for 250 years 1603–1854.
6. In 1657, a major fire ravaged much of the city Edo Castle was destroyed.
7. By the middle of the eighteenth century, Edo was a great city with a large poulation more than one million people.
8. The city was plagued by yet another fire the tragic event occurred in 1872, which devastated the portion of the city known as Ginza.
9. During the period called the Meiji Restoration 1868–1913, Edo was renamed Tokyo, and it became the nation's capital.
10. Since then, Tokyo which also became the nation's capital has been at the forefront of modernization in Japan.

▶ **Exercise 64** Revising to Supply
Brackets Revise the following sentences, adding brackets where appropriate.

1. Their history teacher told them, "For tonight's homework, read the section about America's war with Japan World War II."
2. "Because so few of you speak the language Japanese, I will act as a translator," the tour guide said.
3. Will Adams, an Englishman who came to Japan in 1600, told the great shogun Ieyasu of England's wars with "the Spaniards and the Portugals."

4. At the news conference, the President said, "When he the Japanese Foreign Trade Minister arrives later this week, I hope to discuss the trade imbalance between our two countries."

5. Describing the arrival of Matthew Perry's squadron in Japan, author Noel Busch wrote, "On July 8, his four ships, bristling with bigger guns than any Japanese had seen before, swung . . . into Edo Bay." (using brackets, insert the date 1853)

▶ **Exercise 65** Using Hyphens to Combine Words Copy each of the following items, adding hyphens where necessary. If an item does not require a hyphen, write *correct.*

1. twenty seven
2. self made millionaire
3. happily married couple
4. pre Revolutionary War
5. post modern art
6. multi colored flag
7. two family house
8. one fourth cup
9. North Carolina mountains
10. much needed assistance
11. three hundred forty three
12. one half of the class
13. self cleaning oven
14. South China Sea
15. well done assignment

▶ **Exercise 66** Using Hyphens to Divide Words at the Ends of Lines Assume that the following words fall at the end of a line. If they are properly divided with a hyphen, write *correct.* If the hyphen has been used incorrectly, write the word as it should appear at the end of a line.

1. excit-ed
2. help-ful
3. ha-mmer
4. Ger-man
5. win-ner

6. lo-ose
7. nine-teen
8. Mich-ael
9. si-mple
10. blu-ish

▶ **Exercise 67** Writing Sentences With Parentheses, Dashes, Brackets, and Hyphens Write sentences according to the following instructions.

1. Use parentheses in a sentence about your elementary school.
2. Use dashes in a sentence about two movies you'd like to see.
3. In a sentence describing a person, use a hyphen in a compound adjective preceding a noun.
4. Quote a friend or a family member, adding some clarifying information in brackets.

▶ **Exercise 68** Find It in Your Reading Look through the excerpt from *Hiroshima* in your literature book, and find three examples of the use of dashes, parentheses, brackets, or hyphens. Write down each one, and explain which rule it illustrates.

▶ **Exercise 69** Find It in Your Writing Look through your portfolio for examples of the use of dashes, parentheses, brackets, or hyphens. Determine whether or not these punctuation marks are necessary and, if so, whether they are used correctly. Make all necessary corrections.

▶ **Exercise 70** Writing Application Reread the excerpt from "The Story of an Hour" on page 568, and write a one-paragraph summary of it. In your paragraph, correctly use dashes, parentheses, brackets, or hyphens at least three times.

Apostrophes

Pay close attention to the meaning of each of the following rules for using apostrophes. Then, study the examples illustrating each rule carefully.

Forming Possessives of Nouns

An apostrophe is used to show possession or ownership. The location of the apostrophe depends upon the characteristics of the noun.

Singular Nouns The first rule involves the use of the apostrophe with singular nouns.

> **KEY CONCEPT** Add an apostrophe and *-s* to show the possessive case of most singular nouns. ■

EXAMPLES:
the book of the girl   the girl's book
the leaf of the shrub   the shrub's leaf
the crib of the baby   the baby's crib
the check of the waitress   the waitress's check

Notice that a singular noun ending in *-s* usually uses an apostrophe and an *-s* to form the possessive. The only exceptions are classical and biblical names, which add only an apostrophe to form the possessive.

EXAMPLES:
Moses' brother
Hercules' strength

Plural Nouns Two rules are necessary to form the possessive case of plural nouns. First, there is a rule for forming the possessive case of plural nouns ending in *-s* or *-es*. Second, there is a rule for plurals that do not end in an *-s* or *-es*.

> **KEY CONCEPT** Add an apostrophe to show the possessive case of plural nouns ending in *-s* or *-es*. ■

EXAMPLES:
the shirts of the boys   the boys' shirts
the figures in the charts   the charts' figures
the groups in the classes   the classes' groups

> **KEY CONCEPT** Add an apostrophe and an *-s* to show the possessive case of plural nouns that do not end in *-s* or *-es*. ■

EXAMPLES:
the suits of the men   the men's suits
the toys of the children   the children's toys

Compound Nouns A compound noun contains two or more words. To form a possessive of a compound noun, use the following rule.

▶ **KEY CONCEPT** Add an apostrophe and an -*s* (or just an apostrophe if the word is a plural ending in -*s*) to the last word of a compound noun to form the possessive. ■

The following examples illustrate some of the different kinds of compound nouns commonly used to form possessives.

NAMES OF BUSINESSES AND ORGANIZATIONS:	Major and Marker's baby powder the Red Cross's volunteers Ozu and Sons' Electronics
TITLES OF RULERS AND LEADERS:	King George III's army the Chief Justice's decision Shogun Yoritomo's decree
HYPHENATED COMPOUND NOUNS:	my father-in-law's ranch the secretary-treasurer's report

Expressions Involving Time and Amounts These expressions also require the use of apostrophes.

▶ **KEY CONCEPT** To form possessives involving time and amounts, use an apostrophe and -*s* or just an apostrophe if the possessive is plural. ■

TIME:	a month's vacation three months' work
AMOUNT:	a dime's worth three dimes' worth

💡 **Spelling Tip**

To form the plural possessive of most nouns ending in *ife*, such as *knife* and *wife*, the *ife* is dropped and *ives* is added. An apostrophe follows the *s* to form *knives'* and *wives'*.

▶ **Critical Viewing** Yoritomo was the first shogun—or military ruler. The title then was passed down from generation to generation. Using possessive nouns, describe a possible order of descent. **[Speculate]**

Apostrophes • 581

Joint and Individual Ownership Sometimes people share ownership, and sometimes several people claim individual ownership. The difference affects the use of the apostrophe.

> **KEY CONCEPT** To show joint ownership, make the final noun possessive. To show individual ownership, make each noun possessive. ■

JOINT OWNERSHIP:	Will and Martin's dog, a greyhound, has won a number of prizes.
INDIVIDUAL OWNERSHIP:	Susan's, Marie's, and Alice's papers were graded by the teacher.

> **Exercise 71** **Proofreading to Correct Apostrophes in Possessive Nouns** Revise the following sentences, correcting the possessive form wherever necessary. If a sentence contains no error, write *correct*.

EXAMPLE: I bought five dollar's worth of stamps.
ANSWER: I bought five dollars' worth of stamps.

1. One of natures most destructive forces is the earthquake.
2. Japans' people have been plagued by earthquakes throughout their history.
3. The countries' islands are situated on top of fault lines.
4. Fault lines are areas where the massive portions of Earth's crust, called tectonic plates, bump against each other.
5. The plate's bumping causes shock waves to ripple through the ground, thus creating an earthquake.
6. In 1923, an earthquake ravaged huge parts of Tokyo, Honshu Islands largest city, and the port of Yokohama.
7. The earthquakes' force leveled much of both cities.
8. Peoples' homes were destroyed, and buildings were toppled.
9. Tokyo and Yokohama's casualties numbered more than 100,000.
10. The governments' response was to rebuild the city, engineering most buildings to withstand future earthquakes.
11. The architect Frank Lloyd Wrights Imperial Hotel survived the quake and won praise for its construction technology.
12. Kobes' earthquake in 1995 killed 3,600 people and destroyed 55,000 homes.
13. The earthquake caused more than 100 billion dollar's worth of damage.
14. Businesses, hospitals, and childrens' schools were caught in the devastation.
15. The areas geologic history shows that a powerful earthquake had hit at almost the same spot in 1916.

> **More Practice**
>
> Grammar Exercise Workbook
> • pp. 169–170
> On-line Exercise Bank
> • Section 27.6
>   *Go on-line:*
>   PHSchool.com
>   *Enter Web Code:*
>   efk-1102

Get instant feedback! Exercise 71 is available on-line or on CD-ROM.

Forming Possessives of Pronouns

Two additional rules are needed to show possession with indefinite pronouns and personal pronouns. Indefinite pronouns require the use of an apostrophe and an -*s* to show possession.

▶ **KEY CONCEPT** Use an apostrophe and an -*s* with indefinite pronouns to show possession. ■

EXAMPLES:	nobody's turn	somebody's house key
	one's homework	each other's handkerchiefs
	everybody's friend	one another's bathing caps

Notice in the last two examples that an apostrophe and an -*s* are added only to the last word of a two-word pronoun.

A different rule applies when the possessives of personal pronouns are formed.

▶ **KEY CONCEPT** Do not use an apostrophe with the possessive forms of personal pronouns. ■

The possessive forms of personal pronouns (*his, hers, its, ours, yours, theirs,* and so on) already show possession. Thus, they do not need apostrophes.

EXAMPLES:	*his* old car
	that hobby of *hers*
	its tail
	that house of *ours*
	that paper of *yours*
	that responsibility of *theirs*

Do not confuse the contractions *who's, it's,* and *they're* with possessive pronouns. *Who's, it's,* and *they're* are contractions for *who is* or *who has, it is* or *it has,* and *they are.* Remember that *whose, its,* and *their* show possession.

| PRONOUNS: | *Whose* homes were damaged? |
| | *Its* tremors were felt many miles away. |

| CONTRACTIONS: | *Who's* aware of the extent of the devastation in Kobe? |
| | *It's* the site of a terrible earthquake. |

▼ **Critical Viewing** This expressway was toppled by the Kobe earthquake. What do you think were some of the immediate effects on people living and working nearby? Include possessive indefinite pronouns in your answer. **[Draw Conclusions]**

▶ **Exercise 72** Using Apostrophes Correctly With Pronouns
Copy each of the following sentences, choosing the correct
possessive form from the choices in parentheses.

EXAMPLE: I need (somebody else's, somebody elses')
opinion.

ANSWER: I need somebody else's opinion.

1. While touring the country of Japan, we visited some of
   (its, it's) cultural and historical sites.
2. We went to see the Buddhist temple in Nara, where monks
   practice (they're, their) religion.
3. We tried not to disturb (anyone's, anyones') activities.
4. It is hard to believe that a monk might spend (his, he's)
   entire life there.
5. We also went to see Edo Castle, built by a warlord (who's,
   whose) name I can't remember.

Forming Contractions

A contraction is formed by removing a letter or letters from
a word or phrase and replacing the missing letter(s) with an
apostrophe.

Contractions With Verbs The most common type of contraction involves verbs.

COMMON CONTRACTIONS WITH VERBS		
Verbs with *not*	cannot	can't
	should not	shouldn't
	were not	weren't
	will not	won't
Pronouns with *will* or *shall*	she will	she'll
	we shall	we'll
Pronouns with *would*	he would	he'd
	they would	they'd
Pronouns with *have*	we have	we've
	they have	they've
Pronouns or Nouns With the Verb *be*	I am	I'm
	you are	you're
	she is	she's
	Michael is	Michael's

Notice that *will not* in the preceding chart becomes *won't*, changing
letters as well as replacing letters with an apostrophe.

▶ **More Practice**
Grammar Exercise
Workbook
• pp. 169–170
On-line Exercise Bank
• Section 27.6
  Go on-line:
  PHSchool.com
  Enter Web Code:
  efk-1102

Interactive Textbook

Get instant feedback!
Exercises 72 and 73
are available on-line
or on CD-ROM.

Learn More

For additional infor-
mation about using
possessive pronouns,
see Chapter 22.

KEY CONCEPT Contractions should be used sparingly in formal writing. Reserve them to add flavor to dialogue. In other cases, write out the words. ■

Contractions With Numbers and Poetry Contractions are sometimes used in informal writing to replace the century portion of a year.

EXAMPLES: the class of '03   the blizzard of '98

Contractions are sometimes used in poetry to achieve a poetic effect.

EXAMPLES: e'en (for *even*)   o'er (for *over*)

Contractions With *o', d', and l'* The letter *o* followed by an apostrophe makes up the abbreviated form of the words *of the*. The letters *d* and *l* mean *of* or *of the* when used as a contraction with a proper name, often from a language such as French, Italian, or Spanish.

EXAMPLES: o'clock   O'Sullivan   d'Angelo   *l'Abbe*

These contractions are used most often with surnames.

Contractions in Dialogue When writing dialogue, use any contractions the speaker might use to give the flavor of the speaker's style. You may also want to include a regional dialect or a foreign accent. Because these often include unusual pronunciations involving omitted letters, you may have to insert apostrophes to indicate omitted letters.

EXAMPLES: 'Tis a long way you'll have to be goin'.
              Don' you be afoolin' me.

Overuse of the apostrophe reduces its effectiveness. Thus, you should not overuse it—even in dialogue.

Exercise 73 Using Apostrophes in Contractions Write the contraction for each of the following items.

EXAMPLE: should not
ANSWER: shouldn't

1. should have
2. I am
3. we will
4. he is
5. we are
6. they have
7. would not
8. it is
9. 1957
10. Maggie is

Grammar and Style Tip

When proper nouns contain contractions, always check to make sure they are correctly punctuated and capitalized. Sometimes, a name will contain a capital on both sides of an apostrophe, as in *O'Mara*.

Hands-on Grammar

Contractions Slide

Use a Contractions Slide to review which letters are dropped and where apostrophes belong in common contractions. Start by cutting out three strips of paper, 1" wide and about 14" long; number them *1, 2, 3*. On each strip, print several of the words from the following lists. Make all the letters the same size and equally spaced.

STRIP 1	**STRIP 2**	**STRIP 3**
ISNOT	IHAVE	IWOULD
ARENOT	SHEWILL	YOUWOULD
DIDNOT	WEHAVE	HEWOULD
WERENOT	YOUARE	WEWOULD
COULDNOT	YOUWILL	THEYWOULD

Next, take a piece of 6-1/2" x 8-1/2" paper, and cut three narrow pairs of 1" slits in it about 3" from the right-hand edge. The width of the space between the first pair of slits should be that of one print-ed letter; the second pair, the width of two letters; and the third pair, the width of four letters. (You should be able to weave the strips of paper through the slits.) Then, in the middle of each pair of slits, draw a large apostrophe. (See the illustration.)

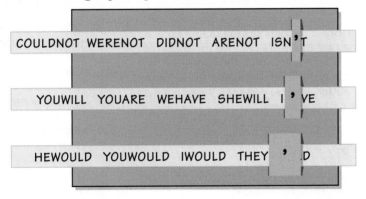

Finally, slide strip *1* through the top pair of slits, stopping each time the apostrophe covers the *o* in not. Repeat with strip *2*, stopping where the apostrophe covers the third and fourth letters from the end; and with strip *3*, stopping when the apostrophe covers the letters *woul*. Each time, what will remain is the proper form of a contraction. Write other words on the backs of the strips, and continue reviewing contractions on your Contractions Slide.

Find It in Your Reading Review a magazine article or short story, and note the frequency and types of contractions used.

Find It in Your Writing Review a piece of your writing, making sure you have used and formed contractions correctly.

Section 27.6 *Section Review*

GRAMMAR EXERCISES 74–78

Exercise 74 **Proofreading for All the Rules for Apostrophes** Revise the following sentences, using apostrophes to form contractions, possessive nouns, and possessive pronouns where appropriate. In addition, revise any incorrect use of apostrophes.

1. Ive had fun in my film class, but now that were studying director Akira Kurosawas movies, Im enjoying it even more.
2. He didnt plan to become one of Japans most important directors.
3. Hed produce fifty years worth of movies before his death in 1998.
4. Its said that his ancestry can be traced back to ancient Japans samurai warriors.
5. However, nobodys certain about this information.
6. Kurosawas best known for the movies *Rashomon, The Seven Samurai,* and *Ran.*
7. Theyll be considered classics long after weve seen them.
8. Kurosawa turned two of Shakespeares plays into movies, and hes also adapted one of Russian author Fyodor Dostoyevskys novels.
9. Weve watched all three of them, and theyve become favorites of ours'.
10. Its obvious that in the film business, everyones always borrowing from somebody elses work.

Exercise 75 **Writing Sentences With Possessives and Contractions** Following the instructions in each item, write sentences that use possessives or contractions. Use apostrophes as needed.

1. Describe the singing voice of a friend, using his or her name.

2. Write a sentence about something you will or would do.
3. Ask a question in an attempt to find out the owner of a lost item. Use the possessive of an indefinite pronoun.
4. Write a sentence announcing that you will arrive somewhere at noon. Spell out the time.
5. Write a sentence describing identical jackets belonging to two friends. Name both friends.

Exercise 76 **Find It in Your Reading** Look around your hometown or school for signs, posters, and other printed materials that might contain apostrophes. Write down five examples and the rules they illustrate. If an apostrophe is used incorrectly, explain why, and then correct the error.

Exercise 77 **Find It in Your Writing** Look through your portfolio for five examples of apostrophes. Write down the sentence in which each word appears, and then trade papers with a partner. Refer to the rules explained in this section, and mark any apostrophes that are used incorrectly.

Exercise 78 **Writing Application** Choose a part of Japanese culture or history mentioned in this chapter that you find interesting. Read more about it in the library or on the Internet, and then write a one-paragraph summary of the information you found. Use at least three apostrophes in your paragraph.

3

Academic and Workplace Skills

Eight A.M., 1993, Andrew Stevivich, Adelson Galleries, Inc.

Academic and Workplace Skills • **589**

Speaking, Listening, Viewing, and Representing

Speaker, 1996, Diana Ong

Written work is only one avenue for sending and receiving information. Much of what you need to comprehend comes to you aurally or through visual representation. To understand and remember effectively, you must learn to listen and view accurately and critically. It is also important that you learn to give information orally and visually. By developing your skills in speaking, listening, viewing, and representing, this chapter will help increase your effectiveness as a communicator.

Speaking
and Listening Skills

Speaking and listening are forms of communication you use every day. In certain situations, however, special skills and strategies can increase the effectiveness of your communication. The concepts and strategies offered in this section will help you improve both your speaking and listening skills.

Speaking in a Group Discussion

A **group discussion** is an informal meeting of people that is used to openly discuss ideas and topics. The group discussions you participate in will, for the most part, involve your classmates and focus on the subjects you are studying. To benefit the most from a group discussion, you need to learn to participate in it.

▶ **KEY CONCEPT** A group discussion is a good way to express your opinions, as well as to hear the opinions of others, in an informal setting. ∎

Communicate Effectively Before you speak, think about the points you want to make and which words will best express them. Organize these points in logical order. Recall examples or supporting facts to illustrate your points as you speak. Also, remember to speak clearly, pronouncing words slowly and carefully.

Ask Questions Asking questions is valuable for two reasons. The first reason is to enhance your understanding of another speaker's ideas. The second reason is to ask questions to call attention to possible errors in other speakers' points.

Make Relevant Contributions Stay focused on the topic being discussed. Relate discussion points to your own experience and knowledge. When you contribute information or ideas, make clear how your contributions are connected to the topic.

▶ **Exercise 1** Holding a Group Discussion With three to five other students, hold a 15-minute group discussion about a topic you are studying in class. Review some relevant material from your textbooks to generate ideas and supporting information for your statements.

▶ **More Practice**

Academic and
Workplace Skills
Activity Book
• p. 1

Speaking in Public

Public speaking usually refers to the presentation of a speech before an audience. Getting a speech ready requires more preparation than is needed for a group discussion. The more time you invest in preparing and practicing your speech, the better your audience will receive it.

Research Tip

Look in encyclopedias or biographical references to learn about great speakers of the twentieth century.

Recognize Different Kinds of Speeches

The kind of speech you give will depend upon your topic, your purpose, and the audience to whom it will be delivered.

> **KEY CONCEPT** Choose an appropriate kind of speech by considering the topic and purpose of the speech, as well as the intended audience. ■

- An **informative speech** explains an idea, a process, or an object. Descriptions and explanations may include technical language or terms.

- A **persuasive speech** attempts to convince the audience to agree with the speaker's position or to take some action. In a persuasive speech, the speaker generally follows the conventions of standard English usage.

- An **entertaining speech** offers the audience something to enjoy. It may be included in other kinds of speeches for variety or emphasis. The language of an entertaining speech is usually standard or informal.

- An **extemporaneous speech** is an informal speech given to suit an occasion, event, or audience. It is presented without the aid of a prepared manuscript.

▲ **Critical Viewing** What speaking and listening skills are being demonstrated in this photograph? **[Draw Conclusions]**

> **Exercise 2** Listening to Examples Listen to a famous speech on CD or audiotape. Identify the type of speech it is by analyzing its characteristics.

> **Exercise 3** Listing Kinds of Speeches Give two examples of topics for each type of speech described above. Then, identify appropriate audiences for each.

Prepare and Present a Speech

Once you know what kind of speech to give and have chosen a topic, you will need to gather information, outline your speech, prepare note cards, and practice your speech.

KEY CONCEPT Follow a series of steps to plan, prepare, practice, and present your speech. ■

Prepare Your Speech

- **Research your topic.** Use the library or other sources to find reliable information to support your claims.

- **Evaluate your material.** Do you think that your material is biased in any way? Make sure that you are giving an accurate, truthful, and ethical presentation.

- **Make an outline.** Include introductory and background material, a logical sequence of major points and supporting details, and an effective summary and conclusion.

- **Prepare numbered note cards.** Use key words and phrases, exact quotations, indentations, capital letters, and other means of highlighting important information.

Present Your Speech

- **Read over your outline and note cards.** Become very familiar with the material.

- **Utilize rhetorical strategies.** Repeat key words and use parallel structure; for example, "We cannot wait; we must take action."

- **Use verbal strategies.** Vary the pitch and tone of your voice. Speak clearly, and project your voice so you can be heard. Slow down or pause to emphasize key points.

- **Take advantage of nonverbal strategies.** Make eye contact with your listeners. Use your posture and gestures to reflect or emphasize your message.

The Baseball Team

A. Why more training is needed
   1. to improve hitting and fielding
   2. to increase endurance

B. What training involves
   1. weight training
   2. cardiovascular exercises
     a. running
     b. biking

C. What training leads to
   1. better win-loss percentage
   2. possible trip to playoffs

Exercise 4 Preparing and Giving a Speech Write a brief persuasive or informative speech on a topic of interest to you. Practice your speech, and present it to the class.

Exercise 5 Receiving and Using Feedback After you present your speech to the class, meet with a small group of your classmates. Ask them to critique your speech. Did it hold their interest? Were there factual errors? Rewrite your speech based on their critiques.

More Practice

Academic and Workplace Skills Activity Book
• p. 2

Evaluate a Speech

When you evaluate a speech, you judge its strengths (which public-speaking skills were successful) and weaknesses (which skills need more work). Work with peers to evaluate one another's speeches. Use the suggestions of your peer reviewers to improve your delivery and content.

▶ **KEY CONCEPT** Evaluate a speech in a way that benefits the speaker and you. ■

The checklist below gives suggestions for evaluating another person's speech:

⟨ᵢ⟩ Learn More

To learn more about persuasive techniques in advertising, review Chapter 8.

CHECKLIST
FOR EVALUATING A SPEECH

☐ Did the speaker introduce the topic clearly, develop it well, and conclude it effectively?

☐ Did the speaker support each main idea with appropriate details?

☐ Did the speaker approach the platform confidently and establish eye contact with the audience?

☐ Did the speaker's facial expressions, gestures, and movements appropriately reinforce the words spoken?

☐ Did the speaker vary the pitch of his or her voice and the rate of his or her speaking?

☐ Did the speaker enunciate all words clearly?

▶ **Exercise 6** Evaluating a Speech Using the checklist in this section, make a detailed evaluation of a speech given in class. List two or more skills used effectively by the speaker, and consider using them in a future speech you will give.

Listening Critically

Speaking is one half of the communication process. The other half of the process is listening. Learning how to become a critical listener is an important step toward comprehension and successful communication.

KEY CONCEPT Improve your critical listening skills through the use of listening strategies and self-evaluation. ■

Learn the Listening Process You are probably already aware that listening means more than hearing sounds. Like all communication, listening is interactive. It requires participation on the part of the listener.

Focus Your Attention The most important step in listening is to focus your attention on the speaker and his or her words. Ignore all people, objects, noises, and thoughts that can distract you from listening. Increase your interest in the subject by acquiring information about it and by finding a connection between the subject and your life.

Interpret the Information When you listen to a speaker and interpret his or her message successfully, you identify and understand important information. Use the following suggestions to guide you:

- Listen for words and phrases that are emphasized or repeated.
- Visualize important statements, and test your understanding by rephrasing them in your own words.
- Write down important sentences, and summarize ideas.
- Watch for nonverbal signals—tone of voice, gestures, and facial expressions—that may alert you to important ideas.
- Link the information currently being given to previous information to form a meaningful pattern.

Respond to the Speaker's Message When you have finished listening, respond to the information you heard. Decide whether you agree or disagree with persuasive messages. Identify which elements of informative messages you find most interesting or useful. If possible, ask questions to clarify your understanding.

▼ Critical Viewing
What listening strategies do you see being used in this photograph? [Analyze]

Exercise 7 Using the Listening Process Apply the strategies on this page as you listen to a speech, a classroom lecture, or a presentation by a classmate. In writing or in group discussions, summarize the speaker's main points and share your response.

More Practice

Academic and Workplace Skills Activity Book
• p. 3

Use Different Types of Listening Different situations call for different types of listening, and part of being a critical listener involves knowing what type of listening is the most appropriate for a given situation. There are four main types of listening: *critical, empathic, appreciative,* and *reflective.*

Types of Listening		
Type	**How to Listen**	**Situations**
Critical	Listen for facts and supporting details to understand and evaluate the speaker's message.	Informative or persuasive essays, class discussions, announcements
Empathic	Imagine yourself in the other person's position, and try to understand what he or she is thinking.	Conversations with friends or family
Appreciative	Identify and analyze aesthetic or artistic elements, such as character development, rhyme, imagery, and descriptive language.	Oral presentations of a poem, dramatic performances
Reflective	Ask questions to obtain information, and use the speaker's responses to form new questions.	Class or group discussions

Ask Different Types of Questions A good listener always clarifies his or her understanding of a speaker's message. The best way to do this is by asking questions, but different questions have different purposes. If you understand the purposes of the following types of questions, you will be able to obtain the information you want to know:

- An **open-ended** question does not lead to a specific response. Use this question to open up discussion. *(Why do you think the school newspaper needs more funding?)*

- A **closed** question leads to a specific response and must be answered yes or no. *(Do you read the newspaper?)*

- A **fact** question is aimed at obtaining a particular piece of information and must be answered with facts. *(How many newspapers did the school print last year?)*

Exercise 8 Using the Different Types of Listening and Questions Identify at least one example of each type of listening and each type of question. Use examples from life, from television, from movies, or from descriptions in stories.

Evaluate Your Listening One way to improve your listening skills is to evaluate them to find out which listening skills work for you and which skills need improvement. Use the following strategies to evaluate your listening skills:

Rephrase and Repeat Statements You can test your understanding of a speaker's statements by rephrasing and then repeating them to the speaker. If the speaker agrees with your paraphrase, you know that you have understood him or her. If, however, the speaker disagrees with your paraphrase, ask the speaker to correct it or to clarify it.

Compare and Contrast Interpretations Write your interpretation of a speaker's message, and compare and contrast it with another student's interpretation. Use a Venn diagram to list the points on which you agree and disagree. Resolve these points of disagreement through discussion and, if necessary, by appealing to the speaker.

Research Points of Interest or Contention Use the library or other reference tools to acquire more information about the speaker's topic or to check questionable facts of the presentation.

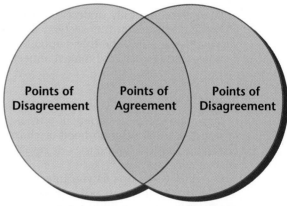

Points of Disagreement   Points of Agreement   Points of Disagreement

Interpretation A   Interpretation B

Exercise 9 Evaluating Your Listening Skills Working with two other classmates, have one classmate read a speech or paper that he or she has recently written.
1. Tell the speaker to pause every paragraph or every few sentences, and take turns with your other classmate rephrasing and repeating the speaker's statements.
2. Ask the speaker to read the entire speech or paper while you and your other classmate take notes. Then, compare and contrast your interpretation.
3. Write an evaluation of your listening skills. Identify areas of strength and areas for improvement.

More Practice

Academic and Workplace Skills Activity Book
• p. 3

Viewing Skills

In today's highly visual world, an understanding of visual representations enhances your ability to receive information.

Interpreting Maps and Graphs

Textbooks, newspapers, magazines, and other written works utilize maps, graphs, and photographs to help convey information. Accurate interpretation of such visual representations increases your ability to understand important information.

▶ **KEY CONCEPT** Analyze and interpret maps, graphs, and photographs in order to become a more knowledgeable consumer of information. ■

To analyze and fully understand visual representations such as those discussed in this section, determine your purpose for viewing them; study the title, caption, and labels; examine symbols and details; and make connections with the text.

Maps

Maps serve a great variety of purposes. They can give the layout of a small neighborhood or chart the skies, indicate changing political boundaries or reveal early human knowledge of geography.

Consider these tips as you interpret maps:
1. Determine the type and purpose of the map.
2. Examine the symbols, scale, orientation, and other pertinent data.
3. Relate the information on the map to any written information accompanying it.

▼ **Critical Viewing**
What kind of a map is the student in this picture using? What kind of information can be obtained from this kind of map? **[Evaluate]**

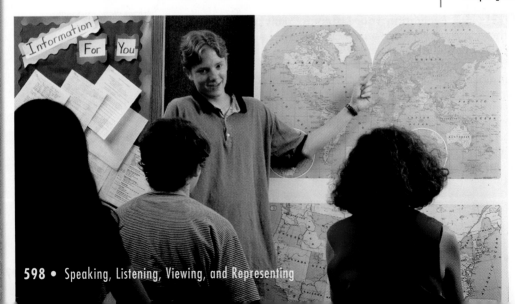

Graphs

Examine the three types of graphs:

Line Graph A line graph shows the relationships between two sets of information; in this case, temperature and time.
1. Read the title. The title summarizes the purpose of the graph and the type of information you will find.
2. Identify the type of information that is shown on the horizontal and vertical data lines.
3. Identify patterns of change, and search the text for possible reasons for the changes.

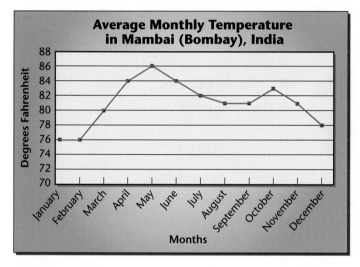

Bar Graph A bar graph compares and contrasts amounts by showing different heights or lengths of the bars.
1. Look across the bottom or at the title to determine the kinds of information being compared.
2. Determine similarities and differences in the data, and search the text for possible causes of the similarities and differences.

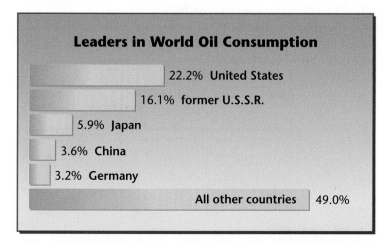

Pie Graph A pie graph illustrates the relationship of parts to each other and to a whole.

1. Read the title to determine what kind of information is being represented and what the whole (100%) stands for.
2. Determine what each wedge represents, and relate the wedges to one another and to the whole.
3. Relate the pie graph information to the text to determine the significance of and possible reasons for the size of each wedge.

United States Occupational Groups by 2005

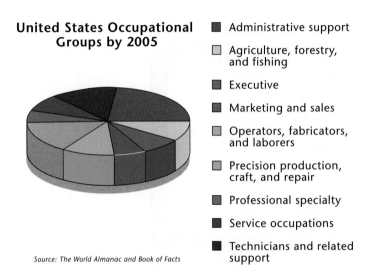

Source: The World Almanac and Book of Facts

- ■ Administrative support
- ☐ Agriculture, forestry, and fishing
- ■ Executive
- ■ Marketing and sales
- ☐ Operators, fabricators, and laborers
- ☐ Precision production, craft, and repair
- ■ Professional specialty
- ■ Service occupations
- ■ Technicians and related support

▶ **Exercise 10** Interpreting Maps and Graphs Using your science and/or social studies text, find two examples of a map, line graph, bar graph, or pie graph. Compare and contrast the types of data represented in each.

▶ **Exercise 11** Creating a Graph Using information from a textbook, an encyclopedia, the sports statistics in the newspaper, or an almanac, create a graph. First, decide which type of graph would present your material most effectively. Then, create your graph.

More Practice

Academic and Workplace Skills Activity Book
• pp. 4–5

Viewing Information Media Critically

Each day, the media send out enormous amounts of information, much of it in visual representations. You must learn to differentiate the various media and critique the information you receive. It is important to distinguish between fact and opinion, accuracy and error, truth and propaganda. Critical observers become alert and responsible consumers of information.

KEY CONCEPT To become a knowledgeable consumer of information, identify and evaluate the different kinds of information and images presented in all media. ■

Recognize Kinds of Information Media Television, documentary films, and the Internet are just a few of the visual media through which information is communicated.

The following chart illustrates several kinds of programs and information found in nonprint information media:

NONPRINT INFORMATION MEDIA			
Form of Medium	Topic(s)	Coverage and Content	Point of View
Television News Program	Current events or news	Brief summaries illustrated by video footage	Gives objective information
Documentary	One topic of social interest	Story shown through narration and video footage	Expresses controversial opinions
Interview	Topics of social interest	Conversations of questions and answers	Presents opinions of interviewer
Editorial	Current or controversial topics	Commentary by a single person supported by statistics or facts	Presents the opinions of a single individual
Commercial	Products, people, and ideas	Short message of images and slogans	Presents information to sell something

Technology Tip

Many television and radio programs have Internet sites where you can get background on a topic. Use the program's title in a key-word search.

Evaluate Persuasive Techniques

The media use certain persuasive techniques to influence your understanding of information. Knowledge of these persuasive techniques, as well as other concepts, will help you become a more critical viewer:

Facts and opinions are two very different types of information. Watch for opinions that are stated as if they were facts.

Bias is a leaning, or partiality, toward a particular viewpoint. Consider whether information is one-sided or allows for several perspectives.

Loaded language and images are emotional words and visuals that make you feel strongly about something—either positive or negative. They are used to persuade you to think and act in certain ways.

Music, slogans, and repetition are often employed to intensify the impact of images and messages you receive. Watch for examples in ads as well as political speeches and campaigns.

Evaluate Information From the Media

Wise consumers must go beyond recognition and carefully evaluate information received through the media. Use the following strategies when evaluating information from the media:

- Be aware of the kind of program you are watching and the kind of information you are receiving. Be alert to the content, purposes, and limitations of the information.
- Be careful to identify facts, opinions, biases, and loaded language and images.
- Check the accuracy of questionable information.
- Use knowledgeable observation to develop your own views about issues, people, and information.

Exercise 12 Analyzing News Coverage Choose a current news event, and observe its coverage on three major newscasts. Take notes regarding the placement and length of each report and the presence of any of the concepts and techniques discussed in this section. Your analysis should compare and contrast the three newscasts, indicating which gave the most objective coverage.

Exercise 13 Analyzing Television Commercials Select a type of product and observe commercials for it presented by three competing companies. Record examples of the techniques discussed in this section, and compare and contrast the techniques used by the different companies. Decide which one presented the most persuasive advertisement, and explain the reasons for your choice.

More Practice

Academic and Workplace Skills Activity Book
- p. 6

Viewing Fine Art Critically

Paintings, drawings, photographs, and other forms of the visual arts present a subjective view of the world. Through line and shape, color and technique, artists capture a vast array of moments and moods. Learning to analyze various elements in a work of art can lead you to a meaningful and personal response.

KEY CONCEPT Analyze and interpret the elements of visual art that lead to a meaningful and enjoyable response. ■

The Reaper, c.1881, Louis C. Tiffany, National Academy of Design, New York City

▲ **Critical Viewing** What are the subject and central focus of this painting? **[Analyze]**

INTERPRETING ELEMENTS OF VISUAL ART

1. What kind of work are you viewing (painting, drawing, photograph, and so on)?

2. What are the subject and central focus of the piece?

3. What mood, theme, or message does the work convey?

4. What techniques does the artist use (color versus black-and-white photography, bold versus impressionistic lines and shapes, vivid versus muted colors, and so on)?

5. Is your overall response to the work more positive or more negative? Why?

Exercise 14 Interpreting Visual Art Consider the questions in the chart Interpreting Elements of Visual Art, and react to the artwork *The Reaper.* Describe your reactions in an essay.

▶ **More Practice**

Academic and Workplace Skills Activity Book
• p. 7

Representing Skills

In this section, you will learn how to represent information using graphic organizers, multimedia presentations, and performances.

Creating Graphic Organizers

Organization skills are crucial when attempting to comprehend or present a great amount of information. Using graphic organizers and other aids to put information in visual format helps make the information easier to understand and remember.

▶ **KEY CONCEPT** To help you comprehend or present great amounts of information, put it into visual formats such as graphic organizers. ■

There are many kinds of graphic organizers, including outlines, flowcharts, webs, Venn diagrams, and timelines. Use the following strategies to create graphic organizers as you read, study, and present information:

- **Identify your purpose.** Determine what information or parts of the text you need to comprehend. This process will help you narrow your focus, eliminate extraneous information, and choose the most appropriate graphic organizer.

- **Utilize text features.** Make use of organizational features in textbooks (titles, headings, subheadings, boldfaced words and phrases) to design a graphic organizer for note taking. Use a web, for example, by placing a section heading in the central circle, subheadings in the radiating circles, and details around each subheading.

- **Examine the kind of information being organized.** This step will help you determine the most appropriate graphic organizer to use. Are you examining chronological events? Use a timeline. Comparing and contrasting? A Venn diagram is a good choice. Analyzing cause-and-effect relationships? Try a flowchart. Looking for the main idea and supporting details? Outlines and webs are helpful.

You can enhance both oral and written presentations by including visual representations like those that follow.

Charts, Graphs, and Tables When you are presenting numbers, statistics, or other complex data, charts, graphs, and tables can help you organize, simplify, and clarify your material.

Maps For many formal and informal uses, maps can provide beneficial visual support. They can be used to depict numerous types of information—from storm tracks to troop movements.

Diagrams, Illustrations, and Pictures Simple line drawings, diagrams, and hand-drawn pictures can visually represent a process or specific features of a topic. A graphic organizer, like the web (or cluster chart) below, can be useful in presenting information.

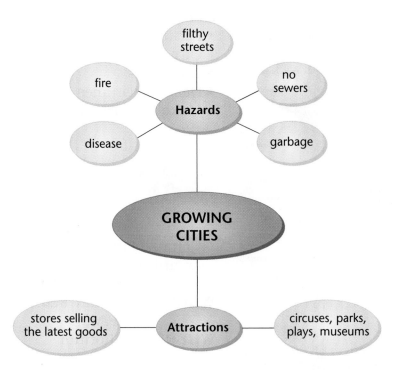

Exercise 15 Creating Graphic Organizers and Visual Aids for Science and Social Studies Select a chapter from your social studies or science textbook, and complete the following activities:

1. Examine the chapter content and determine what types of graphic organizers or other visual aids would best represent the information visually.
2. Create one graphic organizer or aid to illustrate a portion of the chapter, and present this information to your class.

More Practice

Academic and Workplace Skills Activity Book
• p. 8

Using Formatting

With computer technology comes access to a wide choice of creative formats. From boldface to bullets, columns to clip art, word processing offers an abundance of possibilities to design clever, eye-catching visual products. To capture a reader's interest or call attention to key concepts, try some of the following features:

- Capitals or boldfaced type to call attention to headings and key words or ideas

- Italics or underlining to emphasize a line or word

- Numbered lists to indicate steps to be followed in a sequence

- Bulleted lists to highlight items that can be presented in any order

- Creative fonts to make headings or special titles stand out

- Multicolumn format, graphics, borders, clip art, and colored type to enliven any or all parts of the material

Drama Club

Get in on the Action!

Join the Drama Club
- Perform
- Direct
- Build sets
- Design costumes
- Make new friends

Come to our organizational meeting.

WHEN: Wednesday Feb. 12
3:30 P.M.
WHERE: Auditorium

Bring a friend!

▶ **Exercise 16** Using Formatting to Design a Brochure
Select a feature of your school (athletics, student council, or fine arts), a club of which you are a member, or a community group of special interest. Using the technology tips from this section and your own creative ideas, design a brochure to attract and encourage others to become involved.

Working With Multimedia

Enhance an oral report with music, artwork, charts, or a slide show or video, and you have created a multimedia presentation. In this era of advanced technology, the possibilities are limitless. Through careful planning and skillful execution, you can produce a dramatic, dynamic, and distinguished multimedia presentation.

Tips for Preparing a Multimedia Presentation

- Plan and write your presentation.

- Determine what parts of your report you wish to illustrate through the use of media.

- Select one or several media that will enhance your topic and complement each other.

- Make certain that each medium can be seen and heard clearly by all members of the audience. Use large type and images, for example, on an overhead projector, and place charts and posters within sight of everyone.

- Plan how and when you will incorporate the media into your report. Be sure to spread them throughout the presentation. If needed, ask an assistant to run the equipment.

- Write a highlighted outline of the text on note cards indicating the use of each medium.

- Carefully stage and practice the entire presentation several times. To ensure a smooth flow to the presentation, position yourself and all media items so that you can move easily among them.

- Set up in advance, making certain that all equipment is in good working condition, that volume and focus are appropriately adjusted, and that all items are positioned within sight of the entire audience.

- Create a backup plan in case the equipment malfunctions.

Technology Tip

Conduct a technology survey among students and adults. Interview them about the kind of word processor or desktop publisher they use and the features they enjoy most.

▲ Critical Viewing
What kind of medium is this student using in her report? What are some advantages of this medium? **[Analyze]**

> **Exercise 17** Preparing a Multimedia Presentation

Working with two or three classmates, choose a topic of interest from science, social studies, literature, or another school subject. Following the suggestions in this section, prepare, practice, and present a dynamic multimedia report.

> **More Practice**

Academic and Workplace Skills Activity Book
• p. 10

Representing Skills • **607**

Creating a Video

Whether to inform or entertain, videos are powerful communication vehicles. They may vary greatly in length and serve a wide variety of purposes, but whatever their lengths and purposes, effective videos require detailed planning and preparation.

> **KEY CONCEPT** Create an effective video to inform, entertain, or do both. ■

Developing a video of any length involves this basic process:

Tips for Creating a Video

1. Write a shooting script that contains not only the dialogue of the characters but also directions for camera angles, settings, costumes, and props.
2. Create a storyboard. Much like a cartoon strip, a storyboard illustrates the sequence of camera shots.
3. Select and get permission to use specific shooting sites.
4. Obtain costumes, props, music, sound effects, and any other necessities. Line up a crew to assist with any special effects.
5. Cast the roles, and hold rehearsals.
6. Plan a shooting schedule, and distribute it to the cast and crew.
7. Film the scenes. Remember to hold the camera steady, pan and zoom slowly and smoothly, and shoot more than you need. It is easier to cut than to film again.
8. Edit the video.

Storyboard

Production: Portrait of a Winner
Location: High-School Tennis Court
Scene: 2

Wide view of Tom on court practicing serves.
①
Voice-over narrates.

Move in to close-up on Tom.
②
Tom explains his practice.

Close-up on coach.
③
Coach's comments.

> **Exercise 18** Creating a Storyboard and Documentary
Prepare to shoot a 7- to 10-minute documentary. Create a storyboard to illustrate the sequence of events you wish to film. Follow the basic tips discussed in this section, including careful planning and rehearsing, to create a quality documentary.

> **More Practice**
>
> Academic and Workplace Skills Activity Book
> • p. 11

Performing and Interpreting

From ancient times to the present, the performing arts have been a dynamic and moving medium. To be an effective performer requires skill and practice.

▶ **KEY CONCEPT** Plan and present an interpretive performance. ■

Tips for Preparing an Interpretive Performance Use the following strategies when preparing for a performance:

1. Study the text to understand its tone, mood, and meaning. Jot down notes, and highlight the parts you consider especially important.
2. Read the text aloud several times, experimenting with the tone, pitch, and volume of your voice. Vary these elements to achieve the desired moods and effects.
3. Memorize the text.
4. Practice the memorized text, using appropriate postures, gestures, and movements.
5. Incorporate costumes, props, sets, and music to enhance the meaning of the text.
6. Rehearse repeatedly to revise and polish. Ask another person to view your performance and offer suggestions, or make a video and critique yourself.

▶ **Exercise 19** Preparing an Interpretive Performance Use the steps discussed in this section to prepare a 3- to 4-minute interpretive performance of a poem or an excerpt from another work of literature.

▶ **More Practice**

Academic and
Workplace Skills
Activity Book
• p. 12

Reflecting on Your Speaking, Listening, Viewing, and Representing

Review the concepts discussed in this chapter. Write a one-page reflection on your experiences, responding to the following questions:

- How have I increased my knowledge of the importance of good speaking and listening skills?
- What helped me to become more critical in my viewing practices?
- What kinds of visual representations have I found most beneficial in presenting information?
- What activities in this section did I find most enjoyable? Most challenging? Why?

Vocabulary and *Spelling*

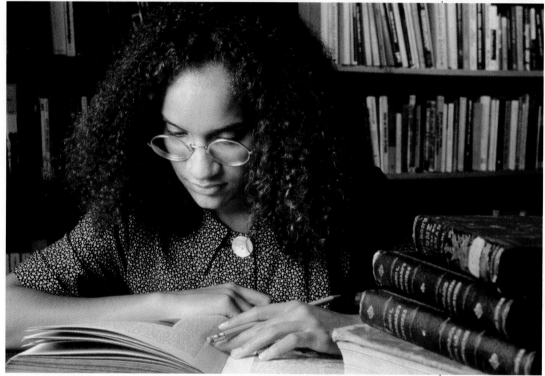

If you compared the vocabulary and spelling abilities you possess today with those of your middle-school years, you would see a significant difference. As your reading has increased, the number of words you understand and are able to spell has substantially increased as well.

Your reading vocabulary—the words you are able to understand from your reading—will almost always be greater than the vocabulary you use in conversation. Working to increase your vocabulary is useful in three ways: You can get information from the textbooks you read, you can use words to communicate effectively in your writing, and you can speak precisely and persuasively. By improving your spelling, you can give your reader a better understanding of your ideas and the message you want to convey.

▲ **Critical Viewing**
In what ways does reading a variety of texts increase your vocabulary?
[Deduce]

Section 29.1 *Developing Vocabulary*

One of the most valuable tools you can ever hope to own is a well-developed vocabulary. Words are for communication, written and spoken. Developing techniques for building your vocabulary is a worthwhile occupation.

Listening, Discussing, and Wide Reading

Whether you know it or not, you have been accumulating words since the day you were born. A child just beginning school has a vocabulary of about 13,000 words. A literate adult speaker of English has a vocabulary of approximately 60,000 words. Most of the new words a person learns are learned through listening, discussing, and reading.

KEY CONCEPT The most common ways to increase your vocabulary are listening, reading, and taking part in conversations. ■

Listen for and Use New Words When you were a toddler, you didn't know very many words. Your vocabulary increased, however, at a rapid pace as you learned words for the things and people around you. First, you heard the words spoken. Then, you learned to repeat them. Eventually, you were able to put the words into sentences and hold conversations.

Listening and discussing are good ways to expand your vocabulary even now. Listening in class, chatting with other people, watching television, listening to the radio, and listening to recorded works of literature and speeches are all ways to expose yourself to new words. When you hear an unfamiliar word, jot it down and look it up in a dictionary. Try to use the word in conversation. This will put it into your vocabulary.

Wide Reading Another excellent way to build your vocabulary is by reading. Try to read a wide variety of books and magazines. When you encounter unfamiliar words or familiar words used in new ways, jot them down and look them up in a dictionary.

Textbooks, newspapers, magazines, novels, and articles on the Internet can all be good resources for extending your vocabulary.

Recognizing Context Clues

The **context** of a word refers to the group of words surrounding it. When you encounter an unfamiliar word in your reading, you can make inferences about its meaning by looking for context clues in the surrounding words.

> **KEY CONCEPT** Use context clues to determine the meaning of unfamiliar words in your reading. ■

Types of Context Clues The following is a list of several types of context clues. Study them, so you can later recognize the ways in which surrounding words can give you clues to the meaning of unfamiliar words.

Formal Definition: Gives the actual meaning of the word.

Familiar Words: Words a reader may know help provide a word's meaning.

Compare and Contrast: Presents an idea or concept that is either clearly similar or clearly opposite to the unfamiliar word's meaning.

Synonyms and Antonyms: Use words with similar meanings (synonyms) or opposite meanings (antonyms) to give the meanings of unfamiliar words.

EXAMPLE: Because the patient was *debilitated* by both the illness and the medication, his doctor recommended physical therapy to strengthen him.

Familiar words in the sentence give clues: *Medication* and *illness* suggest a weakened condition; *therapy* and *strengthen* confirm this idea.

> **Exercise 1** Using Context Clues in General Reading

Use context clues to determine the meaning of each underlined word. Check your answers in a dictionary.

Within the range of written discourse, there are several kinds of writing. One type of writing is called expository because it explains ideas in a sequence. Another kind, a critique, examines the strengths and weaknesses of a specific work.

Another form of writing that is useful in job seeking is called a résumé, which includes information about a job applicant's education and previous employment. Information other than these details is considered peripheral and should not be listed.

Research Tip

Find a book about art history in the library. Locate three sentences in the book that provide context clues that help to determine the meaning of a word. Add the new words to your notebook.

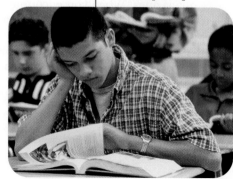

▼ **Critical Viewing** How might a student such as this one figure out the meaning of unfamiliar words in his textbook? **[Infer]**

Denotation and Connotation

Context can help you determine a word's exact meaning. Knowing the denotations and connotations of a word can help you discriminate between shades of meaning.

> **KEY CONCEPT** The denotation of a word is its literal definition. Its connotations include the ideas, images, and feelings that are associated with the word in people's minds. ∎

The dictionary defines a patriot as "one who loves and loyally or zealously supports one's own country." That is just the definition of the word. But what comes to mind when you hear the word *patriot?* You may think of words such as *soldier, pride,* and *self-sacrifice.* You may picture a minuteman in a tricorn hat. You may think of Nathan Hale who regreted that he had but one life to give for his country. You may think of Betsy Ross sewing a flag for a new nation. All of these are connotations associated with the word *patriot.* As you strengthen your vocabulary, be aware of both positive and negative connotations of the words you use.

> **More Practice**
>
> Academic and
> Workplace
> Skills Activity Book
> • p. 14

> **Exercise 2** Discriminating Between Denotation and Connotation Read each pair of sentences below. For each pair, write a sentence explaining the different connotations of the underlined words. Use a dictionary to help you.

1. George Washington <u>implored</u> the American people to accept the new Constitution.
   George Washington <u>begged</u> the American people to accept the new Constitution.
2. Patriotic leaders began a <u>campaign</u> to ensure ratification.
   Patriotic leaders began a <u>crusade</u> to ensure ratification.
3. On foot, on horseback, and by coach, these <u>indomitable</u> men traveled to farms, villages, and cities.
   On foot, on horseback, and by coach, these <u>stubborn</u> men traveled to farms, villages, and cities.
4. They went from town to town to explain the <u>gist</u> of the Constitution.
   They went from town to town to explain the <u>significance</u> of the Constitution.
5. They spread their message with enthusiasm and <u>fervor</u>.
   They spread their message with enthusiasm and <u>eagerness</u>.

Recognizing Related Words

Discovering how words can relate to other words is a good way to increase your vocabulary. For example, many words have *synonyms, antonyms,* and *homophones.*

> **KEY CONCEPT** **Synonyms** are words that are similar in meaning. **Antonyms** are words that are opposite in meaning. **Homophones** are words that sound alike but have different meanings and spellings. ■

Synonyms Synonyms can help you remember the meaning of a word, for it is often easier to remember a one-word synonym than to remember a long dictionary definition. For example, you may be able to remember the word *countenance* by remembering its synonym, *face.*

Antonyms Knowing an antonym for a word—its opposite meaning—can give you a clue about the word's meaning. To remember that the word *fervent* means "impassioned," for example, try to recall that its antonym is *indifferent.*

Homophones It is important to recognize words that are homophones—words that sound alike but have different meanings and spellings—so you can use their correct forms in your writing. You would, for example, want to make sure that you did not confuse the words *waste* ("discarded material") and *waist* (a part of the body). Although the words have the same pronunciation, they have different meanings and spellings.

> **Exercise 3** Recognizing Synonyms, Antonyms, and Homophones Identify each pair of words below as *synonyms, antonyms,* or *homophones.*
>
> 1. garrulous/taciturn
> 2. capitol/capital
> 3. malign/vilify
> 4. rash/calculating
> 5. whole/hole
> 6. frugal/wasteful
> 7. garish/gaudy
> 8. sardonic/cynical
> 9. avid/eager
> 10. relinquish/abandon

Using Related Words in Analogies

Working with *analogies,* a type of word problem often found on standardized tests, strengthens your vocabulary by increasing your understanding of connections between word meanings. It will also benefit you to practice analogies because they are typical items found in aptitude and achievement tests.

KEY CONCEPT **Analogies** present a pair of words that have some relationship to each other. ■

Look at the following analogy, and see whether you can find the pair of words whose relationship is the most similar to the capitalized pair:

EXAMPLE: MYTH : STORY ::
              a. flower : redness
              b. literature : poetry
              c. bonnet : hat

The answer is *C.*

The way to solve analogies is to form a clear idea of the relationship between the capitalized words. In this example, the relationship between the words is *type*—a *myth* is a type of *story.* A *flower* is not a type of *redness. Literature* is not a type of *poetry;* although poetry is a type of literature, that is not what the analogy states. A *bonnet,* however, is a type of *hat.* Other common analogy relationships include *part to whole, defining characteristic, instrument, degree,* and *sequence.*

Exercise 4 **Working With Analogies** First, identify the analogy relationship expressed in the capitalized pair. Then, choose the lettered pair that best expresses this relationship.

1. PEACH : FRUIT ::
   a. vegetable : apple   b. peas : beans
   c. turnip : vegetable
2. BOUQUET : FLOWER ::
   a. key : door   b. chain : link
   c. skin : body
3. JOY : ECSTASY ::
   a. admiration : love   b. life : hope
   c. happiness : sorrow
4. CARPENTER : HAMMER ::
   a. doctor : surgeon   b. woodsman : axe
   c. attorney : judge
5. MARMALADE : ORANGE ::
   a. lemons : fruit   b. ketchup : tomato
   c. jelly : jam

▶ More Practice

Academic and
Workplace
Skills Activity Book
• p. 16

Studying Words Systematically

Using Resource Materials

There are many useful materials you can use, either in print or on-line. In either form, two of the most valuable tools are a dictionary and a thesaurus.

> **KEY CONCEPT** Use a **dictionary** to find the meaning, spelling, pronunciation, and origin of words. Use a **thesaurus** to find words that most precisely express your meaning. ■

Use a Dictionary You should make it a habit to consult a dictionary every time you come across an unfamiliar word. It is a good idea to keep a dictionary nearby, where you can easily access it. When you look up a word in a dictionary, make use of the information that appears with the definition:

- Study the pronunciation given in parentheses after the word. If you can pronounce a word, you are more likely to use it.

- Note the word's part of speech, which appears as an abbreviation (*n.*, *v.*, *adj.*). A word can change its meaning, depending upon its usage.

- Note the origin of the word (its etymology), which usually appears after the part of speech.

- Read all the many meanings given for a word.

Use a Thesaurus A thesaurus helps increase your vocabulary. If you have used the same word several times, you can use a thesaurus to find a new word that is, perhaps, more interesting and more expressive. Be sure to check the meaning of the new word to see whether it fulfills your purpose in writing.

🖥 **Research Tip**

Choose five words, and use a thesaurus to find a synonym for each of them. Then, use a dictionary to see whether there are any subtle differences between each word and its synonym.

▲ **Critical Viewing** What study tools might this student be using? **[Infer]**

> **Exercise 5** Using a Dictionary to Increase Your Vocabulary Look up each word below in a dictionary, and write its definition or definitions.
> 1. trajectory   3. salubrious   5. quiescent
> 2. repudiate   4. impart

> **Exercise 6** Using a Thesaurus to Increase Your Vocabulary In a thesaurus, find a word similar to each word below. Use each new word in a sentence.
> 1. censor   3. benign   5. audacity
> 2. harmony   4. foment

Remembering Vocabulary Words

In addition to a dictionary and a thesaurus, there are other study aids that you can use to add words to your vocabulary.

> **KEY CONCEPT** Use a variety of techniques to remember the meanings of new words. ■

Use a Vocabulary Notebook Divide your page into three columns with the following headings: the *word* you want to learn; a *bridge* word, or hint to help you remember the word's meaning; and the word's *definition*.

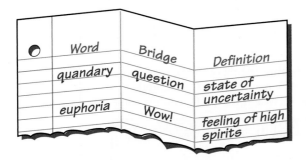

Word	Bridge	Definition
quandary	question	state of uncertainty
euphoria	Wow!	feeling of high spirits

Technology Tip

Find a short entry about an unfamiliar technical subject in an on-line encyclopedia. Find an unfamiliar word, look it up in a dictionary, and add it to your notebook.

Use Flashcards and a Tape Recorder On the front of an index card, write a word you want to remember and a bridge word. On the back, write the definition. Then, flip through the cards, supplying the definitions for the words. Use the bridge word to assist you. Continue in this method until you can correctly define all the words.

Record a vocabulary word into a tape recorder. Leave a space of about five seconds, and then give the definition. Continue in this way with all your words. Then, replay the tape, filling in each blank space with the word's definition. Keep replaying the tape until you can give all the definitions easily.

Work With a Partner Using flashcards and vocabulary notebooks, take turns quizzing each other on vocabulary. In the first round, read the words and have your partner define them. If your partner is slow to respond, provide the bridge word. Repeat the words until your partner can correctly define all of them. In the second round, exchange roles.

> **Exercise 7** Adding New Words to Your Vocabulary
> Identify five unfamiliar words from each of your major subjects. Enter the words and their definitions in your vocabulary notebook. Study the words using one of the above methods. Then, test yourself by using each word in a sentence.

> **More Practice**
>
> Academic and Workplace
> Skills Activity Book
> • p. 18

Studying Word Parts and Origins

You can improve your vocabulary by learning about word structure, or the parts that make up a word. The three word parts that can combine to form a word are a root (such as -*duc*- in pro*duc*tion), a prefix (such as *pro*- in *pro*duction), and a suffix (such as -*tion* in produc*tion*). Many of these word parts come from the Latin, Greek, and Anglo-Saxon languages.

Learning Prefixes

A prefix is one or more syllables at the beginning of a word.

> **KEY CONCEPT** The prefix adds to the meaning of the root. ■

Prefixes Learn the meanings and origins of the prefixes below. The abbreviations *L.*, *Gr.*, and *A.S.* mean Latin, Greek, and Anglo-Saxon, the languages from which the prefixes have come.

TEN COMMON PREFIXES		
Prefix and Origin	Meaning	Examples
ad- (ac-, af-, al-, ap-, as-, at-) [L.]	to, toward	*ad*join, *af*fix, *al*lure, *ap*point
anti- [Gr.]	against	*anti*pathy
com- (co-, col-, con-, cor-) [L.]	with, together	*com*press, *con*tribute
ex- (e-, ec-, ef-) [L.]	forth, from, out	*ex*press, *e*migrate
in- (il-, im-, ir-) [L.]	not	*in*human, *il*legal
inter- [L.]	between	*inter*national
mis- [A.S.]	wrong	*mis*place
mono- [Gr.]	alone, one	*mono*poly
ob- (o-, oc-, of-, op-) [L.]	toward, against	*ob*ject, *o*mit, *oc*casion, *of*fer
over- [A.S.]	above, in excess	*over*flow

> **Exercise 8** Defining Words With Prefixes Using your knowledge of prefixes, figure out the meaning of each word below. Then, check your answers in a dictionary.
>
> 1. *mono*plane
> 2. *inter*pose
> 3. *ad*dendum
> 4. *ob*trude
> 5. *ex*punge
> 6. *mis*anthrope
> 7. *in*expert
> 8. *over*extend
> 9. *inter*changeable
> 10. *con*fabulate

▶ **Exercise 9** Defining Prefixes and Prefix Origins Using a dictionary, write the definition of each prefix and its origin. Then, provide an example for each prefix.

1. ab- (a-, abs-)   3. epi-   5. pro-
2. dis- (di-, dif-)   4. sub- (sic-, suf-, sup-)

Learning Roots

The root of a word contains its basic meaning. Learning roots is the foundation for developing your vocabulary.

▶ **KEY CONCEPT** The **root** carries the word's basic meaning. ■

Roots Roots that stand alone are *free* roots. Roots that need a prefix or suffix are *bound* roots, like most of the roots in the following chart. The abbreviations *L.* and *Gr.* mean Latin and Greek.

TEN COMMON ROOTS		
Root and Origin	Meaning	Examples
-cap- (-capt-, -cept-, -ceipt-, -ceive-, -cip-) [L.]	to take, seize	*cap*able, *capt*ivate, ac*cept*, re*ceipt*, re*ceive*, re*cip*ient
-fac- (-fact-, -fec-, -fect-, -fic-) [L.]	to do, make	*fac*simile, manu*fact*ure, in*fec*tion, de*fect*, *fic*tion
-ject- [L.]	to throw	re*ject*
-leg- (-log-) [Gr.]	to say, speak	*leg*al, *log*ic
-plic- (-pli-, -ploy- -ply-) [L.]	to fold	du*plic*ate, *pli*able, em*ploy*, re*ply*
-pon- (-pos-) [L.]	to put, place	post*pon*e, de*pos*it
-quir- (-ques-, -quis-) [L.]	to ask, say	in*quir*e, *ques*tion, in*quis*itive
-sist- [L.]	to stand	in*sist*
-string- (-strict-) [L.]	to bind, tighten	*string*ent, con*strict*
-vad- (-vas-) [L.]	to go	in*vad*e, e*vas*ive

▶ **Exercise 10** Finding Common Roots Look up each set of words in the dictionary, paying close attention to the word's root, shown in italics. Then, write the basic meaning shared by each pair of words.

1. pro*ced*ure, pro*ceed*   4. ex*ten*sion, ex*tent*
2. pro*duce*, re*duce*   5. trans*fer*, in*fer*ence
3. *puls*ate, pro*pel*

> **Exercise 11** Using Roots to Define Words Write down
each word, paying close attention to the word's root, shown in
italics. Then, write the letter of the word's meaning next to
each word.

1. pro*fic*ient   a. to move something to a different place
2. trans*pose*   b. an introduction to a written work
3. pro*logue*   c. to capture the attention or affection of
4. *capt*ivate   d. to take in or admit
5. re*cept*ive   e. highly competent

> **More Practice**

Academic and
Workplace
Skills Activity Book
• pp. 19–21

Using Suffixes

When a suffix is added to a root, the word's part of speech
usually changes.

> **KEY CONCEPT** The **suffix,** which is added to the end of
the root, can change the word's meaning or part of speech. ■

Suffixes Suffixes are unique in that they change both word
forms and parts of speech. In the chart, the abbreviations *L.*,
Gr., and *A.S.* mean Latin, Greek, and Anglo-Saxon.

TEN COMMON SUFFIXES		
Suffix and Origin	**Meaning and Examples**	**Part of Speech**
-ac (-ic) [Gr.]	characteristic of: mani*ac*, scen*ic*	noun or adjective
-ant (-ent) [L.]	that shows, has, or does: defi*ant*, depend*ent*	noun or adjective
-ful [A.S.]	full of: scorn*ful*	adjective
-fy [L.]	to cause to become: clari*fy*	verb
-ish [A.S.]	of, tending to: fool*ish*	adjective
-ism [Gr.]	act, practice, or result of: tru*ism*	noun
-ity [L.]	state of being: advers*ity*	noun
-ize (-ise) [Gr.]	to make: idol*ize*	verb
-ous (-ious) [L.]	marked by, given to: pomp*ous*	adjective
-tion (-ion, -sion, -ation, -ition) [L.]	state of being: ac*tion*, mis*sion*	noun

Irregular Plurals Irregular plurals are not formed according to the rules on the previous page. If you are unsure how to form a plural, check a dictionary. Irregular plurals are usually listed right after the pronunciation of the word. If no plural form is given in the dictionary, simply add -s or -es to the singular form. Below is a list of common irregular plurals:

IRREGULAR PLURALS		
Singular Forms	Ways of Forming Plurals	Plural Forms
ox	add -en	oxen
child	add -ren	children
tooth, mouse, woman	change one or more letters	teeth, mice, women
radius, focus, alumnus	change -us to -i	radii, foci, alumni
alumna	change -a to -ae	alumnae
crisis, emphasis	change -is to -es	crises, emphases
medium, datum, curriculum	change -um to -a	media, data, curricula
phenomenon, criterion	change -on to -a	phenomena, criteria
deer, sheep	plural form same as singular	deer, sheep
	plural form only	scissors, slacks

Note About *Plurals of Compound Words*: To form the plural of a compound word—that is, a word made up of two or more separate or hyphenated words—add -s or -es to the main noun in the compound word. For example, *rule of thumb* becomes *rules of thumb*, and *editor-in-chief* becomes *editors-in-chief*.

▶ **Exercise 19** Forming Plurals Write the plural for each word. Consult a dictionary if necessary.

1. radio
2. soprano
3. wife
4. fox
5. supply
6. lynx
7. chief
8. son-in-law
9. crisis
10. X-ray
11. tomato
12. waltz
13. rodeo
14. mouse
15. criterion
16. alumnus
17. gratuity
18. fantasy
19. ballerina
20. memorandum

▶ **More Practice**

Academic and Workplace Skills Activity Book
• p. 25

Adding Prefixes and Suffixes

A **prefix** is one or more syllables added at the beginning of a word to form a new word. A **suffix** is one or more syllables added to the end of a word.

▷ **KEY CONCEPT** Adding a prefix to a word does not affect the spelling of the original word. Adding a suffix often changes the spelling of the word. ■

Prefixes When a prefix is added to the word, the spelling of the root remains the same (*in-* + *sincere* = *insincere*; *un-* + *necessary* = *unnecessary*). With certain prefixes, however, the spelling is changed when joined to the root to make the pronunciation easier (*in-* becomes *im-* before *mortal* to form *immortal*).

▷ **Exercise 20** Spelling Words With Prefixes Form new words by combining roots with these seven prefixes. Remember that you may have to change the form of some prefixes. Use a dictionary to check your answers.

ad-, circum-, com-, in-, mis-, per-, pro-

1. -vent
2. -plex
3. -prove
4. -spell
5. -vert
6. -found
7. -pact
8. -missive
9. -scribe
10. -spire

Suffixes Some words require spelling changes when suffixes are added.

Spelling changes in words ending in *y*: Use the following rules for spelling changes of words ending in *y*, paying careful attention to the rule's exceptions.

1. When adding a suffix to words ending in *y* preceded by a consonant, change *y* to *i*. Most suffixes beginning with *i* are the exception to the rule:

   ply + -able = pliable
   defy + -ing = defying
   happy + -ness = happiness
   cry + -ing = crying

2. For words ending in a *y* preceded by a vowel, make no change when adding most suffixes. A few short words are the exceptions:

   annoy + -ance = annoyance
   day + -ly = daily
   enjoy + -ment = enjoyment
   pay + -ed = paid

Spelling changes in words ending in *e*: Use the following rules for spelling changes for words ending in *e*, paying careful attention to the rule's exceptions:

1. For words ending in *e*, drop the *e* when adding a suffix beginning with a vowel. The exceptions to the rule are (1) words ending in *ce* or *ge* with suffixes beginning with *a* or *o*, (2) words ending in *ee*, and (3) a few special words:

   move + -able = movable   drive + -ing = driving
   trace + -able = traceable   courage + -ous = courageous
   see + -ing = seeing   agree + -able = agreeable
   dye + -ing = dyeing   be + -ing = being

2. For words ending in *e*, make no change when adding a suffix beginning with a consonant. A few special words are the exceptions:

   peace + -ful = peaceful   brave + -ly = bravely
   argue + -ment = argument   judge + -ment = judgment

Doubling the final consonant before suffixes: Use the following rules for cases in which a final consonant may or may not change, paying careful attention to the rule's exceptions:

1. For words ending with a consonant + vowel + consonant in a stressed syllable, double the final consonant when adding a suffix beginning with a vowel. The exceptions to the rules are (1) words ending in *x* or *w* and (2) words in which the stress changes after the suffix is added:

   mud + -y = mud dy   submit + -ed = submit ted
   mix + -ing = mixing   row + -ing = rowing
   refer + -ence = ref erence   confer + -ence = con ference

2. For words ending with a consonant + vowel + consonant in an unstressed syllable, make no change when adding a suffix beginning with a vowel. There are no major exceptions to the rule:

   an gel + -ic = angel ic   fi nal + -ize = fi nalize

▶ **Exercise 21** Spelling Words With Suffixes Write the correct spelling for the words below. Check a dictionary.

1. retire + -ment
2. loyal + -ist
3. confer + -ence
4. hurry + -ing
5. rebel + -ion
6. comply + -ance
7. appear + -ance
8. convey + -or
9. abbreviate + -ion
10. imagine + -ary

▶ **More Practice**

Academic and Workplace Skills Activity Book
• p. 26

Spelling *ie* and *ei* Words and Words Ending in *-cede*, *-ceed*, and *-sede*

Words containing *ie* and *ei* and words with the endings *-cede*, *-ceed*, and *-sede* often prove troublesome to spellers.

For most words containing *ie* or *ei*, you can use the traditional rule: "Place *i* before *e* except after *c* or when sounded like *a* as in *neighbor* or *weigh*." For exceptions, as well as for words ending in *-cede*, *-ceed*, and *-sede*, it is often best to memorize the correct spellings.

> **KEY CONCEPT** For *ie* and *ei* words, use the traditional rule after memorizing the exceptions. Words that end in *-cede*, *-ceed*, and *-sede* should also be memorized. ∎

ie and ei Words The *ie* and *ei* rule applies to many words, but like most rules, it has exceptions.

Exceptions for *ie* words: counterfeit, either, foreign, forfeit, heifer, height, heir, leisure, neither, seismology, seize, sheik, sleight, sovereign, their, weird

Exceptions for *ei* words: ancient, conscience, efficient, financier, sufficient

> **Exercise 22** Spelling *ie* and *ei* Words Use *ie* or *ei* to complete each numbered word below.

Even at the (1) h _ _ ght of (2) th _ _ r (3) ach _ _ vement, the (4) _ _ ght athletes (5) consc _ _ ntiously practiced every day. All (6) bel _ _ ved that (7) th_ _ r (8) r _ _ gn as champions would be (9) br _ _ f if they became so (10) conc _ _ ted that they thought they could succeed without hard work.

Words Ending in *-cede*, *-ceed*, and *-sede* The best way to handle words that end with these suffixes is to memorize the correct spelling. The words ending in ***-cede*** are *accede, concede, intercede, precede, recede, secede.* The three words endings in ***-ceed*** are *exceed, proceed, succeed,* and the only word ending in ***-sede*** is *supersede.*

> **Exercise 23** Working With Words Ending in *-cede*, *-ceed*, or *-sede* Write the incomplete word for each sentence, filling in the blanks with *-cede*, *-ceed*, or *-sede*.
> 1. The new regulations super _ _ _ _ the old ones.
> 2. The candidate will not con _ _ _ _ defeat.
> 3. The wedding ceremony will pre _ _ _ _ the reception.
> 4. They probably will suc _ _ _ _ in their new business.
> 5. It is time to pro _ _ _ _ with the meeting.

> **More Practice**
>
> Academic and Workplace Skills Activity Book
> • p. 27

Other Confusing Endings

There are a few groups of suffixes that sound very similar but are spelled differently. For this reason, you should learn to distinguish confusing suffixes and to identify common words that each suffix forms.

KEY CONCEPT Learn to distinguish between confusing groups of suffixes. ■

Learn Confusing Endings There are certain endings that are similar and easy to confuse. Study the following lists, and consult a dictionary.

-able, -ible The suffixes *-able* and *-ible* are often confusing, and it is probably best to check a dictionary if you are in doubt about a spelling. Following is a list of some of the words with these endings.

COMMON WORDS ENDING IN *-able* AND *-ible*

acceptable	imaginable	accessible	possible
believable	probable	flexible	responsible
capable	reasonable	horrible	sensible

-ance (-ant) **and** ***-ence (-ent)*** The most helpful guideline for remembering which spelling to use is that words containing a "hard" *c* or *g* sound usually end with the *a* spelling. Those with a "soft" *c* or *g* sound will usually have the *e* spelling. There are, however, many *-ance* and *-ence* words that do not contain soft or hard *c* or *g* sounds.

COMMON WORDS ENDING IN *-ance* AND *-ence*

abundance	defiance	absence	excellence
acquaintance	importance	convenience	independence
appearance	radiance	patience	correspondence

-ary, -ery There are not many words ending in *-ery* that have the sound *(-airy)*. Most words with that sound are spelled *-ary*.

COMMON WORDS ENDING IN *-ery* AND *-ary*

cemetery	stationery (paper)	dictionary	culinary
millinery	monastery	imaginary	lectionary

Most words with endings that sound similar will have the *-ary* spelling. If you have any doubt whether a word ends in *-ary* or *-ery*, check the spelling of the word in a dictionary.

-cy and -sy Only a handful of English words end with *-sy*. Memorize the words that end with *-sy*, and you will be reasonably safe in using *-cy* for the others.

COMMON WORDS ENDING IN *-sy*

courtesy	ecstasy	fantasy	hypocrisy
curtsy	embassy	heresy	idiosyncrasy

-efy and -ify As with many of the other pairs of suffixes, one of these suffixes is much more common than the other. In this case, the ending -*efy* is rarely used except for the four words in the following chart.

COMMON WORDS ENDING IN -*efy*

liquefy	putrefy	rarefy	stupefy

-eous, -ious, -uous Confusion sometimes arises over the spelling of words ending in -*eous*, -*ious*, and -*uous*. Some of this confusion can be resolved by carefully noticing the pronunciation of the word. Words ending in -*uous*, for example, can be distinguished from the others if they are pronounced carefully. Deciding whether to use -*eous* or -*ious* is more difficult because pronunciation does not help you. It is probably best to memorize these words or check their spellings in a dictionary.

COMMON WORDS ENDING IN -*uous*, -*eous*, AND -*ious*

ambiguous	courageous	righteous	laborious
conspicuous	courteous	anxious	precious
continuous	erroneous	cautious	rebellious
ingenuous	gorgeous	conscious	religious
strenuous	outrageous	delicious	superstitious

▶ **Exercise 24** Writing Words With Confusing Endings Fill in the blanks below. Consult a dictionary if necessary.

1. court _ _ _ s
2. caut _ _ _ s
3. sens _ ble
4. diction _ _ y
5. liqu_fy
6. incred _ ble
7. hypocri _ y
8. correspond _ nce
9. stren _ _ _ s
10. gorg _ _ _ s
11. depend _ ble
12. flex _ ble
13. cemet _ ry
14. radi _ nce
15. independ _ nce
16. station _ ry (paper)
17. station _ ry (unmoving)
18. consc _ _ _ s
19. ecst _ _ y
20. brill _ _ nce

Proofreading Carefully

When you are writing, you are often thinking about the content—the ideas you want to express. However, when you have finished writing, you should proofread for spelling errors.

▷ **KEY CONCEPT** When you proofread your work, focus on each individual word. ■

To discover the proofreading methods that work best for you, use a variety of strategies. Following are some common proofreading strategies:

- Read your work, aloud or silently, to yourself.

- Proofread only one line at a time. Use a ruler or other device to focus on the line you are proofreading and to cover up the lines you are not proofreading.

- Read backwards, from the last word to the first. This forces you to focus only on the words themselves.

- Consult a dictionary when you come across a word that you suspect is spelled incorrectly.

- Check the spelling of proper nouns.

▷ **Exercise 25** **Proofreading Carefully** Write down the correct spelling of all misspelled words in each sentence below (proper nouns are correct). Use a dictionary if necessary.

(1) Within one hundred miles of Washington, D.C., there was a rurual hamlet knoun as Colvin Hollows. (2) It could be reached only by a trial that cut threw the Appalachian canyons. (3) The townspeople were desendants of settlers from a century ago. (4) At one time, the town was completly isalated from the outside world. (5) Families lived in huts and took care of there psycical needs by farming and hunting.

Reflecting on Your Spelling and Vocabulary

Review your personal spelling list, the spelling rules in your notebook, and the methods you use to increase your vocabulary. See whether the spelling lists contain a pattern of the types of words with which you have difficulty. In a journal entry, ask yourself:

- Which words are easiest for me, and which words are most difficult?

- What kinds of spelling errors do I typically make?

- Which method helped me to learn the greatest number of words?

Reading Skills

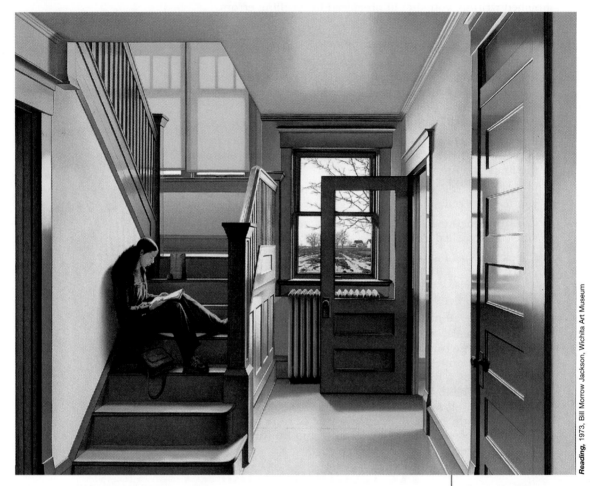

Reading, 1973, Bill Morrow Jackson, Wichita Art Museum

Reading is a visual means of acquiring and retaining information. It is the method by which the majority of students learn best. Reading involves mastering skills in a number of reading-related areas and learning to apply those skills properly. Two of these areas are textbook reading and reading style. By gaining and applying skills in these two important areas, you will become a more efficient and effective reader.

▲ **Critical Viewing**
Why might the girl in this picture have chosen this place in which to read?
[Speculate]

Reading Methods and Tools

As you proceed in life and in school, the material you read increases in quantity and difficulty. Improving your reading skills can improve your performance in your classes. These same reading skills will also increase your enjoyment and appreciation of material that you read on your own.

Reading Textbooks

▶ **KEY CONCEPT** Use textbook reading and study aids to help you understand and remember what you read. ■

Observing Textbook Sections A textbook is structured for comprehension. It contains a variety of reading aids that can help you understand the material with the least difficulty.

TEXTBOOK SECTIONS

Table of Contents This section lists units and chapters with their page numbers. Use it for a quick overview of the book.
Front of the Book

Preface or Introduction This section states the author's purpose in writing the book and may give suggestions for using the book.
Front of the Book

Index This section lists alphabetically all topics covered in the book and the pages on which they can be found. Use it to quickly locate specific topics.
Back of the Book

Glossary This section gives an alphabetical list of all the specialized terms used in the book and defines them. Use it to find definitions.
Back of the Book

Appendix This section includes charts, lists, documents, or other material related to the subject of the book. Use it as a reference source.
Back of the Book

Bibliography This section includes lists of books and articles that the author has used or referred to in writing the book. Use it for follow-up study or for research projects.
Back of the Book

Identifying Textbook Features

Textbooks have special features designed to help you find, organize, and review material:

> **KEY CONCEPT** Use the special features of your textbook to aid your reading and studying of the material. ■

Titles, Headings, and Subheadings Printed in large, heavy type and in different sizes and colors, headings give you an idea of what the material is about. They also divide the material into sections so that you can learn it more easily. Main topics usually have larger and more prominent headings; subtopics have smaller headings.

Overviews Often, a chapter or unit will begin with an overview, outline, or summary of what is to be covered. Use the overview to preview and review the chapter or unit.

Questions and Exercises These are often located at the end of a chapter. Review questions and exercises before you read the chapter to give you an idea of the main points to look for as you read. Afterward, answer the questions and exercises to retain the information you have read.

Pictures, Captions, and Graphics A picture can make a confusing idea clearer. Usually, next to a picture there is a caption—information describing the picture. Graphics such as maps, graphs, and diagrams present complex information in a clear format.

> **Exercise 1** Examining Two Textbooks Select two textbooks in different subjects, and examine them by answering these questions:
> 1. How is the table of contents in each text organized (by theme, chronologically, or by some other method)?
> 2. If the texts contain prefaces, do they explain the books' purposes and give suggestions for using the books? Which preface is more helpful?
> 3. Which text's chapter headings can you more easily turn into questions?
> 4. Are the end-of-chapter questions in each text useful for study? Are the questions in one text more helpful?
> 5. Does each text contain an index, a glossary, an appendix, and a bibliography? How do the elements help you to use the book's material?

Using Reading Strategies

You probably do not have one specific reading style, nor should you. In order to read effectively, you need to know how to pair your reading style with your purpose in reading.

> **KEY CONCEPT** Change your reading style whenever your purpose in reading changes. ■

Vary Your Reading Style

Skimming When you skim a text, you look it over quickly to get a sense of its contents. Look for highlighted or bold type, headings, and topic sentences. Skimming allows you to take in just enough information to get a general idea of the material.

Scanning When you scan a text, you look it over to find specific information. Look for words related to your topic or purpose for reading.

Close Reading When you closely read a text, you read it carefully to understand and remember its ideas. This process involves identifying main ideas, finding relationships between ideas, and drawing conclusions about what you read.

Using Question-Answer Relationships (QARs) You can master answering questions by understanding how they are written. There are four general types of questions. Once you learn these types, you will be able to answer questions more easily.

QUESTION-ANSWER RELATIONSHIPS

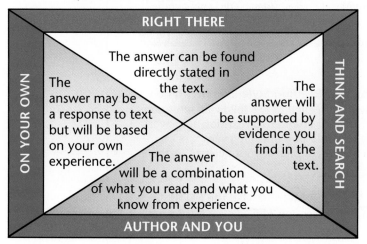

RIGHT THERE

ON YOUR OWN · **THINK AND SEARCH**

The answer can be found directly stated in the text.

The answer may be a response to text but will be based on your own experience.

The answer will be supported by evidence you find in the text.

The answer will be a combination of what you read and what you know from experience.

AUTHOR AND YOU

Research Tip

Keep a log of your reading-style use. During a period of a week or two, note which style(s) you use for different reading materials. Then, determine which style is most useful for each type of material.

Study Aids You can study your textbooks more efficiently by mastering the following six skills: **S**urvey, **Q**uestion, **R**ead, **R**ecite, **R**ecord, and **R**eview. These six skills, abbreviated as SQ4R, will prepare and guide your reading and later help you recall important information.

THE SQ4R METHOD

Survey — Preview the material you are going to read for these features: chapter title, headings, subheadings, introduction, summary, and questions or exercises.

Question — Turn each heading into a question about what will be covered under that heading. Ask the questions *who, what, when, where,* and *why* about it.

Read — Search for the answers to the questions that have been posed in the step above.

Recite — Orally or mentally recall questions and their related answers.

Record — Take notes to further reinforce the information. List the main ideas and the major details.

Review — Review the material on a regular basis, using some or all of the steps above.

> **Technology Tip**
>
> Use a graphics or word-processing program on your computer to prepare an SQ4R form to use as you read. Prepare sections for each of the method's skills, and use the forms as you read critically.

▶ **Exercise 2** Varying Your Reading Style Identify the reading style you would use first in each of the following situations.
1. You are assigned a history chapter to read for homework.
2. You are looking for the date of a specific event.
3. You are taking notes on a chapter of your science textbook.

▶ **Exercise 3** Using the SQ4R Method Use the SQ4R method to study a chapter or section of a textbook that has been assigned to you. Write a brief explanation of how you used the method and the questions you asked.

Distinguishing Between Fact and Opinion

In order to decide whether the material you are reading is reliable, you must be able to distinguish between fact and opinion.

▶ **KEY CONCEPT** Analyze material to decide whether the information presented is reliable. ■

A *fact* is a statement that can be verified, or proved true by objective means. Use records, experimentation, or observation to verify the statement. An *opinion* is a statement that cannot be verified by objective means. An opinion is subjective and must be supported with related facts before it can be accepted as valid. An opinion can express a person's feelings about an idea or a situation. It can also express a judgment or make a prediction based on facts. However, an opinion is valid only if sufficient facts are stated to support it.

FACT:	The actress has appeared in five movies.
OPINION:	The actress is very talented.
SUPPORTING FACT:	The actress has won two Academy Awards.
PREDICTION:	The actress will win an Academy Award for this movie.

▶ **Exercise 5** Analyzing Fact and Opinion Statements Identify the first sentence of each numbered item as *fact* or *opinion*. Tell whether or not the opinions are supported.

1. Camping is a fun way to vacation. Campers can enjoy the outdoors and relax.
2. The word *apnea* means the "suspension of breathing."
3. Many people keep dogs as pets.
4. Everyone should learn to play a musical instrument.
5. Cats are better pets than dogs. Cats are prettier than dogs.

▶ Critical Viewing Many people have strong opinions about pets and endangered animals. Why do you think this is so? **[Speculate]**

Applying Modes of Reasoning

Once you have verified facts and determined that opinions are valid, your next step in critical reading is to analyze the presentation of information. You need to think logically and reasonably about your material in order to draw valid conclusions about it.

KEY CONCEPT Think logically to draw valid conclusions. ■

When you think logically, you use *reasoning* to lead to or support a conclusion. In addition to other forms of reasoning, there are two kinds of formal reasoning: inductive and deductive.

Inductive Reasoning

Moving from specific facts to a conclusion or generalization based on those facts is *inductive reasoning*. A valid generalization is a statement that is supported by evidence and is true in a large number of cases. All generalizations may be open to questioning because there is usually some doubt in reliability—either stated or implied. However, the more evidence you have, the more reliable your generalization will be. If the rules for logical reasoning are not followed, the result is a logical fallacy, or an error in logic.

Deductive Reasoning

Moving from general to specific is *deductive reasoning*. Deduction starts from a general statement that is assumed to be true and applies that statement to specific cases. All of the supporting facts and evidence must be verified before you can consider the conclusion valid.

Analogies

An analogy is a comparison between two things that are similar in some ways but essentially unlike. A *true analogy* compares two different objects or events that are similar in some important way. The comparison relates something unfamiliar to something more familiar. A *false analogy* is one that overlooks essential dissimilarities between the two things being compared. Often, there is some logic in the comparison, but important evidence is omitted. To detect a false analogy, look for provable relationships in a comparison.

🖰 Research Tip

Legal arguments are based on logic. Notice court cases that are summarized in the news or portrayed in movies, books, and television programs. Examine the logic for fallacies and effectiveness.

Logical Fallacies to Avoid

A logical fallacy is a proposition or argument that does not stand up under scrutiny because it is

- not a truthful representation of the facts.
- not a valid interpretation of the facts.

Identifying Hasty Generalizations One example of a logical fallacy is a *hasty generalization*—a statement that is made about a large number of cases or a whole group on the basis of a few examples, without taking into account exceptions or qualifying factors.

EXAMPLE OF A HASTY GENERALIZATION:	Many of my friends are allergic to cats. None are allergic to dogs. Cats cause more allergies than dogs do.

To avoid being fooled by a hasty generalization, ask yourself the following questions:

- How many illustrations or examples are being offered?
- Is it probable that there are many exceptions?
- Does my own experience contradict what is stated?

Recognizing Circular Reasoning Circular reasoning occurs when the supporting facts for an argument are weak or nonexistent. In this case, the original idea is often restated as if it were evidence.

EXAMPLE OF CIRCULAR REASONING:	We have too much homework. I can never get all my homework done at night. Therefore, teachers should give less homework.

To avoid being fooled by circular reasoning, ask yourself the following questions:

- Does the supporting statement add new information?
- Is the support offered strong enough?

▶ **Exercise 6** **Identifying Forms of Reasoning** Identify the form of reasoning or the logical fallacy that applies to each of the following statements.
1. When I sleep fewer than eight hours I wake up tired. Therefore, I probably need eight hours of sleep a night.
2. The new stove must be defective somehow; it either burns the food or leaves it raw.
3. Both passengers are going to Rome; they must be together.
4. The highways of a country are like a circulatory system for goods and materials.
5. Half of the people in my class like spinach, so half of the population probably likes spinach.

Evaluating Word Choice and Language Usage

Language is a tool we use to make sense of the world. Until we can express a thought in words, we usually do not understand the thought and cannot explain it to someone else. In addition to thoughts, we express feelings by means of words.

> **KEY CONCEPT** Learn to identify different uses of language. ■

In your reading, you will find language used in various ways. Recognizing when language is being used to communicate honestly and when it is being used to distort information is an important skill. When you think critically, you need to distinguish between language that presents material clearly and honestly and language that misrepresents ideas and manipulates emotions.

Denotation The denotation of a word is found in a dictionary. It is a word's literal meaning and conveys a neutral tone. Factual or technical information contains denotation—material that is not necessarily meant to pass judgment.

Connotation Words acquire connotative meanings through their usage over time. A word's connotation is its implied meaning; it can take on a positive or negative tone. Certain connotations are emotionally charged and may be used to distort meaning or suggest different interpretations. Generally, the connotation of a word emphasizes certain characteristics or specific information, or it reveals implied or hidden attitudes.

◀ **Critical Viewing** Do newspaper articles depend more on the denotations or the connotations of words? Explain. **[Support]**

Irony Irony is the general term for literary techniques that portray differences between appearance and reality, expectation and result, or meaning and intention.

Understatement When an important idea is played down or treated casually, it is considered to be an understatement.

Inflated Language and Jargon When a writer uses scholarly, technical, or scientific words and overly long phrases, it is considered inflated language. Sometimes, inflated language is used to impress the reader or listener. It can be used to conceal the meaning behind the words.

One type of inflated language spoken by people in a specialized profession or hobby is called jargon. Although jargon appears to be scientific or technical, it often obscures otherwise simple ideas. Jargon can end up making language vague and meaningless.

Euphemism Words and phrases that are considered unpleasant or offensive are sometimes replaced with euphemisms. A euphemism is used to soften the meaning that a more direct word would convey.

Research Tip
Advertising campaigns often capitalize on language use. Observe advertisements in all forms of media, and analyze the language used. Note when language use is effective and when it is misleading.

▶ **Exercise 7** Analyzing and Evaluating Uses of Language
Match each numbered item to the description of language use. Use each letter only once.

1. Reckless spending is the root of the problem.
2. We may downsize to reduce costs.
3. The ratio of personnel to workstations is unbalanced in light of the current space requirements.
4. The change will not be easy.
5. So few people appreciate the benefits of an enforced resignation.

a. Irony
b. Understatement
c. Euphemism
d. Negative connotations
e. Inflated language

Reading Literary Writing

To understand and appreciate works of fiction, you must use your judgment and your imagination. It is just as important for you to respond personally to what you are reading. General reading strategies presented here can be applied to all types of fiction. You will also find specific strategies for reading short stories and novels, drama, and poetry.

Analyzing and Evaluating

▶ **KEY CONCEPT** Use a variety of reading strategies to increase your understanding of fictional works. ■

Establish a Purpose for Reading Before you begin to read a piece, decide why you are reading. Establish a purpose for reading, such as to find out, to understand, to interpret, to enjoy, or to solve a problem.

Ask Questions As you read, question what's going on in the text. For example: *Who* is speaking? *When* and *where* does an event take place? *What* caused it to happen? *Why* does a character say what he or she does? Read to find answers to your questions.

Reread or Read Ahead Reread a sentence, paragraph, stanza, or scene to find the connections among words and ideas. Read ahead to find more information about words and ideas.

Make Personal Connections Use your own experiences to better understand characters, events, and ideas. Think about the ways in which people and events in your own life connect to characters and events in the text.

Read Aloud Use this technique with poetry to hear the sound and rhythm of the lines; use it with drama to appreciate dialogue. Read other works of fiction aloud to gain a better sense of the author's voice.

Analyze You analyze nonfiction for reliability, but you can use the same strategy to analyze fiction to discover the effect of and reason for an author's choices. In addition to understanding specifics, this strategy will give you an overall sense of the piece.

Respond As you read, think about characters, events, conflicts, images, and other literary elements and how you respond to them. When you finish reading, think about what the work means to you, what the theme of the piece is, and how the work has affected your perspective on life.

Reading Fiction

In a great work of fiction—a novel or short story—every word has been chosen carefully to express a precise meaning. A plot has been structured, characters delineated, clues dropped, and themes deliberately implied to create a unique yet believable world. By applying the following strategies, you can more fully appreciate the fictional world a writer has so careful-ly constructed:

Envision the Action in Your Mind A skilled writer describes action clearly and vividly to help you picture the scenes of a story in your mind. Allow yourself to be carried away by the pictures painted by the author's words.

▲ Critical Viewing What clues indicate that this girl is actively involved in what she is reading? **[Analyze]**

Connect the Literature to Your Own Experiences If you empathize, or feel as another does, you'll be able to put yourself in a character's shoes. Imagine yourself in the story's setting and in the character's situations.

Question and Predict In life, you ask yourself questions about people's actions and motivations. What was he *really* doing? Why did she say that? Relate to a work of literature in the same way. Ask yourself why the characters behave as they do. When you find yourself wondering how a series of events will unfold, pause and predict what will happen. When you are trying to predict outcomes, look back, recall, and carefully weigh what you have experienced so far.

Draw Inferences and Conclusions Fictional characters and situations don't come neatly labeled "Villain" or "Disaster" —you have to infer information from the clues you're given. Use a character's attitudes and actions to read "between the lines." When you've finished reading a piece of fiction, reflect on its overall meaning. What general ideas does the writer want you to carry away?

Connect to Historical Context Consider the events and customs of the time in which the work was written. These factors will influence the way an author portrays characters.

▶ **Exercise 8** Reading Short Stories and Novels Read a short story from your textbook or another source. Write a brief explanation of how you applied each of the strategies on this page.

Reading Drama

While plays share many elements with prose, fiction, and poetry, the greatest difference is that a drama is designed to be acted out on a stage before an audience. The story unfolds through dialogue and action and is integrated with the setting that the audience observes—largely from scenery and props. Stage directions indicate when and how the actors move and sometimes suggest sound and lighting effects. When you read a play, you are reading a script; you must always keep in mind that it was written to be performed.

Envision the Action Reading a play without envisioning the action is like watching a movie with your eyes shut. Use scenery and prop descriptions, stage directions, and other details to create the scene in your mind. Where and when does the action take place? How and where do the actors move? What do they sound like? What goes on between the characters, and what do they say to one another?

▲ **Critical Viewing** What stage directions would you expect to find in the written version of this scene from *The Crucible*? What historical details would the playwright have to provide? **[Analyze]**

Connect the Play to Its Historical Context Explore the play's setting. When does the action of the drama occur? What conditions existed during that time period? If the drama takes place in a historical or foreign setting, consider that customs and accepted conduct may differ from those with which you are familiar.

Summarize Dramas are often broken into acts or scenes. These breaks give you an opportunity to review the action. What is the conflict? What happens to move it toward its resolution? Put the characters' actions and words together as you summarize.

▶ **Exercise 9** Reading Drama Read the first act or the first few scenes of a play. List three details describing the play's setting, and elaborate briefly on its historical context; describe the main character(s) in the act or scenes you read; identify two events and the stage directions that indicate them; and describe the action that takes place.

Reading Poetry

Because a poem generally comes at the truth sideways rather than head on, you must use a number of strategies to help you unravel the meaning the poet has hidden within the lines.

Identify the Poem's Speaker Identifying the speaker of a poem is an important first step in gaining insight into a poem. The speaker may be the poet or a fictional character created by the poet.

Engage Your Senses Poems use images—words or phrases that appeal to the five senses—to convey meaning. As you read, picture the visual images in all their detail. Hear the sounds described, and imagine the textures and scents. When you engage your senses, you will find greater enjoyment and meaning in the poem. To help you engage poetry on the sensory level, you may want to use a sensory chart, to which you can add words or images from a poem.

Relate Structure to Meaning Notice where sentences begin and end and how ideas are grouped into stanzas; the start of a new stanza often signals the introduction of a new thought or idea.

Paraphrase Pause occasionally to restate passages in your own words.

Connect to a Historical Context Understanding the social, political, economic, and literary environment in which a poem was written will help you grasp its meaning.

Listen to the Poem To fully appreciate a poem, you must listen to it. Try reading the poem aloud. Analyze the melodies of literary language, paying attention to rhythms and to the repetition of certain sounds. Consider how they contribute to the mood and meaning of the work.

▶ **Exercise 10** Reading Poetry Select a poem from your textbook or personal reading. Read the poem aloud, and listen to its sound. Then, write an analysis of the poem in which you identify the speaker; characterize three images; describe the poem's rhythms and repetition; explain what you think is the poem's meaning; and conclude with a description of the poem's overall effect.

Reading From Varied Sources

Information is made available to you in a wide variety of formats. These sources include—but are not limited to— books, magazines, Web pages, advertisements, newspapers, letters, and speeches. By familiarizing yourself with different types of sources, you will widen the range and type of information you can learn and use.

Read Diaries, Letters, and Journals

Diaries, letters, and journals are firsthand accounts of events or circumstances. Although they are not usually written with publication in mind, they are often published after the writer's death with the permission of his or her family. Some may be written by people whose achievements make them interesting subjects. Others are written by people who lived in interesting times. Keep in mind when you read these primary sources that not all the information in them will be strictly factual. Much of what you read will reflect the writer's personal opinions.

Read Newspapers

Newspapers, which are printed on a daily or weekly basis, are an excellent source of information on current events and issues in your community, in the United States, and around the world. When you read a newspaper, take into account whether the coverage is local, national, or global. Each section of a newspaper has its own purpose. For example, editorial pages offer opinions and evaluations of the topics they cover. Other sections give an unbiased, factual account of the topics they cover. As with all sources, read newspapers critically. Keep an eye out for bias or faulty logic.

Read Transcripts of Speeches and Interviews

A transcript is a written record of what was spoken. You can obtain transcripts of most famous speeches in library resources. Books and other references contain the printed record of what a speaker said. Interview transcripts are usually available through the media that produced the interview. For example, for a transcript of an interview on television, you can write to the television station that produced the program. Speeches and interviews offer one person's perspective on an issue, a situation, or a condition. These thoughts, unlike those set down in diaries or letters, are usually intended for publication. Like diaries and letters, speeches and interviews reveal the person's opinions.

Read Electronic Texts

Web pages, electronic advertising, and e-mail—each of these presents text through an electronic medium. Whether you read text on screen or on a page, read critically. When you read a Web page, consider the source when you evaluate the reliability of the information presented. Look for evidence that the creator of the page has background and expertise in the area. Determine whether the page is sponsored by a company or group that wants to promote a particular point of view. The Internet can be an excellent resource, but as is true with all resources, you must use it with a critical awareness.

▲ **Critical Viewing**
For what types of information might these students be searching? **[Infer]**

Exercise 11 Reading Varied Sources Choose an event or time period from American history, such as the Civil War, the Depression, or the bombing of Pearl Harbor. Find an account of the event or the period in at least three different sources described on these pages. Write a summary of the information you find in each. Then, in a brief evaluation, compare and contrast the type of information you found in each, as well as the unique perspective you gained from reading each source.

Reflecting on Your Reading

After a week of applying reading skills and strategies to both nonfiction and fiction works, think about the experience of using them. Use these questions to direct your reflection:

- Which textbook sections and features do I use most often? For what purpose do I use them?

- Which reading strategies will be most useful to me when I am studying? Which will I use when I am doing research?

- In what ways will the questioning strategies help me analyze and evaluate what I read?

- Which strategies for reading fiction do I find most useful? Which do I find most difficult to use? Which strategies do I want to try to use more often? Why?

Jot down your responses and ideas in a journal or notebook. If you like, compare your thoughts and ideas with those of a partner.

Chapter 31
Study, Reference, and Test-Taking Skills

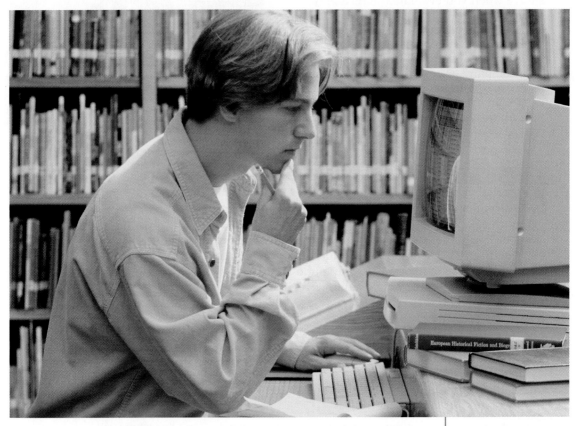

The more skillful you become at studying, the more you will be able to concentrate your efforts on doing your best work. Good study skills can be the key to success in school—you will find that you will need to study less, you will improve your grades, and you will increase your performance on college entrance exams. Overall, your attitude toward school and test-taking will be more positive.

In this chapter, you will learn more about making the most of your study time. You will also learn more about finding information in printed and electronic sources. In addition, you will receive valuable tips that can help you improve your test scores.

▲ **Critical Viewing** On what type of project do you think this student is currently working? On what do you base your answer? **[Speculate]**

Section 31.1

Basic Study Skills

Developing a Study Plan

Time management is essential to your success in school. A study plan can help you to use time to your best advantage.

KEY CONCEPT Develop a study plan in order to manage and use your time most efficiently. ■

Study Area Working in an area that you associate only with studying will enable you to concentrate so that you can do your work better. Set up a study area that is free of distractions, quiet, well lit, and contains all the necessary materials.

Study Schedule Establishing a study schedule will help you fit in all of your assignments and activities. Make a study schedule that will fit your personal needs.

⊙ **Technology Tip**

Create computer forms for your study schedule and assignment book using software such as a word-processing, spreadsheet, or time-management program. You can update and change your forms as your needs change.

MAKING A STUDY SCHEDULE

1. Block out time periods in which you have activities, such as the regular school day, after-school clubs or sports, dinner, etc.
2. Block out study periods of no longer than forty-five minutes each. Take a ten-minute break between each period.
3. Schedule study periods for those times when you are most alert.
4. Plan to study your most difficult subject first.
5. Use study hall and free time at school to complete some assignments.

Assignment Book Keeping track of your assignments in an assignment book will enable you to organize your time to complete both short-term and long-term assignments efficiently. A long-term assignment, such as a research paper, can be divided into short-term goals that you must meet in order to complete the assignment.

Exercise 1 Evaluating Your Study Plan Identify the study skill you need to improve most: setting up a study area, making a study schedule, or keeping an assignment book. Work to improve that skill for one week, and then evaluate your progress.

Taking Notes

Taking notes is an active way to organize and condense material you need to learn. To take useful notes on classroom lectures and activities, as well as on what you read in textbooks, make sure that you have an organized notebook or binder.

- Notes for each subject should be separated by a labeled divider.
- Notes should be neat, with the date and topic on each page.

> **KEY CONCEPT** Use outlines or summaries to take notes while listening or reading. ■

Modified Outline A *formal outline* is a method for taking notes that shows the relationship between main ideas and other ideas that support them (see Section 13.2 for an example). A *modified outline* is a skeleton of the subject—it allows you to organize information quickly. Use a modified outline to record information from lectures, films, discussions, and books. You can also use it to organize ideas before answering questions on an essay test.

In the modified outline below, main ideas are underlined and supporting details are numbered. Notice the short phrases and occasional abbreviations or symbols that are used.

MODIFIED OUTLINE:

> **Technology Tip**
>
> Word-processing programs often have an outlining feature. You may find it helpful to use this feature as you outline material you are studying.

> **Exercise 2** Making a Modified Outline Listen to a television newscast and take notes in modified outline form, using your own words. After the newscast, read your notes, and fill in any information that is needed to make them more clear.

Summary Another useful way to record information is to write a summary of it. In a *summary*, you state the main ideas of a lecture or printed material in your own words, using a few complete sentences. You may take notes in a modified outline and then summarize them, or you may take notes in summary form directly from listening or reading.

Exercise 3 Writing a Summary Write a summary of the notes you took in your modified outline of a television newscast. You may repeat the exercise with another newscast, using summary writing to take notes directly from listening.

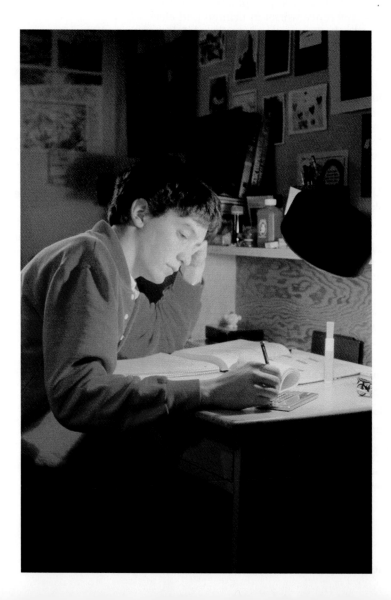

Learn More

Graphic organizers are another excellent tool for taking notes. To learn about using graphic organizers to take notes and present your ideas, see Chapter 28.

◀ **Critical Viewing** Do you think that this looks like an effective study space? Why or why not? **[Analyze]**

Reference Skills

A tremendous amount of information is available through libraries and media centers, as well as through your own computer. This section explores how and where to access the information and how to use the reference sources most effectively.

Using the Library

Libraries, or media centers, are organized carefully to help you find what you need. You will find some, or all, of these resources offered: fiction and nonfiction books, audio- and videocassettes, periodicals (newspapers, magazines, and scholarly journals), microfilm, vertical files, pamphlets and other small printed materials, reference works in printed and electronic form, and access to the Internet and on-line databases.

Using the Library Catalog A *library catalog* is an alphabetically arranged record of books and audiovisual materials that are in the library.

In the past, a library catalog was a system of cards that were filed alphabetically in drawers. You may still find a library catalog that is organized this way, but you are just as likely to find a library catalog organized in printed booklets or in an electronic format.

▶ **KEY CONCEPT** Use the library catalog to find information about a library's books and other materials. ∎

Card Catalog A card catalog lists books, tapes, and CDs on index cards, with each item having a separate *author card* and *title card;* if the book is nonfiction, it will also have at least one *subject card.* Cards are filed alphabetically in cabinets of small drawers.

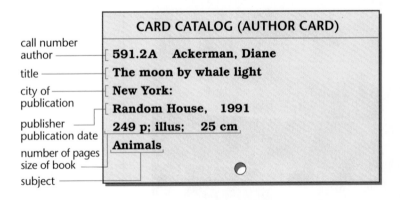

CARD CATALOG (AUTHOR CARD)

call number
author ———— 591.2A   Ackerman, Diane
title ———— The moon by whale light
city of ———— New York:
publication
publisher ———— Random House,   1991
publication date
number of pages —— 249 p; illus;   25 cm
size of book ——
subject ———— Animals

Technology Tip

Ask a librarian whether you can access the library's electronic catalog from a computer outside the library. If so, find out whether you need to download software (usually at no cost) to connect to the on-line catalog.

Printed Catalog A printed catalog lists books on printed pages, with each book listed alphabetically by author, by title, and—if nonfiction—by subject. Often, there are separate booklets for author, title, and subject listings.

Electronic Catalog An electronic catalog lists books in a database that you can access from computers in the library or by using special software on your home computer. Search by typing in the author, title, or subject—often key words or just an author's last name will locate the information you want. Copy status may also be included—whether the book is checked in or available at a branch library or through an interlibrary loan system.

▲ **Critical Viewing** How does this library compare with the one in your school? **[Compare and Contrast]**

ELECTRONIC CATALOG

Author: Ackerman, Diane.
Title: The moon by whale light.
Published: New York: Random House, 1991.
Description: 249 p.; ill.; 25 cm.
Subject: Animals.
Call No.:   591.2A.
Status: On shelf.

▶ **Exercise 4** **Using the Library Catalog** Visit your school or local library, and use the catalog to answer these questions.
1. What kind of catalog does the library use—card, printed, or electronic? Where is it located?
2. Who wrote *The Sun Also Rises?* Is it fiction or nonfiction?
3. What are the titles, subjects, and call numbers of the books in your library by the author Italo Calvino?
4. What are the titles, authors, and call numbers of three books about space exploration published since 1990?
5. What are the titles, authors, and call numbers of two nonfiction books about architecture that are more than one hundred pages long?

Going From Catalog to Shelf

Besides the title and the author, the most important piece of information in a library catalog entry is the *location symbol*. In order to locate an item on the shelf, match the symbols and numbers found in a catalog entry with the symbols and numbers found on the item itself.

Libraries classify books into two main groups: *fiction* (stories created by an author) and *nonfiction* (factual material). Nonfiction includes two smaller groups—*biographies* and *reference books*—that are usually shelved separately.

KEY CONCEPT Use catalog entry location symbols to find materials on library shelves. ∎

Fiction Books Catalog entries for fiction will usually have the location symbol *F* or *Fic*, indicating that the books are located in the fiction section of the library. Some libraries include either all or just the first few letters of the author's last name below the location symbol.

Nonfiction Books Most high-school and public libraries arrange nonfiction books by the *Dewey Decimal System* of classification. This classification system divides knowledge into ten main classes, numbered from 000 to 999. Each of the classes is divided into ten divisions, and each of the divisions is divided into ten subdivisions. When necessary, the subdivisions can be divided even further.

EXAMPLES OF THE WAY NONFICTION BOOKS ARE CLASSIFIED

MAIN CLASS:	600–699	Technology
DIVISIONS:	620	Engineering
SUBDIVISIONS:	621	Applied Physics
FURTHER DIVISIONS:	621.1	Steam Engineering
	621.15	Engines
	621.16	Stationary Engines
	621.165	Turbine Engines

Catalog entries for nonfiction include a *call number* in the location symbol. In a library that uses the Dewey Decimal System, the call number is a Dewey Decimal number. The numbers of the call number are generally followed by the first letter or letters of the author's last name. A library designed for research usually does not contain shelves of books (stacks) for users to browse and locate their own books. In a research library, you submit a call slip to the librarian and get "called" when the book has been retrieved.

Research Tip

Some college and university libraries will allow you access for your research. They may have materials that are not available to you at your school or public libraries.

Locating Biographies and Special Materials

Although biographies can be shelved in the library's history section (the 920's of the Dewey Decimal System) and reference books may be shelved in the specific section that corresponds to their subject, these materials are often found in separate sections.

Biographies The life stories of individual people are marked with the location symbol *B* or *BIO* (for biography) or *92* (short for 920). Biographies are shelved alphabetically by the subject of the book—Franklin D. Roosevelt, instead of by the author of the book (biographer), Doris Kearns Goodwin.

Collective biographies, or books that contain chapter-length biographies about a number of people, will usually be shelved with the library's history section. Their location symbols include 920 through 929 as their call numbers.

Reference Materials Most libraries have an area for reference materials that is separate from the other books. These materials may include booklets as well as books. Any library reference material almost always will carry the letter *R* or *Ref* above the call number. Usually, items that are classified as *Reference* cannot be removed from the library.

Nonprint Materials A variety of symbols may mark nonprint materials—matching the special format of the items. For example, *VC* might be used above a call number to indicate a videocassette. Since most nonprint materials will be kept separately and are often unavailable for direct access, you should ask the librarian for help in finding and using these materials.

▲ **Critical Viewing** Where on these books would you find their Dewey Decimal System identification codes? **[Identify]**

▶ **Exercise 5** **Using Your Library Skills** Follow the steps listed below to prepare a list of materials on a topic of your choice. Then, write a brief paragraph stating how you would like to develop these materials into a research paper.
1. Select a topic for research. It may be a topic that you are researching for one of your other classes.
2. Find ten items in the library catalog related to your topic. Choose a variety of materials, including at least three non-print materials.
3. Copy the essential information from the catalog entry: title, author, and location symbol or call number.
4. Find the materials in the library.
5. Revise your list if any materials cannot be located or do not seem appropriate and useful for your topic.

Using Periodicals, Periodical Indexes, and the Vertical File

Periodical is a term applied to anything published regularly during the year. Periodicals include magazines and journals, but they can include newspapers as well. A *periodical file* lists articles that appear in periodicals by subject and date. In the *vertical file*, you can find the information contained in booklets or pamphlets.

▶ **KEY CONCEPT** Use periodicals to supplement research with specialized or current information; periodical indexes to find articles in periodicals, and the vertical file to find small printed materials. ■

Periodicals Some periodicals are of general interest, while others are devoted to specialized topics. Because of their current nature, periodicals can be a valuable research aid for information that is not available in books.

Periodical Indexes Periodical indexes, which may be published in print or electronic form, are updated regularly and cite articles that appeared during a specified period of time. Many indexes make it possible for you to look up information in periodicals by either subject or author.

SOME COMMON PERIODICAL INDEXES

- *Readers' Guide to Periodical Literature*, often referred to as the *Readers' Guide*, which covers all types of periodicals
- *Art Index, Humanities Index*
- *Business and Technology Index*

Below is a sample entry from the *Readers' Guide*:

SAMPLE READERS' GUIDE ENTRY

subject heading ——————[**TRACK AND FIELD ATHLETICS**

         See also

cross-references ————[Mile running
            [Pole vaulting

subheading ⌐ **Women**   topic clarified in brackets

title of article ⌐ For the record [Joyner-Kersee and F Griffith Joyner].
      illustrated with portraits

author ⌐   K. Casey. il pors *Ladies Home Journal* v116 no 4

name of periodical ——————————   volume and number⌐

pages ————[p. 148-51+ Ap 1999   ⌐date
                └continued at rear of magazine

Research Tip

It is part of a librarian's job to assist the library's users. Do not expect him or her to do your research for you, but take advantage of the librarian's extensive knowledge of the materials that are available. Often, they can guide you to the best sources to meet your needs.

How to Use Periodical Indexes In *printed indexes*, citations are listed alphabetically by subject and sometimes by author. Sometimes, the citations contain abstracts, or brief summaries, of the articles. In *electronic indexes*, citations are part of a database and come up on your screen after you search by typing in specific information, such as the subject, the author's name, or the date; you can also search with key words that will lead you to specific articles. Electronic indexes may also provide full text—an electronic version of the complete articles cited for some or all articles.

Vertical Files Pamphlets are similar to magazines and newspapers in that they often contain current information. Libraries usually store pamphlets in a vertical file—a file cabinet with large drawers. Pamphlets can be found on such topics as welfare, state parks, child abuse, and education. In addition, there may be booklets, folded maps, original newspaper and magazine clippings, and photos. Do not hesitate to ask the librarian whether information on the topic of your research might be found in the vertical file.

▲ Critical Viewing In what types of activities might these students be involved? On what do you base your answer? **[Speculate]**

▶ **Exercise 6** Using Periodicals and Periodical Indexes Visit your school or local library to find answers to these questions about periodicals and periodical indexes.

1. Which printed indexes does the library have? Which electronic indexes are available?
2. Which newspapers does the library carry? Is microfilm or microfiche available for back issues of the newspapers?
3. Give the titles of three news magazines that the library has. In what format are they available?
4. Using the most current issue of the *Readers' Guide*, find an article citation and read the article in a copy of the magazine in the library. (Many libraries will store copies of the most current magazines and newspapers for reference use until they are bound or transferred onto microfilm.)
5. Use an electronic index to locate and find an article for which full text is provided in electronic form. Would you have found that article in the hard-copy material that the library provides?

Using Dictionaries

Of all general reference materials, you probably use a dictionary most often. A *dictionary* is a collection of words and their meanings, along with other information, such as a word's pronunciation, usage, and history. If you refer to a dictionary merely to check the meaning or spelling of words, however, you are not getting all you can out of this valuable resource.

KEY CONCEPT Dictionaries contain a wealth of information about words. Use the dictionary that best suits your needs. ■

Distinguishing Types of Dictionaries There are dictionaries published for almost every audience: for students to use in their studies, for adults to use at home or at work, and for scholars to use in their research. Many dictionaries are available in both printed and electronic form. The following chart describes the three main types of dictionaries.

THREE TYPES OF DICTIONARIES

Unabridged	Exhaustive study of the English language containing more than 250,000 words
Abridged	Compact edition containing listings of 55,000 to 160,000 words
Specialized	Edition limited to words of a particular field, such as foreign languages or mathematics

Exercise 7 Choosing a Dictionary For each situation, answer which kind of dictionary (*unabridged*, *abridged*, or *specialized*) would be the most appropriate.
1. finding special detailed information about a word
2. finding a comprehensive definition of a legal or medical term
3. finding a word's basic meaning
4. finding the origin of a word
5. finding the translation of a foreign word

Research Tip

Unabridged dictionaries are often found on stands in various places in library reading rooms. When you want to look up a word, take a notebook with you because this large dictionary is too bulky to be moved.

Finding Words in Printed Dictionaries A word listed in the dictionary, with all the information about it, is called an *entry*. In printed dictionaries, entry words are arranged alphabetically. To speed your search for a word, some dictionaries provide the following aids:

- **thumb index**—a series of right-hand notches, labeled alphabetically, which indicate the section of entries for words that start with that particular letter or letters
- **guide words**—the two words printed in large type at the top of a dictionary page showing the first and last words covered on the page

To speed your search for a word, use these features:

The Four-Section Approach The four-section approach is a search strategy for finding words quickly. To use this strategy, follow these two steps:

1. Mentally divide the dictionary into the four sections:

ABCD   MNOPQR

EFGHIJKL   STUVWXYZ

2. When you go to look up a word, decide into which section the word falls. For example, if you want to look up *homage*, you know that the word falls near the middle of the second section. If, on the other hand, you want to look up *scabbard*, you know that the word falls near the beginning of the last section.

Finding Words in Electronic Dictionaries In electronic dictionaries, you usually find a word's entry simply by typing the word and having the computer search the dictionary database. If you are unsure of a word's spelling, you can usually type in the first few letters and see a list of words that are similar in spelling.

▶ **Exercise 8** **Working With a Dictionary** Use a dictionary to answer the following questions.
1. In what order would these entry words appear?
   protein—parallel—mortar—cultivate—network
2. Which of the following entry words would appear on a page with the guide words *introduction* and *invention*?
   intrude—introduce—intuitive—invent—inventive
3. What two guide words appear on the page with *midyear*?
4. Which word is not spelled correctly?
   existence—resistance—priviledge—judgment—tranquillity
5. Which word is spelled correctly?
   advisir—accomodate—lightening—fullfill—nickel

Looking at the Parts of a Dictionary Entry In a dictionary, a *main entry* consists of a word and all the information about it. The word (a single word, a compound word, an abbreviation, a prefix or suffix, or the name of a person or place) is called an *entry word.*

Preferred and Variant Spellings English words usually have only one correct spelling, as shown by the entry word. Some words, however, can be spelled in more than one way. The spelling most commonly used is called the *preferred spelling.* A less commonly used spelling is called a *variant spelling.* Most dictionaries provide both preferred and variant spellings.

Syllabification Dots, spaces, or slashes in an entry word indicate where that word may be divided into syllables. When breaking words at the end of a line, remember that you cannot leave a syllable of just one letter on a line by itself. Words with one syllable and contractions are never divided.

Pronunciation Usually appearing right after the entry word, the pronunciation uses symbols to show how to say the word. The syllable that gets the most emphasis has a *primary stress,* usually shown by a heavy mark after the syllable [']. Words of more than one syllable may also have a *secondary stress,* usually shown by a shorter, lighter mark ['].

Part-of-Speech Label The dictionary also tells you how a word can be used in a sentence—whether it functions as a noun, verb, or some other part of speech. This information is given as an abbreviation, usually after the pronunciation.

Research Tip

Unabridged dictionaries frequently include sentences and phrases that show words in context. This feature will help you understand the correct and precise usage of a word.

SAMPLE DICTIONARY ENTRY

① **liv·er·y** (liv′ər ē) *n.*, pl. **-er·ies** [ME, allowance of food, gift of clothes to a servant, thing delivered <OFr *livree*, pp. of *livrer*, to deliver < L *liberare*, to LIBERATE] **1** an identifying uniform such as was formerly worn by feudal retainers or is now worn by servants or those in some particular group, trade, etc. **2** the people wearing such uniforms **3** characteristic dress or appearance **4 a)** the keeping and feeding of horses for a fixed charge **b)** the keeping of horses, vehicles, or both, for hire ☆**c)** LIVERY STABLE ☆**5** a place where boats can be rented **6** [Historical] *Eng. Law* the legal delivery of property, esp. landed property, into the hands of the new owner.

1. Entry Word
2. Pronunciation
3. Part-of-Speech Label
4. Plural Form
5. Etymology
6. Definitions
7. Usage Labels

Plurals and Inflected Forms After the part-of-speech label, the dictionary may also show the plural forms of nouns and inflected forms (past tense and participle forms of verbs) if there is anything irregular about their spelling.

Etymology The origin and history of the word is called its etymology. The etymology usually appears in brackets, parentheses, or slashes near the start or end of the entry. It often uses abbreviations for languages, all of which are explained in the dictionary's key to abbreviations.

Definition The meaning of a word is called its definition. Definitions are numbered if there is more than one. Often, they include an example that illustrates the use of that meaning in a phrase or sentence.

Usage Labels Words labeled *Archaic (Arch.), Obsolete (Obs.), Poetic,* or *Rare* are not widely used today. Those labeled *Informal (Inf.), Colloquial (Colloq.),* or *Slang* are not considered part of formal English. Those labeled *Brit.* are used mainly in countries associated with Britain, not in the United States.

Field Labels Words used in a special way by people in a certain occupation or activity have field labels, such as *History (Hist.), Mathematics (Math.),* and *Chemistry (Chem.).*

Idioms and Derived Words At the end of an entry, idioms—expressions that contain the entry word—may be listed and defined. Derived words, words formed from the entry word (along with their part-of-speech labels) may also be listed.

> **Exercise 9** **Working With a Dictionary** Use a dictionary to follow the directions below.
> 1. Mark the pronunciation for the word *excruciating.*
> 2. What part of speech is the word *concoct*?
> 3. What is the variant spelling of *empanel*?
> 4. Write the plural of the word *parenthesis.* Write the inflected forms of the words *recur* and *control.*
> 5. Describe the etymology of the word *peninsula.*
> 6. Look up *pass* in a dictionary, and write three sentences that use three different meanings for the word.
> 7. Compare and contrast American and British uses of *entrée.*
> 8. Write the definition of *spin* that follows the field label for *flight.*
> 9. Find a dictionary that explains the meaning of the idiom "if worst comes to worst." Describe the meaning of the phrase.
> 10. Look up the word *depressor* in a dictionary. From what word and language is it derived?

◉ Vocabulary Tip

Etymologies are a valuable aid for extending your vocabulary. Knowing a word's origin can help you remember it and can help you unlock the meaning of related words with a common orgin.

Using Other Print References

In addition to consulting nonfiction books and periodicals, take advantage of a library's reference section when conducting research. The materials in a reference section include general references, which cover broad areas of knowledge and usually do not go into great detail, and specialized references, which focus on a specific topic. Be aware that both types of references usually cannot be checked out.

> **KEY CONCEPT** Use general reference works to check basic facts or to explore the range of a topic; use specialized reference books to gather detailed information about one aspect of a broad topic. ■

Encyclopedias General encyclopedias contain articles on a wide range of subjects. The information usually fills a series of books—twenty or more volumes. The alphabetical order and indexes help users find information quickly. Not all topics have a specific article, but the index—usually in one or two separate volumes—directs you to articles that cover particular topics.

Almanacs Almanacs provide up-to-date statistics and other facts on such topics as government, history, geography, astronomy, population, and sports. Relatively inexpensive, almanacs can be found in bookstores as well as in libraries.

Atlases and Gazetteers Atlases include maps accompanied by informative text, such as facts and charts about population distribution, seasonal temperature and rainfall, agricultural and industrial production, and natural resources. When using an atlas, use the index to determine which map you need for a particular place. Unlike atlases, most gazetteers do not contain maps. Instead, they offer brief descriptions of places, arranged alphabetically like entries in a dictionary. In short, gazetteers are geographical dictionaries.

Specialized Reference Works For more detailed information than general reference works provide, there are specialized reference works. These works include specialized dictionaries and thesauruses (or dictionaries of synonyms), specialized encyclopedias, and biographical reference works.

> **Exercise 10** Using Reference Works Use reference works to answer these questions.
> 1. In what country is South America's highest mountain?
> 2. What country did Catherine the Great come from?
> 3. What states border Idaho?
> 4. Who won the Nobel Prize for Literature in 1948?
> 5. What was the purpose of Hadrian's Wall?

Research Tip

Check each of your textbooks for suggestions on appropriate reference works for researching topics for the corresponding classes.

Using Electronic and Media References

In today's world, you are not limited to using books to conduct research. You can take advantage of a wide range of electronic and media resources, including video collections, CD-ROMs, the Internet, and on-line subscription services.

Video References Often, you can get excellent information on a topic by watching a video. Consult your librarian to find out about videos such as the following:

- **News programs** offer current information and insights into how people reacted to historical events as they happened.
- **Documentaries** give in-depth information on specific topics.
- **Special-interest series** provide extended, detailed coverage of many aspects of a topic—for example, the Bill Moyers series on the history of the English language provides valuable insights into how the language evolved.

CD-ROM References Many types of reference works are available on CD-ROM, as well as in printed form.

- **CD-ROM encyclopedias** can provide as much information on a single disc as a twenty-volume book collection. Many CD-ROM encyclopedias also include video and audio segments. To find information, use the search function.
- **CD-ROM atlases** are set up as a database so you can enter a place name or key word to run a computer search for the appropriate map.

Electronic Databases Electronic databases can be found on CD-ROMs or on the Internet. They provide large collections of data on specific topics, and you can search for the data that helps you. The advantages of storing data electronically are that computer disks and servers do not require the space of file cabinets, and the computer searches quickly and thoroughly to give you complete search results in little time.

Technology Tip

Although electronic reference works are valuable resources for your research, your library probably has a limited number of computer terminals for users. Ask the librarian if there is a time when there may be less demand for the computers.

▼ Critical Viewing What are the key differences between conducting research in books and researching on a computer? **[Compare]**

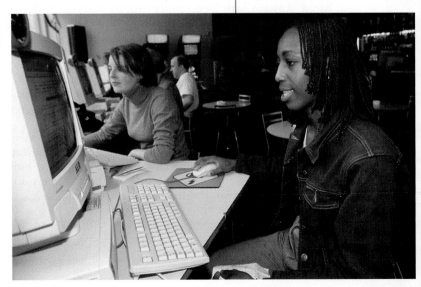

Using the Internet

The Internet is a worldwide network, or Web, of computers connected by phone and cable lines. When you go on-line, or hook up to the Internet, you have access to information at a tremendous number and variety of Web sites. Each Web site has its own address, or URL (Universal Resource Locator). The sites usually consist of several Web pages of text, graphics, and sometimes audio or video displays, which you can download or save on your computer.

▶ **KEY CONCEPT** Use the Internet for all kinds of information, but judge Web sites for reliability. ■

Locating Appropriate Web Sites If you know a reliable Web site and its address (URL), simply type the address into the URL window of your Web browser. If you do not have a specific site in mind, use a search engine, such as *Yahoo* or *Lycos*. Enter key words connected to a topic to find Web sites related to that topic.

- Some search engines are useful for searching broad categories—they allow you to start with broad topics and narrow them down to more specific categories that you might not have considered.
- Some search engines are useful if you already know the specific direction that your search will take.
- Some search engines are "crawlers" that find the top "hits" from other search engines. You may find what you want in the results or determine a particular search engine to use to produce the best results for your search.

Evaluating Web Sites All Internet sources are not created equal. Anyone with a computer and an Internet linkup can transmit data or create a Home Page. As a result, it is essential to critically evaluate any sites you come across. Use the following questions to guide your evaluation.

QUESTIONS FOR EVALUATING WEB SITES
1. What is the source of the information—a respected publisher or organization, a discussion group, or an individual? Are original sources provided?
2. Does the source have credentials—such as experience in the subject or affiliation with a recognized organization?
3. Is the source objective, or is the organization or individual seeking to persuade you to think or act in a certain way?
4. How does the information compare with that presented on other related sites?
5. Is the information up to date?

Technology Tip

Whenever possible, copy and paste URLs from an electronic source to the location (address) line of your browser. This common editing feature allows you to transfer URLs among word-processing programs, e-mail, and the Internet. It's easier, saves time, and there is no chance that you will type one or two letters or numbers of the URL wrong.

Evaluating Information on Web Sites Once you have determined that a Web site is reliable, it is still necessary to look critically at the information it presents. Check to see that each statement that is presented is backed up by evidence. In addition, verify the information using at least one—and preferably two—additional sources. Keep in mind that these sources can be books as well as electronic sources.

Technology Tip

You can often print out a Web page or download it onto a diskette. On a home computer, you can also highlight and copy and paste it into a file in your word-processing program.

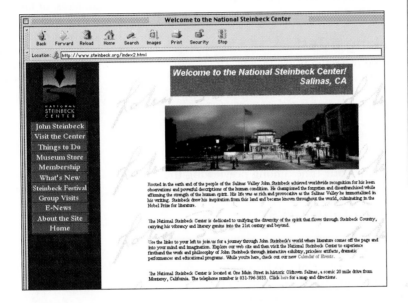

◀ **Critical Viewing** What can you tell about this Web site based on its Home Page? **[Analyze]**

Exercise 11 **Using the Internet** Using a computer in your library, school computer lab, or at home, go on-line and research information to carry out the following research tasks.

1. Use the Internet to find a mailing address for the San Francisco Opera Association.
2. Use the Internet to find the year that the original production of *Death of a Salesman* opened on Broadway, who directed it, and who the major star of the play was.
3. Choose a topic for a literary analysis. List the names and URLs of four Web sites that you think can help you.
4. Find one of Shakespeare's sonnets on the Internet. Record the name and URL of your source.
5. From a reliable Web site, find out about the history of baseball leagues.

Test-Taking Skills

Taking Tests

Tests are an important part of school and can play a key role in determining your acceptance into college, graduate school, and certain occupations. By learning what types of questions are included and by following strategies for approaching a test, you can improve your performance.

Strategies for Taking a Test

Regardless of the type of test you are taking, there are strategies you can use to maximize your performance. The chart below lists some of these strategies, dividing them into tasks to be completed before taking the test, strategies to follow while taking the test, and a proofreading process to follow before you turn in the test.

> **KEY CONCEPT** Divide your time among previewing the test, answering the questions, and proofreading. ∎

🔲 Research Tip

There are many books and computer programs to help prepare students for taking tests. Check your library or media center for these materials, and take advantage of the practice exercises you find in them.

HOW TO TAKE A TEST

LOOK OVER THE TEST

1. Skim the test to get an overview of the types of questions.
2. Decide how much time you must spend on each section.
3. Plan to devote the most time to questions that are hardest or worth the most points.

ANSWER THE QUESTIONS

1. Answer the easy questions first. Put a check next to harder questions, and come back to them later.
2. If permitted, use scratch paper to jot down your ideas.
3. Read each question at least twice before answering it.
4. Supply the single best answer.
5. Answer all questions on the test unless you are told not to guess or that there is a penalty for wrong guesses.
6. Do not change your first answer without a good reason.

PROOFREAD ANSWERS

1. Check that you have followed the directions completely.
2. Reread test questions and answers. Make sure that you have answered all the questions.

Answering Different Kinds of Questions

Familiarize yourself with the features of each type of question so you can answer questions efficiently and accurately when you encounter them on classroom or standardized tests.

KEY CONCEPT Use specific strategies for handling each type of test question to achieve higher test scores. ■

Multiple-Choice Questions Vocabulary and general comprehension are often tested with a multiple-choice format. Three to five possible answers are provided for each question. Typically, only two will come close to being the correct answer.

EXAMPLE: In the following sentence, circle the letter of the underlined word that is used incorrectly.

Tom and <u>me</u> <u>are</u> going to see the movie with <u>her</u>.
a. me   c. her
b. are   d. none of the above

ANSWER: a. (The sentence should read, "Tom and *I* are going to see the movie with her.")

Follow these steps to answer multiple-choice questions:

ANSWERING MULTIPLE-CHOICE QUESTIONS
1. Try answering the question before looking at the choices. If your answer is one of the choices, select that choice.
2. Eliminate the obviously incorrect answers, crossing them out if you are allowed to write on the test paper.
3. Change a question into a statement by inserting your answer. See if the statement makes sense.

Matching Questions Matching questions require you to connect items in one column with items in a second column. The columns may or may not have an equal number of items.

EXAMPLE: Match the words on the left with the definitions on the right by writing the letter of the correct definition in the blank.

_____1. erosion   a. large body of moving ice and snow

_____2. windbreak   b. wearing away of rock and soil on the Earth's surface

_____3. glacier   c. barrier that causes wind speed to decrease

d. ridge deposited by a glacier

ANSWERS: 1: b; 2: c; 3: a

See the chart on the next page for steps for answering matching questions.

ANSWERING MATCHING QUESTIONS

1. Determine immediately if there are an equal number of items in each column and whether the items in the second column may be used more than once.
2. Read all the items in both columns before you try to match.
3. Match easy items first. *Lightly* cross out each used answer.

True-or-False Questions True-or-False questions may appear to be the easiest type of questions. However, it is essential to be aware that just one word can change a true statement into a false one. Read the questions carefully.

Look at the strategies below:

ANSWERING TRUE-OR-FALSE QUESTIONS

1. If a statement seems true, be sure the whole thing is true.
2. Pay special attention to the word *not,* which often changes the whole meaning of a statement.
3. Pay special attention to the words *all, always, never, no, none,* and *only.* They often make a statement false.
4. Pay special attention to the words *generally, much, many, most, often, sometimes,* and *usually.* They often make a statement true.

Fill-in or Short-Answer Questions These questions give you more freedom than other kinds of test questions. There is usually more than one way to state an answer. However, since no answer choices are offered, you must recall the information for the answer.

EXAMPLE: List two ways in which good roads were important to western settlers.

a._____

b._____

▶ Speaking and Listening Tip

In test situations, you may be called on to present oral responses to short-answer questions. Take time to think before you present each answer. Then, try to be as concise as possible, while still providing evidence to back up your points.

Analogy Questions A *verbal analogy* is an expression of a relationship between two words. Analogy questions test your ability to see the relationship between two given words and to apply that relationship to other words.

EXAMPLE: Choose the pair of words whose relationship is most similar to that expressed by the capitalized pair of words.

1. LETTER : WORD ::
   a. club : people   d. homework : school
   b. page : book   e. product : factory
   c. picture : crayon

ANSWER: B is the correct answer because each letter is a part of a word and each page is a part of a book; both relationships are *part to whole.*

There are many other types of analogy relationships. The following chart shows some of the most common ones.

COMMON ANALOGY RELATIONSHIPS	
Relationship	Example
Synonym	joy : elation
Antonym	despair : hope
Quality	library : quiet
Degree (greater or lesser)	shout : speak
Part to whole	page : book
Kind	milk : beverage
Sequence	engagement : marriage
Proximity	shore : water
Device	telescope : astronomer

To answer an analogy question, follow these steps:
1. Define both words in the initial pair. If you cannot define both words, skip the question and go on to the next one.
2. Analyze how the initial words relate to each other.
3. Make certain that you keep each pair of words in the given order. If you reverse the order, you will come up with an incorrect answer.
4. Make certain that the relationship of the parts of speech are the same in the pair you choose as they are in the initial pair.

▶ **Exercise 12** Analyzing Types of Questions Review your old tests, and identify the types of questions that they include. Then, answer the following questions.
1. Is there a type of question you have difficulty answering?
2. Do different subject areas use different types of questions?

Performing on Standardized Tests

In addition to the tests you take in school, there will most likely be many occasions in which you will take standardized tests. These may include state tests, high-school exit exams, and college board tests, such as the SAT and the ACT. The following tips will help you to perform well on standardized tests.

TIPS FOR TAKING STANDARDIZED TESTS

1. **Get plenty of sleep** the night before the test. If you are tired, you will not perform as well.
2. **Eat a healthy meal** before you take the test. It is essential to be well nourished.
3. **Build confidence by preparing thoroughly.** Confidence is one of the keys to success on standardized tests. To build your confidence, prepare thoroughly—if possible, starting weeks—even months—before the test. The more prepared you are, the more confident you will be.
4. **Come prepared** for the test. Find out before you go to the test which supplies—pencils, paper, calculator, and so on—you need or are allowed to bring.
5. **Take care in filling in bubble sheets.** If you skip an item on the test, make sure that you skip the corresponding row on the bubble sheet. Check over your bubble sheet before you turn in your test.
6. **Budget your time.** Know how much time you have for each section; how many questions the section contains; and how much time you can allow for each question. Skip questions you can't answer so that you don't run out of time to complete the test.

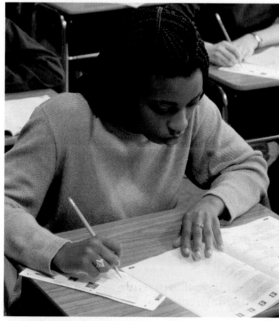

◀ Critical Viewing What is some advice you might offer to this student to help her on the standardized test she is taking? **[Speculate]**

Types of Standardized Tests

Another key to successful performance on a standardized test is being familiar with the test format. Following are standardized tests you might take:

PSAT The PSAT is the preliminary SAT—see the description below. The PSAT is given nationwide and provides students with the opportunity to practice for the SAT. PSAT results determine which students are eligible for National Merit Scholarships. The PSAT has the same basic format as the SAT, except that it does not contain an essay.

New SAT The SAT is used by many colleges as one factor in admissions decisions. It is given nationwide, once a month from October through June except in February. If you are dissatisfied with your SAT scores, you may repeat the test; however, all previous scores will be reported to schools as well as the most recent scores. The new SAT has a math portion, a critical reading portion, and a new writing portion.

The critical reading portion contains sentence-completion questions that test vocabulary and mechanics and contains reading comprehension questions based on short, long, and paired passages.

The writing portion of the new SAT includes a short essay and multiple-choice questions on grammar, usage, and word choice.

ACT The ACT is another test used by colleges as one factor in admissions decisions. The questions—all multiple-choice—focus on English, math, reading, and science reasoning. The English portion asks you to identify errors in grammar, usage, mechanics, logic, and organization. The reading portion presents four passages from different content areas, followed by questions that test your reading and reasoning skills. You can also choose to take the new ACT Plus Writing test, which includes a thirty-minute essay.

ⓠ Learn More

The Standardized Test Preparation Workshops that appear at the end of every chapter throughout this book provide instruction and practice for most of the types of items covered in these tests. The Test Preparation Handbook on pages 688–719 provides instruction and practice for the Writing Section of the new SAT, the Writing Test of the ACT, and the types of Reading Comprehension questions that appear in the reading sections of both exams.

Reflecting on Your Test-Taking Skills

Think about strategies presented in this section and how they apply to you. Use these questions to help you reflect:

- How can I budget my time better while taking tests?

- How can I apply new test-taking strategies when I take tests?

Workplace Skills and *Competencies*

In each new experience, you use your communication skills to gather the information needed to function effectively. In the workplace, good communication skills will help you gather and share the information required for your job, whatever that job may be.

This chapter will help you improve your ability to communicate effectively with others, to set and achieve goals, and to solve problems. There will also be suggestions on how to work more efficiently by budgeting your time and, as you grow more independent, on how to manage your money properly. In addition, you will discover how to learn more about the field of your choice through internships and how math and computer skills help you in your everyday life.

▲ **Critical Viewing**
How do these people use communication skills in their work? **[Analyze]**

Working With Others

You will be expected to interact effectively with people, whether you are pursuing further study or entering the work force. This section offers tips on enhancing your ability to communicate in one-on-one and group situations.

Learn One-on-One Communication

When you apply for a job or for admission to a college, you can make a good impression by learning good one-on-one communication skills. You will then need to refine those skills to work well with the people you meet at work or on campus.

Interviews Learning how to interview properly can increase your chances of being accepted for an internship, hired for a job, or admitted to the school of your choice.

▶ **KEY CONCEPT** An interview requires careful preparation, professionalism, courtesy, and follow-through. ■

🖰 Research Tip

To help plan your career goals, investigate fields of interest at the career center of a local college.

THE INTERVIEW PROCESS

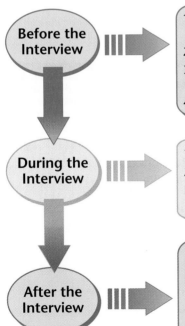

Before the Interview

1. Find out when, where, and with whom the interview is.
2. Gather references, and prepare your résumé.
3. Learn about your potential employer or the college at which you are applying, and prepare questions.
4. Select a neat, appropriate outfit for the interview.

During the Interview

1. Smile and maintain eye contact.
2. Ask and answer questions politely and concisely.
3. Thank the interviewer, and ask when a decision will be made.

After the Interview

1. In a follow-up letter, restate your interest in the internship, job, or college and extend your thanks.
2. When the deadline for a decision arrives, call to check the status.
3. If you are applying for a job and the position has been filled, ask the company to keep your résumé on file.

Successful Interaction Whether you are working on a project with co-workers, speaking to professors, or dealing with clients, the way you present information and ideas affects how they are heard and received by others. It is important to keep in mind that interaction is a two-way street. Listening is as important as speaking.

▶ **KEY CONCEPT** Successful interaction requires sensitivity to and respect for others, as well as the ability to listen. ■

Follow these suggestions for effective interaction:

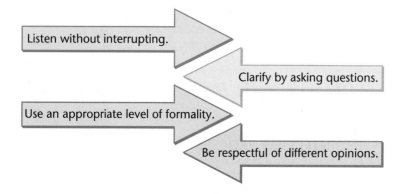

Listen without interrupting.

Clarify by asking questions.

Use an appropriate level of formality.

Be respectful of different opinions.

▶ **Exercise 1** Interviewing at a College or Business Arrange an interview to learn more about a college or business of your choice. Follow the tips in this section to make a good impression. Afterward, tell the class about the experience.

▶ **Exercise 2** Interacting With Others in Various Situations
With other students, role-play the following situations, using the tips for effective interaction as a guide.
1. You must handle a customer who returns merchandise and wants a refund despite the store's no-refund policy.
2. An early riser, you must work out an acceptable living arrangement with your college roommate, who stays up studying half the night.
3. Your colleague at work does not agree with you on an important issue and confronts you at a meeting.

▶ **More Practice**

Academic and Workplace Skills Activity Book
• p. 55

Learn Teamwork

You might work as part of a team to organize a campaign, serve on a committee, or prepare a presentation. Teamwork requires good communication skills. To work well together, group members must know and respect each other's roles.

Roles in Group Discussions A group is typically made up of a facilitator, a recorder or note taker, a timekeeper, and several participants, all of whom must be organized, focused on the discussion, and aware of their responsibilities to be able to succeed at their task. In a group that meets regularly, group members take turns handling the functions of facilitator and other responsibilities.

> **KEY CONCEPT** Members of a group assume distinct, yet equally important, roles to realize a common goal. ∎

The illustration below outlines the roles and responsibilities of individual group members:

Facilitator
Guides discussion from start to finish; mediates disputes

Recorder
Records key points; prepares report of discussion

Timekeeper
Keeps track of time allowed for parts of discussion

Participants
Contribute and debate ideas

> **KEY CONCEPT** Effective participation in group discussions requires an exchange of ideas, constructive debate, and courtesy. ∎

Use the following tips for successful group discussions:

- Listen respectfully to all points of view.
- Share your perspective, and encourage others to do so.
- Work with an agenda.
- Stick to the topic.

Meetings Some discussions are organized as meetings. When you plan a meeting, list the issues and topics to be covered by outlining on an agenda the points to be discussed. Identify any materials or information that will be needed, and decide who will be responsible for this. Assign (or participate in choosing) a facilitator, a timekeeper, and a recorder, or note taker. At the end of the meeting, list follow-up activities and questions. Choose a time, and identify goals for the next meeting.

AGENDA

Planning Meeting
November 3

Attendance: Rebecca, Gregory, Amy, Elaine, Doug, Jeff

Facilitator: Rebecca
Note Taker: Gregory
Timekeeper: Amy

1. Review and amend agenda
   (All — 5 minutes)

2. Brainstorming for ideas
   (All — 10 minutes)

3. Presentation of sales results
   (Elaine — 10 minutes)

4. Discussion of sales results
   (All — 20 minutes)

▼ **Critical Viewing**
What role do you think each person is playing at this meeting? **[Speculate]**

▶ **Exercise 3** **Organizing a Group Fund-raiser** With five classmates, organize a fund-raiser for a class field trip. Make an agenda for the initial meeting, assign roles, hold the meeting, list follow-up questions and activities, and identify goals for the next meeting.

Moving Toward Your Goals

When you dream about something you would like to achieve and you plan to accomplish that dream in a set time, you have set a goal. Goals may focus on improving your interviewing skills, raising your SAT scores, or traveling to another country. Some goals can be achieved in weeks; others take years. When goals conflict with one another, you must decide what is most important to you.

Set Your Goals

Personal goals, such as improving study habits or becoming more physically fit, focus on your development as a person. Professional goals, such as obtaining an internship, focus on your career. Despite their distinctions, personal and professional goals often affect each other. Therefore, you should know your goals and what it will take to achieve them.

To set and achieve a goal, you must define your objective as specifically as possible and map out a time frame in which to complete it.

▶ **KEY CONCEPT** Setting a goal means identifying a specific objective and a time frame in which to complete it. ■

STEPS FOR PLANNING
AND ACCOMPLISHING GOALS

3. As you progress toward the goal, evaluate what is working and what is not. Adjust the steps as needed.

2. Break the goal down into specific steps, each step having a reasonable time frame.

1. Write down the goal as specifically as possible. Consider how your strengths and weaknesses will affect this goal.

Internships One step you can take toward a professional goal is to work as an intern. Internships are positions that employers create for people who want to learn more about a career. The job may entail basic duties, such as running errands and opening mail, or specific skills, such as writing press releases or building theater props. In all cases, the intern, who may be unpaid, learns about a field by working alongside professionals.

▲ **Critical Viewing** How do you think this interview is going to go? Why do you think so? **[Infer]**

Exercise 4 Creating an Action Plan In your notebook, create a detailed plan for accomplishing one of the following goals: begin a career as an electrician or other technically trained professional, gain acceptance to the college of your choice, or take a trip to another country. Find out what is required to attain the goal. Then, include in your plan the steps needed to achieve the goal and the time and resources required for each step.

Exercise 5 Learning About Careers and Internships Select a field in which you are interested. Contact people in that field, and invite them to your class to discuss their occupation. If the organizations they work for offer internships, ask them to explain the responsibilities handled by interns.

Solve Problems

As you work toward your personal and professional goals, you should know how to solve problems that may arise. Effective problem solving involves identifying the problem and generating and evaluating possible solutions. Solving particularly difficult problems often entails creative thinking. Creative thinking can help you generate a variety of possible solutions with which to work.

Creative Thinking There are often several ways to overcome an obstacle. Think creatively to solve a problem; consider unusual or nonstandard solutions.

▶ **KEY CONCEPT** Solving a problem requires a thorough understanding of what's wrong, a number of ideas for possible solutions, and a careful review of each one. ■

Stimulate your creative problem-solving skills by following these suggestions:

- Pose the problem to others, and listen to their advice.
- Imagine how someone with particular talents might solve the problem. What approach, for example, might an inventor take? An artist? A computer specialist?
- Increase the number of solutions by writing down all ideas—however fanciful or impractical. Sometimes, an impractical idea can be made workable with just a few adjustments.
- Interact with people from different cultures and backgrounds to widen your frame of reference and help you generate a greater variety of ideas.

▶ **Exercise 6** Solving Problems With Creative Thinking You want a job as a reporter for a daily newspaper, but you must have published articles to be considered for the position. How do you get published without first having a job? In your notebook, analyze this problem by following the steps to effective problem solving. Come up with three possible solutions by practicing your creative thinking. One idea for getting an article published, for example, could be to volunteer to write press releases for a nonprofit group and to submit them to the local paper.

▶ **More Practice**

Academic and Workplace Skills Activity Book
- page 56

Managing Time

Whether you choose to pursue a bachelor's degree or a plumber's license, you will eventually face a task that must be completed in a set amount of time. Knowing how to use time efficiently can mean the difference between being viewed as a capable person or as one who can't manage the job.

To budget your time, outline appointments and activities and know which are most important. Create "To-Do" lists to remind yourself of important tasks.

🔲 Research Tip

You can find easy-to-understand guides to managing your time and money at your local library.

SAMPLE PLANNER

To-Do List

1. Call Ms. Zimbler for fund-raising information.

2. Pick up art for posters.

3. Drop off brochures at Nancy's.

Mon _9:30 Planning Meeting_

Tues _____

Wed _3:00–5:00 Work_

Thur _7:00 P.M. Baby-sit_

Fri _____

Sat _10:00 Bake Sale_

Sun _____

▶ **KEY CONCEPT** To manage your time, record and prioritize a schedule of appointments, deadlines, and activities. ■

▶ **Exercise 7** **Managing a Schedule** Plan a weekly schedule with the following responsibilities: a job twenty minutes from home from 10 A.M. to 2 P.M., Monday through Friday; college classes ten minutes from home from 6 P.M. to 9 P.M., Monday, Wednesday, and Friday; a daily one-hour workout; and guitar lessons from 1 P.M. to 3 P.M., Saturday. Fit in nine hours of study time, a two-hour dentist visit, a movie with friends, time to write five letters, and a stop at the cleaners. Include a daily to-do list that ranks activities according to importance.

▲ Critical Viewing
Why is managing your time so important? [Analyze]

Managing Money

Money, like time, is limited. A budget will help you manage money wisely. In the workplace, you may be expected to record and manage expenses for your part of a project.

> **KEY CONCEPT** To manage money, record and prioritize a budget of available funds, regular expenses, and projected (or expected) expenses. ■

In most budgets, incoming money, called *credit*, is shown in black. Outgoing money, called *expenses* or *debits*, is usually written in red. For a budget to work, total expenses should not exceed total credits. If they do, the budgeter needs to prioritize and make decisions to cut spending or to come up with ways to increase income.

SAMPLE BUDGET

Drama Club Budget

	Regular Income	Regular Expenses	Projected Expenses
Club Dues	50.00		
From Sponsors	100.00		
Weekly Bake Sale	125.00		
Bake Sale Supplies		25.00	
Posterboard and Paint			10.00
T-shirts for Members			125.00
Weekly Meeting Snacks		15.00	
Total	275.00	40.00	135.00

▲ **Critical Viewing** Why is managing money a difficult thing for many people to do? **[Speculate]**

> **Exercise 8** Managing a Budget Create a budget for a service club. The club has twenty members, each of whom pays $1.00 a week in dues. They hold a weekly car wash, the income from which averages $75.00. The materials for the car wash cost $10.00. The club usually buys pizza for the workers, at a cost of $50.00. The group wants to give $200.00 to a charity. Create a budget for the group, and answer these questions:
>   1. How long will it take for the group to have the $200.00?
>   2. What suggestions would you make for reducing expenses?
>   3. What suggestions would you make for increasing income?

> **More Practice**
> Academic and Workplace Skills Activity Book
> • pages 57–58

Applying Math Skills

On the job, math skills can help you analyze information to make wise decisions about what to buy and what to charge. Whether you work for yourself or someone else, you will need to make these decisions.

> **KEY CONCEPT** Use math skills to determine the best buy for your needs. ■

In life and in the workplace, your math skills can help you to determine the best buy on anything you purchase. For example, one store may advertise paint at $3.00 per gallon when you buy twenty or more gallons. Another may sell paint at 10 percent off the usual price of $4.00 per gallon no matter how many you buy. To decide between paints, you must calculate 10 percent of $4.00, how many cans you need, and which buy is the best for your needs.

> **KEY CONCEPT** Use math skills to determine costs. ■

Math skills can help you figure out how much a job or project will cost. First, figure out the amount of materials or supplies you will need. Then, use math to figure out the total cost of the materials, based on the price per foot, piece, can, or other unit of measurement.

> **KEY CONCEPT** Use math skills to determine the value of your time. ■

When you are offered a salary or a price for a job, use math skills to figure out how much you are being paid per hour. Figure out how many hours the job will take. Then, divide the total pay by the number of hours you will spend on the job. Use this number to determine if you are being paid fairly. For example, if you are offered $50.00 to do a job that will take you approximately 25 hours, you are being paid $2.00 per hour.

> **Exercise 9** Using Math Skills to Give an Estimated Price
A neighbor has asked you to build a fence around her garden. The garden is 10 feet by 12 feet. Use your math skills to estimate how much you will charge her. Figure out the cost of lumber. Estimate how long the job will take you, and calculate your own hourly rate. Then, ask a partner to act as the neighbor, to role-play a negotiation of the price. Write an explanation of how you arrived at the final price.

> **More Practice**
Academic and Workplace Skills Activity Book
• pages 59–60

Applying Computer Skills

Keyboarding skills, knowledge of formatting techniques and other software tools, and the ability to use the Internet to obtain information will benefit you, whether you're working for a grade or a paycheck.

 KEY CONCEPT The computer is a tool that can help you work more efficiently. Employers value employees who are familiar with a variety of computer programs and functions. ■

Like all tools, computers can make a job easier to do. What you use the computer for depends on the job you are doing. The illustration below shows some common computer programs you might use on the job:

Spreadsheets
Word Processing
Internet
Databases

 Exercise 10 Investigating Applications of Computer Skills
Look through the classified ads of your newspaper. Make a list of the computer programs and skills mentioned and the types of jobs that require them. Find out what the programs or skills are, and find out what they are used for. Find out where in your area classes or workshops on these topics are offered.

⊙ Technology Tip

Computer software often has a feature built in that helps you create a résumé. Type in the word *résumé* at the Help command to investigate this feature.

◑ Learn More

To learn what information to include in an effective résumé and follow-up letter, see Chapter 17, "Workplace Writing."

Reflecting on Your Workplace Skills and Competencies

Think about what you have learned in this chapter. Begin by answering the following questions in your notebook:

- In what areas am I strongest? Why?
- What skills should I improve? Why?

Test Preparation Handbook

Preparing for the New SAT® and the ACT®

If you are applying to college, chances are you will take the new SAT®, the ACT®, or both. The new SAT® and the ACT® are standardized tests designed to help colleges compare the abilities of prospective students from all over the world. This Test Preparation Handbook will help you prepare for the Writing Section of the new SAT® and the Writing Test of the ACT®.

The Writing Section

The writing sections on both tests include a timed essay. The new SAT®'s Writing Section also contains multiple-choice questions on grammar and usage. This Test Preparation Handbook will introduce you to each type of grammar and usage question that appears on the new SAT®. It will also be helpful to those preparing for the ACT®, because the same grammar and usage topics are addressed in the English Section of that exam.

CONTENTS

Reading Comprehension Questions

Both the new SAT® and the ACT® test your ability to understand what you read. Reading Comprehension questions typically test these three reading skills:

- Vocabulary in Context: These questions test your ability to understand what a word means from the way it is used in a sentence or passage.

- Finding Information in the Text: These questions test your ability to understand the basic information stated in a text.

- Extended Reasoning: These questions test your ability to infer meaning from a text. You should expect questions that ask about the passage's main idea and details, the author's logic and attitude, and the implications of the author's statements.

The following section contains one example of each type of reading passage presented on the new SAT®. These include the following items:

Short passages	These passages can be as short as one hundred words and are followed by two questions.
Long passages	These passages can be as long as eight hundred words and are followed by as many as thirteen questions.
Paired passages	These consist of two passages and are followed by questions that ask about each passage, as well as questions that ask you to compare and contrast the paired passages.

Please note that on the new SAT®, these passages will be followed by at least two questions. In this Test Preparation Handbook, only one question for each reading passage will be presented along with steps to answer it. It is a good idea to practice further by completing reading comprehension questions from old SAT® or ACT® tests. Your teacher can help you to identify books that contain practice tests. Finally, another excellent way to prepare for the Reading Comprehension section of these exams, and for college, is to read widely and often.

Reading Comprehension

Long Passage

The passage on this page describes the early life of Eleanor Roosevelt.

 STRATEGY **Vocabulary In Context:** Use context clues from the text to figure out the meaning of difficult or unfamiliar words. When you encounter an unfamiliar word in a test passage, you can make inferences about its meaning by looking for context clues in the surrounding words.

▶ **Sample Test Question**

Directions: Read the passage and answer the question that follows; it will be based on stated or implied information.

Eleanor Roosevelt Remembered

1   Eleanor Roosevelt was born to a wealthy and distinguished family. Nevertheless, her childhood was marked by many hardships. She suffered from extreme timidity. Her mother mocked Eleanor for her awkwardness and lack of confidence.

5   When Eleanor was only eight years old, her mother died. Her beloved father died just two years later. As a result of these early losses, Eleanor Roosevelt grew into a woman with profound compassion for the underprivileged.

       When Eleanor Roosevelt was fifteen years old, she traveled

10   to England to attend a boarding school there. For the first time, Eleanor was happy. She was surrounded by friendly girls with whom she could play and learn. Most of all, she found a <u>mentor</u> in the school's headmistress. The headmistress counseled Eleanor, giving her advice and

15   encouragement. She showed Eleanor how to carry herself in many different situations. Eleanor even accompanied the headmistress on trips around Europe. Because of the care shown to her by the headmistress, Eleanor felt special and worthy. Her confidence grew as a result of the attention

20   shown to her. When she returned to New York, she was a graceful, elegant, and poised young woman. Her time in England had given her the confidence to play an important role in history.

TIP: In the actual new SAT®, a long passage will be about fifty lines long. Expect to see questions that test the following skills:

- Making inferences
- Identifying details
- Vocabulary in context
- Drawing conclusions
- Following an author's logic
- Identifying the tone and purpose of the author
- Making predictions

QUESTION: The word *mentor* on line 13 most nearly means

A mother.

B headmistress.

C a good friend.

D advisor.

E companion.

A Word to the Wise
Mentor

The word *mentor* comes from the Latin word *ment,* which means "mind," "thought," or "intellect." A mentor is a person who gives advice, that is, offers the benefit of his or her thought or intellect to another, usually younger, person.

S T E P S

1. **Carefully read the passage to be sure you understand its general meaning.** Then, read the question and the five choices.

2. **Focus on the paragraph in which the word *mentor* appears.** Decide what you believe *mentor* means in this context.

3. **Review the answer choices.** Choice A, *mother,* is obviously incorrect because the headmistress is not Eleanor's mother. Choice B, *headmistress,* is incorrect, too: Eleanor's headmistress was her mentor, but not all headmistresses are mentors. Choice C, *a good friend,* is a plausible choice. However, when we read that the headmistress gave advice to Eleanor and showed her how to behave in many different situations, it seems that there is another dimension to the relationship than just being a good friend. Choice E, *companion,* is another plausible choice because the passage states that Eleanor accompanied the headmistress on many trips. However, the relationship seems to contain aspects that are not captured by the word *companion.* Choice D, *advisor,* is the best definition of the word *mentor.* An advisor or a mentor is someone who encourages and advises a younger person, which is exactly the role that the passage indicates the headmistress played in the life of young Eleanor Roosevelt. Therefore, choice D is the answer.

Reading Comprehension

Paired Reading Passages

The following passages are about Benjamin Franklin. Passage I is a biography of Franklin. Passage II is written by Benjamin Franklin himself.

 STRATEGY **Compare and Contrast:** Most paired reading passages contain questions that require you to compare and contrast the two selections. While reading the two passages, focus on the similarities as well as the differences between the two texts.

> **Sample Test Question**

Directions: Read both passages. Then, answer the questions based on what is stated or implied in the passages.

Passage I

The life of Benjamin Franklin is stranger than fiction. Its realities surpass the idealities of novelists. Imagination would scarcely venture to portray such victories over poverty, obscurity, difficulties, and hardships. The tact, application, perseverance, and industry that he brought to his life-work make him an example for all time. He met with defeats; but they inspired him to manlier efforts. His successes increased his desire for something higher and nobler. He was satisfied only with "going up still higher." He believed that "one today is worth two tomorrows," and he acted accordingly, with the candle shop and printing office for his schoolroom, and observation for his teacher. His career furnishes one of the noblest examples of success for the young of both sexes to study. We offer his life as one of the brightest and best in American history to inspire young hearts with lofty aims.

Passage II

Imagining it may be equally agreeable to you to know the circumstances of my life, many of which you are yet unacquainted with, and expecting the enjoyment of a week's uninterrupted leisure in my present country retirement, I sit down to write them for you. To which I have besides some other inducements. Having emerged from the poverty and obscurity in which I was born and bred, to a state of affluence and some degree of reputation in the world, and having gone so far through life with a considerable share of felicity, my posterity may like to know, as they may find some of them suitable to their own situations, and therefore fit to be imitated.

TIP: The passages featured in Reading Comprehension sections are sometimes written in a very formal, literary style of English. Sometimes the passages are hundreds of years old. Take the time you need to read the passages over until you have a strong sense of their meaning.

QUESTION: Both passages are primarily concerned with

    A   making the reader feel motivated to emulate Benjamin Franklin.

    B   telling a rags-to-riches story.

    C   explaining why Franklin wrote his autobiography.

    D   motivating the reader to learn from Benjamin Franklin's life lessons.

    E   introducing a written version of Benjamin Franklin's life story.

STEPS

1. **Carefully read the passages to be sure you understand the general meaning of each passage.** Then, read the question and answer.

2. **Consider the focus of each passage to determine what these readings have in common.** The first passage describes Benjamin Franklin as a man of exemplary virtue and ends with the statement, "We offer his life as one of the brightest and best in American history to inspire young hearts with lofty aims." The second passage, written by Franklin himself, states his goals for writing an autobiography. Note that both passages seem to introduce the reader to the life story of Benjamin Franklin. They are clearly from the opening paragraphs of a biography or autobiography of Franklin.

3. **Review the answer choices.** Choices A and D seem plausible because both passages mention the possibility that a reader may want to imitate Benjamin Franklin's behavior or learn from his life. However, a close reading of both passages reveals that this is not their main purpose. Choice B is incorrect because although the passages mention Franklin's climb from poverty to success, this progress is not the focus of either passage. Choice C is incorrect because only one of the paired passages is from Franklin's autobiography. The focus of both passages is to frame the introduction of a written account of Franklin's life story. Therefore, the answer is choice E.

Reading Comprehension

Short Passage

The passage on this page discusses the growth of the children's book industry since the 1980's.

 STRATEGY **Make Inferences:** If the answer to a question is not plainly stated in the selection, look beyond the details and information to understand the suggestions and implications of the author's words.

▷ **Sample Test Question**

Directions: Read the passage and answer the question that follows; it will be based on stated or implied information.

The Rise of Children's Books

Prior to the late 1980's, the children's publishing business was a rather slow-moving one. The industry seemed to revolve around classic children's books, most of which had been written decades earlier. The number of new children's books published every year was much smaller than the number of books published every year for adults.

Few predicted the dramatic rise in demand for children's books that occurred in the late 1980's and has continued ever since. By the late 1980's, the generation known as the baby boomers (people who were born from 1946 to 1964), were raising their own children. This large generation of well-educated parents were keen to share a love of reading with their children. This desire produced an unprecedented demand for a wide range of children's books. Today, the children's publishing business is a thriving industry that generates more than a billion dollars of revenue a year.

QUESTION: It can be inferred from the passage that the unprecedented demand for children's books was caused by

    A   the publication of a few popular series, such as *Harry Potter.*

    B   the baby-boomer generation becoming parents.

    C   people getting bored with classic children's books.

    D   the imbalance between the number of books published for adults and the number of books published for children.

    E   the economic boom of the late 1980's.

A Word to the Wise
Infer

The word *infer* comes from the Latin verb that means "to carry in." In English, to *infer* means to conclude from evidence. When you are asked to infer, you are asked to figure something out, using a limited amount of information.

On the new SAT®, the short passage will be followed by two questions.

<u>**S T E P S**</u>

1. **Carefully read the passage to be sure you understand its meaning.** Then, read the question and the five answer choices.

2. **Reread the question.** Notice that it requires you to draw a conclusion about what prompted the rise in demand for children's books. The text states that the demand is related to a well-educated generation becoming parents. These new parents wish to share a love of reading with their children.

3. **Review the answer choices.** Choices A and E include information that is not implied or stated in the text, so they are incorrect. Choices C and D contain information that is stated or implied in the text. However, neither choice C nor D explain the rise in demand for children's books. Notice that the bulk of the passage discusses the rise of children's publishing in relationship to the baby-boomer generation becoming parents. Therefore, choice B is the answer to the question.

Reflecting on Reading Comprehension

Think about the various reading strategies you have studied. Decide which types of reading passages and strategies present the greatest challenge for you. Use these questions to help you reflect:

- What type of Reading Comprehension question do I prefer answering? Why?

- With which type of Reading Comprehension strategy do I most frequently have problems?

- What can I do to improve my performance on these types of test questions?

An excellent resource for improving your performance on Reading Comprehension questions is your teacher. Share your concerns about specific question types and reading strategies with your teacher. He or she can help you improve your skills in these areas. Remember, one of the best ways to improve reading comprehension is to read newspapers and news magazines. The articles in newspapers such as the *New York Times* are often of the same length as those found in short and long passages. Moreover, they contain the same academic vocabulary that appears on standardized tests.

Grammar

Multiple-Choice Grammar Questions

Many students find grammar difficult. However, by focusing on the grammar and usage rules that are most often tested, you can prepare yourself to succeed on this part of the new SAT® or the ACT®. The following section of the Test Preparation Handbook introduces you to some of the most frequently tested grammar and usage topics.

Techniques for Answering Grammar and Usage Questions

Many grammar and usage questions ask you to identify an error in a sentence. Some people can spot grammar and usage errors easily. These people can spot errors because they "hear" the errors as they read. This technique does not work for everyone. If you frequently make grammar and usage errors, it is best to use a systematic approach for answering these questions. This section introduces a step-by-step process for answering the most common types of questions tested in the grammar sections of the new SAT® and the ACT®. By learning these steps, you will prepare yourself for success on this portion of the exam.

As you work through the next section, you will familiarize yourself with some of the most common grammar and usage errors that appear on standardized tests.

Faulty Subject-Verb Agreement

▶ **RULE** A singular subject must have a singular verb, and a plural subject must have a plural verb.

▶ **Sample Test Question**

Directions: Read the sentence carefully. Identify the sentence error from the underlined options. If there is no error, select choice E.

> The <u>federal government</u> <u>have honored</u> Harriet Tubman
>   **A**   **B**
> with a commemorative postage <u>stamp</u> bearing her <u>name</u>
>   **C**   **D**
> and likeness. <u>No error</u>
>   **E**

A Word to the Wise
Agreement

The word *agreement* means "harmony." Subjects and verbs must always harmonize by agreeing in their number, form, and tense.

QUESTION: What is the error in the sentence?

A federal government

B have honored

C stamp

D name

E No error

TIP: Be careful with subjects that are indefinite pronouns. *Each, either, everyone, someone,* and *no one* are always singular subjects. *Few, both, many,* and *several* are always plural subjects.

STEPS

1. **Read the sentence carefully.** Focus your attention on the underlined words or phrases.

2. **Ask yourself: "Does any underlined word or phrase sound wrong?"** If one word or phrase definitely sounds wrong to you, you have probably identified the error in the sentence.

3. **If no words or phrases sound wrong to you, ask yourself: "Does any underlined word or phrase violate a grammar or usage rule that I have learned?"**

4. **Ask yourself: "What is the subject of this sentence?"** The subject of the sentence is *the federal government.*

5. **Decide if the subject is singular or plural.** *Federal government* is a collective noun that takes a singular verb.

6. **Ask yourself: "What is the verb in this sentence?"** The verb—the action of the sentence—is *have honored.* This is a plural verb.

7. **Check that the verb agrees with the subject in number.** The verb in the sentence is plural: *have honored.* It should be singular. Therefore, choice B is the answer to the question.

FOR REVIEW

To review all faulty agreement topics in greater depth, see Chapter 23, Section 1.

Mixed Constructions

▶ **RULE**   Every word in a sentence has a role to play—whether subject, verb, conjunction, or modifier. A single word cannot play more than one role in a sentence.

▶ **Sample Test Question**

Directions: Read the sentence carefully. Decide whether it is correct or needs to be revised. If no revision is necessary, select choice E.

<u>We all know that the facts about heart disease is the</u>

<u>number one killer in America.</u>

A Word to the Wise
Construction

The word *construction* comes from the Latin past participle, *constructus,* meaning "having been built." A construction is something that has been built.

Grammar

QUESTION: What is the best way to rewrite this sentence?

A   We all know it is the number one killer, heart disease, in America.

B   We all know that the facts about heart disease; it is the number one killer in America.

C   We all know that it is the number one killer in America: heart disease.

D   We all know the facts about heart disease. It is the number one killer in America.

E   No revision necessary

S T E P S

1. **Read the sentence carefully.**

2. **Ask yourself: "Does any word or phrase sound wrong?"** If one word or phrase definitely sounds wrong to you, you have probably identified the error in the sentence.

3. **If no words or phrases sound wrong to you, ask yourself: "Does any word or phrase violate a grammar or usage rule that I have learned?"**

4. **Make sure the sentence contains at least one complete thought.** Note that the sample sentence does not complete a thought. It is therefore an error.

5. **Choose the best way to rewrite the sentence.** Choice A omits the relative pronoun *that* and phrase *the facts about*, but misplaces its modifier, *heart disease*. Choices B and C omit the relative pronoun *that* but introduce incorrect punctuation. Choice D correctly omits the relative pronoun *that* and divides the two ideas into separate sentences. Therefore, choice D is the correct answer.

FOR REVIEW

To review words as different parts of speech in greater depth, see Chapter 17, Section 5.

Shifts in Pronoun Person

▶ **RULE**   As part of pronoun-antecedent agreement in a sentence, take care not to shift pronoun person. Such a shift when referring to the same person creates confusion.

Directions: Read the sentence carefully. Identify the sentence error from the underlined options. If there is no error, select choice E.

Psychologists suggest that when you have a problem at

school, <u>you</u> should always talk to a friend, but <u>one</u> should
　　　　A　　　　　　　　　　　　　　　　　B

also find out <u>what</u> a caring adult <u>thinks</u>. <u>No error</u>
　　　　　　　　C　　　　　　　　　　D　　　　E

QUESTION: What is the error in the sentence?

A　you
B　one
C　what
D　thinks
E　No error

S T E P S

1. **Read the sentence carefully.** Focus your attention on the underlined words or phrases.
2. **Ask yourself: "Does any underlined word or phrase sound wrong?"** If one word or phrase definitely sounds wrong to you, you have probably identified the error in the sentence.
3. **If no words or phrases sound wrong to you, ask yourself: "Does any underlined word or phrase violate a grammar or usage rule that I have learned?"**
4. **Identify the pronouns.** Reread the sentence. This sentence introduces the impersonal pronoun *one.* Later in the sentence the impersonal pronoun *you* is used
5. **Check that the pronouns do not shift.** Since the writer has chosen to use the personal pronoun *you* to refer to the person being addressed in the sentence, he or she cannot then introduce the indefinite pronoun *one* to refer to the same person. The pronoun *you* must be used to refer to a person or group throughout the sentence. The error in the sentence is the pronoun shift from *you* to *one*. Therefore, choice B is the answer to the question.

TIP: If there is more than one pronoun in a sentence referring to the same subject, be sure that each pronoun does not shift in number, person, or gender from its first use.

FOR REVIEW

To review all pronoun usage topics in greater depth, see Chapters 22.1, 23.2, and 23.3.

Grammar

Faulty Pronoun Case

RULE Case is the form of a noun or pronoun that indicates its use in a sentence. Pronouns must be in the correct case for the role they play in a sentence.

▶ **Sample Test Question**

Directions: Read the sentence carefully. Identify the sentence error from the underlined options. If there is no error, select choice E.

<u>My</u> mother and <u>me</u> enjoyed the poetry reading of Maya
  A   B

Angelou at <u>her</u> performance marking the reopening of
        C

<u>New York's</u> Museum of Modern Art. <u>No error</u>
   D   E

QUESTION: What is the error in the sentence?

A   my

B   me

C   her

D   New York's

E   No error

STEPS

1. **Read the sentence carefully.** Focus your attention on the underlined words or phrases.
2. **Ask yourself: "Does any underlined word or phrase sound wrong?"** If one word or phrase definitely sounds wrong to you, you have probably identified the error in the sentence.
3. **If no words or phrases sound wrong to you, ask yourself: "Does any underlined word or phrase violate a grammar or usage rule that I have learned?"**
4. **Notice the number of pronouns in this sentence.** This sentence contains three pronouns: *my, me,* and *her.*
5. **Make sure the pronoun is in the correct case.** The pronoun *my* is correct in the possessive case because it refers to the subject of the sentence. The pronoun *her* is correct in the possessive case because it refers to the poetry of Maya Angleou. However, the pronoun *me* is incorrect in the objective case because the pronoun is part of the subject in the sentence. Therefore, the pronoun should be in the nominative case, *I.* The error in the sentence is *me.* Choice B is the answer.

A Word to the Wise
Case

Case is the form of a noun or pronoun that indicates its use in a sentence. The three cases of nouns and pronouns are the nominative, the objective, and the possessive.

New SAT® PREP ACT®

TIP: Its and It's
Confusion between *its* and *it's* is an item consistently on any list of common errors in English grammar. Like *his, its* is used to show possession. Like *he's,* for *he is, it's* is used as a contraction for *it is.*

FOR REVIEW
To review pronoun case topics in greater depth, see Chapter 22.1.

Misplaced Modifiers

▶ **RULE** When a modifier is placed too far from the word it should modify, it can seem to modify the wrong word in a sentence

▶ **Sample Test Question**

Directions: Read the sentence carefully. Identify the sentence error from the underlined options. If there is no error, select choice E.

<u>In the morning light,</u> a small plant <u>sat</u> <u>on the desk</u>
   A   B C
<u>that Sarah had watered</u>. <u>No error</u>
   D   E

QUESTION: What is the error in the sentence?

A In the morning light

B sat

C on the desk

D that Sarah had watered

E No error

S T E P S

1. **Read the sentence carefully.** Focus your attention on the underlined words or phrases.

2. **Ask yourself: "Does any underlined word or phrase sound wrong?"** If one word or phrase definitely sounds wrong to you, you have probably identified the error in the sentence.

3. **If no words or phrases sound wrong to you, ask yourself: "Does any underlined word or phrase violate a grammar or usage rule that I have learned?"**

4. **Identify the parts of speech in the sentence.** The subject, *a small plant*, is followed by the verb *sat*, the prepositional phrase *on the desk*, and the modifying subordinate clause *that Sarah had watered*.

5. **Note that the placement of the subordinate clause suggests that Sarah had watered the desk, not the plant.** Therefore, the modifying clause, *that Sarah had watered*, is clearly misplaced. Choice D is the answer.

[FOR REVIEW]

To review misplaced modifier topics in more depth, see Chapter 20, Section 5.

Grammar

Faulty Word Choice

> **RULE** Words that sound alike or are spelled similarly are easily confused. Such words often have very different meanings.

> **Sample Test Question**

Directions: Read the sentence carefully. Identify the sentence error from the underlined options. If there is no error, select choice E.

Proceeding the trial, the judge conferred with the
   A   **B**
lawyers regarding their clients' cases. No error
       C   **D**   **E**

QUESTION: What is the error in the sentence?

- **A** proceeding
- **B** conferred
- **C** regarding
- **D** clients'
- **E** No error

S T E P S

1. **Read the sentence carefully.** Focus your attention on the underlined words.
2. **Ask yourself: "Does any underlined word sound wrong?"** If one word definitely sounds wrong to you, you have probably identified the error in the sentence.
3. **If no words sound wrong to you, ask yourself: "Does any underlined word violate a grammar or usage rule that I have learned?"**
4. **Ask yourself: "What do the underlined words mean?"** Focus on their meaning in the context of the sentence. Notice that the word *proceeding*, which means "going forward" does not make sense in the sentence. A similar-sounding word, *preceding*, which means "before," would make perfect sense in the sentence.
5. **Review the answer choices.** The error in the sentence is the use of "proceeding" when "preceding" is intended. Therefore, the answer to the question is choice A.

A Word to the Wise
Homophones

The word *homophone* comes from the Greek words *homo,* meaning "the same" and *phono,* meaning "sound." A homophone is a word that sounds the same as another word, even though its meaning is different. Common homophones are *here* and *hear.*

TIP: Studying lists of homophones and commonly misused words will improve your ability to recognize them at exam time. See Chapter 25, Section 2.

> FOR REVIEW

To review word choice topics in more depth, see Chapter 25, Section 2.

Wordiness

▶ **RULE** Every word in a sentence counts. Wordiness or redundance can weaken writing or make the message of a passage unclear.

▶ **Sample Test Question**

Directions: Read the sentence carefully. Decide whether it is correct or needs to be revised. If it does not need revision, select choice E.

The rarely ever disputed contribution of Mark Twain to the ever-changing landscape of American literature is without a doubt affirmed by the long long love affair held by the reader of Twain's *The Adventures of Huckleberry Finn.*

QUESTION: What is the best way to rewrite the sentence?

A The rarely disputed contribution of Mark Twain to the always changing American literature landscape is doubtless affirmed by readers' longest love affair with *The Adventures of Huckleberry Finn.*

B Mark Twain's contribution to the ever-changing landscape of American literature is, without a doubt, affirmed by the readers' long-standing love affair with *The Adventures of Huckleberry Finn,* and seldom disputed.

C Readers' ongoing love affair with *The Adventures of Huckleberry Finn* affirms Mark Twain's rarely disputed contribution to the ever-changing American literature landscape.

D American readers' continuous love affair with *The Adventures of Huckleberry Finn* affirms Mark Twain's seldom disputed contribution to the mutation of the American literature landscape.

E No revision necessary

S T E P S

1. **Read the sentence carefully.**

2. **Ask yourself: "Does the sentence sound wrong?"** If the sentence definitely sounds wrong to you, you have probably identified the error.

3. **If the sentence does not sound wrong to you, ask yourself: "Does the sentence violate a grammar or usage rule that I have learned?"**

> **FOR REVIEW**
> To review wordiness in greater depth, see Chapter 10, Section 4.

Grammar

4. **Ask yourself: "Is every word necessary?"** If a sentence appears long and convoluted, it is most likely an example of wordiness.

5. **Look for redundant words and eliminate them.** Note that the repetition of *long* is redundant; *without a doubt* and *rarely ever disputed* are redundant expressions.

6. **Consider revising complex constructions.** Note that *to the ever-changing landscape of American literature* and *by the long long love affair held by the reader of Twain's* The Adventures of Huckleberry Finn are lengthy prepositional phrases. Replacing them with more concise words or expressions and revising their placement will produce a clearer sentence.

7. **Review the answer choices.** Choice C is the best revision because it uses the fewest words necessary to express the meaning of the sentence. Therefore, the answer to the question is choice C.

Sentence Fragments

> **RULE** A fragment is a group of words with end punctuation that either does not have a subject or verb or does not express a complete thought. Sentence fragments are a common error.

> **Sample Test Question**

Directions: Read the sentence carefully. Then, select the answer choice that best revises the sentence.

> Characters from the plays of Tennessee Williams who are strong-willed and independent.

QUESTION: What is the correct way to write the underlined words?

A Characters from the plays of Tennessee Williams who are weak-willed and unstable.

B Tennessee Williams's characters being weak-willed and unstable.

C Characters from the plays of Tennessee Williams are weak-willed and unstable.

D Weak-willed and unstable characters, being in the plays of Tennessee Williams.

E Characters are weak-willed and unstable being in Tennessee Williams' plays.

A Word to the Wise
Fragments

The word *fragment* comes from the Latin *fragere*, meaning "to break." A fragment is a broken piece of something.

TIP: Two of the most common types of sentence errors are fragments and run-ons.

STEPS

1. **Read the sentence carefully.**
2. **Ask yourself: "Does the sentence sound wrong?"** If the sentence definitely sounds wrong to you, you have probably identified the error.
3. **If the sentence does not sound wrong to you, ask yourself: "Does the sentence violate a grammar or usage rule that I have learned?"**
4. **Ask yourself: "Is this a sentence?"** This is not a sentence. While there is a subordinate clause, *who are strong-willed and independent*, the subject *characters* does not have a verb, and the sentence does not express a complete thought. It is a fragment.
5. **Review the answer choices.** Look for complete sentences that are logical and true to the original test item. Choices A, B, D, and E are all sentence fragments.
6. **Choose the complete sentence.** Use the process of elimination to select the correct answer. Choice C is the only answer choice that contains a complete sentence. Therefore, choice C is the answer.

> **FOR REVIEW**
> To review sentence fragments in greater depth, see Chapter 20, Section 4.

Faulty Parallelism

RULE Parallelism is the placement of equal ideas in words, phrases, clauses, or sentences of similar types.

Sample Test Question

Directions: Read the sentence carefully. Decide whether the underlined portion is correct or needs to be revised.

Sylvia Plath <u>attended Smith College, wrote award-winning poetry, and she married English poet Ted Hughes.</u>

QUESTION: What is the correct way to write the underlined words?

A wrote poetry, received awards and she was married to English poet Ted Hughes.

B married English poet Ted Hughes after she wrote and attended college.

C wrote poetry, received literary awards, and she married English poet Ted Hughes.

D attended Smith College, wrote award-winning poetry, and married English poet Ted Hughes.

E No revision necessary

A Word to the Wise
Parallel

The word *parallel* means "having comparable or identically structured parts." It comes from the Greek roots *-para-*, which means "beside," and *-allos-*, which means "one another."

Grammar

1. **Read the sentence carefully.** Focus your attention on the underlined words or phrases.

2. **Ask yourself: "Does any underlined word or phrase sound wrong?"** If one word or phrase definitely sounds wrong to you, you have probably identified the error in the sentence.

3. **If no words or phrases sound wrong to you, ask yourself: "Does any underlined word or phrase violate a grammar or usage rule that I have learned?"**

4. **Ask yourself: "Are ideas of equal importance expressed in this sentence?"** Check that the grammatical structures are equal. *Attended Smith College* and *wrote award-winning poetry* are phrases, while *she married English poet Ted Hughes* is a clause. The ideas are equal, but the structures are not.

5. **Review the answer choices.** Look for parallel grammatical structure. Choices A, B, and C do not eliminate faulty parallelism. Choice D contains a parallel structure. Therefore, the answer is choice D.

> **FOR REVIEW**
>
> To review faulty parallelism in greater depth, see Chapter 20, Section 6, Section 7.

Comma Splices

▶ **RULE**   A comma splice is two or more sentences incorrectly separated by a comma. This type of run-on sentence can be corrected by introducing a period and presenting two sentences, by using a comma and a conjunction such as *and* or *but*, or by using a semicolon.

▶ **Sample Test Question**

Directions: Read the sentence carefully. Then, select the answer choice that best revises the underlined portion.

For summer reading, our teacher recommended several books, <u>she suggested watching a few movies, too.</u>

A Word to the Wise
Comma

The word *comma* comes from the Greek word *komma,* meaning "a piece cut off." A comma should indicate a piece of a sentence that is cut off from the rest of the sentence by a pause.

QUESTION: What is the best way to rewrite the underlined section?

A   . She suggested watching, too.

B   , but she suggested watching a few movies, too.

C   ; and she suggested watching a few movies, too.

D   , and she suggested watching a few movies, too.

E   , yet she suggested watching a few movies, too.

S T E P S

1. **Read the sentence carefully.** Focus your attention on the underlined section.

2. **Ask yourself: "Does any underlined word or phrase sound wrong?"** If one word or phrase definitely sounds wrong to you, you have probably identified the error in the sentence.

3. **If no words or phrases sound wrong to you, ask yourself: "Does any underlined word or phrase violate a grammar or usage rule that I have learned?"**

4. **Ask yourself: "Are there at least two independent clauses in this sentence?"** If so, make sure they are joined correctly. In this sentence, they are incorrectly joined.

5. **Review the answer choices.** Look for the best option to join the clauses: a comma followed by a matching coordinating conjunction, a semicolon, or a period followed by a separate sentence. Note that in choice A, the second clause is incomplete. In choices B and E, an illogical conjunction is used. In choice C, incorrect punctuation is used before a conjunction. Notice that choice D correctly joins two independent clauses with a comma, followed by the coordinating conjunction "and." Therefore, the answer to the question is choice D.

> **FOR REVIEW**
>
> To review comma splices in greater depth, see Chapter 9, Section 5; Chapter 20, Section 4.

Grammar

Semicolons

▶ **RULE** A semicolon is used to connect two independent clauses that are closely related in thought and structure.

▶ **Sample Test Question**

Directions: Read the sentence carefully. Then, select the answer choice that best revises the underlined portion.

> Langston Hughes published several collections of poetry, <u>and Edgar Allan Poe did not.</u>

QUESTION: What is the best revision of the underlined words?

A , Edgar Allan Poe did not publish several collections of poetry.

B ; Edgar Allan Poe published several collections of poetry.

C like Edgar Allan Poe did not.

D , Edgar Allan Poe did not.

E ; Edgar Allan Poe did not.

STEPS

1. **Read the sentence carefully.** Focus your attention on the underlined section.

2. **Ask yourself: "Does any underlined word or phrase sound wrong?"** If one word or phrase definitely sounds wrong to you, you have probably identified the error in the sentence.

3. **If no words or phrases sound wrong to you, ask yourself: "Does any underlined word or phrase violate a grammar or usage rule that I have learned?"**

4. **Ask yourself: "How many independent clauses are in this sentence?"** Notice that there are two independent clauses, but they are incorrectly joined. The clauses are similar in structure and meaning, though they convey contrasting information. Remember that clauses like these are best joined by a semicolon.

5. **Review the answer choices.** Notice that choices A, C, and D do not use semicolons. Choices B and E use semicolons, though choice B is redundant, repeating an identical structure. Therefore, the answer is choice E.

A Word to the Wise
Colon

The word *colon* comes from the Latin word *colon,* which means "part of a verse." A colon was used to introduce a new part of a verse.

TIP: Colons Colons and semicolons may look similar, but they have very different uses. A colon is most commonly used as an introductory device to point ahead to additional information.

FOR REVIEW

To review semicolons in greater depth, see Chapter 27, Section 3.

Paragraph Structure

▶ **RULE** A paragraph should consist of a main topic sentence and supporting sentences.

▶ **Sample Test Question**

Directions: Read the passage carefully. Then, answer the question below.

> (1) Southern Gothic is a useful literary term for a particular type of fiction. (2) I am happy to report that a Southern Gothic is usually set in the southeastern part of the United States. (3) Often the plot of such a work involves bloody, tragic events and the bizarre relationships of a family or community. (4) The mood of a Southern Gothic is usually dark, though it may be spiced with black humor. (5) Great Southern Gothic writers William Faulkner and Flannery O'Connor have successfully created works that reflect the grotesque, tragic, and grimly humorous southern life.

QUESTION: In context, what is the best revision of the underlined portion of sentence 2 (reproduced below)?

<u>I am happy to report that a Southern gothic is usually set</u> in the southeastern part of the United States.

A	Because of this, a Southern Gothic is usually set
B	As the term suggests, a Southern Gothic is usually set
C	On the other hand, a Southern Gothic is usually set
D	Therefore, a Southern Gothic is usually set
E	As an example, a Southern Gothic is usually set

S T E P S

1. **Read the paragraph carefully.** Focus your attention on the underlined section.

2. **Ask yourself: "Does any part of the underlined section sound wrong?"** If one word or phrase definitely sounds wrong to you, you have probably identified the error in the sentence.

A Word to the Wise
Structure

The word *structure* comes from the Latin word *structura*, meaning "something that has been built."

Grammar

3. **If no words or phrases sound wrong to you, ask yourself: "Does any underlined word or phrase violate a grammar or usage rule that I have learned?"**

4. **Ask yourself: "What is the topic, voice, and tone of this passage?"** This paragraph defines and discusses the term *Southern Gothic*. Except for the underlined passage, the text is written in a formal, objective tone. Choices A, B, D, and E eliminate the informal tone of the underlined text. However, these choices provide no logical connection between the topic sentence and the fact that *Southern Gothic* is set in the "southeastern part of the United States."

5. **Review the choices.** Ask yourself: "Does it support the topic sentence?" The sentence introduction "As the term suggests" in choice C correctly introduces information to support the topic sentence. Therefore, the answer is choice C.

FOR REVIEW

To review paragraph development in greater depth, see Chapter 3, Sections 1 and 2.

Paragraph Coherence

▶ **RULE** In a coherent paragraph, each sentence is essential because it either states or supports the main idea.

▷ **Sample Test Question**

Directions: Read the passage carefully. Then, answer the question below.

> (1) Jazz is often said to be a truly American art form. (2) Its roots have been ascribed to the tribal beats and field hollers of African slaves brought to work in the American colonies. (3) Its true birth as a unique form, however, is reputed by some to have happened the day cornet king Buddy Bolden led his band in improvisation. (4) The exact day is unknown, but the place was New Orleans.

QUESTION: In context, where would the following sentence be best placed in the paragraph above?

Some of America's best-known cities of jazz are Chicago, St. Louis, and New York.

A Word to the Wise
Coherence

The word *coherence* comes from the Latin *cohaer + ere* meaning "to stick." Another word formed from the same root is *adhere*. A coherent paragraph is one in which all the details "stick" together.

A	before sentence (1)
B	between sentences (1) and (2)
C	between sentences (2) and (3)
D	between sentences (3) and (4)
E	No insertion

S T E P S

1. **Read the paragraph carefully.** Focus your attention on the general meaning of the paragraph.

2. **Ask yourself, "What is the topic sentence?"** The first sentence establishes the focus of the paragraph: "jazz . . . a truly American art form." Sentences 2, 3, and 4 clearly address the topic of jazz as an American form rooted and born in America. Each sentence contributes further details to support the topic.

3. **Look for paragraph coherence.** Notice the organization of the paragraph. Determine if each sentence flows into the next and supports the topic. Sentences 2, 3, and 4 clearly follow logically from one sentence to the next.

4. **Consider the best place to insert the new sentence.** Notice that this sentence supports the topic sentence but does not fill any gaps. If placed after sentence 4, it would end the paragraph and provide no closure. The sentence would dangle. Therefore, the correct answer to the question is choice E.

> **FOR REVIEW**
>
> To review paragraph unity and coherence in greater depth, see Chapter 3, Section 3; Chapter 6, Section 4.

Reflecting on Grammar Questions

Now that you have worked through the Grammar section, answer the following questions about your reading and test-taking skills:

- Which grammar and usage topics were you already familiar with?

- Which grammar and usage topics did you find challenging?

Once you have identified areas that you need to work on further, ask your teacher for help in finding materials that you can use to help you improve your skills.

Writing

The ACT® Writing Test

The ACT® Writing Test is optional. If you take this exam, you will be asked to write a persuasive essay explaining your position on an issue.

> **RULE** A persuasive essay presents the writer's point of view on an issue and supports this view with convincing arguments, examples, or details. A persuasive essay urges readers to understand and accept a particular position. It may even encourage readers to take action.

Directions: You have thirty minutes to write an essay on the topic below. Think carefully about the issue presented in the following prompt and complete the assignment that follows.

Sample Writing Prompt

Is it better to be born poor and to attain wealth? Or is it preferable to be born rich and enjoy wealth throughout one's life?
Assignment: In your essay, take a position on this question. You may write about either one of the two points of view given, or you may present a different point of view on this question. Use specific reasons and examples to support your position. You have thirty minutes to write your essay.

How to Succeed on the ACT® Writing Test

1. State a clear position on the issue.
2. Focus on the topic throughout the essay.
3. Support your position with examples.
4. Show logical reasoning through a well-organized essay.
5. Use standard written English.

Studying a Model ACT® Essay

- **Read the essay prompt carefully.**
- **Read the model essay.** Decide whether the student does a good job of writing about the topic.
- **Read the call-outs.** Find out what an examiner might notice about the essay. Pay attention to the elements of the essay that are noted, such as clear and strong introductions and conclusions and the use of details.

Writing the ACT® Essay

1. **After you have reviewed the actual essay written in exam conditions on page 713, try out the prompt on this page yourself.** Give yourself thirty minutes to respond to the prompt.
2. **Make a short outline of what you will write.** Take time to think your plan through carefully as it will drive your essay. This step should take no longer than five minutes.
3. **As you draft, follow your outline to keep yourself on task.**
4. **Allow for five minutes to proofread your essay.** Use the technique on page 719 to proofread your essay quickly.
5. **Once the essay is complete, use the criteria on this page to judge your essay.**

Writing

Model Essay

As children, how many of us wished we had been born to privilege? This wish is an easy daydream, but it might not really make our lives better. It would be far better to be born poor and, through one's efforts, become rich than to be born wealthy. Although I can understand that a wealthy childhood could have many advantages, such as a good education, better nutrition, and wonderful summer vacations, these are not the most important elements of a good childhood. A poor childhood can be valuable if it contains lessons about the importance of love, family commitments, and hard work.

A person who is born rich is enjoying advantages that he or she did not earn. Throughout their lives, people who are born wealthy must feel somewhat unworthy of the advantages that they just happened to be born into. I wonder if you could feel any real achievement when you have had such a head start in life.

On the other hand, some truly remarkable people have been born rich. Bill Gates was born to a wealthy family. He was educated at expensive schools. In addition to this "head start" he was given, Gates certainly has taken the initiative to achieve a great deal in his life. Nevertheless, I would argue that a person who came from a less privileged background and achieved something more modest than Bill Gates may actually be more impressive. To come from nothing and make something of yourself is truly an achievement.

Imagine the pride of people who have achieved wealth after childhoods of economic hardship. One can only point to the determination and hard work of these people for where they are today. They are an inspiration to others. When I think of someone like Oprah Winfrey, who came from so little and has done so much with her life, it makes me think that I can do great things with my own life.

Moreover, I would prefer not to be born wealthy because I think it could make it difficult to imagine what "real life" is like for other people. When you start out poor, you have more respect for poor people. I think that lesson is important to being a kind human being.

In conclusion, it is better to attain wealth than to inherit it. Inheriting wealth and having an easy childhood are appealing because they allow a person to start his or her life with many opportunities. However, a person born poor is able to learn many life lessons through his or her struggle to succeed.

After an interesting introduction, the student uses the language of the prompt to take a position.

Here, the student directly challenges the view opposite to her own.

The student acknowledges a counterexample. Notice how she uses the counterexample to strengthen her overall argument.

The student uses an example of a living person. The student enriches her argument by giving herself something specific to argue against.

The student concludes the essay with a strong restatement of her position on the issue.

FOR REVIEW

To review writing persuasive essays in greater depth, see Chapter 7.

Writing

Writing the New SAT® Essay

The new SAT® essay must be completed in twenty-five minutes. The writing prompt presents an issue. You must develop a position on the issue and write a short essay that supports your point of view.

> **RULE** A persuasive essay opens with a statement of the writer's point of view and supports this point of view with examples or details. The goal of a persuasive essay is to support an opinion well enough to convince readers of its value.

Directions: You have twenty-five minutes to write an essay on the topic assigned below.

Sample Writing Prompt

In order to earn a high school diploma, students need to successfully complete academic requirements. Recently, some high schools have made community service a requirement of earning a diploma. At these schools, even a student who excels at every academic subject cannot earn a diploma unless he or she has also completed a set number of hours of community service.

Assignment: Is community service a fair requirement for high school graduation? Or should high school graduation be based exclusively on academic results? Plan and write an essay in which you develop your point of view on this issue. Support your position with reasoning and examples taken from your reading, studies, experience, or observation.

Studying the Model Essay

Here are some steps to follow to learn from the model essay.

- **Read the prompt and the assignment carefully.** Make sure you understand the issue at hand.

- **Read the model essay.** Decide whether the student does a good job of persuading you, the reader, that her point of view is valid and well thought out.

- **Read the call-outs.** Find out what an examiner might notice about the essay. Pay attention to the elements of the essay that are noted, such as clear and strong introductions and conclusions and the use of many types of examples.

To successfully satisfy the requirements of the new SAT® essay, your essay should

- develop a point of view on the issue.

- use logical reasoning and appropriate examples.

- be well-organized and focused.

- demonstrate good language skills and appropriate vocabulary.

- use a variety of sentences, varying sentence length.

- have relatively few errors of grammar, punctuation, or spelling.

FOR REVIEW

To review writing persuasive essays in greater depth, see Chapter 7.

Model Essay

I believe that high schools ought to require a set number of hours of community service as a requirement for graduation. The goal of high school is to prepare students not only for college, but also for adult membership in a community. Meaningful membership in a community entails donating one's time and effort. Although ideally students would perform community service on their own initiative, it is important to send a clear message to students about the expectations society has of them with regard to community service. Schools can send this message by withholding a diploma from any student who does not adequately participate in community service.

> Student begins her essay with a clear statement about her position on the issue and directly addresses the prompt.

By participating in community efforts, students educate themselves about the world in which they live. They see first-hand some of the challenges facing the least advantaged members of their community, whether it is senior citizens who are confined to their homes, low-income families struggling to put food on the table, or the homeless. Community service can round out an academic education with real-world experience. It is a form of character education that helps young people foster a sense of connection to others and even a sense of how fortunate they are. An example of someone whose life was changed by participation in community service is Barack Obama. In his autobiography, he explains that he was planning on becoming a corporate lawyer but changed his mind after participating in community projects in poor neighborhoods. Today, he is a champion of the underprivileged. In this way, early experiences in community service can help produce a new generation of talented people who dedicate their careers to the public good.

> The student cites an example from an important figure's autobiography. This example makes the essay more sophisticated and compelling.

Moreover, it is in society's best interests that people develop the habit of performing community services when they are young. If people develop a habit when they are young, whether it be playing basketball or participating in community efforts, they are extremely likely to continue this habit in their adult lives. My father became involved with a soup kitchen when he was a teenager. Years later, he works at the same soup kitchen every Saturday morning. It is a part of his weekend routine. By requiring community service from high school students, schools are helping to produce a generation of adults for whom community service is second nature.

> The student transitions cleanly into the next paragraph, where she uses a personal example to reinforce her argument.

Many students feel that their academic requirements keep them extremely busy and that community service is an unmanageable expectation on top of schoolwork. The truth is that students are busy, but we also waste a lot of free time. In my sociology class, I learned that the average teenager spends three hours a day watching television. Community service requirements force students to spend our free time in more productive ways, and that is a good thing.

> The student includes a counterexample to strengthen her essay.

In conclusion, I think that a community service requirement is a fair prerequisite for earning a high school diploma. Community service improves a student's character, contributes to his or her education and establishes a habit of contributing to a community that, with any luck, will persist throughout the student's life.

> The student finishes her essay with a statement summarizing her position and arguments.

Writing

Writing the SAT® Essay

STEPS

1. **Now that you have read a model essay, try out the prompt yourself.** Give yourself twenty-five minutes to respond to the prompt.

2. **Make a short outline of what you will write.** Take time to think your plan through carefully, as it will drive your essay. This step should take no longer than five minutes.

3. **As you draft, follow your outline to be sure you stay on task.** Allow about thirteen minutes for drafting and two minutes for revising your essay.

4. **Allow for five minutes to proofread your essay.** Use the technique on page 719 to proofread your essay in five minutes or less.

   Once the essay is completed, use the criteria on page 714 to evaluate your essay.

Planning the Persuasive Essay

 STRATEGY Spend five minutes making an outline for your essay before you start to write. Make sure your outline includes at least three examples to support your argument.

Directions: You have thirty minutes to write an essay on the topic assigned below. Think carefully about the issue presented in the following excerpt and complete the assignment that follows.

Sample Writing Prompt

An old saying goes, "If at first you don't succeed, try, try again." History is full of examples of determined individuals who never gave up in pursuit of their goals. But persistence alone is not sufficient for success.

Assignment: What is your view of the claim that persistence alone is not sufficient for success? Plan and write an essay in which you develop your point of view on this issue. Support your position with reasoning and examples taken from your reading, studies, experience, or observation.

TIP: Notice that both the new SAT® and ACT® ask you to write point-of-view essays. These are also known as persuasive essays. Your comfort with the requirements of this type of essay will increase your chances for success.

A Word to the Wise
Counterexample

A *counterexample* is an example that runs "counter to" or "against" an argument that a person is making.

S T E P S

1. **Read the prompt and the assignment twice carefully.** Pay attention to the wording of the assignment, noting such details as the direction that you use examples from reading, studies, experience, or observation.

2. **Identify the purpose of your essay—whether to describe, persuade, analyze, or defend.** Note that this prompt is asking for your point of view. You will have to decide whether you are going to argue against the saying, to write in favor of it, or to develop a position in which you find a middle ground.

3. **Consider both sides of the argument.** To get started thinking critically, imagine what a person might say to prove each side. Use a graphic organizer such as the one on page 718 to capture your ideas. Write counterexamples or counterarguments that a person might state to support a position opposite to your own. In your essay, you should use one counterexample and discuss why it does not persuade you to change your position on the issue.

4. **Choose your position.** Review the chart you have completed and decide which side of the argument you will develop in your essay.

5. **Plan examples to support your argument.** A strong essay will support each main point with an example. To best respond to the prompt, consider including three examples: one from your reading (literature); one from your studies (history, science, philosophy); and one from your own experience and observation (current events or something that happened to you or someone you know).

Writing

PRO	CON
1. Persistence enables human beings to accomplish things that seem impossible. **Example from history:** Thomas Edison, inventor of the lightbulb, said, "I have not failed. I've just found 10,000 ways that won't work."	**1.** Persistence is very important, but luck and any other factors play a part in success. There may be a great many people who tried just as hard as Thomas Edison at something but failed.
2. Persistent people don't allow their limitations to stop them from doing things.	**2.** Persistence probably won't matter if you don't also have talent, intelligence, and some friends and family to help you. **Example from history/reading:** Franklin's autobiography shows how having friends in high places and valued skills were key to his success.
3. Even if you try and try and fail, at least you know that you did not give up.	**3.** Sometimes there are good reasons to give up on something. In those situations, "try, try again" might be bad advice. **Example from your own experience:** In junior high, I was a champion gymnast. Then, I had two bad knee injuries. I could have kept trying, but that might have damaged my knee further. I made the decision to give up gymnastics and spend my energy elsewhere.

6. **Use your outline as you write your essay.** Now that you have done the work of making an outline, consult it as you draft. Use it as a checklist to keep you on track and to make sure you are covering your main points and including your three examples.

FOR REVIEW

To review planning a persuasive essay, see Chapter 7, Sections 2, 3.

Proofreading in Five Minutes

 STRATEGY On a timed essay, allow five minutes for proofreading your essay. Since you do not have a lot of time, remember the acronym CUSP to proofread quickly. The letters CUSP stand for . . .

Capitalization: Check that every sentence begins with a capital letter and that proper nouns begin with capital letters. Make sure that no words begin with capital letters unnecessarily.

Usage: Check that your grammar and word choice is correct.

Spelling: Check that all words are correctly spelled.

Punctuation: Check that there are no missing or unnecessary punctuation marks.

Finally, check that your essay is neatly presented. If your writing is illegible, try to make it clearer. Check that any inserted words or sentences are neatly indicated.

TIP: Practice writing essays in your best handwriting. When writing on the test, take care to write neatly.

Reflecting on Test Preparation

Now that you have reached the end of the Test Preparation Handbook, take some time to think about what aspects of test preparation were most challenging for you. Use these tips to get your ideas started.

1. Quickly flip through the pages of the Test Preparation Handbook and jot down reading, grammar, and writing topics that represent a challenge for you.

2. Once you have identified a particular problem area or areas, work through the textbook chapter on the topic. Then, review the Test Preparation Handbook so that you can learn strategies for answering questions on those topics in exams.

3. Ask your teacher for help in building your skills and accessing old standardized tests that you can use for practice.

Citing Sources and Preparing Manuscript

The presentation of your written work is important. Your work should be neat, clean, and easy to read. Follow your teacher's directions for placing your name and class, along with the title and date of your work, on the paper.

For handwritten work:

- Use cursive handwriting or manuscript printing, according to the style your teacher prefers. The penmanship reference below shows the accepted formation of letters in cursive writing.
- Write or print neatly.
- Write on one side of lined $8\frac{1}{2}$" x 11" paper with a clean edge. (Do not use pages torn from a spiral notebook.)
- Indent the first line of each paragraph.

- Leave a margin, as indicated by the guidelines on the lined paper. Write in a size appropriate for the lines provided. Do not write so large that the letters from one line bump into the ones above and below. Do not write so small that the writing is difficult to read.
- Write in blue or black ink.
- Number the pages in the upper right corner.
- You should not cross out words on your final draft. Recopy instead. If your paper is long, your teacher may allow you to make one or two small changes by neatly crossing out the text to be deleted and using a caret [^] to indicate replacement text. Alternatively, you might make one or two corrections neatly with correction fluid. If you find yourself making more than three corrections, consider recopying the work.

PENMANSHIP REFERENCE

For word-processed or typed documents:

- Choose a standard, easy-to-read font.
- Type or print on one side of unlined $8\,^1/_2$" x 11" paper.
- Set the margins for the side, top, and bottom of your paper at approximately one inch. Most word-processing programs have a default setting that is appropriate.
- Double-space the document.
- Indent the first line of each paragraph.
- Number the pages in the upper right corner. Many word-processing programs have a header feature that will do this for you automatically.

- If you discover one or two errors after you have typed or printed, use correction fluid if your teacher allows such corrections. If you have more than three errors in an electronic file, consider making the corrections to the file and reprinting the document. If you have typed a long document, your teacher may allow you to make a few corrections by hand. If you have several errors, however, consider retyping the document.

For research papers:

Follow your teacher's directions for formatting formal research papers. Most papers will have the following features:

- Title page
- Table of Contents or Outline
- Works-Cited List

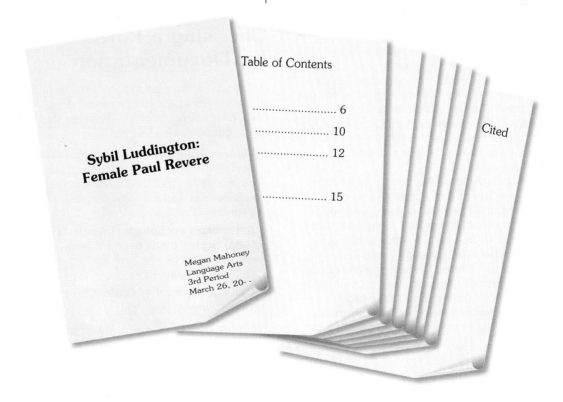

Table of Contents

.... 6

.... 10

.... 12

.... 15

Cited

Sybil Luddington:
Female Paul Revere

Megan Mahoney
Language Arts
3rd Period
March 26, 20- -

Incorporating Ideas From Research

Below are three common methods of incorporating the ideas of other writers into your work. Choose the most appropriate style by analyzing your needs in each case. In all cases, you must credit your source.

- **Direct Quotation:** Use quotation marks to indicate the exact words.
- **Paraphrase:** To share ideas without a direct quotation, state the ideas in your own words. While you haven't copied word-for-word, you still need to credit your source.
- **Summary:** To provide information about a large body of work—such as a speech, an editorial, or a chapter of a book—identify the writer's main idea.

Avoiding Plagiarism

Whether you are presenting a formal research paper or an opinion paper on a current event, you must be careful to give credit for any ideas or opinions that are not your own. Presenting someone else's ideas, research, or opinion as your own—even if you have rephrased it in different words—is *plagiarism*, the equivalent of academic stealing, or fraud.

You can avoid plagiarism by synthesizing what you learn: Read from several sources and let the ideas of experts help you draw your own conclusions and form your own opinions. Ultimately, however, note your own reactions to the ideas presented.

When you choose to use someone else's ideas or work to support your view, credit the source of the material. Give bibliographic information to cite your sources of the following information:

- Statistics
- Direct quotations
- Indirectly quoted statements of opinions
- Conclusions presented by an expert
- Facts available in only one or two sources

Crediting Sources

When you credit a source, you acknowledge where you found your information and you give your readers the details necessary for locating the source themselves. Within the body of the paper, you provide a short citation, a footnote number linked to a footnote, or an endnote number linked to an endnote reference. These brief references show the page numbers on which you found the information. To make your paper more formal, prepare a reference list at the end of the paper to provide full bibliographic information on your sources. These are two common types of reference lists:

- A **bibliography** provides a listing of all the resources you consulted during your research.
- A **works-cited list** indicates the works you have referenced in your paper.

Choosing a Format for Documentation

The type of information you provide and the format in which you provide it depend on what your teacher prefers. These are the most commonly used styles:

- **Modern Language Association (MLA) Style** This is the style used for most papers at the middle-school and high-school level and for most language arts papers.
- **American Psychological Association (APA) Style** This is used for most papers in the social sciences and for most college-level papers.
- ***Chicago Manual of Style* (CMS) Style** This is preferred by some teachers.

On the following pages, you'll find sample citation formats for the most commonly cited materials. Each format calls for standard bibliographic information. The difference is in the order of the material presented in each entry and the punctuation required.

MLA Style for Listing Sources

Book with one author	Pyles, Thomas. *The Origins and Development of the English Language.* 2nd ed. New York: Harcourt Brace Jovanovich, Inc., 1971.
Book with two or three authors	McCrum, Robert, William Cran, and Robert MacNeil. *The Story of English.* New York: Penguin Books, 1987.
Book with an editor	Truth, Sojourner. *Narrative of Sojourner Truth.* Ed. Margaret Washington. New York: Vintage Books, 1993.
Book with more than three authors or editors	Donald, Robert B., et al. *Writing Clear Essays.* Upper Saddle River, NJ: Prentice-Hall, Inc., 1996.
A single work from an anthology	Hawthorne, Nathaniel. "Young Goodman Brown." *Literature: An Introduction to Reading and Writing.* Ed. Edgar V. Roberts and Henry E. Jacobs. Upper Saddle River, NJ: Prentice-Hall, Inc., 1998. 376–385. [Indicate pages for the entire selection.]
Introduction in a published edition	Washington, Margaret. Introduction. *Narrative of Sojourner Truth.* By Sojourner Truth. Ed. Washington. New York: Vintage Books, 1993. v–xi.
Signed article in a weekly magazine	Wallace, Charles. "A Vodacious Deal." *Time* 14 Feb. 2000: 63.
Signed article in a monthly magazine	Gustaitis, Joseph. "The Sticky History of Chewing Gum." *American History* Oct. 1998: 30–38.
Unsigned editorial or story	"Selective Silence." Editorial. *Wall Street Journal* 11 Feb. 2000: A14. [If the editorial or story is signed, begin with the author's name.]
Signed pamphlet	[Treat the pamphlet as though it were a book.]
Pamphlet with no author, publisher, or date	*Are You at Risk of Heart Attack?* n.p. n.d. [n.p. n.d. indicates that there is no known publisher or date]
Filmstrips, slide programs, videocassettes, DVDs, and other audiovisual media	*The Diary of Anne Frank.* Dir. George Stevens. Perf. Millie Perkins, Shelley Winters, Joseph Schildkraut, Lou Jacobi, and Richard Beymer. 1959. DVD. Twentieth Century Fox, 2004.
Radio or television program transcript	"Washington's Crossing of the Delaware." Host Liane Hansen. Guest David Hackett Fischer. *Weekend Edition Sunday.* Natl. Public Radio. WNYC, New York City. 23 Dec. 2003. Transcript.
Internet	"Fun Facts About Gum." NACGM site. National Association of Chewing Gum Manufacturers. 19 Dec. 1999. <http://www.nacgm.org/consumer/funfacts.html>. [Indicate the date of last update if known and the date you accessed the information. Content and addresses at Web sites change frequently.]
Newspaper	Thurow, Roger. "South Africans Who Fought for Sanctions Now Scrap for Investors." *Wall Street Journal* 11 Feb. 2000: A1+ [For a multipage article that does not appear on consecutive pages, write only the first page number on which it appears, followed by a plus sign.]
Personal interview	Smith, Jane. Personal interview. 10 Feb. 2000.
CD (with multiple publishers)	Simms, James, ed. *Romeo and Juliet.* By William Shakespeare. CD-ROM. Oxford: Attica Cybernetics Ltd.; London: BBC Education; London: HarperCollins Publishers, 1995.
Article from an encyclopedia	Askeland, Donald R. "Welding." *World Book Encyclopedia.* 1991 ed.

APA Style for Listing Sources

The list of citations for APA is referred to as a Reference List and not a bibliography.

Book with one author	Pyles, T. (1971). *The Origins and Development of the English Language* (2nd ed.). New York: Harcourt Brace Jovanovich, Inc.
Book with two or three authors	McCrum, R., Cran, W., & MacNeil, R. (1987). *The Story of English.* New York: Penguin Books.
Book with an editor	Truth, S. (1993). *Narrative of Sojourner Truth* (M. Washington, Ed.). New York: Vintage Books.
Book with more than three authors or editors	Donald, R. B., Morrow, B. R., Wargetz, L. G., & Werner, K. (1996). *Writing Clear Essays.* Upper Saddle River, New Jersey: Prentice-Hall, Inc. [With six or more authors, abbreviate second and following authors as "et al."]
A single work from an anthology	Hawthorne, N. (1998) Young Goodman Brown. In E. V. Roberts, & H. E. Jacobs (Eds.), *Literature: An Introduction to Reading and Writing* (pp. 376–385). Upper Saddle River, New Jersey: Prentice-Hall, Inc.
Introduction to a work included in a published edition	[No style is offered under this heading.]
Signed article in a weekly magazine	Wallace, C. (2000, February 14). A vodacious deal. *Time, 155,* 63. [The volume number appears in italics before the page number.]
Signed article in a monthly magazine	Gustaitis, J. (1998, October). The sticky history of chewing gum. *American History, 33,* 30–38.
Unsigned editorial or story	Selective Silence. (2000, February 11). *Wall Street Journal,* p. A14.
Signed pamphlet	Pearson Education. (2000). *LifeCare* (2nd ed.) [Pamphlet]. Smith, John: Author.
Pamphlet with no author, publisher, or date	[No style is offered under this heading.]
Filmstrips, slide programs, and videotape	Stevens, G. (Producer & Director). (1959). *The Diary of Anne Frank.* [Videotape]. (Available from Twentieth Century Fox) [If the producer and the director are two different people, list the producer first and then the director, with an ampersand (&) between them.]
Radio or television program transcript	Broderick, D. (1999, May 23). The First Immortal Generation. (R. Williams, Radio Host). *Ockham's Razor.* New York: National Public Radio.
Internet	National Association of Chewing Gum Manufacturers. Available: http://www.nacgm.org/consumer/funfacts.html [References to Websites should begin with the author's last name, if available. Indicate the site name and the available path or URL address.]
Newspaper	Thurow, R. (2000, February 11). South Africans who fought for sanctions now scrap for investors. *Wall Street Journal,* pp. A1, A4.
Personal interview	[APA states that, since interviews (and other personal communications) do not provide "recoverable data," they should only be cited in text.]
CD (with multiple publishers)	[No style is offered under this heading.]
Article from an encyclopedia	Askeland, D. R. (1991). Welding. In *World Book Encyclopedia.* (Vol. 21 pp. 190–191). Chicago: World Book, Inc.

CMS Style for Listing Sources

The following chart shows the CMS author-date method of documentation.

Book with one author	Pyles, Thomas. *The Origins and Development of the English Language,* 2nd ed. New York: Harcourt Brace Jovanovich, Inc., 1971.
Book with two or three authors	McCrum, Robert, William Cran, and Robert MacNeil. *The Story of English.* New York: Penguin Books, 1987.
Book with an editor	Truth, Sojourner. *Narrative of Sojourner Truth.* Edited by Margaret Washington. New York: Vintage Books, 1993.
Book with more than three authors or editors	Donald, Robert B., et al. *Writing Clear Essays.* Upper Saddle River, New Jersey: Prentice-Hall, Inc., 1996.
A single work from an anthology	Hawthorne, Nathaniel. "Young Goodman Brown." In *Literature: An Introduction to Reading and Writing.* Ed. Edgar V. Roberts and Henry E. Jacobs. 376–385. Upper Saddle River, New Jersey: Prentice-Hall, Inc., 1998.
Introduction to a work included in a published edition	Washington, Margaret. Introduction to *Narrative of Sojourner Truth,* by Sojourner Truth. New York: Vintage Books, 1993. [According to CMS style, you should avoid this type of entry unless the introduction is of special importance to the work.]
Signed article in a weekly magazine	Wallace, Charles. "A Vodacious Deal." *Time,* 14 February 2000, 63.
Signed article in a monthly magazine	Gustaitis, Joseph. "The Sticky History of Chewing Gum." *American History,* October 1998, 30–38.
Unsigned editorial or story	*Wall Street Journal,* 11 February 2000. [CMS states that items from newspapers are seldom listed in a bibliography. Instead, the name of the paper and the relevant dates are listed.]
Signed pamphlet	[No style is offered under this heading.]
Pamphlet with no author, publisher, or date	[No style is offered under this heading.]
Filmstrips, slide programs, and videotape	Stevens, George. (director). *The Diary of Anne Frank.* 170 min. Beverly Hills, California: Twentieth Century Fox, 1994.
Radio or television program transcript	[No style is offered under this heading.]
Internet	[No style is offered under this heading.]
Newspaper	*Wall Street Journal,* 11 February 2000. [CMS states that items from newspapers are seldom listed in a bibliography. Instead, the name of the paper and the relevant dates are listed.]
Personal interview	[CMS states that, since personal conversations are not available to the public, there is no reason to place them in the bibliography. However, the following format should be followed if they are listed.] Jane Smith. Conversation with author. Wooster, Ohio, 10 February 2000.
CD (with multiple publishers)	Shakespeare, William. *Romeo and Juliet.* Oxford: Attica Cybernetics Ltd.; London: BBC Education; London: HarperCollins Publishers, 1995. CD-ROM.
Article from an encyclopedia	[According to CMS style, encyclopedias are not listed in bibliographies.]

Sample Works-Cited List (MLA)

Carwardine, Mark, Erich Hoyt, R. Ewan Fordyce, and
   Peter Gill. *The Nature Company Guides: Whales,
   Dolphins, and Porpoises*. New York: Time-Life
   Books, 1998.

Ellis, Richard. *Men and Whales*. New York: Knopf,
   1991.

Whales in Danger. "Discovering Whales." 18 Oct. 1999.
   <http://whales.magna.com.au/DISCOVER>

Sample Internal Citations (MLA)

It makes sense that baleen whales such as the
blue whale, the fin whale, the bowhead whale, the
humpback whale, and the sei whale (to name just
a few) grow to immense sizes (Carwardine 19–21).
The blue whale has grooves running from under its
chin to partway along the length of its underbelly.
As in some other whales, these grooves expand
and allow even more food and water to be taken in
(Ellis 18–21).

Author's
last name

page numbers
where
information
can be found

Internet Research Handbook

Introduction to the Internet

The Internet is a series of networks that are interconnected all over the world. The Internet allows users to have almost unlimited access to information stored on the networks. Dr. Berners-Lee, a physicist, created the Internet in the 1980's by writing a small computer program that allowed pages to be linked together using key words. The Internet was mostly text-based until 1992, when a computer program called the NCSA Mosaic (National Center for Supercomputing Applications at the University of Illinois) was created. This program was the first Web browser. The development of Web browsers greatly eased the ability of the user to navigate through all the pages stored on the Web. Very soon, the appearance of the Web was altered as well. More appealing visuals were added, and sound was also implemented. This change made the Web more user-friendly and more appealing to the general public.

Using the Internet for Research

Key Word Search

Before you begin a search, you should identify your specific topic. To make searching easier, narrow your subject to a key word or a group of key words. These are your search terms, and they should be as specific as possible. For example, if you are looking for the latest concert dates for your favorite musical group, you might use the band's name as a key word. However, if you were to enter the name of the group in the query box of the search engine, you might be presented with thousands of links to information about the group that is unrelated to your needs. You might locate such information as band member biographies, the group's history, fan reviews of concerts, and hundreds of sites with related names containing information that is irrelevant to your search. Because you used such a broad key word, you might need to navigate through all that information before you find a link or subheading for concert dates. In contrast, if you were to type in "Duplex Arena and [band name]" you would have a better chance of locating pages that contain this information.

How to Narrow Your Search

If you have a large group of key words and still don't know which ones to use, write out a list of all the words you are considering. Once you have completed the list, scrutinize it. Then, delete the words that are least important to your search, and highlight those that are most important.

These **key search connectors** can help you fine-tune your search:

AND: narrows a search by retrieving documents that include both terms. For example: *baseball AND playoffs*

OR: broadens a search by retrieving documents including any of the terms. For example: *playoffs OR championships*

NOT: narrows a search by excluding documents containing certain words. For example: *baseball NOT history of*

Tips for an Effective Search

1. Keep in mind that search engines can be case-sensitive. If your first attempt at searching fails, check your search terms for misspellings and try again.

2. If you are entering a group of key words, present them in order, from the most important to the least important key word.

3. Avoid opening the link to every single page in your results list. Search engines present pages in descending order of relevancy. The most useful pages will be located at the top of the list. However, read the description of each link before you open the page.

4. When you use some search engines, you can find helpful tips for specializing your search. Take the opportunity to learn more about effective searching.

Other Ways to Search

Using On-line Reference Sites

How you search should be tailored to *what* you are hoping to find. If you are looking for data and facts, use reference sites before you jump onto a simple search engine. For example, you can find reference sites to provide definitions of words, statistics about almost any subject, biographies, maps, and concise information on many topics. Some useful on-line reference sites:

- On-line libraries
- On-line periodicals
- Almanacs
- Encyclopedias

You can find these sources using subject searches.

Conducting Subject Searches

As you prepare to go on-line, consider your subject and the best way to find information to suit your needs. If you are looking for general information on a topic and you want your search results to be extensive, consider the subject search indexes on most search engines. These indexes, in the form of category and subject lists, often appear on the first page of a search engine. When you click on a specific highlighted word, you will be presented with a new screen containing subcategories of the topic you chose. In the screen shots below, the category *Sports & Recreation* provided a second index for users to focus a search even further.

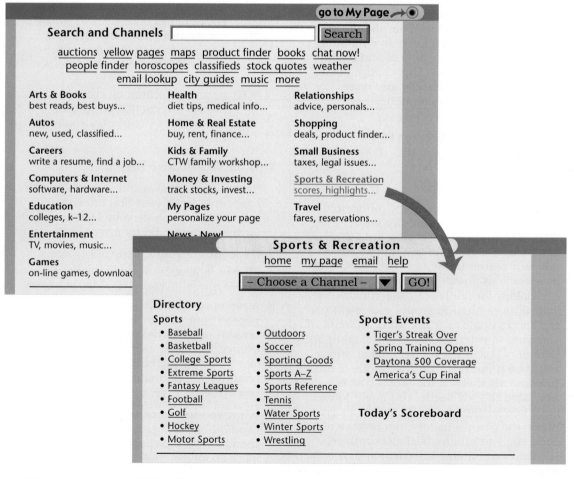

Evaluating the Reliability of Internet Resources

Just as you would evaluate the quality, bias, and validity of any other research material you locate, check the source of information you find on-line. Compare these two sites containing information on the poet and writer Langston Hughes:

Site A is a personal Web site constructed by a college student. It contains no bibliographic information or links to sites that he used. Included on the site are several poems by Langston Hughes and a student essay about the poet's use of symbolism. It has not been updated in more than six months.

Site B is a Web site constructed and maintained by the English Department of a major university. Information on Hughes is presented in a scholarly format, with a bibliography and credits for the writer. The site includes links to other sites and indicates new features that are added weekly.

For your own research, consider the information you find on Site B to be more reliable and accurate than that on Site A. Because it is maintained by experts in their field who are held accountable for their work, the university site will be a better research tool than the student-generated one.

Tips for Evaluating Internet Sources

1. Consider who constructed and who now maintains the Web page. Determine whether this author is a reputable source. Often, the URL endings indicate a source.

   - Sites ending in *.edu* are maintained by educational institutions.
   - Sites ending in *.gov* are maintained by government agencies (federal, state, or local).
   - Sites ending in *.org* are normally maintained by nonprofit organizations and agencies.
   - Sites with a *.com* ending are commercially or personally maintained.

2. Skim the official and trademarked Web pages first. It is safe to assume that the information you draw from Web pages of reputable institutions, on-line encyclopedias, on-line versions of major daily newspapers, or government-owned sites produce information as reliable as the material you would find in print. In contrast, unbranded sites or those generated by individuals tend to borrow information from other sources without providing documentation. As information travels from one source to another, the information has likely been muddled, misinterpreted, edited, or revised.

3. You can still find valuable information in the less "official" sites. Check for the writer's credentials and then consider these factors:

   - Don't let official-looking graphics or presentations fool you.
   - Make sure the information is updated enough to suit your needs. Many Web pages will indicate how recently they have been updated.
   - If the information is borrowed, see whether you can trace it back to its original source.

Respecting Copyrighted Material

Because the Internet is a relatively new and quickly growing medium, issues of copyright and ownership arise almost daily. As laws begin to govern the use and reuse of material posted on-line, they may change the way that people can access or reprint material.

Text, photographs, music, and fine art printed on-line may not be reproduced without acknowledged permission of the copyright owner.

Commonly Overused Words

When you write, use the most precise word for your meaning, not the word that comes to mind first. Consult this thesaurus to find alternatives for some commonly overused words. Consult a full-length thesaurus to find alternatives to words that do not appear here. Keep in mind that the choices offered in a thesaurus do not all mean exactly the same thing. Review all the options, and choose the one that best expresses your meaning.

about approximately, nearly, almost, approaching, close to

absolutely unconditionally, perfectly, completely, ideally, purely

activity action, movement, operation, labor, exertion, enterprise, project, pursuit, endeavor, job, assignment, pastime, scheme, task

add attach, affix, join, unite, append, increase, amplify

affect adjust, influence, transform, moderate, incline, motivate, prompt

amazing overwhelming, astonishing, startling, unexpected, stunning, dazzling, remarkable

awesome impressive, stupendous, fabulous, astonishing, outstanding

bad defective, inadequate, poor, unsatisfactory, disagreeable, offensive, repulsive, corrupt, wicked, naughty, harmful, injurious, unfavorable

basic essential, necessary, indispensable, vital, fundamental, elementary

beautiful attractive, appealing, alluring, exqui-

site, gorgeous, handsome, stunning

begin commence, found, initiate, introduce, launch, originate

better preferable, superior, worthier

big enormous, extensive, huge, immense, massive

boring commonplace, monotonous, tedious, tiresome

bring accompany, cause, convey, create, conduct, deliver, produce

cause origin, stimulus, inspiration, motive

certain unquestionable, incontrovertible, unmistakable, indubitable, assured, confident

change alter, transform, vary, replace, diversify

choose select, elect, nominate, prefer, identify

decent respectable, adequate, fair, suitable

definitely unquestionably, clearly, precisely, positively, inescapably

easy effortless, natural, comfortable, undemanding, pleasant, relaxed

effective powerful, successful

emphasize underscore, feature, accentuate

end limit, boundary, finish, conclusion, finale, resolution

energy vitality, vigor, force, dynamism

enjoy savor, relish, revel, benefit

entire complete, inclusive, unbroken, integral

excellent superior, remarkable, splendid, unsurpassed, superb, magnificent

exciting thrilling, stirring, rousing, dramatic

far distant, remote

fast swift, quick, fleet, hasty, instant, accelerated

fill occupy, suffuse, pervade, saturate, inflate, stock

finish complete, conclude, cease, achieve, exhaust, deplete, consume

funny comical, ludicrous, amusing, droll, entertaining, bizarre, unusual, uncommon

get obtain, receive, acquire, procure, achieve

give bestow, donate, supply, deliver, distribute, impart

go proceed, progress, advance, move

good satisfactory, serviceable, functional, competent, virtuous, striking

great tremendous, superior, remarkable, eminent, proficient, expert

happy pleased, joyous, elated, jubilant, cheerful, delighted

hard arduous, formidable, complex, complicated, rigorous, harsh

help assist, aid, support, sustain, serve

hurt injure, harm, damage, wound, impair

important significant, substantial, weighty, meaningful, critical, vital, notable

interesting absorbing, appealing, entertaining, fascinating, thought-provoking

job task, work, business, undertaking, occupation, vocation, chore, duty, assignment

keep retain, control, possess

kind type, variety, sort, form

know comprehend, understand, realize, perceive, discern

like (adj) similar, equivalent, parallel

like (verb) enjoy, relish, appreciate

main primary, foremost, dominant

make build, construct, produce, assemble, fashion, manufacture

mean plan, intend, suggest, propose, indicate

more supplementary, additional, replenishment

new recent, modern, current, novel

next subsequently, thereafter, successively

nice pleasant, satisfying, gracious, charming

old aged, mature, experienced, used, worn, former, previous

open unobstructed, accessible

part section, portion, segment, detail, element, component

perfect flawless, faultless, ideal, consummate

plan scheme, design, system, plot

pleasant agreeable, gratifying, refreshing, welcome

prove demonstrate, confirm, validate, verify, corroborate

quick brisk, prompt, responsive, rapid, nimble, hasty

really truly, genuinely, extremely, undeniably

regular standard, routine, customary, habitual

see regard, behold, witness, gaze, realize, notice

small diminutive, miniature, minor, insignificant, slight, trivial

sometimes occasionally, intermittently, sporadically, periodically

take grasp, capture, choose, select, tolerate, endure

terrific extraordinary, magnificent, marvelous

think conceive, imagine, ponder, reflect, contemplate

try attempt, endeavor, venture, test

use employ, operate, utilize

very unusually, extremely, deeply, exceedingly, profoundly

want desire, crave, yearn, long

Commonly Misspelled Words

The list on these pages presents words that cause problems for many people. Some of these words are spelled according to set rules, but others follow no specific rules. As you review this list, check to see how many of the words give you trouble in your own writing. Then, read the instruction in the "Vocabulary and Spelling" chapter in the book for strategies and suggestions for improving your own spelling habits.

abbreviate	athletic	catastrophe	curious
absence	attendance	category	cylinder
absolutely	auxiliary	ceiling	deceive
abundance	awkward	cemetery	decision
accelerate	bandage	census	deductible
accidentally	banquet	certain	defendant
accumulate	bargain	changeable	deficient
accurate	barrel	characteristic	definitely
ache	battery	chauffeur	delinquent
achievement	beautiful	chief	dependent
acquaintance	beggar	clothes	descendant
adequate	beginning	coincidence	description
admittance	behavior	colonel	desert
advertisement	believe	column	desirable
aerial	benefit	commercial	dessert
affect	bicycle	commission	deteriorate
aggravate	biscuit	commitment	dining
aggressive	bookkeeper	committee	disappointed
agreeable	bought	competitor	disastrous
aisle	boulevard	concede	discipline
all right	brief	condemn	dissatisfied
allowance	brilliant	congratulate	distinguish
aluminum	bruise	connoisseur	effect
amateur	bulletin	conscience	eighth
analysis	buoyant	conscientious	eligible
analyze	bureau	conscious	embarrass
ancient	bury	contemporary	enthusiastic
anecdote	buses	continuous	entrepreneur
anniversary	business	controversy	envelope
anonymous	cafeteria	convenience	environment
answer	calendar	coolly	equipped
anticipate	campaign	cooperate	equivalent
anxiety	canceled	cordially	especially
apologize	candidate	correspondence	exaggerate
appall	capacity	counterfeit	exceed
appearance	capital	courageous	excellent
appreciate	capitol	courteous	exercise
appropriate	captain	courtesy	exhibition
architecture	career	criticism	existence
argument	carriage	criticize	experience
associate	cashier	curiosity	explanation

extension
extraordinary
familiar
fascinating
February
fiery
financial
fluorescent
foreign
forfeit
fourth
fragile
gauge
generally
genius
genuine
government
grammar
grievance
guarantee
guard
guidance
handkerchief
harass
height
humorous
hygiene
ignorant
illegible
immediately
immigrant
independence
independent
indispensable
individual
inflammable
intelligence
interfere
irrelevant
irritable
jewelry
judgment
knowledge
laboratory
lawyer
legible
legislature
leisure
liable

library
license
lieutenant
lightning
likable
liquefy
literature
loneliness
magnificent
maintenance
marriage
mathematics
maximum
meanness
mediocre
mileage
millionaire
minimum
minuscule
miscellaneous
mischievous
misspell
mortgage
naturally
necessary
negotiate
neighbor
neutral
nickel
niece
ninety
noticeable
nuclear
nuisance
obstacle
occasion
occasionally
occur
occurred
occurrence
omitted
opinion
opportunity
optimistic
outrageous
pamphlet
parallel
paralyze
parentheses

particularly
patience
permanent
permissible
perseverance
persistent
personally
perspiration
persuade
phenomenal
phenomenon
physician
pleasant
pneumonia
possess
possession
possibility
prairie
precede
preferable
prejudice
preparation
prerogative
previous
primitive
privilege
probably
procedure
proceed
prominent
pronunciation
psychology
publicly
pursue
questionnaire
realize
really
recede
receipt
receive
recognize
recommend
reference
referred
rehearse
relevant
reminiscence
renowned
repetition

restaurant
rhythm
ridiculous
sandwich
satellite
schedule
scissors
secretary
siege
solely
sponsor
subtle
subtlety
superintendent
supersede
surveillance
susceptible
tariff
temperamental
theater
threshold
truly
unmanageable
unwieldy
usage
usually
valuable
various
vegetable
voluntary
weight
weird
whale
wield
yield

Abbreviations Guide

Abbreviations, shortened versions of words or phrases, can be valuable tools in writing if you know when and how to use them. They can be very helpful in informal writing situations, such as taking notes or writing lists. However, only a few abbreviations can be used in formal writing. They are: *Mr., Mrs., Miss, Ms., Dr., A.M., P.M., A.D., B.C., M.A, B.A., Ph.D.,* and *M.D.*

The following pages provide the conventional abbreviations for a variety of words.

Abbreviations of Common Titles

Ambassador	Amb.	Lieutenant	Lt.
Attorney	Atty.	Major	Maj.
Brigadier-General	Brig. Gen.	President	Pres.
Brother	Br.	Professor	Prof.
Captain	Capt.	Representative	Rep.
Colonel	Col.	Reverend	Rev.
Commander	Cmdr.	Secretary	Sec.
Commissioner	Com.	Senator	Sen.
Corporal	Cpl.	Sergeant	Sgt.
Doctor	Dr.	Sister	Sr.
Father	Fr.	Superintendent	Supt.
Governor	Gov.	Treasurer	Treas.
Honorable	Hon.	Vice Admiral	Vice Adm.

Abbreviations of Academic Degrees

Bachelor of Arts	B.A. (or A.B.)	Esquire (lawyer)	Esq.
Bachelor of Science	B.S. (or S.B.)	Master of Arts	M.A. (or A.M.)
Doctor of Dental Surgery	D.D.S.	Master of Business Administration	M.B.A.
Doctor of Divinity	D.D.		
Doctor of Education	Ed.D.	Master of Fine Arts	M.F.A.
Doctor of Laws	LL.D.	Master of Science	M.S. (or S.M.)
Doctor of Medicine	M.D.	Registered Nurse	R.N.
Doctor of Philosophy	Ph.D.		

Abbreviations of States

State	Traditional	Postal Service	State	Traditional	Postal Service
Alabama	Ala.	AL	Montana	Mont.	MT
Alaska	Alaska	AK	Nebraska	Nebr.	NE
Arizona	Ariz.	AZ	Nevada	Nev.	NV
Arkansas	Ark.	AR	New Hampshire	N.H.	NH
California	Calif.	CA	New Jersey	N.J.	NJ
Colorado	Colo.	CO	New Mexico	N.M.	NM
Connecticut	Conn.	CT	New York	N.Y.	NY
Delaware	Del.	DE	North Carolina	N.C.	NC
Florida	Fla.	FL	North Dakota	N.Dak.	ND
Georgia	Ga.	GA	Ohio	O.	OH
Hawaii	Hawaii	HI	Oklahoma	Okla.	OK
Idaho	Ida.	ID	Oregon	Ore.	OR
Illinois	Ill.	IL	Pennsylvania	Pa.	PA
Indiana	Ind.	IN	Rhode Island	R.I.	RI
Iowa	Iowa	IA	South Carolina	S.C.	SC
Kansas	Kans.	KS	South Dakota	S.Dak.	SD
Kentucky	Ky.	KY	Tennessee	Tenn.	TN
Louisiana	La.	LA	Texas	Tex.	TX
Maine	Me.	ME	Utah	Utah	UT
Maryland	Md.	MD	Vermont	Vt.	VT
Massachusetts	Mass.	MA	Virginia	Va.	VA
Michigan	Mich.	MI	Washington	Wash.	WA
Minnesota	Minn.	MN	West Virginia	W. Va	WV
Mississippi	Miss.	MS	Wisconsin	Wis.	WI
Missouri	Mo.	MO	Wyoming	Wyo.	WY

Common Geographical Abbreviations

Apartment	Apt.	National	Natl.
Avenue	Ave.	Park, Peak	Pk.
Block	Blk.	Peninsula	Pen.
Boulevard	Blvd.	Point	Pt.
Building	Bldg.	Province	Prov.
County	Co.	Road	Rd.
District	Dist.	Route	Rte.
Drive	Dr.	Square	Sq.
Fort	Ft.	Street	St.
Island	Is.	Territory	Terr.
Mountain	Mt.		

Abbreviations of Traditional Measurements

inch(es)	in.	ounce(s)	oz.
foot, feet	ft.	pound(s)	lb.
yard(s)	yd.	pint(s)	pt.
mile(s)	mi.	quart(s)	qt.
teaspoon(s)	tsp.	gallon(s)	gal.
tablespoon(s)	tbsp.	Fahrenheit	F.

Abbreviations of Metric Measurements

millimeter(s)	mm	liter(s)	L
centimeter(s)	cm	kiloliter(s)	kL
meter(s)	m	milligram(s)	mg
kilometer(s)	km	centigram(s)	cg
milliliter(s)	mL	gram(s)	g
centiliter(s)	cL	Celsius	C

Other Commonly Used Abbreviations

about (used with dates)	c., ca., circ.	manager	mgr.
and others	et al.	manufacturing	mfg.
anonymous	anon.	market	mkt.
approximately	approx.	measure	meas.
associate, association	assoc., assn.	merchandise	mdse.
auxiliary	aux., auxil.	miles per hour	mph
bibliography	bibliog.	miscellaneous	misc.
boxes	bx(s).	money order	M.O.
bucket	bkt.	note well; take notice	N.B.
bulletin	bull.	number	no.
bushel	bu.	package	pkg.
capital letter	cap.	page	p., pg.
cash on delivery	C.O.D.	pages	pp.
department	dept.	pair(s)	pr(s).
discount	disc.	parenthesis	paren.
dozen(s)	doz.	Patent Office	pat. off.
each	ea.	piece(s)	pc(s).
edition, editor	ed.	poetical, poetry	poet.
equivalent	equiv.	private	pvt.
established	est.	proprietor	prop.
fiction	fict.	pseudonym	pseud.
for example	e.g.	published, publisher	pub.
free of charge	grat., gratis	received	recd.
General Post Office	G.P.O.	reference, referee	ref.
government	gov., govt.	revolutions per minute	rpm
graduate, graduated	grad.	rhetorical, rhetoric	rhet.
Greek, Grecian	Gr.	right	R.
headquarters	hdqrs.	scene	sc.
height	ht.	special, specific	spec.
hospital	hosp.	spelling, species	sp.
illustrated	ill., illus.	that is	i.e.
including, inclusive	incl.	treasury, treasurer	treas.
introduction, introductory	intro.	volume	vol.
italics	ital.	weekly	wkly
karat, carat	k., kt.	weight	wt.
left	L.		

Proofreading Symbols Reference

Proofreading symbols make it easier to show where changes are needed in a paper. When proofreading your own or a classmate's work, use these standard proofreading symbols.

insert	I proofred.
delete	I p proofread.
close up space	I proof read.
delete and close up space	I proofreade.
begin new paragraph	¶ I proofread.
spell out	I proofread (10) papers. (sp)
lowercase	I Proofread. (lc)
capitalize	i proofread. (cap)
transpose letters	I proofraed. (tr)
transpose words	I only proofread her paper. (tr)
period	I will proofread⊙
comma	I will proofread and she will help.
colon	We will proofread for the following errors
semicolon	I will proofread she will help.
single quotation marks	She said, "I enjoyed the story The Invalid."
double quotation marks	She said, I enjoyed the story.
apostrophe	Did you borrow Sylvias book?
question mark	Did you borrow Sylvia's book ?/
exclamation point	You're kidding !/
hyphen	online /=/
parentheses	William Shakespeare 1564–1616

Student Publications

To share your writing with a wider audience, consider submitting it to a local, state, or national publication for student writing. Following are several magazines and Web sites that accept and publish student work.

Periodicals

Merlyn's Pen merlynspen.org

Skipping Stones P.O. Box 3939, Eugene, OR 97403
http://www.skippingstones.org

Teen Ink Box 30, Newton, MA 02461 teenink.com

On-line Publications

Kid Pub http://www.kidpub.org

MidLink Magazine http://www.ncsu.edu/midlink

Contests

Annual Poetry Contest National Federation of State Poetry Societies, Contest Chair, Kathleen Pederzani, 121 Grande Boulevard, Reading, PA 19608-9680. http://www.nfsps.com

Paul A. Witty Outstanding Literature Award International Reading Association, Special Interest Group for Reading for Gifted and Creative Students, c/o Texas Christian University, P.O. Box 297900, Fort Worth, TX 76129

Seventeen Magazine Fiction Contest *Seventeen* Magazine, 1440 Broadway 13th Floor, New York, NY 10018

The Young Playwrights Festival National Playwriting Competition Young Playwrights Inc. Dept WEB, 306 West 38th Street #300, New York, NY 10018 or webmaster@youngplaywrights.org

Sentence Diagraming Workshop

Subjects and Verbs

To diagram the most basic subject-verb sentence pattern, draw a horizontal line and place the simple subject on the left and the simple verb on the right. Separate the two with a vertical line.

EXAMPLE: Jerome Martin would have frowned.

Jerome Martin	would have frowned

Adjectives and adverbs are placed on slanted lines below the words they modify.

EXAMPLE: The very tasty dessert had been prepared quite easily.

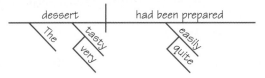

When *you* is understood to be the subject of an imperative sentence, write it in parentheses. Inverted sentences are also diagramed in the usual subject-verb order. The capital letter shows you the word that begins the sentence.

EXAMPLES: IMPERATIVE: Go home.   INVERTED: Will Steve play today?

When *there* or *here* functions as an adverb, put the word on a slanted line beneath the verb. If *there* is an expletive used merely to begin the sentence, however, write it on a horizontal line over the subject. The placement of the expletive is also used for interjections and nouns of direct address.

EXAMPLES:
EXP
There is a park nearby.

INT N of DA
Well, Jan, are you going?

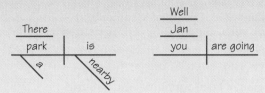

Exercise 1 Diagraming Subjects, Verbs, and Modifiers

Correctly diagram each sentence.
1. Harry skates well.
2. The tiny dancer fell down.
3. There was an extremely severe thunderstorm today.
4. Alice, begin immediately.
5. Did the crowd clap loudly?

Adding Conjunctions

In a diagram, a conjunction is written on a dotted line drawn between the words that are connected by the conjunction. The following example shows how conjunctions are diagramed to indicate the connection between compound adjectives and compound adverbs.

EXAMPLE:
CONJ
CONJ
The tan and white moth fluttered back and forth.

Conjunctions that connect compound subjects and verbs are also written on dotted lines. Notice in the following example how the horizontal line has been split to allow each part of the compound subject and the compound verb to be on a separate line. Also, note how the correlative conjunctions *both* and *and* are placed.

EXAMPLE:
CONJ
CONJ
Both the corn and the tomatoes were planted

CONJ
last spring and have been weeded regularly.

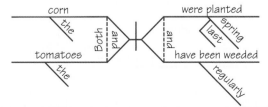

Notice in the last example that modifiers are placed as always under the words they modify. If a word modifies both parts of a compound subject or verb, it is placed under the main line of the diagram. Likewise, if parts of a compound verb share the same helping verb, the helping verb is written on the main line of the diagram.

EXAMPLE: Anxiously, we have been watching and waiting.

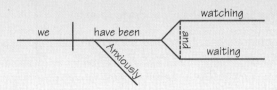

> **Exercise 2** **Diagraming Conjunctions** Correctly diagram each sentence.
> 1. My teacher and her husband live here.
> 2. The burglar entered quickly but silently.
> 3. The bright and witty entertainer will perform tonight.
> 4. The nervous squirrels ran away and hid.
> 5. The sick child was feverishly tossing and turning.

Complements

Because complements complete verbs, they are placed on the predicate side of the diagram. Place the direct object on the main horizontal line following the verb. Separate the direct object from the verb with a short vertical line. Indirect objects are located directly under the verb on a short horizontal line extended from a slanted line.

EXAMPLES: I stapled the papers.   He lent me a pen.

| | stapled | papers | | He | lent | pen |
the   me   a

Objective complements sit on the main line after the direct object. A short slanted line pointing toward the direct object separates them.

EXAMPLE: The club elected her president.

Both subject complements—predicate nominatives and predicate adjectives—are diagramed in the same way. Place them on the same line following the verb. Separate them from the verb with a line slanting toward the subject.

EXAMPLES: The puppy felt soft.   That tree is an elm.

Diagram compound complements by splitting the line on which they appear and adding any conjunctions that connect them.

EXAMPLE: She gave Vic and Mary their coats and hats.

▷ **Exercise 3** **Diagraming Complements** Correctly diagram each sentence.
1. Henry and Mike are practicing their tournament speeches.
2. Carlos intently watched the butterflies and the moths.
3. My dear aunt left me a huge, old desk.
4. The old bridge appears both too narrow and too unsafe.
5. My manager thinks me very efficient and quite reliable.

Prepositional Phrases

A prepositional phrase is diagramed directly beneath the word it modifies. The preposition is placed on a slanted line, and the object sits on a horizontal line. Place any modifiers of the object of the preposition on slanted lines below the horizontal line. If the object of the preposition is compound, diagram it in the same way other compound parts are diagramed.

EXAMPLE: The cup *of hot soup* is sitting *on the table or the stove.*

If a prepositional phrase modifies the object of another prepositional phrase, diagram it below the other phrase as shown in the first example. If a prepositional phrase modifies an adjective or adverb, an extra line is added as in the second example.

EXAMPLES: I ate cereal *with strawberries on it.*

He left early *in the morning.*

When two or more prepositional phrases modify the same word, place them side by side under the word they modify.

EXAMPLE: Go *down the hall* and *to the left.*

▶ **Exercise 4** Diagraming Prepositional Phrases Correctly diagram each sentence.
1. The magazine on that chair has an article about birds.
2. Yesterday, George sent his winter coat to the cleaners.
3. A crowd gathered at the foot of the hill.
4. The detective descended into the basement and disappeared into the great darkness.
5. My mother prepared the blueberry muffins and put them into the oven.

Appositive Phrases

Place an appositive in parentheses beside the noun or pronoun it renames. Position any modifiers of the appositive in the usual way beneath the appositive.

EXAMPLE:

APPOSITIVE PHRASE

My friend, *the one with the suitcase,* is leaving for Greece.

> **Exercise 5** Diagraming Appositive Phrases Correctly diagram each sentence.

1. Our dessert, strawberry crepes with cream, pleased our guests immensely.
2. At her party, she received some placemats, orange ones with yellow borders.
3. My friend Linda plays a good game of charades.
4. They gave the babysitter, a neighborhood girl, a generous bonus.
5. With great delight, the audience watched the movie, a farce about airplane disasters.

Verbal Phrases

As you study the following explanations and examples, remember that a verbal is never diagramed on a single straight line and that any verbal can have a complement.

Participles and Participial Phrases Because a participle functions as an adjective, place it directly beneath the noun or pronoun it modifies. Write it partly on a slanted line and partly on a horizontal line with any modifiers beneath it. When a participle has a complement, such as a direct object, place it after the participle on the horizontal line. Separate the complement from the participle with the usual line.

EXAMPLE:

PARTICIPLE PHRASE

The cars *loudly honking their horns* disrupted my sleep.

A nominative absolute, formed from a noun and participle that are grammatically separate from the rest of the sentence, is positioned above the rest of the sentence.

NOMINATIVE ABSOLUTE

EXAMPLE: *His work finished for the day,* he left.

Gerunds and Gerund Phrases Gerunds used as subjects, direct objects, or predicate nominatives are placed on a stepped line atop a pedestal. If a gerund functions as an appositive, parentheses are placed around the base of the pedestal. Any modifiers or complements are diagramed in the usual way. The example below shows a gerund phrase used as a subject.

GERUND PHRASE

EXAMPLE: *Catching a big fish* was a great thrill.

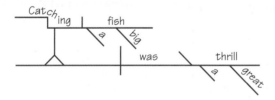

When a gerund or gerund phrase functions as an indirect object or as the object of a preposition, the stepped line extends from a slanted line.

GERUND PHRASE

EXAMPLE: We helped *by carrying the packages to the car.*

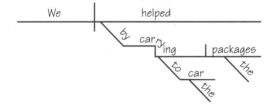

Compound-Complex Sentences Because you now know how to diagram both compound and complex sentences, compound-complex sentences should pose few problems. First, diagram the independent clauses. Then, diagram and connect each subordinate clause as you would if you were diagraming a complex sentence.

EXAMPLE:

ADVERB CLAUSE
When I arrived at work, I had many

disrupting telephone calls, but I still finished

ADJECTIVE CLAUSE
everything *that I had to do.*

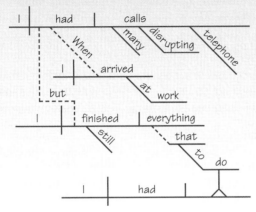

Exercise 7 Diagraming Compound, Complex, and Compound-Complex Sentences Correctly diagram each sentence. The first three sentences are compound, the next four are complex, and the last three are compound-complex.

1. My arms ached, but I continued to swim more laps.
2. The wind dispersed the smog, yet by dusk it had returned.
3. Did Helen attend the concert, or did she get a refund for her ticket?
4. Ursula LeGuin, who writes fantasy stories, will speak to us on Friday.
5. I must get whatever is necessary to repair this lock.
6. Because they had little money, they watched every penny they spent.
7. When you buy a house, look for any railroad tracks in the vicinity.
8. While I watched with interest, the workers measured the carpet, but they miscalculated on the amount needed.
9. She mailed the letter before the sun was up, but by noon she began to regret her decision.
10. If we go to Washington, I want to see the White House, and my sister plans to visit the Smithsonian.

Index

Photo Credits

363: Philadelphia Convention & Visitors Bureau; **364–368:** Corel Professional Photos CD-ROM™; **372:** Texas State Preservation Board; **375:** Corel Professional Photos CD-ROM™; **377:** Pearson Education/PH School; **379 & 388:** Corel Professional Photos CD-ROM™; **399:** Pearson Education/PH College; **400:** Corel Professional Photos CD-ROM™; **403–406:** Courtesy of the Library of Congress; **409:** Ken Karp Photography; **413–424:** Corel Professional Photos CD-ROM™; **426–434:** NASA; **438 & 440:** Corel Professional Photos CD-ROM™; **443:** Pearson Education/PH School; **446:** Florida Department of Commerce/ Division of Tourism; **449–452:** Corel Professional Photos CD-ROM™; **456 & 461:** Courtesy of the Library of Congress; **462:** Massachusetts Development and Industrial Commission; **464:** Courtesy of the Library of Congress; **467:** New York Convention & Visitors Bureau; **468–474:** Corel Professional Photos CD-ROM™; **479:** Pearson Education/ PH School; **483–494:** Corel Professional Photos CD-ROM™; **496–508:** Courtesy of the Library of Congress; **512:** Courtesy of the Library of Congress; **514–537:** Corel Professional Photos CD-ROM™; **540:** Courtesy of the Library of Congress; **545:** The White House Photo Office; **546:** Corel Professional Photos CD-ROM™; **549:** Courtesy of the Library of Congress; **551:** Michael Littlejohn/ Pearson Education/PH College; **552–561:** Pearson Education/PH College; **567–581:** Corel Professional Photos CD-ROM™; **583:** AP/Wide World Photos; **588:** *Eight A.M.,* 1993, Andrew Stevovich, Adelson Galleries, Inc.; **590:** *Speaker,* 1996, Diana Ong/SuperStock ; **592:** Michelle Bridwell/PhotoEdit; **595:** Pearson Education/PH School; **598:** Ken Karp/PH Photo; **603:** *The Reaper,* c.1881, Louis C. Tiffany, oil on canvas, National Academy of Design, New York City; **607:** Ken Karp/PH Photo; **610:** Mark Lewis/Tony Stone Images; **612:** ©The Stock Market/Mug Shots; **616:** Bill Aron/PhotoEdit; **623:** John Brooks/Tony Stone Images; **632:** *Reading,* 1973, oil on masonite, Billy Morrow Jackson, Wichita Art Museum, purchased with funds donated by Mr. and Mrs. Donald C. Slawson; **641:** Tim Wright/CORBIS; **644:** Esbin/Anderson/Omni-Photo Communications, Inc.; **647:** ©The Stock Market/Charles Gupton; **648:** Photofest; **651:** ©1993, Billy Barnes/ FPG International Corp.; **654:** ©The Stock Market/Jose L. Pelaez; **655:** Kevin Morris/Tony Stone Images; **657:** Jeff Greenberg/Omni-Photo Communications, Inc.; **659:** Gary Conner/PhotoEdit; **661:** ©Navaswan/FPG International Corp.; **667:** Inge Yspeert/CORBIS; **669:** ©Stuart Schwartz/The National Steinbeck Center; **674:** ©The Stock Market/Charles Gupton; **676:** Layne Kennedy/CORBIS; **680:** Don Miller/Monkmeyer; **682:** Pearson Education/PH School; **684:** image©Copyright 1998 PhotoDisc, Inc.; **685:** ©The Stock Market/Jean Miele